Dynamic Social Studies for Constructivist Classrooms

Inspiring Tomorrow's Social Scientists

NINTH EDITION

George W. Maxim

West Chester University

Allyn & Bacon

Boston New York San Francisco
Mexico City Montreal Toronto London Madrid Munich Paris
Hong Kong Singapore Tokyo Cape Town Sydney

Series Editor: *Kelly Villella Canton*
Editorial Assistant: *Annalea Manalili*
Development Editor: *Kara Kikel*
Senior Marketing Manager: *Darcy Betts*
Production Editor: *Gregory Erb*
Editorial Production Service: *Publishers' Design and Production Services, Inc.*
Composition Buyer: *Linda Cox*
Manufacturing Buyer: *Megan Cochran*
Electronic Composition: *Publishers' Design and Production Services, Inc.*
Interior Design: *Publishers' Design and Production Services, Inc.*
Photo Researcher: *Annie Pickert*
Cover Designer: *Linda Knowles*

Between the time website information is gathered and then published, it is not unusual for some sites to have closed. Also, the transcription of URLs can result in typographical errors. The publisher would appreciate notification where these errors occur so that they may be corrected in subsequent editions.

Library of Congress Cataloging-in-Publication data unavailable at press time.

Printed in the United States of America

Source for inside cover NCSS Standards: National Council for the Social Studies (1994). Expectations of excellence: Curriculum standards for social studies (Bulletin 89). Washington, DC: National Council for the Social Studies.

Photo credits: Pages xiv, 78: David Mager/Pearson Learning Photo Studio; pp. 7, 166, 204, 225, 270, 327, 384, 420, 444, 446: Anthony Magnacca/Merrill Education; p. 35: Tom Watson/Merrill Education; pp. 39, 44, 90, 103, 136, 207, 308, 340, 356, 368, 376, 381, 409: Scott Cunningham/Merrill Education; p. 62: Laura Bolesta/Merrill Education; p. 69: Pearson Education; p. 115: Timothy P. Dingman/Pearson Education/PH College; p. 128: Pearson Education/Modern Curriculum Press/Pearson Learning; p. 149: Bruce Johnson/Merrill Education; p. 153: Silver Burdett Ginn; p. 154: Courtesy of the Library of Congress; p. 186: Kenneth P. Davis/Pearson Education/PH College; p. 211: Laima Druskis/Pearson Education/PH College; p. 242: Shirley Zeiberg/Pearson Education/PH College; p. 253: Ken Karp/Pearson Education/PH College; p. 275: Marc Anderson/Pearson Education/PH College, p. 303: Patrick White/Merrill Education; pp. 317, 400, 434: Anne Vega/Merrill Education

10 9 8 7 6 5 4 3 2 1 EDW 13 12 11 10 09

Allyn & Bacon
is an imprint of

www.pearsonhighered.com

ISBN-10: 0-13-813243-7
ISBN-13: 978-0-13-813243-9

To Libby, Mike, and Jeff Maxim
I may not always know what to do,
but I always know where to turn.
Thanks for being you!

Contents

Preface

As I worked on this ninth edition of *Dynamic Social Studies for Constructivist Classrooms*, I repeatedly asked myself, "Why are you doing this?" My reason for asking the question over and over again had nothing to do with insecurity or lack of motivation for the job; on the contrary, the process helped me sustain my considerable enthusiasm throughout the revision project. Authors don't simply select a topic to write about and then start punching away aimlessly at the keyboard, but they must discover how to communicate their ideas in ways that capture and sustain a reader's interest. A textbook author's foremost challenge is to inspire students to read what has been written. So, I asked, "Why are you doing this?" because I wanted to find ways to grab your attention, arouse your curiosity, and engage you to continue reading. My answer to the question is also based on a conviction that social studies is crucial for the development of informed, rational, and culturally responsive citizens. I needed to best communicate to you the essential role that social studies plays in bringing pride, responsibility, and meaning to your students' lives as citizens of our nation in the twenty-first century.

This new edition was written with the belief that subject matter is important, and that topics for instruction should be carefully selected and well taught. It is the subject matter that fuels young, inquiring minds. Subject matter should not be considered the only goal of social studies education, however; instead, it should be perceived as the vehicle through which the processes of real-world inquiry and problem solving are carried out. Students who use content in authentic ways learn the subject matter well. Classrooms in which social studies is taught well become places of caring and trust; they engage students in the subject matter in flexible and innovative ways.

That is the basic premise of *Dynamic Social Studies for Constructivist Classrooms*—taking advantage of children's natural curiosity and built-in desire to learn. Because this ninth edition directs primary attention to capturing the natural learning style of children, students will be referred to as "young social scientists." The young social scientists in our classrooms put subject matter to work to find and solve problems just like practicing social scientists do. This kind of teaching does not minimize the subject matter, for social scientists rarely find a powerful and interesting problem without substantial background knowledge. It simply suggests that subject matter can be put to work to stoke the curiosity in our students.

This is not a text steeped in research and theory, although research and theory are an important part of it. Nor is it a "cookbook" text full of delicious classroom recipes, although it does contain a wealth of teaching examples and suggested

strategies. It does build bridges between theory and practice with the hope that future teachers understand that no single method of instruction, by itself, can help us achieve all the important goals of social studies instruction. The text is designed to help you find ways to inspire children to *want* to learn the things they need to know in order to understand and participate in the world around them. To accomplish these goals you must be bold; you cannot be afraid to make mistakes. You must constantly struggle to find the method that works best for your students by seeking out answers that only one question can give: "Why am I doing this?"

What's New to the Ninth Edition?

This new edition maintains the principal focus of previous editions, but it has been thoroughly revised and updated. Each chapter begins with a classroom scenario that captures the chapter's significance. The scenarios, each having taken place in actual elementary school classrooms, work as advance organizers that place the content into a meaningful context. In addition, a number of authentic scenarios are used within the chapters to help you understand and visualize how teachers have actually used suggested teaching strategies in their classrooms. Many of these activities appear as separate highlighted features.

A number of fresh, new visual aids have been added throughout the book. Photographs, illustrations, figures, and tables help to illuminate and reinforce the information presented.

There is an increased attention to literature in this edition. Rather than devote a single chapter to how literature can best be incorporated into social studies instruction, however, you will find suggestions integrated into all chapters. In addition, Appendix A is a summary of quality literature resources used throughout the text.

One of the main changes in this edition is the reorganizing of chapters and arranging them into four thematic sections. Part I deals with *Foundations of Instruction*; Part II addresses the nature of *Classrooms for Young Social Scientists*; Part III describes *Constructivist Approaches to Classroom Instruction*; and Part IV focuses on *Key Instructional Decisions* (planning for instruction). Part IV also includes a chapter new to this edition (Chapter 3): Integrated Learning: Connecting Learning to the Real World.

Several important topics have been expanded on and updated. Throughout the book and specifically in Chapter 2, readers will read about diversity as an underlying premise of instruction; suggestions for helping students live and learn in democratic learning environments have been added to Chapter 5; readers will understand how to introduce and refine inquiry skills through a unique developmental approach to inquiry in Chapter 8; recommendations for technology resources appropriate for today's social studies classrooms have been brought up to date; and Chapter 10 adapts the popular "backward design" strategy of Wiggins and McTighe for planning and carrying out social studies units. And, to the delight and interest of pre-service teachers, additional examples of exciting classroom scenarios have been inserted throughout the text to help highlight and illustrate important professional concepts and skills.

This new edition includes a number of new, helpful instructional tools: MyEducationLab marginal annotations refer readers to online resources that help students virtually observe relevant classroom activities. NCSS standards and sample benchmarks have been listed inside the front and back covers to offer students a handy and highly useful reference; and an NCSS icon has been added in the margin next to each classroom episode to identify the related NCSS instructional standard(s).

Finally, references have been updated throughout the text. The latest ideas from the social studies profession have been included, and appropriate citations were made.

Supplements

Instructor's Manual

For each chapter, the Instructor's Manual contains Key Questions, a Chapter Outline, and MyEducationLab information. It also includes a combination of Print Resources (books, journals, and current event publications), Electronic Resources (websites), Video Resources, and Organizations. There is also a list of the chapters' vocabulary terms and their definitions.

Test Bank

The Test Bank contains multiple choice questions, essay, and true or false questions, as well as the answer keys for each chapter.

PowerPoint

The PowerPoint slides first explain how the books will help you create a dynamic social studies classroom through its features, such as NCSS standards integration, text sets, and classroom activities. Each chapter is then outlined by topics and terms, which you can read to follow along with the book.

PEARSON myeducationlab
Where the Classroom Comes to Life

MyEducationLab (myeducationlab.com) is a research-based learning tool that brings teaching to life. Through authentic in-class video footage, interactive simulations, rich case studies, examples of authentic teacher and student work, and more, MyEducationLab prepares you for your teaching career by showing what quality instruction looks like.

MyEducationLab is easy to use! Wherever the MyEducationLab logo appears in the margins of the text, you can follow the simple instructions to access the

MyEducationLab assets that correspond to the chapter content. These assets include:

Video: The authentic classroom videos in MyEducationLab show how real teachers handle actual classroom situations.

Simulations: Created by the IRIS Center at Vanderbilt University, these interactive simulations give you hands-on practice at adapting instruction for a full spectrum of learners.

Student & Teacher Artifacts: Authentic preK–8 student and teacher classroom artifacts are tied to course topics and offer you practice in working with the actual types of materials you will encounter daily as teachers.

Acknowledgments

This edition would not have been possible without the encouragement and support of my family. Boundless appreciation is extended to my wife Libby, whose loving help was given freely and seized with enormous gratitude; my son Mike, a graduate student, who is spreading his wings and working hard to make his dreams come true; and my son Jeff, a teacher who has allowed the child inside to come out and play. They may not be aware of how much they helped, but I thank them for being my strength.

I am also indebted to my parents, Rose and Stanley Maxim. Their honorable work ethic instilled in me the value of determination in tackling a job as overwhelming as writing a book. Their love of parenthood was an important inspiration for me throughout my life and my career.

I am grateful for the opportunity to work with a highly talented, supportive, and congenial team of editors at Allyn & Bacon: Kelly Villella Canton, Acquisitions Editor; Kara Kikel, Developmental Editor; Darcy Betts, Senior Marketing Manager; Greg Erb, Production Editor; and Lynda Griffiths, Project Manager.

I thank the following reviewers for their helpful suggestions and insights: Thomas B. Goodkind, University of Connecticut; Donna Odom LaCaze, Louisiana State University–Alexandria; Bruce Larson, Western Washington University; Robert L. Osgood, Indiana University–Purdue University Indiana; and Linda J. Reeves, Pennsylvania State University.

Finally, four special friends deserve special thanks for their support and encouragement: Dan Darigan for his inspiration to explore the literacy–social studies connection, John "Pogo" Ogborn for his appreciation of and interest in my professional accomplishments, Charles Spaziani for hanging in there despite not yet achieving his daunting goal: "I'm gonna teach you something, Maxim!" and George White for the times we sat together and shared tales of the authoring process.

About the Author

George W. Maxim began his elementary school teaching career in rural Appalachia and ultimately taught in varied settings and at different levels from preschool through grade 6. After completing a very enjoyable elementary school teaching career, Dr. Maxim pursued a Ph.D. in Elementary Education from Pennsylvania State University, specializing in social studies and early childhood education. He accepted a position at West Chester (PA) University immediately after completing the requirements for the degree, teaching graduate and undergraduate courses in social studies education, creative thinking processes, literacy, and early childhood education. Dr. Maxim served as Director of the Early Childhood program for several years. He lectured, conducted in-service programs, and offered workshops for teachers throughout the country and has been invited to speak to audiences in locations as distant as Seoul, South Korea.

Dr. Maxim is the recipient of a number of teaching awards, including the Certificate of Excellence in (College) Teaching Award from the Pennsylvania Department of Education. As an active member of the National Council for the Social Studies, he has served on the Educational Publishing Advisory Committee and has chaired the Early Childhood/Elementary Advisory Committee. He was instrumental in helping launch NCSS's elementary education journal, *Social Studies and the Young Learner*, serving on its editorial board for several years.

His articles have appeared in *Social Studies and the Young Learner, Social Education, The Social Studies, Childhood Education,* and other relevant professional journals. He has written books other than this text, including *The Very Young, The Sourcebook,* and *Learning Centers for Young Children*. In addition, he contributed a chapter to Loretta MacAlpine's *Inside Kidvid*, a parent's guide to video.

Dr. Maxim's wife, Libby, is a highly accomplished reading coach, having helped scores of children throughout the West Chester area to become successful readers. His oldest son, Mike, is a Ph.D. student majoring in Computer Science at the University of Michigan, and his youngest son, Jeff, is an elementary and middle school teacher at the Gulfstream School in Delray Beach, Florida.

Dr. Maxim enjoys research and teaching; he particularly likes creating new and exciting approaches to classroom instruction. And, as importantly, he will never run away from a good game of golf.

PART I Foundations of Instruction

CHAPTER 1

Dynamic Social Studies

The Subject You Will Teach

What Does Dynamic Social Studies Look Like?

Dorothy Holzwarth's fourth-graders in Upper Darby, Pennsylvania, were about to wind up a thematic unit on their state when Naisha brought in a newspaper story about Maryland having recently adopted the monarch butterfly as its state insect. "Does Pennsylvania have a state insect, too?" inquired several interested youngsters. That was all it took to launch Mrs. Holzwarth's class into one of the most enjoyable social studies learning adventures it had ever tackled.

The students got the ball rolling by looking up information in various books and pamphlets; they found a state flower, a state song, a state tree, a state nickname, and various other official state symbols, but no official "state bug." The children suggested that they should write to the president of the United States to see if they could have one, but Mrs. Holzwarth explained that since this was a state matter they should direct their query to their district legislators in Harrisburg, the state capital.

Before they did so, however, the class decided to conduct a regular democratic election to determine what insect would be the most fitting state symbol. Several insects were nominated and each nominee became the subject of careful study. The students explored the pros and cons of an assortment of bugs such as the praying mantis, dragonfly, ladybug, and grasshopper. After weighing the advantages and disadvantages of each, a class vote settled the matter: The firefly was their selection. Why? One reason was that the scientific name, *Photuris pennsylvanica*, closely resembled the name of their state. Students also liked the fact

that the soft glow of hundreds of these insects dotted their backyards on warm summer evenings, and that they spent many a summer night running around catching these elusive "lightning bugs." (The children had been taught that to catch a firefly and let it walk all over their hands for a while is "okay" but to hurt the insect in any way is very wrong.)

NCSS STANDARDS

III. *People, Places, and Environments*
V. *Individuals, Groups, and Institutions*
VI. *Power, Authority, and Governance*

After the vote, the students were not quite ready to drop the matter. They went on to write a letter to their two state representatives informing them of their actions and asking how they might make their plan official. Both lawmakers were extremely impressed with the children's civic energy and arranged to visit Mrs. Holzwarth's classroom to answer the children's questions and personally thank them for their interest in state issues. The awestruck youngsters listened intently as the legislators discussed the process of introducing a law in the state legislature and advised the students how they might proceed with their project. The children learned that their next step would be to persuade other legislators to support their cause. Undaunted, these 26 children wrote over 250 letters—203 to the House, 50 to the Senate, and 2 to the governor and his wife. The children also learned that they needed popular support from voters in their area, so they canvassed their neighborhoods and shopping malls until they obtained more than 2,100 signatures.

To interest others in their work, the students printed over 600 luminous bumper stickers proclaiming "Firefly for State Insect." They also kept up their letter-writing campaign, asking legislators to vote YES when the bill came onto the floor. The children were invited to Harrisburg for the House Government Committee hearings on their bill, and went to Harrisburg armed with banners on the side of the bus. Instead of the time-honored bus trip favorite, "Ninety-nine Bottles . . . ," the children repeatedly sang an original song they wrote especially for this occasion:

> Oh firefly! Oh firefly!
> Please be our state bug.
> Photuris pennsylvanica,
> You'll fly forever above.
> Oh firefly! Oh firefly!
> You light up so bright.
> It's fun to see such a pretty sight.
> Oh firefly! Oh firefly!

Imagine the thoughts of the children as they arrived in Harrisburg to be met head-on by television crews and reporters from the major newspaper wire services. The hearing itself was held according to established decorum, the children testifying about fireflies for a period of about 2 hours. The committee reported its unanimous support of the bill to the House of Representatives, and eventually the bill passed the House by an overwhelming vote of 156 to 22. Next, the Senate passed the firefly bill by a vote of 37 to 11. When the governor finally signed the bill (Act 59), the children were again in Harrisburg to watch the institution of a new state law. *Photuris pennsylvanica* officially took its place alongside the whitetail deer, ruffed grouse, and Great Dane as official state animals.

For Mrs. Holzwarth's class, this "happening" was much more than an exercise in choosing a state insect. It was an authentic, purposeful learning experience in which the children took direct political action and participated in meaningful legislative processes. They learned about petitioning and writing letters to their representatives, and they saw firsthand how government works. One child noted, "Now we have something to tell our grandchildren." Another, when asked if she would like to get another law passed, blurted, "Darn right! I'd like a law against homework. Homework gives you pimples!"

(As an aside, I recently heard of a group of fourth-graders in another Pennsylvania school district who replicated this adventure by voting for the chocolate chip cookie as the official "state cookie." They diligently followed the process used by Mrs. Holzwarth's class, but the bill died in committee—one of the legislators liked oatmeal/raisin cookies better!)

Social studies can be the single-most thrilling subject in the elementary school, for no other subject helps guide children through the fascinating world around them with such strength and power. Children come to school deeply curious about their surroundings, and social studies provides an ideal setting to utilize their inborn drive to explore and investigate. Social studies teachers understand that elementary school children are the most eager of all learners and that there seems to be a "natural social scientist" living within each. Therefore, their social studies classrooms are richer in variety, richer in stimulation, and richer in challenge than we might find for any other subject.

Good social studies teachers—the "Mrs. Holzwarths" of our world—bring an aura of distinction to their social studies classrooms; they obviously enjoy their work and value the lives they touch. There are no secret recipes or die-cast molds that might help us duplicate these special individuals; each is one of a kind. They know and love our nation and hold bright hopes for its future. Their sense of democratic values influences everything they do in their classrooms. These teachers know that young children are our future and the way they live and learn today becomes the way they will live and learn tomorrow. They expertly handle with keen insight and skill all the subtle professional tasks of a social studies program, and their instructional choices are based on a maze of complicated decisions. They subscribe to Mattioli's (2004) observation: "Teaching is a complex, non-routine and responsive endeavor. . . . As teachers, we have to be constantly aware of what we are doing in the classroom, why we are doing it and why we are doing it the way we are doing it. Teaching is not like Nike. It's not 'Just Do It'" (p. 8). So, teachers,

in order to make a difference in the lives of our nation's young citizens, must attain a wide-ranging collection of professional knowledge and skills.

The physical setting is important, as are the materials used to carry out social studies instruction, but a teacher's professional skills blended together with outstanding personal qualities are the most vital ingredients of good social studies programs. Personal and professional behaviors dictate the tone of the environment and make a lasting impact on the students, on their families, and on society. Few individuals are more significant in the lives of elementary school children than their parents, close relatives, and teachers. As Risinger (2002) so convincingly stated, "Although this may sound corny or naïve, I believe that teaching social studies is more than a job . . . even more than a profession: It's a mission, a calling" (p. 231). For that reason, elementary school social studies teachers should be among the finest people we know, but being a fine person does not in itself guarantee success in teaching. A superior teacher must also possess a set of professional skills founded on sound theoretical and research-based principles.

Successful teachers welcome the challenge of creating superb social studies classrooms and look to sound theory as the basis for their instruction. They deliberately build their programs on their best knowledge of whom they are teaching, what they are teaching, and how they are teaching. Successful social studies teachers have what it takes, in spirit and skill, to tailor-make their classrooms to fit the children who come to them. They demonstrate, without timidity, that they would rather be challenged than safe and bored.

It's a good idea to acquire this can-do spirit early in your career, for succeeding in risky situations may be a more powerful indicator of would-be greatness than any other single personality trait. I once heard that a strong feeling of self-confidence and willingness to take a risk are worth 50 IQ points. So work hard, dream a lot, and muster up the grit to establish a point of view. However, risks cannot, and should not, be taken unless your fundamentals are solid. Good social studies teachers never take risks blindly; their decisions are based on a strong foundation of knowledge and skill. Build that foundation in social studies education and take your risks there; it is the one area of the elementary school curriculum that openly invites the ideas and dreams of adventurous and creative teachers.

What Do You Remember about Social Studies?

Do you remember a "Mrs. Holzwarth" from your elementary school days? Think back to the time when you were an elementary school child. What memories do you have of a social studies teacher doing the things you liked, but also the things you didn't like? Make a list of both kinds of experiences. Share your list with your classmates, perhaps by constructing a group chart listing positive and negative experiences under their appropriate headings. What category of memories generated the most responses? I enjoy doing this activity on the first day of a semester with my classes. It is instructive both for my students and for me. Although I hesitate to describe this category first, the "dislike" category usually includes such memories as reading pages 79 to 81 in the text and writing answers to the questions at the end of the section (while the teacher corrected the weekly spelling tests), listening to the teacher drone on about how a cotton gin works (without benefit of a picture or model), being required to memorize facts about the early explorers of North America (where they came from, when they left their homeland, the date they arrived here, and where they explored), and copying "research reports" directly from the encyclopedia. After looking at and discussing the list of "dislikes," I ask the students to suggest single words that best sum up those types of instructional practices. *Boring, deadly, dull, mind-numbing,* and *humdrum* are some of the terms I remember.

Unfortunately, if their elementary school days had been filled with inconsequential classroom experiences like these, young adults tend to underestimate the hard work that goes into effective social studies instruction: "Is that all there is to it? Why, anybody can teach social studies to elementary school kids! Who can't tell them to take out their textbooks? Read a few pages? Answer the questions at the end of the section? Why does anyone need to take a college methods course to learn to do something so simple?" When faced with such an accusation, the best way to cope is to admit its legitimacy. Anybody *can* tell children to take out their textbooks to read a few pages. And, yes, it's true that anybody *can* ask them the questions printed at the end of a reading selection. The indictments are true, but there is one thing wrong—they miss the whole point of elementary school social studies education. Social studies is not meant to be taught that way; if it were, it's indeed true that there is no point in taking this course.

In contrast to the "dislike" category, the "like" category usually includes memories such as "Writing our own classroom constitution and holding elections," "Making web-based travel brochures to interest students from other states to visit our state," "Using milk cartons to build a model frontier town," "Role-playing a historical figure for a pageant of great people who lived during the Civil War," "Taking a field trip to the seashore to study the shells that washed up," "Cooking venison stew as we read the book *Sign of the Beaver*," "Hearing a Peace Corps volunteer tell of her experiences in Ethiopia," "Making a large mural of the rainforest," "Taking food and clothing to a homeless shelter," "Learning about the history and origin of the families of everyone in the classroom," "Performing a skit about an African naming ceremony," and "Making a large dragon as part of a Chinese New Year celebration." When asked to suggest single words to best sum up these experiences, students regularly come up with terms such as *fun, exciting, interesting, lively, rewarding, active,* and *instructive*. I bring closure to the activity by asking my students to think about these questions: "Which set of words would you want others to use when they describe *your* social studies program?" "What will you need to know or be able to do in order for that to happen?"

The resulting discussion usually draws out questions about the professional know-how required to carry out social studies programs that are fun, exciting, interesting, lively, rewarding, and active, but at the same time, instructive. Some worry that using "fun-type" programs all the time might create serious classroom management problems: "I'd like my social studies class to be fun and exciting, but I'm worried that the children will lose control." "Won't children think of the 'fun' activities as 'play time' and just fool around in class, not learning anything?" Thus, they are worried that a "fun-type" program reduces social studies to a series of insignificant events that most often end up in hard-to-handle behavior problems.

Others are concerned that being strictly serious about the content can do just the opposite—result in a dull and boring fact-filled social studies program: "How do I get across the important social studies content without being run-of-the-mill or ordinary?" "How can I teach content without communicating to the children that I think they're unskilled or ignorant?" They fear that "serious-type" social studies programs can become trivial and tedious for both the teacher and the children and are prone to provoke resentment and hostility in the children. In essence, the question becomes, "How can I make social studies fun and still maintain control over what the children do and understand?" One of the most significant challenges faced by social studies teachers is, on one hand, helping children acquire the knowledge, skills, and values that help prepare them for constructive participation in a democratic society and, on the other hand, organizing and conducting lessons that offer a blend of pleasure, intrigue, variety, active involvement, and excitement.

Back in 1933, John Dewey addressed this dilemma and offered some sage advice that remains relevant even today. In speaking to the serious–fun dichotomy of social studies instruction, Dewey (1933) addressed my students' dilemma when he wrote that if either is used exclusively, "play degenerates into fooling and work into drudgery" (p. 286). Instead of planning instruction at either end of the play–work dichotomy, Dewey recommended a program in which a balance between seriousness and fun is used to help promote learning. That is, teachers should build a personalized approach that brings in the best elements from both types of instruction and blends them in a way that best address the needs and interests of their students. The philosophy of this text echoes Dewey's view; when learning is fun, students become more interested and open to acquiring new knowledge. As a result, they see social studies as an important and fulfilling part of their lives and will strive for serious learning.

A dynamic constructivist social studies classroom helps children look on their world as a never-ending mystery. For many of you, facilitating such a program may require a radical shift in thinking. However, to start you on your way to acquiring a sound plan for teaching social studies, it is important to carefully examine these four fundamental questions:

1. What is social studies?
2. Why is social studies important?
3. What are the major goals of social studies instruction in the elementary school?
4. What is *dynamic* social studies?

What Is Social Studies?

Your first stop on the road of attaining the know-how essential for making content and methodological decisions in elementary school social studies classrooms is to acquire a clear understanding of the subject you will be teaching. Although social studies has been part of the elementary school curriculum for decades, it is not an easy subject to describe. An intelligible description usually begins, however, by exploring the difference between two potentially confusing terms: *social science* and *social studies*. The word *science*, derived from the Latin word *scientia*, means "knowledge." The term *social* has to do with the ways people live with others in human societies. So, putting the terms *social* and *science* together, we can define a *social science* as any of several disciplines that seek knowledge about societies and the relationships of individuals within societies. So, if you're interested in learning about how the people of India are governed, you will need to consult a social science that studies the operation of a society's political system. However, if you want to know where the finest coffee-growing regions of the world are located, you will need to consult a social science that specializes in studying places on Earth and their effects on human activity. Each separate social science has its own

Young children learn social studies by living it.

investigative methodology and specialized field of knowledge related to how people live together in social communities. *Social studies*, on the other hand, is a label for a school subject that integrates, or brings together, the social sciences in a coordinated, systematic fashion to help young people become good citizens in a culturally diverse, democratic society. To help you attain a more comprehensive awareness of the relationship between the social sciences and social studies, each will be discussed in the following sections.

The Six Major Social Sciences

The social sciences are a group of academic disciplines that use the scientific method in the study of humankind. Six major social sciences contribute the knowledge and processes that form the supportive backbone of most elementary school social studies programs: geography, history, political science, anthropology, sociology, and economics. Scientific inquiry is the major method of investigation for social scientists as they examine all aspects of society—from recounting past events and achievements to describing ways our daily lives are influenced by a host of new technologies. Their research provides insights that help us understand how individuals and groups make decisions, exercise power, and respond to change. The work associated with each discipline is distinctive, but specialists from one discipline often find that their research overlaps with work being done in another.

Geography

Geographers study people and places, the natural environment, and the capacity of Earth to support life. They ask questions about places on Earth and their relationship to the people who live in them. The first task in geography is to locate places, describing and explaining their physical characteristics (climate, vegetation, soil, and landforms) and their implications for human activity. Geographic inquiry continues by exploring the relationships that develop as people respond to and shape their physical and natural environments. It permits us to compare, contrast, and comprehend the regions of the world and their various physical and human features and patterns. This knowledge helps us to manage Earth's resources and to analyze a host of other significant problems.

History

Historians systematically investigate, analyze, and interpret the past. They use many sources of information while conducting their research, including interviews, government and institutional records, newspapers and other periodicals, photographs, film, diaries, letters, and photographs. In general, the sources of historical knowledge can be separated into three groupings: what has been written, what has been said, and what has been physically preserved. Historians often seek information from all three. Historians may specialize in studying a certain country or region or a specific time period. Some function as biographers, collecting detailed information on individuals. Others are genealogists, interested in tracing family histories. Some help preserve or study archival materials such as artifacts or historic buildings and sites.

History is an important discipline, but it is considered by some not to be a "true" social science because the processes of scientific inquiry are difficult to apply to the study of the past. This is not meant to disparage the efforts and expertise of historians, but only to indicate that historians are handicapped in their ability to control or reproduce the phenomena they are studying, as scientists do. Instead, historians must reconstruct events of the past from surviving evidence, and resulting interpretations are not always perfect—interpretations change as historians develop more sophisticated techniques of examining evidence and accumulate different kinds of evidence. Consider that, in the 1920s, many historians argued that the first large constructions in the world were the Egyptian pyramids. This contention was disproved in the 1960s with the introduction of carbon-14 dating, which indicated that northern European monuments such as Stonehenge were constructed earlier than most of the pyramids. Today, powerful new methodologies, many using computers, may offer historians the rigorous processes that a true science demands. But for now, history is treated as a discipline wavering somewhere in a misty region between the sciences and the humanities, often being thought of as a link between them, and incorporating methodologies from both fields of study. This is why you may see references to social studies as "history and the social sciences."

Civics (Political Science)

Civics is the study of the rights and duties of citizens. Because citizenship rights and duties are directly related to governance, the origin, development, and operation of governments (political science) are major objectives of the civics profession. The primary emphasis in civics study, then, is given to the role of citizens in the operation of governments. Political scientists conduct research on a wide range of subjects, such as the political relationships between the United States and other countries, alternative forms of government, and the decisions of the U.S. Supreme Court. Political scientists approach their subject through analyses of political institutions or policies, and by means of detailed examinations of the day-to-day workings of contemporary governments. Depending on the topic, political scientists take polls, conduct public opinion surveys, analyze election results, interview public officials, examine the speeches of politicians, study the actions of legislators and judges, and probe the beliefs and personalities of political leaders.

Anthropology

Anthropologists study people to find out about their physical, social, and cultural characteristics. They examine the total pattern of human behavior and its products particular to a special group (language, tools, beliefs, social forms, art, law, customs, traditions, religion, superstitions, morals, occupations, and so on). Anthropologists usually concentrate in one of four specialties—archaeology, sociocultural anthropology, linguistic anthropology, or biological-physical anthropology. Archaeology is the scientific study of earlier civilizations carried out by recovering and examining material evidence of the past, such as skeletal remains, fossils, ruins, implements, tools, monuments, and other items from past human cultures, in order to determine the history, customs, and living habits. Sociocultural anthropology is the study of customs, cultures, and social lives in settings that vary from nonindustrialized societies to modern urban centers. Linguistic anthropology looks at the role of language in various cultures. Biological-physical anthropology studies the evolution of the human body and analyzes how culture and biology influence one another. Most anthropologists specialize in one region of the world. Because of this immense scope of study, anthropology has often been described as a universal discipline, one that comprehensively studies cultures by looking at all aspects of their existence.

Sociology

Sociologists study society and social behavior by examining groups and social institutions, such as the family, government, religion, business, or school. They also study the behaviors and interactions of groups, analyzing the influence of group activities on individual members. Sociologists investigate the values and norms of groups to discover why group members behave as they do. They study how groups form, how they operate, and how they change. The organization of their study of groups centers on many questions, such as "What kinds of groups do people form in any given society?" "What are the expectations of the group members?" "What problems do the group members face?" "How does the group control its members?" To answer these questions, sociologists may visit a particular group, observe what the people in that group do, interview group members, or even live with a group for a short time to more completely understand its nature. The results of a sociologist's research aid educators, lawmakers, administrators, and others interested in resolving social problems and formulating public policy.

Economics

Economists study the production, distribution, and consumption of goods and services. They examine the ways economics affects all of our lives. From youngsters who save their allowance for a special toy, to college students who must scrape together enough money for tuition, through newlyweds who apply for a mortgage as they buy their first home, all people face situations where they attempt to satisfy unlimited wants with limited resources. Referred to as the *scarcity concept*, it is from this idea that a family of economics emerges. Because of scarcity, humans have attempted to find ways to produce more in less time with less material, by which specialization of labor was developed. From specialization has emerged the idea of interdependence, a reliance of people on one another that necessitates monetary, transportation, and communication systems. From interactions of these factors, a market system developed through which buyers and sellers produce and exchange goods or services. Finally, governments, responsible for controlling segments of the market system, ensure the welfare of all their citizens. Information about the economy—including the study of taxation, consumer economics, and economic policy—helps one assess pressing issues of the day.

The Social Science/Social Studies Connection

To understand how social studies gained life as a school subject, we must travel back in time to 1916 when waves of Europeans had arrived on the shores of America ready to find jobs in a recently industrialized nation. In this time of extraordinary social transformation, the National Education Association (NEA) searched for fresh approaches to education that might best assimilate these millions of immigrants and their children. Up to this time, the major purpose of elementary school education was to teach the 3Rs: reading, 'riting, and 'rithmetic. There were no social studies classes in elementary schools; rather, teachers were advised to nurture young citizens by reading stories that stressed such citizenship virtues as courage, honesty, fairness, and obedience. For example, teachers read tales about George Washington's cherry tree chopping (honesty) and silver dollar tossing (strength) exploits to teach children civic virtues. So, students learned about the honorable deeds of important people from the past through moralistic stories. Afterwards, the teacher made sure that the information contained in these stories was "learned by heart and, when forgotten, learned and learned again." The following statement, written by two historians in 1903, furnished support for those educational practices:

> In its effect on the mind, American history is distinctly to be commended. The principal reasons for the study of history are that it trains the memory, . . . exercises the judgment and sets before the students' minds a high standard of character. In all these respects, American history is inferior to that of no other country. The events which are studied and should be kept in memory are interesting in themselves and important to the world development. (Channing & Hart, 1903, p. 1)

The National Education Association established various study committees to examine whether this strong emphasis on factual memorization should remain the central priority of schooling in a "new age," or whether the voice of new, "progressive" educators should be accepted. Look how the following proposal from the emerging progressive educators differs from the quote you just read:

> The one thing that [history] ought to do, and has not yet effectively done, is to help us to understand ourselves and our fellows and the problems and prospects of

> mankind. It is this most significant form of history's usefulness that has been most commonly neglected. . . . It is high time we set to work boldly . . . to bring our education into the closest possible relation with the actual life and future duties of . . . those who fill our public schools. (Robinson, 1912, p. 134)

The NEA established a special committee to study if either of these contrasting philosophies might be more helpful than the other in addressing the twofold needs of assimilating immigrants into a new society and preparing an industrial workforce. After careful reflection, the committee suggested that the school curriculum and instructional practices should be brought more in tune with contemporary society. Supported by the work of leading educators such as Francis Parker and John Dewey, the NEA proposed that our schools should guarantee social efficiency by educating students to understand and resolve social problems; readying students for the job market in a changing world of business and industry; and developing in students practical skills related to health, hygiene, and nutrition. The committee recommended that school subjects should be practical.

To help achieve practical learning, the special NEA committee suggested a brand new school subject—*social studies*—as the major vehicle to help accomplish these goals. Making this proposal was a bold move, since never before had a school subject called *social studies* existed—not in the United States or anywhere else in the world. The only thing that was known was that this completely new subject would be responsible for promoting the idea of "social efficiency" in a rapidly changing society. The NEA (1916) envisioned social studies as "the subject matter related directly to the organization and development of human society, and to individuals as members of social groups" (p. 5). The "subject matter" for this new school subject was to be drawn from the three most influential social sciences of the time—history, geography, and civics—and blended together as one school subject for the purpose of helping children understand our American heritage and acquire the skills and sensitivities basic to constructive participation in our nation's democratic society. (It has now expanded to include the six social disciplines described earlier.) Thus, we can think of social studies as an amalgamation of content and processes from six major social sciences. Social studies, then, is the label used for the school subject that draws its primary content and processes from six social sciences. Rather than focus in depth on any single one, social studies combines each to provide a broad overview of human society, past and present (see Figure 1.1).

Defining the Term *Social Studies*

What could prevent such a deceptively simple idea from becoming immediately embraced by the educational community? An answer to that question was as difficult to arrive at in 1916 as it is today, for over the years splinter groups have presented conflicting views of what this new subject called *social studies* should be. According to some, their efforts have come up empty, for they are said to have

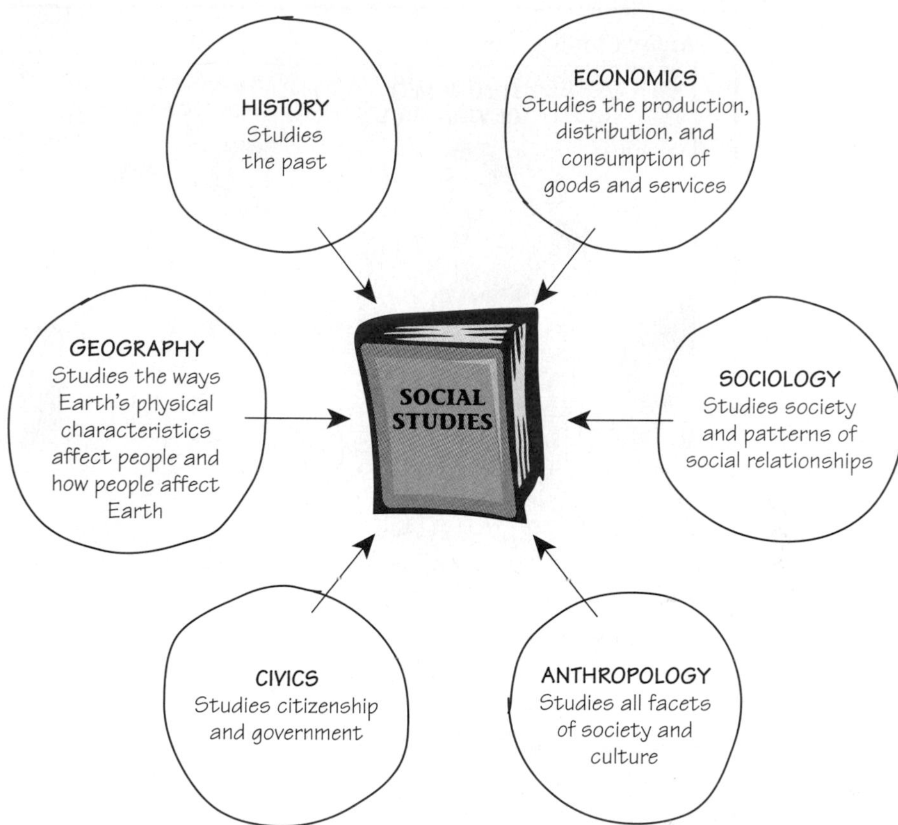

FIGURE 1.1 The Social Sciences

constructed nothing more than an endless maze of ambiguity, inconsistency, and contradiction. Finn (1988) elaborates on this point: "The great dismal swamp of today's school curriculum is not reading or writing, not math or science, not even foreign language study. It is social studies, a field that has been getting slimier and more tangled ever since it changed its name from history around 1916" (p. 16).

Students in social studies methods courses often become confused when they learn of the years of deep internal conflict: "After all these years, why can't social studies educators agree on the nature of this school subject?" To gain some perspective on this question, you must understand that, as with every sensitive educational issue, attempts to reshape social studies are sparked by experts holding strong opinions about how students learn best and what knowledge, skills, and values are most important for active citizenship participation. Such disagreements cannot be quickly resolved; years of controversy, disagreement, and debate are to be expected (see Figure 1.2).

After decades of carefully and patiently gazing at a clouded tangle of puzzle pieces, however, an intelligible, practical image of social studies has begun to

FIGURE 1.2 A Search for Identity

appear. Out of the hazy fog of uncertainty, razor-sharp patterns are beginning to take shape. The leading professional organization for social studies educators—the National Council for the Social Studies (NCSS) (1993b)—helped bring about harmony by aggressively addressing the nature of social studies and ultimately approving the following definition:

> Social studies is the integrated study of the social sciences and humanities to promote civic competence. Within the school program, social studies provides coordinated, systematic study drawing upon such disciplines as anthropology, archeology, economics, geography, history, law, philosophy, political science, psychology, religion, and sociology, as well as appropriate content from the humanities, mathematics, and natural sciences. The primary purpose of social studies is to help young people develop the ability to make informed and reasoned decisions for the public good as citizens of a culturally diverse, democratic society in an interdependent world. (p. 3)

With this NCSS initiative, social studies can now be defined and set apart as a viable school subject. (If you would like to impress your professor, you might like to visit the NCSS website, www.ncss.org, and order a T-shirt with the entire definition printed on the back!) Clearly, the definition has affirmed citizenship education as the primary purpose of social studies instruction, presented an argument for integrated content from the social sciences and other disciplines (expanded from political science, history, and geography), emphasized the need for higher-order thinking skills as opposed to memorization of facts, focused on the need for multicultural understandings, and stressed decision making and personal responsibility as important characteristics of good citizens. We will thoroughly examine these fundamental attributes throughout the remainder of this chapter.

Why Is Social Studies Important?

From the start of public schooling in the United States, the major purpose of elementary education has been to teach children the basic skills of reading, writing, and arithmetic. But, following the NEA's 1916 initiative, social studies took its important place in the curriculum for the primary purpose of preparing our nation's youth for civic participation. Today, it is accepted that our schools must not only help prepare children with the "three Rs" but also with the basic knowledge, skills, and civic virtues essential for active citizenship in the world of the twenty-first century. The survival of our democratic society depends on a citizenry who care for their country and for humanity itself. Will our students be delivered an education that cultivates the moral grit to stand up and cry out for the protection of our nation's future, or one that minimizes civic responsibility and respect for the legacies and principles of our families, neighborhoods, and national communities? How will our future citizens measure the purpose and quality of life in our nation?

Participatory Citizenship

These questions are not new; social studies educators have asked variations of these questions for years. From the first colony at Plymouth Rock to our bustling communities today, educators and community leaders have debated over the best way to fulfill their responsibility to educate America's young citizens. Every generation has experienced deep concern about how to place in its children's collective hands the trust and understanding required to protect peace and freedom and how to teach its youngsters tolerance, cooperation, and the skills of living together in a diverse, democratic society as well as in an increasingly interdependent world. As a nation, we have situated social studies instruction at the core of this responsibility because we are a proud people—a democratic republic of 305 million citizens, each of whom is part of a unique political venture. We prize our political processes, our institutions, our shared heritage, and our freedom.

To preserve and protect this prized inheritance, we call on our schools to fully prepare our youngsters as good citizens—individuals possessing the knowledge, skills, and attitudes required to participate in and maintain our democratic nation. We want our future citizens to respect our past as a democratic society and recognize the rich contributions of all groups who have made modern America a free and powerful nation. We want students to take active roles as champions of

freedom who stand up and cry out for the rights and responsibilities of citizenship. We want students to speak with their voices, actions, and votes for the improvement of the quality of life in our families, neighborhoods, nation, and world. The overriding purpose of social studies should be to provide students with the education required to guard and protect their cultural inheritance, to ready students for the most important duty they will be entrusted with in the new millennium—accepting the post that Thomas Jefferson called *the office of citizen*.

The preservation of our democracy depends on a system of education that prepares its young people to accept responsibility in society, but today's social commentators say we are failing that test. They sadly lament the growing apathy of today's adult citizens, describing our nation as being comprised of "civic couch potatoes." Submerged in public apathy, they reject such basic citizenship responsibilities as volunteering in civic or public arenas (PTA, town council, organizations that feed and clothe the poor); helping solve such real problems as eliminating drug abuse and homelessness; writing letters to the editor; deliberating and debating public policy; working for public interest groups; and voting.

Martin Rochester (2003) tells us that in Ancient Greece the word *idiot* referred to an individual who took no interest in public affairs. Rochester is discouraged that more and more young Americans seem to qualify as idiots in that sense. They are uninterested in political and civic life and have descended into "know-nothingism" and "do-nothingism." In order to produce fewer idiots, Rochester believes that we need to stress the importance of a common base of useful information, skills, and attitudes requisite for producing future citizens to be trustees of our democratic community. As teachers of future citizens, how can we help young adults resist social indifference and accept full responsibility as a stakeholder in our democratic nation?

Preparing students to participate in the political, social, and economic affairs of our democracy and to live together as good citizens in a drastically different world of the future requires a social studies program with citizenship education at its heart. A program centering on participatory citizenship must be made a regular part of school life to help students establish the sense of personal responsibility and accountability that forms a solid foundation to participate as adults in public life. Teachers must provide opportunities for students to go beyond the simple acquisition of facts; they must offer situations where learners use what they know to reason, to analyze, to create, and to evaluate. The NCSS Task Force on Early Childhood/Elementary Social Studies (1989) suggests:

> For children to develop citizenship skills appropriate to a democracy, they must be capable of thinking critically about complex societal problems and global problems. Teachers must arrange the classroom environment to promote data gathering, discussion, and critical reasoning by students. Another important aspect of citizenship is that of decision maker. Children must acquire the skills of decision-making, but also study the process that occurs as groups make decisions. . . . Children need to be equipped with the skills to cope with change. (p. 16)

A significant responsibility of social studies teachers, then, is to offer a sound program that promotes the knowledge, skills, and attitudes necessary for young people to make informed and reasoned decisions for the public good.

What Are the Major Goals of Social Studies Instruction in Elementary School?

As a democratic nation, citizens are expected to be not only knowledgeable but also thoughtful—able to make informed decisions based on national ideals and principles. These demands of democratic citizenship place tremendous demands on our schools: How is it possible for our nation's schools to teach patriotism in an open society? Several professional organizations have issued position statements describing goals outlining precisely how that question might be addressed throughout all levels of schooling, but the NCSS Task Force on Early Childhood/Elementary Social Studies (1989) has compiled a list specifically for the elementary school grades. The NCSS Task Force suggests that the traditional skills of reading, writing, and computing are necessary but not sufficient for young citizens to participate or even survive in a world demanding the kinds of independent and cooperative problem solving required to deal with complex social concerns. Therefore, for the elementary school, the following goals have been identified to help children accomplish what other subjects cannot help them achieve. The specialized social studies goals are divided into three broad areas:

- *Knowledge.* The social studies program should help students construct a rich and accurate background of information about the world at large and the world at hand; the world of the past and the world of the future. This knowledge base will provide the necessary foundation for emerging reflective thought. Even though elementary school children have difficulty with time concepts, they must develop a rich store of knowledge about their country's *history*. *Geography* is equally difficult, but social studies provides continuing opportunities for children to understand the relationships of people with their environment. Concepts from *anthropology* and *sociology* provide understanding of how the multiplicity of cultures within society and the world have developed. Children need to recognize the contributions of each culture and to explore its value system. Knowledge from *sociology, economics,* and *political science* allows children to understand the institutions within the society and to learn about their roles within groups.
- *Skills.* The skills that are primary to social studies are those related to maps and globes, such as understanding and using locational and directional terms. Skills that are shared with other parts of the curriculum but may be most powerfully taught through social studies include communication skills such as writing and speaking; research skills such as collecting, organizing, and interpreting data; and reading skills such as reading pictures, books, maps, charts, and graphs.
- *Values and Beliefs.* The early years are ideal for children to begin to understand core civic principles, or core democratic values (i.e., justice, individual rights,

truth, the common good, equality of opportunity, and diversity), especially in terms of the smaller social entities of the family, classroom, and community. Children can also develop, within the context of social studies, positive attitudes toward knowledge and learning and develop a spirit of inquiry that will enhance their understanding of their world so that they will become rational, humane, participating, effective members of a democratic society.

Effective social studies teaching, then, begins with a clear understanding of the subject's distinctive instructional goals. In general, the goals include the categories of *knowledge, thinking skills,* and *democratic values and beliefs. Knowledge* does not refer to a predetermined collection of facts for students to memorize, but to understandings that students construct by connecting new learning to their previous experiences in and out of school. The *democratic values and beliefs* are drawn from various sources, but especially from the Declaration of Independence and the United States Constitution with its Bill of Rights. These beliefs form the basic principles of our democratic society. Elementary school social studies programs also prepare students to tie together knowledge with beliefs and values using *thinking skills,* such as acquiring and processing information in order to investigate problems and making well-informed decisions that are defensible according to democratic principles.

What Is *Dynamic* Social Studies?

The goals for social studies education in the elementary school are not unlike the goals of social studies education in general, but the environment within which these goals are achieved is much different for these youngsters than for any other level of schooling. Elementary school children come to the classroom with a high degree of natural energy, curiosity, and imagination. They are adventurous, curious, eager to learn, energetic, always in motion, loud, and emotional. Elementary school children are also great socializers and are eager to fit in. Consequently, they like group activities and projects. These are but a few of the characteristics that lead elementary school teachers to establish a one-of-a-kind, developmentally appropriate learning environment for their young learners.

If the young people of our democratic nation are to grow into effective citizens, then social studies must be delivered in a developmentally appropriate way during the elementary years. Knowledge, skills, and attitudes necessary for informed and thoughtful participation in society require an active, engaging, enjoyable, and rewarding system of instruction that results in meaningful and substantial learning. I refer to such a system as *dynamic social studies* largely because it places students in a classroom environment that encourages them to rediscover the "young social scientists" within. Much as adult social scientists, they hold a powerful desire to answer questions about their world and are captivated by spectacular phenomena of their social surroundings. One of the greatest joys of practicing adult social scientists, for example, is to answer a question with the words, "I don't know," because it is exciting to go on and try to discover the unknown. Not knowing is the fuel for their furnace; their joy is in the challenge of finding out something new. And, if the truth is told by my social scientist friends, most would keep doing what they do even if they weren't paid for it. Isn't that just like the natural curiosity of childhood?

We encourage and support this sense of wonder when we open children's minds to the creative spirit that floods the social sciences. Just think about the deep sense of wonder our youngsters display as they operate on their world like "young social scientists": A "geographer" bends down to study the effect of sand sifting through her fingers; an "economist" helps determine how the class will obtain the money necessary to buy a sapling for the school playground; a "political scientist" petitions the principal for a new piece of playground equipment; an "anthropologist" leafs through an old yearbook and marvels at the hairstyle and clothing differences; a "historian" watches and listens as a senior citizen augments stories of World War II with fascinating memorabilia. These children have not acquired the professional credentials of practicing social scientists, but they are curious enough about their social world to act on their curiosities. That is the basic premise of this text: Children are curious about their world and strive to seek answers to their questions so they can obtain knowledge about their wondrous social environment. Anyone who has ever observed children in their private "child's world" must conclude that they are doers and thinkers; in other words, they are natural social scientists.

The model of dynamic social studies that will play a major role in describing the teacher's role as well as in shaping the remainder of this text is shown in Figure 1.3. It is simple, but the model brings together in a clear way the major components of dynamic social studies instruction. The model has five components, each of which must be in place for effective learning to take place: functional content, cross-curricular integration, constructivist teaching practices, intrinsic motivation, and respect for diversity.

Functional Content

Social scientists must be informed, for their inquiries do not spring forth from a knowledge vacuum. Social scientists launch their investigations from a complete and organized knowledge base related to the problems they want to solve. It is when they encounter a new phenomenon that cannot be explained in terms of their organized knowledge base that social scientists become energized to seek new information that might alter or replace their "trusty framework." Think about how this works: The unanticipated discovery of what was going on with Maryland's state insect fueled Mrs. Holzwarth's students' strong interest in learning how to propose one for Pennsylvania. In this case, the youngsters were not completely fulfilled with simply accepting information at face value.

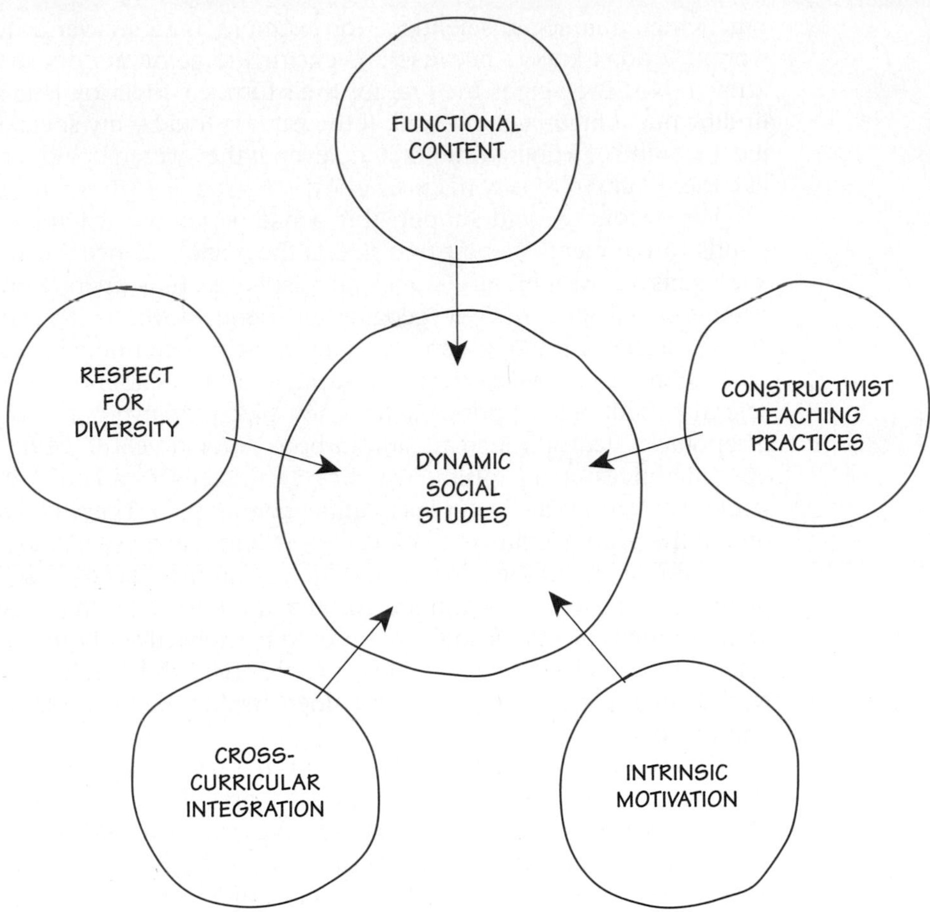

FIGURE 1.3 Dynamic Social Studies

Content knowledge in dynamic social studies programs is not treated merely as facts to be ingested and memorized, but as a base of operation through which questions or problems are explored and confronted. If students are satisfied merely to store the information and retrieve it for others, they could not be considered "young social scientists." If children are to become explorers and questioners rather than passive acceptors of information, they must know enough about something to raise questions, discover something new, or solve a problem. Therefore, dynamic social studies instruction does not stop with the "what" of the social sciences, but continues on with the "how" of the social science disciplines. Students who are learning about geography, for example, must not only have knowledge of geography but also experience how geography works and what geographers do.

The hardest lesson for beginning teachers is to learn that *telling* is not *teaching; told* is not *taught*. Those who consider teaching as information transmission ignore the paramount role of the learner in learning; students will not learn content if they cannot attach meaning to it. Therefore, if children are going to develop the skills appropriate for active citizenship in a democracy, they must be capable of thinking about complex social problems in a classroom environment that promotes decision making and problem solving. Thinking and content are clearly inseparable in dynamic social studies programs.

The most basic responsibility of dynamic social studies teachers, then, is to select "functional content," or a meaningful knowledge core that furnishes the information necessary to become aware of, identify, and solve problems. This component can be thought of as the background of subject area content that spurs the questioning mind and allows one to solve problems or do original work. A firm knowledge background spurs questions, and these questions, in turn, provide the context for obtaining more knowledge.

Curriculum Scope and Sequence

Think for a moment about all the social studies knowledge you have learned over the years. Some facts, such as the name of the seventeenth president of the United States or the major exports of Bolivia, may have been long forgotten but there is probably more that you remember to this day and feel every child should know, too. What five specific facts or understandings do you feel are indispensable for today's youth? Write them down. Compare your list with those of your classmates. Should children learn about important people like Benjamin Franklin, Confucius, and Harriet Tubman; or important places like the Gobi Desert, the Fertile Crescent, and the rain forests of the Amazon? What about important things like pueblos, railroads, and the Great Wall of China; or events such as the Battle of Bull Run, the rise of Christianity, and the discovery of Mohenjo-Daro? Did anyone list significant ideas such as Henry Ford's assembly line, Hinduism, or the Bill of Rights?

When we ask the question, "What content from the social science disciplines should be selected for our social studies program?" we are dealing with the *scope* of the program, or *what* will be taught. A second important question is, "When is the most developmentally appropriate time to teach the selected content?" Answers to this question create the *sequence*, or order, in which the content is treated.

There are a number of possible ways to select and sequence the content but the most traditionally accepted system is referred to as the *expanding environment approach*. No one knows exactly how this system came into existence, but beginning in the 1930s, Lucy Sprague Mitchell (1934) started the ball rolling by proposing that children's understandings of their world developed through a series of sequential stages, beginning with an awareness of what was nearest to them to that which was farthest away—beginning with the "here and now" of their lives and gradually expanding their environments outward. Mitchell pictured a child's growing awareness of her or his world much like the ripples that radiate out after throwing a pebble into a pond. The first ripple can be considered knowledge gained about one's body and the physical characteristics of the immediate surroundings (crib, play area, room, house); the next ripple includes knowledge of the home, family, friends, relatives, and other significant people in the environment; the next focuses on the classroom, school, and other familiar environments such as the street, neighborhood, and the homes of friends and relatives; and, as the child matures, constant investigations open up new environments, so succeeding ripples spread out to the community, the state, the United States, the hemisphere, and the world. Mitchell suggested that social studies content should be organized with respect to this natural progression—begin with the self, home, and school in grade 1, then widen to the neighborhood in grade 2, to the community in grade 3, and systematically outward to the state in grade 4, United States in grade 5, and the Western hemisphere or world in grade 6. In the 1930s, when the new social studies curricula were becoming firmly entrenched, the overwhelming pattern of content selection became the expanding environment approach. Likewise, when textbook companies began to publish their first social studies textbooks, the overwhelming scope and sequence pattern was the expanding environment approach.

Social studies educators favor the "I Like Me" self-concept emphasis early in the expanding environment approach because it is important that children feel good about themselves before they can be expected to learn anything academically. The idea is that if we start early, we can reduce the likelihood that children's self-concepts will become fueled by negative influences. Self-concept can be nurtured in warm classrooms with warm teachers. If we have those things, we maximize the chance that children will grow in a positive direction both intellectually and emotionally. The charming example shown in Figure 1.4 is a free-form poem written in a social studies program that was focused on helping children acquire a positive self-concept and learn to participate as members of a compassionate classroom society. The teacher took deliberate steps to encourage children to be positive, to smile, and to feel special. The poem was Algonquin Patee's heartwarming expression of what that classroom did for him—being unconditionally accepted and loved for one's good (and maybe not-so-good) attributes!

FIGURE 1.4 Self-Concept Poem

Paul Hanna (1963) reaffirmed the concept of expanding environments in an article so influential that his name is most closely associated with the expanding environment approach today. In 1983, the NCSS organized a task force on scope and sequence to study whether the expanding environment approach remained suitable for contemporary times. The task force reaffirmed the merit of the expanding environment approach (shown in Figure 1.5), and it remains the overwhelming favorite among social studies curriculum developers and textbook publishers today.

A dynamic social studies program, then, must provide for consistent and cumulative learning from kindergarten through the middle school years. Content is extended and enriched at each grade level, students building on knowl-

FIGURE 1.5 Expanding Environment Scope and Sequence

Kindergarten—Awareness of Self in a Social Setting
Providing socialization experiences that help children bridge their home life with the group life of school.
Grade 1—The Individual in Primary Social Groups: Understanding School and Family Life
Continuing the socialization process begun in kindergarten, but extending to studies of families (variations in the ways families live, the need for rules and laws).
Grade 2—Meeting Basic Needs in Nearby Social Groups: The Neighborhood
Studying social functions such as education, production, consumption, communication, and transportation in a neighborhood setting.
Grade 3—Sharing Earth-Space with Others: The Community
Focusing on the community in a global setting, stressing social functions such as production, transportation, communication, distribution, and government.
Grade 4—Human Life in Varied Environments: The Region
Emphasizing the region, an area of the earth defined for a specific reason; the home state is studied as a political region where state regulations require it.
Grade 5—People of the Americans: The United States and Its Close Neighbors
Centering on the development of the United States as a nation in the Western Hemisphere, with particular emphasis on developing affective attachments to the principles on which the nation was founded; Canada and Mexico also studied.
Grade 6—People and Cultures: The Eastern Hemisphere
Focusing on selected people and cultures of the Eastern Hemisphere, directed toward an understanding and appreciation of other people through development of such concepts as language, technology institutions, and belief systems.
Grade 7—A Changing World of Many Nations: A Global View
Providing an opportunity to broaden the concept of humanity within a global context; focus is on the world as the home of many different people who strive to deal with the forces that shape their lives.
Grade 8—Building a Strong and Free Nation: The United States
Studying the "epic of America," the development of the United States as a strong and free nation; emphasis is on social history and economic development, including cultural and aesthetic dimensions of the American experience.

Source: Task Force on Scope and Sequence. (1984). In search for a scope and sequence for social studies. *Social Education, 48*(4), 376–385. Reprinted by permission.

edge and skills already learned while receiving preparation for that which is yet to come.

National Curriculum Standards

The expanding environment approach, then, has enjoyed life as the basic curriculum structure that most school districts and textbook companies have used to organize elementary school social studies for well over 50 years. Despite the popularity of the expanding environment approach, however, social studies came under heavy fire during the mid-1980s when all of education was criticized in reports such as *A Nation at Risk* (National Commission on Excellence in Education, 1983): "If an unfriendly foreign power had attempted to impose on America the mediocre instructional performance that exists today, we might well have viewed it as an act of war" (p. 9). For social studies in particular, standardized test results indicated that America's students did not have the knowledge required to make informed decisions about issues that affect them, their families, and their communities. Richard Paxton (2003) reported that these studies produced some fascinating results—for example, 14 percent of U.S. teens identified Abraham Lincoln as our country's first president. The same percentage said that our country celebrates its independence from France each July 4, and 11 percent named John Adams, our second president (succeeding Abe Lincoln?) as the composer of *The Star-Spangled Banner*, while 9 percent believed it was Betsy Ross! In response to these results, some argued that it was the responsibility of social studies programs to move "back to the basics" and teach essential elements of lasting knowledge that children need in order to do well on achievement tests. While the expanding environment approach maintained its popularity as the organizational framework for most social studies curricula, many felt it resulted in school programs that lacked substantial content, especially during the early elementary grades.

By 1990, in reaction to this considerable educational faultfinding, President George H. W. Bush brought together our nation's governors to discuss national educational policy and to determine what might be needed to improve our schools. Their discussions were summarized in the well-known *America 2000*—six national goals for public education. Goal 3, the most noteworthy of all, stated, "By the year 2000, American students will leave grades 4, 8, and 12 having demonstrated competency over challenging subject matter including English, mathematics, science, history, and geography; and every school in America will ensure that all students use their minds well, so they may be prepared for responsible citizenship, further learning, and productive employment in our modern society" (U.S. Department of Education, 1991, pp. 5–6).

A great deal of attention was given to *America 2000*, prompting our nation's leading professional organizations to develop content standards (expectancies of what all students should know and be able to do at the completion of their education) in various subject areas. In addition, most states created their own educational standards and new measures to promote assessment. Initiating a search of your state's department of education website should help access its social studies standards. The NCSS was quick to establish a task force to define what the standards should be for social studies. The central questions guiding the members were: What will students be taught? How will students be taught? How will student achievement be evaluated? Using these three questions as a guide, the task force worked for over one year before publishing *Curriculum Standards for Social Studies: Expectations of Excellence* (NCSS, 1994).

The social studies curriculum standards are expressed as 10 thematic statements that each begin with these identical words: "*Social studies programs should include experiences that provide for the study of . . . .*" For example, the first thematic strand reads, "Social studies programs should include experiences that provide for the study of *culture and cultural diversity*." When presented in list form, this thematic strand is preceded by a roman numeral and shortened thusly, *I. Culture*. Similarly, each of the 10 themes that serve as organizing strands for the social studies curriculum are listed in the same way:

I. Culture
II. Time, Continuity, and Change
III. People, Places, and Environments
IV. Individual Development and Identity
V. Individuals, Groups, and Institutions
VI. Power, Authority, and Governance
VII. Production, Distribution, and Consumption
VIII. Science, Technology, and Society
IX. Global Connections
X. Civic Ideals and Practices

Each of these thematic strands is comprehensively explained in separate chapters of the standards document (see Figure 1.6 for a condensed version). Then, in separate chapters for each of three school levels (early grades, middle grades, and high school), performance expectations and two or three examples of classroom activities are put forward. For example, the *performance expectations* for the first theme, "Culture," are as follows (NCSS, 1994):

How Global is the Curriculum

Go to MyEducationLab, select the topic NCSS Standards, and watch the video entitled "Ethnic Diversity and Standards Planning," and complete the questions that accompany it.

Social studies programs should include experiences that provide for the study of culture and cultural diversity, so that the learner can:

a. explore and describe similarities and differences in the ways groups, societies, and cultures address similar human needs and concerns;
b. give examples of how experiences may be interpreted differently by people from diverse cultural perspectives and frames of reference;
c. describe ways in which language, stories, folktales, music, and artistic creations serve as expressions of culture and influence behavior of people living in a particular culture;
d. compare ways in which people from different cultures think about and deal with their physical environment and social conditions; and
e. give examples and describe the importance of cultural unity and diversity within and across groups. (p. xiii)

FIGURE 1.6 Curriculum Standards for Social Studies

Ten Thematic Strands
Ten themes serves as organizing strands for the social studies curriculum at every school level (early, middle, and high school); they are interrelated and draw from all of the social science disciplines and other related disciplines and fields of scholarly study to build a framework for social studies curriculum design.
I. Culture Human beings create, learn, and adapt culture. Human cultures are dynamic systems of beliefs, values, and traditions that exhibit both commonalities and differences. Understanding culture helps us understand ourselves and others.
II. Time, Continuity, and Change Human beings seek to understand their historic roots and to locate themselves in time. Such understanding involves knowing what things were like in the past and how things change and develop—allowing us to develop historic perspective and answer important questions about our current condition.
III. People, Places, and Environments Technological advancements have ensured that students are aware of the world beyond their personal locations. As students study content related to this theme, they create their spatial views and geographic perspectives of the world; social, cultural, economic, and civic demands mean that students will need such knowledge, skills, and understandings to make informed and critical decisions about the relationship between human beings and their environment.
IV. Individual Development and Identity Personal identity is shaped by one's culture, by groups, and by institutional influences. Examination of various forms of human behavior enhances understanding of the relationships between social norms and emerging personal identities, the social processes which influence identity formation, and the ethical principles underlying individual action.
V. Individuals, Groups, and Institutions Institutions exert enormous influence over us. Institutions are organizational embodiments to further the core social values of those who comprise them. It is important for students to know how institutions are formed, what controls and influences them, how they control and influence individuals and culture, and how institutions can be maintained or changed.
VI. Power, Authority, and Governance Understanding of the historic development of structures of power, authority, and governance and their evolving functions in contemporary society is essential for the emergence of civic competence.
VII. Production, Distribution, and Consumption Decisions about exchange, trade, and economic policy and well-being are global in scope and the role of government in policy making varies over time and from place to place. The systematic study of an interdependent world economy and the role of technology in economic decision making is essential.

VIII.	**Science, Technology, and Society** Technology is as old as the first crude tool invented by prehistoric humans, and modern life as we know it would be impossible without technology and the science which supports it. Today's technology forms the basis for some of our most difficult social choices.
IX.	**Global Connections** The realities of global interdependence require understanding of the increasingly important and diverse global connections among world societies before there can be analysis leading to the development of possible solutions to persisting and emerging global issues.
X.	**Civic Ideals and Practices** All people have a stake in examining civic ideals and practices across time, in diverse societies, as well as in determining how to close the gap between present practices and the ideals upon which our democracy is based. An understanding of civic ideals and practices of citizenship is critical to full participation in society.

Source: Nickell, P. (1995). Pullout feature: Thematically organized social studies. *Social Studies & The Young Learner, 8,* 1–8. © National Council for the Social Studies. Reprinted by permission.

Following a presentation of each *standard* and associated *performance expectations*, the chapters describe *classroom activities* to illustrate how the standards and performance expectations can be applied. For example, to meet performance expectations a, b, and d, the experiences of Carlene Jackson are recounted. Before the first day of school, Jackson examined her class list and inferred from the children's surnames that her class was a rich mix of cultural backgrounds—Mexican, Vietnamese, Korean, African American, and European American. By the end of the first month of school, Jackson and her students decided to study and compare how families meet their basic needs of food, clothing, and shelter in five places: their community; Juarez, Mexico; Hanoi, Vietnam; Lagos, Nigeria; and Frankfurt, Germany. Throughout the unit of study, Jackson and her students read books, looked at photos and slides, watched videos, and talked to speakers from their designated cities. The students honed their reading, writing, speaking, and map-reading skills. They created a chart summarizing the data they collected. You can request a copy of the Curriculum Standards for Social Studies (Bulletin 89) by writing or phoning the National Council for the Social Studies or visiting the NCSS website:

National Council for the Social Studies
8555 Sixteenth Street, Suite 500
Silver Spring, MD 20910
(301) 588-1800
www.ncss.org/links/home.html

As with most breaks from long-established practices, the standards movement brought forth passionate support as well as blistering criticism. In speaking of the

advantages of standards at the time, Resnick wrote "Standards and assessments [will] help bring about better student outcomes—a different quality and higher level of student achievement" (cited in O'Neil, 1993, p. 17). In effect, standards had become "images of excellence" for their proponents.

Supporting this "image of excellence" was the *No Child Left Behind Act of 2001 (NCLB)*, a landmark in educational reform signed into law by President George W. Bush in 2002. President Bush described this law as the "cornerstone of my administration." The legislation called for an accountability system ensuring that all children—including children of color, from low-income families, with disabilities, and of limited English proficiency—are prepared by our schools to be successful, participating members of our democracy. Under No Child Left Behind, each state was required to assess every public school student's progress in reading and math in each of grades 3 through 8 and at least once during grades 10 through 12. By school year 2007–2008, assessments in science were added. These assessments aligned with state academic content and achievement standards and help provide parents with objective data on where their children stand academically.

How Global is the Curriculum

Go to MyEducationLab, select the topic Economics, and watch the video entitled "Theme: Production, Distribution, and Consumption," and complete the questions that accompany it.

Social studies educators supported NCLB's goal of narrowing the achievement gap in reading, writing, math, and science, for they acknowledged that these subjects provide the knowledge and skills necessary for living in a literate and numerate world. However, social studies educators were dismayed that social studies was not included in NCLB's basic program requirements. Sanchez (2007) explained, "These are trying times for the social studies in the elementary school classroom. The current emphasis on reading and math, and more recently science, has had an adverse impact on the instructional time available for quality social studies instruction" (p. P1). Haefner and colleagues (2007) supported Sanchez's conviction: "The reduction or disappearance of social studies from the elementary curriculum is a problem occurring in many states across the nation" (p. 26). Neill and Guisbond (2005) described how the pressures of NCLB have influenced one student's typical school day: "In the morning we read. Then we go to Mrs. Withaus and read. Then after lunch we read. Then we read some more" (p. 31).

According to Pascopella (2005), because social studies has not been included as an area of assessment in NCLB, the targeted assessments have a significantly harmful impact on social studies: "Increased attention to math and language arts under the federal No Child Left Behind law is squeezing out social studies. Many states have standards in social studies so teachers are expected to cover the topic, but without being attached to a high-stakes test, the subject has lost ground. . . . What little social studies is taught usually consists of "laundry lists"—vocabulary words, dates and peoples' names . . . which is just boring" (p. 30).

Mattioli (2004) decries the "second-class" status for social studies and suggests that social studies has more importance as a basic subject in the elementary school curriculum now than ever before:

> What is more basic than giving students the knowledge and skills to function in, care for, and nurture our democratic nation? What is more basic than teaching children about their personal power to impact change in their own lives, this coun-

try and the world? What is more basic than teaching a child to value justice, equality and fair play? What then is more basic than citizenship education? What is more basic than social studies? (p. 7)

The NCLB legislation appears to have created a situation in stark contrast to a report from the NCSS Task Force on Early Childhood/Elementary Social Studies that recommends that, given the importance of social studies in the elementary school, *20 percent of the school day*—which includes reading/language arts, science, mathematics, and the arts—be devoted to social studies instruction. The Working Group of Social Studies Discipline Organizations (2007), including the National Council for the Social Studies, sent a statement to the Senate Committee on Health, Education, and Labor warning that if NCLB continues to ignore social studies in its basic program requirements, an increased "civic achievement gap" will be sure to result:

How Global is the Curriculum

Go to MyEducationLab, select the topic Government / Citizenship, and watch the video entitled "Theme: Civic Ideals and Practices," and complete the questions that accompany it.

> Evidence of the civic achievement gap is rampant. Measures of knowledge and skills reveal lower scores for Blacks and Hispanics, those from single parent families, and those who are poor. Civic attitudes, as reflected in levels of political and social trust, political efficacy, and civic duty are significantly lower for those who are poor and/or of minority or immigrant status. Civic behaviors, including voting, campaign work, and community activity, follow the same pattern. (p. 30)

The working group warned that these indicators of civic engagement need to be addressed to the same extent as NCLB has addressed indicators of the academic achievement gap.

Cross-Curricular Integration

Because the current emphasis on reading and math, and now science, has had such an objectionable impact on the time allotted for quality social studies instruction, frustrated teachers have begun to search for alternative ways to return social studies to its place as a respected component of the elementary school curriculum. In their efforts, most have echoed the words of Sanchez (2007), who suggested that "integrating disciplines is a powerful way to advocate for the social studies because it secures a place for the social studies within the busy school day" (p. P1). So, in their effort to secure a more worthwhile place for the social studies program, teachers are now challenging the traditional practice of separating each school subject into its own detached block of instructional time; in other words, they are questioning the idea of treating reading, writing, math, science, or social studies as separate subjects with very little concern for or attention to the connections they have to one another. Instead, dynamic social studies teachers are seeking ways to connect, or integrate, the subjects. By doing so, teachers are not only able to effectively and efficiently use the allotted amount of time during a busy school day but they are also able to fashion more highly interesting and challenging learning opportunities.

Where does social studies fit into this idea of cross-curricular integration? Advocates for more social studies would lift their voices in a common declaration, "In the forefront!" They contend that social studies is as much of an appropriate setting for integrating the elementary school curriculum as a hardwood floor is for playing basketball. Making sense of the world requires students to *read* about the various people and places that are spread about our Earth; good *literature* transcends time and space as readers learn about and empathize with people whose stories take place in distinctive cultural, historical, or physical settings; *math* helps students understand how numbers assist people to manage the intricacies of their world; the *physical sciences* lend themselves to the same kinds of question asking and decision making as the social sciences, and both are bound together by a problem-centered approach that is used to examine the relationship of people and their environment; and the *arts and humanities* inform students about cultures through the highest forms of personal expression—visual arts, music, dance, and drama. Students not only learn about cultures through the arts but they also have rich opportunities to actively express their own creative ideas. As is plainly evident, the absorbing story of humankind cannot be told without drawing from all areas of the curriculum.

The National Council for the Social Studies (1993a) has supported the integrative nature of elementary school instruction with this declaration from its prominent position statement, *A Vision of Powerful Teaching and Learning in the Social Studies:*

> Social studies teaching integrates across the curriculum. It provides opportunities for students to read and study text materials, appreciate art and literature, communicate orally and in writing, observe and take measurements, develop and display data, and in various other ways to conduct inquiry and synthesize findings using knowledge and skills taught in all school subjects. . . . Particularly in elementary and middle schools, instruction can feature social studies as the core around which the rest of the curriculum is built. (p. 217)

Examine the following classroom scenario to see how one effective, inspired teacher used cultural artifacts as primary motivation for a significant interdisciplinary activity. How many different traditional elementary school subjects can you find integrated into this experience?

> Aba Oshodi introduced his students to the the Igbo (or Ibo) people of southeastern Nigeria by reading Ifeoma Onyefulu's award-winning book, *My Grandfather is a Magician: Work and Wisdom in an African Village* (Frances Lincoln). This is the story of a little Nigerian boy who is confused about what kind of job he would like to do when he grows up. He is exposed to several role models—his father is a teacher, his mother owns a bakery, his aunt is a doctor, and his uncle is a blacksmith. But his grandfather seems wiser and stronger than any of them, for he is a traditional healer who knows about the special medicinal powers of plants and trees. In addition to anticipating the

NCSS STANDARDS

I. *Culture*
III. *People, Places, and Environments*
IX. *Global Connections*

little boy's decision, the children enjoyed learning about many interesting facets of Igbo village life.

To capitalize on his students' newfound interest in African village life, Mr. Oshodi took his fifth-grade students on a field trip to an Igbo arts exhibit at a local cultural museum. The exhibit displayed more than 100 objects produced by Igbo artists and craftspersons. The items at the exhibit included wooden totemic sculptures, pottery, textiles, examples of painting and body adornment, and a variety of masks. Although wood predominated, as it does in most African art, the exhibit also included objects of bronze, iron, and ivory.

The purpose of the visit was to stimulate further interest in the Igbo through the beauty of their creative arts. Mr. Oshodi's goal appeared to have been achieved as the students returned full of questions ripe for investigation: "Why are the small totemic figures important to the Igbo?" "What was the purpose of those elaborate masks on display?" Returning to the classroom, Mr. Oshodi capitalized on the students' spontaneous interests and established research groups that ventured into the world of the Igbo through visits to Internet sites, informational books, newspapers, and other references, including informational pamphlets from the exhibit.

A whole new world opened up to Mr. Oshodi's students—they learned that Igbo art forms were a direct expression of their culture. For example, the small wooden totemic figures (ikenga) symbolized traditionally masculine attributes such as strength, courage, and aggressiveness. These carved figures were kept in the men's meetinghouse. Among women, body jewelry such as ivory and brass anklets symbolized prestige and social position. The masks played a major role in the Igbo's masquerades in which male performers acted out different aspects of their spiritual ideals.

The Igbo culture became more clearly understood and appreciated each day as its rich heritage and creativity came alive in the classroom. After the children had amassed sufficient information to fulfill their curiosities, Mr. Oshodi suggested a number of models or displays that the groups might generate to share what they had discovered. One group created jewelry for a mini-display; another made a model of an Igbo mask; a third designed calabashes with intricate geometric designs; a fourth assembled a replica ikenga. Each group described its project by writing a short informational outline with the following information:

- What is the item?
- From what is it made?
- How is it used?
- What do we have in our culture that compares to this item?

Each group demonstrated and described its item to the class. At the conclusion of the experience, Mr. Oshodi asked his students what they had learned about the Igbo culture from the items they researched. Through the group assessment tasks, the children became creators of original art forms that communicated the discoveries they made as captivated learners.

By integrating subject areas in the elementary school, teachers help establish an environment that engages students in highly focused and meaningful learning experiences. Children strive for and flourish in such an environment, for the very nature of childhood fuels active curiosity. The integrated curriculum not only helps satisfy such natural curiosity but it also helps build connections among the things the children experience. Additionally, as important as these outcomes can be in the overall developmental scheme of childhood, the integrated curriculum helps preserve a place for social studies in the elementary school curriculum.

Constructivist Teaching Practices

The importance of a curriculum that integrates social studies among the other disciplines cannot be overstated, but an equally significant issue that continues to engage the minds of social studies educators is, "What is the best way teachers might carry out instruction in such a program?" Competing theories and philosophies of learning and teaching have been proposed throughout the years, but the *constructivist* model has convincingly burst to the forefront today and will serve as the model for dynamic social studies instruction in this textbook. Constructivism isn't new or radical or revolutionary. Jean Piaget and Lev Vygotsky developed the theories to support constructivism almost 70 years ago. John Dewey advocated an instructional system we now call constructivism back at the turn of the twentieth century; Jerome Bruner did the same a few decades later.

In a nutshell, constructivists believe that children build their own knowledge of the world as they attempt to establish connections between what they already know and that which is new to them. Sometimes, children can smoothly fit the demands of a new learning task into their existing cognitive frameworks. When that happens, the children enter a state of "cognitive comfort" because they were able to successfully apply their background of existing knowledge in their effort to make sense of the learning task. At other times, the children's existing conception of the world can be so far removed from the new learning experience that it creates a state of "cognitive distress"—the children have some difficulty associating what they already know and cannot use their existing knowledge to immediately unlock meaning from a learning task. It is at this point that children become driven to resolve the difference: "Why doesn't this new information fit in with what I already know?" When this discrepancy challenges their expectations, children will try to unearth the requisite knowledge to aid them in reconstructing their existing model of the world (making sense out of the learning task). Building new concepts by altering existing cognitive structures is at the center of what constructivism is all about.

If you think deeply about this constructivist portrayal of the learning process, it is evident that the emphasis on constructive mental activity corresponds very closely with the way practicing social scientists carry out their investigations (although with more highly coordinated and unified processes). Puzzling problems that grow from a conflict between what the social scientist already knows and what she or he is confronted with creates an element of interest that launches a social scientist's inquiry. Once the problem is recognized and captures a social scientist's interest, she or he sets in motion a series of powerful investigative processes until the conflict is resolved and new understandings are constructed.

Constructivists refer to "interest" as the energy required to set off the constructive process. To make constructivism work in social studies classrooms, then, teachers must be able to create and present *intriguing situations* (challenging tasks, questions, or problems) that inspire our young classroom social scientists to want to figure something out. For these intriguing situations to work properly, teachers must be clearly aware of what their students already know and what they are able to do. If children are confronted with something too far removed from their current level of understanding, for example, they will become frustrated and bewildered. Obviously, they will be unable to successfully participate in the learning task. Conversely, if the intriguing situation lies comfortably within the children's existing cognitive framework, they will be unchallenged and uninspired to explore the situation any further. The key to effective instruction is to gear the intriguing situation slightly in advance of the children's existing level of cognitive development. It is within this region that children are challenged to learn, and teachers are confident that children are experiencing challenges that are neither too easy nor too difficult.

In addition to organizing intriguing situations, teachers in constructivist classrooms must also function as facilitators or guides to make certain that the children can capably navigate their way through the learning experience. Because teacher assistance is essential, constructivist learning can be thought of as having both cognitive and social components. The cognitive component describes learning as the process of resolving intriguing situations; however, that resolution process is rarely accomplished in isolation. It is difficult for children to change their thinking on their own; intriguing situations alone are not enough. Children need to see things in new ways. Therefore, it is important for children to enter into educational dialogues with the teacher or other children. Language passing back and forth among individuals in written and oral forms is viewed as indispensable for learning in a constructivist classroom.

Children construct new knowledge as they collaborate with adults or peers to work their way through puzzling tasks or problems. Constructivism begins with the principle that the primary role of teaching is not to lecture, explain, or otherwise attempt to pass on knowledge, but to guide, facilitate, and support children as they pull together their own ideas and conclusions. One the most familiar strategies used by teachers to assist children in connecting their current knowledge to a new learning experience is teacher facilitated discussions. The following classroom exemplar demonstrates how one teacher used an anticipation guide during a facilitated discussion to help her students connect their current understandings of the topic to any new information contained in the learning experience.

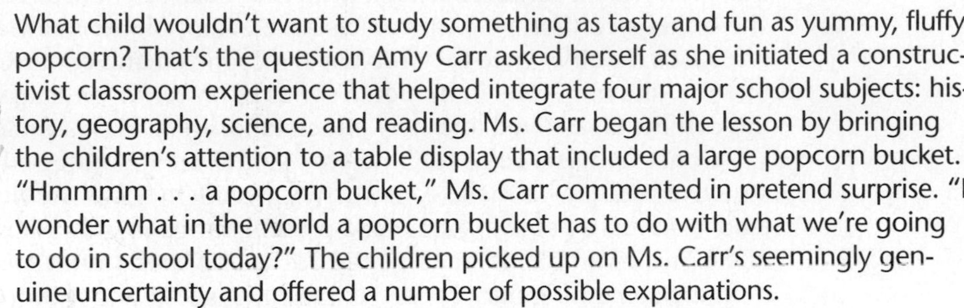

What child wouldn't want to study something as tasty and fun as yummy, fluffy popcorn? That's the question Amy Carr asked herself as she initiated a constructivist classroom experience that helped integrate four major school subjects: history, geography, science, and reading. Ms. Carr began the lesson by bringing the children's attention to a table display that included a large popcorn bucket. "Hmmmm . . . a popcorn bucket," Ms. Carr commented in pretend surprise. "I wonder what in the world a popcorn bucket has to do with what we're going to do in school today?" The children picked up on Ms. Carr's seemingly genuine uncertainty and offered a number of possible explanations.

Then, holding the bucket on her lap so that all could see, Ms. Carr reached in and held up a cup of popcorn kernels. "Look," suggested Ms. Carr. "What could you tell me about this?" To help them keep track of all their suggestions, Ms. Carr recorded the students' comments on a knowledge chart: "Those little yellow things are called kernels." "That's what popcorn looks like before you pop it. It's fluffy white after you pop it." "Some people put butter on it." "I like lots of salt on mine." "I think the American Indians invented it." Ms. Carr listed everything they knew (or thought they knew) about popcorn in a column labeled "What We Know about Popcorn."

NCSS STANDARDS

I. *Culture*
II. *Time, Continuity, and Change*
VIII. *Science, Technology, and Society*

Ms. Carr then pulled a picture book out of the popcorn bucket, introduced it, and read aloud *The Popcorn Book* by Tomie de Paola (Holiday). It is a delightfully illustrated picture book that tells children everything they want to know about popcorn. The book takes them through the history of popcorn, tells where it is grown, explains how the Native American Indians made popcorn, and describes how Native Americans in Massachusetts brought bowlfuls of popcorn to the first Thanksgiving potluck feast. It even reveals the secret of how those hard little kernels suddenly burst into the feathery globules we call popcorn. After the book was read, Ms. Carr coordinated a group discussion during which the children talked about all that they had learned. Ms. Carr helped the students record their new information in the second column ("What We Learned about Popcorn") and corrected any information in the first column that was inaccurate.

The book experience satisfied the need to know for some youngsters, but there remained several who were personally driven to find out even more information about popcorn. Ms. Carr directed them to the classroom computers where they explored a wealth of information obtainable from the Jolly Time® popcorn company (www.jollytime.com). All the relevant information they uncovered was added to the information chart.

Teachers in constructivist social studies classrooms do not commit themselves to any single method as the exclusive "right way to teach." They understand that there are many ways to help children unlock the mysteries of life and that the heart of solid social studies instruction is balance and proportion.

Knowledge is constructed by learners as teachers facilitate their active investigations into the mysteries of our world.

Intrinsic Motivation

Certainly, interest is a prerequisite for children in their efforts to resolve intriguing situations in social studies classrooms. The interest might come entirely from the children as they act on their spontaneous intriguing situations, or the children might accept a contrived interest and make it their own. Whatever the source, if children find classroom activities interesting, meaningful, and worthwhile and take great effort to construct knowledge and intelligence, we say they are *motivated* to learn. In other words, motivation can be thought of as a strong internal desire that rouses us to action or keeps us absorbed in certain activities until we accomplish our goals. For example, in recent years I have learned to play fantasy sports on the Internet. I am not addicted to the game as I understand many are, but I love drafting teams, trading players, and fighting for league championships (yes, I've won a few). I take part in fantasy sports not because someone has told me I must, but because I enjoy it. Certainly, the T-shirts that come with league championships are a special reward for doing well, but I enjoy the competition whether or not it results in a championship or a T-shirt. To me, the activity is pleasurable and worthwhile in and of itself. What activities do you engage in on a regular basis simply because

you enjoy doing them? Intrinsic motivation is what leads you to action and keeps you engaged in those activities.

There are some activities I engage in that are not so enjoyable, but I do them anyway because they bring me things I do enjoy. Washing my car is an example. It's not something I yearn to do during my free time; I don't particularly like doing it. However, my family and I do appreciate a clean, shiny automobile. The motivation to wash my car is the same as mowing my lawn or shoveling the snow from my driveway. The push to do these is called *extrinsic motivation* because the desire to complete these chores does not come from within. The activities themselves are not enjoyable, but the rewards are—a shiny car, a clean yard, and a clear driveway. Likewise, a child who searches a number of trade books to find out how it might have felt to leave home at the age of 12 to work as an apprentice in colonial America because he or she is genuinely interested in finding out is *intrinsically* motivated, whereas the child who researches the topic just to get a good grade or a teacher's praise is *extrinsically* motivated. The interest, enjoyment, and satisfaction is in the work itself when one is intrinsically motivated; when one is extrinsically motivated, the driving force is outside pressure or reward. No activity in itself, however, is intrinsically motivating for everyone. Fantasy sports are fun for me, but I'm sure there are some of you who would rather watch paint dry than play fantasy sports on the computer. The same is true for any activity; it can be motivating only to a particular person at a particular time.

What are some of the factors that motivate learning? First, you must be aware that the social climate of the classroom is significant. If students can think of the classroom as a caring, supportive place where learning is considered to be important, they will tend to become more fully involved in the learning process. Eager learners must be fed by wholesome encouragement and support. Second, the demands of a learning situation also influence a student's motivation to learn. If tasks are too easy, students will soon become bored and withdraw from participating. If they are too difficult, students will become frustrated and refuse to see a task through to completion. The key is to apply what we know about constructivist classrooms: Students will seek out activities and persist longer with them if the instructional tasks are challenging but achievable. Third, the significance of a learning task also promotes motivation. Students must be helped to see how any particular learning can be applied in the real world. They are more motivated by something they know can be applied to their own lives than by something with no perceived value. Fourth, the learning task must be pleasurable. Youngsters tend to become more engaged in the experience when they are upbeat about and thrilled with the subject matter content or learning task. Last, extrinsic rewards, on the other hand, should be used with caution, for they have the potential for decreasing intrinsic motivation.

By getting the children involved in enjoyable and instructive activities where they collaborate with each other while deciding what to do and how to do it will be more interesting and personally relevant. And, as lessons become more interesting and personally relevant, the more motivating they will be. Dorothy Yohe, a first-grade teacher, subscribes to the idea that the more interesting a classroom activity is, the more likely children are to throw themselves into it and stick with it through completion. In the following scenario you will see how excitement runs high as children are led by "Econ" through an informative journey in "The Land of Economics."

"Econ" is a fuzzy toy spider who bounces on an elasticized string wrapped around Mrs. Yohe's finger while cheerfully inviting the children to come with him on a voyage to his kingdom, The Land of Economics. Econ's kingdom consists of 26 towns, each beginning with an economic alphabet letter name. In each town live producers whose occupations begin with the town letter. A-Town, for example, is the home of artists, actors, and accountants; B-Town houses barbers, bankers, and butchers; in C-Town live car dealers, carpenters, and coal miners. Econ and his spellbound travelers spend several days in each town where children learn about occupations starting with that letter. Dorothy Yohe invites parents to class to describe their occupations—for example, Isaiah's mother, a landscaper, visited during L-Town week, and Rita's father, a computer programmer, shared his story during C-Town week. Visiting parents become members of the VIP (Very Important Parent) Club, and all are encouraged to visit during the weekly studies.

NCSS STANDARDS

IV. *Individual Development and Identity*

VII. *Production, Distribution, and Consumption*

Mrs. Yohe is occasionally challenged to stretch the limits of her creativity as she tries to make certain that each occupation has only one VIP guest (if there are two beauticians ready to come to the classroom, for example, one could be the "beautician" and the other a "hairdresser"). VIPs are classified as either producers of goods or providers of services. Appropriate storybooks, videos, field trips, and other sources of information help fill in the content while students visit a specific town; creative dramatics, art projects, writing activities, and reinforcement games supplement instruction and provide for information processing and enrichment.

As the journey through the economic alphabet comes to an end, usually before the busy holiday weeks early in December, Econ welcomes the children to a beautiful shopping mall, disappointingly not completed because of an unfortunate strike. Econ leads the children in a discussion of some of the causes and effects of strikes. Even though the strike has now been settled, it will take more workers to complete the mall in time for the holiday shoppers. Econ asks the children to work for him.

Children work and plan the shopping mall with Econ's help. He hires them to build the shops, paying them in play money. After the stores and shops are constructed, the children switch roles. They now become transformed into clever consumers at the lavish new shopping mall. One day, half the class is assigned to work in the shops while the other students are consumers. The next day, the groups reverse roles. The shopping mall incorporates a bank in which students may deposit and withdraw the play money they earn in class. Stores include a restaurant, card and gift shop, travel agency, bank, flower shop, food market, jewelry store, shoe store, and a clothing shop. The story of a pizza shop illustrates how one business was created.

After a field trip to a local pizza shop, Mrs. Yohe's children were ready to transform an unoccupied store space into their own pizza restaurant. Their first task in setting up the restaurant was to arrange the tables and chairs for the customers and make sure the "kitchen" was ready to begin producing pizzas. Once that was accomplished, some children thought some special touches were needed: flowers for the tables, pictures on the walls, a telephone for reservations, and even wallpaper to brighten up the space. Crews went to work on each project, taping up their own artwork for pictures, getting the play telephone from the kindergarten room, using sponge printing to create several sheets of patterned "wallpaper," making flowers from pipe cleaners and tissue paper, and selecting easy-listening music for the diners.

Next, the children thought about a name for their pizza restaurant and constructed signs, menus, and a logo. They decided that "Pizza Shop" would be a fine name for their restaurant. Mrs. Yohe set up a long sheet of butcher paper and poster paint for the children to make a large sign. They decided to use a pizza slice as a logo and painted one next to the name. Other groups made "restroom," "no smoking", "exit," "open/closed," and "please wait to be seated" signs.

After carefully inspecting the sample menu from the pizza restaurant they visited, the children decided to use it as a model for their pizza menu. They looked through old magazines for pictures, but ended up drawing their own and putting the prices next to an illustration of each food and drink item. Mrs. Yohe cut some sponges into the shape of their logo, and the children stamped the logo onto the menu, plain white napkins, take-out boxes, place mats, and order pads.

Now the children used their pizza restaurant to dramatize the roles of producers and consumers. Some were customers and sat at the table ("Do you take credit cards?"). Others put on aprons to take orders ("Hello. My name is Chris. What can I get for you?"). No one seemed to notice that most of the orders were taken down in scribble writing. Two children donned chef's hats and pretended to flip and spin pizza crusts.

The pizza restaurant is but one example of the kinds of activities you would find if you visited Mrs. Yohe's first-grade social studies classroom. As a matter of fact, Mrs. Yohe's children began another project immediately after their interest shifted from the restaurant to Gerald, who came to school donning new eyeglasses. You guessed it—a field trip to the ophthalmologist and the assembly of an eye care facility was next, complete with an eye chart that helped some children read and write the alphabet and a section that displayed pipe cleaner "designer frames." Exploring the fascinating effect of lenses also captivated the children's interests.

The restaurant and eye care center were two areas that the children came back to visit over and over again. As they added other stores, they took great pride in giving tours to parents, other classes, and building visitors. It became the catalyst and context for the study of neighborhoods and communities throughout the year.

To summarize, students are more likely to display a high level of intrinsic motivation when they find the subject matter they are studying to be interesting, when they like what they're doing, when they feel they are capable of accomplishing a task, and when they believe they have some control over the learning situation. The ability to motivate students is a basic skill for teachers in dynamic social studies classrooms, for all students must feel they are capable of learning and that you are there to help. Toward this goal, Bennett (2007) advises social studies teachers:

> Make a conscious effort to find what motivates your students and connect them to the social studies curriculum. Watch how students interact. Survey the class to learn about students as individuals. Use this information as you plan for daily activities and social studies lessons. Continually engage in community building activities that help students become part of the learning community so they will feel comfortable sharing experiences and opinions. Most of all, let your students see you enjoying the content of social studies. You and your students will learn and grow together throughout the year. (p. 6)

Respect for Diversity

Have you ever been involved in a situation where you had more difficulty doing something than anyone else? Plait fancy braids? Play a musical instrument? Ride a unicycle? Speak a foreign language? Memorize something? Maybe you were the only one who had problems. How did you feel? How would you have felt if every day when you came to school you were the only one who couldn't perform certain tasks that could be completed by others with relative ease?

Now reflect on whether you have ever been involved in a situation where you were able to do something more easily and quickly than anyone else. How did you feel then? What could be done in school to keep you from becoming miserably bored? What could be done to best help you work toward fulfilling your unlimited potential?

Creating a context for learning in dynamic social studies classrooms starts with genuine respect for the cultures of all learners.

Like any of us who have been in these situations, all children come to school with varied strengths and limitations to form a classroom community consisting of unique backgrounds, talents, and skills. Teachers achieve quality in the dynamic social studies program when they deliver the best for each youngster and make the most of their time with everyone in their classrooms. Effective teachers adapt instruction to meet the special needs, talents, and interests of all their students. The quality of their dynamic social studies programs is distinguished by a keen awareness and consideration of each youngster as a distinct individual, including those

whose backgrounds or exhibited needs are not shared by most others. These children may exhibit specific developmental disabilities, speak a home language that does not match the school's, come from diverse cultural or ethnic backgrounds, or possess unique gifts and talents. Whatever the circumstance, the field of elementary school social studies education should be consistently responsive by offering appropriate experiences to fully develop their native capabilities.

At the heart of this topic is a concern about equity and fair treatment for groups that have traditionally experienced discrimination because of race or ethnicity, language, gender, or exceptionality. Because of the wide range of diversity in contemporary society, all teachers must become instructionally effective with diverse groups of students. Children in today's schools come from an enormous range of backgrounds, languages, and abilities. To meet their educational needs, dynamic social studies teachers must derive instruction from our pluralistic society as well as our membership in a global community. Ukpokodu (2006) describes the importance of establishing such culturally conscientious classrooms:

> The increasing diversity . . . of American society demands that classroom teachers prepare students for national and global citizenship. Students of the twenty-first century need to cultivate . . . knowledge, intellectual skills, and democratic attitudes and values needed to successfully navigate diverse cultural, social, economic and political contexts. Tomorrow's adult citizens will need to reconstruct their communities and the world to become more just, humane, and peaceful. (p. 4)

As an example of how cultural conscientiousness can work in dynamic social studies classrooms, Rosee Arya asked her young children to identify what they considered to be the most important characteristic they could use to define themselves. She offered them several examples of characteristics that were descriptive of her: female, ex-athlete, teacher, and mother. Then, in pairs, Ms. Arya had the students share stories about when they felt especially proud to be associated with the characteristic. Next, the students were asked to write and illustrate a short story that explained the characteristic they selected. Amy, proud of her Jewish background, used it to define herself. Then, because this activity took place in early December, she told the story of Hanukkah, which is also referred to as "The Festival of Lights." See Amy's story in Figure 1.7.

Multicultural education helps students to understand and appreciate cultural and ethnic differences and similarities and to become aware of the accomplishments of the diverse groups within our society.

Teachers in cognitive constructivist social studies classrooms do not commit themselves to any single method or source of information as the exclusive "right way to teach." They recognize that there are many ways to unlock the mysteries of life and that the heart of solid social studies instruction is balance and proportion. Sometimes they will "bring the action to the children," demonstrating, assisting, and explaining in order to help their students construct concepts or refine skills. At other times, they will allow the children to "initiate the action," supporting students emotionally and intellectually as they independently strive to explain a puzzling

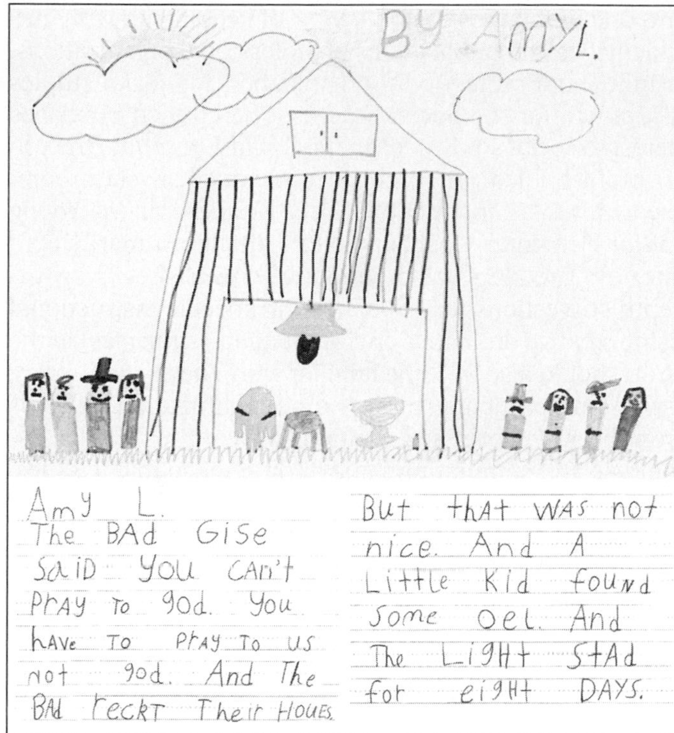

BY AMY L.
Amy L.
The BAd Gise
SAID You CAn't
PrAy To god. You
hAve To PrAy To US
not god. And The
BAd reckT Their Houes.
But thAt WAS not
nice. And A
Little Kid found
Some oel. And
The LigHt StAd
for eigHt DAYS.

FIGURE 1.7 Lower-Grade Personal Story

question or problem. Regardless of how they approach it, good social studies teachers involve children in doing something—discovering, processing, and applying information; talking, listening, writing, reading; manipulating, building, doing; investigating, exploring, probing; collaborating, cooperating, team building. Effective social studies teachers design, make, and use a variety of strategies and materials that help children learn about their social world in an engaging and instructive way.

A Final Thought

At the roots of a democracy are knowledgeable and thoughtful citizens. Of course, they have many other qualities, too, but high on the list of behavior for democratic citizens is thinking for themselves. Democracy requires individuals who are able to search for and examine the facts whenever they must make up their minds about important issues. These issues might relate to one's personal life or to complex international concerns; regardless, the protection of our freedoms lies in the hands of rational people. Such skills must be learned during the early years with a dynamic social studies curriculum that offers meaningful experiences to all.

All youngsters must find something to excite their interest and stimulate their thinking. A one-dimensional approach to social studies instruction cannot do this. We fail our children with our narrowness; if our myopic view of teaching has caused them to feel stupid or to be bored, we have lost. Learning for an informed citizenry is too important to be thought of as something that everyone must be able to do in any single way. The danger to our future is great when we restrict the adventuresome, "can-do" spirit of childhood. Therefore, dynamic social studies programs must employ various teaching strategies and promote functional thinking skills. The probing, wondering mind of childhood must be freed. Our society of tomorrow starts in your classroom today.

The complexities of the twenty-first century may dictate a quality and quantity of education far different from what we can currently imagine. You must take your emerging view of what social studies is and constantly search for ideas that help construct new roles for teachers in a new century. In addition to what we have considered up to this point, one of the most helpful ways of keeping up with current trends is to review the activities and publications of professional organizations.

The largest and most influential professional organization for social studies educators is the National Council for the Social Studies. The council publishes several publications of interest to social studies teachers: *Social Education,* the primary journal, focuses on philosophical, theoretical, and practical classroom-application articles involved with K–12 instruction; *Social Studies and the Young Learner,* a separate journal for elementary teachers, offers articles primarily concerned with teaching strategies. The NCSS also periodically publishes "how-to" pamphlets that offer in-depth suggestions for implementing specific instructional responsibilities (such as using creative dramatics or current affairs strategies) in the social studies classroom. You should also become familiar with *The Social Studies,* a journal not associated with any particular professional organization. It deals with classroom practices on the K–12 level and contains a wealth of articles describing ideas for classroom use and stimulating thought on philosophical issues. The relevant addresses follow.

National Council for the Social Studies
8555 Sixteenth Street, Suite 500
Silver Spring, MD 20910
(301) 588-1800

The Social Studies
1319 Eighteenth Street, NW
Washington, DC 20036

REFERENCES

Bennett, L. (2007). Motivation: Connecting each student with the world. *Social Studies and the Young Learner, 19,* 4–6.

Berg, M. (1988). Integrating ideas for social studies. *Social Studies and the Young Learner, 1,* unnumbered pull-out feature.

Bruner, J. (1960). *The process of education*. New York: Vintage.

Channing, E., & Hart, A. B. (1903). *Guide to the study of American history*. Boston: Ginn and Company.

Clark, D. C., & Cutler, B. C. (1990). *Teaching*. New York: Harcourt Brace Jovanovich.

Dewey, J. (1933). *How we think*. Boston: D.C. Heath & Company.

Finn, C. E. (1988, May). The social studies debacle among the educationaloids. *The American Spectator,* 15–16.

Haefner, T. L., O'Connor, K. A., Groce, E. C., Byrd, S., Good, A. J., Oldendorf, S., Passe, J., & Rock, T. (2007). Advocating for social studies: Becoming agents for change. *Social Studies and the Young Learner, 20,* 26–29.

Hanna, P. R. (1963). Revising the social studies: What is needed? *Social Education, 27,* 190–196.

Hirsch, Jr., E. D. (1987). *Cultural literacy: What every American needs to know.* Boston: Houghton Mifflin.

Howard, R. W. (2003). The shrinking of social studies. *Social Education, 67,* 285–287.

Mattioli, D. (2004). The power of one: Making a difference in a changing world. *Social Education, 68,* 7–8.

Mitchell, L. S. (1934). *Young geographers.* New York: John Day.

National Commission on Excellence in Education. (1983). *A nation at risk: The imperative for educational reform.* Washington, DC: Author.

National Council for the Social Studies. (2002). Creating effective citizens. *Social Education, 65,* 319.

National Council for the Social Studies. (1993a). A vision of powerful teaching and learning in the social studies: Building social understanding and civic efficacy. *Social Education, 57,* 213–223.

National Council for the Social Studies. (1993b, January/February). Definition approved. *The Social Studies Professional, 114,* 3.

National Council for the Social Studies. (1994). *Curriculum standards for social studies: Expectations of excellence* (Bulletin 89). Washington, DC: Author.

National Council for the Social Studies. (1981). Essentials of the social studies. *Social Education, 45,* 163–164.

National Council for the Social Studies Task Force on Early Childhood/Elementary Social Studies. (1989). Social studies for early childhood and elementary school children preparing for the 21st century. *Social Education, 54,* 16.

National Education Association. (1916). *The social studies in secondary education. Report of the Committee on Social Studies* (Bulletin 28). Washington, DC: Bureau of Education.

Neill, M., & Guisbond, L. (2005). Excluded children, lost learning: The costs of doing business with NCLB. *Social Studies and the Young Learner, 17,* 31–32.

Ochoa-Becker, A. S. (2001). A critique of the NCSS curriculum standards. *Social Education, 65,* 165–168.

O'Neil, J. (1993). On the new standards project: A conversation with Lauren Resnick and Warren Simmons. *Educational Leadership, 50,* 17–23.

Pascopella, A. (2005). Staying alive: Social studies in elementary schools. *Social Studies and the Young Learner, 17,* 30–32.

Paxton, R. (2003). Don't know much about history—never did. *Phi Delta Kappan, 85,* 264–273.

Peterson, P., & Knapp, N. (1993). Inventing and reinventing ideas: Constructivist teaching and learning in mathematics. In G. Cawelti (Ed.), *Challenges and achievements of American education* (pp. 134–157). Alexandria, VA: Association for Supervision and Curriculum Development.

Risinger, C. F. (2002). Two different worlds: The dilemma facing social studies teachers. *Social Education, 66,* 231–233.

Robinson, J. H. (1912). *The new history* (pp. 17–18, 134). New York: The Macmillan Company.

Rochester, M. (2003). The training of idiots. In J. Leming, L. Ellington, & C. Porter-Magee (Eds.), *Where did social studies go wrong?* [Online] Available: www.coreknowledge.org/CKproto2/about/CommonKnowledge/V16ivOctNov2003/V16ivOctNov2003_where_ss_wrong.htm.

Sanchez, R. M. (2007). What we treasure and who we are. *Social Studies and the Young Learner, 20,* P1–P4.

Ukpokodu, O. (2006). Essential characteristics of a culturally conscientious classroom. *Social Studies and the Young Learner, 19,* 4–7.

U.S. Department of Education. (1991). *America 2000: An education strategy.* Washington, DC: Author.

Working Group of Social Studies Discipline Organizations. (2007). Working Group of Social Studies Discipline Organizations joint statement on NCLB. *Social Studies and the Young Learner, 20,* 30–31.

CHAPTER 2

Diversity in the Classroom
The Children You Will Teach

What Does Diversity in the Classroom Look Like?

Ten-year-old Graciela flew into her house one day after school and declared to no one in particular, "I know just what I'm gonna bring in. This is gonna be so cool!" What Graciela was so excited about was a social studies family museum project designed to highlight the cultural diversity in her classroom. That afternoon in school, Mary Novak read to her fifth-graders Patricia Polacco's book, *The Keeping Quilt* (Aladdin), which tells the story of a beloved quilt that is passed along from generation to generation. It is made from the clothing of family members who came to this country as immigrants from their Russian homeland. Following a short discussion of the story events, Ms. Novak and the children talked about the idea that everyone has a family history and about how interesting it would be to bring into the classroom something special, like Polacco's quilt, representing each child's heritage.

To begin the project, Ms. Novak sent letters home with the children asking parents to help select an item of special cultural significance that their children could bring to school. This artifact should reflect the beliefs and traditions of their families and have been in their family for more than one generation; it should have a long story to tell. To model for the class what to bring, Ms. Novak shared her own family artifact. "I have found that children find it difficult to develop a strong interest in a museum project unless they think that family history is fun. If children find that family history is fun and informative, they will be eager to plunge in."

Ms. Novak started by referring to her relatives from the past as her "ancestors" and showed on a map where they came from. She then described some distinctive family traditions and shared a favorite family heirloom: "I remember as a child your age how I loved to go through my mom's family keepsakes. There were all kinds of keepsakes covering three generations—as far back as my great-grandparents. The stuff may not have been worth much money, but it was important to our family in other ways."

NCSS STANDARDS

I. *Culture*
II. *Time, Continuity, and Change*
IV. *Individual Development and Identity*

Then, holding up a cloth doll for all to see, Ms. Novak continued:

"Here is a story to illustrate my point. This is my great-grandmother Julia's doll. It is a cloth doll dressed in a traditional Polish folk costume that was made in Poland during the 1890s. The doll was given to my great-grandmother in 1903 when she was just 7 years old. After her oldest sister Helen got married and moved from Poland to the United States, the doll became Julia's best friend. A short time later Julia, too, got married and moved to the United States where her husband found work on the railroad. Julia packed up the doll and brought it to the new land with her. Later, she had two little girls and the girls loved to play with the cloth doll, too. They played with it so much, however, that the doll eventually became threadbare and torn. My great-grandmother Julia eventually put it away in a storage chest. Great-grandmother Julia's two daughters ultimately raised their own families and the tattered doll in the chest seemed to have been forgotten by all.

"When I was just a little girl in 1980, my great-grandmother Julia died. When they were going through her things, my mother found the doll and began asking all the relatives questions about it. She brought the doll home and showed it to me, explaining what she uncovered about the doll's history. A couple of years later, I had the doll repaired and now it sits in a child's rocker in my living room for all the family to see when they come to visit. I make sure that my family knows the story of great-grandmother Julia's doll, and of its place in our family's history."

After her story, Ms. Novak went on to explain, "Almost all of your families came from other countries, too, and have interesting stories to tell about special family relics, which we can learn about by interviewing them just like newspaper and television reporters do." Ms. Novak clarified that interviewing is a good way to learn new information and that most interviews are based on *Who, What, When, Where*, and *Why* questions. Together, the children developed a list of six possible questions that might help better understand their families. Ms. Novak recorded the students' suggestions on the chalkboard:

- Did our family live in another homeland before moving to the United States?
- Why did our family come to the United States?
- When did our family move to the United States?

- What are some customs that are distinctive to our culture or family?
- What artifact holds special meaning to our family? Why is it important to our family?
- Is there a favorite family story that is connected to the artifact?

Ms. Novak's story helped make children aware of how a family's history and culture can be rooted in an artifact. As the children brought their artifacts to school, they told the keepsakes' stories by patterning Ms. Novak's model presentation with information gathered from their interview questions: what it is, where it came from, how it is used, who it has belonged to, and how old it is. After the presentations, Ms. Novak took a digital photo of each student holding his or her artifact and arranged the photos in a *Family Artifact Gallery*. A "museum card" containing the information about the artifact was attached below each photo.

On the day of their presentations, the students took turns sharing their family artifacts and reading from a "museum card" the story of its significance. Graciela, the excited student from the start of this chapter, read this report about the pair of colorfully decorated maracas she was so anxiously planning to share:

"My family lived for many generations in a tiny village in the Andes Mountains of Peru. My ancestors were farmers who planted gourds in a large section of the farm. When they are dried, gourd shells become very hard and can be used for many things, including bowls or bottles and containers for storing salt and spices. Peruvian artists carve and paint special designs on the gourds. These old maracas were made out of gourds, too. My grandfather told me why these maracas are important to our family. He said that around 200 years ago, people from his tiny village began making regular trips to other villages to trade their gourds, corn, and beans for other goods. One day they met gourd carvers from another village. They taught my ancestors how to carve and decorate gourds. For generations after that, my family's gourds were thought to be the best in all of Peru. When my grandfather and his family moved to the United States, they brought along samples of their work, including these maracas."

In like manner, other students came to the front of the class, presented a family keepsake, and read about its significance from the "museum card." Included were a chunk of ceramic tile from Italy, kente cloth from Ghana, a wood carving from Indonesia, an intricately embroidered shirt from Russia, and a cookbook from Greece. The class sat spellbound as each artifact was shared; they asked spontaneous questions about each.

Following the artifact presentations, Ms. Novak helped the students process the information they had collected. First, the students had drawn a large world map and displayed it on an open wall. Each child sketched a self-portrait on an index card, printed her or his name on it, and taped it to the wall around the map. Then each student took a piece of red yarn to represent her or his father's lineage and a piece of yellow yarn to represent her or his mother's. The students connected both pieces of yarn to their index cards and to the countries of their ancestors' origin. The map and the museum were both on display for parents during a late autumn open house. Ms. Novak asserts that one of the most compelling outcomes of this project is its power to build a sense of community in the classroom.

As an important note, teachers like Ms. Novak realize that family history projects can be extremely difficult for children whose families have been touched by adoption, divorce, or death of a parent, or those from blended families, families with same-sex partners, and so on. The very idea of a family's history can raise questions of belonging and relatedness, and cause divided loyalty, confusion, and, in rare cases, embarrassment. As a result, some youngsters may struggle with the assignment or refuse to participate. Ms. Novak anticipated these possibilities, so she made sure to telephone the parents of children who might have difficulties before she sent home the initial letters. The parents were appreciative of her consideration. One set of adoptive parents encouraged their daughter to research her birth family, and one blended family refused their child permission to participate in the project. Students and their families have a right to choose how they want to become involved. Carl, whose parents are divorced, now has a stepmother. He decided to bring in two artifacts—one representing each family structure. By offering suitable help and understanding, teachers can demonstrate a deep respect for their students and their families' privacy.

What Is Multicultural Education?

Ms. Novak includes multicultural experiences as an integral part of her total curriculum, establishing an all-inclusive learning environment that nurtures mutual trust and respect for all people. She operates with a strong conviction that children who are equipped with a knowledge of and appreciation for the glorious diversity among people will more likely be wise citizens who respect our nation's rich milieu of cultures, heritages, abilities, and interests.

The cultural and ethnic composition of our schools has become increasingly diverse and, as you would expect, mirrors the changing nature of American society. To provide effective and successful classroom instruction, Ms. Novak understands and commits to practices that confirm and build on the backgrounds of her students. Knowledge of a family's culture as well as expectations for its children provides her with information that enhances the development of effective classroom interactions and instructional practices. Some long-established models of education tend to overlook the ways cultural conditions can impact the lives of children; therefore, they operate with a conviction that there is "one best path for all." Ms. Novak, however, asserts, "The belief that a singular approach is applicable to all cultural groups tends to render education practically useless to all but the most assimilated groups."

As a nation, we prize our cultural and ethnic diversity. We are of many colors, speak many languages, and observe many distinctive customs and traditions. All of us contribute to our nation's rich and wonderful diversity, whether our ancestors are from any of the more than 100 ethnic groups represented in the United States.

During the first decade of the twentieth century, the United States was in the middle of receiving the largest influx of immigrants in the nation's history—about 18 million immigrants between 1890 and 1920. Steamers pulled into Ellis Island and other American ports filled with Irish, Germans, French, English, Italians, and Eastern Europeans. Absorbing these various ethnic cultures was a highly complex and confusing predicament. Eventually, however, the term *melting pot* (or crucible) gained popularity as a term to describe the process by which people of different nationalities, cultures, races, and religions could be dissolved, mixed, and blended. As a result, they would lose their discrete identities and become fused into a new product that was quite different from the original components—the amalgamated American citizen:

> America is God's great Crucible, a great Melting Pot where all races of Europe are melting and reforming! . . . Germans and Frenchmen, Irishmen and Englishmen, Jews and Russians—into the Crucible with you all! God is making the American. . . . The real American has not yet arrived. He is only in the Crucible, I tell you—he will be the fusion of all races, the coming superman. (Zangwell, 1909, p. 37)

Proponents of the melting pot idea believed that all ethnic groups possessed strengths and that, as the "Crucible of America" merged them into a single alloy, a new and greater culture would be cast. The melting pot, then, was not meant to destroy cultural diversity per se, but to combine the strengths of many cultures into something new and unique: "The new emerging American culture must be built not on the destruction of the cultural values and mores of the various immigrant groups but on their fusion with the existing American civilization. . . . In the burning fires of the melting pot, all races were equal—all were reshaped, and molded into a new entity" (Krug, 1976, p. 12).

Today, our nation is experiencing a second wave of immigration, a movement of people with profound implications for our nation's schools. The new immigrants come to our shores not mainly from Europe this time, but from Asia and Latin America. Today, the Hispanic population is the fastest-growing ethnic group in the United States. The U.S. Bureau of the Census (1996) reported that in 1996, Hispanics comprised 11 percent, Asians comprised 4 percent, and whites of European descent made up 73 percent of the population. The Bureau estimates that by 2050, these demographic figures will change so that Hispanics will make up 25 percent of the population, the Asian proportion will double to 8 percent, and the whites of European descent will experience a swift decline to 53 percent. To complicate this population shift, Rong (1998) adds, "There are many forms of diversity among the new immigrants. To begin with, 'Hispanic' and 'Asian' are umbrella terms for large groups of people who differ substantially among themselves. . . . [For example,] 'Hispanic,' or alternately 'Latino,' is a category including people of various races, cultures, religions, and residencies across broad geographic areas" (p. 396).

This radical shift challenges the suggestion of a melting pot, or central national identity. Most observers now feel that it is impossible to combine people of so many diverse cultures into one new culture. Instead, some expect that the United States will gradually break up into several disconnected groups of people. Or, perhaps it will evolve into a pluralistic society that shares some core citizenship ideals, but with minimal interaction among groups. However these trends emerge, we can be certain that our schools, as has our society in general, will have discarded the idea of a single "American" alloy emerging from a great melting pot. *Cultural pluralism* is the philosophy that now describes American society; the United States is viewed as a multitude of cultures, each with its own distinctively rich uniqueness that contributes to the larger culture. Instead of a melting pot or crucible, our society has been likened to a salad bowl, a mosaic, or a patchwork quilt where each culture retains its unique characteristics that are still identifiable within the larger design. The foundation of social studies instruction is based on this idea of cultural pluralism—becoming sensitive to and respecting the contributions of each group to society as a whole.

With our nation's increasing ethnic and cultural diversity, educators have seriously questioned the relevancy of a traditional social studies curriculum. Ukpokodu (2006) proposes, "Given the increasing diversity in today's student populations, the traditional social studies classroom is no longer appropriate or capable of preparing all students, especially minority/urban students, for effective citizenship in a multicultural democracy" (p. 4). Therefore, we have an obvious need for cultural relevancy in our social studies programs. Although citizenship values and traits such as democracy, loyalty, and justice will remain important instructional considerations, associated content must be taught in ways that are relevant to all students. Teachers will need to find ways to adapt instructional strategies so that all children feel connected to the learning experience.

The concept of diversity is extremely broad and impossible to treat in one chapter of this book. For that reason, this chapter will focus only on students from various ethnic, cultural, special needs, and gender backgrounds. Social studies programs that are responsive to these multiple perspectives are commonly referred to as multicultural programs, or *multicultural education*. Although many definitions of multicultural education dot the educational literature, this definition will guide content presentation in this chapter: *Multicultural education is an approach to classroom methodology and content selection that recognizes and values the complex dimensions of American cultures and society.*

What Is Culture and Ethnicity?

All individuals belonging to a group—whether an ethnic group, religion, peer group, or family—have a culture, or a system of behaviors, beliefs, customs, and attitudes. Culture is reflected in the group's artwork, literature, language, clothing, inventions, and traditions. Cultural differences are widespread, in both the overt (clothing, hairstyle, language, naming ceremonies) and the subtle (how one speaks to an elder). Culture consists of all the accepted and patterned ways of a group's behavior. It is a body of common understandings. It is the sum total of the group's ways of thinking, feeling, and acting.

Cultures have similar needs, but often choose to satisfy them in dissimilar ways. For example, let us look into a need that all cultures have in common—food. All groups must eat food in order to survive, but what we eat, how we eat, where we eat, and when we eat is determined by our culture. The basic ingredients, the way food is prepared, served, and preserved, and the tastes we enjoy vary depending on our cultural background. Some groups, for example, acquire protein from various animal sources—cows, pigs, horses, dogs, cats, mice, snakes, or beetle grubs. Other groups eat no meat, poultry, or fish—"nothing with a face." Some groups may reject certain foods because of their cultural values and beliefs: Muslims and Orthodox Jews do not eat pork; Hindus do not eat beef; some East Africans find eggs unfit for human consumption; and some Chinese do not drink milk. As Confucius once said, "A man cannot be too serious about his eating, for food is the force that binds society together."

How Global is the Curriculum
Go to MyEducationLab, select the topic Multicultural Perspectives and Ethnic Studies, watch the videos entitled "Incorporating the Home Experience of Culturally Diverse Learners" (Parts 1-4), and complete the questions that accompany it.

What foods do you think of as "multicultural"? Are they foods from other countries, such as *deok* (traditional Korean rice cakes) or *dodo* (a Nigerian fried plantain or banana) or *won ton* (Chinese dumplings)? Are they foods from different regions of the United States, such as smoked salmon (Northwest), collard greens and grits (Southeast), Navajo fry bread (Southwest), or New England clam chowder (Northeast)? Each of our cultural backgrounds and life experiences shape the way we think of food.

In our contemporary global community connected by the Internet, cell phones, and convenient travel, it is easy to network with a broader variety of people and learn about their culture. With regard to our food theme, for example, 25 years ago it would have been difficult to imagine going to a major league ballpark and eating anything other than hot dogs, peanuts, and popcorn. Now those items are often gloriously joined by nachos, fajitas, burritos, sushi, hummus, Asian stir fry, Swedish meatballs, pizza, tortilla chips with salsa, and an assortment of pasta and salads. And, consider the variety of ethnic produce in our nation's supermarkets as an indication of the degree to which traditionally ethnic groups now influence the general eating habits of the United States. Whether we choose to compare and contrast food, religion, holiday customs, clothing styles, or any other of the array of cultural traits, the unique beliefs and behaviors of any distinct culture provide its members with a feeling of group identity (ethnicity). See Figure 2.1.

FIGURE 2.1 Cultural Diversity

Source: Turner, M. (1980). *Social studies and the young learner, 5*, 2. © National Council for the Social Studies. Reprinted by permission.

An *ethnic group*, according to Bennett (2007), "is a community of people within a larger society that is socially distinguished or set apart, by others and/or by itself, primarily on the basis of racial and/or cultural characteristics, such as religion, language, and tradition" (p. 55). Examples of ethnic groups are Native American, Mexican American, German, Polish, African American, or Greek. *Ethnicity*, then, involves a deep feeling of personal attachment to an ethnic group and greatly influences the standards its members use to judge themselves and others, as well as its beliefs about what is worthwhile, satisfying, or important. Strong feelings of ethnicity determine the ways we think, feel, and act.

Sometimes, cultures become convinced that their own behaviors and beliefs are the proper and best ways of thinking and acting. A characteristic found in most cultures, this phenomenon is referred to as *ethnocentrism*, or the tendency to view one's own culture as the absolute best and the standard against which all others are judged. Although it is proper to respect one's own culture, ethnocentrism carried to an extreme makes it impossible to view another culture objectively through its "cultural lens." As a result, it prevents one culture from understanding, coexisting with, or appreciating another. Cultural narrow-mindedness often results, a condition especially worrisome today in light of the need for interdependence among countries and the importance of establishing positive ties among all cultural groups. Banks (2009) advises teachers to view the curriculum from diverse ethnic and cultural perspectives so that feelings of ethnocentrism will be minimized: "Individuals must clarify their own ethnic and cultural identities before they can relate positively to people who belong to different racial and ethnic groups. Educators need to foster the development of self-acceptance but discourage ethnocentrism. Diversity and unity in a delicate balance should be fostered by the schools" (p. 26).

While considering the nature of ethnic and cultural group membership, it must be noted that the labels used to organize this chapter are merely social constructions that cannot possibly embrace the defining characteristics of any single individual. For example, a person might not only be "White Anglo-Saxon Protestant," but also French, southerner, farmer, hearing impaired, female, and lower-middle class. This person's group memberships, as is true for most people, include race, ethnic group, region, occupation, religion, disabled or nondisabled, gender, and social class. Many aspects of one's life are shaped by membership in several groups, making this woman a much different person than an intellectually gifted African American male doctoral student from a large eastern city who grew up in a crowded high-rise apartment, or a female Navajo physician whose family makes its home in a pueblo in the southwest desert. Groups can be defined along many different lines, and everyone is a member of an assortment of groups, each of which creates its own culture (knowledge, rules, values, and traditions that guide its members' behavior).

All of this is not meant to confuse you, but only to emphasize that the children you teach are not only Haitian, female, French speaking, Roman Catholic, nor gifted learner; they are uniquely complex individuals who have become who they are through the interaction of many intricate genetic, cultural, and environmental factors. The labels we choose to describe the groups they belong to are not meant to stereotype, but only to provide insight into the best practices for dynamic social studies instruction.

All children come to school with strong cultural and ethnic identities, whether those identities are typical or extreme. Their identities must be accepted and respected by the teacher and used to form the starting point for all that goes on in the classroom. Bennett (2007) advises, "Multicultural education . . . is an approach to teaching and learning that is based on democratic values and beliefs and affirms cultural pluralism within culturally diverse societies. . . . In a pluralistic democracy such as the United States . . . the primary goal of public education is to foster the intellectual, social, and personal development of *all* students to their highest potential" (p. 4). Banks (2009) stresses that multicultural education must be conceptualized broadly; it must include information and strategies for teaching about white ethnic groups such as Italian Americans or Irish Americans as well as about ethnic groups of color such as African Americans, Mexican Americans, or Asian Americans. Banks adds, "To conceptualize ethnic and cultural studies more narrowly will result in curricula that are too limited in scope and that will not help students understand fully both the similarities and differences in the experiences of the diverse groups in the United States" (p. 16).

How Global is the Curriculum *Go to MyEducationLab, select the topic Multlcultural Perspectives and Ethnic Studies, watch the video entitled "Multicultural Perspectives in a Classroom," and complete the questions that accompany it.*

How Are Multicultural Perspectives Incorporated into the Social Studies Curriculum?

Over the years, classroom teachers have attempted a variety of strategies to incorporate ethnic perspectives into their social studies programs. Perhaps the earliest variety and still most widely used is commonly referred to as the *tourist approach*. Tourist approaches, although carried out with the best of intentions, rarely broaden children's understandings of people and cultures. They are characterized by offering special activities or projects only when a significant cultural holiday or special observance comes up—such as performing a dragon dance only during the Chinese New Year, reading a book about Amelia Bloomer only during Women's History Month, teaching a unit on Mexican Americans only during early May (Cinco de Mayo), reading books about important African Americans only during the month of February, or playing the dreidel game only during Hanukkah. Certainly, learning about those cultural elements is important and should be given a special place in dynamic social studies programs, but limiting instruction to such events shortchanges the true multicultural spirit. Tourist-type experiences might make students a bit more aware of the world around them, but genuine understanding comes from all that children do during the day and throughout the school year.

Educators today recommend moving away from tourist approaches because they are too limited in scope and fail to help students acquire an overall view of the role of various ethnic groups in the evolution of United States society. Banks (2009) labels the tourist approach the *contributions approach* and asserts that although it is "the easiest approach for teachers to integrate ethnic content into the curriculum . . . it has several serious limitations, including not helping students to attain a comprehensive view of the role of ethnic and cultural groups in U.S. society. Rather, they see ethnic issues and events primarily as an addition to the curriculum and thus as an appendage to the main story of the nation's development" (pp. 18-19).

Banks (2009) suggests that reform can be better accomplished by incorporating ethnic content, perspectives, and frames of reference into the total curriculum instead of simply making appendages to the curriculum. He suggests that this process could be most effectively accomplished by mixing and blending four approaches into actual teaching situations: (1) the contributions approach, (2) the additive approach (3) the transformative approach, and (4) the social action approach.

The Contributions Approach

Because the *contributions approach* is basically another label for the tourist approach, it has identical shortcomings. Despite its flaws, Banks suggests that the approach is possibly the most convenient way to bring in ethnic content because it allows teachers the opportunity to add ethnic content to the curriculum without investing the time, effort, and training needed to rethink and restructure the entire program of study. To illustrate, examine Saul Greenberg's plan to include information about Cinco de Mayo (5th of May) in his social studies curriculum because it is an important day marking the date of an important battle between the Mexican Army and the French Army at the Battle of Puebla (*Batalla de Puebla*). The holiday commemorates the initial victory of Mexican forces at Puebla, and even though the battle merely delayed the French invasion of Mexico City, it has become a symbol of Mexican heritage and pride. The holiday is more of a Chicano (Mexicans living in the United States) celebration than a Mexican one; it is a time for parades, mariachi music, folk dancing, special meals, games, and other types of festive activities.

Mr. Greenberg understood that it would be foolish to celebrate Cinco de Mayo in his classroom without the children knowing why, so he first shared Janice Levy's picture book, *Celebrate! It's Cinco De Mayo* (Whitman). The book tells the story of a young child and his family celebrating the holiday while a simple history of the holiday is intermingled with the plot. After the book discussion, Mr. Greenberg helped the children play a game popular among Spanish-speaking children (Perez, 1993) called "Los Colores" ("The Colors"). The game is a lot like the popular childhood game you may have played as a child, "Red Rover."

In this game, one child is chosen to be St. Guadalupe and another is chosen to be Mother-of-Color, or Rainbow. All of the other children are given color names, each one assigned by Rainbow. (You may use English color names only, or create an opportunity to teach Spanish color names: rojo = red, verde = green, azul = blue, amarillo = yellow, negro = black, and blanco = white.) All the colors belong to Rainbow, and they line up behind her, across the play space from St. Guadalupe. St. Guadalupe's area is designated as "Home Base." St. Guadalupe then initiates the dialogue:

NCSS STANDARDS

I. *Culture*
IV. *Individual Development and Identity*
IX. *Global Connections*

St. Guadalupe: "Knock, knock!" (Child pretends to knock on a door.)
Rainbow: "Who is it?"
St. Guadalupe: "St. Guadalupe."
Rainbow: "What do you want?"
St. Guadalupe: "I want a color."
Rainbow: "What color?"
St. Guadalupe: "Rojo!"

When St. Guadalupe calls out a color, all the children assigned that color name must attempt to reach "Home Base" without being tagged by St. Guadalupe. If they reach "Home Base" safely, they get ready to go again. Those who are caught help St. Guadalupe tag other players until everyone (including Rainbow) is captured. Then the game is over.

As you can easily see, the holiday activity, although useful for integrating ethnic content into the curriculum, was basically tacked on rather than highlighting a major story of America's development.

The Additive Approach

Banks considers the *additive approach* as the first phase of restructuring and integrating the total curriculum because it advances from the "tacked-on" contributions approach by inserting several alternative ethnic perspectives and viewpoints into the traditional curriculum, without going through a major revision of the entire program of study. The major shortcoming of this approach is that the incorporated ethnic content is viewed primarily from the perspective of the mainstream ethnic or cultural groups rather than from the viewpoints of the diverse groups in U.S. society. People from various ethnic groups are included in the curriculum, yet racial and cultural inequities or injustices are not comprehensively addressed.

NCSS STANDARDS

I. *Culture*
III. *People, Places, and Environments*
IX. *Global Connections*

To exemplify the additive approach, we will visit the third-grade classroom of Mary Gilland who is convinced that the study of folktales is one of the most valuable ways to teach students about diverse cultures. She determined that a cross-cultural study of folk literature could help her children discover universal qualities shared by all cultures. For instance, well-behaved people reap rewards while greedy, disobedient behavior receives punishment. Her aim was to have the children compare the characters, story structure, and moral dilemmas in the different versions.

Mrs. Gilland selected six books for this cross-cultural experience:

Folktale	***Country of Origin***	***Reward***
Cinderella (North-South)	France/USA	Marries prince
Yeh-Shen (Putnam)	China	Marries king
Mufaro's Beautiful Daughters (Lothrop)	Zimbabwe	Marries king
The Egyptian Cinderella (HarperTrophy)	Egypt	Marries Pharaoh
Princess Furball (HarperTrophy)	Germany	Wins a prince
Cendrillon: A Caribbean Cinderella (Aladdin)	Caribbean	Becomes a princess

To begin, Mrs. Gilland read the most common *Cinderella* variant to her students—the Charles Perrault version. She designed a large wall chart and printed the book title at the top. She added the areas for comparison along the side. After she read the book, Mrs. Gilland offered timely questions and prompts that helped the children fill in the needed information:

- Who were the main characters in the story? What were they like?
- Where did the story take place? When?
- Summarize the major events on a "story mountain" (see Chapter 4).
- What problem did Cinderella face?
- What kind of magic helped solve the problem?
- What was Cinderella's reward for proper behavior?

Mrs. Gilland followed the same sequence for the remaining five *Cinderella* variants, adding a new variant each day. Figure 2.2 illustrates how her students compared two *Cinderella* variants. Through this sequence, Mrs. Gilland helped the children see that people may differ in some ways, but important values and beliefs are often shared.

The additive approach offers ethnically diverse learning opportunities by modifying the curriculum with culturally relevant instructional activities and materials. The content is expanded to include contributions from all groups so that the curriculum presents multiple perspectives of the community, nation, and world.

FIGURE 2.2 Chart Comparing Two *Cinderella* Variants

	Cinderella	Yeh-Shen
Characters	Stepmother, 2 stepsisters, prince, fairy godmother, and beautiful Cinderella	Stepmother, stepsister, king, and beautiful Yeh-Shen
Setting	"Once upon a time" long ago in Europe	Long ago in China
Problem	Stepmother and stepsisters mistreat Cinderella. She is not allowed to go to the ball.	Stepmother forces Yeh-Shen to do the heaviest work. She kills Yeh-Shen's pet fish. Yeh-Shen is not allowed to go to the big festival.
Magic	Fairy godmother turns a pumpkin into a gleaming coach and rags into clothes, including glass slippers.	The bones of Yeh-Shen's dead fish give her a dress and slippers.
Events	Cinderella goes to the ball, loses a glass slipper while rushing to return by midnight; prince finds the slipper, Cinderella tries it on, and marries the prince.	Yeh-Shen goes to the festival, loses a slipper, returns home. King finds slipper and searches for owner; Yeh-Shen tries on the slipper and it fits. Her rags become a gown. Yeh-Shen marries the king.

The Transformative Approach

The *transformative approach* employs strategies that enable students to view concepts and issues from multiple points of view. This means that we not only add new content about various ethnic groups, heroes, themes, or problems but we also infuse their various perspectives and points of view. The challenge of this approach is that it requires a complete makeover of the curriculum. Banks (2009) suggests the use of sophisticated problem-solving and decision-making skills to examine historical and social events from different points of view that he refers to as *insider* and *outsider* perspectives: "People who have experienced a historical event . . . such as discrimination . . . often view the event very differently from people who have observed it from a distance" (p. 20). Doris Wadwa used the story of Nellie Bly to help her students vicariously explore the dynamics of sexism through the eyes of a brave female.

A powerful account of sexism was employed by Doris Wadwa to help her students employ critical thinking skills to situations involving gender bias by reading *Stop the Presses, Nellie's Got a Scoop!* by Robert Quackenbush (Simon and Schuster). The story centers on a boy and girl who found an old suitcase in the attic. While rummaging through its contents, the two young investigators discover a relic telling of the life of Elizabeth Jane Cochran, nicknamed "Pink" because she liked wearing that color as a child, and they reflect from a contemporary perspective. When Pink was 18 years old she wrote an anonymous letter, signed "Lonely Orphan Girl," to the editor of the *Pittsburgh Dispatch* to condemn a sexist editorial. The managing editor of the *Dispatch* was so impressed by Pink's forthright style that he ran an ad asking her to identify herself. Instead, she showed up in person and convinced the editor to hire her. Pink had landed her first job as a journalist! Since it was considered quite improper for a woman to write for a newspaper at that time, women customarily used pen names. After several suggestions from newsroom workers, Pink and the editor chose *Nellie Bly*, the character in a popular song written 35 years earlier by Stephen Foster.

NCSS STANDARDS

- **I.** *Culture*
- **III.** *Time, Continuity, and Change*
- **V.** *Individuals, Groups, and Institutions*

Not interested in writing fluffy women's interest stories or columns about fashion, Nellie immediately took on meaty stories about social issues—working women, female prisoners, poverty, women's rights, divorce laws, and factory conditions. Her work, controversial at times, sparked social reforms that had been considered necessary for years.

As they learned about the tumultuous life of this vocal spokesperson for women, the children wrote entries into a double-entry journal. In the left column, they jotted down brief notes about significant events in Nellie Bly's life. Then they recorded their feelings in the right hand column. (See an example in Figure 2.3.)

FIGURE 2.3 Double-Entry Journal for Nellie Bly

Nellie Bly's Life Events	My Feelings
Born in Cochran's Mills, PA	Look out world!
Nicknamed "Pink" as a child	I like the color pink, too.
Wrote a letter to a newspaper editor in Pittsburgh complaining about a sexist article	She was brave because women weren't respected then.
Editor asked her to join the paper	I'm glad he liked her "spunk."
Took the name "Nellie Bly"	Women writers could not use their real names.
Wrote articles about women factory workers	She was brave.
At age 21 she went to Mexico and wrote articles criticizing the Mexican government	I would be afraid to get arrested.
Nellie moved to New York City where she wrote about the horrid conditions in women's insane asylums	This brought Nellie lasting fame.
In 1888, Nellie took a trip around the world in 77 days—a world record back then	Nellie became a role model for women everywhere.
In 1894, Nellie retired from journalism and became an industrialist and was president of the Iron Clad Manufacturing Co.	Wow! Now she's a leading women's industrialist. What a woman!
Nellie died in 1922 at age 57	Nellie died young, but had a very full life.

Teachers planning to use a transformative approach to instruction weave a range of unique and important cultural perspectives throughout the social studies curriculum. Doris Wadwa awakened the social consciousness of her students through the eyes of an individual having the passion to challenge inequitable social conditions and bring about social justice. By presenting critical issues and multiple perspectives through powerful resources such as children's literature, teachers help all children learn that people can truly make a difference.

The Social Action Approach

The *social action approach* to teaching about ethnic groups takes in all the elements of the transformative approach, but adds a component that requires students to take social action related to the concept or issue being studied. Mirka Warczka siezed an opportunity to empower his students to be social agents of change when conditions related to a current local construction project were reported by the media.

NCSS STANDARDS

- **I.** *Culture*
- **II.** *Time, Continuity, and Change*
- **III.** *People, Places, and Environments*

Mirka Warczka's sixth-graders became quite troubled after they read a newspaper story about the accidental discovery of a mass grave while a construction crew was excavating a site for a new office complex. After a great deal of careful research, a university professor found that the remains were all that was left of 57 Irish immigrants who died of Black Diphtheria while working as railroad laborers in the late summer of 1853. Their job was to use their picks and shovels to clear and straighten out a portion of hilly land through which a set of new train tracks were to run. It was grueling, dangerous work, and these men labored from dawn to dusk during their 6-day workweek. Unfortunately, a combination of unhealthy conditions and terrible accidents helped contribute to a familiar expression of that time: "An Irishman buried under every tie."

The 57 Irish immigrants had been working here only six weeks before they got sick with Black Diphtheria and died. They were callously dumped in a mass grave between two of the hills they worked to clear. This location was now at the center of a busy crossroad where the office complex was going to rise.

"I can't believe it," blurted Charles. "Those poor men didn't mean anything to the company that hired them."

"Yeah," agreed Katrice. "They were wiped off the face of the Earth and nobody even cared."

"It's like they were treated worse than animals. They were willing to work hard, and look how bad they were treated!" protested Tyreke.

"I wish there was something we could do to give them the respect they deserve," offered Diane.

"Maybe there is," suggested Mr. Warczka. "Let's think about it."

The students researched the situation a bit further and found that a group of interested people had planned to gather at a dedication ceremony in about a month to honor the workers. The group's goal was to locate as many of the workers' remains as possible and provide the men with a proper burial near the construction site.

Today, there is a small plot of land near the office site where the 57 Irish workers are buried. The stones surrounding the tiny burial ground are the exact blocks the workers put down as the base for the tracks. The students attended the dedication ceremony and were given permission to plant an oak sapling at the site to commemorate the occasion. It now grows proudly next to a dignified historical marker that honors the workers.

"To know and to not do is to not know" is a very old Chinese proverb that sums up the situation that attracted the attention of these students. What the old saying means is that if these children were aware of this tragic injustice and failed to respond to it, then they may as well have not known about it at all. Children must be helped to become knowledgeable of ethnic and cultural issues, pay attention to them, and embark on a path of participation that leads to positive change through action: "I wouldn't have known how much a kid like me could help if we didn't have a chance to read about the Irish railroad workers," reflected Freddy.

It is probably unrealistic to expect teachers to make an immediate jump from the contributions approach to a social studies curriculum that focuses on decision making and social action. Instead, it is more reasonable to use the contributions approach for a while and, once teachers feel comfortable with the content and materials, progressively advance to the increasingly sophisticated demands of the succeeding approaches. Despite the challenges of using the various approaches to infusing multicultural content into the curriculum—it can take time, energy, and a great deal of work—Cumming-McCann (2003) believes that the potential rewards are significant:

> Learners seeing themselves in the curriculum, their voices being heard and valued in the classroom. Students feeling a part of the educational process, learning and obtaining the high expectations that are set for them, and beginning to believe that they belong. Imagine students feeling informed, competent, and able to make decisions that have an impact on their lives, their children, and generations to come. Multicultural education holds the power to transform, it provides hope at a time when the future is unclear, and, perhaps most importantly, it provides an opportunity for us to imagine the world as a fair, equitable, and just place in which to live and work. (unnumbered page)

What Are the Goals of Multicultural Education?

Banks (2009) advises that "concepts, content, and teaching strategies [for multicultural education] cannot be identified and selected until goals are clearly defined" (p. 25). In order for all children to reach their greatest potential, then, teachers must begin any instructional decision-making process by asking the fundamental question, "What are the broad outcomes to be achieved, or targets to be reached, as a result of instruction?" The answer to this question will help teachers settle on the methods and materials they will use to prepare their students with the knowledge, skills, and values required to participate as reflective citizens in a diverse, pluralistic society.

The National Council for the Social Studies (1991) has stated that multicultural goals should attempt to attain a delicate balance of diversity and unity, for we are one nation that respects the cultural rights and freedoms of its many peoples. As schools embark on educational programs that reflect multiculturalism, they must demonstrate a commitment to these goals:

1. Recognize and respect ethnic and cultural diversity;
2. Promote societal cohesiveness based on the shared participation of ethnically and culturally diverse peoples;
3. Maximize equality of opportunity for all individuals and groups; and
4. Facilitate constructive societal change that enhances human dignity and democratic ideals. (www.socialstudies.org/positions/multicultural/, unnumbered online page)

The NCSS (1991) advises that multiculturalism should promote neither ethnocentrism nor nationalism. Rather, personal ethnic identity and knowledge of diverse ethnic identities is considered indispensable for promoting understanding and respect.

Teaching in Culturally Diverse Settings

To work effectively with the diverse populations that now characterize our nation's schools, teachers must make certain that the curriculum reveals meaningful, fair, and accurate content while encouraging meaningful and motivational learning experiences. If that extra effort is not made, multicultural programs can often turn

Teachers must help promote understanding, respect, and acceptance of people from diverse racial and ethnic groups.

into *culturally assaultive* experiences instead of culturally responsive ones. To explain what it means to be culturally assaultive, pretend for a moment that you are observing a classroom where children are learning about rituals and ceremonies of various Native American tribes. These rituals and ceremonies often included special headdresses and clothing; symbolic chanting, singing, and dancing were done to the rhythm of drums, rattles, and flutes or whistles. Today, a teacher wants the children to understand that in August, when it is particularly dry in the Southwest, Native American tribes used to perform a rain dance for the water that was so essential to their crops. To help the children understand what a rain dance was, the teacher directed them to form a circle and stand quietly until she gave them actions to mimic. The teacher started by swishing her palms together to imitate the sound of a light drizzle. She turned toward the child at her right who then mimicked the teacher's action until the "drizzle" was passed one by one, all around the circle. Next, the teacher snapped her fingers, then patted her thighs to indicate the growing "rainstorm" and passed the signals on around the circle. Finally, the group stomped its feet to indicate a downpour. The process was reversed to end the rainstorm. Thus, the class participated in a "Native American Rain Dance." Although various interpretations of "rain dances" can be found in Native American cultures, I have yet to find a ceremonial dance with these movements.

This example paints a clear picture of how disrespectful and offensive culturally assaultive teaching can be. It has no place in dynamic social studies classrooms. In its place, we must use *culturally responsive teaching*, defined as having these characteristics:

- It acknowledges the legitimacy of the cultural heritages of different ethnic groups, both as legacies that affect students' dispositions, attitudes, and approaches to learning and as worthy content to be taught in the formal curriculum.
- It builds bridges of meaningfulness between home and school experiences as well as between academic abstractions and lived sociocultural realities.
- It uses a wide variety of instructional strategies that are connected to different learning styles.
- It teaches students to know and praise their own and each others' cultural heritages.
- It incorporates multicultural information, resources, and materials in all the subjects and skills routinely taught in schools. (Gay, 2000, p. 29)

Although most educators agree that there is a significant need for culturally responsive education, they advise that the revised curriculum must not be centered on any particular racial, religious, or ethic group. It is without question that our nation's schools have been guilty of shortchanging the treatment of ethnic minority groups; to meet everyone's needs is unquestionably fundamental and necessary. The tendency of some curriculum developers, however, is to turn around the traditional Eurocentric emphasis to focus on certain ethnic minority groups such

as Mexican Americans or Asian Americans. Banks (2009) warns that to conceptualize ethnic and cultural studies that narrowly "will result in curricula that are too limited in scope and will not help students understand fully both the similarities and differences in the experiences of the diverse groups in the United States" (p. 16). He further asserts, "Mainstream perspectives should be among many different perspectives taught in various content areas" (p. 20). Children must learn to look at culture from many different perspectives: European Americans must learn about Hispanics, African Americans must understand and appreciate the contributions of Native Americans, Asian Americans must examine and value the lives of Arab Americans, and likewise in various alternative combinations. Although it would be impossible to include content about every ethnic group, Banks (2009) recommends that "each curriculum should focus on a range of groups that differ in their racial characteristics, cultural experiences, languages, histories, values, and current problems. . . . The curriculum can be transformed only when events, concepts, and issues are studied from the perspectives of a range of ethnic, cultural, and religious groups" (p. 16).

Characteristics of Culturally Responsive Teaching

The concept of culturally responsive education is based on the premise that ethnic and cultural content is fundamental to curriculum reform and that culturally responsive materials and activities not only help to develop a greater awareness of one's own cultural, racial, and ethnic identity but they also help students respond positively to individuals from groups other than their own. Thus, culturally responsive education places students in classroom settings that recognize and respect their own cultural backgrounds and uses their backgrounds as a foundation on which to build cultural consciousness, intercultural competence, and multicultural perspectives. Below are several principles that exemplify a culturally responsive social studies classroom.

Establish a Democratic Learning Community

A vision of culturally responsive instruction cannot become a classroom reality unless it is firmly supported by a foundation of democratic principles—liberty, freedom, justice, fairness, equality, and equal opportunity. A culturally responsive and supportive classroom environment celebrates diversity, respects human differences, and eradicates racial, ethnic, cultural, and gender stereotypes. Culturally responsive classrooms are settings where students live productively in a democratic learning community. Most teachers would support the idea that children must be active members of a democratic classroom community; this is and has been an important goal of education. Yet, the question of how to accomplish this goal has been challenging, to say the least. Certainly, telling children all about respected democratic principles is not enough. If all children are to actually learn what it means to be active citizens of a democratic community, then these principles must become part everyday classroom life.

Gimbert (2002) advises that in democratic classroom communities students must feel respected and be respectful to others. Students must feel accepted and appreciated as individuals but, at the same time, they must be aware of their place in the group. Democratic classroom communities must try to be like all that we value in our nation's democratic society. Basic to Gimbert's approach (see www.responsiveclass.org) are seven *guiding principles*:

1. The social curriculum is as important as the academic curriculum.
2. How children learn is as important as what they learn. Process and content go hand in hand.
3. The greatest cognitive growth occurs through social interaction.
4. There is a set of social skills children need in order to be successful academically and socially: cooperation, assertion, responsibility, empathy, and self-control.
5. Knowing the children you teach—individually, culturally, and developmentally—is as important as knowing the content you teach.
6. Knowing the families of the children you teach and inviting their participation is essential to children's education.
7. How the adults at school work together is as important as individual competence. Lasting change begins with the adult community.

Gimbert's approach also contains six *practical teaching strategies*:

1. *Morning Meeting:* A daily routine that builds community, creates a positive climate for learning, and reinforces academic and social skills
2. *Rules and Logical Consequences:* A clear and consistent approach to discipline that fosters responsibility and self-control
3. *Guided Discovery:* A format for introducing materials that encourages inquiry, heightens interest, and teaches care of the school environment
4. *Academic Choice:* An approach to giving children choices in their learning that helps them become invested, self-motivated learners
5. *Classroom Organization:* Strategies for arranging materials, furniture, and displays to encourage independence, promote caring, and maximize learning and positive social interaction.
6. *Family Communication Strategies:* Ideas for involving families as true partners in their children's education.

Ukpokodu (2006) advises that concepts of democracy and community are significant underlying components of culturally responsive classrooms:

> Specifically, the teacher structures the learning community to empower all students to experience belonging, autonomy, and competence. . . . To accomplish this, ample opportunities should be provided for students to work together consistently and systematically, through frequent partnership and cooperative learning activities. . . . These methods foster bonding, as students learn to give and take, appreciate each other, and develop a sense of interdependence. (p. 5)

Functioning much like Dewey's concept of a "laboratory of democracy," the classroom can be thought of as a place where students can manage their own affairs and distribute authority among all its members. How can this shared authority be exercised? R. A. Simmons used the following activity to help answer that question.

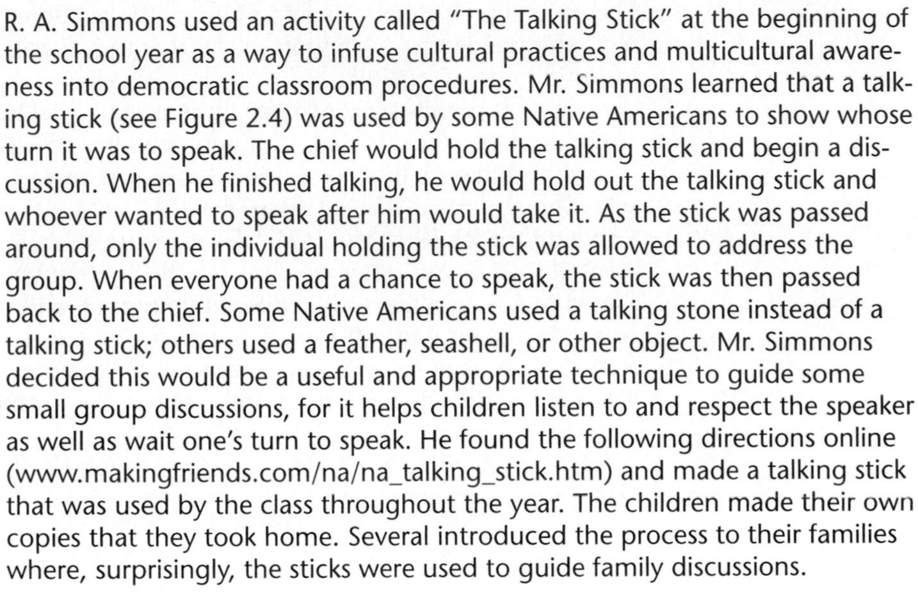

R. A. Simmons used an activity called "The Talking Stick" at the beginning of the school year as a way to infuse cultural practices and multicultural awareness into democratic classroom procedures. Mr. Simmons learned that a talking stick (see Figure 2.4) was used by some Native Americans to show whose turn it was to speak. The chief would hold the talking stick and begin a discussion. When he finished talking, he would hold out the talking stick and whoever wanted to speak after him would take it. As the stick was passed around, only the individual holding the stick was allowed to address the group. When everyone had a chance to speak, the stick was then passed back to the chief. Some Native Americans used a talking stone instead of a talking stick; others used a feather, seashell, or other object. Mr. Simmons decided this would be a useful and appropriate technique to guide some small group discussions, for it helps children listen to and respect the speaker as well as wait one's turn to speak. He found the following directions online (www.makingfriends.com/na/na_talking_stick.htm) and made a talking stick that was used by the class throughout the year. The children made their own copies that they took home. Several introduced the process to their families where, surprisingly, the sticks were used to guide family discussions.

NCSS STANDARDS

I. *Culture*
V. *Individuals, Groups, and Institutions*
VI. *Power, Authority, and Governance*

Talking Stick Directions: You need

- Stick
- 1 yard suede cord
- One yellow pony bead symbolizes sunrise (The East)
  One red pony bead symbolizes sunset (The West)
  One white pony bead symbolizes snow (The North)
  One green pony bead symbolizes grass (The South)
- 1″ strip of faux fur as a reminder to speak softly
- Feather as a reminder to be wise as an eagle
- Bear claw bead as a reminder to be strong like a bear
- Tacky glue
- Scissors

FIGURE 2.4
Native American Talking Stick

Instructions: Cut a 1″ × 6″ strip of faux fur. Wrap it around the end of a stick, gluing in place. Wrap the bottom with a piece of suede cord to secure. Trim. On the other end, wrap another piece of suede cord securing one end and leaving the other end dangling. Tie on a bear claw bead. Slide on the pony beads. Dab the end of a feather in glue and push it up into the bottom pony bead.

Begin with the "Here and Now" of the Students' Lives

If you plan to turn your classroom into a place where cultural responsiveness is a reality, start with a focus on the cultural and ethnic groups represented by the school population. Teachers with a multicultural perspective know that, because they cannot possibly offer equal treatment to the hundreds of microcultures in this country, they must begin by developing an understanding of and sensitivity and respect for the various cultures of the families served by the school community. For example, in urban Los Angeles or in El Paso, Texas, a teacher could start with the Mexican American culture, and in rural Lancaster County, Pennsylvania, a teacher would find it beneficial to start with the Amish culture. In other areas of the country, schools should focus on the character of the groups represented in the community. These cultures should become an integral part of social studies, expanding the standard curriculum with diversity and multiple perspectives. Cultural diversity must be infused into the social studies program and become the lens through which the pluralistic nature of our nation can be focused.

The students, community, and families your school serves should be the primary starting point for culturally responsive instruction, but this is often a daunting prospect for many teachers. They may be at a disadvantage because they may not live, nor have they ever lived, in the community where they teach. In most instances, they have not been in their students' homes nor have they been active in community activities. It is no easy task to incorporate cultural knowledge into one's teaching when personal experiences are limited, so how does a teacher begin to learn about other cultures? Gollnick and Chinn (2002) explain:

> Using the tools of an anthropologist or ethnographer, we could observe children in classrooms and on playgrounds. We can listen carefully to students and their parents as they discuss their life experiences. We can study other cultures. We can learn about the perspectives of others by reading articles and books written by men and women from different ethnic, racial, socioeconomic, and religious groups. Participation in community, religious, and ethnic activities can provide another perspective on students' cultures. (p. 320)

The knowledge you uncover about the community in which you teach and about the rich cultural backgrounds of the families served by your school should help you make the content you are teaching more meaningful by making the children's own experiences the center of the educational process.

A prerequisite for meeting the needs of all families is the belief in their dignity and worth. Researchers have found that "to the extent that the home culture's practices and values are not acknowledged or incorporated by the school, parents may find that they are not able to support children in their academic pursuits even when it is their passionate wish to do so" (Florio-Ruane, 1989, p. 169). Be especially willing to listen as well as talk to the parents of your students—make sure that they understand your program's goals. Find out what they would like their children to learn about their own culture and other cultures. To teach multiculturally requires starting where students are. By finding out where the children are, you may find that the values and expectations of some families may differ markedly from your own. Convinced that the need for understanding and accepting the strengths and differences among her students was never more important, Helen Nguyen regularly offers multicultural experiences so that each child will feel included and valued.

To motivate her fourth-graders to celebrate their own ethnicity through the concreteness of personal experiences, Helen Nguyen had her students create name acrostics—poems in which the first letter of each line spells out a word or phrase. Ms. Nguyen directed the students to print their first and last names vertically on a sheet of paper. For each letter of the first name, the children wrote a word or phrase that described them personally. For each letter of their last name, they wrote a word or phrase that had meaning for their ethnic group. A copy of Lorena Silva's (a Mexican American student) acrostic is shown in Figure 2.5.

FIGURE 2.5 Name Acrostic

Lively	Spanish-speaker
Outgoing	Independent
Reader	La Familia
Enjoys singing	Virgin of Guadalupe
Never sad	Arts
Always happy	

After completing and sharing their personal acrostics, the students were assigned to read a biography about a prominent person from their ethnic or racial group and devise an acrostic for that individual. When all were completed, the acrostics were shared with the class and displayed in a special section of the room.

Ukpokodu (2006) supports this personal approach as a starting point for learning: "To motivate students in the social studies classroom, the teacher must begin from where the students are in their lives, and then connect this reality to the curriculum. Culturally conscientious teaching affirms the lived reality of the everyday lives of students" (p. 6). In Ms. Nguyen's classroom, students will be motivated to explore the contributions of their own and other cultures because they were helped to connect their unique life experiences to subsequent instructional strategies and learning activities.

Regardless of how assimilated the students in your classroom might be, it is your responsibility to ensure that they understand cultural diversity and know the contributions of members of minority as well as dominant groups.

Use Numerous and Varied Instructional Resources

Teachers can uncover abundant instructional resources by seeking input from students, parents, and the local community. Oral and local histories, family records, and cultural museums can be extremely useful. Realia—such as multiethnic dolls, examples of Japanese calligraphy, tortilla presses, kimonos, cowboy boots, nesting dolls, chopsticks, bongo drums, serapes, and tie-dyed cloth from Africa or Asia—fascinate children and encourage interest in people. Inviting people from the community who are willing to come to your room and share something of their culture is a splendid addition to any multicultural program. Resource people can demonstrate a special craft or talent, read or tell a story, display and talk about an interesting artifact or process of doing something, share a special food or recipe, teach a simple song or dance, or help children count or speak in another language. If you arrange for visits from different people throughout the year, then your children will begin to respect and value all cultures. Children should be helped to understand that the arts reflect culture, and that one cannot fully appreciate the value of any

These middle schoolers demonstrate with their mariachi instruments that the arts can bring to life the study of every culture.

art without some understanding of the culture from which it grew. Conversely, one cannot fully appreciate a culture unless one values the creative efforts of its members. Wachowiak and Clements (2006) explain: "One important way for transmitting, maintaining, and analyzing any culture is through the visual arts; hence, art plays an important role in social studies education. . . . The arts are integral to the study of culture, and they are a common denominator in world civilizations" (p. 91).

All social studies programs have the responsibility to provide quality educational experiences that help children become compassionate individuals who feel comfortable with their identities and sense their unity with other people. We must create positive environments where children learn to accept others with cultural differences and begin to develop the skills of living cooperatively in a culturally diverse nation.

Draw from the vast resources of the arts, such as music, art, and literature, which offer some of the most valuable multicultural experiences, as they know no cultural boundaries. The common expressions of human feeling found in these art forms can be used effectively to develop children's capacities to identify with their own and other groups—indeed, the totality of human civilization.

Music It is never too early to introduce young children to the music of various cultures. Songs, rhymes, and chants evoke pleasure and enthusiasm from the very young in kindergarten and first-grade classrooms. Take your children to musical events having distinct cultural characteristics—the varied pitches and subtle differences in intonation of African music, the sophisticated harmonics of traditional Chinese music, Russian religious and folk tunes, the panflutes of the Andes region of South America, and expressive Yiddish melodies complete with laughing and weeping.

Visual Art and Crafts Pictures, arts and crafts, puppets, and other forms of creative expression add zest to the early grades. Seeing the beautiful handmade crafts (pottery, silver and turquoise jewelry, and baskets) of the Hopi and Zuni, for example, helps students understand important aspects of these cultures. Invite guest speakers to demonstrate their special art techniques—Amish quilt making, Inuit soapstone carving, Chinese paper cuts, Patachitra paintings from India, or Plains Indian pictographs.

Literature and Storytelling Read, tell, or dramatize folk stories of various cultures. Good children's literature tells the story of the lives, culture, and contributions of diverse cultural groups in the United States. Through sharing carefully selected literature, students can learn to understand and appreciate a literary heritage associated with many diverse cultures.

Make every effort to expand your students' knowledge of ethnic and cultural groups in American society by exposing them to quality literature—fiction, biography, and folktales. It would be enjoyable and instructive for everyone in your class to visit the library to find one good children's book with an interesting story about her or his ethnicity or culture. Celebrate the diversity in your classroom by presenting a brief book talk and a few sample illustrations or photos from each book.

Use Assorted Instructional Strategies

Children differ from one another from the time they enter this world, and they grow increasingly more unique as they mature through childhood. They vary in physical appearance, emotional makeup, interests, likes, dislikes, gender, ethnicity, race, and countless other characteristics. They vary, also, in the way they learn. Any teacher having a deep interest in children can tell you how important it is that teachers take these individual differences very seriously. Some teachers, however, operate with a conviction that all children should adjust to the teachers' preferred instructional strategies; when it comes to teaching, "one size fits all." Ukpokodu (2003) states,

> We can shortchange many students when we teach to a handful of students while failing to recognize the multiple ways in which diverse learners learn. . . . Such teachers continue to plan and implement curricular and instructional activities that meet the needs of "the average" learner, while assuming that those who do not learn and achieve have no one to blame but themselves. . . . As a result, they often experience disconnection from the learning experience. Today's teachers need to recognize that in any given classroom there is an array of learners who think, process information, and perform in different ways. (p. 31)

Although teachers have informally recognized these differences among children for years, formal theories of different kinds of intelligences are fairly new. One of the most recognizable of these theories has been the *theory of multiple intelligences,* developed by psychologist Howard Gardner in *Frames of Mind: The Theory of Multiple Intelligence* (1983) and *Intelligence Reframed: Multiple Intelligence for the 21st Century* (1999). Gardner's theory suggests there are at least 10 distinctive ways by which people learn about the world:

- *Logical-Mathematical Intelligence.* Children with this strength are good problem solvers, so they enjoy being involved in logical thinking and scientific investigations. These students are very curious and ask endless streams of questions. They like to think abstractly and welcome challenges associated with numbers, patterns, and relationships.
- *Linguistic Intelligence.* Children with this strength are endowed with a mastery of language. They love the sound and rhythm of words and enjoy listening to, reading, and making up stories, poems, jokes, and riddles. They learn new vocabulary or a second language easily. These children are good at expressing themselves with words and are sensitive to the different functions of language.

- *Musical Intelligence.* Children with this strength enjoy producing or listening to music and appreciate various forms of musical expressiveness. You will find them singing, dancing, playing musical instruments, and composing.
- *Visual-Spatial Intelligence.* Children with this strength are able to manipulate and create mental images; they are good at visualizing and are artistically inclined. They will draw and paint superbly, enjoy building things with a variety of construction materials, and will have an easy time interpreting and constructing maps and models.

How Global is the Curriculum *Go to MyEducationLab, select the topic Diverse Learners, and view the Lesson Plan entitled "Using a Multiple Intelligences Approach in Middle Grades."*

- *Bodily-Kinesthetic Intelligence.* Children with this strength are good at movement or other physical activities. They love to be involved in large motor activities such as sports and dance or use their fine motor dexterity to build and fix things. These children want to move all the time.
- *Interpersonal Intelligence.* Children with this strength are outgoing and very tuned into other people's feelings and emotions. They can recognize the moods and feelings of others, empathize with them, and respond appropriately. They understand other people and work effectively with them. These children appear to be "natural leaders."
- *Intrapersonal Intelligence.* Children with this strength are inner-directed. They understand things about themselves—their own strengths, weaknesses, and motivations. These children appear introverted and prefer working alone; they have great confidence in their own ability to get things done.
- *Naturalist Intelligence.* Children with this strength are able to recognize flora and fauna, to make other consequential distinctions in the natural world, and to use their ability in hunting, farming, and the biological sciences.
- *Existential Intelligence.* These children possess sensitivity and capacity to tackle deep questions about human existence, such as the meaning of life, why we die, and how we got here.
- *Moral Intelligence.* This is the final intelligence in Gardner's list to this date. It has to do with a concern for rules, behaviors, and attitudes that govern the sacredness of life—in particular, the sanctity of human life and, in many cases, the sanctity of any other living creatures and the world they inhabit.

Traditionally, schooling has heavily favored the verbal-linguistic and logical-mathematical intelligences, so Gardner suggests that we must modify our teaching approaches to better meet the needs of all our students. The role of teachers is to identify their students' strengths and make use of as many of these intelligences as possible in the materials and activities they select for their students. Naturally, every daily social studies lesson will not lend itself to the utilization of each intelligence, but all should be in plain sight regularly throughout the school year. Culturally responsive social studies instruction requires the selection of activities that work across a great number of children's intelligences. "It is not enough to plan one activity and expect that everyone will experience success engaging in it," warns Ukpokodu (2003). "One size does not fit all. This understanding creates the capacity to bridge social and ethnic gaps. . . . However, this does not mean that teachers should create lower expectations for diverse learners" (p. 32).

It makes sense, then, that culturally responsive teaching strategies should be as variable as the children we teach. Sometimes, instructional outcomes are best accomplished through teacher direction and control of the focus of attention. The lesson follows a logical sequence of activities beginning with an attention-grabbing introduction and ending with an activity to reinforce learning or apply concepts and skills. Although the teacher assumes primary responsibility for structuring the lesson, she or he will modify instruction to meet the needs of individual children. Often, a satisfying and pleasurable teacher-guided lesson will evolve into an inquiry episode by inspiring spontaneous questions of personal interest.

A wide variety of strategies and materials can be used to teach multicultural concepts and sensitivities. They are comprehensively described throughout the remainder of this book.

Understand and Recognize Language Diversity

How Global is the Curriculum *Go to MyEducationLab, select the topic Multicultural Perspectives and Ethnic Studies, watch the video entitled "Teaching Bilingual Students," and complete the questions that accompany it.*

It is logical to assume that when teachers work with children from diverse ethnic and cultural backgrounds, they will encounter an assortment of languages. Hand-in-hand with the rich diversity of cultures in the United States is a grand assortment of languages and dialects. According to the 2000 U.S. Census (2003), over 18.4 percent of American children between 5 and 17 years are from non-English–speaking homes and, in California, 42.6 percent are from non-English–speaking homes. At least 10 million immigrants have come to this country during the past three decades and a great majority are Hispanics. At least 10 million immigrants have come to live in this country during the past three decades and well over 70 percent of these new immigrants are Hispanics, most having settled in California, Arizona, Texas, and New Mexico. As teachers, we must be aware of how these changing demographics will continue to influence the student composition of our classrooms.

Concerns about the goals and purposes of educating non-English–speaking students date back to the Revolutionary War, when school was taught in any of 18 languages spoken by the colonists—English, German, Scottish, Irish, Dutch, French, Swedish, Spanish, Portuguese, and others. As the colonies eventually blended into a new nation, however, English became the dominant language in public education. The freedom to use other languages has become a matter of unrelenting conflict since that time. In 1907, for example, President Theodore Roosevelt made this comment about immigrants and language: "Any man who says he is an American, but something else also, isn't an American at all. . . . We have room for but one language here, and that is the English language." Through the early part of the twentieth century, nearly all bilingual education initiatives had been destroyed.

Although there has been evidence of the sporadic use of languages other than English in our nation's schools, the widespread use of bilingualism (teaching in two languages) did not occur until the 1960s, when the civil rights movement brought attention to discriminatory practices throughout society. In 1968, the Elementary and Secondary Education Act (ESEA) provided funds for schools wanting to provide bilingual education for language-minority students. Also known as the Bilingual Education Act of 1968, it is regarded as the first official federal recognition of the needs of students with limited English speaking ability. Since 1968, the act has undergone several changes reflecting the shifting needs of these students and of society in general. In 1988, Congress passed a new plan for bilingual education, the fourth reauthorization of the original Bilingual Education Act of 1968, in which there was mandated a controversial three-year limit on bilingual education; after three years, students must attain English fluency and schools. The old Bilingual Education Act ran its course until 2002, when it was replaced by the English Acquisition Act of 2002, part of President Bush's No Child Left Behind legislation (also known as Title III). Unlike the Bilingual Education Act, individual states were given the responsibility to support the education of English language learners (ELLs). However, accountability provisions and English assessments were mandated, measurable achievement objectives were in place, and schools were to be held accountable for demonstrating academic progress in English.

If teachers are to experience success in bilingual education, they must have access to the best research-based classroom practices as well as a wealth of information about strategies that meaningfully engage parents as important partners in the learning process. When applied productively, these prerequisites can help make instruction more successful. Bennett (2007) informs that the design of bilingual education programs vary according to the philosophy of a local community or state. She classifies them into three categories: (1) English as a second language (ESL) programs, which use only English as a medium of classroom instruction and communication; (2) two-way bilingual education, which pairs up children who speak different home languages and work together and communicate in their home languages (the goal is to learn each other's language); and (3) maintenance or developmental programs, which help children achieve academic success in both their native language and in English. The goal of dual-language instruction is to teach English while helping the child maintain a sense of ethnic identity.

Using only English in the classroom has its critics. Crawford (1992) describes the effect of this practice on children:

> To devalue a minority child's language is to devalue the child—at least, that's how it feels on the receiving end. The longtime policy of punishing [Hispanic/Latino] students for speaking Spanish is an obvious example. While such practices are now frowned upon, more subtle stigmas remain. Children are quick to read the messages in adult behavior, such as a preference for English on ceremonial occasions or a failure to stock the school library with books in Chinese. . . . Whatever the

> cause, minority students frequently exhibit an alienation from both worlds. Joe Cummins calls it bicultural ambivalence: hostility toward the dominant culture and shame toward one's own. (pp. 212–213)

Despite the fact that most bilingual education advocates echo Crawford's sentiments, Arizona has become the second state to adopt an English-only schools initiative. Proposition 203, modeled on a California measure adopted in 1998, prohibits instruction in any language other than English, even in programs designed to teach them a foreign or Native American language. Such students are to be placed in a structured English immersion program not normally intended to exceed one year.

The more common alternative to submersion in English is bilingual teaching—that is, using two languages as vehicles of instruction. The primary goal of bilingual programs is not to offer instruction in English per se, but to teach children in the language they know best and to reinforce their understandings through the use of English. Grant and Gomez (1996) explain:

> The core curriculum in public school bilingual classrooms is the same as that for any other classroom. The only significant curricular difference is the focus on language development (ESL and the appropriate native language) and attention to the cultural heritage of the targeted language minority group. Besides teaching language, science, math, social studies, art, and music, bilingual teachers must facilitate language learning in everything they do. They are concerned with how best to teach non-English–speaking students the full range of subjects while developing native and [English language] skills. (p. 118)

If you visited an elementary school social studies classroom with a bilingual program, you would likely see an English-speaking teacher and a teacher or aide fluent in a native language. Their preferred teaching approach follows Scarcella's (1990) preview/teach/review format. In this design, the content of the lesson is previewed in English, the body of the lesson is taught in the student's native language, and then the lesson is reviewed in English. This approach is often used when two teachers—one English-speaking teacher and one fluent in the native language—collaborate in a team effort. In addition to Scarcella's preview/teach/review format, Freeman and Freeman (1993) recommend the following guidelines for bilingual instruction:

1. *Environmental Print.* Children learn to recognize words written in both English and their native language when they see print in a number of environmental contexts—magazines, newspapers, telephone books, menus, food packages, street signs, days of the week, classroom posters, labels, nametags, charts, bulletin boards, and other interesting sources. Words should be printed both in English and the children's native language.
2. *Culturally Conscious Literature.* Classroom use of multicultural literature written in the students' native language helps strengthen cultural values and

beliefs. Quality books are now being written for children in a number of languages and are becoming increasingly available throughout the United States. For example, Carmen Lomas Garza's bilingual book, *Family Pictures: Cuadros de Familia* (Children's Book Press), is an authentic portrayal of what it is like to grow up in a Mexican American family in south Texas (Rosalma Zubizerreta authored the Spanish version). If you cannot afford to purchase a number of such books, parents or other members of the community might be willing to lend books written in the children's native language. Having a parent or other volunteer come to school and read from these books adds respect and appreciation for the native language.

3. *Language Buddies.* Learning a second language is enhanced greatly when students are paired up with English-speaking classmates who speak the native language fluently. English proficiency is promoted by the classmate's careful explanations, modeling, and assistance with new words.

Bilingual education, like all dimensions of multicultural education, is based on a commitment to school success for all of our nation's children. A bilingual curriculum should provide students with educational opportunities that are meaningful, compassionate, and challenging—to develop the full range of oral and written language necessary to function in school and as a citizen in our democratic society.

What Other Inequities Must Be Addressed by Our Schools?

In addition to ethnic diversity, our nation's schools must consider the kinds of classroom practices that best address inequities related to special needs and to gender. An appropriate response to these issues can help each child achieve to her or his fullest potential.

Educating Children with Special Needs

Nearly every day, you will come into contact with individuals who fall into one or more categories of exceptionality. Anyone who has spent time with children knows that there are many ways they are all alike and some ways they stand apart from one another. It is important to keep this perspective in mind, for children with disabilities are similar in many ways to children without disabilities. Wolery and Wilbers (1994) clarify:

> All children share needs for food and shelter, for love and affection, for affiliation with others, for opportunities to play and learn, and for protection from the harsh realities of their environments. All children deserve freedom from violence, abuse, neglect, and suffering. All children deserve interactions and relationships with adults who are safe, predictable, responsive, and nurturing. All children deserve oppor-

> tunities to interact with peers who are accepting, trustworthy, kind, and industrious. All children deserve . . . educational experiences that are stimulating, interesting, facilitative, and enjoyable. (p. 3)

In addition to sharing a set of basic needs, all children go through similar stages of development. Although the timing will not be exactly the same for each, children throughout the world move through predictable patterns of motor development (they will walk before they run), language development (they will babble before they speak in sentences), cognitive development (they will want to explore their surroundings with their hands and fingers before they will try to read a book for information), and social-emotional development (they will scream to get their own way before they ask permission for things). Chandler (1994) explains that children with special needs may develop at a rate different from that of more typical children, but the sequence of development remains the same:

> For example, we know that children learn to sit before they stand, stand before they walk. This sequence is the same whether a child is nine months old or three years old. If three-year-old Amanda is unable to walk, we consider her a child with special needs. However, our knowledge of child development still tells us that she first needs to sit, and then stand, before she can walk, even though her development of these skills is delayed. Again, understanding typical development provides the information needed to teach and care for the child with special needs. (p. 21)

Despite these commonly shared needs, children with special needs are different in some ways from children without disabilities. Wolery, Strain, and Bailey (1992) explain: "They need environments that are specifically organized and adjusted to minimize the effects of their disabilities and to promote learning of a broad range of skills. They need professionals who are competent in meeting the general needs of . . . children and are competent in promoting learning and use of skills important to the specific needs of children with disabilities" (p. 95). It is estimated that between 10 to 12 percent of all children in the United States fall into the children with special needs category; they deviate far enough from the typical in at least one respect that an individualized school program is required to address their needs. Who are these children with disabilities? Public Law 101–476, the Americans with Disabilities Act of 1990, defines children with disabilities as those:

> A. With mental retardation, hearing impairments including deafness, speech or language impairments, visual impairments including blindness, serious emotional disturbance, orthopedic impairments, autism, traumatic brain injury, other health impairments, or specific learning disabilities; and B. who, by reason thereof, need special education and related services.

The Concept of Inclusion

Much effort these days is being directed toward inclusion. Inclusive classrooms operate with a conviction that it is discriminatory not to include all students in a regular classroom regardless of handicapping condition. The inclusion movement was initiated over 30 years ago with Public Law 94–142 (the Education for All Handicapped Children Act), signed into law in 1975, and implemented in the fall of 1978. It was a valuable outcome of the many social efforts during the early 1970s to prevent the segregation of any child from regular classrooms, whether because of special needs or race. Specifically, Public Law 94–142 made free public education mandatory for all children older than age 5 who were identified as having special needs. Such education was to take place within a "least restrictive environment," defined as a place where the same opportunities as those available to any other child are offered to children with special needs (those who need special attention to overcome conditions that could delay normal growth and development, distort normal growth and development, or have a severe negative effect on normal growth and development and adjustment to life).

A comprehensive educational, medical, sociocultural, and psychological evaluation by a multidisciplinary team determines the extent of a child's disability. From there, possible remediation strategies are proposed. Schools do this by scheduling a meeting with the prospective teacher, the child's parents, a representative

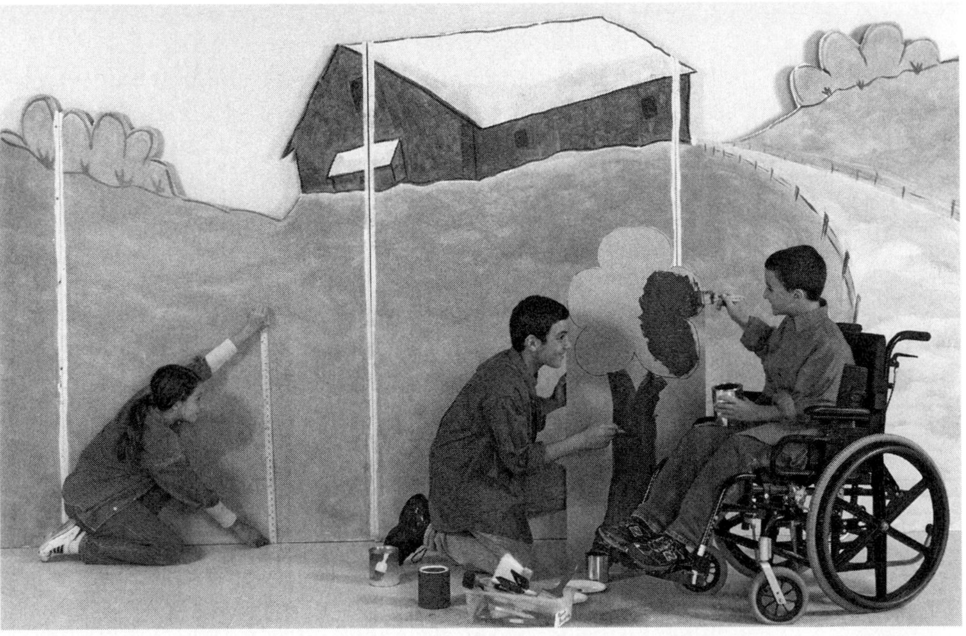

Inclusion is the idea that all children, regardless of their strengths or disabilities, can learn in a regular classroom.

from the school district (usually a special educator), and a member of the assessment team. All information about the child is shared and a personalized education plan, the individualized education program (IEP), is unfolded.

In 1990, Public Law 101–476 amended Public Law 94–142 in several very important ways. First, the legislation clarified what parents could demand for their children with disabilities. It reinforced the idea that all children with disabilities between the ages of 3 and 21 should receive a free and appropriate public education in a "least restrictive environment (LRE)" with their nondisabled peers. In addition to expanding and clarifying special education services for children with disabilities, the legislation replaced the title of PL 94–142 (Education for All Handicapped Children Act) with a new one (Individuals with Disabilities Education Act—IDEA). IDEA has been revised many times over the years; the most recent version was passed by Congress in 2004 and published in 2006.

The 2004 version of IDEA operates with the conviction that it is inappropriate to place all children with disabilities in the regular classroom but to have a "continuum of placements" available. These placements may range from the regular classroom to residential settings. The goal is to place each child in a setting that is specifically suited to her or his unique needs. However, the original intent of IDEA remains the same—to educate as many children with disabilities as possible in the regular classroom while still meeting their individual needs.

Teaching Children with Disabilities

The inclusion of children with disabilities into regular elementary school classrooms has presented a major challenge to teachers. An important consideration in meeting that challenge is to acquire a positive attitude toward inclusion and the individual needs of all students. While recognizing that there are no simple answers, consider how you would feel and what you would do in each of the following situations:

- Sarah has a convulsion and you are the only adult around.
- Alejandro is lost and cannot hear you calling him.
- Jessica seems unable to sit still; she constantly interrupts other children in class.

It might surprise you that the way most people choose to "deal" with problems like these is to avoid them. How many of us tend to steer clear of children with disabilities because we feel inadequate or insecure? You cannot take this approach as a teacher of elementary school children today. You must replace your feelings of inadequacy by confronting your uncertainties and replacing them with confidence based on accurate knowledge. To effectively implement the spirit of inclusion, all professionals must learn something about how it operates; doing so may alleviate many fears and make those involved in the process feel more secure. The following suggestions are general and should be adjusted in consideration of each unique situation.

Learn about Each Specific Disability You have a good start toward understanding children with disabilities if you know about child development. After all, children with disabilities are children. It is important to know that children with disabilities are more like other children than they are different from them. Therefore, your first step in working with children with disabilities is to establish a framework with a solid understanding of child development.

When a child with developmental disabilities enters your classroom, take time to meet and get to know something about her or him. You might invite the family to visit your classroom, or find it instructive to visit the child at home. Whatever the choice, you will need a great deal of background information about the child. Other sources of background information include past teachers or other specialists who have previously cared for the child.

Certainly, it is not possible to know everything about all the special needs you will meet during your teaching career, but you will have to learn a lot about each as you encounter it. That is why the relevant public laws stipulate that a team of specialists must be involved in the formulation of each IEP. However, you should become familiar with the ways one can accept, understand, and become sensitive to the needs of every child. To help in this regard, search through many professional journals, books, and videos available through professional organizations or publishers of special education materials. Get to know each child well.

Once you gather basic information about a specific need, you have taken the first step in working with a child. Solit (1993) uses the case of Marie to describe how this knowledge background fits into the total scheme of planning a program for children with disabilities:

How Global is the Curriculum *Go to MyEducationLab, select the topic Students with Special Needs, watch the video entitled "SmartBoards for Children with Hearing Impairments," and complete the questions that accompany it.*

> The teacher learns that Marie has a moderate hearing loss, with no developmental or cognitive delays. Marie wears hearing aids. The audiologist taught the teacher how to check the hearing aid to ensure it is working. The teacher learns that the hearing aid will make sounds louder, but it will not necessarily clarify speech. The parents explain that Marie uses American Sign Language to communicate. The [principal] decides to find a volunteer who can sign to Marie, communicate with the teacher, and also be a role model for Marie. The teacher also receives release time to attend sign language classes.
>
> The audiologist explains how to adapt the classroom environment so there are less auditory distractions for Marie. The teacher learns that many aspects of the program do not need to change because Marie will benefit from the high quality . . . classroom that is already in place. (p. 133)

Maximize Interactions between Children with Special Needs and Nondisabled Children It is important for children living in a pluralistic society to develop relationships with children who experience a wide range of disabling conditions. That way, children will learn to accept differences at an early age. You can help in this regard by giving simple explanations about a child's disability when she or he comes to your classroom. Youngsters are curious; they want to know about a new child and will be satisfied with a short, open, honest explanation ("Russell's legs don't work well, so he needs a wheelchair"). Encourage the children with disabilities to share their strengths. For example, Russell can help another child in a project that involves the use of his hands (such as building a diorama or drawing a picture), while nondisabled learners may assist Russell with his special needs. In his classroom, for example, Russell regularly joins his classmates on the playground for recess. One of their favorite games is kickball. To play, Russell selects a "designated kicker" to kick the ball for him; after it is kicked, he speeds around from base to base in his wheelchair. Social acceptance and cooperation help support students with diverse abilities. Think about how much more beneficial Russell's experiences are than the experiences of Gerald's, a fourth-grader who was involved in regular classroom activities but not in a constructive way.

Gerald was turned off to school. He achieved well below grade level, rarely responded to his teacher's questions, could barely print legibly, and was seldom included in activities by his peers. Although his teacher accepted Gerald and valued him as a person of worth, he rarely assigned him a useful role in group projects.

One day, Gerald and three other members of his group were involved in an origami project in which they were required to read and follow illustrated directions showing how to fold an 8-inch square piece of paper several times until it turned into a cup. Two of Gerald's partners were high-achieving students, one was an average student overall but extremely gifted as a problem solver, and then there was Gerald.

NCSS STANDARDS

I. *Culture*
IV. *Individual Development and Identity*

Qing Yu, the highest achiever, was the best reader in class and was assigned the group role as "direction-reader/clarifier." Darnell, the other high achiever, was the group manager. He was responsible for making sure everyone stayed on task and had the necessary materials. Felice, the average achiever/top problem solver, was there to help out if anyone experienced difficulty completing the task. Gerald, reacting as he normally did, drew away and went to work on his own. The three others tried their best, but became completely lost in the directions; they followed each other along a path of confusion.

At the same time, alone and overlooked, Gerald had successfully completed seven of the eight steps and was about to finish the last. However, his attention was unexpectedly sidetracked as he heard Qing Yu call to the teacher, "Help! We're lost!"

Not paying attention to Gerald, the teacher addressed the troubled students. As the teacher suggested that the students go back to the beginning, reread the directions more carefully, and study the illustrations, Gerald made the last fold and clutched a cup ready for service. But no one noticed; the confusion continued. As the teacher stood near and offered encouragement, Gerald slowly slipped the cup below his desk out of sight of everyone (assuming someone might actually want to see it) and waited until it was time to move on to something else.

Individualize Your Program Start where the child is and plan a sequential program to encourage him or her to build one skill on another. Visit classrooms where children with disabilities have been successfully included. Look for ways teachers individualize their instruction. How is peer interaction stimulated? Are parents involved in the classroom activities? Are peer questions about a child's disability answered openly and honestly?

Assess Your Classroom Environment Helping children with special needs feel comfortable in your classroom involves some very critical considerations. Overall, the inclusive classroom should contain the same materials and activities suggested for general social studies programs, but these offerings must be enhanced with opportunities to meet the needs of children with disabilities. It helps to include photographs or pictures of people with disabilities participating with nondisabled people on the job or in a variety of other activities. Be sure the learning materials are accessible to all the children. Some children will need Braille labels to help them locate things; others may require ramps to move from one area to another. Whatever the case, be sure to explain to the other children why these special adaptations have been made ("This ramp helps Francine get to the top level when she is in her wheelchair"). Invite adults with disabilities to share their special talents and interests with your students. In short, the classroom should offer a safe environment where all children feel accepted, whatever their capabilities or special needs. Despite the fact that some adjustments must be made, each child should be empowered to gain skills and understandings in all areas and to reach her or his full potential.

Choose Books That Help Children Learn about and Appreciate Diversity Many good children's books offer information about disabilities, explain difficulties youngsters with disabilities often encounter, and tell stories about people who serve as positive role models for children with disabilities. Marc Brown's *Arthur's Eyes* (Little, Brown), for example, tells of how a little boy learns to cope with teasing about his new eyeglasses. Ada Bassett Litchfield's *A Button in Her Ear* (Albert Whitman) explains deafness and how hearing aids help children who have hearing losses. Lucille Clifton's *My Friend Jacob* (Dutton Juvenile) portrays a relationship between a young boy and his older friend with a learning disability. Maxine B. Rosenberg's *My Friend Leslie* (Lothrop) is a photographic essay of a young girl with multiple disabilities.

Literature can be one very important path to understanding and acceptance. This point can be illustrated clearly through this episode from the life of Helen Keller (1920), who lost her sight and hearing after a fever at the age of 19 months. The following high point in Keller's life occurs when her teacher, Anne Sullivan, places the hand of her then 7-year-old pupil under the spout of a pump:

> Someone was drawing water and my teacher placed my hand under the spout. As the cool stream gushed over one hand she spelled into the other the word water, first slowly, then rapidly. I stood still, my whole attention fixed upon the motions

> of her fingers. Suddenly I felt a misty consciousness as of something forgotten—a thrill of returning thought; and somehow the mystery of language was revealed to me. I knew then that "W-A-T-E-R" meant the wonderful cool something that was flowing over my hand. That living word awakened my soul, gave it light, hope, joy, set it free! (pp. 23–24)

Keep many types of stories available and use them to promote questions, conversations, and empathy for children with developmental disabilities.

Inclusion involves changes in attitudes, behaviors, and teaching styles. Plan your inclusive social studies program to fit your children's needs. No single chapter in a textbook can hope to give you a complete idea of the responsibilities involved in doing so, but if you truly want to be a standout teacher, you must begin with sensitivity to the world of all children.

Gender and Classroom Instruction

How Global is the Curriculum *Go to MyEducationLab, select the topic Multicultural Perspectives and Ethnic Studies, watch the video entitled "Caring, Flexibility," and complete the questions that accompany it.*

The image each of us acquires about our masculine or feminine character and the various behaviors and attitudes normally associated with being male or female is called *gender identity*, or *gender typing*. Like most other aspects of child development, gender identity emerges from dynamic interactions of biological and environmental forces. There is no question, for example, that there are basic genetic and physiological differences between males and females; biology sets the stage for gender identification. However, biology alone does not determine gender-specific behavior. From birth, many families begin to show us in subtle ways exactly what it means to be masculine or feminine. For example, little girls are most often dressed in something pink and frilly, whereas boys are routinely clad in blue. Boy babies are commonly referred to by such terms as *big* or *tough*, whereas girls are quite often described as *pretty* or *sweet*. From these early days on, choices of toys, clothing, and hairstyles supplement verbal messages to influence gender identity.

Through environmental manipulation, children unwittingly acquire a gender frame of reference that explains what it means to be a boy or girl. This happens at about the age of 2; from that point on, children work hard to fit into their gender roles. By age 5 or 6, they have already learned much of the stereotypical behavior of their gender. "Appropriate" behaviors are reinforced throughout the early years of life by internalizing the attitudes and responses of such environmental influences as family, relatives, peers, and the media. In other words, little girls who are rewarded for playing with dolls, read books about girls playing with dolls, and see girls playing with dolls on television will be more likely to play with dolls than with trucks. Likewise, little boys who have similar experiences with trucks will be more likely to play with trucks than with dolls. It would seem, then, that if gender-specific behaviors are influenced by such environmental phenomena, children raised in bias-free environments would not exhibit a preference for stereotypically gender-specific toys. However, a phenomenon referred to as *developmental sexism* seems to crop up despite our most systematic attempts to shape a nonsexist environment. This means that young children grow to be enormously sexist in their perception of gender roles and choice of play activities (most boys choose to engage themselves as cowboys while girls play house) even if they have been brought up in a nonbiased environment.

This concept of developmental sexism is supported by Kohlberg's (1992) idea of *gender constancy*. That is, children learn early in life that they permanently belong to a category called "boy" or "girl"—their gender cannot change. Once children grasp the concept that they cannot be transformed from girl to boy and back again, they organize the world into "girl" or "boy" categories and become powerfully attached to their gender. Such a strong attachment to one's gender continues to grow through the early elementary grades, cementing the peer solidarity that influences behaviors compatible with society's expectations for males and females.

Gender-role stereotypes seem to be markedly decreasing in our elementary schools, but they continue to be a problem. Although books appear to be fairer and more inclusive than in the past, Sadker, Sadker, and Klein (1991) believe that teachers prefer to read the books they grew up with; many of these older books represent highly traditional gender roles. Therefore, even today, the influence of sexist books can be found in some classrooms.

In addition to problems with books, Sadker and Sadker (1986) suggest that girls are shortchanged during classroom interactions. Elementary school teachers ask boys more questions, give them more precise feedback, criticize them more frequently, and give them more time to respond. The teacher's reaction may be positive, negative, or neutral, but the golden rule appears to be that boys get the most attention from teachers in elementary school classrooms.

Additionally, the American Association of University Women (AAUW) has reported, "There is clear evidence that the educational system is not meeting girls' needs. Girls and boys enter school roughly equal in measured ability. In some measures of school readiness, such as fine motor control, girls are ahead of boys. Twelve years later, girls have fallen behind their male classmates in key areas such as higher-level mathematics and measures of self-esteem (1992, p. 2).

Although most of the research into gender bias in schools has been centered on the unfair treatment of girls, Campbell (1996) cautions, "It is boys who lack role models for the first six years of schooling, particularly African American, Latino, and Asian boys. While young, European American girls benefit from their female-centered primary school experience, children of color—particularly boys—fail. It is boys who encounter the most conflicts and receive the most punishments in school and most often get placed in special education and remedial programs" (p. 113).

Gender stereotyping can be tied to many influences and conditions, but teachers must take a positive role in recognizing bias and replacing it with equitable expectations for all children. This means eliminating one's own biases of gender-associated behavior and stereotyped notions about gender roles. This can be done by providing males and females with appropriate instruction and by avoiding gender-role stereotyping. Some guidelines to avoid sexism in teaching follow.

Avoid Stereotyping Masculine and Feminine Roles Examine ways you might be limiting the options open to boys and girls. During class discussions, for example, many teachers attempt to reason with young children in order to create more objective attitudes about gender roles. When a child says, "Only boys can grow up to be truck drivers," teachers are tempted to reply, "That's not true. Women can be truck drivers, too." This approach often fails. The young child's way of classifying the world into male and female is new and not open to exceptions. A child may even become upset that the teacher fails to see the world in the same light and defend his or her case even more strongly. A teacher can compound the problem, then, by trying to reason with a child. First, let the children know you understand and accept their unique system of trying to make sense of the world. Instead, you might say, "I know you've never seen a woman truck driver before, so it's hard to understand that women can drive large trucks, too." However, trying to reason with a child through comments such as, "It's okay for women to be truck drivers, too. Many women are very good at driving large trucks," often elicits a response such as, "Well, they shouldn't be!"

Stereotyping should be avoided at all costs. This advice extends not only into how females are featured but also into whether men are depicted in traditionally male roles and careers.

Use Gender-Free Language Whenever Possible Through words and actions, teachers assume the position of a positive role model. Be sensitive to your choice of masculine terms to refer to all people; for example, *police officer* replaces *policeman*, *firefighter* replaces *fireman*, and *mail carrier* replaces *mailman*. If your children use labels such as "fireman" frequently, begin a discussion with a comment such as, "Saying the word fireman makes it sound like only men fight fires. Do you think that's true?" Then introduce the word *firefighter* and point out that men and women (and boys and girls) can do the same kinds of jobs. Additionally, be aware of how actions can convey ideas of gender-role coequality. For example, the children may learn to interpret gender roles less rigidly if they see their teachers, male and female, displaying characteristics typically associated as either masculine or feminine—for example, being assertive and forceful, sensitive and warm, depending on the situation.

Make Sure Your Classroom Materials Present an Honest View of Males and Females Just as you lead young children toward understanding the idea of equality through your words and actions, the activities and materials you choose for your classroom should resist gender stereotyping. Books such as *Heather Hits Her First Home Run* by Phyllis Hacken Johnson (Lollipop Power Books) and Charlotte Zolotow's *William's Doll* (HarperTrophy) are sensitive books that address stereotypes. *William's Doll* takes a look at a situation many little boys face:

> William would like a doll so he could play with it like his friend Nancy does with her doll. At the very thought of a little boy with a doll, his brother and friend call

> him creep and sissy. William's father buys him a basketball and a train, instead of a doll. William becomes a very good basketball player and he enjoys the train set, but he still longs for a doll. Finally, when William's grandmother comes for a visit, she buys him a doll and explains to his father that having a doll will be good practice for him when he grows up and has a real baby to love. (Raines & Canady, 1989, p. 50)

Teachers who wish to build a good classroom collection of gender-fair books will need to look for books that show children and adults engaged in a variety of activities, regardless of gender.

A program offering opportunities for both sexes to participate in positive classroom experiences should transcend obsolete sex-role expectations such as boys taking the lead when mathematics skills are required, and girls dominating when sewing or cooking activities are needed for a project. Encourage the boys to wash the art table after completing a salt-and-flour relief map and the girls to hammer the nails needed to hold together a model clipper ship. If this doesn't happen freely, discuss the situation with your students. Say, "I notice that in most social studies projects the boys build the model. This seems to exclude the girls. Why do you think that is happening?" Invite equal access to activities by encouraging children to engage in a wide range of experiences that are free of gender stereotypes.

Balance the Contributions of Men and Women in the Social Studies Program All students should be exposed to the contributions of women as well as men throughout history. Students are being cheated of a wealth of information about the majority of the world's population when women are not included as an integral part of the curriculum. Banks (1994) suggests that women can be virtually ignored in written history. Citing the Montgomery, Alabama, bus boycott of 1955 as an example, Banks maintains that most textbook accounts emphasize the work of men such as Martin Luther King Jr. and Ralph D. Abernathy, or organizations headed by men, but virtually ignore the work of women. He uses the memoirs of Jo Ann Gibson Robinson, president of the Women's Political Council of Montgomery, as an example. The council was started in 1946 to "provide leadership, support, and improvement in the black community and to work for voting rights for African Americans" (Banks, 1994, p. 6). The council received numerous complaints concerning bus driver offenses against African Americans who were asked to give up their seats on crowded buses to whites. On December 1, 1955, Rosa Parks was arrested for refusing to give up her seat. Disgusted by such hostile encounters with bus drivers, the council distributed leaflets that called for a boycott of city buses. Referring to Rosa Parks, Robinson's leaflet read in part: "This woman's case will come up on Monday. We are, therefore, asking every Negro to stay off the buses Monday in protest of the arrest and trial. Don't ride the buses to work, to town, to school, or anywhere else on Monday" (Garrow, 1987).

Although most textbook accounts credit King and Abernathy for the Montgomery bus boycott, plans to end bus segregation with a boycott were actually instituted two years earlier, in 1953, by Robinson's Women's Political Council. The Parks case in 1955 just happened to be the "right time" to implement the boycott. The situation seems to be improving in recent years, but the work of historically significant females such as Jo Ann Gibson Robinson still must find its way into our nation's textbooks. This does not mean we must sit back and wait for that day; it will take a great deal of scholarly effort to uncover their stories, but the experiences of women from all walks of life must be highlighted in the social studies curriculum.

Schools that foster positive gender roles will help children value the likenesses and differences in themselves, thereby taking an important step toward alleviating the damage resulting from long-ingrained patterns of sexism in our society. It is this unconditional positive regard for children that lies at the heart of social studies education.

A Final Thought

Good social studies teachers always impress me with the warmth they connect to the special moments they share with their students. The expressions on children's faces when they learn something new, the excitement shown by parents as their children make progress during the year, just being with children and knowing that there is a common bond of affection, the children's unspoiled enthusiasm—such experiences revitalize teachers and can strengthen their commitment to the profession. Many teachers find great joy in the candid individual expressions that mark each child's uniqueness: "Henry came up to me holding his finger as if it were hurt. When I asked him what was the matter, he replied, 'An elephant bit my finger,' and then turned and walked away!" These are the special moments of satisfaction awaiting a teacher of elementary school children. You will find extraordinary joy, affection, excitement, and personal satisfaction as you meet challenges each day.

Children thrive under good teachers who delight in children being who they are. These teachers adapt the social studies classroom to meet every child's ethnic, cultural, linguistic, and special needs. This includes providing the child with the time, opportunities, resources, understanding, and affection to achieve the important goals of social studies education. To affirm individual differences, teachers must eliminate bias from the elementary school environment. Every child must know he or she is appreciated and respected by the teacher and needs experiences that reflect an understanding and appreciation for individual and cultural differences. These experiences are not only memorable and pleasurable, but they also last a lifetime—they help make our world.

REFERENCES

American Association of University Women. (1992). *How schools shortchange girls*. Washington, DC: Author.

Banks, J. A. (2009). *Teaching strategies for ethnic studies*. Boston: Pearson.

Banks, J. A. (1994). Transforming the mainstream curriculum. *Educational Leadership, 51*, 4–8.

Bennett, C. I. (2007). *Comprehensive multicultural education: Theory and practice*. Boston: Pearson.

Campbell, D. E. (1996). *Choosing democracy: A practical guide to multicultural education*. Upper Saddle River, NJ: Merrill/Prentice-Hall.

Chandler, P. A. (1994). *A place for me: Including children with special needs in early care and education settings*. Washington, DC: National Association for the Education of Young Children.

Clark, L., DeWolf, S., & Clark, C. (1992). Teaching teachers to avoid having culturally assaultive classrooms. *Young Children, 47*, 5.

Crawford, J. (1992). *Hold your tongue: Bilingualism and the politics of English only*. Reading, MA: Addison-Wesley.

Cumming-McCann, A. (2003, February). *Multicultural education connecting theory to practice*. Retrieved from www.ncsall.net/?id=208.

Florio-Ruane, S. (1989). Social organization of classes and schools. In M. Reynolds (Ed.), *Knowledge base for beginning teachers* (pp. 163–172). Oxford: Pergamon.

Freeman, D. E., & Freeman, Y. S. (1993). Strategies for promoting the primary languages of all students. *The Reading Teacher, 46*, 552–558.

Garcia, R. L. (1991). *Teaching in a pluralistic society: Concepts, models, and strategies*. New York: HarperCollins.

Gardner, H. (1999). *Intelligence reframed: Multiple intelligences for the 21st century*. New York: Basic Books.

Gardner, H. (1983). *Frames of mind: The theory of multiple intelligences*. New York: Basic Books.

Garrow, D. J. (1987). *The Montgomery bus boycott and the women who started it: The memoir of Jo Ann Gibson Robinson*. Knoxville: The University of Tennessee Press.

Gay, G. (2000). *Culturally responsive teaching: Theory, research, & practice*. New York: Teachers College Press.

Gimbert, B. (2002, September). *New horizons for learning*. Retrieved from www.newhorizons.org.

Gollnick, D. M., & Chinn, P. C. (2002). *Multicultural education in a pluralistic society* (6th ed.). New York: Macmillan.

Grant, C. A., & Gomez, M. L. (1996). *Making schooling multicultural: Campus and classroom*. Upper Saddle River, NJ: Prentice-Hall.

Keller, H. (1920). *The story of my life*. Garden City, NY: Doubleday.

Kohlberg, L. (1992). In G. R. Lefrancois, *Of children*. Belmont, CA: Wadsworth.

Krug, M. (1976). *The melting of the ethnics*. Bloomington, IL: Phi Delta Kappa.

National Council for the Social Studies. (1991). *Curriculum guidelines for multicultural education*. Retrieved from www.socialstudies.org/positions/multicultural/.

Perez, J. (1993). Viva la differencia. *First Teacher, 14*, 24–25.

Public Law 101–476, October 30, 1990, Stat. 1103.

Raines, S. C., & Canady, R. J. (1989). *Story s-t-r-e-t-c-h-e-r-s: Activities to expand children's favorite books*. Mt. Ranier, MD: Gryphon House.

Rong, X. L. (1998). The new immigration: Challenges facing social studies professionals. *Social Education, 62*, 393–399.

Sadker, D., & Sadker, M. (1986). Sexism in the classroom: From grade school to graduate school. *Phi Delta Kappan, 68*, 512.

Sadker, M., Sadker, D., & Klein, S. (1991). The issue of gender in elementary and secondary education. In G. Grant (Ed.), *Review of research in ed-*

ucation. Washington, DC: American Educational Research Association.

Sadker, M., Sadker, D., & Steindam, S. (1989). Gender equity and educational reform. *Educational Leadership, 46,* 44–47.

Scarcella, R. (1990). *Teaching language minority students in the multicultural classroom.* Upper Saddle River, NJ: Prentice-Hall.

Solit, G. (1993). A place for Marie: Guidelines for the integration process. In K. M. Paciorek (Ed.), *Early childhood education 94/95.* Guilford, CT: Dushkin Publishing.

Stearns, P. N. (1996). Multiculturalism and the American educational tradition. In C. A. Grant & M. L. Gomez (Eds.), *Making schooling multicultural: Campus and classroom* (pp. 17–33). Upper Saddle River, NJ: Merrill.

Ukpokodu, O. (2006). Essential characteristics of a culturally conscientious classroom. *Social Studies and the Young Learner, 19,* 4–7.

Ukpokodu, O. (2003). Meeting the needs of diverse learners. *Social Studies and the Young Learner, 16,* 31–32.

U.S. Bureau of the Census. (2003). *Summary tables on language use and English ability: 2000 (PHC-T-20).* Washington, DC: U.S. Government Printing Office.

U.S. Bureau of the Census. (1996). *Current population reports—Population projections of the United States by age, sex, race, and Hispanic origin: 1995–2050.* Series P-25-1130. Washington, DC: U.S. Government Printing Office.

U.S. Office of Education. (1977). Education of handicapped children. *Federal Register* (part 2). Washington, DC: Department of Health, Education and Welfare.

Wachowiak, F., & Clements, R. D. (2006). *Emphasis art.* Boston: Pearson.

Wolery, M., Strain, P. S., & Bailey, D. B. (1992). Reaching potentials of children with special needs. In S. Bredekamp & T. Rosegrant (Eds.), *Reaching potentials: Appropriate curriculum and assessment for young children, Vol. 1.* Washington, DC: National Association for the Education of Young Children.

Wolery, M., & Wilbers, J. S. (Eds.). (1994). *Including children with special needs in early childhood programs.* Washington, DC: National Association for the Education of Young Children.

Zangwell, I. (1909). The melting pot (A Play). Quoted in D. M. Gollnick & P. C. Chinn (1983), *Multicultural education in a pluralistic society.* St. Louis: Mosby.

CHAPTER 3

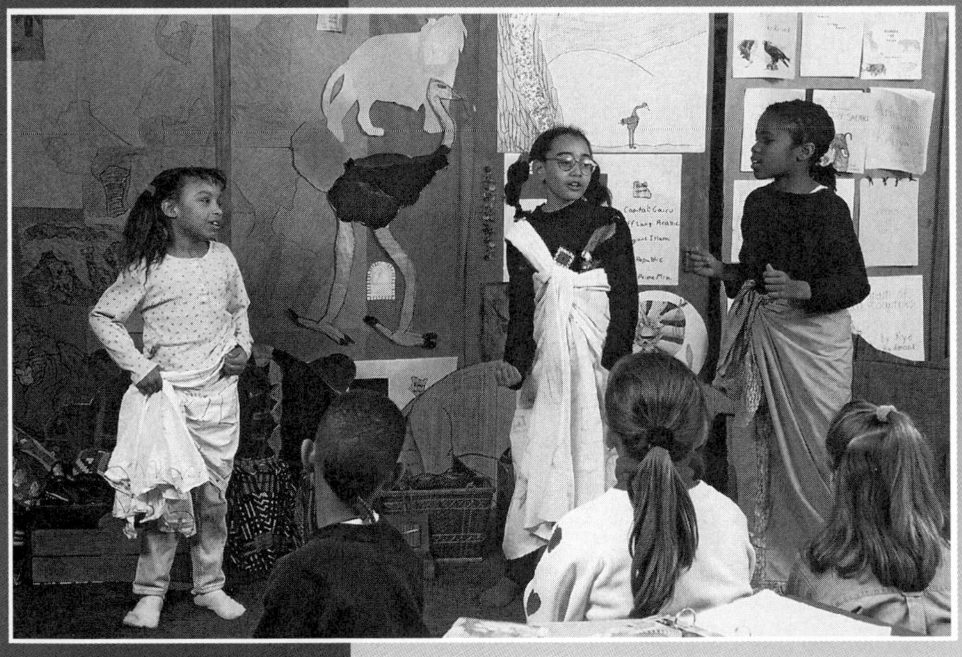

Integrated Teaching
Connecting Learning to the Real World

What Does Integrated Learning Look Like?

At the start of a late-November thematic unit dubbed "December Holidays," Anna Garber prearranged a number of attention-grabbing items on a large table at a classroom interest center, above which was draped a banner bearing the word *Kwanzaa* (a Swahili term meaning "First Fruits"). Kwanzaa is a week-long festival honoring one's African American heritage and is celebrated for seven days beginning December 26. The classroom table was covered with a green tablecloth and accessorized with red and black cloth mats—the three colors of the African American flag. A number of items commonly used in Kwanzaa celebrations were displayed on the table. After the children had an opportunity to explore the items, Mrs. Garber brought the class together and read the book *The Gifts of Kwanzaa* by Synthia Saint James (Albert Whitman). The book clearly and interestingly explained each of the items on display. Afterward, Mrs. Garber led a discussion of the story, focusing on the relationship between the items on the table and the experiences of the people in the book, as well as on similarities and differences between Kwanzaa and other traditional December celebrations.

On succeeding days, Mrs. Garber offered these learning experiences:

- She arranged candles on a *kinara* (candleholder supporting the seven candles representing the Kwanzaa principles) so that a black candle was in the middle, red candles on the left, and green on the right. Each day, a candle was lit and Mrs. Garber and the children talked about the associated principle of Kwanzaa.

- Mrs. Garber invited parents, grandparents, and members of the community into the classroom to share a family photo album or some valued articles that were passed down from generations past. And, since music, song, and dance are important to the celebration of Kwanzaa, some guests were able to demonstrate musical instruments with African or African American roots.
- Mrs. Garber showed the children examples of beads that were worn by some Africans for adornment, ceremonies, and religious purposes. The children learned that in some tribes, the patterns or colors of strings of beads could carry very special meaning. The children strung their own colored wooden beads that were worn during Kwanzaa week and others that were to be given as gifts during the classroom's planned Kwanzaa festival.
- The class played the West African game called "Snake" (*Da Ga*). It is similar to our game of "Tag."
- Mrs. Garber taught the children songs from West Africa with a recording called *Multicultural Rhythm Stick Fun* (Kimbo). The children listened to the rhythmic melody and responded to the simple directions with rhythm sticks.
- The class tried the traditional African art of tie-dye as they fashioned their own *dashiki* (de-SHE-ke), or traditional shirt for African men, and *gele* (GAY-lay), or women's traditional headwrap.
- In keeping with the spirit of Kwanzaa, the children created a simple but natural "gift of the heart" for the animals near their school. They threaded popcorn and fresh cranberries on long strands of string. Later, they would drape the food-covered strings on trees or bushes as a holiday treat for the animals.

How Global is the Curriculum
Go to MyEducationLab, select the topic Cross-Curricular Connections, and watch the video entitled "Opportunities for Learning," and complete the questions that accompany it.

NCSS STANDARDS

I. *Culture*
V. *Individuals, Groups, and Institutions*
IX. *Global Connections*

Mrs. Garber and the class were so pleased by what they had learned about Kwanzaa that they wanted to invite the students' families to a classroom Kwanzaa celebration, or *karamu* (kah-RAH-mu). The karamu would serve not only as an excellent review of all the learning experiences that had taken place beforehand but it also would also provide an interesting and authentic way to share what they had learned with others. To begin, the students placed two large tables in the center of the room. They positioned an unlighted *kinara* at the center of each table and spread 20 ears of corn (one for each child in the home or, in this case, the classroom) on each. Since the *mazao* (fruits of the harvest—usually corn, grapes, bananas, apples, and pears) is an important element of the Kwanzaa table, each child brought to school two pieces of fresh fruit and worked together with their classmates to put together a nutritious "First Fruits" salad. On a smaller table, the children arranged their Kwanzaa gifts—beads for family members in attendance and the popcorn string for the birds.

The celebration began with a welcome to all and a brief explanation of Kwanzaa. The boys were elegantly clad in their *dashikis*; the girls were attractively adorned in their *geles* as they told the story of Kwanzaa. Each family member in attendance received a student-constructed booklet explaining the seven Kwanzaa principles; the class and the adults in attendance joined together to read aloud the principles and meanings together. Then, the "First Fruits" salad and other nutritious treats were enjoyed by all. Following the celebration, the children performed their rhythm stick activity and demonstrated how to play the game of *Da Ga*. Last, the children presented their parents with the gift of beads and, together, the children and their parents took the popcorn strings outdoors and placed them in trees and on bushes for the animals to enjoy.

Sometimes a project like this can bring about some very unexpected and prized outcomes. For example, after the classroom celebration had ended and guests were leaving the school, a set of parents approached Mrs. Garber and thanked her for the opportunity to participate in the *karamu*. They disclosed having known very little about Kwanzaa before this experience, but that having the opportunity to join together with their children and other families in such a meaningful way convinced them that celebrating Kwanzaa in their own home would be a tradition they wanted to establish. Since the school calendar made it necessary for the class to celebrate Kwanzaa prior to its normal dates in late December, the parents had plenty of time to prepare for their own celebration at home. Certainly, the major goal of this learning experience was to help children understand holiday traditions and be respectful of diverse customs and beliefs, but it also encouraged quality lifelong practices. Meaningful activities often grow far beyond the limits imposed by classroom time and space.

Anna Garber was an incredible teacher with many years of experience when I first met her. A model professional in every way, Mrs. Garber had a tremendous influence on my teaching career (and I'm sure many others). I was sold on the way this remarkable person motivated children to do great things. Using what seemed like magical ease and ability, Mrs. Garber skillfully facilitated their curiosities, interests, and persistence in digging up solutions to life's mysteries. If you were lucky, somewhere along the line you had a Mrs. Garber, too. Someone who made the sun come up. Someone who smiled and was patient. Someone who wouldn't let you quit. Someone who told you that all things really are possible. Someone who inspired you to reach for the stars.

Like me, everyone sitting in your classroom has a teacher to thank. You've all had that special person in your life who you could count on—a special individual who was able to discover that delicate balance between fun and seriousness that was the key to unlocking your world. If it's possible, take the time to revisit that once-in-a-lifetime individual and let her or him know just how much she or he mattered.

The "Mrs. Garbers" of our world realize that the goal of dynamic social studies education is to develop informed, caring citizens who will one day make a difference in our country. To help attain this goal, our Mrs. Garbers make social studies a subject that children can sink their teeth into. They believe that elementary school children are naturally inclined to dive headlong into whatever excites their curiosity and that teachers should be a little more flexible, a little more spontaneous, and a little more willing to depart from the commonplace to help students explore their world. "If teachers are reluctant to take risks," Mrs. Garber shrewdly challenged me one day, "how can they ever hope to inspire that ideal in their students?" Our Mrs. Garbers are sensitive to the fact that as children's interest in their world expands, a wealth of stimulating learning experiences must be employed to heighten their discoveries. When your first class comes eagerly marching into your classroom, whom will they face as their teacher? Will you turn out to be a Mrs. Garber in their lives? Or will you be satisfied to be counted among the ordinary?

Many feel that today's obsessive demands for addressing academic standards and achieving lofty standardized test scores cheat teachers of their dream-building time and may eventually lead to the extinction of our Mrs. Garbers. It is no secret that teachers today are so overwhelmed by standards expectations in reading, writing, and math that social studies has become one of the school subjects likely to be postponed, shoved to the end of the day, or forgotten about altogether. Jennings and Rentner (2006) report, "To find additional time for reading and math, . . . 71% of districts are reducing time spent on other subjects in elementary schools. . . . The subject most affected is social studies" (p. 111). If social studies does happen to get squeezed into a day's schedule, the children are often led through a quick oral reading of a few pages in the textbook followed by a question-answer session "just to get it in."

"When can I possibly find the time to teach social studies the way I'd like to?" these teachers implore. "I just can't find one more minute in my day to fit everything in! Besides, our school district isn't required to test for proficiency in social studies as we do for the other subjects, so we aren't rewarded for giving much effort there. Why take the time?" Consequently, we find that "in some places, instructional time for social studies is as little as twelve minutes per week" (VanFossen, 2006, pp. 376–403). This all seems to indicate that nontested school subjects such as social studies seem to be pushed aside or forgotten about altogether in this current high-stakes accountability environment.

As a result of these "reforms," teachers appear to have little motivation to experience the kinds of joy, creativity, and innovation that can be found in teaching social studies. But, by denying our youth quality social studies instruction, we starve them of the knowledge, skills, and attitudes prerequisite of effective citizenship in our proud democratic society. Mary Vanderslice (2007), a fourth-grade teacher, agrees: "Social studies has taken a place 'on the back burner' for much too long. It is time to pull it off the stove and serve it up to our students in the most creative fashion we can imagine" (p. 5). In their quest to "pull social studies off the back burner," teachers have begun to bring together the various elementary school subjects to create interesting and challenging learning opportunities. Therefore, they might choose to combine history with the literacy program by having children read and write biographies and historical fiction. They could bring map skills to math class as children compute distances between locations. And, the arts can take on new life as the students sing slave spirituals or dramatize the Boston Tea Party. Referred to as *integrated learning*, the practice of joining together elementary school subjects is based on the idea that the real world doesn't compartmentalize life into subject matter categories; life demands that we all must use a complex network of entwined skills and information to take on real issues.

In today's schools, teachers have found integrated learning a perfect framework for keeping social studies an active subject in the elementary school classroom. Vanderslice (2007) explains, "I can honestly say that if I did not integrate . . . social studies into math and literacy, this area of study [social studies] would more than likely go untouched" (p. 4). Stevens and Starkey (2007) found that integrated learning experiences not only kept social studies alive in their classrooms but it also produced outstanding achievement results: "Our students improved their literacy scores on average by at least two levels and gained [social studies understandings as well]. In an age of pressure to achieve well on high-stakes tests, we think we have arrived at a way of teaching that not only satisfies literacy requirements, but also teaches students in a lively way about the world in which they live" (p. 10).

What Is Integrated Learning?

The concept of curriculum integration is nothing new. It has been around in one form or another since the 1800s, and has been supported over the years by prominent educators such as John Dewey. By its very nature, integrated learning is designed to break down the barriers among school subjects in an attempt to make learning more substantial for students. Through Mrs. Garber's classroom example at the beginning of this chapter, it is easy to see how an integrated curriculum accesses knowledge from all of the traditional subjects without labeling them as such—children experienced learning as a unified whole rather than having it broken down into separate subjects such as history, math, art, music, or reading.

Mrs. Garber adopted the integrated learning philosophy after her first few years of classroom teaching. At the end of her first year, she recounted to me, while she was constantly thinking about the apparent connectedness among the various school subjects, Ms. Garber began to ask some interesting *"Why"* questions: *"Why* is it that when my students read a story about Sojourner Truth at nine-thirty in the morning and I follow that up with a creative art project, it is called reading?" *"Why* is it that when we read about Sojourner Truth at two-thirty in the afternoon and I follow that up with a dramatic skit, it is called social studies? I'm essentially doing the same thing!" As I thought about what she had said, I wondered how anyone could possibly teach social studies without teaching reading, too (and vice versa). Certainly, reading skills are utilized and strengthened as the children read about all the fascinating people, places, and events that have shaped our world and, conversely, our insights into all the fascinating social characteristics of the world are enhanced as we read about them.

Those who support curriculum integration contend that schools must think of education as a process of getting children ready to successfully tackle real-world issues of the twenty-first century, rather than as an assortment of discrete, compartmentalized subject matter that children must burn into their brains. Risinger (2005) criticized the current emphasis of high-stakes testing as a means of assessing the level to which curriculum standards are being addressed by school districts, and he called for social studies educators to expand the use of integrated curriculum projects and instruction. He defended his position with this strong support: "Research suggests that students learn more, enjoy classroom activities, and do as well or better on tests when they are shown how different subjects (such as science and social studies) are related" (p. 149).

In summary, an integrated social studies curriculum:

- Draws from all subjects taught in the traditional elementary school curriculum
- Makes use of integrative learning materials and activities
- Places an emphasis on projects
- Organizes instruction around a designated theme or topics, such as "Democracy in Greece" or "Deserts Around the World."

Drawing from Other Subjects

Dynamic social studies programs do not exist merely to transmit a massive data package that often results in a partial or shallow understanding of our world. Instead, the best programs offer comprehensive and interconnected experiences that enlighten students' understandings of humanity past and present. They pull from many areas of the curriculum to present a cohesive, absorbing awareness of the world.

The Arts

Although involvement in the arts can be both pleasurable and instructive, the arts have often been unfairly and narrowly characterized as simply an "added fun" part of the elementary school curriculum. However, the arts are much more than a curriculum frill; they are an indispensable element of the human experience.

Can you think of a better way to understand and appreciate ancient Japanese culture than through their magnificent kabuki theater, kana characters (writing), kites, folktales and folk songs, origami (paper folding), men's and women's kimonos, temples, statues, pottery, and poetry? The arts inform us about so much that they may well tell the most complete story of any civilization. I like to make the argument that it is not possible to know about and appreciate any culture without an awareness of their arts. The social sciences communicate insight and wisdom through their distinctive methods of investigation and special bodies of knowledge, whereas the arts articulate the emotion and the spirit of the people through their observations and imaginations in art.

Horace Pippin, a celebrated African American folk artist, expressed his memories of World War I with his first oil painting, *End of the War: Starting Home*. In this 1930 painting, Pippin portrays a battle between German and American soldiers when he fought as a member of the African American Infantry division nicknamed the Harlem Hell Fighters. His oil painting communicated content and feeling that would be impossible to duplicate through other forms of information exchange. The arts tell us about people—how they feel and what they value.

As with Pippin, Isadora Duncan, a renowned dancer, once commented, "If I could tell you what I meant, there would be no point in dancing." Through dance, Duncan was able to communicate emotion as few dancers had done before her, as well as instruct about history and culture. She accomplished all of this using a special "language" comprised of a series of graceful movements. (The story of this talented dancer is portrayed in Rachel Isadora's splendid book, *Isadora Dances* [Puffin].) If Duncan were unable to express her message through dance, and Pippin through oil painting, whatever they wanted to convey would have been lost forever. A wealth knowledge is available through the arts to help children understand the human condition both intellectually and emotionally. Every child should have opportunities to explore the arts as "language of civilization," for the arts may well provide us the most powerful imprint of any society. Thus, the social sciences inform us, whereas the arts impassion us.

The term *the arts* has been assigned a range of meanings throughout the years, but in this text *the arts* will include the visual arts, music, dance, and drama. Although the visual arts and music have traditionally received the most attention in social studies instruction, all four components must be treated equally. And, as you explore opportunities to include the arts in your social studies program, it is important to recognize that children must not only learn to examine and appreciate the arts of any culture, but must have significant opportunities to (1) recreate what they have observed and (2) originate their own creative expressions.

Because the processes of recreating the arts and originating personally creative expressions are intended to strengthen concepts of any culture, authenticity and accuracy are of extreme importance. If the the primary purpose of reproducing a Kachina is to "expand children's understandings of Kachina dolls as religious items of the Hopi people," for example, then your students must use precise detail in recreating the dolls. To explain, a rain cloud design on the face of a

Kachina is a symbol of distinct significance—its purpose is to seek out spiritual help for rain and fertility. The children, then, must use this symbol only if they intend to convey that exact meaning. Likewise, all symbols and markings on Kachinas have relevance—the sun, clouds, moon, stars, and lightning. Certain objects such as feathers, bells, boughs, beads, and shells suggest specific meanings, too. Frivolous designs, such as baseballs or musical notes, have no place in recreating Kachinas because they are not authentic symbols of the Hopi culture.

Although a major aim of the arts in social studies is to help children gain and express knowledge of their world by recreating the works of a culture, a quality arts program offers children opportunities to originate their own creative expressions, too. To illustrate, let us return to the Kachina doll example. Just suppose that you have carried out instruction as was recommended in the preceding paragraphs—(1) your students learned about real Kachinas and then (2) they made accurate reproductions or models to communicate what they had learned. Now you wish to have your children personalize the information by creating original symbols for Kachina dolls. However, this should be done only if the artifact lends itself to such original expression. Interestingly, there are over 1,000 documented Kachinas, and new ones are regularly invented or created by Hopi people. Because of this spirit for continuous originality, it is considered proper to encourage your students to fashion new Kachinas. Therefore, those baseballs and musical notes that were discouraged in the preceding paragraph take on new life now that originality becomes the central purpose of the artistic experience. John Dewey once made a clear connection between these three complementary aspects of the arts when he said, "A beholder must create his own experience." Children must be given opportunities to enrich and express what they learn about the arts through as many expressive experiences as possible, for students who study the arts are also more likely to display originality and creativity in all of their social studies work.

Contrast the concern for accuracy in carrying out the Kachina-related learning experiences to a teacher who asked his students to construct model colonial log cabins with pretzel sticks and peanut butter, or the teacher whose students constructed tipis (conical structures intricately made of animal skins or birch bark by the Native Americans of the Great Plains) with painted construction paper cones. How could these "learning activities" possibly help students gain an understanding of how log cabins were built from logs laid horizontally and interlocked on the ends with notches? How would students understand that, despite their appearance, tipis were not just simple tents or that the way the shelters were constructed communicated important expressions of spiritual beliefs and cultural values? These kinds of activities commonly appear in idea resource books, but they create a weak connection between the experience and an understanding of people. This word of caution is not meant to stifle your eagerness for a "hands-on" arts component of social studies instruction, but rather to point out your responsibility to organize and coordinate meaningful knowledge through the arts.

Wachowiak and Clements (2006) warn that both bad art instruction and bad social studies instruction can easily result from the sloppy integration of those two curriculum areas: "Stereotypes emerge all too readily from carelessly planned lessons, and hasty assignments result too often in look-alike exercises such as sketchily colored-in outlines of one's palm and fingers for a Thanksgiving turkey. It goes without saying to eschew stereotyped, impersonal activities, such as photocopied patterns of pilgrims and presidents' profiles. . . . Do not use art exercises just as a way to fill an unplanned fifteen minutes" (p. 96).

The Visual Arts

Dynamic social studies teachers operate with a conviction that the visual arts must play a significant role in instruction if students are truly to understand and appreciate any culture. As students explore the visual arts of various peoples of Africa, for example, they are eager to try their hands at tie-dye, weaving, mask construction, or sculpture. Likewise, you help enhance the study of Greece by having students experience its architecture, sculptures, paintings, and pottery. Enliven a unit on medieval Europe by having children study and recreate coats of arms, stained glass, and castle design. You can use the arts of Gyokatu (fish printing), block printing, kite making, batiks, and folded-paper design to introduce students to Asian cultures. Native American sand paintings, blankets, bead working techniques, textiles, pottery, and basketry help students learn about the earliest cultures in North America. Pysanky (intricately designed Easter eggs) and flax (straw) dolls bring to life important aspects of Ukrainian culture. The potential is unlimited for integrating the visual arts and social studies. When children become aware of art as something valuable that people do in real life to communicate ideas and feelings, they are inspired to create their own.

Although dynamic social studies programs offer countless opportunities to involve children in standard art experiences such as dioramas, murals, mosaics, and collages, the most popular art process used in elementary social studies classrooms seems to be illustrations. You may have children replicate the collage technique as modeled by Eric Carle, make a picture book of animals common to the tropical rainforest, draw a product map of China, or paint a scene showing the landscape of the high Andes Mountains. There are literally hundreds of possibilities.

The benefits of art can best be summarized through the words of a fifth-grader named Wylam who, when asked how he liked the recent study and recreation of ancient cave paintings, responded, "I learned all the stuff you have to know and all the work you have to do to make a beautiful rock painting. It's not as easy as it looks. The part I liked best was doing the painting. The part I didn't like was when we had to write about it in our journals. It was fun working with rock painting. It was COOL!!!!"

Music

People have sent messages across distances by pounding on drums. They have gone off to war to inspiring military marches. They have walked onstage to receive their diplomas to the joyful strains of *Pomp and Circumstance*. They have raised their voices while singing national anthems. They have sung work songs or chants to keep their work rhythm as they pulled in nets or pried rails back into line. People have sung songs of worship in camp meetings and cathedrals, and they have welcomed harvests with celebratory dances. They have communicated their grief in tender ballads and rocked their babies to sleep with gentle lullabies. Wherever and whenever possible, people have expressed patriotism, joy, grief, love, fear, pleasure, and joy in making music for themselves and for others. Music, without question, has the power to bring forth and communicate powerful emotions.

How can you help children understand all of this? Certainly, young social scientists must have experiences with many kinds of music. Different people and faraway places may be abstract notions for some children, but they can be made more concrete by forging a relationship with music and social studies. Of all types of music, exposure to folk music is one of the most fitting mediums for teaching social studies. Folk music started long ago, at a time when the role of music was to tell a story about work and life and to help people get through life. Folk music is an important cultural form through which people tell of and maintain their own histories in the face of changing social conditions. Whether they are spirituals sung by African American slaves or Appalachian bluegrass fiddle music, folk songs draw on the life experiences of ordinary men and women and reflect their struggles as well as their achievements.

Creative Movement and Dance

Dance, usually with the accompaniment of music, is an art form in which the human body is used as a vehicle of expression. Dance has existed since the beginning of humankind, before verbal and written communication was developed. It was the first form of communication used by humans to interact with others and to make meaning of their world. Likewise, moving rhythmically seems to be innate in young children and seems to help them better understand themselves and the world in which they live. Because movement as a form of self-expression seems to be fundamental to our existence as human beings, dance should be considered an important part of a dynamic social studies program. Dance helps young social scientists use movement to creatively uncover and come to understand and appreciate diverse cultures. As students examine the role of dance in different cultures, they learn to connect with other people and respect their diversity.

Until recently, dance was taught mainly as an activity included in the physical education curriculum. It is now recognized as an art form comparable to music, drama, and the visual arts, and equally worthy of inclusion in an integrated social studies curriculum.

To ensure that children acquire accurate concepts of any culture, it would be helpful to invite resource people who can demonstrate dance movements into the classroom to share their talents with the children. If you are unfamiliar with the specific movements of a particular dance, it would be important to invite someone into the classroom who has that knowledge or to seek information that will help you learn (a gym teacher or dance school instructor can help). However you address the issue, the important consideration is that performances must be done without error or they would be considered very disrespectful by the group being represented.

Making the most of the value of dance and movement in social studies makes obvious to children that music is an integral part of people's lives rather than a form of expression engaged in by a talented few.

Drama

Like music, people have used drama to reveal their innermost feelings of conflict, despair, truth, beauty, hope, and faith since the dawn of civilization. Drama brings out the essence of a culture clearly before one's eyes and is an excellent vehicle to challenge students to think about and appreciate diverse cultures. Drama is a vital aspect of a culture; by its very nature, drama is an important kind of social communication. For primitive humans, it was a ritualistic effort to communicate with magical spirits; through ceremonial rituals, while dressed in masks and skins, groups would try to seek cooperation with the spirits to control certain events (a good hunt, the power of thunder, fertility). As humans began to settle in regular communities and rely more on agriculture, their greatest fears became bitter weather and a failed harvest, so special dances and rituals were created to appeal to the controlling spirits. From these early forms, drama developed into a stylized form of communication with intricate dialogue, disguises, and symbolism.

Dramatizations should emerge from the social studies content. The students' concern for elaborate scenery and costumes should not take precedence over the concepts or ideas the play is designed to convey, however. Simple objects can effectively represent more intricate items; for example, a mural or bulletin board can serve as a backdrop, a branch in a big can filled with dirt makes an excellent tree or bush, your desk becomes a cave, chairs placed in a straight line can be seats on a train or airplane, a pencil can become a hand-held microphone.

Until you try this art form in your own classroom, it is impossible to comprehend how highly effective drama can be as a hands-on activity in social studies. The children must not only research their characters but they must also become familiar with a myriad of other information, including the clothing they should wear. Consequently, children develop an increased understanding of and interest in cultures and discover many fascinating things about the history of their community, nation, and world. In addition, drama truly ignites the interests of children and enhances their interest in uncovering information about people, places, and things.

Always the highest form of creative expression of any culture, the arts teach us about people through their visual arts, music, dance, and drama. The arts are considered essential to understanding cultures, both past and present; the arts open up children's worlds and minds. Certainly, learning through the arts can bring social studies to life. In addition, we must offer children the opportunity to represent what they have learned, thus achieving greater comprehension and retention of the discovered knowledge. To truly benefit from an integrated arts experience, children must not only learn through the arts, but they must have abundant opportunities to actively produce their own creative work. The following classroom scenario illustrates how these two important facets of the integrated arts program go hand in hand.

NCSS STANDARDS

I. Culture
IX. Global Connections

New Year, the most important of the traditional Chinese holidays, begins each year on the first day of the first lunar month. In 2008, that day fell on February 7, a time when George White, a third-grade teacher, wanted to offer a meaningful, integrated, arts-based learning experience that would help his students understand and appreciate the ancient holiday. To help them acquire a basic background of information, Mr. White read aloud the beautifully illustrated book, *Chin Chiang and the Dragon's Dance* by Ian Wallace (Groundwood). The book tells the story of young Chin Chiang who dreamed of dancing the Dragon's Dance on New Year since he was as high as his grandfather's knees. But, now that the holiday was approaching, the young boy worries that he might not be able to dance well enough to make his grandfather proud of him. Eventually, though, a friend helps Chin Chiang discover the confidence he needs to perform the dance with skill and pride.

The book is a fascinating story that highlights the importance of the holiday as well as the meaning of the Dragon Dance, a dance that is believed to bring Chinese people strength, wisdom, and good fortune. The children learned that dragon dances are performed at New Year to scare away evil spirits. They watched an actual Dragon Dance on their computers after Mr. White found an appropriate Internet site (www.youtube.com/YiDaoLiondance). They loved seeing the dragon dancers raise and lower the ornate dragon rhythmically as nearby musicians supplied the pulsating accompaniment. The class learned that dragons used in dragon dances vary in length and that longer dragons are thought to be luckier than shorter ones.

The children were enthralled with the story and video and begged Mr. White to let them make their own moving dragon to celebrate the holiday. Of course, he welcomed their enthusiasm and guided their initial efforts to construct a sturdy frame for their dragon. The children covered the frame with cloth that was painted and decorated to resemble a dragon's head and body. Because the length of the dragon is associated with the luck it brings, the children decided that they wanted a very long dragon.

To perform the Dragon Dance, the young dancers carried the dragon's representation on poles. The lead dancers lifted, dipped, and shook the dragon's head while those who followed imitated the rhythmic movements of

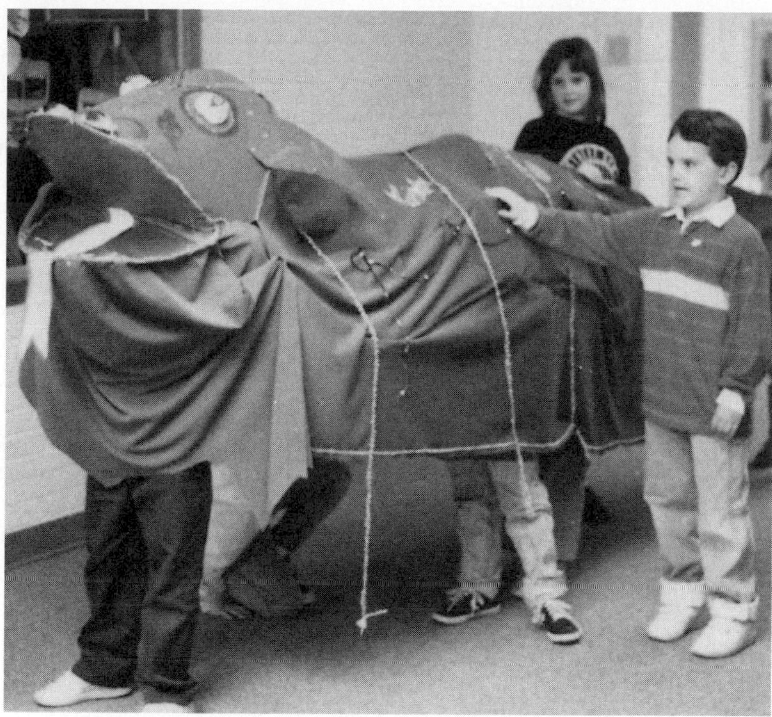

The arts offer children a valuable way to express what they have learned.

the dragon in a rising and falling manner. Accompaniment was supplied by a number of student "musicians" using traditional drums, cymbals, and gongs.

To add some festive pizzazz to the classroom in recognition of the Chinese New Year, the children made colorful hanging paper lanterns and suspended them throughout the classroom. They also devoured some tasty fortune cookies Mr. White shared with them; they especially enjoyed pulling out the slips of paper and reading the words of wisdom or prophecy.

How Global is the Curriculum
Go to MyEducationLab, select the topic Literature Connections, watch the videos entitled "Reading for Information" and "Literary Elements" and complete the questions that accompany them.

Reading

Presently, there is significant disagreement over whether textbooks or trade books should serve as the principal reading resource in social studies classrooms. Some teachers feel that textbooks are written too unimaginatively for their students; their heavy load of facts and carefully controlled vocabulary result in bland and voiceless reading. "Just the size and weight of the text are turn-offs for my students," reported one teacher. "I can't imagine any of them being excited enough about their social studies text that they would want to curl up on the couch to read it!" Other teachers counter that most social studies texts are easy to use and offer a carefully researched instructional package, including manuals complete with goals, objectives, lesson plans, activities, and tests. "Our school's social studies program is based on the social studies textbook," explains another teacher: "How else would any teacher know what was done in the earlier grades and what will be expected in later grades? And, the manuals offer marvelous instructional support." A textbook program is mostly prized by first-year social studies teachers who find it helpful to have a textbook's organized content, concise lessons, and suggested reading strategies as they find their way in the classroom. As they gain experience, however, these teachers often seek to "spread their wings" and begin to allocate an equal place for trade books and textbooks in their social studies programs. Neither textbooks nor trade books form the foundation of their curriculum; both are incorporated among an extensive mixture of other possible learning resources.

With these considerations in mind, what should teachers of dynamic social studies do? Use trade books only, textbooks only, or a combination of both? The point of view of dynamic social studies is that students need a wide variety of reading materials in their social studies program, including both well-written textbooks and quality trade books. Each has the potential to extend and enrich learning, if used properly.

Textbooks

Oftentimes, when teachers are asked to describe their social studies curriculum, they will tell you all about their textbooks. Principals regularly introduce new teachers to the school's social studies curriculum by informing them, "Here's the textbook. You should get to know it; it will be your best friend." I would estimate that 90 percent of all classroom instruction in social studies is regulated by textbooks. Most educators agree that textbooks are important tools of instruction but that they should not dominate everything that goes on in the social studies classroom; they should be considered only one of many useful teaching tools. When textbooks are used as the major medium for learning in social studies classrooms, for example, a teacher's role becomes a bit prescribed—a coach or mentor who carefully scaffolds learning. When teachers scaffold learning, they must use all the specialized techniques that help bridge the gap between students' backgrounds of experiences and the demands of the textbook reading material. This important role involves much more than telling the students to open up their books to a certain page and then asking them questions about what they had just read. Because this scaffolding role is quite complex and is used for many kinds of learning experiences other than textbooks, the teacher's role is treated as a separate topic in Chapter 7.

Trade Books

Disenchanted by the dryness that has often been associated with the "assign-question-and-answer" approach to textbook-driven instruction, more teachers than ever before are using a variety of texts (print sources) in social studies. Although these texts may include such sources as newspapers, magazines, diaries, primary resources, and a number of other print learning tools, the present center of attention will be on trade books.

Most of us have shared our childhood with a menagerie of trade book friends, and there are many that we remember with special delight. Their adventures and misadventures were sources of great enjoyment, and the thoughts of missing out on the exploits of Harry Potter, Amazing Grace, Winnie-the-Pooh, Strega Nona, Madeline, or Tom Sawyer is unthinkable. It seems that very little burns itself so lastingly into our minds as the storybook characters we met during our childhood. First and foremost, then, good literature brings charm and pleasure to childhood. But literature can also educate at the same time it entertains.

Trade books (both fiction and nonfiction) contribute much to the social studies program; they present information about people, places, events, and times in inspiring, memorable, and relevant ways. But implementing a trade book–based social studies program means that teachers must be familiar with the books that can help students explore a theme or topic. The range of trade books is enormous, spanning all types of topics. But four types (genre) of books are especially useful in dynamic social studies classrooms: informational books, historical fiction, biographies, and folk literature.

Informational Books A good informational book enlightens. Informational books support social studies instruction by supplying facts, concepts, and ideas for children's research and projects. Informational books also serve as strong models for children's expository writing projects, such as reports. These books are not designed to entertain; they deal exclusively with factual material. Many teachers have stereotyped informational books as being dry and dull; however, there are scores of informational books that adhere to finer literary standards and catch our eyes and hold our interests just like a good novel. As Darigan, Tunnell, and Jacobs state, "The writer of compelling [informational books] does not simply collect and display facts but weaves information and details into a vision that reveals the subject in a way readers find irresistible" (p. 330).

Informational books should supply an ample amount of details so the children are able to easily comprehend the concepts presented, but not be so intricate that they are frustrating for children of the intended grade level. A good informational book should provide factual information in an interesting and instructive way. One rule of thumb is to examine the cover and sample pages from the beginning, middle, and end of the book. Does it appear to be dull and lifeless? If it does, it will be even more unexciting to a child; children will reject books that do not immediately capture their attention. Illustrations and photographs should clarify the text as accurately and realistically as possible. And, advanced technology has made it possible to fill informational books with helpful graphics. Be careful with this graphics element, though. An overabundance of graphics may divert children's attention from the written text itself. Authors and illustrators should also avoid stereotypes in informational books. All books should feature both children and adults of different racial and ethnic backgrounds.

Historical Fiction The purpose of both history and historical fiction is to recount past events as accurately as possible, but historical fiction is designed to augment truthful historical detail with a story. Therefore, historical fiction can be defined as stories of historical figures or events told in precise and fact-based historical settings, but the author often takes liberty with character dialogue or may add fictional characters. It is important to stress that stories in this genre, although considered fictional, do accurately capture the spirit, behavior, and social conditions of the people and time they depict. But they go beyond the events, dates, and details of history by telling a story that captures young readers and transports them vicariously to the past. As they take this journey, students enter into the lives of the characters and make personal connections to the past.

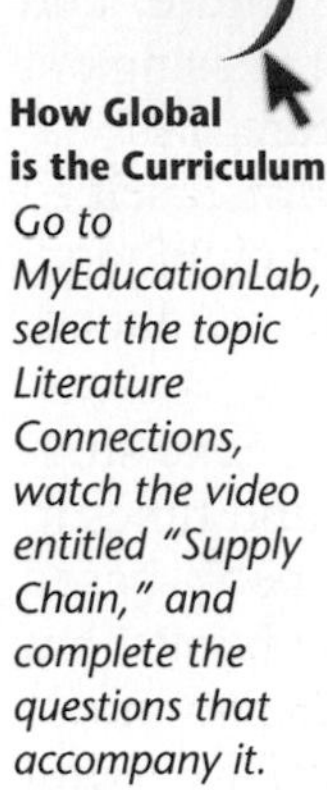

How Global is the Curriculum *Go to MyEducationLab, select the topic Literature Connections, watch the video entitled "Supply Chain," and complete the questions that accompany it.*

A picture book like Donald Hall's *Ox-Cart Man* (Viking) can give younger children a personal glimpse of life in early nineteenth-century New England as it tells about a man who lives on a farm with his wife, daughter, and son. The book begins with the family packing a two-wheeled wooden cart with the various goods they have to sell—mittens, shawls, and birch brooms. Next, the man travels on foot to Portsmouth where he sells the goods, the cart, and his beloved ox. With money earned from the sale, the man buys an iron kettle, an embroidery needle for his daughter, a knife for his son, and two pounds of wintergreen peppermint candies. The man then strolls home where he is lovingly welcomed by his family. Together, as the seasons pass, they work on the new mittens, shawls, and brooms they will sell again next year in Portsmouth.

Older children will learn about the offensive institution of slavery by reading the historically accurate events and characters described in James Lincoln Collier and Christopher Collier's book, *Jump Ship to Freedom* (Dell Yearling). The book tells the story of 14-year-old Daniel Arabus and his mother, slaves owned by Captain Ivers of Stratford, Connecticut, during the mid-1780s. They had always dreamed of buying their freedom and, by law, they should be free. Daniel's father had fought in the Revolutionary War and had earned enough in soldier's notes to buy his freedom. But now Daniel's father is dead and his valuable Revolutionary War notes had been stolen from his mother by Mrs. Ivers. Daniel daringly decides to steal them back, but an enraged Captain Ivers discovers the theft, suspects Daniel, and locks him away on a ship bound for the West Indies where he will be forced to work in the notorious sugar cane fields. On way to its destination, however, the ship is damaged by a treacherous storm and must dock in New York City for needed repairs. While in New York, Daniel cleverly becomes involved in a series of captivating events that eventually lead to his freedom.

It is very difficult, even for professional historians, to know exactly what happened in the past, for ongoing research and study regularly result in new interpretations of what went on in earlier times. Stories in this genre, although fictional, are based on the best of what is known about historical fact and offer readers a glimpse of what the past was like through engaging and informative stories. Because children are more likely to become absorbed in history when it comes to them as a story, historical fiction should be a component in all contemporary social studies programs.

Biographies The stories contained within this genre are written accounts of someone's life. Like historical fiction, biographies must be rooted in accurate historical fact; the authenticity of time and place must be truthful and precise in all good written biographies. And, like historical fiction, biographies must engage young readers in a spellbinding story that brings to life the main character portrayed in the book. Children enjoy learning about well-known and extraordinary people; biographies offer great insight into who they are and what makes them important. Take, for example, *Anne Frank's Story: Her Life Retold for Children* by Carol Ann Lee (Troll). Most of us have heard about or read Anne Frank's classic diary that chronicled 25 months of her fearful life hiding in a warehouse in Nazi-occupied Amsterdam from 1942 to 1944. But this carefully researched book provides much more information about Anne's life before, during, and after her time she went into hiding. The book includes lucid recollections from Anne's family and friends and includes rare black-and-white photos of Anne and her family.

Folktales A genre as old as language itself, folktales are "stories of the people" that were originally passed down orally from one generation to the next. They often taught special lessons, thereby effectively becoming part of a culture's traditional values and customs. Among the numerous "lessons" that were taught through the fundamental nature of the stories were those of good and evil, wisdom and foolishness, beauty and unattractiveness, age and youth, stinginess and charity, or being rich or poor. Folktales are simple stories of simple people; they express the customs, beliefs, and traditions considered important by a particular folk culture. They teach important lessons in clear and convincing ways, helping prepare children to live well with their fellow human beings.

Successful social studies instruction can be accomplished in many ways, such as by providing your students opportunities to interact with a variety of people, by traveling to fascinating places, or by searching the Internet for specific knowledge and unique perspectives on the world. As important as any form of instruction, however, is the role of good literature. Good literature not only instructs but it also reflects the values and beliefs of any culture. Therefore, it is important that teachers integrate good trade books into the social studies program and make first-rate stories an element of the normal daily routine.

Mathematics

Teaching in ways that integrate mathematics and social studies is often acknowledged as a major goal of instruction. The National Council for the Social Studies (NCSS) encourages such practice; the National Council of Teachers of

Mathematics (NCTM) advises math teachers to "enhance students' understanding of mathematics by using other disciplines as sources of problem solving" (2000, p. 278). Regrettably, however, the connections between these two subjects are not often as clear as we would like them to be. Some subjects seem to blend together without a glitch; merging social studies with literature or even the arts is fundamentally natural and uncomplicated. But incorporating mathematics into social studies planning causes some teachers to throw futile questions of "Why me?" into the void. Their uncertain efforts to satisfy the goal of curriculum integration seems to wrap up with such dubious solutions as a file of word problems having a weak social studies connection: "In the last mayoral election, Smith received 56% of the votes and Jones received 44%. If 8,000 votes were cast, how many votes did each candidate receive?" Word problems like these can be appropriate and useful following an actual election, but to try forcing connections outside of meaningful contexts does not help the curriculum integration process. Integrating mathematics into social studies must not be artificial, but accomplished in such a way as that the combination more clearly describes our world: "If all . . . teachers in a school do their best to connect content areas, mathematics and other disciplines will be seen as permeating life and not as just existing in isolation" (NCTM, 2000, p. 279).

It seems that as teachers deepen their understanding of how to support student learning through curriculum integration, they frequently identify more and better ways that social studies and math jointly contribute to their students' understanding of our world. As they do this, both subjects take on a livelier, more accessible nature and become more personally meaningful for the students. By understanding the sophisticated interactions of math and social studies, teachers learn to build creative learning activities that help students develop and communicate key ideas rather than just providing them with disconnected facts and skills. Think about the many concepts that involve combining math and the social sciences: population changes, population density, distribution, growth rates, GDP, per capita income, the stock market, production and consumption of resources, mapping and graphing data, analyzing data, comparing the sizes of states in the U.S. or countries in the world. What could you add to this list?

Simply knowing the related content appropriate for curriculum integration does not complete the job of teaching for a math–social studies connection. Equally as important is selecting and developing activities and materials designed to help the students successfully achieve the targeted goals. In considering those activities, teachers must first judge whether the activity has the potential to deliver goal-relevant benefits and then decide whether or not the students will find the activity interesting and enjoyable. In an effort to make learning more connected and meaningful, Jamie Schenskie organizes instruction so that curricular areas are linked in meaningful contexts.

Jamie Schenskie became increasingly concerned as her students behaved day after day as though she had misjudged their ability to understand calendar time, a part of her math program. Just today, for example, Armand flashed a blank look while attempting to explain why today was all of these things—Wednesday the 20th of October, 2008. Was the process of learning concepts associated with calendar time too difficult for her fifth-graders? Were the ideas too abstract? And, to add to her anxiety, school district standards for history included chronological thinking, or understanding when events occurred in the past and in what sequential order. Chronological thinking is considered fundamental to historical reasoning. Was she expecting her students to behave day after day as though they knew something even if they didn't have a clue? Ms. Schenskie began to detect the potent connection between history and math. If her students were unable to apply chronological thinking to the use of calendars, it would hinder their ability to grasp the concept of past, present, and future—the heart of historical reasoning.

NCSS STANDARDS

I. *Culture*
II. *Time, Continuity, and Change*
IX. *Global Connections*

As with all abstract concepts taught in her classroom, Ms. Schenskie knew that she must approach the topic of chronological thinking with materials and activities that were attention grabbing, authentic, and understandable. Reviewing the days and dates on a commercially available calendar didn't seen to address these criteria, so, to reawaken their interest for a November calendar, Ms. Schenskie decided to use an activity she had experienced in a professional workshop: the talking calendar. The workshop presenter described how the introduction of sound to motion pictures became a powerful cultural phenomenon, and suggested that applying the concept of talking pictures ("talkies") to calendars would be capture the children's interest and curiosity. Ms. Schenski agreed.

To begin, Ms. Schenskie drew the outline of a calendar on a large sheet of yellow paper covering a bulletin board. In the space where a picture or illustration normally appears on a commercial calendar, she added beads, feathers, and multicolored fall leaves. At the center of the space, underneath a stick in which she had cut ten notches, Ms. Schenskie printed this title:

Moon of Falling Leaves
A November Talking Calendar

Ms. Schenskie selected this title and decorative accessories because her students had been making headway through a unit on Native Americans and recently learned about the moon-based calendar system of the Lakota Sioux. Although they understood that the Plains Indians did not have a calendar system like ours and their "moons" system of marking the passage of time did not actually correspond with our system of months, Ms. Schenskie decided, for simplicity, to begin the "Falling Leaves" full moon with the first day of our traditional month of November. She often chooses a good book to introduce new ideas. In this case, she read Eve Bunting's sensitive picture book, *Moonstick: The Seasons of the Sioux* (HarperTrophy). The book matched perfectly with this project; it described the 13 moons of the Sioux year and how they are marked on a "moonstick," a stick that has been decorated with painted symbols and beadwork. A new notch is cut into a stick as each moon passes, 13 notches marking the course of each year.

Ms. Schenskie was careful to describe how the Lakota marked time by observing nature closely and naming the passing moons according to seasonal qualities—"Planting Moon," "Hunger Moon," "Thunder Moon." Because the moon labels explained the qualities of nature at the time, they occasionally changed from year to year depending on such things as weather variations or food supply. That is why "Moon of Falling Leaves" may correspond with our month of October one year and with November the next. Regardless, Bunting's book is a sensitive portrayal of the Lakota way of recording changes that occur in nature and in life.

Next, Ms. Schenski cut rectangular pieces of white drawing paper so that, when folded horizontally in the middle, the resulting squares would fit the boxes for the numbered dates on the calendar outline. On the top fold of one square, she printed the Sioux word for *one:* "wanji." She attached it to the calendar square immediately beneath the label "Tuesday," the first day of the month of November.

The students examined the new calendar carefully and questioned Ms. Schenski about the whereabouts of their regular calendar. "We're going to try something new this month," announced Ms. Schenski. "So I've put away the old calendar and thought we'd make a special talking calendar this month. Want to give it a try?"

"Sure," the students declared in agreement. "But how do we make a calendar talk?"

"It's easy," reassured Ms. Schenskie. "All we have to do is come up with some important things to say about the Sioux. To start, think about what the buffalo provided the early Sioux."

"The stomach was sometimes used as a water bucket," suggested Tyree. Ms. Schenskie printed his idea on a large sheet of chart paper. Quickly, other ideas flowed: "The hide was used for blankets." "The bones were used to make tools." "The Sioux made yellow paint from gallstones." Each contribution was added to the chart paper.

When the students ran out of ideas for the ways buffaloes were used, Ms. Schenskie brought out another sheet of chart paper and asked, "What are some items you would find in an early Sioux home?" That was followed by questions that helped categorize additional information about the Sioux—their food, spiritual life, and crafts.

After all the ideas were offered, Ms. Schenskie informed the students that their information would be used for the talking calendar. "Here's how it works," she said. "First, look at my square with the word *wanji* (wahn-chee) on it. Wanji is our 'one' in the Lakota number system. I've decorated the square with a moon because it illustrates that the Lakota used moons as a way to mark the passage of time. Now I'm going to select something from our information bank that tells about the importance of moons in the lives of the Sioux. Here it is:

Today is wanji,
the first day of the Moon of Falling Leaves.

Ms. Schenskie lifted up the top square on which the numeral was illustrated and revealed a vibrant crayon drawing of leaves that illustrated the two-line bit of information. "That sounds great!" the students agreed. "And it looks great, too!" (See Figure 3.1.)

Ms. Schenske next gave the students a blank piece of paper like hers and assigned each a number. "Use the ideas we came up with on the charts to

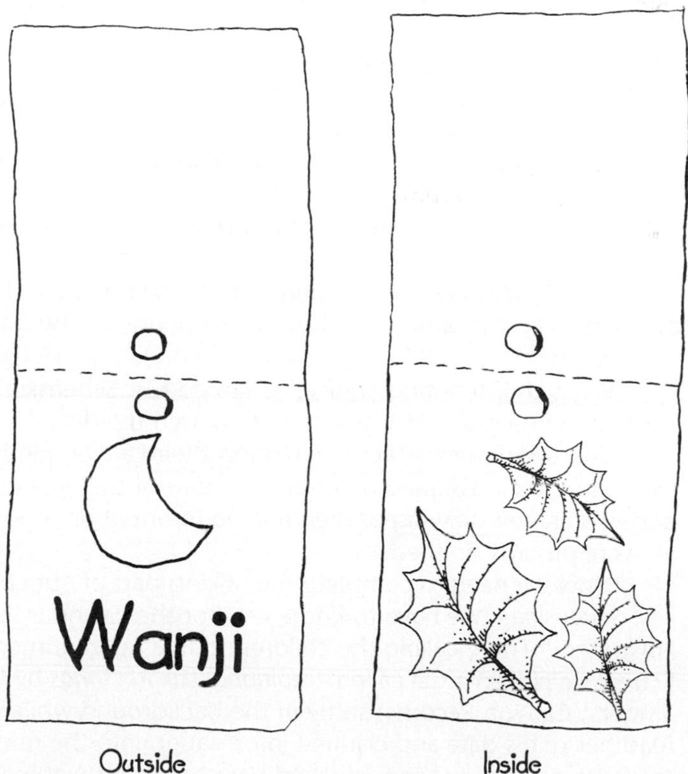

FIGURE 3.1 Sample Calendar Card

come up with a design for your date," she directed. "First, however, we must learn about the Lakota number system. It is somewhat similar to our base-ten number system, but it is important to know the correct pronunciation. Stressing the unique vowel sounds and other special sounds, Ms. Schenske introduced the numbers from one to ten: wanji (wahn-chee), nunpa (noon-pah), yamni (yahm-nee), topa (toh-pah), zaptan (zahp-thahn), sakpe (shahk-peh), sakowin (shah-koh-ween), saglogan (shah-gloh-gahn), napciyunka (nahp-chee-yuhn-kah), wikcemna (wee-cheh-mnah). The children recited the names as Ms. Schenske mounted numeral cards on the wall. The children next learned how to count from 11 to 19. "Wikcemna" (ten) is understood, so it is not spoken when counting from 11-19; to say eleven, the children simply say the word *ake* (ah-keh), which means "plus" followed by the number of units. For example, "ake wanji" is 11 and "ake sakowin" is 17. The twenties get somewhat trickier. Now, "wikcemna" must be expressed: wikcemna nunpa = 10 × 2, or 20; wikcemna nunpa ake yamni = 10 × 2 + 3 = 23. Can you figure out how to express 25 or 31 in the Lakota number system?

The air grew still as the eager young minds went to work. After a few minutes, Hannah's hand shot into the air as she proudly announced:

Today is saglogan, or November nine,
My arm band is made from quills of porcupine.

"That's wonderful!" Ms. Schenskie and the children declared. "And it rhymes like some poems, too!"

"Wait . . . I've got one," shouted Harry with great pride:

Today is yamni, the third day of Falling Leaves Moon,
Each person in our camp eats about three pounds of buffalo meat each day.

"What an interesting choice," beamed Ms. Schenskie. "I like the way you used the same number in your fact to match the date."

Soon everyone was at work writing their Lakota numbers and creatively illustrating their assigned dates on the front of the drawing paper. They added a crayon drawing of their related information inside. In a short time, all were proudly finished.

"Now we need to complete the talking part of our calendar," announced Ms. Schenskie. "We have to find a way for the calendar to say what you have illustrated." Then, calling the children to line up in numerical order, Ms. Schenskie played a CD called *Traditional Lakota Songs* by the Porcupine Singers (Canyon Records) softly in the background while each child, in turn, read her or his date and clarified information into the microphone of a tape recorder. Each child then attached her or his card within the appropriate square on the large bulletin board calendar. The colorful illustrations brightened the room and captured the children's attention: "That's the most beautiful calendar I've ever seen," gushed Juanita.

For the last phase, Ms. Schenskie invited the children to sit attentively and listen as the calendar "talked." With the tape recorder hidden in back of her desk, Ms. Schenskie secretly pushed the "play" button and, to the children's complete surprise, the calendar began to talk! As each child's piece was read, Ms. Schenskie opened the paper to reveal the drawing inside.

The talking calendar brought vitality to Ms. Schenskie's math and social studies program in ways that she never thought possible. The talking calendar became an important part of the daily routine as Ms. Schenskie played the recording, stopping at the day's date and propping open that day's drawing for all to observe and appreciate. Buoyed by her success, Ms. Schenskie expanded the interdisciplinary calendar curriculum each month to include calendars from other cultures: a Roman version complete with Roman numerals for the dates and Latin names for the month (*Februarius*) and days of the week (*Dies Saturni* for Saturday), a Mayan calendar adaptation, and an Egyptian version.

In addition to expanding and reinforcing important skills, math is essential if we expect our students to have a meaningful grasp of important social issues, too. Is it possible to fully comprehend the national budget, the appeal to help more Americans pay for basic private health coverage, or the shift in population among the top-ten U.S. cities from 1995 to 2009 without integrating math and social studies? The same is true with other social, ecological, and cultural issues: Everyone needs mathematics to have a deep grasp of homelessness and poverty, the effects of deforestation on global warming, the struggles of Native Americans whose heritage appears to be disintegrating, and the feasibility of efforts for comprehensive immigration reform. Math helps us all better understand these social issues and the innovative solutions that have been proposed to turn these problems around.

Science

How Global is the Curriculum *Go to MyEducationLab, select the topic Cross Curricular Connections, watch the video entitled "Questioning, Investigating and Observing," and complete the questions that accompany it.*

Suppose you were among the first group of settlers to step onto the shores of this country. You would undoubtedly be overwhelmed by the incredible beauty of this vast, unspoiled land. You marvel at the sparkling clear water in the streams, observe abundant natural wildlife, peer into the bright blue skies, and inhale a lungful of pure fresh air. In just over 300 years, we have taken that pristine terrain and turned it into a natural time bomb that poses a volatile threat to the survival of life and beauty on this planet. Burning fossil fuels in our cars and trucks release toxic air pollutants; across the Americas, the last snippets of wild nature are being wiped out by chain saws and bulldozers; Earth's atmosphere has become congested with heat-trapping carbon dioxide, threatening large-scale global warming; contamination of our streams and lakes; and uncluttered landscapes are rapidly becoming a memory. Every day, Earth becomes more and more polluted.

This is where a major social studies–science connection comes in. Social studies teachers must realize that understanding and appreciating our *cultural roots* is an important overriding goal of social studies instruction, but, equally as important, students must understand and appreciate their *natural roots*, too. Children must be helped to recognize that Earth is a habitat shared by people and other living things and that its survival depends on a complicated relationship between delicate cultural and natural systems. Margaret Mead (1978), a distinguished anthropologist and deeply committed social activist who wrote about many contemporary issues, hoped that schools would help children both learn about themselves and their culture as well as work toward a more humane and socially responsible society: "If children feel themselves as part of the living world, learn respect for it, and their uniqueness in it, they will have a foundation for growth into responsible citizens who will be able to discriminate and make decisions about science used for constructive purposes and the science used for destructive purposes." Therefore, contemporary social studies programs, through sound interdisciplinary planning, must enhance our students' understandings of the complexity of contemporary natural problems and help them achieve a sense of responsibility required to restore and preserve our natural environment.

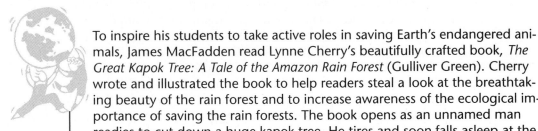

To inspire his students to take active roles in saving Earth's endangered animals, James MacFadden read Lynne Cherry's beautifully crafted book, *The Great Kapok Tree: A Tale of the Amazon Rain Forest* (Gulliver Green). Cherry wrote and illustrated the book to help readers steal a look at the breathtaking beauty of the rain forest and to increase awareness of the ecological importance of saving the rain forests. The book opens as an unnamed man readies to cut down a huge kapok tree. He tires and soon falls asleep at the base of the tree. One by one the animals enter his dream to plead with him not to destroy their home and try to convince him about how important every tree is in the rain forest. When the man awakes and sees the silent, somber expressions on the animals' faces around him, he silently drops his axe and walks away.

NCSS STANDARDS

- **III.** *People, Places, and Environments*
- **VII.** *Production, Distribution, and Consumption*
- **VIII.** *Science, Technology, and Society*

The students had participated in prior learning experiences about endangered animals and rain forests, so, before reading this book, Mr. MacFadden wanted to make connections to what they already knew. He called their attention to the large wall map of the world's major rain forest regions that the students had previously made and helped the students review the layers of the rain forest and the variety of life in each layer.

When the book was finished, the students found plenty to talk about. After spending several minutes conducting a passionate informal discussion of the book, Mr. MacFadden directed the students to a wall chart on which all the speaking animals in the book were listed. To complete the chart, he asked the students to list the reasons each of the animals gave for not cutting down the kapok tree. He asked, "Do you think the animals really talked to the man, or was it all a dream?" He also asked the students to talk with a partner about the meaning of several of the animals' reasons. For example, they discussed what the anteater meant when he said to the man, "Senhor, you are chopping down this tree with no thought for the future. And surely you know that what happens tomorrow depends upon what you do today." He concluded the discussion by asking, "What do you think would have happened if the man had not listened to the animals?"

Once the activities were completed and the students' interests remained high, Mr. MacFadden chose to use their energy to engender a schoolwide awareness of the plight of endangered animals through a unique mural project. In advance, he located several informational books about endangered animals and located several appropriate websites. The books were displayed on a large table and the students had access to computers as they needed them. Then the students were divided into several small work groups, each having these responsibilities:

1. The groups were to select at least five endangered animals. Using a variety of arts and crafts materials and a length of butcher paper, the students were to depict the animals and the habitat in which they lived.

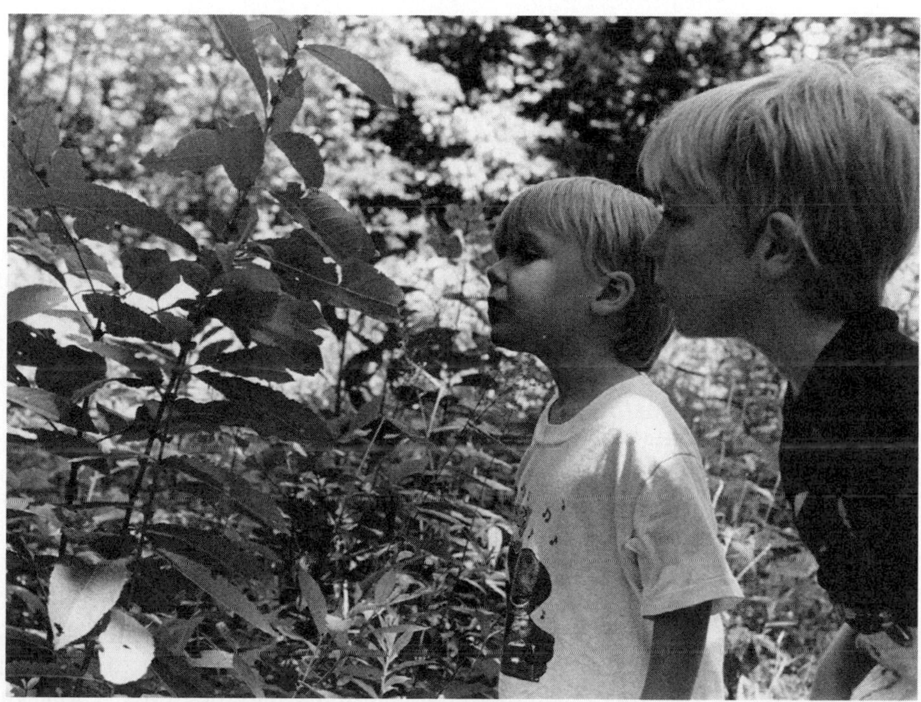

By integrating science and social studies, children learn that decisions made by human beings can influence the survival of all living things.

2. The groups were to prepare a written script describing its mural. The script must have included at least two sentences about each animal and a clear description of the habitat.
3. Each group recorded its script onto a tape recorder. The students were to take turns reading portions of the script.
4. The murals were mounted on the walls of the school's multipurpose room and a tape recorder was placed on a small table beneath each. Other classrooms were invited to visit the talking mural.

Our youth of today must be convinced that saving Earth is important and that they can make a big difference in preserving our planet. Through appropriate integrated experiences, students must be helped to realize that many of the things they can do will be fun, but others will require a lot of work. Regardless of whether their efforts are thought of as being fun or work, however, we want them to muster the courage and passion to step forward and make a difference.

Integrative Learning Materials and Activities

The process of selecting first-rate learning materials and activities with integrative potential is an often understated but demanding task. That is, some teachers become so obsessed with the idea of selecting "perky" materials or activities that they often use but a single criterion for selecting classroom experiences—ones that can be described as "cute." As a result, their social studies classrooms tend to offer "cutesy" activities that are likely to distort the focus of instruction. For example, in a unit on famous artists, is it really necessary to slip in math by measuring the area of Andy Warhol's paintings? Forced connections run the risk of glossing over important concepts that result in little or no meaningful learning. This practice is often described as a "cookbook" approach, where commercially produced teacher idea books appear to serve as the chief curriculum guide. As in planning a menu, however, the individual recipes may be mouth-watering and appetizing, but when combined into one meal, the mishmash could be stomach-turning. Rather than limit instruction to "cookbook recipes," it is important to know what makes learning materials and activities work. Knowing how to bring about productive learning is a much tougher task than simply leafing through the pages of a single resource. Here are a few questions to ask yourself as you ponder the use of any materials or activities for your social studies program.

- Do the materials/activities address performance expectations as outlined in NCSS and/or state/school district social studies standards?
- Are the materials/activities appropriate for the developmental makeup of the targeted group of students? Do they have a solid theoretical base?
- Does the material/activity effectively contribute to the development of cognitive abilities and problem-solving skills?

- Does the material/activity engage students as active learners? Will it arouse interest and pleasure in learning?
- Can the materials/activities carry on over several lessons as a reasonable series of interrelated experiences?
- Will the material/activity present opportunities for cross-curricular integration?
- Is the material/activity free of bias?

Hands-On Learning

Because children of all ages learn best when involved in experiences where they can actually manipulate something, a crucial responsibility of dynamic social studies teachers is to make available fascinating learning materials and activities: strutting about in adult clogs from the Netherlands, pulling out Russian Matryoshka (nesting) dolls to reveal a smaller figure of the same type inside, or exploring ancient Chinese tangrams, 7-piece puzzles that fit together to form a shape of some sort. Hands-on learning has become the familiar phrase to describe experiences like these, but like many other recurrent terms and phrases, there are discrepancies about what "hands-on learning" really means. Rather than enter into a debate about the issue, we will simply operate with the idea that *hands-on learning* by and large refers to any activities in classrooms that use real materials (*realia*)—a Nigerian calabash, a Korean 1,000-won note or 50-won coin, or a genuine Navajo rug. In addition to cultural objects, students should also have many opportunities to handle specialized tools of social studies investigation—maps, globes, compasses, computers, timelines, charts, graphs, timing devices, cameras, and calculators. The concept of hands-on social studies is based on the belief that children should learn with the methods of natural exploration they typically use while trying to make sense of the world around them.

John Ogborn introduced his fifth-graders to Chinese tangrams by reading Ann Tompert and Andrew Parker's picture book, *Grandfather Tang's Story* (Dragonfly). This is a folktale in which the illustrator, Robert Andrew Parker, uses watercolor washes and novel tangram patterns to help the author retell a traditional Chinese tale about two shape-changing fox fairies. The story opens with Grandfather Tang and Little Soo sitting under a peach tree in their backyard. Grandfather Tang tells Little Soo a story about two friendly foxes, Chou and Wu Ling, who were always trying to outdo each other. When Wu Ling becomes a rabbit, for example, Chou becomes a dog who chases him, and so on. Parker illustrates seven "tans" (pieces of a tangram square) to represent the various characters in the story. As Mr. Ogborn read the story aloud, he manipulated his own set of tangram pieces on an overhead projector to show his students how each animal was formed in the story. (See Figure 3.2.)

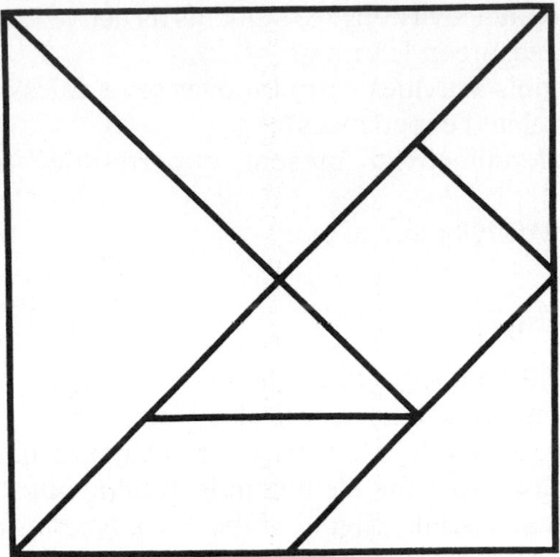

FIGURE 3.2 Chinese Tangram

After the story was read and discussed, Mr. Ogborn challenged his students to search the Internet for information regarding the origin of tangrams in Chinese society. The students uncovered several accounts and legends, but the one they liked the best told of a tiny village that wished to honor its emperor. The finest craftspeople set about to fashion a beautiful glazed tile. As a servant of the emperor was carrying the ceramic tile, he tripped over a stone in his path and fell, shattering the extraordinary tile into seven pieces. In a panic, the servant and the villagers desperately tried to reassemble the tile into a square, but could not. Dejectedly, they went before their emperor. But, before they could explain what happened to the tile, the emperor discovered that many other shapes could be formed from the pieces. Absorbed in arranging and rearranging the pieces, he thought the villagers had made him a magnificent puzzle!

NCSS STANDARDS

I. *Culture*
II. *Time, Continuity, and Change*
IX. *Global Connections*

After their research was completed, Mr. Ogborn gave each student a set of 7-piece tangrams and challenged each to use his or her pieces to create interesting objects or animals. Then the students were placed in random groups and asked to write a second story using their group's own tangram creations.

There is one fundamental way that we use the term *hands-on learning* in social studies education today. It refers to a particular instructional strategy where students manipulate and work with materials that instruct. "Hands-on" plainly means having students manipulate the things they are studying and providing opportunities to handle the specialized tools used by social scientists. So, in a more general sense, hands-on learning can be thought of as being synonymous with the expression learning by doing.

Field Trips

Field trips are first-rate learning adventures for any age—kindergartners, uppergraders, high school or college students, and adults. Who doesn't learn best when taken to a firsthand source of information? Good field trips for elementary school youngsters involve students as active participants. A trip to the automobile museum during which children are lectured to by a guide or are required to be silent observers is not as good as a trip that allows them to get into an automobile, sit in the driver's seat, talk to the owner, listen to the engine's roar, and possibly even be taken on a short ride on a protected course. A trip to the bakery where the children can merely look at something being prepared is not as good as a trip that allows them to measure and mix the ingredients for a batch of healthy muffins that they will gulp down later. A good field trip must envelop elementary school children in opportunities for direct, meaningful involvement.

At no time was this point clearer than when Erika Ziegler heard a discussion about firefighters among a small group of her first-graders as they were exploring a book in the library corner. Because she was planning to introduce firefighters as part of their year-long study of community workers, Ms. Ziegler listened as the children talked excitedly about the big rubber boots and hard yellow hats the firefighters wore in the pictures. Seizing the moment, she suggested that it might soon be fun to visit some firefighters at the fire station near their school. "We could really go there?" asked Chin-Jen. "Wow, that would be fun!" exclaimed Sarah. Ms. Ziegler had no doubt that interest was high, so she called the fire department to ask if the class could visit. She was told that not only was such a visit possible but that arrangements could also be made for two firefighters to take them for a short ride on a truck.

NCSS STANDARDS

III. *People, Places, and Environments*
V. *Individuals, Groups, and Institutions*
X. *Civic Ideals and Practice*

On the day of the trip, the children eagerly got off the school bus when it arrived at the fire station. Their anticipation grew into excitement as they peered in at the bright red and silver truck parked in the garage. Keeping the children well in control, Ms. Ziegler reminded them to stay behind her and the parent volunteers until the firefighters explained what to do. When two firefighters invited them to enter, the children gingerly approached the vehicle. The firefighters showed the children all their paraphernalia and explained their jobs. "The truck is shiny," remarked Rebecca. "Yeah, and look at those big hoses!" shouted Ben. "That fireman is a lady. Wow, a lady fireman!" shouted Denise, all agog. "Do you have to go to college to learn how to be a firefighter?" asked Caio. The children watched, listened, commented, and asked questions as they tried on the hard hats and floppy boots, stared at the dazzling lights, and listened to the firefighters talk. The most adventurous youngsters even accepted an invitation to climb up into the cab and sit in the fire truck. All this wonderful activity culminated in a slow, well-supervised, short trip around the parking lot on the back of the truck.

Ms. Ziegler was rewarded by the fact that this learning experience was thoroughly enjoyed by the children, and that they had learned a great deal about a valuable community service.

When they returned to school, Ms. Ziegler brought the children together as a group to talk about their experiences at the fire station. They then drew pictures and wrote about their favorite experiences. (See Figure 3.3.) Later that day, the children dictated a thank-you note that was mailed to the firehouse.

Ms. Ziegler's field trip was successful because she always followed a set of specific guidelines whenever she planned field trips for her students. She learned that appropriate field trips include the responsibilities as shown in Figure 3.4.

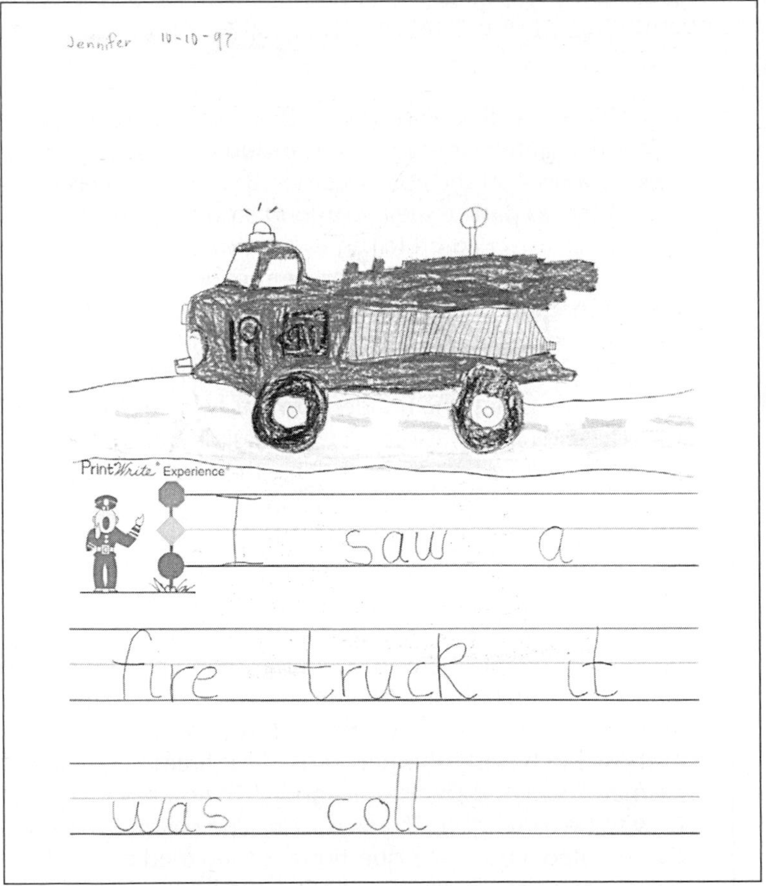

FIGURE 3.3 A Student's Response to a Field Trip

FIGURE 3.4 Field Trip Checklist

1. Address logistical concerns associated with the trip:
   - Have you taken the trip beforehand?
   - Have you made all necessary arrangements at the field trip site—what time you will arrive, where the restrooms are located, accommodations for children with special needs, places for lunch and snack?
   - Are there any special rules or regulations that must be followed at the site?
   - Have parental permission slips been signed (even if the school uses a blanket permission form)? Do not take children who haven't returned them.
   - Has transportation been arranged? (For liability reasons, a school bus is much better than a private car.)
   - If private cars are to be used, have you verified that each driver has adequate insurance and a valid driver's license? Have you provided each driver with a map and precise directions?
   - Have you planned proper supervision? (I always felt a 4:1 child-adult ratio was maximum.)
   - Are chaperones informed about what you expect of them? Do they know the behaviors expected of the children?
   - Do parents understand what clothing is appropriate for their children?
   - Do the students understand the expected standards of conduct? (Children respond better when they have a voice in determining these.)
2. Establish a clear purpose for the trip; be sure the children understand clearly why they are going ("What are we looking for?" "What do we want to find out?"):
   - Read books, share brochures or posters, and talk about what to expect at the site. Give the children an idea of what to expect.
   - Involve children in planning the trip.
3. Prepare for the trip:
   - Use name tags (including the school name and teacher's name). This helps if a child gets lost, as well as assists volunteers when they need to call a child by name.
   - Assign a partner, or buddy, for each child. Explain why it is important to stick together.
   - Divide the class into groups. Give each student a specific responsibility (recorder, photographer or illustrator, organizer, and so on).
   - Show the students how they will record information from the trip (worksheet or guidesheet).
4. Take the trip:
   - Be sure to take roll when you leave and each time you depart or return to the bus.
   - Take along a basic first-aid kit (or nurse). Several wash cloths or paper towels will be needed if a child gets sick on the bus.
   - Arrive on time.
   - Keep the children who will need your attention close to you.
   - Introduce your class (but not each individual child) to your guide, if there is one.
   - Enjoy the experience!
5. After the trip:
   - Have the children write (or dictate) thank-you notes, or draw pictures expressing their appreciation to volunteers and field site personnel.
   - Talk with the class about what they liked best.
   - Provide enrichment activities—draw pictures, write stories or poems, create a dramatic skit, make a map, or conduct any related activity to help the children deepen their understanding of the trip.
   - Have the students evaluate the trip: Did they accomplish the purposes identified at the beginning of the trip?

Classroom Visitors

Classroom visitors are individuals from the world outside of school who come into your classroom to share some specialized skill or knowledge with your students. They fulfill essentially the same educational purposes as field trips but, instead of leaving school, visitors bring the action to the children. As with field trips, though, the classroom visitor should not be a talker who simply delivers a speech while the children serve as a captive audience; the children must be involved in the action.

Although not as patently irresistible as leaving school for a part of the day, children do enjoy contact with outside visitors and their interesting ideas and materials. Care must be exercised in the way classroom visitors are selected, however. The safest approach seems to be asking for recommendations from other teachers, informed parents, and other school personnel.

Charles Spaziani wanted to introduce his fifth-grade students to American history in a new way. "If you eat soup for lunch each day, you never get to try anything new," he avows. So, when it came time to study the accomplishments of Teddy Roosevelt, Mr. Spaziani contacted the local history museum for suggestions of a guest speaker who might present the major highlights of Roosevelt's life in a fresh, attention-grabbing way. The question barely cleared Mr. Spaziani's lips as the museum director blurted, "Ed Crocheron! Call Ed Crocheron!" The director went on to explain that Ed was a local resident and amateur historian who became fascinated with the life of Teddy Roosevelt. After completing years of research, Crocheron now brings Roosevelt to life as a realistic, attention-grabbing recreator. He looks like Roosevelt, complete with the droopy mustache and undersized spectacles that make Teddy Roosevelt instantly recognizable. Ed even dresses in the cowboy image of Teddy Roosevelt, complete with vest and weather-beaten hat.

When Ed Crocheron entered Mr. Spaziani's classroom, he became instantly transformed into Teddy Roosevelt. He began by holding up a large, old, grainy photo and explaining: "My earliest recollections were as a young boy. My most noteworthy early memory was viewing the funeral procession of Abraham Lincoln from the upstairs window of our family home in New York City."

Crocheron, complete with illustrative props, continued telling about the early life of Roosevelt, until his voice suddenly turned somber. "On Valentine's Day in 1884, when I was only 22 years old, I was at the center of one of the cruelest twists of fate ever. On that day—on Valentine's Day, no less—my wife Alice died during childbirth. On the same day, in the same house, my mother died of typhoid fever." Displaying a reproduction of the

NCSS STANDARDS

- **II.** *Time, Continuity, and Change*
- **VI.** *Power, Authority, and Governance*
- **X.** *Civic Ideals and Practice*

actual document, Crocheron sadly went on to exhibit a facsimile of a page from Roosevelt's diary of that day. Covering the page was a black X, two lines high. Then "Roosevelt" went on to read the few words that were entered on that page: "The light has gone out of my life." "Roosevelt" paused for a second or two, regained his composure, and explained that he spent much of the next two years on his ranch in the Badlands of Dakota Territory. There, he overcame his sadness as he learned to ride horses, rope, drive cattle, and hunt big game. "The other cowboys called me a dude," the reenergized speaker joked.

"Some of my proudest achievements were my conservation projects," "Roosevelt" detailed as he displayed large picture prints of national parks in the United States. "In 1908, I set aside 800,000 acres in Arizona as Grand Canyon National Monument to protect it from developers."

In much the same way, "Roosevelt" moved on to shed light on his career in politics and describe an African safari (decked out in a yellow pith helmet). He concluded his riveting presentation by describing an event that occurred in 1912, when he ran for President of the United States on the Progressive ticket: "When I was campaigning in Milwaukee, I was shot in the chest by a fanatical saloonkeeper. The bullet didn't kill me, but it did become lodged in my chest. I was saved only because the bullet hit both a steel eyeglass case I was carrying and a copy of the speech I had in my jacket. (Crocheron displayed facsimiles of both.) I went on to deliver the speech and, afterwards, a doctor's exam confirmed that I was not badly wounded. The doctors agreed that it would be more risky to remove the bullet than to let it stay in my chest." "Roosevelt" explained that he soon recovered, but the words he spoke at that time would have been appropriate at the time of his death in 1919: "No man has had a happier life than I have led; a happier life in every way."

Ed Crocheron stopped at this point and asked the children if they had questions. Hands anxiously flew into the air as the children promptly requested information on a number of topics: "What would you do about the war in Iraq if you were president now?" "Are Teddy bears really named after you?" Of course, Crocheron's responses were conveyed in the manner of "Teddy Roosevelt."

Careful planning and organization are required if teachers anticipate fruitful classroom visits such as the one provided by Mr. Spaziani. The following questions are offered to assist you in establishing a productive course of action.

- Is the speaker really necessary? Does she or he address standards or educational objectives in ways that other sources fall short?
- What would you like to have addressed in the presentation? Inform the speaker about the topic of study and how she or he can contribute to it.

- Have you offered the speaker suggestions on what it takes to involve your students in an appropriate and enthusiastic presentation? Advise the speaker to bring real, touchable items or visual aids. Let her or him know how important it is to include students in demonstrations or other activities. Also, suggest that the speaker move around the classroom so the children will feel personally involved. And, let the speaker know that it helps to ask students questions once in a while, too.
- What is the date, time, and location of the visit? How long do you want the visitor to talk? (The speaker will want to match the presentation to the attention level of the children—about 20 minutes for K–2 children and 30 minutes for grades 3 and up.) Contact the classroom visitor and clarify, well in advance, the details of the presentation.
- Does the visitor know where to report and where to park? Be sure she or he knows how to get to your school; send a map or written directions. Most schools will require all visitors to report to the main office, so be sure to meet and greet the speaker there (perhaps with a student from your class).
- Have the students been prepared for the classroom visitor? Clarify precisely who the guest is and why she or he will be visiting. Include student involvement in all phases of planning, including setting up desired behavioral expectations.
- Does the speaker welcome student-generated questions? Although questions may arise during the presentation, it is useful to help students prepare appropriate questions in advance.
- Is your attention focused on the speaker? It is important for the teacher to model appropriate behavior during the presentation.
- What is the teacher's role at the conclusion of the presentation? Thank the speaker for the visit, focusing on the new content and insights that were furnished. Discuss the visit with the students, making sure to associate new understandings with the established purposes for the visit. Help the students compose a thank-you note for the visitor; you must promptly mail the speaker a professionally suitable letter of thanks, too. Plan a follow-up experience with activities that summarize, reinforce, or highlight key outcomes. These might include an art activity, dramatic skit, or other suitable experience.

Computer-Based Multimedia

The multimedia revolution in our nation's schools involves multiple technologies, but the computer is at the heart of this revolt. Whether using CD-ROM encyclopedias, word-processing tools, educational software, interactive CD-ROM worktexts, or various online opportunities, computer-based learning plays a huge role in many social studies programs. Computer-based learning can be used in combination with most other subjects or methods of instruction, so it can be considered an exceptional curriculum integration medium.

The Internet

Connections to the Internet are providing access to vast outside sources of information and creating new opportunities for interdisciplinary learning. Some teachers utilize Internet resources to such a degree that they hail the Internet as a new era in learning. Katherine Nell (a teacher in Philadelphia, PA) maintains that her online connection has revitalized her teaching and motivated and excited her students. One of the greatest benefits cited by Ms. Nell is the capacity for collaborative research; through planning and sharing with their online peers, students find that the information they exchange has meaning—an instantaneous and utilitarian motive. She and her students have joined other classrooms around the country to investigate everything from the weather to prices for consumer goods. The major complaint voiced by Ms. Nell is that there just are not enough online classrooms to make a comprehensive exchange of projects and ideas possible.

How Global is the Curriculum *Go to MyEducationLab, select the topic Technology, watch the video entitled "Social Learning (with Computers)," and complete the questions that accompany it.*

For some teachers, it's a challenge to bridge the gap between traditional instruction and technology. However, as many teachers have learned, tapping into the Internet helps children benefit from a rich source of new ideas, friends, and experts. Blagojevic (1997) describes several categories of project ideas that were carried out in classrooms using the Internet:

- *To Make New Friends.* Using e-mail, children from Maine exchanged letters with Icelandic children.
- *To Extend the Curriculum.* After listing favorite storybook characters, children from Sacramento and Baltimore initiated a "story swap." Each group created and e-mailed original stories to each other.
- *To Build Cross-Cultural Comparisons.* Children from Oregon worked with children from Florida, Arizona, Japan, Russia, and South Africa on a collaborative book. Each location responded to the question "How do you like to play?" The children assembled a *How We Play* book of stories and drawings.
- *To Produce Information.* After a bee stung young Ted on the leg one day, his classmates suggested they build a web page that would educate people about bees. They researched bees and added their own drawings to the informational pages.
- *To Learn More.* A week after creating their web page, the class received an e-mail message from a bee expert. He pointed out that their bee was actually a yellowjacket wasp and explained the difference between bees and wasps. The children used this information to correct their page.
- *To Meet New People.* While they were studying penguins, a group of children electronically "met" a class of second-graders from Dunedin, New Zealand. They were awed to learn that their New Zealand friends could walk a half mile down the road to see penguins in the bay.

- *To Explore the World.* The Internet allows children to break out of the walls of their classroom to interact with people all over the world.

As fascinating as the Internet world can be, it can also confront you with a few problems. Perhaps the greatest is the availability of material not suitable for children. The Telecommunications Act requires Internet services to keep such material away from children, but nothing substitutes for careful supervision. Online services provide controls that allow you to limit what your children can access. Software such as Cybersitter or Surfwatch lets you supervise visits to the Internet.

Hypermedia (Presentation Software)

A special computer application that has contributed greatly to social studies programs today has been the use of hypermedia, a communications tool that combines video, graphics, animation, and text. Known as *presentation software,* hypermedia authoring programs enable students to organize and communicate information in innovative and thought-provoking ways, accessing and integrating information from such diverse sources as the Internet, sounds or clip art pulled from public domain software, photographs from a digital camera or scanner, and clips from a video camera or CD-ROM. Three widely used presentation software programs are HyperStudio, ClarisWorks, and, especially for the younger set, the SlideShow portion of KidPix. These are not the only hypermedia tools available to teachers and students, but they are excellent examples of how such programs work.

I once heard a computer expert say, "To be truly literate, one must learn to communicate in the dominant system of a culture." At no other time was this truism clearer to me than when I visited an elementary school "History Fair" and examined all of the wonderful projects. Every display attracted a great deal of attention, but one stood out above all the others. I was made aware of this special display by a neighbor who turned to me and asked, "Can you believe what Michael did on the computer?"

I walked over to Michael's space and was met with eye-popping graphics, clear text, dazzling animation, and breathtaking audio. Telling about the life of Harriet Tubman, Michael's project gave every impression of a professional presentation. Scanned photos from literature sources, spoken text that highlighted the key events in Harriet Tubman's life, recorded spirituals, and the culminating video clip of Martin Luther King Jr.'s "I Have a Dream" speech made the presentation a special occurrence. The "flash" was not the priority in Michael's presentation; the message was certainly the important element. However, the presentation software added much more to Michael's research than if he had simply put together an oral or written report.

NCSS STANDARDS

II. *Time, Continuity, and Change*
VIII. *Science, Technology, and Society*
X. *Civic Ideals and Practice*

Some presentation software systems contain special "buttons" that allow the user to immediately access another part of the presentation by clicking on a prompt. For example, Michael's presentation included a button at the point in Harriet Tubman's life when she gave slaves secret directions on how to flee to the North. By using the mouse to click the button, the user could listen to the song "Follow the Drinking Gourd" while looking at an illustration of the Big Dipper.

If students find learning more interesting and engaging as a result of creating an interactive project, then computers have served their purpose. Presentation software creates increased excitement about doing research because students know that their final report is going to look good and be fully interactive. Presentation software is readily available, relatively inexpensive, and not difficult to use. Teachers should use this practical technology application and demonstrate modern, effective communication techniques to their students.

Blogs and Podcasts

The present-day blog evolved from online diaries where individuals would keep a written account of their personal lives. Blogs have now become expanded into websites where people contribute written observations or news on any particular topic such as American history, politics, or local news. A typical blog blends text and images, as well as links to other blogs, web pages, or media related to its topic. The ability for readers to leave comments or additions in an interactive format on free online blog sites is a vital part of many blogs. Students can discuss important topics, ask questions, and receive feedback from other students. Most blogs are primarily textual, and can be created and updated with minimal technological expertise.

Teachers are finding blogs very useful in their social studies programs. If you've never before entered a blog site, try www.escrapbooking.com/blogging/index.htm. It offers helpful advice for setting up blogs and examples of how blogs can be used productively in the social studies classroom.

A podcast is a collection of audio (sometimes video) files that are distributed over the Internet and downloaded to portable media players (such as an MP3 player) or personal computers. Subscribing to and listening to podcasts requires no special equipment; they are simply downloaded and listened to, much like a radio show. Unlike radio shows, however, podcasts are not "real time." That means that the material is prerecorded and users can listen whenever they wish. Users can listen to these episodes one at a time or they can subscribe for free to the entire podcast series using software on their computers. With a subscription, all new shows are automatically downloaded to a computer as soon as they are available.

Podcasting's original function was to offer a medium to distribute individual "radio shows," but the system quickly became used in a wide variety of other ways. For example, the *New York Times, CNN,* and the 300+ stations of *National Public Radio* all provide podcasts on latest news stories. World news, sports, comedy, food, politics, music, books, walking tours; the students pick the topic and they'll find podcasts about it. They can even learn Chinese with daily audio podcasts (ChinesePod). Just like you use a web search to search for web pages, you can use a podcast search to find podcasts. A good place to start is a site like Yahoo! (podcasts.yahoo.com).

Podcasts are becoming progressively more accepted in social studies education. In addition to listening to podcasts on boundless topics, podcasts can be created by social studies teachers and students as a way to communicate information with anyone at anytime. An absent student can download the podcast of the recorded lesson. Students can listen to a teacher's podcast as they review an assignment or study for a test. But perhaps the most popular use of podcasting in schools is to publish student oral presentations. All you need is a microphone and a script; then, just download the free, easy-to-learn software, Audacity, and use it to produce and edit audio files. Sound effects and music can be easily inserted. The simplest way to make the podcast available is to link from a web page to your audio file.

The format of a podcast can be anything you like, but one that works especially well for a large number of social studies teachers is the news/talk-show format: "My name is Farrell Pelensky, and this is your favorite podcast site right here in Cedar City Elementary School." (Changing the host for each podcast generates greatest interest.) "Hope you're having a good day and are ready to listen to the top school news of the week as voted on by the fifth-graders of Cedar City Elementary. Here it goes!" As Farrell and his classmates talk, a sound effect CD provides the teletype background. News items often range from actual current events to special school events or projects, special student accomplishments, local tours, oral history, and other local happenings. Commercials may be interjected to promote items such as a school band concert, the school store, and so on. Some children enjoy creating parodies of actual commercials. The talk-show format may conclude the broadcast as the host interviews a local popular figure, teacher who has taken an interesting trip, or a student who has won a special prize.

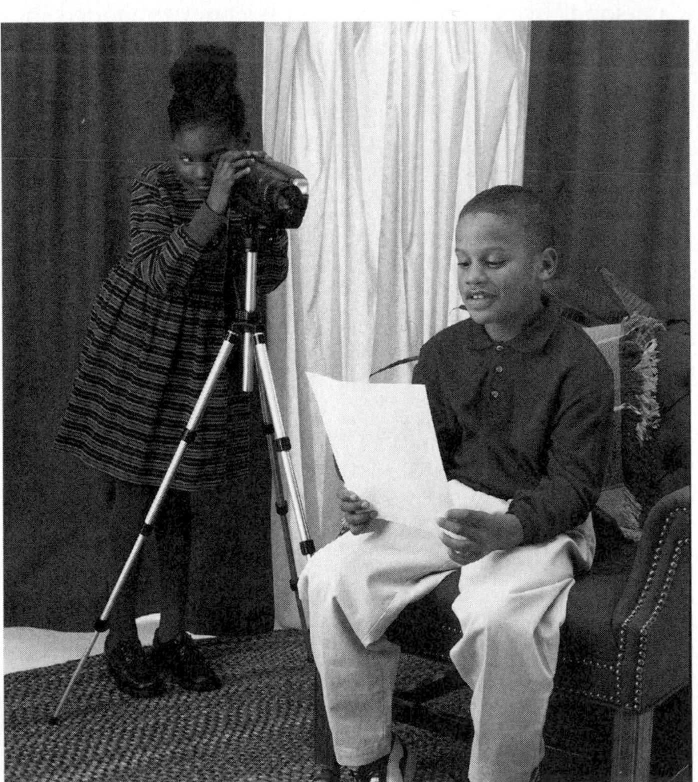

Podcasting provides an exciting way to explore and deliver social studies content.

Blogs and podcasts are quite appealing to students who enjoy working with computers. Creating either will expand their audience and allow them to enter into global communication. So, as blogs offer student opportunities to communicate widely through print, podcasts provide the opportunity to communicate through the spoken word.

Projects

The use of projects represents one of the most up-to-date integrative trends in elementary school social studies today. Good and Brophy (2003) define *projects* as "relatively long-term, problem-focused, and meaningful [modules] of instruction that integrate concepts from a number of disciplines or fields of study" (p. 234). Although the project approach is currently receiving significant attention from social studies educators, the idea is hardly new. For almost a century now, the value of projects has been endorsed in professional journals and books. It all started with John Dewey and his work at the famous experimental school at the University of Chicago. Dewey's philosophy was based on answers he constructed for this critical question: "How can teachers bring the school into closer relationship with the home and neighborhood life, instead of the school being a place where the child comes solely to learn certain lessons?" Dewey's methods included projects that encouraged students to investigate their own interests through meaningful dialogue and collaborative problem solving.

Key Events of a Project

Projects usually start with an *opening event*, which serves to stimulate initial interest in the topic. The opening event might come from primary sources such as classroom guests, field trips, real objects, special events, or illustrative processes. Or, they might be secondary sources such as books, magazines, photos, maps, and videos. Whatever the source, the idea of the opening event is to help students develop a strong attachment to the topic and to associate their past experiences to it. Therefore, you will want to encourage your students to recall any previous experiences related to the opening event. As students begin to come up with questions they would like to investigate, write them down and post the list so they can guide future data-gathering efforts. In effect, students should examine what they already know, and decide what it is they want to know. Many teachers like to use charting techniques during the opening event as a way of listing questions as they arise and organizing what the students already know (or think they know) about the topic. Webs and K-W-L charts work well; see Chapter 7 for a detailed explanation of those techniques.

During the second event, the students will become engaged in *investigating* and *producing* something. Teachers help students investigate their problems by making available a variety of resources—real objects, books, Internet sites, and other research materials. It is crucial to provide a wealth of research materials, but extremely critical for social studies projects to involve students in fieldwork or to arrange for them to speak with experts. The students will search for information to solve their problem by conducting an experiment, directly observing a phenomenon, or interviewing someone, to name a few potential investigative strategies. As the students work, their teachers will help them apply research skills such as collecting, organizing, and interpreting data. Although most of the work in any project is done by the students, they often require substantial guidance from their teacher to execute their plans and ideas.

How Global is the Curriculum *Go to MyEducationLab, select the topic Assessment, watch the video entitled "Using a Culminating Event as an Evaluative Tool," and complete the questions that accompany it.*

During this second event, it is important that the students not only conduct the research but also reflect on their findings in order to create something that represents what they have learned. Some children need time to reflect on new knowledge in order to understand it fully in their own terms, so don't hurry students through this segment. Imaginative activity can be very challenging for some children. As the students ponder what they should do, the teacher can offer them imaginative ways of personalizing their new knowledge through print, art, drama, and community action:

- Publishing-related experiences (newspaper, magazine, book, letter, poem)
- Art experiences (illustration, diagram, model, collage, mural, mobile, diorama)
- Drama experiences (reader's theater, play, skit, video presentation, puppets)
- Community action (petition, service project, letter to newspaper)

The culminating event involves communicating or sharing with others the work of the project. This provides an excellent opportunity to review and evaluate all that has been going on during the past days or weeks. Usually there is too much to share, so the class has to be selective in deciding what would best to tell the story of their project to other classes, the principal, or the parents. Finally, the teacher can use children's ideas and interests to make an evocative transition between the project being concluded and the next topic of study.

This summary has offered an explanation of the general features of projects, but it is important to think of each project as being distinctive. The teacher, the children, the topic, and the location of the school all contribute to the uniqueness of each project. An example of a social studies project that started out through interest generated by a fifth-grade teacher, Carmie Keiser, is described here.

Ms. Keiser's students liked to take virtual trips on the Web and showed a lot of passion for travel. So she decided to capitalize on their enthusiasm and put them to work as intern travel agents for the classroom-based World Wide Travel Agency. To create interest, Ms. Keiser and her students received a pretend letter one day from Mr. John Doe, an imaginary client who planned to do some extensive traveling throughout the United States in the near future, and wished to arrange his itinerary through the World Wide Travel Agency. The students were impressed with the potential business this new client could bring to the agency, but were a little unsure if they could handle it. They wanted to help this important client, but needed to get some information about what travel agencies do. No problem here; Donyelle's mother ran the local travel agency and was more than happy to arrange a visit to her place of business. The students returned to the classroom teeming with posters, pamphlets, guidebooks, and brochures. These materials helped the students understand the kind of information tourists need. They learned first-hand about the travel business and what it takes to promote trips to the different places in our country.

NCSS STANDARDS

III. *People, Places, and Environments*

VII. *Production, Distribution, and Consumption*

Ms. Keiser and her students agreed that it would be in their best interest to designate sections of the classroom as separate "travel agency offices," one to deal with each region of the United States. After the students were divided into small groups, each came up with its own office name and displayed a business sign. The separate offices displayed a map of the United States that included the names of its region: Middle Atlantic States, Great Lakes, and so on.

The travel agency offices thought they were nearly ready for business, but then someone pointed out that they needed to design an advertising package for their respective regions with resources similar to those they brought back from their trip to the real travel agency. They decided it would be best to produce a guidebook, travel poster, travel brochure, magazine advertisement, and a radio/television campaign.

Before they began their task, Ms. Keiser asked the students in each travel agency office to focus its research activities on the kinds of attractions its region was noted for: sandy beaches, scenic mountain trails, historic sites, industry, or agriculture. Some groups found information in magazines and books, others decided to watch a video, but all found a wealth of information on various Internet sites. After they finished, each group illustrated a large poster and used a few well-chosen words as a caption (for example, the group investigating America's Southwest focused on the Grand Canyon and used the caption, "A Grand Adventure!").

The brochures were eye catching, too. Patterned after commercial brochures, each contained colorful illustrations and captions on the front. For example, a steaming loaf of bread dominated the front of the group responsible for enticing visitors to "The Central Plains: Our Nation's Breadbasket." The children chose six important features of the region to highlight on the inside, each feature accompanied by text and illustration. The back of each brochure included a small map of the region, directions on how to get there, and sources of further information.

The purpose of the magazine ads and radio/television campaigns (a 30-second spot using the classroom video camera) were similar—to draw visitors by describing the important features of the region. Students were advised that each form of advertising needed a concise message so potential customers wouldn't be bored by excessive detail.

The guidebooks were much more comprehensive. Ms. Keiser showed commercial guidebooks that students used as models to create their own. Each guidebook had these features:

- A preface that briefly promoted the attributes of the region
- An introduction that served as a slightly more comprehensive guide to the region's attractions, climate, geographical features, chief products, and so on
- A history section that included significant dates and events as well as the important people who have lived in the region
- A calendar of events that highlighted fairs, celebrations, and seasonal attractions
- A places-to-see section that included the capital, information about major cities, museums, parks, zoos, recreational activities, historical sites, and businesses
- A food and shelter section that provided information about hotels, restaurants, and campsites, as well as their costs

To culminate the activity, Ms. Keiser requested that each travel agency office share its advertising campaign with the other offices in the World Wide Travel Agency. Parents were later invited to visit the classroom to enjoy the students' work. All children learned a great deal about the various regions through participating in this enjoyable, creative project.

The project approach to geography is an appropriate teaching strategy that confronts students with geography-related problems that serve as a focus for research activities. Project activities can involve the whole class or small groups; they can extend over several months or take as little time as a day. Regardless, children take the initiative in completing projects. The teacher sets the scene and falls into the role of a facilitator, supporting the children's efforts. Projects can be initiated from the children's spontaneous interests or they can flow from an interesting experience provided by the teacher. The current interest in projects stems from our growing knowledge about the probing, wondering minds of the children we teach. Social studies projects are a source for nurturing their natural responsiveness and interest in the world around them.

Thematic Units

Although spontaneous projects work for many teachers, some teachers are not completely comfortable with the approach. They insist that projects are too difficult to manage. Not knowing in advance where the project will take the class or how long it will go on worry those who need more structure in their professional lives. They grumble in frustration, "I have to address so many other curriculum requirements that I don't have time for projects." They complain that it is unreasonable to expect teachers to have a "bagful of tricks" on hand at all times to adeptly take advantage of when a child may become interested in a new topic. Besides, a large majority of school districts supply curriculum guides for teachers that specify grade-level topics around which teachers are expected to plan their instruction. Teachers are permitted to extend and enrich the specified topics, but the basic subject matter and sequence of those subjects must be followed. "I prefer this kind of curriculum structure," asserts one teacher. "The students of my colleagues who rely on a spur-of-the-moment, project-based curriculum gain only small fragments of knowledge on a whole host of matters. They lack an overall sense of direction in what they learn."

Teachers distrustful of the spontaneous nature of projects maintain that a lack of curriculum structure jeopardizes their ability to make available subject matter considered essential for understanding our world: "What happens if my students never develop a natural interest in China? Does that mean they will miss out on all the interesting discoveries associated with this rich land and glorious civilization?" Certainly not, mediators maintain; the motivation might not be as high as when children discover something by themselves, but if they are allowed to actively pursue what the teacher brings to them, students will become interested in it and be eager to learn. The idea is that concepts worth knowing about should be developed in a variety of ways; children need a mixture of direction and freedom. A learner's spontaneity should be encouraged and exploited, but teachers must also organize materials and situations to provide well-designed learning opportunities for their students.

One currently popular method for organizing prearranged social studies instruction is the thematic plan, or thematic unit. *Thematic plans* are extended blueprints of instruction created by teachers around a central idea; they contain an orderly sequence of lessons that provide a sense of cohesiveness, or unity, to classroom instruction. Experiences cut across traditional subject lines and are comfortably integrated with other subjects.

The actual form of thematic units varies from teacher to teacher; for some a thematic unit may be fundamentally a chapter from the textbook augmented with a few additional activities, whereas for others it may be an all-inclusive design that incorporates content and strategies across subject lines—from math, science, literature, creative writing, music, art, and others. Integrating other subjects into the development of social studies thematic units, however, makes most sense to young children; it is an idea that centers education in a true "child's world" where children are able to attach what they're learning to the real world. An integrated thematic unit offers a variety of "happenings" designed to satisfy and extend a child's natural sense of wonder.

The differences between thematic units and projects are quite small, but think of thematic units as being planned primarily by the teacher. The teacher selects the content, learning experiences, and length of time for the thematic units. On the

other hand, the interests and problems of the children drive projects. You don't know ahead of time where projects will take your class or when they will end.

Thematic instruction can be a potent tool for teaching social studies and for eliminating the isolated, disjointed nature of the elementary school curriculum. Successful implementation calls for a great deal of detailed preliminary planning because the best thematic units do not happen by chance; they are the result of hard work and attention to every detail. For that reason, the topic of thematic planning is much too comprehensive to be detailed here. Instead, Chapter 10 is intended to offer the type of comprehensive help that teachers seek out as they plan and implement theme-based instruction.

A Final Thought

How Global is the Curriculum *Go to MyEducationLab, select the topic Teaching Strategies, watch the video entitled "Succeeding in Your First Year of Teaching," and complete the questions that accompany it.*

The heart of dynamic social studies instruction is balance and proportion. As important as they are, these elements do not normally emerge as part of a teaching personality during a student's undergraduate certification program, during student teaching, or even after a year on the job. They often emerge after repeated successes with textbook-based instruction. You will not rely on textbooks to guide you throughout your entire teaching career; a feeling of unrest and a strong desire to "spread your wings" will begin to entice you to expand your repertoire and experiment with varied instructional materials and activities during your earliest years of teaching. In a time-honored description of teacher development, Katz (1972), explains this professional evolution as a stage-related process:

- *Stage One:* You are preoccupied with survival. You ask yourself questions such as, "Can I get through the day in one piece? Without losing a child? Can I make it until the end of the week? Until the next vacation? Can I really do this kind of work day after day? Will I be accepted by my colleagues?" Textbooks are useful tools that help teachers gain the confidence necessary to manage the routines causing most of the anxiety during this stage. (*First year*)
- *Stage Two:* You decide you can survive. You begin to focus on individual children who pose problems and on troublesome situations, and you ask yourself these kinds of questions: "How can I help the shy child? How can I help a child who does not seem to be learning? What more can I do for children with special needs?" (*Second year*)
- *Stage Three:* You begin to tire of doing the same things with the children. You like to meet with other teachers, scan magazines, and search through other sources of information to discover integrative projects and activities for the children. You ask questions about new developments in the field: "Who is doing what? Where? What are some of the new materials, techniques, approaches, and ideas? How can I make social studies more dynamic?" (*Third and fourth years*)

According to Katz's developmental theory, then, new teachers cannot be expected to move away from a deliberate textbook-based routine until sometime during the third year of teaching. At first, you will feel more comfortable teaching with the help of textbooks and with ideas learned from others. The need to grow and learn will become evident as an inner drive gives you no other choice but to branch out. You should then begin to formulate and refine a personal philosophy of instruction that will serve as a foundation to support all professional decisions in the future. The difference between teachers who are good "technicians" and those who are educational leaders appears to be their willingness to constantly think about and work toward methods based on a sound personalized philosophy of teaching and learning.

You will use textbooks, then, and they will contribute immeasurably to your social studies program. But the emphasis of your instruction should be on variety. Continually confront youngsters with significant experiences so they get to know our world and build the qualities that help them become constructive, active citizens. The kinds of citizens our boys and girls grow up to be is determined to a great extent by the ways they live and grow in school.

REFERENCES

Blagojevic, B. (1997). Internet interactions. *Scholastic Early Childhood Today, 11*, 47–48.

Chard, S. C. (1998) *The project approach: Making curriculum come alive*. New York: Scholastic.

Darigan, D. L., Tunnell, M. O., & Jacobs, J. S. (2002). *Children's literature: Engaging teachers and children in good books*. Upper Saddle River, NJ: Merrill/Prentice-Hall.

Good, T. L., & Brophy, J. E. (2003). *Looking in classrooms*. Boston: Allyn & Bacon.

Jennings, J., & Rentner, D. S. (2006). Ten big effects of the No Child Left Behind Act on public schools. *Phi Delta Kappan, 88,* 110–113.

Katz, L. G. (1972). Developmental stages of preschool teachers. *Elementary School Journal, 73,* 50–54.

Mead, M. (1978). Creating a scientific climate for children. In C. Charles & B. Samples (Eds.), *Science and society: Knowing, teaching, learning*. Washington, DC: National Council for the Social Studies.

National Council of Teachers of Mathematics. (2000). *Principles and standards for school mathematics.* Reston, VA: Author.

Risinger, C. F. (2005). Social studies, interdisciplinary teaching, and technology. *Social Education, 69,* 149–150.

Steptoe, J. (1987). *Mufaro's beautiful daughters: An African tale*. New York: Lothrop, Lee & Shepard.

Stevens, R. L., & Starkey, M. (2007). Teaching an interdisciplinary unit on shelter. *Social Studies and the Young Learner, 20,* 6–10.

Vanderslice, M. (2007). Keeping social studies alive with a heritage activity. *Social Studies and the Young Learner, 20,* 4–5.

VanFossen, P. J. (2006). Reading and math take so much of the time . . . An overview of social studies instruction in elementary classrooms in Indiana. *Theory and Research in Social Education, 33,* 376–403.

Wachowiak, F., & Clements, R. D. (2006). *Emphasis art*. Boston: Allyn & Bacon.

PART II Classrooms for Young Social Scientists

CHAPTER 4

Young Historians

Learning to Unlock the Past

What Does Today's History Look Like?

Reginald Garrett, a fifth-grade teacher, put his young historians to work one day when a question for serious consideration burst forth from a quite unlikely source. A group of students was reading a magazine article describing fads of youth today—their clothing styles, favorite television shows, most popular entertainers, and so on. An extended conversation about whether the poll accurately reflected "kids of today" got nearly everyone involved. As the students talked about and sometimes questioned the article's accuracy, one student looked at Mr. Garrett and abruptly shifted the direction of the conversation. "Mr. Garrett," she asked, "what fads were popular when *you* were a kid like us?"

Realizing that the spark for historical inquiry often comes from personally activated questions, Mr. Garrett seized the moment and shared a few of his memories. He was surprised to see that the class remained quite interested throughout his discourse. Without having pre-planned a historical inquiry experience for his students, Mr. Garrett unexpectedly found himself in the midst of one. He started by writing the students' original problem on the board in an *IWW* . . . format: "I wonder what fads were 'cool' with the fifth-graders of the 1980s."

An attention-grabbing problem or perplexing question, then, becomes the initial spark that ignites the children's inner drive to resolve the uncertainty. Mr. Garrett's young historians are ready to go; it is now time to spring to action. As his young historians considered alternative sources of information about the state of affairs "long ago," they determined that three might match up best to their

present needs: *oral history, written resources,* and *artifacts*. Knowing that time prohibited their using each of these sources, the students decided that their best alternative was to draw together an oral record of the 1980s. They planned to interview family members and neighbors, many of whom were elementary school students during that era. The students planned a written list of questions they would use as a source of their data.

Mr. Garrett's students summarized and rank-ordered the responses to each interview question on a large chart. The results are shown in Figure 4.1. Mr. Garrett helped his students make descriptive statements of the data by asking questions such as, "What did you discover about fads of the 1980s? How does this list compare to present-day fads? Why do you think this has happened? How might this list change in the future? What makes you think so?"

NCSS STANDARDS

- **I.** *Culture*
- **II.** *Time, Continuity, and Change*
- **IV.** *Individual Development and Identity*

The class concluded their study by planning an "'80s Day" at school, coming to school dressed in the fashion of the day, listening and dancing to period recording artists such as Men at Work, and probing the popular toys and games of the time such as Pac-Man. Parents prepared some special snacks for the "time travelers," including fondue and powdered juice drinks, which were all consumed during a videotape showing of an episode from TV's most popular program of the 1980s, *The Cosby Show.*

Mr. Garrett bases his overall approach to teaching history on a conviction that history cannot be restricted to memorizing "who did what to whom, when,

FIGURE 4.1 Summary of Interviews

Savings	Toys	Clothing	Entertainers	Sports Stars	TV Shows
Awesome	Cabbage Patch Kids	Camouflage clothes	Bill Cosby	Mary Lou Retton	Cosby Show
Rad	He-Man	Fingerless gloves	Michael J. Fox	Walter Payton	He-Man: Masters of the Universe
Cool	Transformers	Legwarmers	Ralph Macchio	Greg Louganis	Punky Brewster
	My Little Pony	Jams	Madonna	Larry Bird	The A-Team
	G.I. Joe	Parachutes pants	Wham!	Evelyn Ashford	Webster
	Stickers	Cutoff shirts	Emmanuel Lewis	Pete Rose	Who's the Boss?
		Collars turned up	Ricky Schroder	Kareem Abdul-Jabbar	Silver Spoons
		Checkered shoes	Gary Coleman	Carl Lewis	Knight Rider
		Jeans	Mr. T		Family Ties
		Belts below the waist	Michael Jackson		
			Sylvester Stallone		

and where" or to a chronological listing of events commonly found in textbooks. He believes history can be found everywhere—homes, museums, newspapers, and so on. It can be found in a box of old receipts; in games children play; in stories people tell; in paintings, clothes, tools, furniture, books, letters, and diaries. Wherever we look, we can find clues to our past. Mr. Garrett wants his students to know that the past is not just a list of names and dates, but is a captivating story of life in other times.

How Global is the Curriculum *Go to MyEducationLab, select the topic History, watch the video entitled "Theme: Time, Continuity, and Change," and complete the questions that accompany it.*

Unfortunately, not all children experience history like Mr. Garrett's students. When asked to share their feelings about history, many children echo Henry Ford's contention that history is "bunk"; they don't like history because they say it is "boring." Mr. Garrett, however, helps to steer clear of this view of history by addressing the goals of historical study in a much more inspired way. His young historians learn history, but the part they like best is the "story" of history—Mr. Garrett's history is today's history.

The National Standards for History (National Center for History in the Schools, 1996) reinforces Mr. Garrett's convictions. This influential document proclaims history, along with literature and the arts, as the most enriching studies in which elementary school students can be engaged. "History connects each child with his or her roots and develops a sense of personal belonging in the great sweep of human experience" (p. 2).

What Is History?

Simply put, *history* is considered a narrative (story or explanation) of the past. Anything that has a past has a history—and a story. People who study the past to establish what happened, how it happened, and why it happened are called *historians*. Connecting these two thoughts, I like to refer to elementary school students engaged in getting to the bottom of the mysteries of the past as "young historians." Young historians, like all historians, look at the past as a puzzle to be solved. They ask questions of the past and look for answers in the evidence left by people who lived before them.

Historians, then, tell a story of what has gone on in the past by investigating and interpreting anything that has somehow survived over the years. The approach they use is commonly referred to as the *historical method,* which generally entails three separate tasks: (1) uncovering important information about the past, (2) verifying the accuracy of the information, and (3) organizing the information into an informative historical narrative.

To carry out their duties, historians seek out evidence from a variety of sources, both written and nonwritten. *Written* sources include books, journals, almanacs,

letters, diaries, songs, speeches, poems, court records, cookbooks, traveler's reports, advertisements, memoirs, government publications, land surveys, account books, and campaign slogans. They also include the gravestones, old calendars, posters, maps—anything with writing on it. However, written sources go back only to about 3000 BC. when the Sumerians developed a pictographic type of writing known as cuneiform. Writing made it possible for people to keep records, compose poems and stories, or inscribe a treaty—all potential sources of information for historians. The past before the development of writing is called *prehistory*.

Nonwritten sources include *physical artifacts*, such as tools, weapons, jewelry, machines, toys, uniforms, masks, utensils, furniture, monuments, buildings, clothing, photographs, statues, and cookware; *visual images*, such as photographs, videos, paintings, sculptures, and cave drawings; and *oral and audio histories*, such as a culture's oral tradition—stories such as folktales and myths that have been passed down from generation to generation by word of mouth—and live interviews or audio recordings.

Historical evidence that existed during the historical period under study is called a *primary source*. Anything produced at a time later than the historical period under study is called a *secondary source*. To illustrate, the written memoirs of Susan B. Anthony are considered primary sources, whereas Martha E. H. Rustad's children's biography, *Susan B. Anthony (First Biographies)* (Capstone Press) is a secondary source. Newspapers from September 1862 describing the battle at Antietam are primary sources for the study of the Civil War, but a video recreation of the battle must be considered a secondary source. Primary sources are considered to be among the most indispensable learning resources in elementary school classrooms because they give our students firsthand, genuine insight into the past; they are the most important tools anyone can draw on while probing a historical event. Secondary sources, however, also hold an important place in elementary school social studies programs. For example, children will want to use a secondary source such as a reference book or website if they need to retrieve a specific piece of information quickly. (Try the Click2 History website www.awesomestories.com/history/ to learn the story behind famous historical events.) Such resources help children quickly find out when Benito Juarez lived, where Wilbur and Orville Wright's first successful flight took place, and who was president when the United States entered World War I. Secondary sources, such as the treasure trove of children's literature, are also useful in helping children learn more about something from the past.

The historical method, then, begins with a historian's attempt to use primary and secondary sources to tell a truthful story about the past. But, because no evidence from the past is self-revealing (the evidence can't tell its own story to a historian), it is open to interpretation. Therefore, we say that history is *subjective*. A historian studies the evidence, determines its accuracy, and then pieces it together to the best of her or his ability as a written narrative. Because this is an extremely delicate process, our views of history are constantly changing as new findings are uncovered and revised interpretations of old evidence are made.

New challenges often confront established views of history and add controversy to any historian's story of the past. Was Christopher Columbus a heroic explorer or a liar and a crook? Did Mrs. O'Leary and her cow cause the Great Chicago Fire or is this merely a nineteenth-century legend? Did John Hancock help organize the Boston Tea Party to protest lack of representation or because British taxes threatened his tea business? Did the redcoats really fire the first shot at Lexington? Did Edwin Stanton, Secretary of War at the time of Lincoln's assassination, actually plot to kill President Lincoln? Was Mary Todd Lincoln bright, vivacious, and politically astute or was she high strung, hot tempered, and not especially sold on the concept of honesty? Our views of history constantly shift as the interpretation of new and old evidence disputes the legitimacy of earlier explanations.

Why Is History Important?

One of the most hopeful signs in social studies education during the past decade has been the widespread and growing support for more history in our schools. Proponents are not supporters of the kind of history that demands memorizing a bunch of facts, but rather the history that makes the past seem real—the history that captivates young historians and activates them to weave together various pieces of information in the best tradition of a storyteller. Taking on the role of young historians helps students recognize their place in history, realizing that their lives will be part of a yet unrecorded history.

The most common rationale for including history as a central part of social studies is that, by studying the past, our young citizens will be better prepared to judge the present and the future. To help clarify this point, it would be instructive to think about what response you might make when asked these two questions: What is prerequisite to understanding any present social condition? What is prerequisite to effectively making decisions about the future? To many, both questions can be acceptably answered using but a single word: *knowledge*. If knowledge is our selection, then, there can be only one place to find it—in the past. Why? I once heard it said that the future is unknown, the present is momentary, and everything else is history. So, where else but the past does one come across the knowledge needed to understand and confront great issues? The experiences of other times enlighten us with the knowledge required to figure out solutions to present and future challenges.

The National Center for History in the Schools (1996) supports these views with the argument that *knowledge of history is the precondition for political intelligence*:

> Without history, a society shares no common memory of where it has been, of what its core values are, or of what decisions of the past account for our present circumstances. Without history, one cannot undertake any sensible inquiry into the political, social, or moral issues in society. And without historical knowledge and the inquiry it supports, one cannot move to the informed, discriminating citizenship essential in the democratic processes of governance and the fulfillment for all our citizens of the nation's democratic ideals. (p. 1)

What Should Students Know or Be Able to Do?

If our goal as social studies educators is to prepare informed, reflective, and active citizens, then history must be transformed from a subject that operates mainly as a storehouse of information. Barbara Wisdom (a great name for a teacher, don't you agree?), a fifth-grade teacher, explains that when we teach about the *Westward Movement in the United States*, we must include names and dates and places and battles.

"Although memorizing names and dates is not the overriding purpose of history instruction," Ms. Wisdom suggested, "important facts and concepts must be considered an essential part of any history program. The reason is obvious—we can't teach our children how to think as young historians unless they have something worth thinking about."

The argument that we can teach students how to understand the world of the past without conveying to them the events and ideas that have brought it into existence is a weak argument. One of the reasons why history is so tricky to teach is that students are not interested in learning facts unless those facts are embedded in challenging or engaging contexts, but they cannot comprehend the contexts without knowing the facts. Therefore, if history is to be taught properly, teachers must enable students not only to recount the past, but also to analyze issues and problems faced by people at critical moments in the past.

The National Center for History in the Schools (1996) adds that

> true historical understanding requires students to engage in historical thinking: to raise questions and to marshal solid evidence in support of their answers; to go beyond the facts presented . . . and examine the historical record for themselves; to consult documents, journals, diaries, artifacts, historic sites, works of art, quantitative data, and other evidence from the past, and to do so imaginatively—taking into account the historical context in which these records were created and comparing the multiple points of view of those on the scene at the time. (p. 59)

With this important perspective in mind, the National Center for History in the Schools (1996) established a list of five interconnected dimensions of historical thinking that are meant to serve as outcomes that students need to achieve during their elementary school years. Known as the Five Sets of Standards in Historical Thinking, these statements are intended to help teachers develop instructional plans and guide students through challenging programs of study in history:

- *Standard 1:* The student thinks chronologically.
- *Standard 2:* The student comprehends a variety of historical sources.
- *Standard 3:* The student engages in historical analysis and interpretation.
- *Standard 4:* The student conducts historical research.
- *Standard 5:* The student engages in historical issues-analysis and decision-making.

Direct encounters with the art and architecture of the medieval world are exciting for young learners and enhance their growth in historical thinking.

In General, How Should History Be Taught?

How Global is the Curriculum
Go to MyEducationLab, select the topic History, and view the lesson plan entitled "Ideas for the History Classroom," and complete the questions that accompany it.

Although the National Standards for History pinpoints the standards for an elementary school social studies program, the National Center for History in the Schools (1996) does not ignore the important matter of instructional methodology. The group stresses that teachers can bring history alive in the classroom largely by using "stories, myths, legends, and biographies that capture children's imaginations and immerse them in times and cultures of the recent and long-ago past" (p. 3). Teachers should work closely with their school media specialists to determine which books hold greatest potential for energizing history instruction. When selected, these books should be displayed engagingly, used regularly, and discussed as a part of the regular classroom instructional routine.

The National Center goes on to recommend that "in addition to stories, children should be introduced to a wide variety of historical artifacts, illustrations, and records that open to them first-hand glimpses into the lives of people in the past: family photos; letters, diaries, and other accounts of the past obtained from family records, local newspapers, libraries, and museums; field trips to historical sites in their neighborhood and community; and visits to "living museums" where actors reenact life long ago" (p. 3). Furthermore, special experiences help breathe life into history. Examples include field trips to museums and historical sites,

historical craft and model-building experiences, National History Day projects, and the experience of constructing an oral history of some local "big event." Critically important to a vital history program, then, is to engage children in historical thought through the use of a wide range of artifacts, including tangible items and written documents. We will examine these vital resources in the following sections.

Investigating with Historical Artifacts

Several years ago, my great-grandfather's treasured pocket watch was handed down to me shortly after he had passed away. The watch was extraordinarily special to him because it was the first item of material worth he had bought for himself after selling his cow and using the money to escape his peasant's life in Ukraine to find a job as a railroad worker in the United States. My great-grandfather had already retired from his unskilled railroad job by the time I was a youngster, but one of my earliest and fondest boyhood memories is admiring the intricate design on the watch's shiny gold cover and watching the delicate second hand rotate in a steady beat on the watch's immaculate face. I remember studying my great-grandfather's routine of slowly sliding out the watch from his faded coverall pockets as I sat with him on his front porch and listened to stories he told in broken English about his early life in Ukraine. I'm still not sure if he really needed to know the time or whether the watch was a satisfying reminder of the path he had traveled in life, but the obvious pleasure that surfaced on his mustached face is still firmly etched on my mind. Naturally, I was thrilled as a young man to have inherited the gold pocket watch because it helped me remain in touch with my great-grandfather, and his stories, even though he was physically no longer with me.

As I think more deeply about my great-grandfather's pocket watch, I cannot help but think about how important it is to teach history to children through the stories that are connected with items from the past. It is much as Potter (2003) so thoughtfully reflected: "[Primary sources] are part of the past; they are with us today; and touching them allows us, quite literally, to touch and connect with the past" (p. 372).

Like my great-grandfather's pocket watch, primary sources of historical evidence have the power to arouse a meaningful curiosity in and imagination of the past. Remnants of the past help connect students to earlier times and virtually set fire to their interest in days gone by. In speaking of the advantages of using primary resources in social studies classrooms, Simpson (2005) stated, "In the field of history education, great strides have been made in using primary sources as a means of engaging students, thus enabling teachers to avoid the pitfalls of simply teaching to the text and deadening effects of 'drill and kill' pedagogy. Programs that encourage the use of primary sources . . . have grown spectacularly" (p. 353).

Primary sources (*artifacts*) serve to ignite the interests of students and play an important role in helping them master essential historical concepts and processes. *Artifacts* are objects that actually existed at the time historical events occurred. They may include either (1) *tangible items,* such as works of art, furniture, tools, utensils, and weapons, or (2) *written documents from the past*, such as letters, diaries, journals, newspapers, speeches, interviews, memoirs, documents, cookbooks, and photographs. Artifacts serve as the raw material to help us understand the past; when they are used in combination with written interpretations of the past (such as trade books or textbooks), we generate a sound blueprint for carrying out historical investigations in the elementary school social studies classroom.

Tangible Items

Students are naturally curious about and fascinated by things that they can see, touch, and explore, so tangible items help history come alive in a very concrete way. One of your primary responsibilities as a teacher of history, then, is to collect historical items (or reproductions) based on the historical events, themes, or periods you will be teaching. What kinds of objects should you consider gathering? Anything that helps your children gain a sense of history—artwork, letters, diary entries, cookbooks, photo albums, clothing, musical instruments, utensils, tools, music, toys, currency, report cards. Anything hands-on that brings relevance and meaning to the study of times past qualifies.

Where can teachers locate artifacts for their social studies classrooms? Gray and Owens (2003) acknowledge there is no sure-fire way of uncovering artifacts, but offer a number of suggestions on how to start. First, look in your own attic, garage, or basement (or grandma's and grandpa's). It's amazing what old things you'll find—toys, household items, clothing, sports equipment, immigration papers, old photos, letters, postcards, diaries, and other useful memorabilia. Flea markets or yard sales, too, are excellent sources of inexpensive artifacts that are suitable for social studies classrooms. It's rare to visit one of these places without running into fellow teachers who are there for the same reason you are. Arrive early! In addition to those potential sources of historical artifacts, parents of your children are often willing to lend or donate items for classroom use. Either make an announcement explaining your needs at an open house meeting or send home a note requesting specific materials for a topic under study and you will certainly receive more than you might expect. Reproductions of tools, clothing, or other items can be found online through vendors who sell to historical reenactors (see www.cwreenactors.com/index.php). In addition, one of the best ways to find historical documents related to a person or event is through an Internet search. The National Archives Digital Classroom (www.archives.gov/digital_classroom) and the Library of Congress American Memory Collection (memory.loc.gov/ammem/amhome.html) are two excellent sources.

Last but not least, you might want to check with a local historical society, museum, or library. Their archives contain a rich source of artifacts related to local people, places, and events. Most of the items in local archives are unavailable from other sources, so if an awareness of your local or cultural heritage is an important part of your curriculum, take advantage of the benefits these local institutions may offer. In addition to their educational exhibits, many of these local or regional institutions now lend artifact kits to schools. Their kits offer original items

and replicas from specific time periods that help arouse the children's interest in local, state, and regional history. The Colorado Historical Society, for example, offers a number of historical kits. Their *Cliff Dwellers* kit is packed with artifacts and activities related to excavating prehistoric artifacts buried in sand. Check with your local museums or libraries and, if available, check out a kit like this for your children. Their faces will beam with each thrilling discovery.

Tangible items can be used singly (a colonial salt box), or they can be placed together into special collections, boxes, or kits related to historical topics or themes. One teacher, for example, assembled an artifact kit on colonial kitchens. The goal of compiling the kit was to illustrate that early colonial homes for common people were very simple places. So, the kit consisted primarily of wooden ware—bowl, trencher, tankard, spoon, salt box, and candle box. Other than the iron cooking pot, these were among the most important items in a colonial kitchen. A pewter tankard was added, but just to illustrate that metal was valuable and rarely found in ordinary homes. Creating a collection to represent a particular historical period or event authenticates the experience for children and helps them deal with abstract historical concepts. Teachers report that tangible items increase students' interest, enhance their understanding, and make classroom discussions more meaningful and interesting.

Higgs and McNeal (2006) assert that if tangible items are to be properly used in history programs, they should not be simply put on display with a "look but don't touch" warning. Instead, they must be a part of quality learning experiences during which children purposefully manipulate the items while constructing meaningful historical concepts. Higgs and McNeal go on to recommend the following sequence as a recommended strategy to guide children as they examine objects from any collection or kit:

1. Assemble or obtain a kit of items (or reproductions) that clearly represent an era or culture under study. Write a printed description of each item and keep it concealed from the children until a later time. Arrange a table display containing samples of modern implements so that comparisons to contemporary cultures or times can be made at a later time.
2. Pair up the children and place a different item on each pair's desk.
3. Invite the children to explore their items. They should be encouraged to use all their senses, but the materials should never be placed into their mouths. Then, as young historians, they are directed to write down their observations on an "Observation Log." The children should not "guess" what the items are at this point; they only record descriptions.
4. After the descriptions are recorded, the pairs brainstorm and record on their Observation Logs what they think their item might have been used for. The children must supply reasons for each assumption: "Why do you think this is so?" "What is your evidence?" Some items, like a clay pot or coin from colonial times, will be fairly straightforward to identify, whereas others, such as a Jacob's Ladder or Jack Straws, will be much more difficult.

5. Direct the children to retrieve a printed description of their item that you had previously arranged on a table. The descriptions may or may not verify the children's previous assumptions. The descriptions should be added to their Observation Logs.
6. The children must match their items to the modern counterparts that would do similar work. If the children feel that none of the displayed counterparts fulfill this purpose, they are encouraged to suggest their own. The pairs discuss the comparisons and enter their interpretations on the Observation Logs.
7. Have the children speculate about what people are represented by the items: "Who used these items?" "What evidence helped you make this decision?" The children should record their suppositions and write a few sentences of explanation on their Observation Logs.
8. The pairs share their decisions with the class; the class deliberates as a whole to determine the actual event, era, or culture represented by all the items. If they have difficulty arriving at a consensus, the teacher could add information to help the class arrive at a sound conclusion.

Tangible items can knit strong and powerful links to the past. Each has its own story and effectively weaves a potent hands-on connection to people from other time periods. Unfortunately, in many classrooms, real objects are thought of much as museum pieces—too valuable to touch so they are kept under lock and key. However, tangible items help children realize that history is the story of real people and serve as potent hands-on catalysts for meaningful ways to explore the past.

To help introduce children to the process of using tangible items, it is best to begin with materials that are meaningful to the children themselves or to someone in their family—items such as jewelry, clothing, utensils, or musical instruments. Children like to tell stories about themselves, so ask them to bring to school and share their personal or family objects at a classroom display area I like to call a *Family Artifact Museum*.

To set off the process in her classroom, Yvonne Perry-Segarra read to the class Bonnie Pryor's book, *The House on Maple Street* (HarperTrophy). In the story, an ancient arrowhead and broken china cup from early times are unearthed in a contemporary child's yard. The story of the two objects is used to help connect the past to the present for two little girls in the house on Maple Street. The story introduced the idea of a treasured individual or family item to the children, and their budding perception of the concept was extended through a helpful follow-up discussion. All agreed that a good working definition for *artifact* would be "something important from long ago that is very special to you or your family." Ms. Perry-Segarra then introduced the Family Artifact Museum project by sharing a personally treasured relic—her teaching certificate (housed in a protective frame). The children were

allowed to inspect the certificate as Ms. Perry-Segarra explained how she earned it and why it is important to her and her family. She answered the children's eager questions as the certificate made its trip around the riveted group. Throughout this process, Ms. Perry-Segarra modeled an artifact sharing presentation the children would soon be responsible for carrying out.

NCSS STANDARDS

I. *Culture*
II. *Time, Continuity, and Change*
IV. *Individual Development and Identity*

Ms. Perry-Segarra next presented details about the classroom artifact project. That evening at home, with the help of a family member or close adult, she suggested, the children were to look through the mementos of their lives and find something important to them or their families—a photograph, a letter, a toy, food, a religious object—anything significant that would bring a touch of their past to school. Then the children were to prepare a short oral presentation during which they explained what type of artifact they brought to school, how old it is, what it is used for, and who it belonged to, and told a short story about its importance to the child or family. A letter was sent home detailing the project and asking parents or close adults to help their children select an artifact that has been in their family for a long time and has special importance to their family.

The next day, all but one of 18 children brought a tangible item to school; the child who couldn't share was raised in the foster care system and was not familiar enough with any family's history to meaningfully share an artifact. Enrique, however, brought a photo of a "Welcome to Arizona" sign. He explained it was taken by his Grandpa Erubiel when he emigrated from Mexico and searched for a piece of land near Tucson. Grandpa Erubiel eventually found suitable ground and part of the Chavez family still lives in the little adobe farmhouse he built on it.

"My grandmother made this clay storyteller doll for my father," reported Luz. (Navajo storyteller dolls are a rather contemporary addition to traditional Navajo pottery. These handmade clay figurines depict a Navajo storyteller with little children gathered tenderly in her or his arms, telling stories that serve to pass on knowledge and cultural values from one generation to the next.) "The storyteller is telling stories of our Hopi people to the little babies in her arms," explained Luz. "Our Navajo people mixed their craft skills with their love of storytelling to make these storyteller dolls. The dolls are very popular and are becoming more valuable every day."

Alicia struggled to hoist an old manual typewriter onto the sharing table. (For those who don't remember, a typewriter is a mechanical device with a set of keys that, when pressed, prints characters and words on paper!) "My grandma used this typewriter in a business office when she was a secretary," Alicia reported. Alicia went on to provide a short demonstration of how typewriters work. "Now computers and printers have taken the place of these old typewriters," Alicia explained.

Other technological phenomena seemed to capture the interest of the children: Ivan demonstrated a hand-held console that created quite a buzz: "Here's a Nintendo Game Boy with a Tetris game cartridge. My big brother in college got this one in 1989 when he was just a little boy. I think it was the first year they made the Game Boy and he said they were very popular."

As the presentations continued, the children were surprised to see how much they had in common; they remarked time after time that these presentations really helped them to get to know each other. The artifacts, along with their explanations, effectively generated great interest in the cultural heritage of the class. To conclude the presentations, Ms. Perry-Segarra sought additional feedback on how the children viewed this activity: "Was anyone unsure about what kind of object to share?" "How did you feel about the actual act of sharing your item with the class?" "Was anyone concerned about what your classmates might think of you after they heard you tell about your item?" "What did you learn about your family as you were selecting an to bring to share?" "What did you learn about others as you heard them share their objects?"

Most of the tangible items were much too prized by the families for them to remain on display in school beyond the day of the presentation, so Ms. Perry-Segarra took digital photographs of each and mounted them on a bulletin board display. The children filled out information cards that described the artifacts—where they came from, how old they were, who they belonged to, and what they were used for—and attached the cards next to the photos. The exhibit proudly became known as the classroom *Family Artifact Museum*.

Artifacts are among the most important resources historians use to deepen their understanding of the past. They can be experienced on field trips or in the classroom.

Living Museums The world outside the classroom is rich in historical learning experiences, and offers excellent hands-on resources to engage the children more completely in exploring tangible items. By taking trips outside of school, students experience things firsthand that are impossible in the classroom. Visiting museums and "living history" sites to observe the clothing, houses, furnishing, tools, and other artifacts both enlighten and enrich understandings of any historical period.

A list of places to visit can range from A to Z—from antique shops to the zoo. Regardless, the challenge is to effectively draw out student understandings from wherever you choose to go. A fifth-grade teacher, Soojeong Kim, who was teaching a unit titled "Colonial Life in America," makes the value of such trips crystal-clear. She realized that her students' failure to comprehend time and place concepts might stifle their curiosity and interest in studying colonial America, so she arranged a trip to an authentic living museum in Cooperstown, New York.

The children's spirits were instantly aroused as the class walked up the path connecting the parking lot to the restored colonial village called "The Farmers' Museum." Authentic in every detail, the village was an actual working farm in which people dressed in period garb and used authentic implements to perform the duties of colonial farmers. About halfway up the path, the class fixed their eyes in horror as a farmer led a huge ox hauling a cart directly toward them. None of the children had ever before seen a real ox; few knew exactly what an ox was. "Let me outa here!" shrieked Frank guardedly as the snorting animal, covered with flies and oozing slobber, ambled up and stopped next to him. The farmer invited Frank to pat the ox, but Frank was too scared to try.

"I never knew an ox was so big," Lois marveled as she reached up and patted its wet nose.

Following Lois's lead, several classmates approached the ox, some patting it and others commenting on its size, smell, and drawing power for flies. Some children were satisfied to simply look at the ox, while others ran away from it when it made the slightest movement; one or two even made faces at it—they did all sorts of things. The farmer told the class about the importance of oxen to colonial life and they were enthralled with his story. He thanked them for stopping by and told them that his tired animal needed to go to the barn for a rest.

From that day on, all the children knew exactly what an ox was. Pictures of oxen, stories of oxen, or a video of oxen could never hope to approach the sounds, smells, sights, and tactile sensations of the real animal.

The ox experience seemed to transform the students from audience to actors. "That was awesome," shouted Tahben in anticipation. "What else is there?"

NCSS STANDARDS

I. *Culture*
II. *Time, Continuity, and Change*
III. *People, Places, and Environments*

The first building the students came to was a school, where a "school marm" taught them about the ABCs exactly as a teacher would have done in colonial times. Spirits soared as the children went to the barn, where workers involved them in the entire process of making linen from flax. (Ms. Kim was as fascinated by the process as the children. She, too, had never before seen linen made from flax even though she taught the concept from textbook diagrams for years.) By now, it was getting late and Ms. Kim tried to get the class to move on to the tanner, wigmaker, blacksmith, gunsmith, cooper (barrel maker), and glass blower, but the children insisted on staying at the barn for the corn husking bee and gunnysack race. At every stop, the children had an opportunity to touch, handle, and use; Ms. Kim had a tough time pulling them away from each stop so they could visit the next exhibit. It was very apparent that Ms. Kim and her students were quite new to this world of the past, not old hands who have "been there" and "done that." And, they were thrilled to be placed in the role of "historians," passionately and actively exploring the past.

The next day, when the students came back to their classroom, they were primed and ready to go to work. Ms. Kim involved the class in several learning activities that focused on the events at The Farmers' Museum.

How Global is the Curriculum *Go to MyEducationLab, select the topic History, watch the video entitled "First Person Presentation," and complete the questions that accompany it.*

The world outside the classroom is a stimulating place for young historians. Explore your community for these "hidden" resources and even you might learn new knowledge beyond "the here and now."

Oral History Bringing to school or visiting someone who can tell stories of personal experiences related to historical people or events is an idea with exciting possibilities. Referred to as *oral history*, these tales are not necessarily treated as major classroom productions; all that is needed is someone interesting to spin a yarn of times gone by. Take the time Jim Mosteller, a sprightly 93-year-old, visited a fifth-grade classroom and mesmerized the children with firsthand accounts of turn-of-the-century life.

"When we got automobiles around here, you couldn't use them in the winter. There weren't any paved roads in town!" Mr. Mosteller chortled. "My father had one of the first cars in town. It was one of those open cars with leather seats and brass lamps. I'll never forget one Sunday—we had eleven flat tires!"

Mr. Mosteller had the children's undivided attention when he told what a dollar would buy: one dozen eggs, a loaf of bread, a pound of butter, and a half-pound of bacon. He also told the children about a whistle-stop campaign during which Teddy Roosevelt visited town in 1912 ("I can see

him to this day") and the transfer of the Liberty Bell on a flatbed car from Philadelphia to San Francisco for safekeeping during World War I.

Mr. Mosteller went on to capture the children's interest with other enchanting anecdotes about his early years: The average wage was $.22 per hour, there was no Mother's Day or Father's Day; and most women washed their hair only once a month. The stories stimulated the children's curiosities about the past to such a degree that their teacher decided to launch a "One Hundred Years Ago" investigation. The children were assigned to research separate topics (such as clothing, games, songs, lifestyle, or school) and used library and Internet resources to uncover attention-grabbing information about the world of 100 years ago. They composed short illustrated stories that were bound together into a book titled *If You Lived One Hundred Years Ago*.

NCSS STANDARDS

I. *Culture*
II. *Time, Continuity, and Change*
VII. *Production, Consumption, and Distribution*
VIII. *Science, Technology, and Society*

Although oral history chats like Mr. Mosteller's provide students a very helpful inside look into what it was like to live during a particular time, those that are supplemented with suitable artifacts help students develop even clearer insights into the historical period under study. Wade, Gardner, Doro, and Arendt (2007) refer to the relationships resulting from involving senior citizens in such meaningful history exchanges as "intergenerational friendships." They advise that "intergenerational friendships can provide a 'real life' connection to the study of history" (p. 28). Our intergenerational friends have many useful tales to tell; historians have long recognized the value of oral history and fear that if we do not appreciate and preserve these stories, they might disappear forever.

Often a teacher can arouse strong interest in history by simulating the narrative of someone who lived in the past. The teacher-as-historical figure creates a window into the past by using simple costumes, props, and spoken words or gestures to reach beyond the boundaries of immediate time and into the world of the past. Schreifels (1983), for example, brought life to one of her history topics by taking on the role of a famous explorer:

> The day I discovered my fifth-grade class had no idea who Vasco da Gama was—and cared less to find out—I vowed to come up with some way to provoke interest in historical personalities. If da Gama and the rest of the early explorers were to become more than hard words to be stumbled over in a textbook, I realized, something drastic—and dramatic—had to be done.
>
> The next morning during social studies class, I slipped into the hall, plunked an old beehive hat on my head, swept a wraparound skirt over my shoulders and reappeared as an unreasonable facsimile of Vasco da Gama, fifteenth-century sea captain. I introduced myself with my best Portuguese accent and invited questions.
>
> At first there were merely giggles, until I threatened to make every student walk the plank unless I got some proper, respectful questions. The first was about how I got there (via a time machine that just happened to look like a filing cabinet). Eventually someone wanted to know just who I was.

> "I'm Vasco da Gama, and I'm very famous."
>
> "For what?" they all demanded.
>
> I then proceeded to regale them with stories of my sailing prowess. Ever since that time, I've found I need only lean on the filing cabinet to get everyone's undivided attention. "Is the time machine going to bring us another mysterious person?" students plead. Quite often the answer is yes. And although these time machine visitors may have fuzzy historical memories, they serve to stimulate real interest in people of the past. (p. 84)

As Schreifels advises, you need not "go overboard" to involve students personally and motivate them to learn. Some of the most effective techniques require very little extra teacher preparation time to organize.

Interviews Conducting interviews is a superb way to introduce children to the process of collecting hands-on historical data. Most children are familiar with interviewing; they see people interviewed on television nearly every day. Help beginning classroom interviewers understand how to conduct an interview by videotaping a television interview and then discussing what an interviewer does. Emphasize the types of questions an interviewer asks; some questions are designed to gather facts, while others are intended to find out about personal feelings and opinions. Since children seem to ask many questions that elicit yes or no answers, point out that an interviewer asks very few, if any, of those questions because questions like that do not result in much useful information. *Why*, *how*, and *what* questions produce much more. You can provide your young historians an opportunity to act as interviewers by showing them an interesting object and encouraging them to keep asking questions until they get at the story behind the object. Play the "interviewee" role as the children assume the job of "interviewers."

Teachers are able to capture children's interest and attention by introducing history in an entertaining and captivating way.

When children are comfortable asking good questions, have them plan an interview with a person who might contribute new insights into an historical topic.

Mario Fiore asked his students to brainstorm a series of questions they might ask their grandparents to find out what life was like when they were in elementary school. Each suggested question was written on an index card. The students examined the collection of index cards, discarding those requiring simple yes or no answers and keeping those that stood the best chance of drawing out the more detailed information they were looking for.

Once the cards were arranged in a useful questioning order, the students were set to conduct their interviews. Some grandparents lived in the same community as the students, but others lived far away so they had to be interviewed by phone or e-mail. Students were free either to use a tape recorder or to jot down notes to help them remember what was said during the interview, but most found that the tape recorder worked best. The children listened carefully to their grandparents' responses to determine whether the desired information was being gathered. If not, they asked probing follow-up questions to clarify points or elicit additional information. Next, Mr. Fiore's young historians wrote individual accounts of their interviews. Each was read in class, and one set of copies was bound into a class book. A sample is shown in Figure 4.2.

NCSS STANDARDS

II. *Time, Continuity, and Change*

Historical Photographs and Paintings Similar to the many types of important hands-on historical artifacts we have inspected to this point, photographs and paintings, too, can surrender priceless data about the past. Just think—if it were not for photographs and paintings, how else could we build a clear image of earlier period architecture, fashion, hairstyles, transportation, family life, or agriculture? The people of the past and the environment in which they lived as depicted in photographs and paintings offer children views of the human condition unattainable through other forms of communication.

Old photographs can help children either acquire information on a specific topic under investigation or ignite a deep inner need to find out more. Take, for example, this circa 1907 photograph of a woman dressed in period clothing using a newfangled "candlestick" telephone (courtesy of the Library of Congress). To a child growing up in an era of wireless technology, it may seem strange to see someone communicating with separate transmitter and receiver components connected by a wire. But just like the contemporary cell phone and computer, the advent of the telephone during the late 1800s

Interview

My interview is with my grandfather whom I call "Grampy." Grampy was born in 1912 in Rathmel, PA. Grampy is 80 years old and is my father's father. He is the oldest member in my family. Counting him he has 8 brothers and sisters. Three of them are still alive. He now lives in Sayre, PA, alone, with his fat cat named "Mama Cat." Grampy loves to tell jokes and tells them all the time. My dad usually calls him at night and Grampy always has a joke.

Question: What kind of hobbies did you have when you were 12?

Answer: He liked to go fishing and hunting. He couldn't get a hunting license untill he was 12. Most of his time he worked on the slackpile. His job was helping the family. Once and a while he went swimming. He paid $.10 for a movie. His brother would take them in his Model-T-Ford. He still fishes but does not hunt.

Question: What was your first car? How much did it cost?

Answer: Grampy's first car was a 1929 Essex. It cost him $500 to get it. He was 23 years old when he got it.

FIGURE 4.2 A Student's Interview with His Grandfather

and early 1900s brought forth much magic and excitement; people would stop whatever they were doing just to gawk at it: How could these complicated devices make it possible for people to hear voices coming out of nowhere? For the first time in history, telephone lines made it possible for people to carry on direct long-distance communication between homes and businesses. Certainly no means of communication had revolutionized the daily lives of ordinary people during the early twentieth century as much as the telephone.

As you examine this old photograph, it should be easy to appreciate the often-quoted Chinese proverb, "A picture is worth ten thousand words." What evidence does the photograph contain that helps make it a valued element of the history of early technology? What information does the photographer communicate about the conditions of life in the early twentieth century? What can be learned about clothing or hairstyles of the people during this time? Photographs can, with careful teaching, present children with a wealth of useful historical data that could otherwise take written resources pages after pages to describe.

Historical Paintings In much the same way as photographs supply a powerful link to the past, paintings, too, can transport children to another time to tell a story, express a feeling, or send a message. Just inspect Pieter Bruegel the Elder's 1565 painting, *The Corn Harvest (August)*, a painting that depicts field workers, including a reaper, relaxed and resting from their morning labors (www.abcgallery.com/B/bruegel/bruegel94.html). The painting has been used as the cover for this book. Does the painting make you wonder who these people are, where they lived, what their lives outside the fields were like, or what they believed in? What does this painting tell you about farming methods in the sixteenth century? How have the land and the farming methods changed since the painting was done? How has Bruegel's depiction of this rustic seasonal activity affect the observer's feelings about the minor significance of people within the enormity of nature?

Elementary school children particularly enjoy forms of artwork like Bruegel's *The Corn Harvest* because they can easily identify the objects or events being represented. Wachowiak and Clements (2006) explain, "The child believes the purpose of art is to represent something. He or she wants objects that look real, with clarity and good definition. Indeed, the more realistic and clear the artworks, the better the artworks are liked. . . . They do not care for pictures showing anything weird or ugly" (p. 192).

Children don't have to wait until art class to experience great art. Carry the excitement of great art to your social studies classroom by welcoming into your classroom some of the great artists of the past. You won't need to build a cave or mock art museum to house copies of their works, but when you're studying the Civil War, why not set aside a little alcove to display the works of Thomas Nast (*Nast's Nook*) or Winslow Homer (*Homer's Hovel*)? If you're teaching a unit on Colonial America, think about turning a small corner of your classroom into a Benjamin West display. (West was a painter of historical scenes, mostly portraits, around and after the time of the American War of Independence.) Whether or not you like these specific suggestions, convert a small corner of your classroom into *something* at least twice a year so your children can step back, look at, and explore great art. Setting up a mini-gallery doesn't need to be expensive. You might be able to purchase prints with funds from your principal's petty cash account or they can be bought online or at local bookstores very reasonably. If that's not possible, try to borrow prints from your local library. You will find that a love for social studies will grow as children experience the greatness of the arts.

In order to fully realize the potential of historical photographs and paintings in social studies classrooms, teachers must help children learn to read them with the same insights and drive that they use to teach children to read the printed word. So, as you share a photograph or painting with your children, remember that they will vary in their ability to extract meaning in much the same way as they vary in their ability to comprehend the printed word. Some children will be able to function only at the *literal level* of interpretation. That is, they will be able to tell you only what they see—naming and listing specific details and facts related to what is being observed. Others will operate at the *inferential level*, where they can to use clues from the photograph or painting to access its hidden meanings. Most students will be able to talk about the specific, directly observed details in the photograph or painting, but fewer will be able to make inferences, searching for meaning that is indirect rather than specifically observed. Even a smaller number of children will be able to function at the *critical level* of interpretation. That is, they will find themselves puzzled, confused, and frustrated when asked to probe deeper into the photograph or painting for the purpose of raising questions, making decisions, or assessing the value of what they see.

As you lead a group discussion about a historic photograph or painting, be sure to use prompts of varying levels of difficulty. This will give children an opportunity for success at their individual levels and expose less able children to the higher-level thinking of their classmates. Sample prompts follow.

Literal Prompts

- "Let's talk about what you see here."
- "Describe what is happening."
- "Can you explain what is happening in your own words?"
- "Can you explain what happened when . . . ?"
- "Who is (are) the main character(s) in the photograph?"
- "Can you find an example of a(n) ____________________?"
- "What is ____________________?"
- "Can you name the ____________________?"

Inferential Prompts

- "I wonder why that happened."
- "Why do you suppose the person did that?"

- "Can you provide an example of what you mean?"
- "What might happen next?"
- "How is this similar to . . . ?"
- "What could have happened after ____________________?"
- "What are some of the possible consequences of ____________________?"

Critical Prompts

- "Can this be done a better way?"
- "What is the value of ____________________?"
- "Defend your position about ____________________."
- "Do you think ____________________ is a good or a bad thing?"
- "How would you have done it differently?"
- "What changes would you recommend?"
- "How would you feel if ____________________?"
- "What do you think about ____________________?"

Written Materials

Put a copy of *The New York Times* from October 30, 1929, in the hands of an enthusiastic young historian and the events that led to the Great Depression spring to life. As your young historians read a copy of Richard Nixon's 1974 snappish letter of resignation, they will erupt with questions and comments about one of the most controversial events in our nation's history. Reading the words contained in the "stuff of history" helps bring children to the action. It's like taking a seat in a time machine and traveling back, if only for a few moments, to explore the intriguing lives of our ancestors.

Letters Personal letters give us a window into history through the eyes of people who lived long ago; they offer firsthand historical insight into the past. The topics covered by historical letters are diverse. They can describe eyewitness accounts of famous battles, nuances of family life, or details of an invention. Despite their value, however, many potentially useful letters have been discarded, misplaced, or destroyed through the years. Fortunately, however, many have survived and now help tell the tale of the lives of our ancestors, including both the famous and not-so-famous. Consider, for example, just how much Benjamin Franklin's letters have helped us gain insights into his life. Among other interesting revelations, Franklin's surviving letters have helped us learn that he was vigorously opposed to the bald eagle as our national symbol. Franklin had considered the turkey as a far more appropriate symbol of the newly formed United States. After examining past records, historians learned that Franklin was actually in France when Congress designated the eagle as our national symbol in 1782. Annoyed at their decision, Franklin put pen to paper and composed a harsh letter of opposition to their deed. Of the eagle, Franklin wrote, "He is a bird of bad moral character; he does not get his living honestly; you may have seen him perched on some dead tree near the river, where, too lazy to fish for himself, he watches the labour of the fishing-hawk; and when that diligent bird has at length taken a fish and is bearing it to his nest for the support of his mate and young ones, the bald eagle pursues him and takes it from him. Besides, he is a rank coward; the little kingbird, not bigger than a sparrow, attacks him boldly and drives him out of the district."

Franklin continued, "The turkey is in comparison a much more respectable bird, and withal a true original native of America. . . . He is . . . a bird of courage, and would not hesitate to attack a grenadier of the British Guards who would presume to invade his farmyard with a red coat on."

You may have heard stories of Franklin's dissatisfaction with the bald eagle as our national symbol, but don't you agree that reading his actual words adds a great deal of substance and interest to the matter? Think about the degree to which actual letters, or exact replicas of them, would enliven the investigative efforts of your young historians, too.

A wealth of surviving letters appropriate for use in social studies classrooms is available online from the National Archives at www.archives.gov/research/arc/. In the late 1970s, the National Archives pioneered a new program to make federal records available to classrooms and to encourage teachers to use archival sources as learning tools. Responding to their availability in her classroom, Celia, a fifth-grader commented, "I love the artifacts they have, especially the letters. They show us what people were really thinking about back in the old days."

Journals and Diaries One of my favorite literary passages is the diary entry my wife wrote the day we were married. As she described her typical wedding fears, such as tripping up the aisle or drawing a blank while reciting our vows, and told how planning the wedding grew into the most frenzied nightmare of her life, I wondered how she possibly survived everything to write in her diary that day. Despite all her qualms, at the end of the entry she made a short remark that I carry with me to this day: "These worries don't mean a thing. I'll still be marrying the man I love and nothing is more important than that."

Through the years, my wife continued writing daily entries in her diaries, recording the major joys and successes of our lives and also the things that went wrong. Her writing "tools" were a low-priced ballpoint pen and a traditional, marbled black-and-white covered composition notebook that she changed each year. These tools were not important; it was the five or ten minutes she squeezed out of each day to sit down with her ballpoint pen and composition book that helped her (and me) distinguish what was truly important in life. (Times have changed, though. Now, instead of taking out the time-honored ballpoint pen and composition book, my wife's daily five or ten minutes are spent adding to a web-based blog!)

Obviously, diary keeping is nothing exclusive to our family; it has existed throughout the world in one form or another for hundreds of years. Most people today use the words *diary* and *journal* interchangeably, but some prefer using the term *diary* only for dated entries that contain personal information and beliefs. *Journal*, on the other hand, is used for entries that objectively document specific observations or events, not necessarily on a daily basis; personal feelings and beliefs are not supposed to be recorded in journals. In this book, the currently popular practice of using these two terms interchangeably will be followed.

Consider both journals and diaries to be personal records of happenings, experiences, and personal reflections. In the past, because there were few other ways to keep a record of important daily events, journals or diaries occupied both the grand and the ordinary people. Historians have recognized journals and diaries as being among the finest resources for adding to our understanding of the past. In fact, it is by examining individual diaries that have uncovered information about significant past events that would have been impossible to uncover in any other way: "What was it really like to ride on the Oregon Trail?" "What were some of George Washington's official activities as our nation's first president?"

Examine the following entry from Catherine's diary to read a gripping account of her Oregon Trail experience.

> August 1st we nooned in a beautiful grove on the north side of the Platte. We had by this time got used to climbing in and out of the wagon when in motion. When performing this feat that afternoon my dress caught on an axle helve and I was thrown under the wagon wheel, which passed over and badly crushed my limb before father could stop the team. He picked me up and saw the extent of the injury when the injured limb hung dangling in the air.
>
> In a broken voice he exclaimed: "My dear child, your leg is broken all to pieces!" The news soon spread along the train and a halt was called. A surgeon was found and the limb set; then we pushed on the same night to Laramie, where we arrived soon after dark. This accident confined me to the wagon the remainder of the long journey. (www.isu.edu/~trinmich/00.n.diaries.html)

Catherine and her six siblings were eventually orphaned along the Oregon Trail. Despite these misfortunes, Catherine maintained her diary throughout the entire trip, recording both the good times and bad. It is now available, along with many others, on a website designed specifically for teachers designed by Mike Trinklein and Steve Boettcher, creators of *The Oregon Trail*, a documentary film that aired nationally on PBS. During the three years spent researching the film, Trinklein and Boettcher uncovered a wealth of great material for teachers, so they built the following website to make it all available: www.isu.edu/~trinmich/00.n.dairies.html.

There are many other good websites that offer good original diaries for classroom use. The DoHistory website (www.dohistory.org/interests/i_teaching.html), for example, not only brings a diary's words directly to your students but it also uses a special "magic lens" that changes the diary from a handwritten to a transcribed version as it is moved over the handwritten version. This is a very useful tool, since many historical diaries have been written in a script that is very difficult for elementary school children to read. Children simply use the computer's mouse to move the lens around the diary page to see the "magic" transcription of the handwritten diary page. There are also many other unique historical documents that have been scanned in and transcribed on this site, along with examples of how historians use such documents in their investigations. In addition to quality websites, there are also many good examples of diaries and journals in children's literature. A few examples are listed here:

Kristina Gregory. *Across the Wide and Lonesome Prairie: The Oregon Trail Diary of Hattie Campbell, 1847*. Scholastic.

Ellen Emerson White. *Voyage on the Great Titanic: The Diary of Margaret Ann Brady*. Scholastic.

Anne Frank, Mark Falstein, and Steve Moore. *Anne Frank: The Diary of a Young Girl*. Tandem Library.

Richard Platt. *Castle Diary: The Journal of Tobias Burgess*. Candlewick.

Historical Newspapers As they relate to history, the pages of old newspapers contain a wealth of information—firsthand accounts of major events, fashion trends, real estate, government and politics, reform movements, businesses, sports and recreation, health and medicine, entertainment, industry, technology, and weather. Newspapers portray the attitudes, values, and beliefs of different times.

Several online resources have made the availability of historical newspapers much more effortless than in the past. One site of particular promise is the ProQuest Historical Newspapers™ project (www.ancestry.com/learn/library/article.aspx?article=3252) that will initiate the digitization of newspapers dating from the nineteenth century to the present—in most cases, full runs of newspapers. The historical archives will digitally reproduce every issue from cover to cover—not just the news stories and editorials, but also the photos, graphics, and advertisements. Also, the Library of Congress and the National Endowment for the Humanities announced the availability of "Chronicling America: Historic American Newspapers" (www.loc.gov/chroniclingamerica/). "Chronicling America" is an Internet-based, searchable database of U.S. newspapers with select digitization of historic pages as well as information about newspapers from 1690 to the present.

Consider the newspaper advertisement for a runaway indentured servant from 1843 as shown in Figure 4.3. Among the advertisements in old newspapers, you will often find reward notices that offer interesting clues to nineteenth-century life. Such advertisements usually include data such as the clothing the runaway wore and comments on his appearance and temperament. With their "striped row trousers," "gingham roundabouts," "brown flannel jackets," "old straw hats," or "dark fustian pantaloons," these "remarkably ugly fellows" may have "lost two of their fore teeth" or "had three fingers cut off at the first joint on the right hand."

RUN AWAY
on the 1ſt of March inſtant,
an Indentured Servant
boy to the
Boot and Shoemaking Buſineſſ,
named Marble Laplant:
he iſ between 16 and 17 yearſ of age,
dark complexion
haſ a ſcar on hiſ right cheek,
and iſ a Remarkably Ugly Looking Fellow.

FIGURE 4.3 Ad for a Runaway

These descriptions provide remarkable portraits of indentured servitude during the colonial days.

During our nation's early history, most indentured servants in the colonies were enlisted from among the mounting number of pitiable underprivileged street people of the urban areas in England. Helpless to find work, many of these hungry and thirsty victims eagerly signed contracts of indenture over a fine dinner and much liquor. Children as well as adults were valued labor resources; children were easily enticed into servitude with candy and other treats. Indentured servitude was such a common practice at this time that it is commonly believed that up to one-half to two-thirds of all immigrants to Colonial America arrived as indentured servants.

By contract, indentured servants were required to furnish unpaid labor for four to seven years. The masters needed only to feed, clothe, and lodge them. Supposedly, an indentured servant's work was to be equivalent to that of an apprentice, but indentured servants had few rights. They could not vote and were not allowed to marry without permission from their masters. They were often subject to violence by their masters—being regularly lashed and beaten for very little reason. Most who served their time obediently were freed; the master was required to provide his former servant only with minimal survival necessities—clothing, a few tools, and either a small amount of money or land.

Your children can be helped to analyze the evidence contained in historical period newspapers by asking questions like these designed for the runaway ad; of course, the questions must be adjusted for the type of newspaper section under consideration:

- Why did the indentured servants run away?
- What hardships did they face?
- Why did people want to be indentured servants?
- Were indentured servants mostly men and boys?
- How valuable was an indentured servant to his master?

Historical Narratives The notion that historical narratives play an important role in social studies education is certainly not a new or novel idea. Actually, historical narratives have been regarded as the lifeblood of elementary school history programs for quite some time. Basically, *historical narratives* are written accounts of actual events that are communicated in such a way as to tell a story. Narratives have the power to reveal the motives and intentions, values and ideas, and the hopes, doubts, fears, strengths, and weaknesses of people who have lived before us.

Three major types of historical narratives—*historical fiction, biographies,* and *folk literature*—help reconstruct the past for elementary school children by dramatizing and humanizing the sterile facts of history. They vicariously transport young historians to the past and enable them to more clearly understand that today's way of life is a continuation of what people did in the past, and that the present will influence the way people live in the future. A history textbook tells; a quality piece of literature not only tells but also has the power to evoke emotion. Perhaps 10-year-old Regina's reaction to history in textbooks summed it up best: "You can't imagine yourself there!" Textbooks confine students to the classroom; gripping stories from good books transport them to new and exciting worlds filled with individual heroism and epic events, evoking emotions rarely found in textbook passages—compassion, humanness, misfortune, happiness, awe, and grief. Consider, for example, how historical fiction enlivens the events surrounding the Great Chicago Fire of 1871. Here is a description of the event as you might read about it in a typical social studies textbook.

> Just after 9 o'clock on Sunday evening, October 8, 1871, a fire broke out at 13 DeKoven Street in the barn behind the home of Patrick and Catherine O'Leary. Precisely how the fire started remains a mystery after all these years, but the O'Leary cow often is assigned the blame. After two days of raging flames, on the morning of October 10, 1871, the fire finally died out. At least 300 people had died, a third of the population was homeless, and approximately $200 million worth of property was destroyed. Seventy-three miles of streets and 17,450 buildings had been destroyed; 3½ square miles of Chicago's central business district were reduced to rubble. The fire ranks among the most incredible events of Chicago's history, and is recognized as one of the most extraordinary reconstructive ventures in the United States.

The paragraph, although informative, offers the main facts of the event without giving us an idea of the emotional scars suffered by the people who experienced the fire. In her book, *Children of the Fire* (Aladdin), Harriette Gillem Robinet

does not simply chronicle a series of events as we might find in such a customary textbook treatment. Robinet goes beyond the basic historical facts in her spellbinding account of the fire as witnessed by an orphaned 11-year-old girl named Hallelujah. The daughter of an escaped slave, Hallelujah wanders through city streets to watch the blaze from its inception. Early excitement grows into fright as the worried little girl watches rows of buildings become consumed by flames and realizes how many people are losing their homes and their possessions. As she weaves throughout the city, Hallelujah meets several other "children of the fire," each of whom represents dissimilar racial, ethnic, and economic backgrounds. During the next few hours, Robinet (2001) describes how Hallelujah and a raggedy little girl named Rachel not only experience the horror of the fire but they also learn an important lesson: Although people may come from varying backgrounds, they become equals in the midst of disaster:

> They crossed Jefferson Street and gazed back. The fire was a massive yellow brightness that had burned a square block of shanties and sheds. Low flames licked up at the wooden crumbs behind them like mice creeping out after supper.
>
> Ahead of them wind fanned flames like a yellow fire-breathing monster. It was leaping toward the sky and gobbling up more dry wooden shanties. . . .
>
> "All them folks' homes," said Rachel sadly. She sighed.
>
> Hallelujah said nothing. She was thinking that all the junky wooden sheds and smelly cow barns and shanties were better burned down. Maybe they would stink less. (p. 23)

If you truly want your students to understand people and to enliven the historical period in which they lived, good narratives are a must. Young historians need to be exposed to a wide variety of historical narratives, but exposure to good books is only half the story. If students are going to function as true young historians in the classroom, they must have a chance to write their own narratives in addition to reading those written by others. Actually, this is not that hard for them to do, as most elementary school children are natural storytellers. Just take some time to listen carefully to their casual conversations and you will hear youngsters spinning yarns about what is happening in their lives and describing the importance of those events. Their narratives could be about either the past or the present, but sometimes they venture into the uncertainty of their future, too. Like historical narratives, young people's narratives include stories of successes, dreams, and heroism, as well as of sadness and pain. Narratives bring to light the "stuff" of history—the important incidents, events, and accomplishments that help illuminate both the past and the present.

Three types of trade book–based literature seem particularly adaptable to the social studies program: *historical fiction, biographies*, and *folk literature*. In addition, we can include the use of textbooks as a type of historical narrative, since they, too, provide accurate accounts of past events written by authorities in the field.

Historical Fiction Historical fiction is a category of realistic stories that are set in the past; the facts are accurate but the characters are fictional (although they sometimes interact with actual historical figures). Historical fiction offers children opportunities to vicariously experience the past by entering into a convincingly true-to-life world of people who have lived before them. By being transported to the past through the vehicle of literature, students enter into the lives of the historical figures and, through mental imagery, become moved to attach emotion to their condition.

It is easy to see how good historical fiction makes history seem real. Note how Patricia Beatty brings to life a young boy's struggles in her book, *Charley Skedaddle* (1987). The story is set during the Civil War when 12-year-old Charley Quinn, a member of the Bowery Boys (the toughest street gang in New York City), vows revenge for his brother's death at Gettysburg and plans to enlist in the Union Army. One day, he sees Con, an old friend, marching along a street in New York City with other soldiers of the Union Army:

> "Take me along with you, Con, please!"
>
> For a moment the man's face twisted in thought, then he boomed, "Sure, Charley. Why not? I got five days' cooked rations with me. Ye can share 'em."
>
> A short man with brown sideburns and a dark face in the ranks next to Con said, "He's only a shirttail kid, Con."
>
> "No matter, Jem Miller. The Army's got uses for kids. Ye keep up with us men, Charley, ye hear. Ye let go of me now."
>
> "I'll keep up, you bet." As Charley trotted past the Bowery Boys, he waved his hat and shouted, "I'm off to join the Army!"

Unfortunately, when the horrors of war became a reality and he sees his best friend killed, Charley is terrified. He "skedaddles" away from the Union Army. Eventually, though, while still a deserter, an act of courage far from the battlefields proves to Charley that he's not the coward he thought himself to be. Beatty brings the Civil War to life for elementary school students by telling about its horrors through the experiences of someone who thinks of life the same way they, as 12-year-olds, do.

A teacher's obvious interest in and use of historical fiction strengthens the appeal of the past. Suddenly, through story, the magnitude of humanity's accomplishments is revealed, arousing the imagination and interest of the reader.

If written well, historical fiction offers children fuller understandings of human problems and human conditions. The historical fiction you choose should:

- Tell an interesting story. The book should practically "set the reader on fire."
- Portray realistic characters and authentic settings. The historical period should be so precisely described that the people within the book "walk right into the room."
- Cleverly infuse accurate historical facts and illustrations.

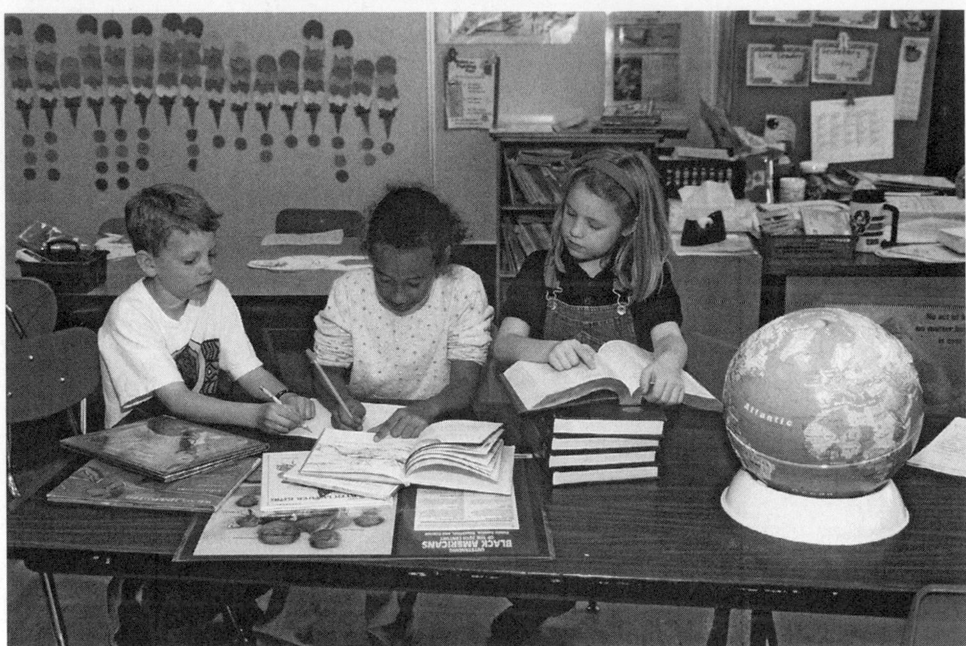

Quality historical fiction illuminates a time period for children by telling a good story of the past.

- Reflect the spirit and values of the times. The stories cannot be made to conform to today's ethical values (such as contemporary points of view concerning women and minorities).
- Contain authentic language. The spoken words should give the flavor of how people actually talked.

Biographies Biographies are much like historical fiction in that they are based on documented information, but rather than telling stories of fictional characters, biographies are stories of the lives of real people. The work of Esther Forbes offers an excellent comparison of a biography and historical fiction. In 1942, Forbes won the Pulitzer Prize for her adult biography, *Paul Revere and the World He Lived In*. While she was researching the book, she discovered several interesting stories about the lives of Boston's young apprentices. As a result, she wrote a book for children, *Johnny Tremain* (Houghton Mifflin); it won the Newbery Medal in 1944. The book is about a fictional silversmith's apprentice to Paul Revere, who lived in Boston in the days leading to the American Revolution. A skilled craftsperson, Johnny becomes one of the best at his trade. But a practical joke backfires, and Johnny's hand becomes maimed for life. Johnny then becomes involved in pre-

Revolutionary War activities. The book captures nearly every student's interest and remains one of the most popular works of historical fiction to this day.

In recent years, there has been a nationwide interest in teaching and learning values, or principles that society agrees helps distinguish right from wrong or good from bad. Reading about heroes has been an important part of this interest because heroes embody the values we seek out in real life. Heroes are brave, compassionate, loyal, tolerant, and fair. They are willing to stand up for what they believe. And, for children, biographies of exemplary heroes provide superb models of citizenship. Heroes are special people; their behavior seems to invite emulation. Children need heroes because heroes inspire them to similar rightness. In contrast to the past, however, when heroes could do no wrong, modern biographies show their human side, informing young historians about their weaknesses as well as their strengths. Children relate more closely to heroes when they can be accepted as real people, complete with doubts, discouragement, mistakes, conflict, and frustration.

The best biographies for young historians, then, portray the main character as true-to-life, neither flawless in character nor disgraceful and humiliating. Heroes should be recognized as real human beings with both strengths and limitations. Jean Fritz has been especially effective in creating remarkably true-to-life portraits of famous figures. In Fritz's (1979) absorbing biography, *Stonewall*, she depicts one side of Confederate General Thomas "Stonewall" Jackson as a hard-working but underachieving young cadet at West Point. No one ever thought he would grow up to be one of the greatest military leaders in America:

> But however determined he was, no one watching him struggle would have guessed that Tom ("The General" as they called him) could have survived four years at West Point. Indeed, he could hardly get through a recitation. When called on to answer a question or solve a problem, Tom sweated so profusely his classmates joked that one day he would drown them all. (p. 26)

On the other hand, Fritz describes how Jackson's determination to succeed served him well:

> Inch-by-inch Tom pulled himself through. Near the bottom of his class at the end of his first year (fifty-first in a class of seventy-two), he rose to seventeenth by the end of his senior year, and his classmates, who had grown fond of him, said it was a pity there wasn't a fifth year at West Point. Tom would have graduated top man. (p. 26)

By examining Stonewall Jackson's character at various points throughout the story, students learn to appreciate one of the nation's most brilliant and heroic leaders as well as one of its oddest heroes.

The same guidelines used for selecting historical fiction apply to biographies. Be sure the story is a well-researched, carefully documented account of the person's life with fast-moving narrative and a clear, readable writing style.

Folk Literature Fables, myths, legends, and folktales belong to the great component of literature called *folklore*. In essence, these are the stories that began with illiterate people and were handed down orally by storytellers for generations. Originating wherever people gathered—in marketplaces, during tasks such as weaving or sewing, in taverns, or around the hearth—the stories were told not only for the entertainment of the listener but often as an expression of cultural beliefs. The rich oral tradition of these stories was kept alive by generations of storytellers; the tales eventually found their place within printed literature.

Because folktales have been retold from generation to generation within every culture, they effectively reflect any culture's beliefs, values, lifestyles, and history. An authentic tale from China, for example, will include references to the land on which the people lived, their food, their homes, their customs, and their beliefs. Take, for instance, this passage from Ann Grifalconi's *The Village of Round and Square Houses* (Little, Brown), an African folktale that helps explain why the village of Tos, where women live in round houses and men in square houses, is like no other village in the world:

> Supper might be fish or rabbit or ground-nut stew or yams—
> But always I would be the one to pound and soften the white cassava root,
> To make the *fou-fou* we eat at every meal.
> Then Mama would cook the *fou-fou* and beat it 'til it was white and fluffy
> And she would pile the food into big bowls with round handles—
> Just right for our small hands to hold.
> Then we would march into the big round room—
> Our bare feet gripping the earthen floor. . . .
> And I would come in last bearing the fou-fou! (pp. 5–7 of an unnumbered text)

Grifalconi's careful research (she visited Tos and learned the story from a woman who lived there) paints a vivid picture of what life long ago was like in the Cameroons in Central Africa. Children not only look forward to understanding why the men and women live in differently shaped houses but they also enjoy learning about the history and culture of Tos, an isolated village on the slope of an extinct volcano.

Teachers using any type of literature in their history programs must remember that they have a responsibility to encourage students to reflect on what they read. They can use a variety of strategies, many of which are described throughout this text—stories, poems, journals, descriptions, words, illustrations, and graphic organizers.

Folk literature has deep roots in all cultures. Through this genre, students broaden their understandings of those cultures, as well as sense the common bonds that have linked together cultures for centuries. Countless books have memorable impact and may serve as the substance around which you could plan multiple learning opportunities in history.

To ensure that important benefits actually emerge from the use of all three types of historical literature in your classroom, you must carefully research the story content so that you are able to place the students into an accurate time and place context. For example, I recall observing a field experience student read Elizabeth George Speare's *The Sign of the Beaver* (Yearling) to a group of fourth-graders. She did a good job during the introductory phase, informing the students that the story took place long ago in the Maine wilderness where Matt is left by his father to tend a new cabin while he returned to Massachusetts for the rest of the family. The students located Maine and Massachusetts on a map and traced the probable route Matt's father had taken. That was good, but to further establish the story background, the field experience student went on to display a large illustrated portrayal of a village in which Native Americans of the past might have lived (because their interactions with Matt are central to the story). The idea was very nice, but the story is an eastern woodlands story. The illustration, however, depicted a buffalo hunting camp of the Cherokee (Plains Indians) with its cone-shaped tepees. The student complicated her error by referring to the Cherokee shelters in the print as "wigwams." As the regular classroom teacher stepped in to help correct the error-filled introduction, I couldn't help wonder about how preservice teachers might be convinced of the need to confirm the accuracy of what they are teaching.

You must understand that the many benefits of historical literature can be realized only if you place the story content in an accurate context. Historical fiction is based on a strong background of fact and should be used as a vehicle to enlighten, not confuse. Some helpful resources for assessing and selecting quality sources of historical narratives follow:

- *Notable Children's Trade Books for Young People*, compiled annually since 1972 by the Children's Book Council in cooperation with the Book Review Committee of the National Council for the Social Studies (NCSS). The annotated book list is published once a year in *Social Education*. To obtain a single copy, send a check for $2 payable to the Children's Book Council, along with a self-addressed, 6-by-9-inch envelope with 3 ounces of postage to the Children's Book Council, 12 West 37th Street, New York, NY 10018. The list may be downloaded from the CBC website (www.cbcbooks.org).
- *Social Studies and the Young Learner*, a quarterly magazine published by NCSS, features a regular article on books appropriate for elementary social studies as well as suggestions for use. To subscribe ($15/year), contact the National Council for the Social Studies, 3501 Newark St. NW, Washington, DC 20016; (202) 966-7840.
- *An Annotated Bibliography of Historical Fiction for the Social Studies, Grades 5–12* by Fran Silverblank, published by Kendall/Hunt for the National Council for the Social Studies.

The following classroom episode illustrates how José Zabala was able to engage his children's historical thinking, when the source of instruction was a historical narrative.

The purpose of Mr. Zabala's lesson was to help students understand the major factors that transformed many of the colonists from loyal British subjects to dissidents on the verge of revolution. He began by announcing to the class that the school district budget just bottomed out and very little money was available to purchase the supplies necessary to finish out the school year. A committee of teachers had met to study the problem and decided that a good source of revenue would be to have students pay a small fee each time they put something into the wastebasket, used the restrooms, got a drink of water, or sharpened their pencils. Mr. Zabala asked the students if they thought this was a fair solution to the district's money crisis, especially since they had never before been required to pay such a "tax." He also raised the question of whether teachers had the right to impose such a tax on students. Mr. Zabala involved the students in an active debate of the options available to them (avoid paying the fee, boycotting classes, protesting the plan, complaining to the local newspaper) and the consequences of their actions.

Mr. Zabala then encouraged the students to recall that the Seven Years' War drained the treasury of Great Britain, so the government was in desperate need to raise money, just like the students' teachers. Britain began to do something it had never done before—it decided to impose taxes on the colonies. The class drew parallels between the British taxation plans to their tongue-in-cheek classroom "tax." Then, to begin the day's textbook reading assignment, Mr. Zabala invited guesses about what the British might tax in the colonies and how the colonists might react to those British taxes. After the students exhausted their ideas, Mr. Zabala directed them to read sections from a source of children's literature (*The American Revolution* by Alden R. Carter [Franklin Watts]) to find out (1) what the British decided to tax, (2) the colonial reaction to each British tax, and (3) the British response to the colonists' reactions. After a short discussion of the reading selection, the students summarized the three British taxes described in the textbook selection: (1) the Stamp Act, (2) the Townshend Duties, and (3) the Tea Act (see Figure 4.4). Mr. Zabala directed the students to chart each on a graphic organizer. (Note how the organizer directly relates back to the stated purposes for reading.)

Communicating through Historical Narratives

Why should students write in social studies? Although seemingly complex, this question is easy to answer: Social studies is a curriculum area "that is as appro-

FIGURE 4.4 Graphic Organizer

priate for writing as the gym is for basketball" (Murray, 1987 p. 54). The social studies curriculum offers rich and varied contexts in which students are able to write frequently and purposefully—an environment in which writing in different forms can be perceived as necessary and useful. In this section, we will explore how writing can be employed in dynamic social studies classrooms and, specifically, we examine the many ways we can enhance learning in history through writing.

When children read a wide variety of historical narratives, they will develop an interest in using the styles of their favorite authors as a model to write their own narratives. This predilection for imitation is important because replication plays a productive role in students learning to write in any genre. All writers, either by accident or design, begin by imitating the style and content of other writers. Take advantage of this imitative urge and encourage it; your students will soon begin to develop their unique "writing personalities." Conducting the research required to complete their original narratives and putting thoughts together to form a written narrative help students better understand the people who have made history. One student's biographical sketch of Sacagawea is shown as an example in Figure 4.5.

It should be clear by now that one of my major beliefs is that literacy can be a significant part of social studies education. By using the writing process in a content subject such as history, children become more aware of what they know and begin to feel comfortable drawing from their knowledge to express growing ideas through print. Surely, children do not learn to write only during that part of the day designated as "writing class" but also write while involved in subjects such as social studies, which offer a rich content framework that serves to facilitate various kinds of writing.

It is best to set up students for success as they first begin writing in these new forms. Be sure to review the components of the writing process before you start and plan to model and demonstrate the techniques associated with each writing form. Remember, too, that imitation plays a large part in other forms of prose writing just as it does in writing historical narratives. So, as you share real diaries, newspapers, historical journals, and other primary sources of written historical evidence with your students, they will be most highly motivated to imitate what they see and

Mike

Sacagawea

She was a Shoshoni Indian Woman
who guided Lewis and Clark, She
was helpful because her presence was a
Sign of peace to different tribes.
they encountered. She could find many
plants and herbs to eat. She wanted
to see the Pacific Ocean and
the whales, Clark took her all
the way to the Great Stinking Pond,
The trip took two years and 6 months.
Sacagawea was a brave woman,

FIGURE 4.5 Biographical Sketch

try their hands at creating their own versions. Take advantage of this inclination to imitate the style and structure of other writers and encourage it.

Period Newspapers

Period newspapers offer a thought-provoking writing form appropriate for the study of history because they help students express the content of what they are learning as well as influence the attitudes and beliefs of others through such tactics as political cartoons or editorials.

A trip to a newspaper publisher and a careful inspection of the local newspaper can help the children understand how newspapers are operated. Although newspaper staffs differ among newspapers, all generally include the following positions which many teachers have challenged their students to imitate in the classroom:

- *Publisher.* Owner or person who represents the owner; responsible for the overall operation of the newspaper.
- *Editors.* Responsible for several facets of newspaper production, such as deciding what goes into the newspaper, assigning reporters to cover events, determining where to position the stories, and writing their opinions of significant events (editorials).
- *Reporters.* Cover the stories by digging up the facts and interpreting them.
- *Feature Writers.* Produce special columns such as jokes and riddles, lost and found, recipes, and so on.

- *Copy Editors.* Examine stories for mistakes and adjust length to meet space requirements.

There are several types of stories the students will be interested in writing for their period newspaper. Depending on the era being studied, some possibilities include:

- *Front-page story* about a national/world/local event from the period
- *Editorial column* responding to an event
- *Original political cartoon* about an event
- *Sports section* with stories about popular sports or athletes of the day
- *Real estate section* original advertisements showing what homes were like at the time
- *Help wanted section* showing the kinds of jobs the people had
- *Classified section* exhibiting the kinds of things people might be selling or wanting to buy
- *Movie review* assessing a movie or illustrating a movie poster from the time
- *Fashion page* containing illustrations and descriptions of the styles of the period
- *Food guide* write a food column describing the recipes and/or meals that were popular
- *Advice column* describing the types of problems people had and offering counsel

After assigning the students to the news-gathering, writing, and illustrating jobs, you will want to get the rest of the class involved in the "behind the scenes" departments. As an example of one group's efforts to publish a period newspaper, consider Curtis Yannie's fifth-graders who fashioned a newspaper set in Revolutionary War times. Mr. Yannie's students were involved in a study of the Revolutionary War. Their front-page stories took form beneath these blaring headlines: "British Evacuate Boston," "Grand Union Flag Unfurled Over Boston," "Redcoats Invade New York," "Congress Approves Declaration of Independence," and "Washington Stuns Hessian Fighters." Feature articles detailed such items of interest as quilting, candle-making, and the steps of drying food for winter. An advertising section offered articles for sale (spinning wheels, bed warmers, teams of oxen, pewter tableware, flintlock rifles, wigs). An employment section listed such jobs as post rider, saddler, tanner, wigmaker, tavern keeper, chandler, mason, cooper, hatter, and printer. An editorial page displayed a political cartoon showing a crowd of Continental soldiers pulling down an equestrian statue of King George III as they celebrated the signing of the Declaration of Independence in Philadelphia, and an editorial solicited funds for the relief of widows and children of the patriots "murdered" at Lexington. There was a book review of Thomas Paine's *Common Sense*, and a sports section detailing the results of such popular events as stool ball, quoits, arm wrestling, and gunny sack races. When finished, the

period newspaper was sent to the production department where illustrations were created. It was then typed and copied, assembled, stapled together, and distributed to the other fifth-grade classrooms.

Diaries

Diaries fascinate elementary school students because they are real and personal; young historians not only experience the cold facts of an historical event but they also come into contact with human emotions, values, and attitudes. For example, in the summer of 1863, a young woman joined her uncle's family in their migration from Ohio to the Idaho Territory. Her name was Lucia Darling. During the course of the three-month journey, Lucia kept an extensive diary. The diary recorded camp life, daily activities, encounters with other wagon trains, interactions with Native Americans, and landmarks along the route.

After having the students examine selected pages from Lucia's diary, a teacher might ask them to imitate the writing style by pretending to be a friend of Lucia and writing a page about the character's chores and responsibilities, hardships, and other experiences. Imaginatively placing themselves in the shoes of real people can serve as a strong stimulus for diary writing. The following diary entries were written by a student pretending to be a sailor on one of Magellan's ships that was unable to complete the circumnavigation of the globe in 1522:

> Day 10. The storm lasted two days and two nights. I never saw waves so high or the wind blow so hard. Our ship was thrown against huge rocks and was smashed to bits. We held onto our lifeboats for longer than I could remember—every sailor was scared stiff. We finally spotted some land. . . .
>
> Day 11. Fresh water is disappearing. Our captain divided us into four groups. Each group was to go in a different direction to search for fresh water. In mid-afternoon the fourth group found a freshwater spring on the west side of the island. . . .

Letters

Letter writing offers another major type of writing option for social studies classrooms. If students have had an opportunity to invent diary entries, then letter writing is a reasonable next step. Friendly letters and diaries are conversational in style and express the writer's account of important events as well as emotions attached to them. And, as with all other writing forms, models of letters from the past are necessary to help youngsters analyze the conversational style as well as the format of the times. If writing a simulated letter to your own father during colonial days, for example, the proper greeting would be *Honour'd Sir* and a proper ending would be *Your Dutiful Daughter (or Son)*. Also in keeping with authenticity, students should write with the implements commonly used at the time. A letter during colonial times would have been written with quill pen—a goose, peacock, pheasant, or wild turkey feather. Ink was made by crushing and boiling down such natural vegetation as cranberries or walnut shells. This may be difficult to do in typical elementary school classrooms; educational supply companies, though, sell small colonial writing kits containing a goose feather and dry ink for about $3 each. There were no envelopes during colonial times, so students should simply fold the letter and seal it. A blob of hot sealing wax was used during colonial days, but pressing a small ball of clay to seal the simulated letter would work fine.

How Global is the Curriculum *Go to MyEducationLab, select the topic Literature Connections, watch the videos entitled "Pre-Writing in the 6th Grade" and "Peer Editing," and complete the questions that accompany them.*

Klaus Hubben offers a fine example of imaginative letter writing. When his fourth-graders were learning about Christopher Columbus, he asked them to pretend to be Columbus writing a letter to Queen Isabella requesting support for his explorations. See Figure 4.6 for an example of an imaginative letter.

Writing Stories

In composing their own stories, children must learn that all historical narratives—including biography, historical fiction, and folktales—have a *setting*, which is usually described early in the story and helps the reader create vivid pictures of distinctive times (stories can take place in the past, present time, or the future) or

FIGURE 4.6 A Student's Letter Written from the Perspective of a Historical Figure

Dear Queen Isabella, Oct. 1491
If you'll give me financial help I can prove that this world is round I have been studying sailing since the age of 13 years old and am a very experienced sailor I could get my crew and me out of any storm we run in to.
I can bring you back spices, treasures and any thing else I may find on this voyage. I have been sailing from a young age and should be successful I hope you'll consider my request.

Your Loyal subject,

C. Columbus, Navigator

places (stories can take place anywhere). They learn that the second element of historical narratives is comprised of the story *characters*. What are their physical and emotional attributes—how do they look, dress, and feel? What do the characters say? What do the characters think? Third, they learn that the story has a *plot*, or sequence of events. The plot describes the action—what the characters do and what happens to them. In most picture books, the plot is relatively simple with one main sequence of events, but in chapter books, the plot becomes more complex with one or more subplots that underlie the main events.

In most cases, the stories written by elementary school children will have relatively simple plots. Their stories usually contain a single episode, but in a few instances, two or three episodes might follow one another, building on each other as the story takes form. Regardless of the number of episodes, however, the plot is more than a sequence of events. To engage the reader, a good plot must have a tension-building conflict, a difficulty to rise above, or an engaging problem to solve. It is to discovering how these complexities are resolved that captures the reader and makes her or him want to keep reading to the end of the story. The plot usually has three parts: (1) a problem, conflict, or difficulty (with nature, with society, between characters, or within the character); (2) roadblocks (the character faces obstacles in an attempt to solve the complexity); and (3) the solution (a turning point in the story where the roadblocks are overcome). The solution brings a simple but satisfying ending to the story that is either anticipated by the reader or surprises the reader with an unexpected twist.

Writing historical narratives is an especially relevant form of writing in history because narratives necessitate conducting research and personalizing the data to provide an accurate account of the major events of the time. In helping students understand how to express themselves through this genre, it is always a good idea to use high-quality trade books as models.

Beginning any piece of written work is a challenge for all writers; however, starting an historical narrative can be especially difficult for children. Because many children have trouble establishing an historical frame of reference for a story's setting (both time and place), they can be unsuccessful in their attempts to establish believable characters, a distinctive time frame, and a realistic setting. As a result, it is not unusual for a child's historical narrative to begin with "Once upon a time, far, far away, there was a (person) named . . . ." To help students overcome such difficulties and write successfully in the narrative form, teachers find it valuable to infuse meaningful historical content within a proper writing framework.

In the following illustrative account, Maria Stanitis used the *Storypath* approach as the framework of instruction to support her young historians as they worked to complete a historical narrative about the winter of 1777 when George Washington and his troops camped at Valley Forge.

The Storypath Approach The instructional approach used by Ms. Stanitis is built on the principle that, for instruction to be meaningful, children's enthusiasm for a story should be used to teach important concepts and skills in history. In her

Storypath curriculum, students contribute to the development of a story as they acquire new and deeper understandings about the topic under study.

The Storypath approach was originally developed in Scotland during the 1960s, and has been popularized in the United States during the past few years by Margit McGuire at Seattle University. Each Storypath unit begins by helping children establish the setting and characters for their class story. Then, students are confronted with a critical problem that sets in motion the plot of the story. The Storypath episodes are shown in Figure 4.7.

Ms. Stanitis regularly begins any Storypath by having the students, working together in small groups, create a setting for the topic under study; in this case, the class is learning about the Revolutionary War—more specifically, the winter spent by George Washington and his troops at Valley Forge. Ms. Stanitis began the Valley Forge Storypath by telling the students they will be writing a story that takes place in 1777 in a well-known location in southeastern Pennsylvania. To prepare, she asked the students to locate Valley Forge on a map depicting significant Revolutionary War events. This first step helped orient the students to the setting of the story. Ms. Stanitis then went on to help her young historians build a somewhat deeper understanding of the setting. The students, in small groups, were to create a mural based on a brief description she read aloud to the class.

After Ms. Stanitis read the description, the student groups met together to talk about the landscape features that would comprise their mural. Some decided that the snow-covered rolling hills of Valley Forge would amply illustrate the setting, but

FIGURE 4.7 Episodes of a Storypath Unit

Creating the Setting

Students create the setting by completing a mural or other visual representation of the topic they will be studying.

Creating Characters

Characters are added to the mural or visual representation.

Context Building

Students are involved in activities that stimulate them to think more deeply about the people and place they have created. Important concepts are deepened and reinforced.

Critical Incidents

Characters confront a problem characteristic of those faced by people of that time and place.

Concluding Event

Students plan and organize an event that brings closure to the unit.

others insisted that that tents, log huts, campfires, bare-branched trees, heavy gray clouds, and large boulders would make the scene more complete. Still others thought it would be a good idea to add the Schuylkill River in the background, as smithy's shop in a dell, and a few muddy roads. One group decided that a cutaway view of a log hut should be central to its design. In a short time, all were satisfied with their plans and went to work building their murals.

The focus of this mural activity was not to make an exact replica of the military camp, but to help students express their own ideas of the time and place. There is a tendency on the part of some teachers to give their students too much detailed information. When they receive too much, the students tend to merely duplicate what they saw, read, or heard instead of build their own unique mental picture of the landscape features. Ms. Stanitis does not underestimate what young students can do by themselves; she is aware that the process of designing a mural and talking about it prior to writing is a "rehearsal" process for the actual writing act, not an end in itself. Before many children write, they like to draw a scene and talk about it. Then they write about the scene they drew. Called *pictorializing*, this appears to be a useful preparation (or rehearsal) strategy many young writers use before putting words on paper.

After the students pulled together the landscape for their murals, Ms. Stanitis led a discussion with the framework of prompts below:

- What do you imagine life was like in this camp?
- How might it feel to live in this camp?
- How did the weather affect the living conditions?
- What might a historian say about the events at Valley Forge?

Next, the young historians brainstormed a list of words that they felt adequately described the Valley Forge landscape. Using a black marking pen, the students wrote their words—*freezing, snowy, bitter, dangerous*—on index cards (one word to a card). The cards were posted around the mural to create a sizable word bank. To better connect her students to the place they created, Ms. Stanitis asked each group to use the words and the mural to write a paragraph or two describing the scene depicted. One group wrote this about its scene: "The Army was camped on a plateau overlooking a small valley. The place was called Valley Forge. It was wintertime and very cold. They lived in tents for awhile but George Washington gave the troops orders to build log huts. Twelve men lived together in a 16 × 14 foot log hut. It was much smaller than our classroom. Each hut had a stone fireplace. Most of the huts were built about 2 feet down in a hole in the ground but were about 6 feet high. They had dirt floors. The huts were drafty, cold, smoky, and awfully unhealthy."

Ms. Stanitis explained that now that the setting for their story was firmly in mind, her young historians must next describe the characters. The groups went to work talking about the people who occupied the camp, what they looked like, and the work they would have been doing. Ms. Stanitis found that some students were interested in conducting additional research to make their characters as true to the time as possible, while others were satisfied to simply capture the overall flavor of the era. Ms. Stanitis acknowledged each of these approaches and found that both were productive. She did, however, provide a wide range of resources, including trade books and appropriate websites, to help them gather necessary data.

Once the students were satisfied with their research, they added characters to their landscape murals. The groups named their characters and completed a short biographical description for each. Danusia wrote this character sketch, for example, to describe a pitiful character she painted on her group's mural: "Thomas Gates was in miserable shape. He looked like a skeleton—pale, sick, and sad wrapped in a thin blanket. He was sitting next to a smoky fire. He didn't have a coat or a hat or shoes. Just after Christmas his feet and legs froze so bad that they turned black. A doctor had to cut them off." Few descriptions were as heartrending as Danusia's, but most were quite descriptive of the squalor and suffering the troops were forced to endure. Ms. Stanitis went on to encourage the students to think about how these single character descriptions might be connected with others to create interesting story ties.

The next Storypath episode required the students to establish a deeper understanding of the events at Valley Forge. Ms. Stanitis presented a list of suggested topics for the students to research and about which to write a one-page report. Some possible choices were *What the Troops Ate, Getting Supplies to Valley Forge, Sanitation and Personal Hygiene,* and *Leaving Valley Forge*. Suggesting research topics might be considered to be a bit too structured for those who believe that students write better reports if they select the topic, but Ms. Stanitis decided that specifying the topics would be a better approach for this particular unit. (She will make every effort to meet the varied needs and interests of her students with less structured research activities in forthcoming units.)

Obviously, social studies teachers do not simply assign students a report to write and send them on their way. They must model the process of report writing. So, to help them begin their reports, Ms. Stanitis led a discussion about where the students might locate information for their various topics. (The Internet offers many excellent sites for this topic.) She then modeled how the students could take notes from a source of information and organize the notes for the report. Ms. Stanitis introduced a graphic organizer to show how she takes information from her notes and organizes it into paragraphs having a main idea and supporting details (see Figure 4.8). Just as the act of pictorializing (constructing the mural) served as a rehearsal tool during the initial phase of Storypath, Ms. Stanitis used a graphic representation as a rehearsal technique to help students consider what information they wanted to use in their stories and how they should organize the information.

When the students completed their graphic organizers and written reports, they were asked to prepare a short oral presentation so that everyone would know more about the Valley Forge experience. In reporting on the morale at Valley Forge, for example, Chelsoon's group wrote the following information: "Washington was a great general, but the spirits were very low and there wasn't very much military skill at the Valley Forge camp. There was a lot of gambling and fighting. Some men even walked away from camp when they wanted to. The men were brave, but they

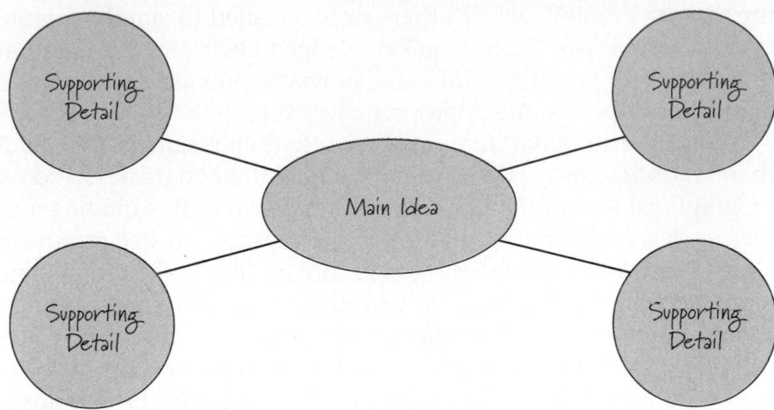

FIGURE 4.8 Organizing an Informational Paragraph

didn't know how to march together or even how to move on the battlefield. They knew how to use their bayonets more for cooking over a fire than for fighting. All this changed when Baron von Steuben arrived in February. The men loved Baron von Steuben. He drilled the men and trained them until they were a mean fighting machine. The men had new pride and their spirits grew because of von Steuben."

How Global is the Curriculum *Go to MyEducationLab, select the topic History, watch the video entitled "Making Presentations," and complete the questions that accompany it.*

Convinced that her students were now at the point where they had ample information regarding the setting, characters, and events at Valley Forge, Ms. Stanitis asked them to recall the three story elements: "Let's think of the three elements that make up historical stories, or narratives." A recorder wrote each on the board as the elements were suggested: (1) an engaging setting, (2) strong characters, and (3) an exciting plot. Ms. Stanitis helped the students combine the three elements into a descriptive sentence: "We include three important elements in the stories, or narratives, we write in social studies: setting, characters, and plot."

"Once I have the setting, characters, and events in mind," explained Ms. Stanitis, "I try to think of a problem that would be appropriate for the main character. Then I ask myself, 'How can I help my character solve this problem?' 'Do I need other characters to create a good ending?' 'What course of action might have helped my character rise above her or his problem?'" The students suggested several different problems: "How did this ragged and poorly fed army get through the winter?" "How did this ragged army become victorious?" From there, the students worked cooperatively to complete their historical narratives. Now that her students had something to say, Ms. Stanitis guided them through the rest of the writing experience with strategies used by experienced writers when they compose something for a specific audience. Called the *writing process* approach, Ms. Stanitis organized her classroom as a writing workshop where children functioned as real authors.

It is beyond the scope of this text to go deeply into the writing process; you will find it useful to read the appropriate sections in the book used for your literacy courses. But it is important at this point to describe how Ms. Stanitis brought closure to this writing experience. She knew that her young historians enjoyed publishing their own books, and did so for many of the writing projects in which they were involved throughout the school year. It was apparent that publishing was valued by looking at a corner of the room where the sign "GoodBook Publishing Company" was clearly visible. After the writers completed their Valley Forge manuscripts, they took their stories to the classroom publishing company where they were polished and printed by a staff of expert workers. The class loves to be involved in these behind-the-scenes publishing departments:

- *Production Department.* Puts pictures and stories together and gets them ready for printing (Students who know how to use the word processor, or have a desire to learn, can make special contributions here.)
- *Art Department.* Designs book covers; illustrates stories, if necessary
- *Advertising Department.* Creates ads (with pictures) that highlight new books
- *Mechanical Department.* Runs the printer or copier, collates the pages, staples them, and gets them ready for distribution (Many books are produced with hard covers.)
- *Circulation Department.* Places the books in the classroom library and delivers first print copies to the principal, other teachers, and classmates

How Should Chronology Be Taught?

Up to now, we have looked at the kinds of classroom experiences appropriate for helping elementary school children construct historical knowledge and thinking behaviors. However, there is one additional area of historical thinking that we have not yet addressed—chronological thinking—a process that is at the very heart of history. Students understand the chronological organization of history when they know how to order events and people into major periods of time and to identify and explain historical relationships. In its *National Standards for History*, the National Center for History in the Schools (1996) made a strong case for teaching chronological thinking in our schools: "Without a strong sense of chronology—of when events occurred and in what temporal order—it is impossible for students to examine relationships among those events or to explain historical causality. Chronology provides the mental scaffolding for organizing historical thought" (p. 62).

Chronological thinking is the process of acquiring a sense of historical time—past, present, and future—and the ability to identify the sequence in which events occurred. Young historians must understand that human events take place over time, one after the other. It is important to establish this linkage in order to reconstruct events and tell the stories that establish relationships between important events. Young historians must learn the measures of time that all historians use—day, week, month, year, decade, and century. Using the calendar is one way to do this, but strategies for teaching calendar-related skills is a topic that goes beyond the scope of this text. We will look at timelines, however—a specialized tool that allows young historians to place historical events in meaningful chronological order.

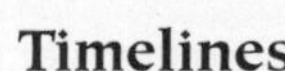

Timelines

Timelines are graphic representations of historical events, constructed by dividing a unit of time into proportional subdivisions. As children study the past, timelines help them put events into perspective. Timelines are a very helpful way of teaching about the past. However, simply furnishing your students with a previously made timeline and asking them to interpret it will not teach an appreciation for history or an understanding of the chronology of events. They will learn more from timelines if they construct the timelines themselves.

For the very youngest children, construct timelines on topics related to their immediate experience. Illustrate routines of the daily schedule, for example. Have the children talk about what they do in school each day and select an illustration (or photo) that shows it. The children can arrange the illustrations or photos in sequence according to which activity takes place first, second, and so on.

Extend their ability to sequence major daily events to something else that has great meaning in children's lives—holidays and school vacations. Cut out a symbol for each major holiday and vacation period. These will vary, depending on the culture of your school and the nature of cross-cultural holidays as you learn about them. The children can use clothespins to clip the symbols in temporal sequence (see Figure 4.9). The children must decide which symbol comes first, second, and so on, as they place the symbols in proper sequence.

After your students have sequenced major events such as these, they should be ready to create their own timelines of slightly longer spans of time—perhaps a timeline highlighting the stages of a human's life span, of the children's lives, their families' histories, or their community's history. These timelines can be as simple or as sophisticated as your students' abilities will dictate. For example, Silas Dillman read Tomie de Paola's book *Now One Foot, Now the Other* (Puffin). It is a touching story that describes what it is like to be young and old and finally to die. After a short discussion, Mr. Dillman organized his students into small groups and asked each group to draw an sketch on a sheet of $8\frac{1}{2} \times 11$ inch drawing paper that illustrated one of the significant life stages: "Birth," "Learn to Walk," "Learn to Talk," "Ride a Bike," "Go to Kindergarten," "Enter Fourth Grade," "Go to Middle School," "Enter High School," "Graduate from High School," and "Go to College" or "Go to Work." After they were done, Mr. Dillman took the students to the playground. Those holding the "Birth" card were the starting point for the timeline. Next, the children thought about the age at which they began to walk. Mr. Dillman instructed the children holding the "Learn to Walk" card to begin at the "Birth"

FIGURE 4.9 Sequencing Holidays

point and evenly pace the number of steps it would take to get from birth to walking. He used the same process for each of the other illustrations. When the chronological sequence was complete, Mr. Dillman led the students in a discussion of the uneven distances among the various cards.

Mr. Dillman extended this strategy to demonstrate the sequential nature of historical events. His young historians were first asked to read Jackie Robinson's autobiography, *I Never Had It Made* (Putnam), written with Alfred Duckett. Then small work groups were directed to illustrate sheets of drawing paper with the major events from Jackie's life. Next they went to the playground and walked off one step for each year between events.

You could try a similar strategy after bringing the timeline illustrations back to the classroom from the playground. If students are asked to walk off years between events like they did on the playground, they will quickly learn that taking one step for each year will cause them to bump into walls. They will soon discover that a smaller unit of measure is necessary for their classroom timelines, perhaps one or two inches to represent a year rather than one step.

When working with smaller-scale timelines in the classroom, emphasize accuracy. An inexact scale distorts time relationships and interferes with true chronological thinking. Sequencing the major events in a famous person's life is a good way to introduce smaller-scale timelines. Let us consider Horacio, a student from Mr. Dillman's classroom who read the autobiography of Jackie Robinson. He wanted to create a smaller-scale timeline of Jackie's life, so he selected and summarized the important life events in sequence.

Horacio was quite familiar with computer applications and enjoyed using the computer to assist in social studies projects, so he searched approved Internet sites for access to a timeline generator. He found one at www.teach-nology.com/web_tools/materials/timelines and used it to create a timeline, as shown in Figure 4.10. Horacio encountered a slight problem as he attempted to transfer the data from his summary list to the timeline, however. He had selected 10 highlights to summarize Jackie Robinson's life, but the timeline generator allowed Horacio only eight cells. Horacio studied his 10 events carefully and eliminated 2 from the list so he could complete the computer-generated timeline. So, as you can see, the timeline construction process involves much more than the perfunctory task of arranging events in sequence. Important problems must be solved and critical decisions must be made all along the way.

R. T. Cerovich tried the following problem-solving, manipulative timeline activity with his students: Mr. Cerovich organized the class into groups of three, asked each group to divide a sheet of drawing paper into eight squares, and to sketch on each square an invention that Mr. Cerovich had randomly passed out to each group, such as false teeth, electric fan, personal computer, aspirin, ice cream cone, laser, video camera, Barbie doll, and Ferris wheel. The students created a "Prediction Timeline" by cutting out the squares and attaching them to the places on a timeline to indicate the years when they thought their inventions were made. Mr. Cerovich then had the students research their inventions, learn the story of each, and verify the year when their inventions were actually produced. Each

The Life of Jackie Robinson	
1919	• Jackie Robinson is born
1941	• Won letters in four sports at UCLA
1945	• Jackie joins the Kansas City Monarchs
1946	• Jackie scores winning run in "Little World Series"
1947	• Jackie plays for Dodgers. Is named Rookie of the Year
1957	• Jackie retires from baseball
1962	• Jackie is inducted into the Baseball Hall of Fame
1972	• Jackie Robinson dies at age 53

FIGURE 4.10 The Life of Jackie Robinson

group's contributions to the preliminary timeline were adjusted properly and all of the inventions were sequenced accurately to form a long "Invention Timeline."

Timelines are a great way to place in perspective the accomplishments of a renowned historic figure or stories of important events. Some schools purchase commercially prepared timelines to serve as reference points for important social studies themes or topics. If these are displayed on the wall or on the floor, students will be able to determine the sequence of major events at a glance. They not only help students bring chronological awareness to history but they also establish a rich framework on which historical narratives can be summarized or created.

A Final Thought

History has long been a valued part of schooling in America; it continues to exert a major influence on what and how social studies is taught in our nation's elementary schools. Many have praised its value for producing good citizens over the years, but none has done so more eloquently than Winston Churchill, who once proclaimed, "The further backward you look, the further forward you are likely to see." Such statements underscore the importance of developing the skills and sensitivities of historical consciousness in our schools. In a society steeped in triumphs and tragedies, knowledge of our past helps us to develop pride in our successes and discontent with our errors.

We cannot, however, expect children to become interested in the study of history when all we ask them to do is memorize facts from a textbook. Surely, content is an important part of history, but we must also be aware of the processes of history. Young historians must have regular opportunities to explore history rather than simply be exposed to it. We must lead students to perceive the nature of history itself. Those strategies will help students acquire a more balanced sense of history—it is not only something one knows but also something one does.

REFERENCES

Beatty, P. (1987). *Charley Skedaddle*. New York: Troll Communications.

Chicago Daily News. (1910). DN-0008720, Chicago Daily News negatives collection, Chicago Historical Society. http://memory.loc.gov/cgi-bin/query/D?cdn:2:./temp/~ammem_TNiR.

Cruz, B. C., & Murthy, S. A. Breathing life into history: Using role-playing to engage students. *Social Studies and the Young Learner, 18*, 4–8.

Darigan, D. L., Tunnell, M. O., & Jacobs, J. S. (2002). *Children's literature: Engaging teachers and children in good books*. Upper Saddle River, NJ: Merrill/Prentice-Hall.

Eisenberg, L. (1991). *The story of Sitting Bull, great Sioux chief*. New York: Dell.

Forbes, E. (1943). *Johnny Tremain*. Boston: Houghton Mifflin.

Fritz, J. (1979). *Stonewall*. New York: Putnam.

Fritz, J. (1982). *Homesick: My own story*. New York: Putnam.

Freedman, R. (1989). *Lincoln: A photobiography*. New York: Clarion.

Gray, T., & Owens, S. (2003). From attics to graveyards: How to locate primary documents for your classroom. *Social Education, 67*, 386–388.

Grifalconi, A. (1986). *The village of round and square houses*. Boston: Little, Brown.

Higgs, P. L., & McNeal, S. (2006). Examining a culture from museum artifacts. *Social Studies and the Young Learner, 16*, 27–30.

Milton, J. (1987). *Marching to freedom: The story of Martin Luther King, Jr.* (pp. 4–5). New York: Dell.

Murray, D. (1987). In N. Atwell, *In the middle*. Portsmouth, NH: Heinemann/Boynton Cook.

National Center for History in the Schools. (1996). *National standards for history*. Los Angeles, CA: Author.

Potter, L. A. (2003). Connecting with the past. *Social Education, 67*, 372–377.

Ravitch, D., & Finn, C. (1987). *What do our 17-year-olds know? A report on the first national assessment of history and literature*. New York: Harper and Row.

Robinet, H. G. (2001). *Children of the fire*. New York: Aladdin Paperbacks.

Schreifels, B. (1983–1984, March). Breathe life into a dead subject. *Learning*.

Simpson, M. (2005). Editor's notebook. *Social Education, 69*, 353.

Taylor, M. D. (1992). *Mississippi bridge*. New York: Penguin.

Wachowiak, F., & Clements, R. D. (2006). *Emphasis art*. Boston: Pearson.

Wade, R., Gardner, D., Doro, P., & Arendt, S. (2007). Bridging the years: An intergenerational history project. *Social Studies and the Young Learner, 19*, 24–28.

CHAPTER 5

Young Geographers
Exploring the People–Place Connection

What Does Today's Geography Look Like?

At the beginning of November, Gloria Robertson launched her third-graders into one of the most enjoyable and instructive projects they had participated in during the year. She began by reading the book *Flat Stanley* by Jeff Brown (HarperCollins). In the book, Stanley Lambchop is a perfectly typical young boy until one morning at home he was flattened by a falling bulletin board. Although Stanley is very flat (he was not hurt), he discovers there are many advantages to being four feet tall and half-an-inch thick. Stanley can slide under doors, go down into sidewalk grates, and even be folded up small enough so that his parents could stuff him into a large envelope and mail him off to California to visit some friends. Stanley fully enjoys his flatness until his brother finds a way to help him become well rounded again. After reading the book, Ms. Robertson kicked off the Flat Stanley project by asking her students to design, make, and send their own Flat Stanleys out from Rochester, New York, into the wide, wide world (cooperating classrooms around the country).

Each young geographer began the project by drawing, coloring, and cutting out a paper Flat Stanley and printing her or his name, school address, and classroom e-mail address on the character's back. The children made a small notebook for their Flat Stanleys; on the cover they printed the words "Flat Stanley's Travel Journal." They wrote a brief statement on the first page describing what the project was all about: "I am sending you a Flat Stanley and his journal. Please write down some things about your community and school and what you do

each day with Flat Stanley. Thank you." Then, for two days, the children wrote about their community and some of the major events in Flat Stanley's school and home life. Their journal entries were to provide a model for Flat Stanley's hosts. For example, one day Jerome wrote: "We took Flat Stanley to the Susan B. Anthony House today. He learned about Susan B. Anthony's fight to gain voting rights for women." After two journal pages like this, the children wrote a guidance page for Flat Stanley's hosts: "Dear Friend: Please finish my journal. Include places I've been and sights I've seen. An inexpensive souvenir, or best yet, a photo of you and me together at a special place we visited, would be nice! Sincerely, Flat Stanley. P.S. Would it be possible to send my owner a postcard from your town?"

NCSS STANDARDS

III. *People, Places, and Environments*
IX. *Global Connections*

Each Flat Stanley, journal, a photo (a class photo showing the students holding their Flat Stanleys at the Susan B. Anthony House), an inexpensive souvenir (a "Failure is Impossible" pencil from the Susan B. Anthony House), and a self-addressed envelope with return postage were inserted into oversized envelopes (just like in the Flat Stanley story) and sent from Rochester, New York, to participating classes around the country. A send-off party, which included music and food, was a huge success. Each student shared a moment alone with his or her Flat Stanley before saying good-bye. A small spray of confetti was thrown on the box holding all the envelopes and a thunderous "Bon voyage!" was shouted before the students took them to the post office to be mailed.

Online and paper maps became important reference tools for Ms. Robertson's young geographers as they sought out the route their Flat Stanleys would take to get them to their destinations. For example, locating Fargo, a small city in eastern North Dakota, wasn't a problem for Jack but that didn't stop him from worrying about his little guy: "Look where my Flat Stanley is going," he remarked. "I should have dressed him warmer!"

After about a week, Margaret received the first return postcard. It was sent from Flat Stanley's host in Greenville, Mississippi; the entire class wanted to know just where Greenville was located. They looked through the detailed wall map and placed a pin on the map to mark the location of this first reply. Markers were added to designate each location visited by the Flat Stanleys as the latest envelopes were received. Some hosts sent e-mail messages to Flat Stanley's original owners, detailing his new adventures as well as providing information about the weather/climate, local landmarks, population, industries, seasonal activities, and so on. After about three weeks, most of the Flat Stanleys had returned from their trips. The journals were full of marvelous information about their exciting adventures. The envelopes contained modest souvenirs—a small red plastic lobster from Bangor, Maine, and a miniature bag of peanuts from the site of the "World's Largest Peanut Boil" in Luverne, Alabama. Ms. Robertson's social studies class spent an entire week of school reading through the journals and recording the path of each Flat Stanley's travels. The class honored the Flat Stanleys who had not yet returned with a "Missing in Action" poster, complete with photos of the absent Flat Stanleys and their owners.

The project ended as Ms. Robertson's students wrote thank-you letters to Flat Stanley's hosts. This fabulous project helped the young geographers in Ms. Robertson's room learn much about our country and its geography.

Gloria Robertson continually strives to provide the best possible learning experiences for her students. During this quick look into her classroom, it was easy to see how she stirred the students' curiosity about the world with a wonderfully inspiring, developmentally proper interdisciplinary project. Ms. Robertson doesn't confine geography to memorizing where places are located. Although she understands that it is important to know where places are (especially if you want to find your way back home after school), she knows it is even more important to understand why places are located where they are and how they got there. So, Ms. Robertson constantly challenges her students to think about things such as how and why their school was built where it is, where the shoes they are wearing came from and how they got there, and why maple trees rather than palm trees grow in their community. So, in Ms. Robertson's approach to teaching, students are helped to think of geography not only as a source of information about the world but also as a way of thinking and acting. They are helped to comprehend basic geographic information—facts about location and place—as well as the more complex understandings related to human interactions with the environment. Although some teachers think it's proper to teach geography by handing out a worksheet and having the students locate the major cities of California or assigning country reports (that will surely be copied from an encyclopedia or a website), Ms. Robertson is convinced that such uninspired "teaching" will not only fail to meet her district's geography standards but it will also result in yet another generation of students oblivious to the excitement that geography can offer. Gilbert M. Grosvenor (2007), Chairperson of the Board of the National Geographic Society, supports the contentions of teachers like Gloria Robertson: "Young learners . . . find geography engaging. . . . I have seen it with thousands of schoolchildren in the classrooms I have visited for more than 20 years promoting the discipline across the country. Taught well, geography . . . should be the most popular subject in school" (p. 4).

What Is Geography?

You may have no clue as to where Turkmenistan is or whether Zzyzx is a community in the United States or an animal at the zoo, but geography is standing by ready and willing to help you find out. What is geography? I don't want to get too finicky about a definition for the discipline at this time because, as with history, every geographer will give a slightly different version of what the discipline is or should be. For use in this text, however, *geography* will be defined as "an integrative discipline that brings together the physical and human dimensions of the world in the study of people, places, and environments. Its subject matter is the Earth's surface and the processes that shape it, the relationships between people and environments, and the connections between people and places" (Geography Education Standards Project, 1994, p. 18). In short, geography can be thought of as the science of space and place—the study of Earth's natural environment and how it influences people.

How Global is the Curriculum *Go to MyEducationLab, select the topic Geography, watch the video entitled "Theme: People, Places, and Environments," and complete the questions that accompany it.*

As is true of history, all informed citizens must know geography. There is no doubt that a strong grasp of geography equips people to make better-informed decisions about how to use Earth's resources; for example, geography helps us answer such questions as "Are there any positive consequences of floods?" and "Is this the best location for the proposed sewage treatment plant?" Grosvenor (2007) argues that today's young learners absolutely need geographic knowledge and skills to succeed in the future: "In a world increasingly defined by a global economy, cultural migration, and mounting environmental challenges, geography is an ever more important prerequisite to citizenship and success in the future" (p. 4).

In dynamic social studies, young geographers learn how to describe places on the Earth's surface, explain how these places came to be, and appreciate the delicate bond between humans and their physical environment. They learn geography by asking the same questions professional geographers ask: Where is it? Why is it there? How did it get there? What is the relationship between the people and this place?

Each element of our definition of geography has been expanded on to this point, but before we go on to another topic, I want to make sure that we address the element that was stated in the first three words of the definition—that is, geography is *an integrative discipline*. It is interesting to note that, of all the disciplines contributing to the elementary school curriculum, geography is probably the most open and accepting to incorporating the content and processes of the other disciplines. A deep curiosity about our world motivates geographers to communicate with anybody who might help them better understand the world. We only have to look at the way geography and history can work together to more clearly explain the integrative nature of the discipline. For example: "How did New Orleans' location on the Mississippi River help it become the nation's fourth-largest city in 1830?" "Why was the Erie Canal built between Albany and Buffalo during the early 1800s?" "What geographic obstacles did the railroad workers face in building the transcontinental railroad during the 1860s?" Cooperating with various disciplines is a vital dimension of comprehending Earth as the home of people. An example from Kayla Lavender's classroom helps illustrate the integrative nature of geography in elementary school classrooms.

Kayla Lavender finds it hard to understand why so many teachers hesitate to use interdisciplinary learning strategies in their classrooms. "Research findings aside," Ms. Lavender asserts, "It takes only a drop of common sense to figure out that children learn best when they are helped to make connections among the different areas of learning." Practicing what she preaches, Ms. Lavender has integrated almost every subject area of her fourth-grade curriculum, and her students are reaping the rewards.

NCSS STANDARDS

III. *People, Places, and Environments*
VIII. *Science, Technology, and Society*
IX. *Global Connections*

Today, Ms. Lavender has decided to kick off a new interdisciplinary unit by using a highly enjoyable and appropriate picture book, an instructional resource fundamental to all of her teaching plans. In preparation, Ms. Lavender printed address labels for each child in her classroom and attached them to business-size envelopes. She put the envelopes into a cloth shoulder bag that she designed and sewed together to look like a mail carrier's sack. She then randomly selected one child and asked him to act as a mail carrier and deliver the contents of the bag. The children each received envelopes with their names and addresses on them. Ms Lavender asked, "How did the mail carrier know where to deliver the letters?" The children had no difficulty responding, "Our names are on the envelopes. He looked at our names."

"Yes," Ms. Lavender concurred. "What question, then, does the first line of the address answer?"

"Who gets the letter," the children responded nearly in unison.

"What's on the next line?" Ms. Lavender continued.

"It's my house number and street," countered Sanjay in an instant.

"Yeah, ours, too," the children agreed.

"What question does the second line answer?" asked Ms. Lavender.

"Where we live," answered Jason.

"It tells where our houses are. The street address," added Damares.

"What about the next line?" continued Ms. Lavender.

"It tells the town and state we live in. The third line tells where we live, too," offered Elsa.

"What do you think would be on the next line of the address if we moved from our state?" challenged Ms. Lavender. "If you think you know, write it in the space below your city, state, and zip code."

Offering hints along the way, Ms. Lavender continued to challenge the children to add lines to their envelopes. Many added country and continent, a few added the hemisphere, and only one or two included our planet Earth, solar system, or galaxy in the address.

At this point, Ms. Lavender introduced the book of the day to the children: *My Place in Space* by Robin Hirst, Sally Hirst, Roland Harvey, and Joe Levine (Orchard Books). In the book, Henry Wilson and his sister Rosie ask the bus driver to take them home. The bus driver inquires where they live, teasing that they probably don't know the address. Henry shrewdly tells the driver exactly where he lives and offers a brief description of each part of his growing address: 12 Main Street, Gumbridge, Australia, Southern Hemisphere, Earth, solar system, solar neighborhood, galaxy and supercluster to which Earth belongs. As darkness descends during Henry's humorous explanation, we are offered a glimpse of several interesting astronomical phenomena. The book offers a richly illustrated and entertaining description of our "where we are" as well as an indication of the incredible distances involved.

After completing the book, Ms. Lavender helped the children chart their expanding universe on a large wall exhibit and directed them to add the relevant information underneath their addresses on the envelopes. The students were enthralled with the length of their final addresses and couldn't wait to get home and share it with their families.

Although the distance numbers in the book were far too abstract for most of the children in the classroom, Ms. Lavender challenged the more talented children with this problem: Suppose you were in a vehicle traveling at 60 miles per hour. How long would it take you to get from our school to the center of Australia (the setting of the book)? Around Earth at the equator? At the center of the solar system? Then, to reinforce some of the information in the book, the children went on a virtual field trip of our solar system with *National Geographic's* virtual solar system http://science.nationalgeographic.com/science/space/solar-system and took an interactive trip through our solar system with "Arty the Part Time Astronaut": www.artyastro.com/artyastro.htm.

It would be instructive for you and your classmates to carefully analyze Kayla Lavender's instructional episode to determine how many separate disciplines were involved in this integrative experience. It's a given that science and geography were there, but how many others could you find? An interdisciplinary curriculum teaches content, skills, and thinking processes by taking advantage of natural connections among the disciplines. It has proven to have a positive impact on learning, and teachers often report renewed energy when using this fresh approach. Grosvenor (2007) reported on two *National Geographic* interdisciplinary initiatives intended to improve overall achievement in elementary schools. The first, called *GeoLiteracy*, integrates the study of reading, writing, and geography with students in grades 3 through 7. Controlled testing showed that students who were instructed using this program had significant gains in reading comprehension. Moreover, teachers reported that the approach helped them teach both subjects more effectively. A second project, called *GeoMath*, generated learning materials for kindergarten through grade 8 that integrated geography and math. Tests showed that students demonstrated strong geographic achievement and significantly improved their math learning. It appears, then, that integrated geography instruction can improve overall achievement among elementary school children. Through curriculum integration, teachers can make geography an important part of every classroom and, at the same time, help children find answers to the fascinating questions they have about the world around them.

Why Is Geography Important?

What's the point of teaching geography in the elementary school? There is no question that we are now living in an interconnected world and that virtually every aspect of life can be placed in a global perspective. For that reason, it is very important to know about people and places around the world, and geography can help us effectively face the challenges of our time. A good geography program helps students better understand their community and our nation, and their relationships to other places and cultures. Geography also gives us tools we need to help us move from place to place in the world and to make rational decisions about our environment. Succinctly, the Geography Education Standards Project (1994) advises that students need to study geography for reasons that range from the most profound to the most utilitarian:

- *The Existential Reason.* Humans want to understand the intrinsic nature of their home—that pale blue dot in the vastness of space. Geography helps them understand where they are.
- *The Ethical Reason.* Life is fragile; humans are fragile. Geography provides knowledge of Earth's physical and human systems and of the interdependency of living things and the physical environment. This knowledge, in turn, provides a basis for people to cooperate in the best interests of our planet.
- *The Intellectual Reason.* Geography focuses attention on exciting and interesting things, on fascinating people and places, and on things worth knowing because they are absorbing and because knowing about them lets humans make better-informed and, therefore, wiser decisions.
- *The Practical Reason.* With a strong grasp of geography, people are better equipped to solve issues at not only the local level but also at the global level.

In summary, geography has the power to help students acquire knowledge of our planet Earth and where important places are located. It also stimulates student interest in their surroundings, develops an awareness of the variety of human and physical conditions around the world, and promotes a sense of wonder at the splendor of the physical environment. And, perhaps most importantly, geography helps students build up an informed concern about the quality of the environment, thereby advancing their sense of responsibility for the care of Earth and its people.

What Should Young Geographers Know or Be Able to Do?

The most helpful steps to improve the teaching of geography have been efforts of the National Geographic Society, the National Council for Geographic Education, and the Association of American Geographers. Offering strong leadership and direction, these professional groups have published guidelines proposing what should be taught to our nation's children. The guidelines have been widely circulated and subsequently utilized for curriculum development purposes in school districts throughout the United States.

The first significant contribution to the improvement of geographic education was originated in 1984 by the National Council for Geographic Education. Its Committee on Geographic Education (1984) issued a publication entitled *Guidelines for Geographic Education*, the contents of which became widely known as the "Five Themes of Geography." The themes offered a design of five big ideas around which geographic instruction should be organized: *location, place, relationships within places, movement,* and *regions*.

The Five Themes of Geography

Given the option of anywhere in the world, where would you choose to live? It's a tough choice because all locations on Earth have their advantages and disadvantages with regard to human habitation; one person's like is another's dislike. I once asked my class this question and was surprised by their different responses. One student said Salt Lake City was her "dream location" because she was an avid skier and would love to ski all winter long on the powdery snow for which Utah is so famous. She loved everything about winter and had longed for years to live in such a "perfect" place. On the other hand, another student selected Santa Barbara, California, where he said everything is "perfect." He pointed out that days are usually mild all year long, with clear blue skies filled with bright California sunshine. Because there is no real "off-season," this student boasted that he'd be playing beach volleyball in January and enjoying temperatures in the 70s while the other student will be freezing on the snowy slopes of Utah.

Whatever location you've chosen as your "perfect" place to live, the key is that several factors would have played a huge part of your decision. Those factors are quite probably aligned with the five themes (see Figure 5.1 on page 198) selected by the National Council for Geographic Education, the framework on which the content of geography should be taught.

How Global is the Curriculum
Go to MyEducationLab, select the topic Geography, watch the video entitled "Salt Maps," and complete the questions that accompany it.

1. *Location: Position on the Earth's Surface.* Location answers the question, "Where are we on the Earth's surface?" Location may be absolute or relative. *Absolute location* refers to a specific position on the Earth's surface by using such identifiers as latitude and longitude or a street address: "The Great Salt Lake is in Northern Utah," pinpoints the location of a place as does, "Santa Barbara is 34° North latitude and 119° West longitude." *Relative location* means to locate a place respective to other landmarks—the direction or distance from one place to another. For example, "Salt Lake City is southeast of the Great Salt Lake," or "Beachside Santa Barbara is the hub of a large coastal California county lying northwest of Los Angeles, just off Highway 101."

2. *Place: Physical and Human Characteristics.* All places on planet Earth have unique characteristics that distinguish them from other places. *Physical characteristics* include such features as rivers, lakes, mountains, wildlife, soil, precipitation, beaches, and the like. For example, "Wasatch Mountain snow has been called 'The Greatest *Snow* on Earth!'" *Human characteristics* deal with the changes that people have made to the environment. For example, Santa Barbara didn't exist until pioneers settled the area: "On a spring day in 1782 the Padre Presidente of the California Missions, Father Junípero Serra, and the Spanish Governor de Neve founded the mission of Santa Barbara."

3. *Relationships within Places: Humans and Environments.* The physical features of a location affect people in different ways. An explanation of those ways can be divided into three parts: How people have been changed by the environment; how the environment has been changed by people; and how people depend on the environment. *How people have been changed by the environment* is often called *adaptation.* Whenever people move into a location, they often make lasting changes there because of the nature of the environment. For example, if a city is located on a fertile plain, it may become the hub of a thriving agricultural center. And, if a city is located near a fault (break, or crack, on Earth's surface), it may experience earthquakes. Therefore, people in Santa Barbara will explore different construction materials, shapes, and design options that affect the durability of their buildings. *How the environment has been changed by people,* or *modification,* is the way people alter their surroundings to satisfy themselves. In Salt Lake City, for example, large water projects are in the works to divert water from nearly 100 miles away because the growing population is exhausting the existing water supply. And in Santa Barbara, the Gibraltar Reservoir has been built on the Santa Yves River as a source of water for the community. *Depending on the environment* is when people rely on their environment for something important, such as the use of trees as material to build new houses, or oil to run our vehicles and factories, or rivers to transport goods and natural resources. Geographers look at all the effects—positive and negative—that arise when people establish relationships within places. Sometimes a human act, such as damming a river to prevent flooding or to provide irrigation, requires consideration of all the possible consequences. For example, dams offer many advantages. They are used to generate electricity through water power, to boost water-supply systems, and to create artificial lakes for recreation. However, dams can also harm the environment. They can interfere with fish migration and damage the habitats of other wildlife by reducing water flow.

4. *Movement: Humans Interacting on the Earth.* People network with other people, places, and things almost every day of their lives. They travel from one place to another; they communicate with each other by phone or e-mail; and they

rely on products, information, and ideas that come from far beyond their home locations. Students should be able to recognize where resources are located, who needs them, and how they are transported over the Earth's surface. The theme of movement helps students understand how they are connected with, and dependent on, other regions and other people in the world. For example, southwest of Salt Lake City are the Oquirrh Mountains, the site of the largest open-pit copper mine in the world. The mine produces copper that is shipped to all areas of the United States as well as throughout the world. And when you arrive in Santa Barbara, traveling around town is a breeze. Most of the major attractions are in a compact downtown where, if you don't feel like walking, you can grab a pedicab (Santa Barbara's answer to the rickshaw).

5. *Regions: How They Form and Change.* A basic unit of geographic study is the region, an area on Earth's surface whose characteristics make it different from other areas. The unifying characteristics may be physical, political, or cultural, but through the concept of regions, geographers are able to separate the world into manageable units for study. Geographers divide the world into many different regions, depending on what they are interested in studying. They may define regions according to types of land, climate, or characteristics of people. Therefore, we have land regions such as the Central Plains, the Great Plains, the Appalachian Highlands, and the Pacific Coast. Using a land region classification scheme, then, we are able to assign Salt Lake City to our nation's Great Basin and Santa Barbara to the Pacific Coast region. We have 12 climate regions on Earth, including tropical wet climates that are hot, muggy, and rainy the year round and desert (arid) climates that receive little or no measurable rainfall. We have regions defined by people speaking the same language or having the same religion. There are all sorts of regions that geographers will bicker about, and proclaim that a certain place should or shouldn't be included in some region. In what region is your college or university located? What are its characteristics? How many other regions could it be a part of?

How Global is the Curriculum
Go to MyEducationLab, select the topic Geography, watch the video entitled "Cause-Effect in Geography," and complete the questions that accompany it.

Now that you have learned a little about the five themes, think about how you might be able use them. Imagine for now that you are a television reporter. A team of geographers has just discovered a lost land and you have been assigned to interview them. What are some of the questions you might ask the geographers about this new place? If you are familiar with the five themes of geography, it will help to ask important questions from each. Here are some questions to get you started:

- Where is it?
- What does it look like?
- How many people live there?
- What kind of climate does it have?
- What are the natural resources and how are they used?
- What kind of houses do the people live in?

That is just a start to the questions you will use during the interview, and the questions you will ask as you prepare your geography curriculum. However, the answers will yield only the barest information about places on our planet. Keeping in mind the five themes, what are some other questions you might add?

National Geography Standards

Ten years after the release of the five themes, an alliance of four professional groups calling itself the Geography Education Standards Project (1994) released a set of National Geography Standards titled *Geography for Life. Geography for Life* tried to replace the well-respected "five themes of geography" with a proposal it called the "six essential elements of geography." Actually, the six essential elements consisted of similar items as the five themes; however, they were more comprehensively described and were referred to by different terminology: *the world in spatial terms, places and regions, physical systems, human systems, environment and society*, and *the uses of geography*. Although the two documents used contrasting terminology and varied in depth, they were quite consistent with one another in terms of content. The standards did not supplant the five themes of geography (*location, place, human/environment interaction, movement*, and *region*). The five themes have remained a useful tool for organizing geographic instruction, and can be used jointly with the standards to offer broad guidelines for state standards documents and school district curriculum guides. A publication prepared by the National Geographic Society and available from the National Council for Geographic Education, entitled *Key to the National Geography Standards*, provides a useful summary of the standards and of how the themes relate to them.

The National Geography Standards' six essential elements and 18 standards are reproduced in Figure 5.1.

Because the social studies program in her school district is standards-driven, Becca Jones, a fifth-grade teacher from Flagstaff, Arizona, has developed new ways to think about geography and its key skills. And, as a dedicated teacher, Ms. Jones was eager to incorporate the standards into her instructional plans. She realized that implementing the standards would require adding new activities and strategies to her professional repertoire but, because adjustments take time, effort, and careful personal reflection, her principal recommended that the district's teachers implement only one or two new changes to their teaching each semester. This semester, Ms. Jones chose to focus the second essential element: Places and Regions. Her goal was to meet this standard by offering her students interesting, hands-on activities and by encouraging them to think deeply about their surroundings as well as the physical and human characteristics of other fascinating places on Earth. One way this was accomplished was through an activity Ms. Jones called the "Exchange Package."

NCSS STANDARDS

I. *Culture*
III. *People, Places, and Environments*

FIGURE 5.1 Geography for Life: National Geography Standards

The World in Spatial Terms

Geography studies the relationships between people, places, and environments by mapping information about them into a spatial context.

The geographically informed person knows and understands:

1. How to use maps and other geographical representations, tools, and technologies to acquire, process, and report information from a spatial perspective
2. How to use mental maps to organize information about people, places, and environments in a spatial context
3. How to analyze the spatial organization of people, places, and environments on Earth's surface

Places and Regions

The identities and lives of individuals and peoples are rooted in particular places and in those human constructs called regions.

The geographically informed person knows and understands:

1. The physical and human characteristics of places
2. That people create regions to interpret Earth's complexity
3. How culture and experience influence people's perceptions of places and regions.

Physical Systems

Physical processes shape Earth's surface and interact with plant and animal life to create, sustain, and modify ecosystems.

The geographically informed person knows and understands:

1. The physical processes that shape the patterns of Earth's surface
2. The characteristics and spatial distribution of ecosystems on Earth's surface

Human Systems

People are central to geography in that human activities help shape Earth's surface, human settlements and structures are part of the Earth's surface, and humans compete for control of the Earth's surface.

The geographically informed person knows and understands:

1. The characteristics, distribution, and migration of human populations on Earth's surface
2. The characteristics, distribution, and complexity of Earth's cultural mosaics
3. The patterns and networks of economic interdependence on Earth's surface
4. The processes, patterns, and functions of human settlement
5. How the forces of cooperation and conflict among people influence the division and control of Earth's surface

Environment and Society

The physical environment is modified by human activities, largely as a consequence of the ways in which human societies value and use Earth's natural resources, and human activities are also influenced by Earth's physical features and processes.

The geographically informed person knows and understands:

1. How human actions modify the physical environment
2. How physical systems affect human systems
3. The changes that occur in the meaning use, distribution, and importance of resources

The Uses of Geography

Knowledge of geography enables people to develop an understanding of the relationships between people, places, and environments over time—that is, of Earth as it was, is, and might be.

The geographically informed person knows and understands:

1. How to apply geography to interpret the past
2. How to apply geography to interpret the present and plan for the future

Source: Geography Education Standards Project (1994, pp. 34–35).

To begin, Ms. Jones asked her students to assemble a number of inexpensive objects that could help explain life in Flagstaff. The objects would be placed together in a package and sent to fifth-grade students in a friend's classroom located in Elmira, New York. The students deliberated for quite some time until they selected a small chunk of volcanic cinder to represent Sunset Crater; a branch of ponderosa pine and a pine cone to represent Coconino National Forest, the world's largest contiguous ponderosa pine forest; a piece of wood, toy train engine, and plastic cow to represent the lumbering, railroad, and ranching early economy of Flagstaff; a pair of mittens to represent the outstanding skiing and snowboarding at the Arizona Snowbowl; and a small piece of silver jewelry with turquoise stones to represent native culture. Everyone seemed content with the collection until Claire shouted, "I just thought of something!" The children stopped what they were doing and peered at Claire in anticipation of her great revelation. "The Purina Company has a big pet food factory here," she continued. "We should put something in the package to show that a lot of people from Flagstaff work there." The children breathed a collective sigh. "Not bad, Claire," they responded with a level of enthusiasm a few notches below hers. "What do we put in, a dog biscuit?" Marvin asked drolly. "Good idea!" Claire agreed, as Marvin stared in disbelief, "The dog biscuit is perfect." The dog biscuit received a place among the other relics as the students wrote a letter explaining each. Figure 5.2 shows one paragraph of the letter; it describes the significance of including the pair of mittens. The students from Elmira arranged a package of items and explanatory letter that characterized their city and region and sent it back to their new friends in Flagstaff.

The National Geographic Society's *Xpeditions* has a new series of web pages containing splendid resources for using the standards; there is a link to each standard with related classroom activities (www.nationalgeographic.com/xpeditions/).

In Flagstaff it snows a lot during wintertime.
Sometimes it snows as much as 2 feet.
There are many winter sports in Flagstaff.
People especially like to go to the Mountains
to snow ski. I like to go snowboarding.
Jeffwan

FIGURE 5.2 Student Letter

It is well worth a look at Xpeditions for its useful explanations of the geography standards and its suggestions for put the standards into action.

The themes and standards are applicable to all school districts in the United States, but districts are encouraged to adjust each to local interests and needs. To illustrate how this process can work, let us examine the following example; it outlines the positive results that can easily be achieved with a little careful planning and a commitment to geography on a daily basis (O'Mahony, 2003).

Perry Elementary School in Erie, Pennsylvania, could be a typical inner-city school, just like other schools with social issues, cultural diversity, and ethnic challenges caused by immigration and poverty. It has the same stats as other problematic neighborhood schools. But Perry Elementary is different. Poised on the cutting edge of a growing geography reform movement in the United States, Perry integrates geography throughout the curriculum. Teachers use geography as a springboard for launching instruction in reading, literature, science, match, and history. All the while, they are emphasizing the "Five Themes of Geography."

How does Perry build enthusiasm for geography schoolwide? Here are some geo-friendly examples:

- Students eat lunch in a geocentric decor featuring the 50 states and an enormous map of the world. One wall of the cafeteria is emblazoned with lists of the "The Ten Most Populous Countries," "The Ten Largest Countries," and "The Ten Longest Rivers." Another showcases pictures of children from around the world in native dress. An electronic sign flashes the geography question of the day.
- The school's hallways flaunt murals depicting scenes from Australia, China, Japan, and other far-from-Pennsylvania lands. Flags of many nations hang from the rafters. A poster in a much-traveled stairwell proclaims, "Vexillology—the Study of Flags and Their Origin."
- Perry has forged "sister-school" relationships with schools in Japan, Canada, the People's Republic of China, the United Kingdom, and Australia.
- During morning announcements, a grade-specific geography question is posed over the public address system, with a free pizza for the class whose representative is first to arrive in the office with the correct answer. (No running allowed!)
- With hats from around the world, a map-rug instead of chairs, scales to weigh yourself in stones and kilograms, a large-screen TV for viewing nature films set in international locales, and maps, maps, and more maps, the Gilbert M. Grosvenor Geography Learning Lab was designed to be an "inviting place that students couldn't wait to visit and hated to leave," according to Perry's Principal Grode.
- Even the Perry mascot embraces the schoolwide theme: Toby the Traveling Bear has been all over the world. He's visited Russia, China, Europe, Australia, and Africa. Toby once got lost in Frankfurt Airport and has climbed to the top of Mount Kenya.

Clearly, Perry's geography-immersion education is working. Its students—an ethnically and socioeconomically diverse group, one-quarter of whom receive special education—consistently rank above average in state and national standardized tests. And they're geographically literate. Just ask Gilbert Grosvenor, a man who knows a little something about geography. (He's chairman of the board and former president of the National Geographic Society.) After visiting Perry Elementary School, Grosvenor offered this assessment: "I'd bet second-graders there would score better on geography tests than students at Ivy League schools."

In General, How Should Geography Be Taught?

By preparing students with the knowledge and sensitivities to make wise judgments about their environment, you will be developing caring citizens and powerful decision makers. That's certainly a worthy ambition for the future of our nation and the world, but one very important question begs to be answered before we can hope to achieve it: How does a society that has not learned geography well teach it to a new generation? A step in the right direction would be to make the subject more interesting and more worthwhile for our students. Professional education is the key to helping teachers master the specialized content of geography and the distinctive teaching methods that engage students in active learning. If teachers do not receive the necessary training in the content and processes of geography, they run the risk of teaching it like they might have been taught in elementary school—memorizing state capitals and the major exports of a country. As one of a new generation of teachers, you must stand ready and willing to take on the role of "expert" in the field. But there is more than knowing the content and processes of geography and mastering the recommended strategies for teaching them. You must help children understand that our Earth is shared by people and other living things and it must be carefully maintained. You must also recognize the need for geography in a contemporary world where our continued existence hinges on the attitudes of our nation's young citizens toward our fragile planet.

Implementing an instructional program in the elementary school that places students in the role of young geographers requires an understanding of five phases that underlie geographic study: (1) observing, (2) speculating, (3) investigating, (4) extending and reinforcing, and (5) evaluating.

Teacher-Guided Discovery

Teachers who prefer to use teacher-guided discovery strategies assume the role of facilitator, modeling and leading the way for their students. A detailed classroom example of teaching the five phases of geographic investigation is described here.

Observing

The process of geographic understanding begins with observing an actual geographic feature (such as a pond, building, or road) or a representation of an

environmental feature (such as a video, photograph, or illustration) and answering the question, "What do you see here?" These observations are designed to help students describe and define places, so you might begin by having them write about or draw simple maps and illustrations to record their observations. Unquestionably, the most ideal geographic learning experiences begin by engaging students in direct observations of locations within their environment and recording what they observe.

Certainly, it is impossible for teachers to take their students to every location under study. No one would expect teachers from Boise, Idaho, or Caribou, Maine, for example, to take their students to Amazonia so they could directly observe the natural beauty of the world's largest rain forest. Therefore, teachers must use multiple resources for instruction: primary documents; photos; videos; maps, globes, atlases, and charts; informational books; periodicals with numerous pictures and maps; textbooks; and virtual field trips on the Internet through such sites as *The Field Trip Website* (www.field-trips.org/trips.htm).

Ernest Frombach, for example, initiated a thematic study of "Homes Around the World" by inviting his fourth-graders to draw models and tell stories about their own homes and families. He wanted to connect the concept of homes with the students' own backgrounds of direct experience. After discussing the likenesses and differences of the homes in their classroom, Mr. Frombach displayed large study prints of homes from around the world and guided the observation and discussion with these questions: "What kinds of homes do you see here? In what ways are these homes like your homes? In what ways are they different?"

Convinced that field trips are valuable observational experiences that can assist young learners to gain a better understanding of geographic concepts, Mr. Frombach provided his students with regular opportunities to observe and experience things firsthand in on-site situations, too. For this unit on "Homes Around the World," some types of homes could not be observed directly (adobe homes and yurts, for example), so field observations were unimaginable. However, Mr. Frombach knew it was possible to take a trip to Hoopes Park so the children could study the oldest still-standing structure in the community—a well-preserved stone farmhouse originally built in 1738. This stone farmhouse, built by Thomas Hoopes using stone from an adjacent quarry, is very important to the community and can be found nestled in a grassy plot at the center of the park that bears his name. The children enjoyed visiting this site and learned a great deal about the property's charm as they examined its original architectural details.

According to local historian Craig Moore, the house is one of just 47 known still-standing stone houses that were built by the late eighteenth century in their part of the county. The students stood in awe of three stone fireplaces (two more are still hidden behind plaster walls), a stone wall that separated the main house and the kitchen, original wide-plank oak floors, raised six-panel doors, and deeply recessed window sills. They also loved the simple closed staircase that led to the second floor and an original plank door with a 200-year-old wrought-iron thumb latch that opened to the basement.

"It's a real piece of history," gushed Jill, who had never been inside a house as old as this.

"There's nothing else like it," agreed Anthony.

When included as observational experiences, Mr. Frombach found that field trips benefit his geography program in these ways: (1) hands-on learning permits students to interact with real things rather than try to learn from abstract examples, (2) students develop a greater appreciation of the environment that they will investigate, and (3) examples observed in the field can be related to other classroom work. In order to increase the potential benefits of field trips, however, there needs to be careful preparation. Before the trip, help the children think about, discuss, and record what they are likely to see. Encourage them to ask questions they will want to investigate. Talk about whom they may want to interview at the site or what would be possible to bring back to the classroom.

When your class goes to a site, the students should take field notes and make sketches of what they are most interested in or what they would like to learn more about when they return to school. When the children return to the classroom, it is important to discuss the field trip—what happened, whom they spoke to, what they saw, and what they learned. Sketches or field notes become the basis for detailed illustrations or for the construction of models; field notes are used to write summary accounts of or narratives about the trip.

It is a fact of life, though, that regardless of how well you plan the trip, many "unexpected surprises" as well as "unexpected benefits" will be sure to crop up. For example, on this trip, Ethan yanked on Jamielle's homemade necklace and sent beads rolling in every direction, and midway through the visit, Carl was terrified by a goat's loud bellow and screeched, "Get me outa here! I wanna go home!" After Mr. Frombach took care of those troubles, Carrie spilled her snack and drink all over herself. And when the class returned to school, individual letters of thanks revealed some interesting "confessions":

> Dear Sir:
>
> I am sorry about the way our class acted on our trip to your park, but I did not personally curse or anything. I hope you let us come back. Our friend who pulled down his pants is sorry!

> Dear Sir:
>
> I am sorry that our class was bad on its trip to the park. I apologize for exposing myself. I hope you let us come back. (P.S.—I am a boy.)

Speculating

Geographic investigations begin with observation, but they don't stop there. Observation lays the foundation for more complex understandings such as why things are where they are and how they got there: "Where is it located? Why is it there? What do you think has caused it to look this way?" Students must not stop the

Observational experiences lead to the construction of geographical intelligence.

process of learning about a geographic location simply by looking at and describing it; they must speculate about possible answers to "where" and "why there" questions.

Mr. Frombach, continuing the topic of "Homes Around the World," asked his young geographers to look for clues in the pictures and during the field trips so they could think about how climate, natural resources, and other physical features of locations might have influenced the selection of building materials as well as the design of a home. He asked, "How have the people adapted their homes to the environment?" This process should not be pure guesswork, but rather a systematic form of deductive reasoning that calls on students to use previously acquired understandings and experiences to make reasoned inferences. These inferences, in turn, will next be tested by the students while they uncover supportive data.

Investigating

In this third phase of geographic inquiry, young geographers gather information about locations as well as about the human characteristics of those places. To answer geographic questions, students must be helped to gather information from a variety of sources in many ways. In the earlier elementary grades, literature, videos, resource persons, Internet sites, or any other suitable informational sources might do this. In the middle and upper elementary grades, students can engage in these and other investigative activities such as fieldwork (taking photos, distributing questionnaires, conducting interviews, collecting samples, reading and interpreting maps), or library research.

Because of the wealth of information on each type of home, Mr. Frombach decided it would be most efficient to subdivide his class into specialized research groups such as "yurts" (Mongolia), "adobe homes" (American southwest), and "leaf huts" (Central African rain forest). Mr. Frombach visited each group and used timely prompts to direct and extend thinking. For example, while visiting the adobe group, he offered prompts like these: "What kind of homes are these? Where are they found? What are they made of? How were they made? Why are they made this way? How do these homes compare with ours? Why are adobe homes so popular in different parts of the world? Do you think that homes in these areas will always be built this way?"

Regardless of the grade level, *something* constructive must be done with the results of the students' research. Mr. Frombach felt it was important to first help each group organize its research into an informational paragraph or two. We will study what he did with the adobe group as an example.

Mr. Frombach began the process by asking the students to list on a chart all of the factual data they uncovered about adobe homes around the world. When the chart was filled with many words and phrases, he asked the students to study it carefully and think about this question, "Do any of these items seem to belong together?" As the students studied the chart, they circled their selections with a black marker. Mr. Frombach then asked, "Why did you group these items together?" and invited the students to explain the common characteristics of all the items in the group. Next, Mr. Frombach asked the students to come up with a label that encompassed the characteristics of all the items in the group. Since the students had circled places around the world where adobe homes can be found, they simply called this group "Places."

Mr. Frombach then explained, "We are now going to use the information you circled to write a paragraph." Then, with the understanding that many informational paragraphs begin with the main idea, he asked, "Please say in one sentence what all these items seem to be telling us."

There was no response for what seemed like an eternity because this was a very difficult responsibility. Then Amanda suggested, "You can find adobe houses all around the world."

"Yeah," agreed Yanming, "they're all over."

"Good thinking," praised Mr. Frombach as he wrote the suggestions on the chalkboard. "This is a great way to start our paragraph. Let's examine the two ideas closely and try to combine them into one sentence to begin our paragraph."

Again, there was a constructive lull in the classroom as the children thought hard about their charge. Eventually, several suggestions were made; the children settled on "The world is full of adobe houses." The group scribe then recorded the first sentence on a large sheet of chart paper.

"Now that we have our topic sentence," instructed Mr. Frombach, "we'll need to focus on the underlined items in order to add details to the paragraph." After

deciding on the order that the supporting details should be written, the "adobe group" drafted this paragraph:

> The world is full of adobe houses. The most adobe buildings can be found in the southwestern part of the United States. Especially in the desert areas of New Mexico and Arizona. These include both homes and missions. Adobe homes can be found in other Spanish-speaking countries like Mexico, Peru, and Bolivia. Surprisingly, adobe homes can be found in the arid regions of western China, in Iran, and on the island of Cyprus. Depending on the location, adobe homes can be found in all kinds of different shapes, sizes, and colors.

Next, the group studied its paragraph and reworked it under the guidance of Mr. Frombach. For example, they realized that "Especially in the desert areas of New Mexico and Arizona" was an incomplete sentence so it was combined with other ideas into a complex sentence: "Most adobe buildings can be found in the southwestern part of the United States, especially in the desert areas of New Mexico and Arizona." Likewise, they edited the rest of the paragraph and wrote the final copy on chart paper. Appropriate illustrations then were added.

Later, responding to a similar instructional sequence by Mr. Frombach, the students circled in red those items dealing with history of adobe building, in blue those items dealing with the building process, and in green those items dealing with the advantages and disadvantages of living in adobe homes. Each subsequent paragraph was added to the first chart and displayed in the group's work area to summarize what it had learned about adobe as a building material. It is obvious that the students were not only learning about homes around the world but were also refining specific writing skills, such as writing an informational paragraph.

Extending and Reinforcing

You may extend and reinforce the children's learning by using small group writing activities, constructing models, making maps, studying tables and graphs, or examining all kinds of literature. Having had such a stimulating data-gathering experience, children will have much to share. For example, Mr. Frombach wanted to take the unit beyond the ordinary to where the action is. During his unit on "Homes Around the World," students had learned that early Pueblo Indians, the Anasazi, built adobe homes by using the "puddling method." They built walls by placing handfuls of wet adobe on a mound, letting it dry, and adding another layer. They would add layer after layer rather than stacking bricks. The Spanish introduced adobe bricks to the Pueblo Indians, and, because of its many favorable properties, adobe remains a building material of preference today. To help his students understand how to build with the adobe material, Mr. Frombach adapted the adobe brick-making process he discovered on the Internet. The students mixed earth, straw, and water to create the mud *(zoquete)*, packed it tightly into a wooden mold, and allowed it to thoroughly dry in the sun for three or four days. When the mud turned into hard brick, the students took the form by the handles and released the adobe.

"Congratulations, class," smiled Mr. Frombach wryly. "Only 6,000 more and we'll have enough to construct our own *casita*!"

Like Mr. Frombach, social studies teachers around the country have developed significant learning situations in which their children are actively and directly involved in doing something real.

Evaluating

The final phase of geographic inquiry is making personal judgments about the situation: "Have the people been wise in using the environment in such a way? Is this the most productive use of the land or its resources?" All personal opinions must be supported with sound reasons: "If not, why not? If so, why?" Since so many conditions of our world are intimately associated with the wise use of our physical environment, skills in this realm are of primary importance to children, the adult citizens of the future.

It is this physical environment–people linkage that makes geography such a valued component of today's dynamic social studies. Geographic terms and place locations are important; students need to know and use correctly the appropriate

Children conceptualize geographic information as they construct a three-dimensional map of a traditional African village.

geographic terms and concepts. However, to become truly geographically literate, students must apply their basic skills and understandings to discovering relationships among people, places, and other phenomena. For example, generalizations about the influence of weather on homes or elevation of a region on agriculture are fundamental geographic relationships necessary for increasing geographic literacy.

Maps: The Tools of Geographers

Maps are all around us today. Who among us has not used such popular websites as Google Earth, Google Maps, or MapQuest or a GPS unit to get somewhere? These are all fantastic systems that assist us in finding a location no matter where we are in the world. Adults and children find them to be enjoyable as well as highly useful. But we shouldn't be lulled into complacency. Regardless of how functional a GPS might be or how serviceable an online map has been, we must possess some basic map skills and understandings before we are able to use them. Although often taken for granted, success in reading and using maps is fundamental to our lives, regardless of our age.

As in our daily lives, it is impossible to teach or learn geography without using a map or even several maps simultaneously. Maps are absolutely necessary for collecting and interpreting data about places on Earth. Thus, desk maps, wall maps, online maps, globes, and atlases are essential requirements for all dynamic social studies classrooms. The Committee on Geographic Education (1984), the same group that outlined the five fundamental themes of geography discussed earlier in this chapter, emphasized the importance of maps in the social studies classroom: "Reading, interpreting, and making maps are skills integral to geographic education and to acquiring geographic knowledge" (p. 2). The Geography Education Standards Project (1994) added: "Making maps should be a common activity for all students. They should read (decode) maps to collect information and analyze geographic patterns and make (encode) maps to organize information. . . . For students, making [and using] maps should become as common, natural, and easy as writing a paragraph" (p. 43). One of your major tasks in developing a solid geography component in your social studies program is to help children acquire the basic skills necessary to construct and interpret maps.

What Is a Map?

What is a map? This can be a misleadingly simple question for anyone who has used such helpful tools as road maps to find the way from one place to another or weather maps to plan daily activities. Maps are so much of our lives that we often take them for granted. But allow yourself a few moments now and truly think about an answer to the question: "What is a map?" Isn't the job much more difficult than you first expected? It's hard to believe how often the familiar becomes more complex as we think more deeply about things. Nonetheless, having a good idea of what maps are is fundamental if you plan on teaching them to elementary school children.

Although there is no standard answer to our question among social studies educators, several components are commonly found in accepted definitions of what a map is. For our purposes, then, we will join together those common components into this definition: *A map is a flat representation of the Earth's surface (or portion of it) as seen from above. Drawn to scale, maps use colors, symbols, and labels to represent the Earth's surface features.* No one knows for sure who drew the first map or when it was drawn, but very long ago some clever individual came up with the idea of scratching a stick through dirt to show the way to the best hunting ground in the world or poking dots in the soil to indicate the position of remarkable stars in the dark night sky. Now people make maps for many reasons—to find a hotel or restaurant, to show variations in terrain, to establish the locations of major battles, or to indicate the distribution of votes for each party from the last presidential election. Maps show a host of other things, too, but even the best maps are worthless unless the user knows how to make or read them. For that reason, one of the most important skills specifically associated with geography is to help students develop the competencies that will enable them to communicate with maps.

Maps as Models of Our World

When we teach children about maps, it is reasonable to begin with the question that started this section, "What is a map?" There are many who think they have found the answer by trying to convince children up to the age of 6 or 7 that a map is a representation of the Earth that one would see if looking down from the sky, or "a bird's eye view." This could be a constructive approach for older children, but for kindergartners or first-graders, the top-down image is quite confusing. Piaget tells us that this confusion results from the children's natural egocentricity during the early grades; that is, they see things pretty much from one point of view—their own! They just can't understand that everyone else can't see things the same way they do.

Piaget conducted a classic study, called the *mountain study*, to investigate this phenomenon. He devised a square table with three distinctly different plaster mountains arranged as shown in Figure 5.3. The mountains would look quite different from each of the four sides of the table. Each mountain was slightly different in size and shape, and each had a different symbol on top—a house, a cross, and a church. Piaget then positioned children in front of the simple mountain range and asked them to select from among four drawings the view that they presently observed. Next, he introduced a doll who took a leisurely "walk," stopping at each of the three remaining sides of the square table. The children remained seated at their original chair and were asked to select the drawing depicting the doll's viewpoint at each stop. Not surprisingly, the younger children were unable to visualize the display from the doll's changing perspective. They kept picking the drawing showing the mountains from where they were sitting; older children

FIGURE 5.3 Piaget's Mountain Arrangement

(past the age of 7) chose correctly what the doll would see from its perspective. This showed that children younger than age 7 or 8 have a self-centered perception of the world.

It appears, then, for younger children, thinking of a map as a representation of the Earth from a bird's-eye point of view simply does not work. Ekiss, Trapido-Lurie, Phillips, and Hinde (2007) add that "younger children also find it hard to relinquish what they may consider to be the defining features of some objects (such as legs on a table) even if they are not visible to the child when looking down" (p. 7). In other words, the child wants to represent what she knows rather than what she sees. The aerial view alone doesn't capture what the child knows about tables, so she draws four legs sticking out the sides like a spider even though she cannot see them. She knows they are there and is compelled to represent them.

Instead of expecting children to do something beyond their capabilities, then, it would be more instructive if teachers used activities matched to the developmental uniqueness of the children. Best practices for teaching very young children are based on the premise that active involvement with hands-on, concrete materials eventually help to lay the groundwork for work with abstract ideas. Gandy (2007) supports this opinion: "Young children learn geographic skills primarily through play, rather than formal instruction. Playing with toy trucks and cars on the carpet or in the sandbox, moving furniture around in a dollhouse, and building designs with blocks develop perceptions and skills that can apply to more abstract concepts in later years" (p. 31). Through play, children gradually learn to transform mental images, or internalized ideas of things such as a house or bus they have acquired through direct experience, for example, into symbolic representations of those ideas (a block arrangement, drawing, or even a printed word that represents the internalized idea). This complex ability to interpret or create symbols that represent something real does not happen overnight; it takes time for children to master their ability to understand how symbols can be used to represent what they know about their growing world. The first leg on this long road toward understanding the symbol system of maps involves helping the child understand that one thing can stand for another. As far as map reading is concerned, this goal is best accomplished through active engagement and experimentation with blocks and other play materials.

Representing the World through Block Play

Many hands-on play materials—blocks, boxes, wooden or plastic people and animals, simple machines, vehicles, and paper and crayons—must be made available to children so they can use them to represent their expanding world. For the very youngest, their representations will be something basic, like pushing a block across the floor, while screeching, roaring, and sounding the horn just like a noisy 18-wheeler does as it hauls a heavy load through the neighborhood. The center of attention for this child is mainly on the physical aspect of the activity, or the *doing* component of constructive play. That doesn't mean there is no meaning associated with the activity. A little comment or question from the teacher often is enough to offer insight into what is going on in the child's mind:

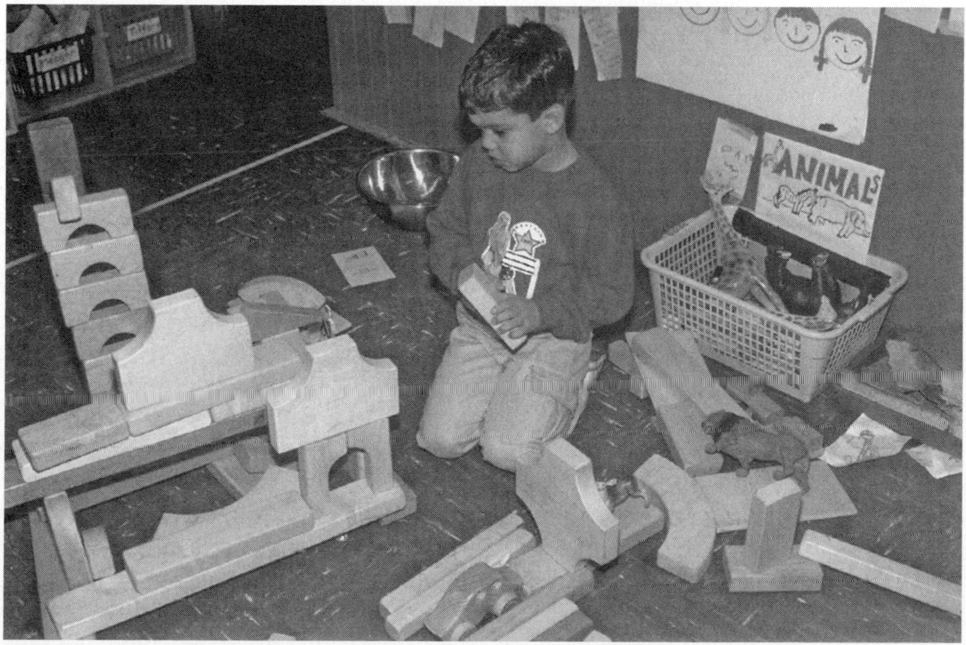

Block structures offer the most valuable premapping representational experiences for young children.

Teacher: Tell me about your truck.
Child: It's my big tractor trailer.

Teacher: Is it going somewhere?
Child: To the store.

Teacher: What kind of store?

Child: To Toys 'R Us store. My favorite.

Teacher: Is your truck bringing something to the store?
Child: Lotsa, lotsa, lotsa toys! B-r-r-r-m-m-m! Ha-a-a-r-r!"

Do you recall that the child's truck was a single block in this example? The "store" was simply four blocks arranged as a square. Being aware that blocks represent something real is why teachers must encourage young children to talk about what they are building. It not only increases the children's interest in the activity and helps them clarify their thinking but it also makes teachers more aware of how the children's structures represent the real world even if the symbols are not immediately recognizable.

When they have many opportunities to play, children will gradually become more concerned about making their symbolic representations more authentic. They still enjoy the *doing* component of play, but they give increased attention to accuracy of representation and become more specific in their buildings. Pushing around a block just won't do, neither will using four blocks to make a store. The older children have a greater understanding of their world, so they set about selecting and arranging blocks and other building materials in ways that they believe more clearly depict what they know. Having explored their real environment in kindergarten and first grade, these youngsters are now better able to systematically organize their experiences into increasingly more complex structures. They will not only build an impressive veterinarian's office, but will add accessories that make it seem more authentic—computers, examination tables, toy animals, doctor's kit, leashes, clothing, and so on.

Certainly, experiences with hands-on materials help satisfy the child's natural drive for physical activity, but they also stimulate cognitive growth through the questions and situations that often come up during their use. While pretending to fight a fire in their block-built shopping center, for example, a group of first-graders suddenly wondered aloud, "Hey, how's the water get in the hose?" The study resulting from this spontaneous request for information took them to the street to look at the fire hydrants and eventually to the town's reservoir where they saw the source of water and the massive pumps that send the water through a pipeline maze to their streets. Naturally, when they returned to the classroom, the children were determined to represent the reservoir with a large sheet of blue bulletin board paper and add a series of plastic pipes that carried the water to their building block "hydrants." Their block structure became an increasingly detailed symbolic representation of real places in their environment and, in essence, that's what a map is. The structure became a concrete connection to something real; therefore, these children, like all children, found it helpful to build and play before abstract map concepts were introduced. Cognitive development does not happen independently of physical action for young children.

You can learn a lot about children by watching and listening. Then, by offering judicious prompts, you can help them think about their structures and find new relationships among established ideas. As children get older and mature, their representations will take on greater depth. An urge to depict greater reality will be a driving force for them, and progressively their simple little buildings will grow into organized neighborhoods and communities complete with battery-operated traffic signals and street lights or elevators set in motion with strings and simple pulleys. It is when the children's structures become this enriched, extended, and refined that they are entering into a period of growth when systematic learning experiences could be employed to help them understand the abstractions associated with maps.

Children's First Maps

If there is a single area of controversy that stands out above all others in map reading instruction, it is agreeing on the most appropriate time to move from the kinds of unstructured, open-ended construction activities we have examined so far to more systematic instruction that enables children to comprehend the abstract concepts related to the symbol systems of maps. Although social studies textbooks and scope and sequence charts often include various map basics as early as kindergarten or first grade, Piaget's description of egocentricity fuels considerable disagreement about whether children are cognitively ready before second grade. Despite this ambiguity about the best time to begin map instruction, there is general consensus that when instruction is developmentally suitable, children are capable of learning about maps.

The fundamental prerequisite for crafting a suitable instructional program is to identify the specific skills necessary to read and make maps. Designing appropriate instructional activities is usually not difficult when teachers are on familiar terms with the basic skills central to producing and reading maps:

- *Locating Places.* Finding the exact position of a place
- *Reading Cardinal and Intermediate Directions.* North, south, east, and west as well as northeast, northwest, southeast, southwest
- *Recognizing and Expressing Relative Location.* Where something is in relationship to something else
- *Interpreting Map Symbols.* Knowing that signs and colors represent real things, such as buildings, mountains, roads, bridges, and rivers
- *Understanding Map Scale.* The relationship between distance on the map and distance on the Earth (e.g., one inch equals one mile)
- *Knowing That the Globe Is the Most Accurate Representation of Earth's Surface.*

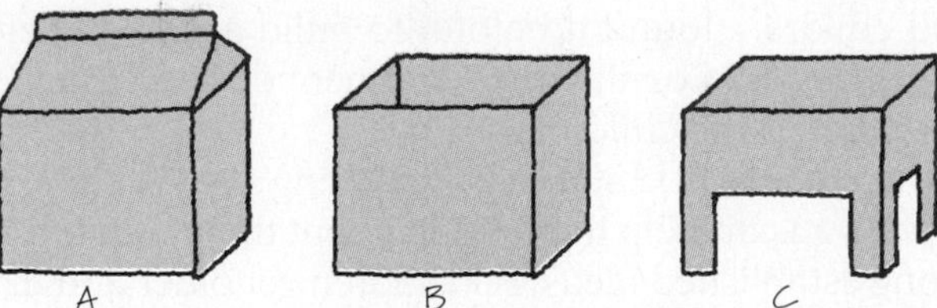

FIGURE 5.4 Milk Carton Desks

Maps Representing the Classroom

Initial mapping experiences should be carried out in a place where the children are able to directly observe what is to be mapped. The mapping activity itself should not be totally removed from the block constructions the children had been making up to this time. Fertig and Silverman (2007) advise, "When teaching geography to students in the [early grades], we should provide firsthand experiences that young children need to make meaningful sense of their world. First- through third-graders are not ready developmentally to learn how to identify species of animals living in a rain forest or to color code Earth's five oceans and seven continents" (p. 15). Distant places and abstract concepts are a better fit for third grade and higher. Sobel (1998) calls this the "small world approach," suggesting that teachers in the early grades design instruction to help students understand the environment that is closest to them. If it's true, then, that formalized map skills instruction begins most effectively within a "small world," then the most logical place to start appears is the classroom.

Launch your classroom map-making project (it usually works best with middle-of-the-year or late-year second-graders) by obtaining white half-pint dairy cartons available online from most packaging companies at a reasonable price for school projects. Direct the children to cut off the tops so that they end up with a square, open-top box. Turn the box over so it is standing on the open end and then cut away parts along the sides with scissors so that the cartons appear to have legs (see Figure 5.4).

Discuss the cardboard desks with the children, focusing on how they serve as models, or representations, of their actual desks. The children next paint the desks with tempera paint, make and glue construction paper books or pencils on top, put their name cards on the fronts of the desks, and add any other features that would authenticate the experience.

When the desks are finished, ask one child to locate her desk on a large sheet of cardboard (such as a side of a refrigerator packing box) that you have placed on a worktable or on the floor. Explain that the cardboard represents the classroom floor, but on a smaller scale. Encourage the child to carefully locate her desk in the actual classroom and then study the sheet of cardboard to determine the most appropriate spot for her milk carton desk. Once this first desk has been placed correctly on the sheet of cardboard, the rest of the construction process will move along quickly. To start, a child who sits next to the first child will be invited to place his desk "next to Margaret's." As children take turns placing their desks on the classroom model (use terms such as *in front of, next to, in back of,* and so on), they are primarily using three of our basic map-reading skills:

1. Understanding that their milk cartons represent their real desks (*interpreting map symbols*)
2. Deciding where their desks should be placed (*locating places*)
3. Determining the placement of individual desks in relationship to the other desks (*recognizing and expressing relative location*)

Next, ask the children to bring to school empty boxes they might have around the house, from small jewelry boxes to boxes about the size of a toaster. Divide the class into small groups, each of which will now be responsible for selecting a box the group thinks most closely resembles the piano, book shelf, teacher's desk, or whatever. Since some young children find it difficult to work with others, you might want to have small individual projects such as the classroom waste basket or computer. Keep a careful eye on the children as they select the boxes to represent their classroom features. It seems to never fail that the group responsible for the teacher's desk will select the largest box, even though the teacher's desk is far from the largest classroom feature. The children consider their teacher to be such an important person in their lives that anything less than the largest box would be discourteous! If this happens (chances are that it will), you should persuade the children to look carefully at their own real desks and compare them to the teacher's real desk; then discuss the relationship. In due course, they will select a box that more closely represents the true size relationship. The children will explore, investigate, manipulate, test, and adapt the whole way through the process of selecting and designing the boxes to represent real classroom features. This is a primary advantage of using the classroom as the children's first mapping experience; basic skills are acquired and deepened as children go back and forth from map to real classroom, deciding how the features should be represented.

Sometimes the end result of their efforts generates the kinds of humorous episodes that all teachers hold dear. For example, one teacher found that every group and individual had finished its assigned classroom feature, so it was time to place the representations on the growing three-dimensional map. But Alice was still at her workstation busily working on her model wastebasket. When the teacher approached Alice to see what was causing the holdup, she found that the little girl was cutting, folding, and crunching dozens of tiny pieces of paper for her wastebasket. The job was taking forever! It seems that the actual classroom wastebasket was packed with scraps from the mapping project and, in her drive to represent the model as accurately as possible, Alice took it upon herself to miniaturize each piece.

As the students complete their assigned features, they will be ready to add them to the three-dimensional classroom map. This phase of map construction is critical, as it contributes to the emergence of the "bird's-eye-view" concept—forming a mental picture of something as if it were viewed from above, much like the way a bird might view something as it flies over. You can help children acquire this bird's-eye-view perspective by advising them to look at their model classroom feature from directly above as they arrange them on the map. That way, they will see only the tops of the desks, tables, file cabinets, and so on, and begin to understand that paper maps are created from this viewpoint of Earth. Notice that during this phase of construction, the three previous map-reading skills are extended and reinforced, and a new skill is introduced: *developing an idea of relative size and scale*.

Once the model classroom has been accurately arranged, you can further extend and reinforce map skills by using their map as a learning tool:

Locating Places

"Put the teacher's desk where it is located in our classroom."
"Where would you place the piano? The file cabinet?"
"Point to the box that shows the puppet stage . . . the worktable . . . the teacher's desk."
"James, can you find Michelle's desk? Put your finger on it."
"Put your finger on the aquarium. Now trace the path you would take to answer the door."

Recognizing and Expressing Relative Location

"Whose desk is closest to the coat rack?"
"Trace the shortest path from the reading corner to the door."
"Which is closer to the door, the science center or the teacher's desk?"

Interpreting Map Symbols

"Pick up the box that represents the puppet stage."
"What does the red box stand for?"
"How can we show the coat rack on our map?"

Developing an Idea of Relative Size and Scale

"Which is larger, the file cabinet or the piano?"
"Which box should be smaller, the teacher's desk or the worktable?"
"Point to the smallest (or largest) piece of classroom furniture."

Because constructing the classroom map should be considered only the beginning of a comprehensive instructional program, it should now be used as the major learning tool to introduce and reinforce each of the specific map skills. Through appropriate learning experiences, these skills can be developed and strengthened in a rewarding and satisfying manner.

Map Symbols

The three-dimensional model of the classroom can be easily transformed into a flat paper map by following a few simple procedures. First, provide a large sheet of craft paper exactly the same size as the cardboard base of the three-dimensional model. Explain that this large piece of paper will be used to make a flat map of the classroom. Dividing responsibilities, ask the students, one at a time, to remove their desks from the three-dimensional model. Direct them to stand directly above their model desks, slide a piece of construction paper beneath the desks, and trace around the outer perimeter with a crayon. The children cut around the resulting outlines and label them with their names. Before the three-dimensional desks are placed back on the model, help the children compare the piece of construction paper with the desk models to notice how a flat symbol can represent an object when looking from the top. The flat desks are then glued in their correct places on the large sheet of craft paper. Be sure not to hurry the children through this process; use the same prompts to help them place their desks as you did while constructing the three-dimensional model. Also, follow the same procedure while representing the other three-dimensional classroom features: file cabinet, piano, computer center, and so on. The three-dimensional map gradually becomes transformed into a flat map as colorful traced outlines replace the three-dimensional models. For the children to understand how the flat map functions in the same way as the three-dimensional map, ask questions like those used for the three-dimensional map. Effective discussion is as important for this flat map phase as for the three-dimensional phase.

To reinforce what has been accomplished so far with map symbols, write the word *desk* on the chalkboard and lead a short discussion about the physical characteristics of their actual classroom desks. After the students have shared their thoughts, emphasize that the written word *desk* stands for their real desk in the same way as the spoken word and a map symbol do. Ask the children to think about what the symbol for *desk* might be in the special language of maps. Follow this procedure while helping the children make up their own symbols for the other features on the large classroom maps. Don't be overly concerned if their symbols are not the same as standard map symbols; at this point you are more concerned with the overall concept of symbolization than the conformity of representation. Place the model desk from the three-dimensional map on a worktable for all to see; then, on a card next to the model desk, draw its agreed-upon symbol, and then print its word name on another card. Do this for each separate classroom feature. Now follow this chain (*the feature or its photo or picture—symbol—word label*) whenever new map symbols are introduced in your classroom.

The children should now realize that the special set of symbols people use to communicate ideas is called a *language*. In the United States, most citizens use the English language to communicate orally and in print. In school, we learn English as our main language, but we also learn other languages, including the language of maps.

At this point, inform the children that one of the most important elements of a map is its *legend,* and that maps would be worthless unless people understood the meaning of the various symbols drawn on the map. A map legend is usually positioned in a small box in the corner of the map and contains information that informs the map reader what the symbols mean. Show the children a legend on a pictorial map of a familiar location such as a park or zoo (see Figure 5.5). Pictorial symbols are most appropriate because nearly all children come to school with a variety of experiences involving pictures—storybooks, television, movies, cereal boxes, magazines—so the idea that pictures represent ideas and information is not new to them. Therefore, using maps that look like a "picture of a place" provides a better foundation for instruction than trying to get children to understand that a real map is an aerial view of a place on the Earth's surface. Young children already possess knowledge of the immediate world around them; therefore, richly illustrated pictorial maps are considered appropriate at this time of map instruction. Once the children understand how legends are displayed on the pictorial maps, they will be quite interested in adding legends to both their large flat classroom map and the smaller individual maps they will be drawing shortly.

Cardinal Direction

The best method of introducing young children to the concept of cardinal direction is the same as we have discussed for all other related map concepts—through direct experience. Primary-grade children enjoy going outdoors with simple compasses to find the cardinal directions (north, south, east, and west). Explain to the

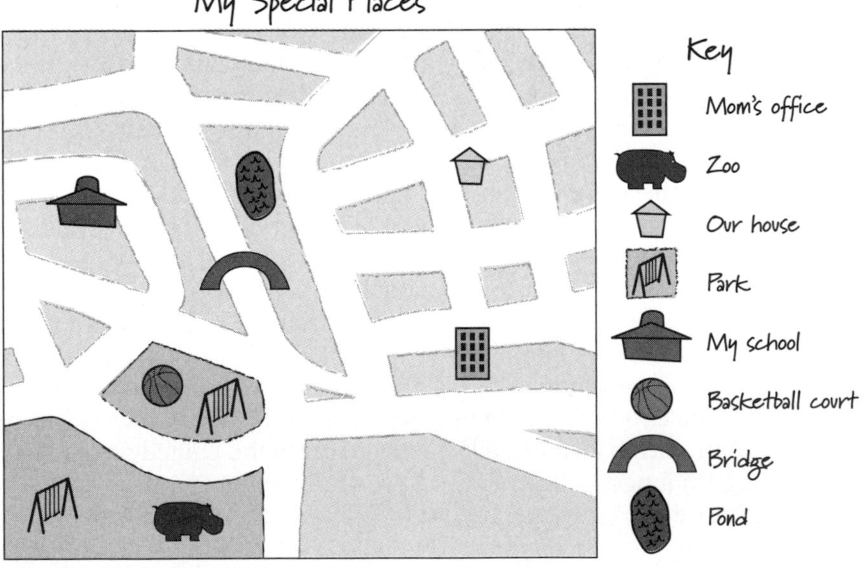

FIGURE 5.5 Early, Grade Pictorial Map

students that a direction is the point or line toward which something lies or faces. Ask all the students to face forward, and explain that forward is a direction. Do the same as you have them to face backward. Both of these requests involve the children responding to a direction. Explain that maps have very special words to describe directions—*north, south, east*, and *west*. They are the four basic points on a compass. North and south are at the top and the bottom, and east and west are on the right and left sides of a compass.

The children should be helped to locate a point to the north with the compass. They will soon see that south is behind them, east is to the right, and west is to the left. If the children are outside at noon on a sunny day, they will find a new clue for determining direction—in our northern hemisphere, at noon, their shadows will point in a northerly direction. Once they determine north this way, the other directions will be easy to find. To help them remember the other directions, ask the children to search for outstanding physical landmarks. Have one child face in a northerly direction and select the first obvious feature, such as a large building. Give the child a card labeled "north" and ask her to stand facing in that northerly direction with the card in her hands. Then select a second child to stand back-to-back to the northerly child. Ask the children what direction he is facing. If no one says "South," tell them. Ask the second child to find an outstanding physical feature to the south (such as a large tree) and give him a labeled card to hold. Repeat this procedure when explaining the east and west directions. Do this again with other children until you are satisfied that the children understand. When they connect landmarks with directions, the children begin to understand that directions help us locate places in our environment. You may ask, for example, "In what direction must I walk if I want to go to that water tower?" To help reinforce these directional skills, provide a number of follow-up activities. For example, "Simon Says" can be adapted to a directional format—"Simon says, 'Take three steps west,' " "Simon says, 'Turn to the south.' "

After the children have had this fundamental introduction to direction, extend the understandings to their classroom map constructions. When they return to the classroom with their compasses and direction signs, have them repeat the process for finding north. Then, attach the "north" card on the north wall. On which wall should the south card be placed? East? West? Now, have the children determine how the walls of their classroom maps should be labeled.

After finding the classroom directions by using the compass, teach the children to orient maps in the proper direction whenever they use them. North on the map should always face north in the classroom. This may involve turning chairs or sitting on the floor; however, by always turning themselves and their maps in the direction of true north, children avoid the widespread misconception that "north" is the direction toward the front of the room.

Map Scale

The idea of scale should be introduced in a general way rather than in a mathematical sense in the early primary grades. Map scales can be extremely confusing

to young children because they find it difficult to associate the size of a map to the real dimensions of a physical feature in the environment. However, children must realize that maps need to be small enough to be easily carried and handy to use. To illustrate this point, with the three-dimensional classroom map and large flat map still on display, give the children a sheet of $8\frac{1}{2} \times 11$ inch drawing paper and, using their special legend that was previously developed, draw a smaller version. Some children will immediately reduce the size of the classroom features proportionately. Others will have greater difficulty trying to reproduce the large classroom features on their smaller papers. Some start by drawing one feature as big as it is on the large map and then wonder why they don't have room to include all the rest. Remember that children's sense of proportion, like other perception skills, are yet unrefined. Through trial-and-error exploration, the children will soon learn to make their individual maps smaller than the classroom model and large flat map. Each of their maps, according to Ekiss, Trapido-Lurie, Phillips, and Hinde (2007), "should have the following map elements: Title, Orientation, Author (cartographer), Date, and Symbols . . . , which create the acronym TOADS" (p. 8).

Model Neighborhoods and Communities

Using the small-world approach to map instruction should not stop at the classroom door. During grades 2 or 3, children should be engaged in representing other meaningful places in the local environment. The process of building a model neighborhood or community, for example, is a thrilling and challenging mission that presents a way for students not only to learn about their neighborhood or community but also to master beginning map skills as well.

As with the model classroom, most materials for the model neighborhood or community consist of packaging items easily found around the house. Oatmeal boxes and toilet paper or paper towel rolls are excellent building materials for trees, cylindrically shaped buildings, silos, or structures such as large oil storage tanks; cereal boxes, tissue boxes, candy boxes, and pasta boxes easily represent tall buildings, apartment houses, or stores; and different-sized milk or juice cartons make nice houses with peaked roofs. All you need to do is provide the proper work materials (construction paper, tempera paint, crayons, marking pens, school glue) and the children will go right to work.

I like to start the actual model with something the children can directly observe—the school building. Walk around the outside of the school and carefully note its shape and size. Then, encourage the students to look over the boxes and decide on one, or combination of, boxes that might most accurately represent their school. Discuss the colors of paint or construction paper that might work best to cover the box as well as any possibilities to highlight special features (trees, flagpole, parking lot) so it would look as much like the real school as possible. Toy cars, school buses, bicycles, and other vehicles also add to the realism.

A model neighborhood or community can expand outward from the school as students visit the immediate neighborhood, a shopping center, the zoo, community services buildings, and so on. You might limit the project to the immediate school neighborhood, or extend it throughout the year as the children learn about all the elements of communities.

Story Maps

Good children's books offer fabulous opportunities for exposure to early mapping activities. Some books are perfect; chain stories that the children (or teacher) can illustrate easily are excellent selections. For example, in Eric Hill's popular "lift-the-flap" story *Spot's First Walk* (Putffin), a curious puppy meets all kinds of new animal friends as he wanders behind fences, by a chicken coop, and near a pond on his first venture away from home. As you read the story, invite the children to predict whom they might meet under each flap. When the story is finished, have the children draw pictures of the snail, fish, bees, hen, and other friends Spot met along the way. Their simple illustrations can be arranged as a floor display, creating a sequence map of Spot's travels. The children can retell the story by explaining what happened at each point as they walk along their "map." It might be fun to cut out "puppy footprints" from construction paper and have the children place them on the floor to trace Spot's footsteps (pawsteps?) as they travel from place to place. Other stories appropriate for story maps include *Katie and The Big Snow* by Virginia Lee Burton (Houghton Mifflin), *Rosie's Walk* by Pat Hutchins (Macmillan), and *Harry the Dirty Dog* by Gene Zion (HarperTrophy). A sample story map for the traditional tale, *The Three Billy Goats Gruff*, is shown in Figure 5.6.

The Globe

Since the early primary-grade child's concept of the planet Earth in space is quite limited, planned instruction in related concepts is not particularly successful. Nonetheless, you should not totally do away with globe activities in the primary-grade classroom. With simplified 12-inch globes, children can understand that the globe is a representation of Earth, much like the three-dimensional models were representations of their classroom. Have the children examine their three-dimensional classroom map and talk about how their classroom map is a model of their classroom—a place in the real world. Next, talk about how it would feel to be an astronaut and to be able to look at Earth from way above, like they were able to view their classroom model. Show a satellite image of Earth (http://earth.google.com/) and ask the children describe what they see. Focus on some broad attributes, such as how the land masses and bodies of water look. Show the children a globe and discuss how it is a model of the earth, just like their three-dimensional representation was a model of their classroom. The globe should include a minimum amount of detail and, if at all possible, should show the land masses in no more than three colors and the bodies of water in a consistent shade of blue. Only the names of the continents, countries, largest cities, and largest bodies of water should be labeled. Globes that show more detail easily confuse the very young child.

FIGURE 5.6 Story Map

Emphasize the utility of maps by trying to jam the globe into your pocket or purse. Talk together about the difficulties of the task. Ask what the problem would be if the only thing we had to find our way around the Earth was a globe that we carried in our pocket or purse. Thankfully, we learned that it would be much easier to slice off a section of the globe and flatten it out so it would be much easier to carry around. Compare a flat map to the globe, associating the pairing with the three-dimensional classroom model and large flat map of the classroom.

Globes can become important informal teaching tools in your early-grade classroom. When reading stories, children may wish to know where their favorite characters live; you can show them the location. For example, if you are reading the children a story that is set in Los Angeles, you may want to show them where Los Angeles is located in relationship to your community. However, even this would be meaningless unless you relate it to the children's own experiences. Say, "A globe tells you where places are. Pictures tell you what the place is like." After pointing out where Los Angeles is located, show some photos or illustrations of familiar features or landmarks. Familiarize young children with the globe and with the fact that they can use the globe to locate special places. The basic globe concepts for development in the primary grades are (1) to understand the basic roundness of the Earth, (2) to understand the differences between land and water areas, and (3) to understand that Earth is mostly made up of water and seven large land areas known as continents. The students should know that our country is called the United States of America and that it is located on the continent of North America. North America is made up of several countries: north of the United States is Canada; south is Mexico; the Atlantic Ocean is east of the United States, and the Pacific Ocean is west. The United States is made up of 50 states; most touch each other. Two states that don't are Alaska and Hawaii. By the end of the primary grades, children should locate their home state on a map of the United States.

The aim of beginning map instruction is to make it possible for young children to learn about maps through informal, open-ended, learning experiences. To supplement these indispensable experiences, it is wise for teachers to read to their children among from the many children's books that offer information about maps and mapping:

- Joan Sweeney's *Me on the Map* (Dragonfly): A young girl starts with crayon drawings of her bedroom and house and then expands to street, town, and eventually a map of the world as she informs us all about cartography.
- Tish Rabe's *There's a Map on My Lap!* (Dragonfly): Dr. Seuss's famous Cat in the Hat introduces the reader to a wide variety of maps and map formats in Seuss's traditional lyrical rhyme.
- Jack Knowlton's *Maps and Globes* (HarperTrophy): This book offers a brief history of mapmaking, explains how to read maps, and introduces readers to a variety of maps.

Map Instruction in the Middle and Upper Grades

The map and globe skills that we will teach in the middle and upper elementary school grades are exactly the same as the ones we used throughout the early grades. Obviously, however, they will need to be applied in much more complex settings and used for increasingly varied purposes. While in the early grades, children acquired basic map concepts and skills by representing what they knew about the real world through constructed models and pictorial maps, each supplemented with helpful, reinforcing teacher-initiated questions and prompts. They also made use of prepared maps that (1) were highly pictorial in nature or quite uncomplicated; (2) often represented a directly observable environment such as the school, park, zoo, or neighborhood, or an imaginary place such as "Candyland" or "Spaceland"; and (3) gradually expanded their horizons to include more distant locations such as the community, state, the United States, North America, seven continents, and major bodies of water.

Now, as they enter the middle elementary school grades, the children will not only build on and refine these skills but their map making and map usage

experiences will help them arrive at new and important understandings. A trip to Bynam Faw's fifth-grade classroom illustrates how map construction remains an important process in the upper elementary grades, for visually representing the new content helps trigger the use of background knowledge while it builds and uses important map reading processes.

Bynam Faw's fifth-grade social studies curriculum integrates geography and history while teaching about the major regions of the United States. The region currently under study is the Great Plains. Students have been captivated by stories of how settlers pushed west into the Great Plains during the 1860s and settled what are now Kansas, Nebraska, South Dakota, and North Dakota. They learned that wheat grew very well in the rich soil of the Great Plains and became the most important crop of the region. However, they also found out that early farmers faced many challenges that often ruined or damaged their crops—storms, dry spells, insects, blizzards, and floods. Nevertheless, the pioneers were relentless and worked hard to build successful farms throughout the region.

NCSS STANDARDS

II. *Time, Continuity, and Change*

III. *People, Places, and Environments*

One of the major resources for the study of this region was the collection of "Little House" books by Laura Ingalls Wilder. The students had learned that Laura's childhood was spent traveling by covered wagon west from Wisconsin to Indian Territory in Kansas and eventually to Dakota Territory. Most recently, the class had been reading *Little House on the Prairie* (HarperTrophy), a story filled with the challenges faced by the pioneering Ingalls family as they moved to the Kansas prairie in the late 1800s, built their own home, and established a successful farm. Wilder offers a lasting storybook depiction of pioneer life in Kansas by including trips to Independence, the nearest town to their farm. Laura makes it seem like the town is much farther away from the farm than the 13 miles it truly is, but to a little girl seated on a bone-jarring buckboard, that can seem like a long way to go. Today, Mr. Faw planned to help his students explore the kinds of buildings the Ingalls family might have found in Independence: "Imagine that you are going with the Ingalls family on a trip from their farm to Independence, Kansas. What do you expect to find there?" After a brief discussion, Mr. Faw divided the students randomly into teams of two and assigned each team to a center dealing with a major building: one-room school, church, hotel, general store, livery stable, blacksmith shop, jail, lumberyard, barbershop, cooper (barrel maker), and saloon. The students were advised that they would become "experts" on these places by examining a website Mr. Faw had accessed for each group (hoover.archives.gov/LIW/pioneertown/activities_pioneertown.html).

After the students completed their research, they were directed to write a short descriptive paragraph on index cards detailing what they uncovered. The "One-Room School" team, for example, wrote this narrative:

Schools in early prairie towns were one-room school houses. There you could find students ages 6 to 16 and eight grades in one room. There was one teacher for all of them, and older students often helped the younger ones.

The index cards were displayed on a large chart to summarize the kinds of buildings that would be found in small prairie towns of the 1860s. Next, students were instructed to use any of a number of cardboard boxes that Mr. Faw gathered beforehand, along with construction paper, paint, crayons, and other art materials, to construct a model of their buildings. First, Mr. Faw reviewed with the students the materials that the pioneers used to construct these buildings and advised them that they were free to use the computer, encyclopedia, textbook, or any library references to gather any additional information. The students went right to work. After the models were constructed, they were arranged on a tabletop display (with the index card information chart behind them). The groups were eager to function as tour guides, telling "sightseers" about their pioneer town as other classes came to visit throughout the day.

As you read about how these fifth-graders mapped their pioneer town, did you sense how their construction activity was similar to the representations, or models, assembled by children during the early elementary grades? Teachers do not discard basic map skills instruction after the early grades, but rather adjust instruction within appropriate contexts in an effort to help children refine and strengthen their

A selection of high-quality maps and globes furnish teachers with powerful geographic tools.

thinking and comprehension processes. Upper-grade map skills are best acquired as a result of continuous, developmental instruction by teachers ready to reinforce and extend what has been accomplished during the early grades.

In addition to map construction, children in the upper elementary school grades are helped to acquire the insights and understandings vital to drawing out meaning, relationships, and ideas from increasingly detailed and abstract maps. Comparing this process to reading a book, you might say that children are taught to read stories in first grade but for the most part by using picture books having simple text. Later, as the children mature and become more skillful, they read progressively more challenging materials such as chapter books. Likewise, the delightfully picture-like representations on the maps the children create or use during the early primary grades gradually evolve into more abstract representations such as road maps or topographical maps.

It is important to provide a wide variety of maps for your young geographers, both as sources of information and as models for their own map construction:

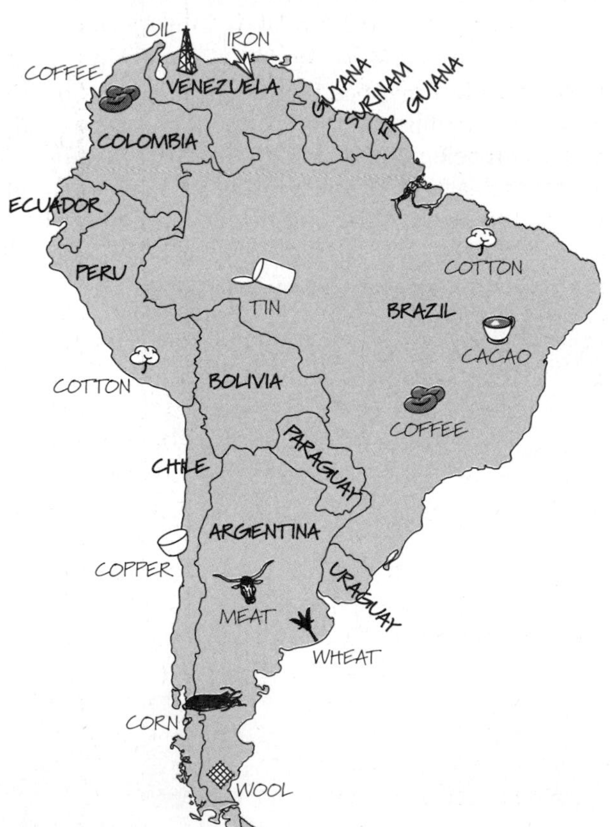

FIGURE 5.7 Product Map of South America

- *Political maps* show the line boundaries between countries, states, cities, and other human-made features.
- *Physical maps* show landforms and waterways, such as deserts, islands, forests, rivers, lakes, mountains, straits, and bays.
- *Product maps* show agricultural or manufactured goods in a region, such as dairy, corn, oil, wheat, or automobiles. (See Figure 5.7.)
- *Tourist maps* show the major attractions in an area—resorts, hotels, entertainment, buildings, and other sights. Tourist maps are usually rendered as a three-dimensional view of a place, but look more like works of art than actual maps.
- *Raised relief maps* are molded vinyl three-dimensional maps with bumpy surfaces that help children feel and see the differences in mountains, hills, plateaus, and plains. These are ideal for tactile learners.
- *Climate maps* show a region's general pattern of weather conditions, seasons, and weather extremes like hurricanes, droughts, or rainy periods. Have you ever wondered why one area of the world is a desert, another a plain, and another a rain forest and why are there different types of life in each area? The answer is climate.

- *Historical maps* show what places were like long ago and how they changed over time. They may show the routes of the explorers to North America, for example, or what the original 13 colonies looked like. They could show the United States in 1861 when the Civil War began. The map may show the states that wanted to break away from the Union and become their own nation (Confederate States of America) and the northern states (the Union). The 1861 map may also show that not all the land was yet organized into states—the Dakota Territory and New Mexico Territory, for example.
- *Road maps* are maps that help us figure out a good route between two places. If you want to travel from Boston to Atlanta, a good road map will tell you how far and in which direction you must travel.

Students must be helped to understand that they can learn many things about our planet from different types of maps, and also that they are able to communicate to others what they know about a place by constructing many kinds of maps of their own. If elementary school students are going to acquire geographic competency, they must acquire the necessary tools and techniques to think geographically. Geographic information is compiled, organized, and stored in many ways, but to think geographically, maps are central to understanding and analysis. If we expect children to use these increasingly complex maps successfully, we must help them arrive at deeper understandings of and insights into the six basic map skills.

Advanced Map Reading Strategies

The overriding purpose of teaching children to make and use maps in the elementary school is to help them acquire the knowledge and the thinking processes essential for understanding the world around us. Such a goal requires that teachers understand the fundamental ways children build higher-level map skills so they can create productive, developmentally suitable learning experiences. Earlier in this chapter, you learned the six basic skills that define map skills instruction. The key to effective upper-grade instruction is to provide the children with a wide range of instructional experiences that are directly associated with the new and advanced components of these skills as the children progressively confront them. Each of the new and advanced components will be described next.

Map Symbols

The map genre most frequently used with upper elementary children is the topographic map. Topographic maps come in many varieties; they can represent roads, rivers, buildings, camping areas, parks, and native vegetation—almost anything natural or made by humans. Learning how to interpret the increasingly abstract symbols used to represent these features is the first step in using topographic maps in the upper elementary grades. This does not happen as soon as the children step foot an the higher-grade classroom, however; their first maps will use pictorial

symbols similar to those used in the lower grades and gradually become more abstract as the children transition into the upper grades. During their earliest experiences with topographic maps, for example, the children will find that the symbol used for a camping site will be a tent, or the symbol for an oil-producing area an oil derrick. (Figure 5.7 is a good example of showing such symbols.) Progressively, the symbols will become more abstract. On some maps, for instance, stores, churches, schools, and other buildings will be indicated by various geometric shapes, point symbols (dots, circles, or stars, for example) will show cities, and colors will designate features such as vegetation (green) or water (blue).

We do not now fully understand the mental processes involved in learning to understand these increasingly abstract symbols; theoretical work in this area has been meager at best. With the exception of Piaget's insights, little research has been carried out that can be applied directly to map learning. What the slight research does indicate, however, is that once they move through the upper elementary grades, children's lack of success in reading maps becomes one of the most predictable outcomes of map instruction. Bednarz, Acheson, and Bednarz (2006) report that "assessments indicate that students are not competent map users. An analysis of the National Assessment of Educational Process (NAEP) geography exam revealed that at every grade level (grades 4, 8, and 12) test items that required students to use and interpret maps were the most challenging" (p. 399). Among the reasons offered for these low scores is that hands-on and active learning opportunities experienced during the earlier grades tends to level off once the children are faced with the kinds of nonrepresentational symbols they encounter on more complex maps. Bednarz, Acheson, and Bednarz (2006) advise, however, that the children's difficulties are not limited to the increasingly abstract symbols they now encounter. For some reason, they appear to be confused even in dealing with pictorial map symbols. Consider, for example, how a drawing of a cow, intended to represent a cattle-raising area, can puzzle some children. Some think that it represents the existence of one giant cow in the location rather than a cattle-raising region. A car symbol intended to represent an automobile-manufacturing location has been interpreted as the location of a parking lot or traffic jam. Color is often interpreted incorrectly as well. The green commonly used to designate low elevation is often thought to represent grassland or forest. Mark Twain's *Tom Sawyer Abroad*, originally published in 1894, brings these symbol interpretation problems to light with the kind of humor we can associate only with the author. In the book, Tom Sawyer and Huckleberry Finn set sail for Africa in a professor's futuristic hot air balloon. As they awake on the second day of the journey, the boys shared some interesting ideas regarding maps.

> ". . . we ought to be past Illinois, oughtn't we?"
>
> "Certainly."
>
> "Well, we ain't."
>
> "What's the reason we ain't?"
>
> "I know by the color. We're right over Illinois yet. And you can see for yourself that Indiana ain't in sight."

"I wonder what's the matter with you, Huck. You know by the color?"

"Yes, of course I do."

"What's the color got to do with it?"

"It's got everything to do with it. Illinois is green, Indiana is pink. You show me any pink down here, if you can. No, sir; it's green."

"Indiana pink? Why, what a lie!"

"It ain't no lie; I've seen it on the map, and it's pink."

You never see a person so aggravated and disgusted. He says:

"Well, if I was such a numbskull as you, Huck Finn, I would jump over. Seen it on the map! Huck Finn, did you reckon the States was the same color out-of-doors as they are on the map?"

"Tom Sawyer, what's a map for? Ain't it to learn you facts?"

"Of course."

"Well, then, how's it going to do that if it tells lies? That's what I want to know."

"Shucks, you muggins! It don't tell lies."

"It don't, don't it?"

"No, it don't."

"All right, then; if it don't, there ain't no two States the same color. You git around that if you can, Tom Sawyer." (pp. 42–43)

Bednarz, Acheson, and Bednarz (2006) go on to say, "One explanation for these [symbol interpretation problems and] low assessment scores is that few

Constructing three-dimensional models in the upper grades helps reinforce the idea that maps are representations of real places in the environment.

social studies teachers . . . are prepared and motivated to teach about and with maps" (p. 399). Despite this apparent apathy, the writers suggest that instruction can make a difference; children's understanding of maps and how to use them can be improved with suitable instructional practices. One suggestion offered by the writers is that teachers maintain the practice of having children construct maps in the upper elementary grades like they did in the earlier grades, for most maps can be tied directly into the subject matter under study. Consider, for example, Paul Revere's famous ride. It becomes much more dramatic and vivid if fifth-graders construct a map of the event showing the starting point, route traveled, and eventual destination. A second recommendation was to encourage the use of online maps such as Google Earth. These aerial and satellite produced images are widely available and easy to use.

Place Location and Relative Location: Grid Systems

Sometimes people become confused when they hear the geographic terms *place* and *location*: "I thought they meant the same thing! You mean they're not? Well, what's the difference between place and location?" Because these terms are used interchangeably in our daily lives, people find it difficult to understand why they have different meanings when used by geographers. To be true young geographers, children should realize that these two terms have different meanings for professional geographers. *Location* tells you where things are, while *place* tells you what they are like (the physical and human characteristics). If someone asked me, for example, "Where do you live?" I could say, "I live at 123 Main Street." The *location* of my house is 123 Main Street. But if I wanted to clarify the location, I might add, "It's the beige stucco house with green shutters." With that brief explanation, I described some distinct physical characteristics that helped distinguish my *place* (house) from other places (houses) on the block. Likewise, on maps, there are many places (deserts, mountains, rivers, highways, trees, factories, coffee-growing regions) that children must learn to locate. Locating places is the basic responsibility of being a young geographer.

Upper grade children would find it very difficult to locate specific places on most of the wide selection of maps they will be using without understanding grid systems, which are characteristic of the maps and mapping experiences they will now encounter. Map grids consist of a pattern of rows and columns that form quadrilateral (usually square or rectangle) grid sections. Most times the lines that form the quadrilaterals are straight but occasionally they are curved. Each vertical column on many map grids is designated with a letter, while the horizontal rows are numbered. (On some maps this arrangement may be reversed.) Any location can be then be found by finding the quadrilateral named with a paired letter and number.

As with the early grades, upper grade children must be offered a number of experiences and activities to help establish and reinforce newly introduced skills and concepts. One that I especially like to use is called Guess Who.

Guess Who. Arrange student desks in rows. Attach a letter of the alphabet, starting with *A* at the front left desk, *B* to the front desk of the next row, and so on. These letters should be plainly seen by someone standing at the front of the room. Display a numeral for each column, starting with *1* at the first desk, *2* at the desk behind 1, and so on, again making sure it can be clearly seen from the front of the room. Randomly select five children and have them go to the front of the room and stand with their backs turned and eyes closed. Select five more children to sneak to the front, each tap one child lightly on the shoulder, and return to their seats. Then, the children in the original group open their eyes and try to guess who tapped them by calling out a grid square—for example, "*C-5* tapped me." Alternate places each time you play and make sure everyone gets a chance to be in both groups.

Latitude and Longitude

In the upper elementary grades, children use a very special grid system to help them answer the important geographical question, "Where am I?" That logical grid system is called the *latitude and longitude system*. This system consists of east-west lines called *parallels of latitude* and north-south lines called *meridians of longitude* (see Figure 5.8).

The parallels of latitude are imaginary lines that encircle the Earth horizontally. They measure distances in degrees north or south of the equator (designated as zero degrees latitude). The parallels grow smaller in circumference as they approach both poles, but each degree of latitude is approximately 69 miles apart. The vertical longitude lines run from pole to pole around the earth and measure distances in degrees east or west of the prime meridian (designated as zero degrees longitude). The distance between the longitude lines is about 69 miles at the equator and gradually gets shorter until the lines meet at the poles. Because they are all exactly the same, any of the longitude lines could have been selected as the prime meridian, but Greenwich, England, was arbitrarily established as the site of the prime meridian by an international conference in 1884.

In mathematics, circles are measured in degrees, and since the Earth is basically circular, it was decided to measure latitude and longitude in degrees, too. To

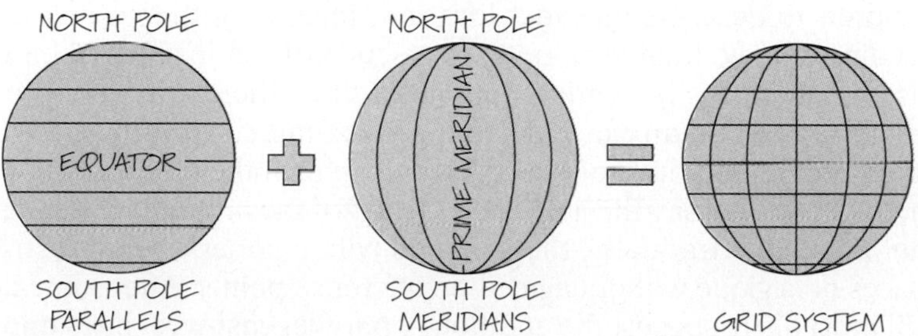

FIGURE 5.8 The Earth's Grid System

be precise in locating places on the Earth's surface, degrees of latitude and longitude have been divided into minutes (60 in a degree) and seconds (60 in a minute). So, the location of Paris, France, would look like this: 48° 52′ N, 02° 20′ E (48 degrees and 52 minutes north of the equator and 2 degrees and 20 minutes east of the prime meridian).

Latitude and longitude lines provide us with the *absolute location* of a place on the earth's surface. For example, the absolute location of the White House is established as 39° N and 77° W, a set of coordinates referred to as a *location's map address*. A location's map address is one kind of absolute location. Oftentimes people regard street address as another kind of absolute location, but others argue that grid coordinates should be considered the only exact form of absolute location. For elementary school purposes, I like to recommend using both map addresses and street addresses as types of absolute location. In addition to its map address, the absolute location of the White House could also be established as 1600 Pennsylvania Avenue NW, Washington DC 20500. *Relative location*, on the other hand, is determined by locating one place in relationship to another place or to nearby landmarks. For example, if we say that the White House is located in Washington DC, situated on the banks of the Potomac River and bordered by the states of Virginia to the west and Maryland to the east, north, and south, we're describing the city's relative location. Relative location describes the location of one place on the Earth in relationship to one or more other places. Relative location is not as precise as absolute location, but it is useful for describing where places or things are or to offer a general idea of its geographic location. If I just simply tell you that Washington DC was located at 39° north, 77° west, you probably couldn't picture its location quite as well as if I told you that it was in the Middle Atlantic states, bordered by Maryland and Virginia. Or, if someone asked you directions to the site of the world's largest fiberglass fish, it would be more helpful to say, "Go through two traffic signals and turn left onto Flounder Street. It's next to the first gas station on your left," than to give its coordinates, "It's located at the intersection of 45° north latitude and 91° west longitude."

The importance of a grid system such as latitude and longitude as a means of absolute location can be illustrated to the children with a large, unmarked ball. Lead a discussion comparing the similarities of the large ball and Earth as represented by the classroom globe. Glue a small plastic ship to the ball and ask the children to describe its exact location, imagining themselves shipwrecked and needing to radio their location to be rescued (the ship marks their wreck). They will discover that this is nearly impossible, since there is no point of reference from which to describe an exact location. For example, if the children say the ship is located on the front side of the ball, you can turn the ball and the statement will be incorrect. If they say the ship is on the top of the ball, turn it back again to the original position. Gradually, the students will experience the frustration of locating places on a globe without agreed-on reference points. After some deliberation, they will most likely suggest the addition of parallel east-west lines and instruct the rescue squad to search an area "three lines down from the middle line."

On closer examination of this arrangement, and after high-level interactions with their teacher, the children will discover that the rescuers need to travel all around the world along the "third line down from the middle line" to find them unless given even more precise locations by devising meridians, or north-south lines. The rescue squad then only needs to find where the two points meet. Eventually, the children can be led to locate many well-known places in the world using latitude and longitude. Determining precise locations by using actual degrees of latitude and longitude may be beyond the capabilities of most fourth- and fifth-grade children. Guide them, however, in using latitude and longitude for locating general areas, such as the low latitudes (23½° north and south of the equator), the middle latitudes (between 23½° and 66½° north and south of the equator), and the high latitudes (between 66½° north and the North Pole and 66½° south and the South Pole). Children can generalize about the climatic similarities within these areas. In which latitudes are most cities located? Where is the weather warm (or cold) throughout most of the year? Show them how to find places east or west or north or south of their location by using meridians. After careful observation, they may find many surprising facts. For example, Rome, Italy, is nearer the North Pole than is New York; Detroit is north of Windsor, Ontario; Reno, Nevada, is farther west than Los Angeles, California; the Gulf of California does not touch California at any point; and the Pacific Ocean is east of the Atlantic Ocean at Panama.

Recognizing and expressing absolute and relative location is a sophisticated map skill because it involves not only finding places on a map but also understanding interrelationships among geographical features, such as the influence of rainfall on the vegetation of a region. For example, when examining a rainfall map of Africa, shown in Figure 5.9, children should be able to determine the type of vegetation that might grow in each region and how this influences the ways people live. So, children will find that maps are used for much more than just locating a place or to find the route one must travel to reach a destination. By combining different thematic maps, children will soon learn to discover connections among

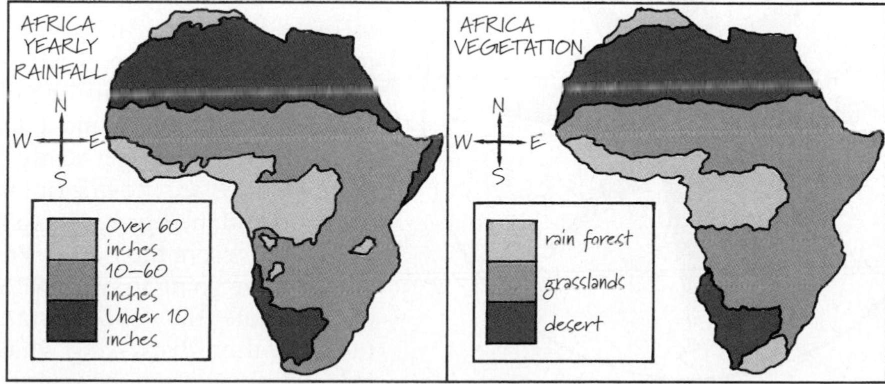

FIGURE 5.9 Rainfall and Vegetation Maps of Africa

phenomena: Where would you expect to find fishing villages in Maine? By recognizing connections among phenomena, children can learn to find answers to questions that are not directly given on a single map.

Cardinal and Intermediate Direction

During the early elementary grades, children formed accurate and clear understandings of the cardinal directions (north, south, east, and west) by participating in suitable map use and map construction activities. And by constructing and using varieties of maps, the children began to understand that, to ensure conformity, cartographers draw maps with north at the top and east at the right. Thus, the younger children acquired the basic understandings that standard placements of cardinal directions, combined with an arbitrary system of logical symbols, establish the underpinning of a graphic system designed to inform people how to locate places in the world.

Now, in the upper elementary grades, the children will be introduced to *intermediate directions* (also called *ordinal* or *intercardinal directions*). The children learn that when they move in directions between north, south, east, and west, they are going in one of the four intermediate directions. Each of the intermediate directions is located between the cardinal directions: northeast, southeast, southwest, and northwest. The children should notice that each of the intermediate directions begins with either north or south and adds either east or west to put together an intermediate direction.

Most of the maps the children used in the lower elementary grades printed the cardinal directions on the four sides of the map. In the upper grades, most maps will do away with those direction tags and, instead, supply a direction indicator called a *compass rose*. A compass rose is a small figure on a map displaying the cardinal directions and sometimes the intermediate directions. An illustration of a compass rose is shown in Figure 5.10.

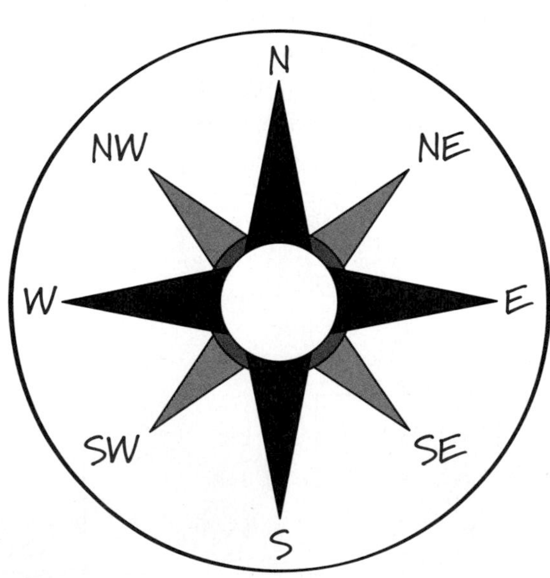

FIGURE 5.10 Compass Rose

The compass rose is one of the three basic features the children must familiarize themselves with as they get ready to study a map. The other two are the *title* (it tells what the map is about) and the *legend* (it explains the symbols used to represent the Earth). For example, if the students are going to work with a political map of their state, they should start by reading the title and then discussing what they think the map will show. Then they should look at the legend. They will notice that on a political map the legend will show different lines that indicate county, state, or international borders as well as the symbols used to indicate major and minor cities. Finally, the children should locate the compass rose and determine which direction is north on the map. The map should then be oriented so that north on the map will be facing the same direction as north on the compass. (You must label the walls of your classroom to reveal the actual directions those walls face.) These three elements should be checked each time the children use or make a map.

Notice how Erma Moonflower uses a road map to help reinforce her fourth-grade students' understanding of three of the six map reading skills: *direction, symbol*, and *place location*.

To start, Ms. Moonflower arranged the students into groups of two. She distributed to each pair a road map of the United States showing two major types of roads: interstate highways and U.S. highways. Today, the students were going to focus on interstate highways; tomorrow they will deal with U.S. highways. To initiate the lesson, Ms. Moonflower displayed a sample sign for each of the two major highways (see Figure 5.11).

Ms. Moonflower asked the students to use the compass rose to orient their road maps, check the title to see what kind of map it was, and examine the legend to determine which of the two sample signs represented an interstate highway. They had no trouble finding the information on the legend. Orel added that he knew the first sample sign represented interstate highways because he saw those signs on summer vacation with his family. Yolanda was even more insightful: "My road map shows that the first sign is on the roads that go through two or more states. Interstate means traveling between two or more states, so the first sign must be an interstate sign."

The teacher then asked her students to carefully examine the map of the interstate highway system to see if they could uncover any pattern in the numbering of the highways. In a flash, Ricardo noticed that interstate highways running east and west were numbered evenly while those running

FIGURE 5.11 Interstate and U.S. Highway Signs

north and south had odd numbers. Ms. Moonflower passed out a yellow marker to each group and asked the students to highlight each north–south highway. After each group did so, Ms. Moonflower asked the students to start in the north and identify the states through which each interstate highway passed. She then challenged them to see if they could find another pattern, this time using only the highlighted north–south interstate highways. This challenge took a little time, but the students eventually discovered that the higher the number, the farther east the highway: for example, Route 95 runs north and south along the east coast while Route 15 does the same in the west.

Next, Ms. Moonflower passed out an orange marker to each group and asked the students to highlight the east–west interstate highways. In like manner, she directed the students to identify the states through which each passed and challenged them to uncover a numbering pattern. They found that the highest even-numbered interstate highways were in the north and the numbers gradually got smaller as one traveled south. For example, Route 90 was northernmost on their maps while Route 40 was southernmost.

Ms. Moonflower then assigned each group a pair of cities and directed them to use a marking pen to trace the interstate highway that would connect each pair. The children were required to explain the direction they needed to travel as well as compute the distance between the city of origin and destination.

To culminate the lesson, Ms. Moonflower asked the students to reexamine their road maps of the United States to recommend a route for a new interstate highway, number it according to the pattern revealed previously, and provide good reasons why the highway would be useful or helpful.

Teaching with and about maps must be carried out in various contexts. Textbooks, worksheets, and workbooks offer a number of interesting and productive activities and lessons, but it must be stressed that hands-on experiences along with various reasoning and problem-solving contexts should continue throughout the elementary and middle school grades.

Scale

Cartographers draw topographic maps to scale when they reduce the size of every real feature an equal percentage to accurately portray the Earth. Simply defined, then, *scale* is considered the relationship between distance on the map and distance on the Earth. Let us say that the distance between Community A and Community B is 5 miles. To show this relationship on a paper map, we could draw the communities 1 inch apart. Once we decide on this proportional representation, or map scale, it must remain constant for all other points on the map. So, all other features that are 5 miles apart in the world must also be 1 inch apart on the map;

those 10 miles apart on Earth must be 2 inches apart on that map. The scale of the map is determined by the amount of real-world area covered by the map and the size of the paper used to render the map. Whatever the map scale selected, however, it is usually located in the legend box, which describes the symbols and provides other important information about the map.

Basically, map scale can be expressed in three major ways. Our example expressed scale as a verbal scale. *Verbal scales* are word statements that tell what distance on the map is equal to what distance on the ground, such as, "One inch equals 5 miles" or "One centimeter equals 5 miles." Although verbal scales may appear to be fairly uncomplicated, they are not often found on the topographic maps our upper elementary grade children will be using. Instead, a second type of scale, the graphic scale (sometimes called the *bar scale*) is more widespread. A *graphic scale,* as shown in Figure 5.12, uses a bar or line with separations marked by smaller intersecting lines, similar to a ruler, to help measure straight-line ground distance. By measuring the distance between two points on a map, and then referring to the graphic scale, it is easy to calculate the actual distance between those two locations. First, lay a straight-edged piece of paper on the map so that the ends extend beyond both points. Make a mark on the edge of the paper at each point (see Figure 5.13). On the map of Florida, for example, a student wishes to calculate the distance between Port St. Lucie and West Palm Beach, so she makes a mark on the paper at each of those points. To calculate the straight-line ground distance, she then moves the paper down to the graphic scale and aligns the left mark with zero then looks carefully at the point where the right mark aligns. In this case, it falls slightly past 50 miles, so the student can estimate the distance between Port St. Lucie and West Palm Beach to be approximately 55 miles. Because it is the most uncomplicated of map scales, the graphic scale is the recommended option for use at the elementary school level.

The third common approach to stating map scales is the *representative fraction* (or *ratio*) scale, which indicates how many units on the earth's surface is equal to one unit on the map. See Figure 5.13. It can be written as 1/100,000 or 1:100,000. In the metric system, the representative fraction could be interpreted as one centimeter on the map equals 100,000 centimeters (1 kilometer) on the Earth. Or, in standard measure, it could indicate that one inch on the map is equal to 100,000 inches on the land (about 1.6 miles). The interesting thing about representative

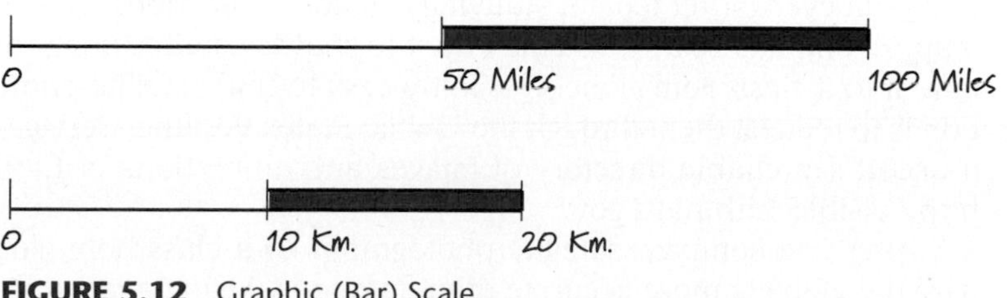

FIGURE 5.12 Graphic (Bar) Scale

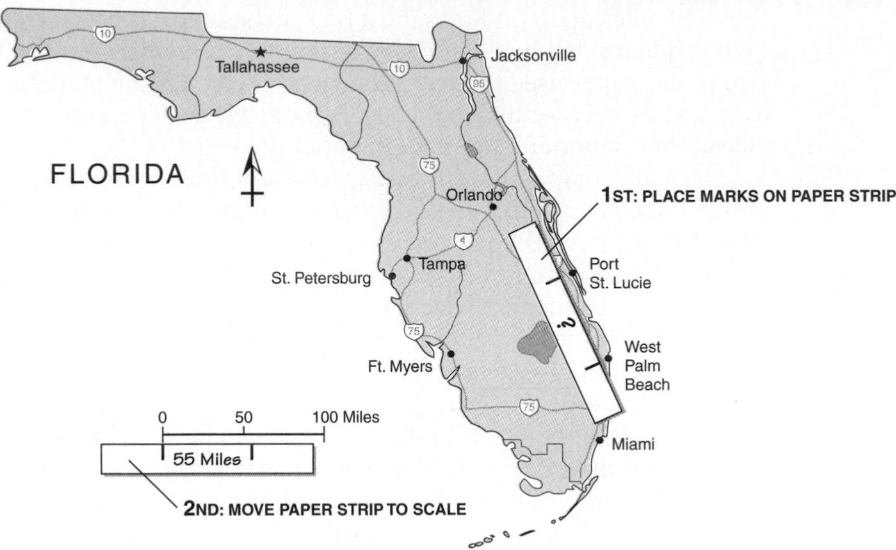

FIGURE 5.13 Using a Graphic Scale

fractions is that the scale does not necessarily need to be represented by regular measuring systems. So, if a child wanted to invent a scale where 1 paperclip on the map is equal to 100,000 paperclips on Earth, it is entirely proper and useful. Although the representative fraction scale is useful on many maps, it can be confusing to many upper elementary grade children because they have difficulty conceptualizing the large ratios.

The Globe

Recall the basic globe-reading skills we discussed for the early grades: informal instruction aimed mainly at helping the children realize that the globe is a model that represents Earth. Their major formal map-reading experiences up to this time dealt with flat maps on which they located cities and other places of interest. They learned how to tell direction and how to compute the distance between one place and another. Now they must learn that a globe is the only accurate map of Earth, and is an even better tool for studying locations, directions, or distances than a flat map. To emphasize this, you may want to show a satellite image of Earth and compare it to a classroom globe. It is fairly easy to find satellite photographs; one option is to request them through the United States Weather Service. Also, NASA has a useful searchable directory of images and animations of Earth on its website http://visibleearth.nasa.gov.

After you compare satellite photographs to a classroom globe, illustrate just why the globe is more accurate than flat maps. Using a large, thin rubber ball or a globe made from papier-mâché, cut the ball in half and draw an outline of North America (or any random shape) on the ball. Have the children apply hand pressure to flatten the ball and discuss the resulting distortions. Then use scissors to cut through the ball along lines that represent longitude lines. Have the children try to flatten the ball again. Although the ball flattens more easily, the drawn outline still becomes distorted. Help the children discover that this is a major problem faced by mapmakers (cartographers) when they attempt to make flat maps of places on the Earth (see Figure 5.14).

Globes help to show shapes of areas exactly as they would appear on the Earth's surface. Unfortunately, maps are not able to do this. Representing a curved surface precisely on a flat map has confounded cartographers for years. A classroom globe shows shapes and areas more accurately than maps. Therefore, globes and maps should be used reciprocally while developing the skills outlined in this chapter.

Many activities can be used to familiarize the children with the globe, the countries of the world, and their locations. For this first activity, you will need an inflatable globe. Start the game by tossing the globe to a child and hope that she or he catches it! That child is responsible for locating a country beginning with the letter *A*. When this child finds one, she or he calls out the country's name, "Angola!" That child then tosses the globe to another child and calls out the letter *B*. That child must then find a country beginning with the letter *B* and call it out, "Bolivia!" Continue in this manner, challenging the children to work through the alphabet: Canada, Denmark, Egypt, Finland, Greece, and so on. If anyone has difficulty, it is helpful to consult a list of countries arranged alphabetically. An alphabetical listing of countries, along with their flags, can be found at the Wikipedia website: http://en.wikipedia.org/wiki/List_of_countries.

Children's books, used in partnership with globes, offer another fun and unique way to learn about the countries of the world. One example is *Humpty Dumpty Sat on the Globe: Geotales from Around the World* by Fereydoun Kian (Wonderglades Kids). On one page Kian shows a map of a country or continent with a list of informative facts (for example, Egyptians invented bowling, Persians invented pants). A character is illustrated on the opposite page in the actual shape

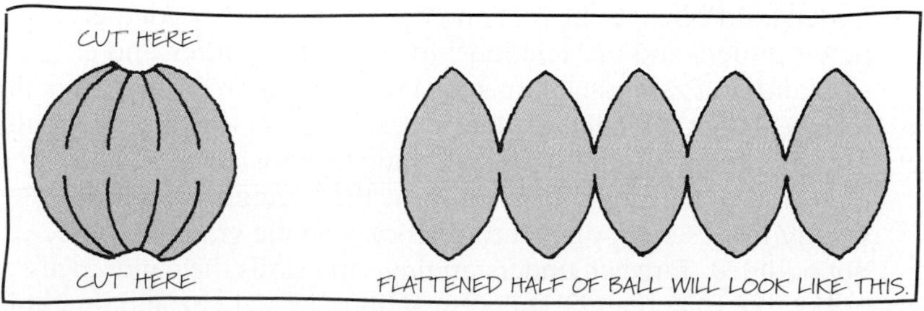

FIGURE 5.14 The Globe as a Flattened Ball

of the country or continent (for example, Italy is a boot, Cuba is an alligator, Africa is a zebra's head) and a clever story ties it all together. A book like this can be an excellent model for upper grade children to use as they rewrite the story. Students can work alone or in a group to play with the illustrations, language, and writing pattern that the author and illustrator used. Their text and illustrations will present additional factual information about Earth within a story format. For example, Gabriele wrote this about her country beneath its map: "Russia has the most movie theaters in the world." Then, on a separate page, she drew a picture to illustrate a connection between a map of Russia and an animal or person shape. She reproduced a famous art print from 1869 showing a Russian man in traditional clothing carrying a huge bear on his back. The way they mixed together formed the outline of Russia. The children gathered all their pages together, added a cover and title page, took turns sharing their contributions, and added the book to their class library.

A Final Thought

A great deal has changed in the field of geography education in recent years. Geography is once again recognized as a core curriculum subject in our elementary schools. New professional standards for teaching geography have joined the five themes as guidelines for what American children should learn in kindergarten through grade 12. Many state departments of education and local school districts now use these standards and themes as guidelines for instruction and for curriculum development. However, the most dramatic changes affecting geography education are changes in the world itself. Many countries do not have the same names they once had, borders have changed, and some countries have dissolved while others have blossomed into existence. Advanced communication makes it possible to become instantaneously connected to people all over the world. The global economy has become increasingly competitive, and precious natural resources are becoming scarcer. The environment becomes more fragile with each passing day.

How can geography help us successfully face these challenges? Studying geography helps develop the skills and understandings that enable us to become geographically informed. That is, geography's tools and techniques help us to better understand where things are and how and why they got there. Geography helps us better understand our relationships to other cultures and environments. Such vision and understanding forms the basis for making reasoned political decisions on all levels, from global trade to the best location for a new community high school.

This chapter introduced wide-ranging considerations fundamental to effective map and globe skills instruction in the elementary school. Because they vary greatly from school district to district, specific grade-by-grade expectancies were not outlined. Targeted understandings and skills the children are expected to know or be able to do can be found in school district curriculum guides. Those guides will also offer activities and resources that are considered a useful part of their social studies program.

From creating community maps to deciphering road maps and satellite images, this chapter offered simple, enjoyable suggestions to teach young geographers the fundamentals of geography. As the power and beauty of geography are unlocked in dynamic social studies classrooms, children can much more clearly see, understand, and appreciate the web of relationships among the people and places on Earth.

REFERENCES

Alibrandi, M. (2005). Elementary how to do it: Online interactive mapping. *Social Studies and the Young Learner, 17*, 1–2.

Augustin, B., & Bailey, M. (2001). Adobe bricks: Building blocks of the Southwest. *Middle Level Learning, 12*, 4–9.

Bednarz, S. W., Acheson, G., & Bednarz, R. S. (2006). Maps and map learning in social studies. *Social Education, 70*, 398–404, 432.

Committee on Geographic Education. (1984). *Guidelines for geographic education: Elementary and secondary schools*. Washington, DC: Association of American Geographers.

Ekiss, G. O., Trapido-Lurie, B., Phillips, J., & Hinde, E. (2007). The world in spatial terms: Map making and map reading. *Social Studies and the Young Learner, 20*, 7–9.

Fertig, G., & Silverman, R. (2007). Walking and talking geography: A small-world approach. *Social Studies and the Young Learner, 20*, 15–18.

Gandy, S. K. (2007). Developmentally appropriate geography. *Social Studies and the Young Learner, 20*, 30–32.

Geography Education Standards Project. (1994). *Geography for life: National geography standards 1994*. Washington, DC: National Geographic Research & Exploration.

Grosvenor, G. M. (2007). The excitement of geography. *Social Studies and the Young Learner, 20*, 4–6.

National Geographic-Roper 2002 global geographic literacy survey [Online]. (2002), Available: www.nationalgeographic.com/education/teacher_community/pdf/NGS-Roper-GeoLitReport2002.pdf.

O'Mahony, K. (2003, March). Transforming geography in our schools. New horizons for learning [Online]. Available: www.newhorizons.org/trans/omahony.htm.

Sobel, D. (1998). *Mapmaking with children: Education for the elementary years*. Portsmouth, NH: Heinemann.

Twain, M. (2001). Tom Sawyer abroad. Available: http://books.google.com/books?id=hI8DGkScAvUC&vq=Tom+Sawyer+Abroad.

CHAPTER 6

Young Political Scientists
Citizens in Action

What Does Today's Civics Look Like?

Helena Rubin's students are gathered around a worktable at the back of the classroom. Anna Mae carefully measures one turtle while Bradley weighs another on an electronic scale. They and their classmates are finding out that learning can be useful—and fun. Ms. Rubin's classroom became one of the first classrooms around the country to become involved in a long-term project to save Vietnam Pond turtles threatened with extinction. These Southeastern Asian turtles are now considered extinct in their home habitat in a very small area of Central Vietnam. Their natural habitat was either destroyed by the chemical Agent Orange used during the Vietnam War or has been converted to rice fields. Because there is no protection program in their homeland, the Asian Turtle Consortium has tapped several schools nationally to help address the plight of this species. The schools will help to breed a new generation of these turtles in the United States and send them back to conservation sites in Vietnam.

Ms. Rubin's class received its 10 turtles in October and has been faithfully feeding, weighing, and measuring them since then; they have kept careful records of the turtles' development. The turtles were about $1\frac{1}{2}$ years old when they arrived, and the five largest will be sent back to Vietnam at the end of the school year. "It's a big responsibility," commented Marisol. "I was really excited when I found out the importance of this project. When I was little, I always wondered what I could do to help animals in danger of extinction. Now I know I can make a difference."

Buoyed by the feeling of responsibility they acquired while working with the turtle project, Ms. Rubin's students have been inspired to tackle additional opportunities for community volunteerism as they have arisen. They adopted a local park and pledged to keep it clean, packed breakfasts for the homeless as part of a Martin Luther King Day service project, collected funds for the March of Dimes, made placemats and took them to a local nursing home to decorate meal trays on Valentine's Day, and raised $200 for a classmate's family whose house was damaged by a terrible fire. Through their incredible thirst for involvement, Ms. Rubin's young citizens took their first ambitious steps into the realm of real-life learning called *service learning*. Service learning encourages active assistance through student projects that meet the needs of groups or individuals within the community. It helps students become engaged in community matters as conscientious citizens and helps give students the assurance that they can make a difference in their communities. Although service learning cuts across all curricular areas, it is a big part of the discipline known as *civics* (sometimes called *political science* or *government* in high school or college).

NCSS STANDARDS

- **III.** *People, Places, and Environments*
- **VI.** *Power, Authority, and Governance*
- **IX.** *Global Connections*
- **X.** *Civic Ideals and Practice*

What Is Civics?

Civics is the study of political and legal systems, about our rights and responsibilities as citizens, and about how our government works. Specialists who study governments and the obligations of citizenship are called *political scientists*. In this chapter, elementary school students will be referred to as *young political scientists* or *young citizens* because, in dynamic social studies classrooms, they participate in citizenship education activities throughout the year, applying their civic knowledge to the solution of real problems—just like professional political scientists and active young citizens. Their role in the classroom is based on the belief that education in a democracy must be what Alexis de Tocqueville called "an apprenticeship in liberty."

An unquestioned goal of public education over the years has been to prepare students for effective citizenship. The National Council for the Social Studies (2001) has defined an effective citizen as one "who has the knowledge, skills, and attitudes required to assume the 'office of citizen' in our democratic republic" (p. 319). The idea of the "office of citizen" was first proposed by Thomas Jefferson, third president of the United States and leading political thinker, whose life and thought has begun to regain interest from the American public. As a political philosopher, Jefferson captured the spirit of representative democracy and the rights of citizens. He believed that in a representative democracy, citizens must feel that they hold highest political office in this country—the "office of citizen." As "office holders" in our representative democracy, citizens must not only be well informed about their individual rights and the issues of the day but they must also accept the responsibility of performing civic duties. The National Council for the Social Studies (2001) advises that schools must prepare students to assume the "office of citizen" by creating well-planned and organized citizenship education programs in which activities "expand civic knowledge, develop participation skills, and support the belief that, in a democracy, the actions of a person makes a difference. Throughout the curriculum and at every grade level, students should have opportunities to apply their civic knowledge, skills, and values as they work to solve real problems in their school, the community, our nation, and the world" (p. 319).

Why Is Civics Important?

In 1782, few believed that a unified nation could be created out of a collection of "free and independent states" spread out over a vast expanse of land. Each state had incredibly diverse economic interests, was fearful of an overly strong federal government, and remained fiercely loyal to established regional, ethnic, and religious ties. The newly independent states often fought each other over land and money, and, to add fuel to an already blazing fire, there was no national political organization with the power to settle their disputes. Over the next five years, the chaotic state of affairs became so alarming that many people agreed that the new union of states could not survive without a strong federal government. Therefore, in the hot summer of 1787, 55 delegates from 12 of the 13 states gathered in Philadelphia for the "Grand Convention," which was charged with the daunting task of creating a strong federal government while, at the same time, protecting the rights of the states and individuals. The delegates, known as the *framers*, took four months to draw up the plan—the United States Constitution, a document that described the government of a new nation. It was from this unsettled start that the seeds of one of the grandest political experiments of all time sprouted its roots—a republic with a representative democracy.

By the late 1700s, after the Constitution was ratified, many of the early disputes among the states began to fade and a new feeling of patriotism emerged. It was especially fitting that education was considered an important factor that would guide the country and its people into the future. Central to the framers' conception of a successful representative government was an informed public citizenry capable of exercising their rights and responsibilities in an informed and meaningful manner. And this potential, according to Thomas Jefferson, grew from civic education. Civic education would provide the knowledge and courage to "enable every man to judge for himself what will secure or endanger his freedom." If citizens did not know the Bill of Rights, for example, how could they weigh individual freedoms against the needs and welfare of the common community?

So, from the beginning of our nation's history, civic education has been, and continues to be, central to public education and essential to the survival of American democracy: "'Government of the people, by the people, and for the people,' in Lincoln's phrase, means that the people have the right to control their government. But this right is meaningless unless they have the knowledge and skills to

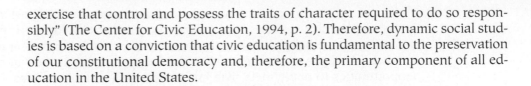

exercise that control and possess the traits of character required to do so responsibly" (The Center for Civic Education, 1994, p. 2). Therefore, dynamic social studies is based on a conviction that civic education is fundamental to the preservation of our constitutional democracy and, therefore, the primary component of all education in the United States.

What Should Young Political Scientists Know or Be Able to Do?

The goal of civic education is the development of informed, responsible citizens committed to the principles of American constitutional democracy. Their effective and responsible participation grows from the acquisition of a body of knowledge and a set of applicable participatory skills. Toward this goal, the Center for Civic Education (1994) established a set of standards specifying what students should know and be able to do in civics. The K–4 standards are summarized in Figure 6.1. The standards are not intended to be used as a basis for a national curriculum in civics, but simply as a guide to teachers so they know what they should teach their students and as a framework for curriculum developers on which they might build high-quality civics programs.

Because her school district has implemented a standards-driven social studies curriculum with a strong emphasis on civics, Claire Boyer, a second-grade teacher at Media Elementary School, was responsible for using the civics standards as a guide for planning classroom instruction. She always enjoyed taking the study of local government beyond the textbook to where the action was, so she turned her students loose on a civics adventure that was firmly grounded on the recommended standards. Specifically, Ms. Boyer hoped to have her students actively engaged in understanding how the well-being of communities is established and maintained as well as simulating civic life in the community. Guiding her efforts were the following standards.

- I.A. "What is government?"
- I.C. "Why is government necessary?"
- I.D. "What are some of the most important things governments do?"
- I. E. "What are the purposes of rules and laws?
- III.D. "What are the major responsibilities of local governments?"

For her special standards-driven civics project, Ms. Boyer challenged her young political scientists to build a town for themselves and run it. To start the project, she asked her students to pretend to be adult citizens in their community of Media 30 years in the future. To draw them into the future, she read them a "letter from the Environmental Protection Agency" dated 30 years from now demanding that all families move from Media as soon as possible due to severe and irreversible toxic waste problems. The families, traveling together in search of a new place to settle, were led to a large,

FIGURE 6.1 Civics Content Standards

I. What Is Government and What Should It Do?

A. What is government?
B. Where do people in government get the authority to make, apply, and enforce rules and laws and manage disputes about them?
C. Why is government necessary?
D. What are some of the most important things governments do?
E. What are the purposes of rules and laws?
F. How can you evaluate rules and laws?
G. What are the differences between limited and unlimited governments?
H. Why is it important to limit the power of government?

II. What Are the Basic Values and Principles of American Democracy?

A. What are the most important values and principles of American democracy?
B. What are some important beliefs Americans have about themselves and their government?
C. Why is it important for Americans to share certain values, principles, and beliefs?
D. What are the benefits of diversity in the United States?
E. How should conflicts about diversity be prevented and managed?
F. How can people work together to promote the values and principles of American democracy?

III. How Does the Government Established by the Constitution Embody the Purposes, Values, and Principles of American Democracy?

A. What is the United States Constitution and why is it important?
B. What does the national government do and how does it protect individual rights and promote the common good?
C. What are the major responsibilities of state governments?
D. What are the major responsibilities of local governments?
E. Who represents you in the legislative and executive branches of your local, state, and national governments?

IV. What Is the Relationship of the United States to Other Nations and to World Affairs?

A. How is the world divided into nations?
B. How do nations interact with one another?

V. What Are the Roles of the Citizen in American Democracy?

A. What does it mean to be a citizen of the United States?
B. How does a person become a citizen?
C. What are important rights in the United States?
D. What are important responsibilities of Americans?
E. What dispositions or traits of character are important to the preservation and improvement of American democracy?
F. How can Americans participate in their government?
G. What is the importance of political leadership and public service?
H. How should Americans select leaders?

empty room in the school basement made available just for their project. To keep track of the victims of this unfortunate plight, the "citizens" were required to fill out Official Community Census Forms. After they completed the census, the citizens of this new town (named "New Media" by vote) built homes for themselves from large packing boxes put aside from a shipment of new furniture the school received that summer. The citizens painted and pasted until they were satisfied the boxes looked like "real houses" and brought a sense of reality to the empty room. Streets were laid out and named. A street sign bearing the name "Dunlap Street" was a tribute to Mr. Richard Dunlap, the principal of Media Elementary School, but no one was quite sure of the inspiration for Grape Road or Ice Road. A town newspaper was launched to chronicle the daily progress of New Media's citizens and to keep its populace informed. "Toxic Waste Forces Townspeople to New Land" blared the headlines on January 7, the first day of the project. An accompanying story read, "Townspeople Paint the Town," in reference to the construction of new homes.

NCSS STANDARDS

III. *People, Places, and Environments*
VI. *Power, Authority, and Governance*
X. *Civic Ideals and Practice*

The day after the families completed their homes, they held a town meeting to discuss potential community problems, with Ms. Boyer presiding for the first meeting only. As is often the case with youngsters this age, they could foresee no problems in particular. However, Ms. Boyer was quick to suggest some—fires, crime, and problems that might arise if she could not lead future town meetings. Discussion led to the establishment of police and fire departments and an election for mayor. The children quickly set up minimum qualifications for voter registration and went about soliciting candidates for the mayoral position. Seven candidates immediately announced their intent to run, but three dropped out of the race the following day because they were too busy. Campaigning and debating began as students forged their platforms: Alex promised a cleaner environment, and Curtis vowed gun control. Candidates then planned campaign strategies, showing that political make-believe mirrors political reality. There was, to be specific, the "great cookie caper," involving Alex and her closest opponent, Curtis. On the last day of campaigning, Alex distributed "Vote for Alex" pamphlets decorated with paper hands grasping real chocolate chip cookies. Curtis's followers quickly cried "Bribery!" and complained that Alex was trying to buy votes. The matter went to the election board, which found that "no influence was obtained through the distribution of the cookies."

Following her landslide 14–2 victory, Alex immediately appointed Curtis as chief of police and presented him with his first book of tickets. Using his tickets to control the breaking of laws such as speeding (running in the halls), littering ($100 fine), and loitering (daydreaming), Curtis eventually learned the powers of his position. Through it all, Alex made new friends, was subject to the pressures of old ones, and generally learned that a position of authority has its rewards as well as its pitfalls. "I learned I'm never gonna be the real mayor," she reflected. "Even just pretending to be the mayor is a tough job."

Alex and her council members provided crucial leadership as the town began to grow through its hectic early days. Other classrooms acquired a sense of civic responsibility and offered to contribute to the growth of New Media. The first-graders, studying the topic "Needs of People," contributed a food store and displayed the products themselves (Bob's California watermelon: $20 a pound). The third grade, studying "What Towns Need," built an electric power station, stringing yarn lines from one cardboard tube light pole to another all around town. The fourth grade, not involved in a relevant social studies topic at the time, demonstrated the interrelatedness of the physical and social sciences. They wired up streetlights by connecting batteries to light bulbs, thus applying their knowledge of energy to making lives better for people. The fifth grade, anxious to contribute with the rest, made a trash truck (complete with oatmeal-box "trash cans" for the customers) and a bus from cardboard boxes. Finally, the kindergarten class spruced up the entire town with pink, white, and red paper flowers.

The entire village of New Media grew through the remainder of the school year as the children added new features to coincide with what they were studying. The students served as perfect hosts as visitors from area elementary schools came to Media Elementary School to witness the expansion of New Media.

In this exemplary classroom experience, Ms. Boyer set in motion a carefully selected project intended not only to address the targeted standards but also to achieve an important educational aim recommended by the NCSS (2001) in its position statement, *Creating Effective Citizens*: "Students are provided with opportunities to participate in simulations . . . and other activities that encourage the application of civic knowledge, skills, and values" (p. 319). Simulations and other activities that directly involve the students in the responsibilities of citizenship provide a rich course of action for standards-driven civics instruction. Even during the early grades, children should experience civics by simulating the duties of public officials in their own communities. As citizens of their community, they can vote, propose public policy, follow rules, make sound judgments, and practice most citizenship responsibilities found in a democracy. The ultimate goal of these experiences is to inspire young citizens so they will in time participate actively in the public life of their communities throughout their adult years.

In General, How Should Civics Be Taught?

As we have learned, U.S. public schools bear a significant and historic duty to enhance the acquisition of civic knowledge and civic responsibility in our nation's youth. Most teachers and parents would agree that, since children are not born with instinctive predispositions for democracy, teaching them the traits and responsibilities of active citizens is an important goal of education. Yet, knowing how to accomplish this goal, given all the demands related to accountability measures presently heaped on teachers, is challenging to say the least. Kahne and Middaugh (2008) state that the challenge "is the belief by some that civics instruction is relatively less important than, and takes time away from, subjects such as math, science and reading" (p. 34). As a result, social studies (including civics) has become the curriculum area where most reductions have taken place. The authors add that, despite this emphasis on math, science, and reading, little or no progress has been shown in those areas since 1990. Meanwhile, however, the authors report that the level of student civic knowledge, commitment, and participation has been declining. The *Social Education* staff of NCSS (2005) emphasized, "It is vital that the civic mission of schools be a focus of attempts to improve our nation's educational system, and that it should not be shortchanged by ongoing educational initiatives" (p. 414). How can teachers meet this challenge and create an optimal classroom environment for citizenship education?

How Global is the Curriculum
Go to MyEducationLab, select the topic Government/Citizenship, and view the artifact entitled "Purposes of State Government," and complete the questions that accompany it.

Although most teachers rely on social studies textbooks as their most frequent source of instruction, Alleman and Brophy (2002) support other options. Speaking of textbooks, they explain, "Elementary social studies textbooks tend to sprinkle bits and pieces of the topic of government across chapters. . . . The content tends to be far removed from the children's lives. . . . Overall, textbook treatments focus on branches of government, government leaders and what they do, patriotism, rules and laws, problem solving, and voting. While most of the content . . . is worthwhile, the approach seems to lack the grounding and context that defines government within children's own world" (p. 7). It is for that reason that teachers should be encouraged to use active strategies that involve their children in direct personal experiences that focus on potential life applications.

Kahne and Middaugh (2008) suggest, "When schools provide the kinds of opportunities that allow students to learn and practice a variety of civic skills, learn about how government works, see how others engage civically and politically, and grapple with their own roles as future citizens, then we see increases in both students' commitment to and capacity for [civic learning]" (p. 38). A realistic elementary school model designed to promote these desired civic outcomes would likely consist of four major components: (1) engage children in citizenship processes, (2) teach subject matter content through interesting topics and active processes, (3) inspire the actions and attitudes of civic responsibility, and (4) help children examine and analyze the values our democratic society shares and holds dear. If children are to truly learn what it means to be active citizens in a democratic society, democratic living must be experienced as a distinctive and fundamental piece of daily classroom life. When that happens, children are supplied with a context in which academic standards and caring relationships combine to exemplify democracy is in a realistic and meaningful way. So, democratic classrooms must have teachers who are able to use integrative, creative, and active strategies not only to help construct meaningful citizenship skills and understandings but also to establish an environment where children practice the general values that are part of democratic citizenship—liberty, equality, justice, freedom, tolerance, responsibility, and community.

Engaging Children in Citizenship Processes: The Democratic Learning Community

We should not think of childhood as a time during which children prepare to *become* citizens, apparently when they reach voting age, but as a time when children truly function as active citizens in a number of groups, including their family, classroom, and school. Children do not need to wait until they're 18 years old to experience what it means to be a citizen; citizenship awareness can start on the very first day of school. The elementary school is an ideal place for early and meaningful experiences in responsible citizenship, for no other setting offers young children as much fodder for citizenship participation. Parker (2006) commented that when children go to school, they are immersed in a social culture which teaches a great deal: "Its power at least matches that of the school's formal curriculum because the children experience it day after day. It's the 'air they breathe' there, so to speak, in the classrooms, hallways, playground, cafeteria, the principal's office, everywhere. In key ways . . . it shapes who they become" (p. 12).

How Global is the Curriculum *Go to MyEducationLab, select the topic Government / Citizenship, watch the video entitled "Sunnyville," and complete the questions that accompany it.*

At no other time during the school year do optimism, anticipation, and hope soar so high as on the first day of school. Returning from summer vacation, most children are renewed and energized—raring to go and excited to start a fresh, new school year. Sadly, one of the first things some teachers do to nullify this enthusiasm is to inform the children without delay who is boss: "Read them the 'riot act' as soon as they step inside the door," some insist. "You've got to jump on them for every little misbehavior; if you don't, it only gets worse as the year goes on!" These teachers seem to demonstrate little regard for their students' feelings through their unkind comments: "I make sure I do not smile until at least Thanksgiving—you've got to intimidate them or they'll run all over you."

These teachers believe that children need someone stern, someone with a firm hand to show them direction—fear is their motivator. Such teachers may demonstrate one of several different personalities. Have you met one of these teachers anywhere in your schooling?

- *The Commanders.* Their stern, direct orders force children to behave: "Stop that right now!" "I'm the captain of this ship and what I say goes!"
- *The Intimidators.* They sound a lot like the Commanders, but they add disturbing penalties: "If you cannot stay quiet, I'll make sure you go home with social studies homework tonight!" "Since Gerald cannot keep his pencil quiet, we'll all stay inside for recess."

- *The Unresponsives.* They remain aloof and unapproachable when children have problems: "No, I'm not going to tell you again. I gave the directions once and you chose not to listen." "No, I cannot help you. You're old enough now to tie your own shoes."
- *The Judges.* They specialize in put-downs that chip away at a child's self-esteem: "You're acting like little babies today." "You're always the one who starts trouble around here." Or, as one teacher said to me in a moment of slight irritation, "Maxim, you'll never amount to anything!"
- *The Labelers.* They enjoy attaching insensitive names to their put-down statements: "You tripped again? You're such a klutz, Anthony." You forgot your homework again, Katina? You'll always be an airhead!"

I hope you never had one of these teachers because the encounters they have with children are often upsetting, and they slowly chip away at their fragile shell of self-respect. The effect of biting criticism and sarcasm is humiliation; children will end up feeling bad, stupid, dishonest, or irresponsible. And, what recourse does a teacher have when these verbal indignities become so habitual that children start to tune them out? It seems that their only alternative is to turn the power up a notch and dole out increasingly callous remarks. But all forms of punishment, including verbal attacks, tend to be ineffective; if they do work, their effect is only temporary: First, *punishment is subject to intensification*. For example, a teacher may give a single child a homework assignment while the others have none. This may work the few first times it's tried because not many children want to be the only one with homework. But, at some point, the child is going to say, "I don't care. This doesn't bother me anymore," and the teacher will have to find something a little more unpleasant to control the child's behavior. Therefore, punishment must keep on escalating to maintain its effectiveness. Second, *punishment often mimics an online auction*. The child is forced to make a choice as to whether the punishment is worth the risk. The choice of behavior is determined by whether the misbehavior is worth the mental anguish or even physical discomfort that may result. Third, *punishment destroys the adult–child relationship*. I know of very few elementary school children who come to school with the goal of making their teacher's day as miserable as possible. Most seek the affection and support caring adults provide in a nurturing environment. When they see an angry face, hear a sharp voice, or become the target of an icy glare, they feel more pain and sadness than we can imagine. Our hurtful feedback to children cuts deeply because they are at a point of life when they need our acceptance and our support so much.

Not surprisingly, democratic teachers thoroughly reject this insensitive approach. "That's ridiculous advice," they counter. "Children should see their teacher as a positive influence, not as someone to keep clear of. Teachers need to smile, not scowl. If you don't smile until Thanksgiving, neither will the children!" They add, "Instead of scaring children, we need to help them acquire an understanding of their rights and responsibilities in a democratic learning community." For new teachers, though, the idea of establishing a democratic classroom is easier said than done because they often misconstrue democratic classrooms for laissez-faire classrooms. They may have witnessed how some teachers manage their classrooms at the opposite end of the spectrum from the autocratic approach. Called *permissives,* these teachers believe any form of corrective response has the potential to inhibit their children's behavior and cause them to fear or resent adult power. Permissives also worry about losing their children's friendship or even dipping in popularity; some are driven by their desire to be thought of by the children as being "cool." Clearly, permissive teachers empower children to "rule the roost" by giving them all the freedom they seek. Not surprisingly, permissive classrooms are loud, confusing, disorderly, and dangerous. In the long run, children will lose respect for their teacher and begin to wonder, "Will I be safe here?" "Is my teacher competent enough to protect me?"

A democratic learning community, however, is not a place where the teacher is powerless and without control. Because of school welfare policies, teachers must always be in control. However, as a democratic teacher, you establish the conditions for democracy to exist—a place where children are helped to establish the rules, take responsibility for their own behavior, and discover they do not need a dictator but rather a facilitator—someone who helps people work together. Taken a step further, a democratic teacher is an *authoritative* (not authoritarian) facilitator—an adult who can be trusted and turned to in full faith, and a caring individual who knows how to say the right word or do the right thing at just the right time. Authoritative teachers do not use gruff voices, nor do they scowl at children to control them; they do not ridicule, yell, or threaten. Likewise, they do not seem so disinterested and so removed from situations that the children feel alone. Authoritative teachers are neither feeble nor overbearing. Instead, they hold children in deep regard; they never shrink from the responsibility to lead when the children need their help. They are firm when they need to be, and they are gentle, too.

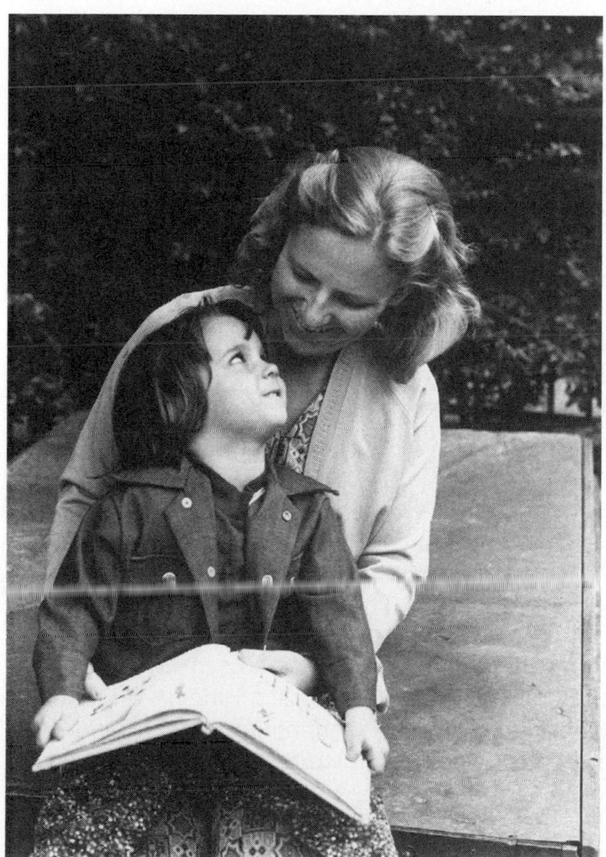

Democratic teachers effectively meet every child's needs for dignity, respect, and acceptance.

Democratic teachers facilitate the children's self-control. They help children understand the difference between right and wrong, good and bad; they encourage children to make their own decisions and correct their own mistakes. Helping children acquire self-control through democratic leadership, however, is a very challenging assignment. Think about how much simpler it is to gain

instantaneous obedience by yelling across the room, "Quiet down right now! You know I don't tolerate loud talking in this classroom," than to take the time and effort to help the children manage their own behavior. Democratic leadership requires sensitivity, determination, and a good bit of professional insight, for in democratic classrooms the authoritative teacher must blend a style that mirrors fairness, respect, and sensitivity, encouraging self-reliant behavior while simultaneously guiding students with reasonable limits and controls. In other words, the children have rights that must be respected by all and protected by the teacher.

The students will not think of their classroom as a democratic society simply because you tell them it is. Rather, they have to learn that it is a type of social structure where everyone has been brought together as a community of learners, where everyone is expected to share the common goals and behavioral standards that lead to academic and social success. The students are encouraged to be cooperative, polite, respectful, and caring in their classroom because traits like these shape the common good of their learning community. By building a democratic learning community, teachers create a common cultural experience that helps children feel connected to one another and eager to build positive interpersonal relationships: "We are all here to help each other live and learn."

At the beginning of the school year, then, teachers make every effort to establish trusting relationships with their students, making them feel that they are on their side, and that everyone is worthy of respect. Democratic teachers know children come to school anxious about issues such as whether they are going to fit in, be accepted by their peers, have friends, or experience academic success. Students who sense that they are accepted and valued are ready to take on these challenges and welcome a new social experience in their lives—the democratic learning community.

Teachers start building a democratic learning community far before school is scheduled to begin. Arranging the classroom attractively and functionally; learning about the children, including those with special needs; and planning opening-of-school activities are some important first steps. Because children are often a bit on edge the first day of school, involving them in group icebreaker activities can help relieve the anxiety.

The First Day of School

A familiar picture is painted on the first day of school in every community around the country: Children, some smiling and some with blank stares on their faces, all toting an assortment of packs on their backs, cautiously stepping off a large yellow bus and marching excitedly through a set of welcoming doors. The day brings out a range of emotions in children, teachers, administrators, and parents—it is a huge day in everyone's school year.

Whether you are teaching kindergarten or fifth grade, there are many simple things you can do to help prepare children for this new adventure in life. From the beginning, let your children know that you care about them by greeting them at the door, smiling (yes, even before Thanksgiving), using eye contact when saying hello, and offering a personal comment that shows you are interested in them ("I'm happy to see you. Welcome to *our* (not *my*) room." A warm welcome goes a long way toward starting the year out right.

Once a class of younger children is settled in, read them an appropriate book with a "first day of school" theme. For this example, I will use the popular favorite, Margaret Wise Brown's *The Important Book* (HarperTrophy). In a predicatively repetitive pattern, the book explains the "important thing" about all sorts of objects such as a spoon, apple, or shoe. After you read the book, help your students discover its recurring pattern. Do this by rereading a page of the book and helping the children determine the author's writing style. Then share something about yourself that you have written in the author's style—your own "most important" page: "The most important thing about Mr. Bullock is that he loves to teach. Mr. Bullock has a basset hound, plays golf, and loves to travel. But the most important thing about Mr. Bullock is that he loves to teach." A teacher sharing information about himself or herself is something that often gets overlooked in opening-day activities. Although the students may recognize your name, they know very little additional information about you. Tell them where you grew up, where you went to school, your teaching background, and how long you have been teaching. Give them ideas about your interests, hobbies, and special talents.

Modeling the author's style, help the class write its own page for a class *The Important Book*. Use a digital camera to photograph each child. Print the photos and mount them on each child's page. The children will love this earliest illustrated book of the year. It is also handy for substitute teachers who come to your class throughout the year. They will appreciate being able to match faces with names with the help of this resource.

A large variety of get-acquainted games and activities like this are available for the first day of school. Upper grade students become inquisitive sleuths in an informative, entertaining get-acquainted game called "Two Truths and a Lie." To play, group the students by fours and ask everyone to come up with three interesting but little known facts about themselves, one of which must be untrue. For example, I could say: "I have a pilot's license." "I am the youngest of 9 children." "I have a tattoo on my back." It is best to list these three facts on an index card. Allow the children about 5 minutes for listing the three facts, for this can be a difficult task for some. As a matter of fact, you will probably need to push along a few.

Advise the children that everyone will now take turns sharing their three statements with their small groups. The other group members will ask questions about the statements in an effort to determine which one is the lie. Allow about 5 minutes to share and then ask the group members vote on which statement they believe is the lie: "I have a pilot's lesson. Who thinks that's the lie?" "I am the youngest . . . ?" After each group completes its interrogation session, bring the class back together and discuss the question, "What interesting things did you learn about your classmates?"

The children enjoy this game so much that I have recommended this adaptation to my social studies methods classes: Have your children read biographies or selections from historical fiction. Then, play the game as described, but have the children take on the identity of their historical characters.

Do not expect your students to become a cohesive, caring democratic community after only one or two of these cooperative activities, however. A close community takes time to build—do not rush or become impatient.

Establishing Rules (Standards) for Classroom Behavior

How Global is the Curriculum *Go to MyEducationLab, select the topic Teaching Strategies, watch the video entitled "Classroom Rules," and complete the questions that accompany it.*

The collaborative design and implementation of group behavioral standards (classroom rules) is a distinguishing goal of democratic teachers and democratic classrooms. This task is considered an indispensable component of successful democratic learning communities. Safe environments, where clear boundaries describe individual rights and responsibilities, are basic to the process of working together. "We need to know how to act in our classroom," Darius explained, "so we can have a safe place for everybody to live in and learn." One of the most basic characteristics of a democratic learning community, then, is the development of class standards that everyone agrees to follow—the rules that inform children about what is expected of them and what the consequences of their behaviors will be. When children have a voice in this rule-making process, they develop a sense of ownership and pride that sets the tone for the rest of the school year. Teachers find that children work best when they have a hand in making the rules and are more inclined to remember the rules, respect the rules, follow the rules, and take a role in group problem solving if classmates have trouble following the rules. Most importantly, the process of collaboratively defining classroom rules builds skills in and respect for democratic processes.

Although this rule-making process may not be the right time to bring in such documents as the United States Constitution or its Bill of Rights, it is important to help students understand that classroom rules, like the laws of our land, are made to ensure that individuals will not be deprived of their rights and that everyone is obliged to respect the rights of others. In democratic learning communities, then, students know that their voices are listened to and respected. They feel valued as individuals but understand that their behavior cannot infringe on the rights of their teachers or classmates. The community environment not only provides a preparation for life in a democratic society, it is life in a democratic society.

Margaret Chou used a collaborative rule-making approach to creating classroom rules much in the way she would use the collaborative process for any typical lesson throughout the school year. The only difference is that this is going to be their first lesson. To begin, Ms. Chou tapped the rich storehouse of children's literature, using Marie Winn's book, *Shiver, Gobble, and Snore* (Simon & Schuster), a particularly suitable story for helping students grasp the importance of rules. It focuses on a funny king who made silly rules. In his kingdom lived three unhappy subjects: Shiver, who was always cold; Gobble, who was always hungry; and Snore (guess what he liked to do). Many of the king's rules severely limited the cravings of these one-of-a-kind characters, so they decided to move away to a place where there would be no rules. Alas, the three friends discovered that disputes could not be resolved in their new land—because they had no rules! They finally decided that to live peacefully, they must make reasonable rules.

Following up on the book's theme of how difficult life could be if there were no rules, Ms. Chou involved the children in a fun-filled discussion technique (Lindquist, 1995) to encourage children to think about classroom rules:

NCSS STANDARDS

V. *Individuals, Groups, and Institutions*
VI. *Power, Authority, and Governance*
X. *Civic Ideals and Practice*

> I often start out in September by asking the class to brainstorm all the things we can do to make our classroom a terrible place, a place where no one would want to come, a place where we could guarantee no learning would occur.
>
> As we list the surefire ways to kill a classroom, each suggestion more outrageous than the last, we begin to build a community. Eventually, when we have exhausted our efforts, most sincere and many hilarious, I ask the class to picture [and talk about] a room like the one we've just described. (p. 35)

After listening to the book and having a conversation like that, it's not difficult to persuade the children to focus on the importance of rules and how rules could help make their classroom a happy, productive environment where all students will feel safe and respected. Ms. Chou divided her class into small discussion groups and directed each group to suggest what the children learned about the process of making good rules. Here are the edited suggestions that Ms. Chou wrote down on a large sheet of chart paper:

- The rule should be clear so everyone knows what it means.
- The rule must be fair, so everyone can do what is expected.
- The rule must explain what happens if someone doesn't follow it.
- The list of rules should be kept short.
- Everyone should have a part of making the rules.

The next day, Ms. Chou continued exploring the topic of rules with another informal discussion: "Tell me some rules, or laws, that citizens of our community must follow. Why are these rules important? Who made these rules?" The reason for this discussion was to help the children understand that a classroom community, like a public community, functions much better when people agree to a set of behavioral standards. Ms. Chou then made a direct connection to their classroom: "Do you suppose rules are important for our classroom community? Why are they important? Who should make these rules?" The discussion ended with agreement that rule setting should be a shared process. Ms. Chou was happy this suggestion came from the children, for they tend to accept ownership of the rules when they have a voice in making them rather than think of classroom rules as the teacher's rules.

Ms. Chou started the process of shared rule making with a direct question: "What are some important rules that can help us live together safely and happily in our classroom community? How should we act so that our classroom is a good and safe place for everyone?"

"You mean like no chewin' gum?" Danylo mumbled as he struggled to speak with a wad of gum pocketed inside one cheek.

"Like no pushing and hitting?" wondered Lisa.

"Yes," responded Ms. Chou, knowing that she must be nonjudgmental at this point of the process. "We have a very good start."

Next, Ms. Chou divided the class into small groups and suggested that the groups brainstorm a list of other possible classroom rules. The groups deliberated for about 30 minutes as they carried out their task. Ms. Chou then randomly selected one group to write its first two suggestions on the chalkboard as the other groups crossed off similar items from their lists so they would not be repeated. The groups, in turn, repeated this process until they exhausted their lists—over 40 proposals! The class looked carefully at each proposal, most of which were stated in negative terms: "Don't fight," "No talking out loud unless you raise your hand," "Don't take things without permission." Groups tended to recommend a negatively stated rule for every imaginable situation ("Don't look out the window during class"). Ms. Chou suggested that rules beginning with "no" often seem insensitive to her, so she requested that the students to rephrase any negatively stated rules as affirmative ones: "Raise your hand if you want to talk."

Next, Ms. Chou and the students reviewed their lengthy list and concluded that it violated one of their important rule-making guidelines: "The list of rules should be kept short." To help the students trim down the list, Ms. Chou asked the question, "Do any of these rules look like they mean the same thing?" She offered an example: "Let me show you what I mean—'Don't talk out of turn' sounds almost like, 'Raise your hand when you want to talk."' The students used colored chalk to underline those they thought might go together well. Ms. Chou now challenged the students to defend their choices: "What makes you think these rules go together?" To further develop this idea, Ms. Chou challenged the students to form one big rule to replace all the little rules they merged together. Five general rules remained. For example, one merged group contained these small rules that they combined into one eventual big rule: Be polite and considerate to others:

- Raise your hand to speak.
- Listen when someone is talking.
- Follow the teacher's directions.

- Call people by their right names.
- Use our inside voices.
- Use helpful words instead of hitting if you have a disagreement with someone.
- Use words to let others know what you need or want.

This final task involved making a permanent poster displaying the classroom rules. Each child and Ms. Chou signed it, and displayed it prominently in the classroom. Here is the list Ms. Chou's students constructed:

- Be polite and considerate to others.
- Respect the personal space and belongings of others.
- Respect school property.
- Solve disagreements ourselves. If we cannot, we will ask the teacher for help.
- Follow all classroom procedures.

Ms. Chou considers the rule-making process to be serious business and expects that the rules made collectively must apply to her as well as to her students. She thinks about their rule about being polite and considerate to others, for example, when she sees a fellow teacher sit at his desk, head down, feverishly writing a note to a friend while a little girl tries to ask him to clarify a question on a test. He seems highly irritated at the loss of his private time and utters a one- or two-word response, so unmindful to the situation that he is completely unaware of whom the child is. "Why do we so often demand politeness and consideration from students and grant immunity to teachers?" Ms. Chou wonders. Teachers should never forget that they are powerful role models for their students. Because they shape student behaviors by their own example, teachers should hold themselves to the same standards for civility and respect that they expect of their students. If a classroom rule states, for example, "In this classroom, we use a respectful tone of voice," the rule applies equally to students and teachers. To quote Ms. Chou, "In the classroom, teachers should aim to treat others consistently, fairly, and respectfully. We are mirrors for our students!"

How Global Is the Curriculum
Go to MyEducationLab, select the topic Teaching Strategies, watch the video entitled "Meet the Teacher-Ms. Trask-Tyler," and complete the questions that accompany it.

Ms. Chou recognizes that the greatest end product of teaching cannot be limited to the subject matter her students may master, but includes what they value and how they act. Long after her students forget math operations or grammar rules, they will remember what Ms. Chou said and how the she related to them. So, a basic consideration of democratic learning communities is that the teacher must talk and act as she would like her students to talk and act. Do you want your students to be respectful, honest, tolerant, or courteous? These things will not happen simply by giving orders; you need to model these ideals and behaviors to the best of your ability. If children are to experience what it is like to live in a democracy, then the values associated with democratic living must guide the behaviors of everyone in the classroom, including their teachers.

Class Meetings

Have you had a recent squabble with a friend? What about confronting a member of a class workgroup who fails to do her or his part? We've all have had experiences that make us realize just how stressful and complicated human relations can be. If they are that difficult for adults, think about how complicated relationships can be for young children who may be egocentric and impulsive by nature. Oftentimes our youngsters are thrust together with potentially incompatible classmates and find themselves in situations where they have little, if any, control. Picture the anxiety and stress these children face—assignments that are too difficult, children picking on each other, too much homework, bullies, wondering how they fit in; the list is monumental. McClurg (1998) recommends, "At the year's beginning the teacher's first job is to reduce anxiety and reassure each child that his or her needs and point of view will be recognized and valued in this new place. That is the role and purpose of a regular, formalized [classroom] meeting" (p. 30). The purpose of classroom meetings is to find constructive solutions to student problems. Because class meetings comprise another reasonable facet of democratic learning communities, students must be introduced to the classroom process meetings during the first weeks of school.

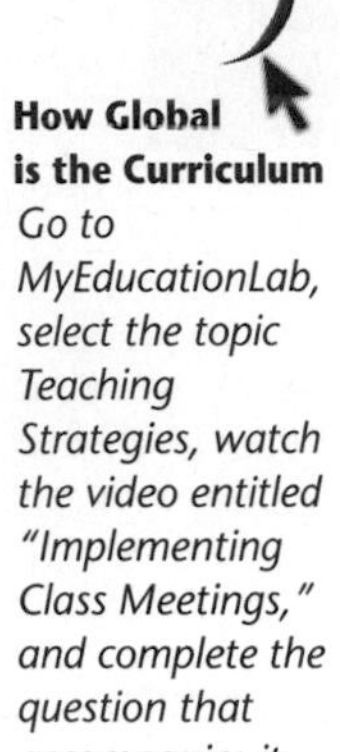

How Global is the Curriculum *Go to MyEducationLab, select the topic Teaching Strategies, watch the video entitled "Implementing Class Meetings," and complete the question that accompanies it.*

The younger the children are, the more difficult it is for them to think of things from another's perspective, so it takes great effort on the part of the teacher to get classroom meetings to run smoothly. A teacher's role will vary according to grade level, but a few guidelines help make meetings function constructively. Class meetings are best carried out in an environment where children can share freely and where they realize that what each has to contribute is worthwhile. A positive, supportive atmosphere is basic to smoothly operating class meetings. Sitting in a circle, semi-circle, or oval provides the greatest attention and maximum participation, as children are able to see one another when they talk and listen. Class meetings should be held on a regular basis, perhaps about three times a week. It is helpful to use sentence starters as a springboard for interactive discussion if the children have never participated in a class meeting. Some sample sentence starters are "Something I like about this classroom . . . ," "Something I think would improve our classroom . . ." "An important decision I think we should make . . ." or "I wonder why . . . ."

When the children reach the point where they can address important class problems competently, a student can add an item to the meeting agenda by putting a piece of paper inside an agenda box or writing it on the chalkboard. The issue, which includes the student's name and date, makes up the agenda for the class meeting. A group leader, the teacher first serving as a capable model early in the year, helps the children grasp the class meeting procedure. After a few practice meetings, students will become interested in taking over; each interested student should have an opportunity to be a meeting leader throughout the school year. The meeting script follows:

- *Clearly present the topic of discussion for the meeting.* Make sure everyone understands what the problem is. Problems are usually of two major types: (1) those dealing with schoolwork and (2) those having to do with difficulties among students. Class meetings should address only those problems affecting the entire class. Those involving two or three children are best handled in other ways (unless they affect the entire class).
- *Implement recommended group problem-solving strategies.* Clarify the problem, analyze causes, identify alternatives, assess each alternative, choose a solution, implement the solution, and assess whether the solution was helpful.
- *Establish the rules of good discussion.* Signal when you want to speak, listen carefully to others, and be respectful of everyone's opinions (no put-downs, complaining, or fault finding).
- *Use active listening strategies.* Paraphrase a student's comments or ask clarifying questions.
- *Summarize what has been said.* All of the ideas should be quickly repeated: "Let's go back and recall what was said."

The students should be helped to come up with constructive solutions to problems rather than suggest any kind of punishment. Teachers should show confidence in the students' decisions and make an effort to give their ideas a try, even if their proposed solutions appear to have a good chance of failing. By doing this, teachers communicate a very important message: "I know you will do your best and I have faith that you'll do what's right." However, if it is obvious that someone or something could be hurt or offended as a result of the class decision, the teacher should exercise her or his veto power. But, because a major goal of class meetings is to help students make caring decisions, teachers should not use their veto power unless it is vitally essential. Students will learn from their mistakes.

Although most class meetings will be set up to address behavioral issues, they should not be limited solely for that reason. Classroom meetings can be used to evaluate classroom rules or establish standards for a field trip. They can be used to share feelings of appreciation or to offer compliments for something the students admire about a person or policy. Regardless of how they are used, class meetings help students learn that their ideas are appreciated and valued and that they have a stake in working together as democratic citizens. Class meetings establish a feeling of trust and respect among teacher and students, and help students accept responsibility for what goes on in their classroom—the ultimate goal of democracy in the classroom.

Classroom Symbols

One of the factors contributing to the eventual bonding together of states into our new nation was the planning and designing of patriotic symbols—the American flag, the bald eagle, the great seal, *The Star-Spangled Banner,* and so on. Surprisingly, some of these key symbols could be unfamiliar to a few young children in your classroom, and other children will have difficulty grasping the ideals the symbols stand for. So, it is important to start the discussion of classroom symbols by helping the children recognize well-known national symbols and appreciating the ideal represented by each.

Explain that a symbol is a mark or representation that stands for something else. Our flag is a national symbol. Like our flag, many other symbols are used to represent the United States of America. Have the students brainstorm other national symbols. You will want to demonstrate or display several: the Statue of Liberty, the Liberty Bell, the bald eagle, a rose (national flower), Mt. Rushmore, the White House, *The Star-Spangled Banner*, and the United States Capitol. What do these symbols represent? For example, the bald eagle represents freedom, liberty, and strength. Help the children understand the symbols by carrying out short mini-lessons.

In groups, students should be challenged to create and design symbols for their democratic learning community—for example, a flag, song, motto, great seal, flower, animal, tree, class cheer, and so on. What does each symbol represent? All suggestions should be welcomed and the class should vote to determine the preferences in each category. Design each symbol and display or use them proudly throughout the year. The class song may be sung on Monday mornings or Friday afternoons; the class cheer can be used to reward outstanding accomplishments; and the great seal may be used on classroom stationery. Sometimes, students even like to select a classroom name that they will be known by throughout the year—two that I remember well are "Mr. Beam's Dreams" and "The Nova Superstars." It is surprising how much of a community spirit can be generated by involving children in choosing these special symbols.

Civic Knowledge: Comprehending Fundamental Information and Ideas

When children have the opportunity to participate meaningfully as citizens in supportive democratic learning communities, they tend to develop a deeper interest in exploring the content of civics and in acquiring the knowledge essential to eventually become involved in the civic life of their local, state, national, and global communities. Civic knowledge is a vital part of the elementary school curriculum, for without knowledge of citizenship and government there is no underpinning for significant civic participation. The future energy and strength of our democracy is in the hands of a new generation of young people convinced about the critical importance of attaining a deep understanding of civics knowledge. Lesser (2006) goes so far as to propose that "the teaching of civic knowledge is the bedrock of civics education" (p. 300). The Center for Civic Education, in its influential *National Standards for Civics and Government* (1994), supports the importance of meaningful civics subject matter content: "Formal instruction provides a basis for understanding the rights and responsibilities as citizens in American constitutional democracy and a framework for competent and responsible participation" (p. 1).

How Global is the Curriculum *Go to MyEducationLab, select the topic Literature Connections, watch the video entitled "Reading for Information," and complete the questions that accompany it.*

Civics, then, furnishes the essential content base for the support and construction of desirable democratic beliefs and attitudes. The associated facts and concepts, however, must not be vague, ill defined, or simply committed to memory—for example, "The federal system of government divides power among the executive, legislative, and judiciary branches"—without regard for what they mean. Students often find instruction that is limited to rote memorization to be trivial and uninteresting because they fail to see the relevance of memorized facts to their lives. Instead, civics instruction must embrace the processes associated with active learning—discovering, constructing, and applying functional information. It is important at this point to stress that active learning does not confine itself to physical action (bodily movement and manipulation of hands-on materials). It also involves all the genuine and significant mental activity that helps children make important intellectual advancements. Therefore, active learning methods have both mental and physical components. You will have no trouble locating instructional resources and strategies suitable for active learning; they include children's literature, online searches, group discussions, problem-solving experiences, role playing, the arts, writing assignments, and collaborative or cooperative learning groups. You will see how these and other techniques can be used by teachers to create intriguing situations that encourage the construction of key civics concepts such as the Constitution, how a bill becomes a law, the branches of government, and the rights and responsibilities of citizens.

The United States Constitution

Federal legislation passed in 2004 requires that all schools receiving federal assistance teach students about the United States Constitution on Constitution Day, September 17. This law does not distinguish among elementary, secondary, or college-level institutions, so it has been interpreted to apply to all levels. Lesser (2006) suggests that all social studies teachers should look forward to Constitution Day with excitement: "Constitution Day must be seen as an opportunity. This is our moment. . . . For this one day, [social studies teachers] are in the spotlight" (p. 294). Since the law does not specify what the educational program should consist of, social studies teachers are being looked to for their leadership; this is our opportunity to take hold of the lead and provide the guidance for those who would like to teach with appropriate and meaningful methods.

Notwithstanding the Constitution Day directive, learning about the U.S. Constitution has been and remains an important part of the elementary school social studies program in most school districts. The children learn that the Constitution is the cornerstone of our government—the basic and supreme law of the United States. In 4,543 words, including the signatures, the Constitution outlines the structure of the U.S. government and the rights of all American citizens. It was written in 1787, when delegates from 12 of the 13 states met in Philadelphia in what is now called Independence Hall to discuss improvements to the federal government (Rhode Island chose not to participate). The resolution calling the convention specified that its purpose for convening was to respond to dissatisfaction with the weak Articles of Confederation and the need for a stronger federal government. At first, delegates from only Virginia and Pennsylvania chose to attend,

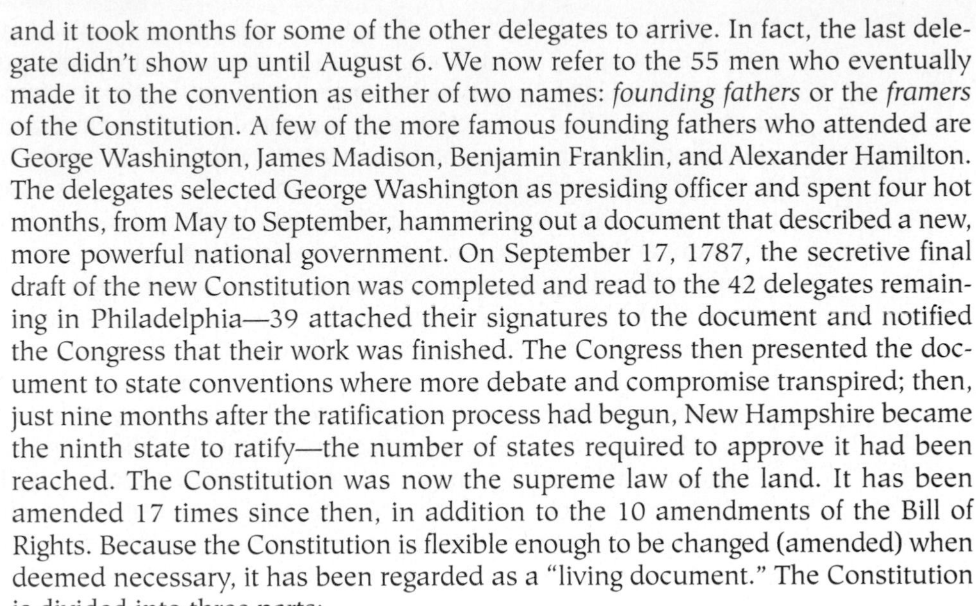

and it took months for some of the other delegates to arrive. In fact, the last delegate didn't show up until August 6. We now refer to the 55 men who eventually made it to the convention as either of two names: *founding fathers* or the *framers* of the Constitution. A few of the more famous founding fathers who attended are George Washington, James Madison, Benjamin Franklin, and Alexander Hamilton. The delegates selected George Washington as presiding officer and spent four hot months, from May to September, hammering out a document that described a new, more powerful national government. On September 17, 1787, the secretive final draft of the new Constitution was completed and read to the 42 delegates remaining in Philadelphia—39 attached their signatures to the document and notified the Congress that their work was finished. The Congress then presented the document to state conventions where more debate and compromise transpired; then, just nine months after the ratification process had begun, New Hampshire became the ninth state to ratify—the number of states required to approve it had been reached. The Constitution was now the supreme law of the land. It has been amended 17 times since then, in addition to the 10 amendments of the Bill of Rights. Because the Constitution is flexible enough to be changed (amended) when deemed necessary, it has been regarded as a "living document." The Constitution is divided into three parts:

- *Preamble.* This explains the purpose of the document.
- *Articles.* These describe the structure of the government (legislative, executive, and judicial branches) as well as the process for amending the document. There are seven articles.
- *Amendments.* These are the changes made to the Constitution. The first 10 are called the Bill of Rights; there are a total of 27 amendments approved since 1791.

Karla Griffin realized that deciphering the parts of the Constitution was not at the top of her students' "to-do list" and that her first step as a teacher was to somehow create a spontaneous need and desire to figure them out: "One of my biggest challenges as a teacher," Ms. Griffin muses, "is to know how to arouse and appeal to the interests of my students." Continuing this trend of thought, Ms. Griffin wondered aloud, "How can they learn the content without simply 'transmitting' the facts to them? To complicate matters, the language used in the original Constitution places such difficult reading demands on my fifth-graders!" After spending a great deal of time and effort on these dilemmas, Ms. Griffin finally decided to carry out the learning experiences in a social situation, emphasizing a literature-based approach highlighted with collaborative learning efforts among the children and between herself and the children.

Obviously satisfied with her decision, Ms. Griffin's broad smile and look of anticipation for what was to come fashioned an image of enthusiasm that her students would undoubtedly find infectious. "One of the keys to

NCSS STANDARDS

II. *Time, Continuity, and Change*
VI. *Power, Authority, and Governance*
X. *Civic Ideals and Practice*

achieving success with any strategy you make up your mind to use," Ms. Griffin acknowledged, "is to demonstrate to the children that you can hardly wait to use it. When you demonstrate sincere passion for any teaching responsibility, they often look forward to it as a pleasurable, productive, and stimulating learning experience."

Ms. Griffin understands that she must start any new instructional sequence by activating the children's existing knowledge of the content, so she and the class spent a little time discussing their experiences as citizens of their democratic learning community and how, to fulfill their responsibilities as good citizens of that community, they were expected to carry out a number of distinctly significant responsibilities. The children were then helped to connect the idea that just as they are responsible and respectful citizens of their classroom, they also are expected to assume a responsible and respectful role in their growing communities—school, neighborhood, municipality, state, or nation. The students concluded that, just like their classroom community, each expanding community requires rules and responsibilities to keep everyone safe and protect individual rights. How do individuals carry out the responsibility of being good citizens in these various communities?

Central to the concept of democracy in our national community is the U.S. Constitution. Like the rules established for citizens of their democratic learning community, the standards that define what it means to be a good citizen of our nation are outlined in this revered document. Ms. Griffin introduced her students to the Constitution by displaying an art print of the signing of the United States Constitution (available from www.foundersofamerica.com/CONSTITUTION_DAY/). She asked them to think about what was going on in the picture: "What comes to your mind as you look at this picture? What do you suppose is happening? When did this event take place?" Ms. Griffin recorded their responses on the chalkboard. She then displayed a large poster print of the U.S. Constitution and explained that this is a clue about how the men in the picture solved a very important problem. She invited the students to examine the document quickly and asked, "What came to your mind when you saw the three large words at the beginning of the document, 'We the people . . .'" Again, she recorded their responses on the chalkboard. Finally, Ms. Griffin focused the discussion on both the picture print and the copy of the Constitution: "Based on our discussion, do you have any new ideas about what was going on in the picture?" Then, to help the children judge the accuracy of their responses, Ms. Griffin passed out copies of *Shh! We're Writing the Constitution* by Jean Fritz (Putnam). In a very engaging style, Fritz transports the reader back to the Constitutional Convention in Philadelphia to tell the story of the birth of our Constitution. Smartly entwined into the account of how the framers carried out their task are some wonderful little anecdotes that are sure to capture the children's imagination. The text of the Constitution is reproduced in the book.

Fritz's simplified but accurate story of how the Constitution shaped a new nation makes this a superb option for introducing young readers to the intricacies of the document. Although the literary quality of this book by itself makes it an excellent choice, Ms. Griffin's main reason for choosing it was to communicate important content in ways that made the "long ago and far away" seem more realistic. Some teachers mistakenly attempt to draw out knowledge after reading stories like this by asking "dead-end" questions, or simple questions that may (1) disregard the development of personal meaning from the material, (2) prove to be irrelevant or too difficult, (3) require answers that must be restated precisely from the book, or (4) fail to help children cope with or resolve problems. Oftentimes such discussions can be thought of as "inquisitions":

- Where was the Constitutional Convention held? When was it held?
- How many states sent delegates? Which state chose not to attend?
- Name some famous "framers" who attended the Constitutional Convention.
- How many states were required to ratify the Constitution?
- What three branches of government are established by the Constitution?

Holding an inquisition with a list of questions like these serves to fulfill only one purpose—cementing the children's boredom. How can teachers, in bright elementary classrooms brimming with eager young learners, do things like this?

To help her students unlock the specifics of the U.S. Constitution itself, Ms. Griffin used a technique she referred to as a poster session. Ms. Griffin began dividing the class into several groups of three and assigning them to the following parts of the Constitution: Preamble, Article 1, Article 2, Article 3, Article 4, Bill of Rights (first 10 amendments), and Amendments 11 through 27. Each group was directed to create a visual portrayal of its part of the Constitution on a large sheet of poster board. Their portrayals could include drawn illustrations, words, pictures from magazines, printed images from the computer, or any other representations that communicated the associated content and spirit. The posters were positioned on the walls around the classroom and a short narrative describing each was attached. Other fifth-grade classrooms were invited to examine the display, circulating from poster to poster. Ms. Griffin passed out post-it notes to all visitors and asked them to provide feedback for each poster. After this poster session, Ms. Griffin brought the class together and led a discussion about what the children had learned and what they considered to be the most valuable outcome of the project.

In addition to this introductory experience, Ms. Griffin carried out varied active instructional strategies designed to support in-depth learning. For example, when studying the Bill of Rights and succeeding amendments, Ms. Griffin divided the students into pairs and had them access the Web in order to complete a Bill of Rights Scavenger Hunt. She gave the students a sheet of paper containing situations that could be illustrative of the amendments—for example, "A group of fifth-graders write a letter to the school principal complaining about a lack of playground equipment." Ms. Griffin is watchful that the scavenger hunt includes the foremost provisions of each amendment, and not minutiae or trivial issues. The students seek relevant information by searching various websites such as the National Constitution Center's interactive Constitution (www.constitutioncenter.org/constitution/), the National Archives' (www.archives.gov/exhibits/charters/charters.html), actual images of the Constitution as well as a readable history of the creation of the Constitution, and Justice Learning's useful guide to the Constitution (www.archives.gov/exhibits/charters/charters.html). After the students complete the scavenger hunt, Ms. Griffin reviews the amendments that have just been cited.

Ms. Griffin used learning experiences like these to introduce current controversial issues that have arisen with the different parts of the Constitution. One day, for example, the newspaper had an account describing the neglect of a dozen dogs that were terribly mistreated by their owner. A photo accompanying the story depicted several of the incredibly undernourished, scrawny, sickly dogs. The students spent some time discussing the ways these dogs in particular, and animals in general, are sometimes mistreated. "It's like they need a Constitution!" blurted Charlie.

"Not a bad idea," chimed in Jaung.

Seizing the opportunity, Ms. Griffin divided the students into three groups. Each group was to use the simplified U.S. Constitution as a model and work together to write a "Preamble" and "Bill of Rights" for an "Animal Constitution." When they finished, the groups compared their "Preambles" and "Bills of Rights," eventually merging them into a single document designed to protect the rights of all animals.

Teachers serious about helping students understand the Constitution look for any opportunity to relate its principles to their lives. Rather than limiting instruction to the memorization of First Amendment rights, for example, Yvonne Jordan encouraged her students to compile a "First Amendment Diary" to personalize what they learned about the rights guaranteed under the First Amendment.

First, Ms. Jordan's students read Sy Sobel's straightforward overview of the United States Constitution, *The U.S. Constitution and You* (Barron's Educational Series), and how it protects the rights of citizens. They learned that when the Constitution was ratified in 1789, some states refused to go along with it because they were concerned that it did not protect certain freedoms. They thought the Constitution should be amended, or changed, to protect these freedoms, so they introduced a Bill of Rights. The Bill of Rights is made up of 10 amendments; the First Amendment is:

> Congress shall make no law respecting an establishment of religion or prohibiting the free exercise thereof; or abridging the freedom of speech, or of the press; or the right of the people peaceably to assemble, and to petition the government for a redress of grievances.

So that the students operated from a common understanding of the First Amendment, Ms. Jordan helped the class rewrite the Bill of Rights in their own words:

NCSS STANDARDS

IV. *Individual Development and Identity*
VI. *Power, Authority, and Governance*
X. *Civic Ideals and Practice*

> People are free to practice any religion they want. The government cannot stop citizens from saying or writing what they want. The people have the right to gather together to discuss problems they have with the government and to inform the government of their problems.

The students then recalled the freedoms guaranteed by the First Amendment: freedom of religion, freedom of speech, freedom of the press, and freedom of assembly. Each of these freedoms was listed horizontally along the top of a grid titled "First Amendment Diary." Underneath each heading, students were asked to list the protected activities they were engaged in over a weekend, such as "Attended a soccer game" or "Went to church with my family." On Monday, Ms. Jordan helped her young political scientists compile a class list of all the entries, and led a discussion of the data with questions like these:

- How many times did you rely on your First Amendment rights?
- How might your weekend have changed without the First Amendment rights?
- Which rights were exercised most? Least?

Through this activity, Ms. Jordan not only demonstrated that civic knowledge is indeed important but that it also must have relevance to the students' lives. Civic education is something more than studying flowcharts of "How a Bill Becomes a Law" or reading a textbook chapter on the "Separation of Powers." Students more clearly understand civics by participating in the processes they are learning about.

As children experience the dynamics of a democratic learning community and learn about the United States Constitution, they could become involved in activities that help them combine both. For example, citizens of both our democratic society and the classroom are bound by the rules and laws fairly established by its members. To help connect these ideas, one teacher invited the students to use the U.S. Constitution as a model to compose their own classroom constitution (see Figure 6.2).

National Symbols

Among the actions that helped forge a sense of national identity and spirit following the Revolutionary War was the introduction of special national symbols. These

FIGURE 6.2 Classroom Constitution

Grade 6 Constitution

We the students of Grade 6, Room 14, in order to form a more perfect class, do establish this Constitution of the Sixth Grade.

Article I. Officials

1. There will be two branches of our government: the executive branch and the legislative branch.
2. The executive branch is made up of the President, Vice President, Secretary, and Treasurer.
3. The legislative branch is made up of all the rest of the members of the class.
4. Two candidates each for the offices of President, Vice President, Secretary, and Treasurer shall be nominated the Friday before the third Monday of each month.
5. Election of officers shall take place the third Monday of every month by secret ballot.
6. A student may hold a term of office only once.

Article II. Qualifications of Officers

1. Everyone automatically becomes a member of the legislative branch when entering Room 14 as a student
2. Students must have these qualifications to be an officer:
   a. must be a member of Room 14 for at least two weeks.
   b. must be honest and trustworthy.

Article III. Duties of Executive Branch

1. President
   a. The President shall run all class meetings.
   b. The President shall take charge of the class in the teacher's absence.
   c. The President shall help the substitute (show him or her where things are).
   d. The President shall appoint class helpers.
2. Vice President
   a. The Vice President shall help the President when necessary.
   b. In the absence of the President, the Vice President shall take over.
3. Secretary
   a. The Secretary shall take notes at all class meetings.
   b. The Secretary shall take care of all class mail (letters, thank you notes, and so on).
4. Treasurer
   a. The Treasurer shall take care of all class funds.

Article IV. Duties of Legislative Branch

1. To approve, by majority vote, class helper assignments.
2. To approve, by majority vote, any decision for which the class is responsible.
3. To volunteer for class helper assignments:
   a. clean chalkboard
   b. feed fish
   c. water plants
   d. pass out papers
   e. take lunch count
   f. serve as class librarian
   g. greet room visitors
   h. keep art materials orderly
   i. check attendance
   j. run errands
4. To approve, by two-thirds vote, any amendment to this constitution.

Article V. Presidential Vacancy

The Vice President shall take over if the President's office is vacant, followed by the Secretary, and then the Treasurer.

Article VI. Class Meetings:

Meetings shall be held each Friday from 2:30-3:00 p.m.

Article VII. Amendments

1. An amendment may be proposed by any member of the class.
2. An amendment must be approved by two-thirds vote of the legislative branch.

Amendments

Amendment 1.
An elected official shall temporarily give up any classroom helper jobs held during his or her term of office. (Approved: February 10)

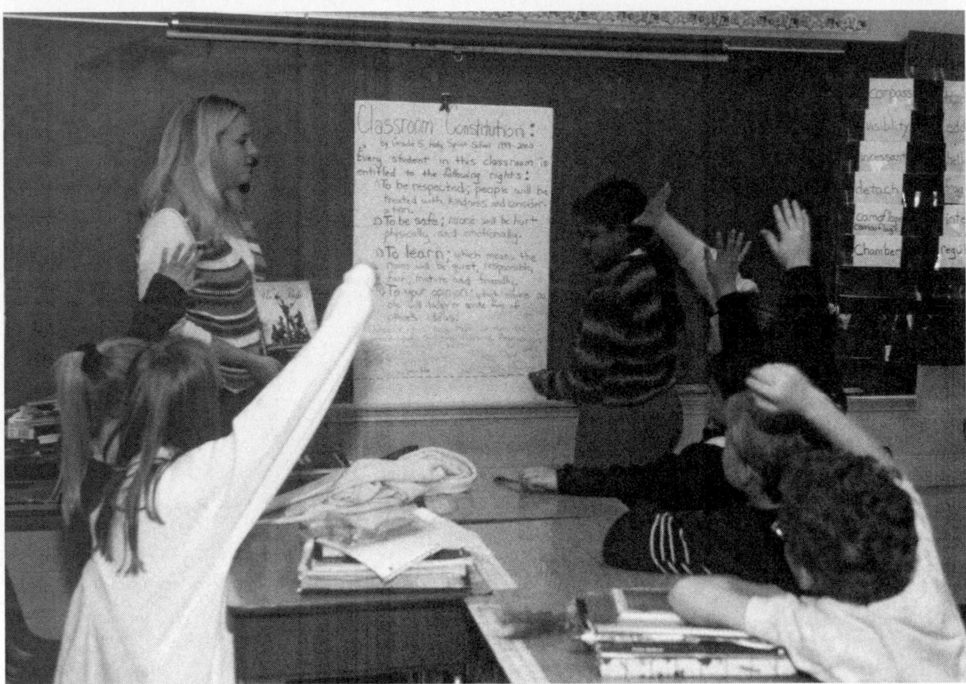

Children take turns signing their classroom constitution.

helped define America as a new nation and became representative of a new history and culture. National symbols have evoked a sense of unity and patriotism since the birth of our nation. Think back to the tragic terrorist attack on the United States on September 11, 2001, for example. Many Americans turned to the American flag as a symbol of strength and unity and hoped that such patriotism would not end with the events of September 11. An understanding of and respect for national symbols have undergone renewed importance in democratic learning communities.

Students in Isabel Tarango's fifth-grade classroom gathered around a yellow rug they called their "Conversation Station." The Conversation Station was a meeting place where everyone gathered whenever there were special ideas to discuss. Ms. Tarango chose this distinctive place to get together because she believes that children attach more importance to classroom events when they are held in special places. Today, Ms. Tarango wanted the class to meet at the Conversation Station to begin a new topic of study: "Major Flags throughout American History." Before starting any new topic, Ms. Tarango makes sure her students are able to connect their previous knowledge and experiences to the new information, so she unfurled the present flag of the United States and asked the students what they knew about the colors, stars, and stripes: "What do you see here? What colors are on the flag? How many stars are there? How many stripes can you count?" Inform the students that the colors and shapes have special meaning. Ask them to explain why there are 50 stars (50 states) and 13 stripes (original 13 colonies) on the flag. Discuss why the colors red, white, and blue were selected for our flag. Here is where it gets a little tricky, though, because no one knows for sure why those three colors were chosen. George Washington is often credited for explaining: "We take the stars from Heaven, the red from our mother country, separating it by white stripes, thus showing that we have separated from her, and the white stripes shall go down to posterity representing Liberty." But, as you can see, Washington's statement doesn't account for the color blue. However, the three colors were also used in the great seal, first used publicly in 1782, so an idea of the specific meaning of each can be gathered from the words of Charles Thompson, Secretary of the Continental Congress. Reporting to Congress on the meaning of the colors on the great seal, Thompson explained: "White signifies purity and innocence, Red, hardiness and valour, and Blue . . . signifies vigilance, perseverance & justice." Many people accept Thompson's statement as an accurate explanation for the colors on our American flag.

NCSS STANDARDS

II. *Time, Continuity, and Change*

X. *Civic Ideals and Practice*

Since the major emphasis of this study was going to be research and writing (finding out and informing), Ms. Tarango felt that her students required a model of expository writing; they tend to write better original pieces while trying to write like the models they see in books. Therefore, she brought to class the book *Flag Day* by Dorothy Les Tina and illustrated by Ed Emberley (Crowell). Another very appropriate children's book is Lloyd G. Douglas's *The American Flag* (Children's Press). Tina's book tells the controversial story of Betsy Ross and describes ways to honor the flag, then goes on to describe related symbols: The Star-Spangled Banner, the Pledge of Allegiance, and others. Ms. Tarango read the first six pages of the book, which gave a short history of flags, and helped her students analyze the story structure.

Realizing that the topic of major flags in U.S. history was too expansive for one written report, Ms. Tarango broke it down into small, manageable divisions for separate small group investigations: "British Union Jack," "Grand Union Flag," "Betsy Ross's Flag," "The Star Spangled Banner," "Flag of 1818," "Flag of 1912," and "Today's Flag." The plan was for small groups to investigate separate flags, write a short report, share the reports orally, and compile the small reports as separate chapters of a class book, *Flags throughout American History*.

The next stage of the research project involved developing a list of questions that the students should ask about their specific flag. Ms. Tarango's class decided that each small group should answer the same questions as modeled in Tina's book, *Flag Day:* What colors were used? What symbols were used? When was it adopted? Why was it changed? The questions provided a starting point for further research and served as a focus for the students' writing.

Next, the students searched through a variety of reference materials, including Internet sites (www.foundingfathers.info/American-flag/). Ms. Tarango monitored this portion of the research process carefully, for she feels that children must learn to choose relevant information and avoid word-for-word copying from a book, encyclopedia, or other source of information. "Nothing can be more deadly," growls Ms. Tarango, "than to allow a child to stand in front of a classroom and read a report that was copied word-for-word. You'll hear frequent pauses, the child will speak in a monotone, and she or he will often struggle to pronounce unfamiliar words."

To help them organize their reports, Ms. Tarango gave the students a number of index cards. She explained that these would be referred to as *information cards* because each would be divided into two major sections: a large circle at the top of the card represented the dot of the letter *i*, and the bottom rectangular section represented the stem. The students then printed the main idea (usually the first sentence of a paragraph) on the top section (the dot of the *i*); in the bottom section they listed all the supporting details (see Figure 6.3). This visual aid helped the children summarize the information effectively and guided them as they wrote their reports.

For the sharing stage, Ms. Tarango used a tactic she called the "TV News Magazine." In a television news magazine format, an "investigative reporter" from each research group set up an area of the classroom where he or she shared the group's written piece with an audience of four or five classmates (or children from other classrooms). Several investigative reporters

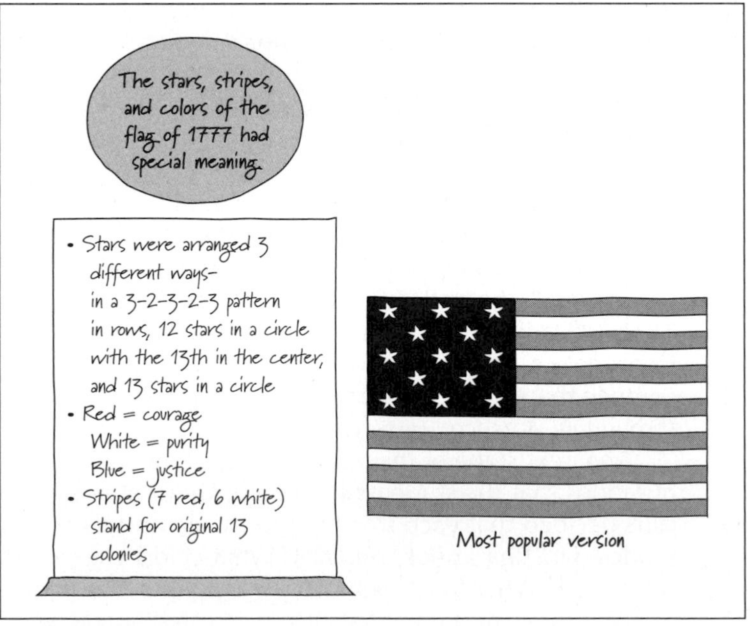

FIGURE 6.3 A Sample Information Card

functioned simultaneously and repeated their presentations as their classmates revolved from one reporter to the next. Ms. Tarango's investigative reporters donned simple costumes and used simple props to help the audience get a feel for the historical era. For example, the investigative reporter presenting the "Grand Union Flag" wore a pair of glasses pulled down over his nose like Benjamin Franklin, and the reporter who told of the "Betsy Ross Flag" arranged a number of five-pointed stars among some simple sewing implements.

As part of its presentation, each group displayed a model of its selected flag and read a short report describing the flag's historical significance. Figure 6.4 is an example of the report that was read aloud by the first group for our colonists' earliest flag, the "Grand Union Flag."

After researching several other national symbols in like manner (Uncle Sam, the bald eagle, *The Star-Spangled Banner*), Ms. Tarango helped the students connect their new understandings to their own lives. Comparing life in their classroom with our nation, Ms. Tarango divided the class once more into small study groups.

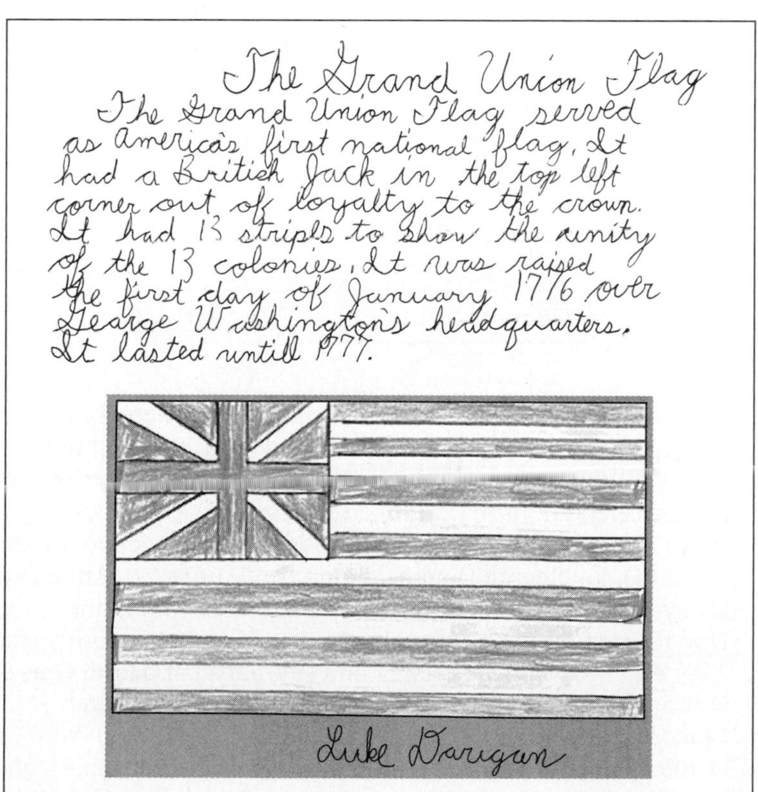
The Grand Union Flag

The Grand Union Flag served as america's first national flag. It had a British Jack in the top left corner out of loyalty to the crown. It had 13 strips to show the unity of the 13 colonies. It was raised the first day of January 1776 over George Washington's headquarters. It lasted untill 1777.

Luke Darigan

FIGURE 6.4 Student Flag Report

National Holidays

National holidays are a significant part of every nation's culture, and the Congress of the United States has set aside a number of special days to remember and honor noteworthy historical events or individuals as well to pay tribute to significant national or cultural beliefs and customs. Most U.S. citizens look forward to the celebrations that are such an integral part of these patriotic national observances—speeches, music, symbols, special foods, art, drama, or literature. Federal government offices are always closed on federal holidays; schools and many businesses close on major holidays such as Thanksgiving, Christmas, and New Year's Day but may not always be closed on other days such as Presidents' Day or Veterans' Day. At present, Congress has designated 10 legal holidays:

New Year's Day	January 1
Martin Luther King Day	Third Monday in January
Presidents' Day	Third Monday in February
Memorial Day	Last Monday in May
Independence Day	July 4
Labor Day	First Monday in September
Columbus Day	Second Monday in October
Veterans' Day	November 11
Thanksgiving Day	Fourth Thursday in November
Christmas Day	December 25

Only legal federal holidays have been listed here, but there are dozens of other holidays that Americans look forward to each year. Although not acknowledged as legal national holidays, these special cultural and ethnic observances prompt unique celebrations in the United States: (1) *federal observances*, such as Earth Day (April 2), Arbor Day (date varies), Mother's Day (second Sunday in May), Flag Day (June 14), Juneteenth (Emancipation Day) (June 19), Armed Forces Day (third Saturday in May), Father's Day (third Sunday in June), and Citizenship/Constitution Day (September 17); *cultural, ethnic, and religious observances*, such as Chinese New Year (between January 21 and February 19), Mardi Gras (February or March), Orthodox Christmas (January 7), St. Patrick's Day (March 17), Easter (date varies), Cinco de Mayo (May 5), Rosh Hashanah (date varies), Yom Kippur (September or October), Chanukah/Hanukkah (date varies in December), and Kwanzaa (December 26–January 1); and *fun days*, such as Groundhog Day (February 2), Valentine's

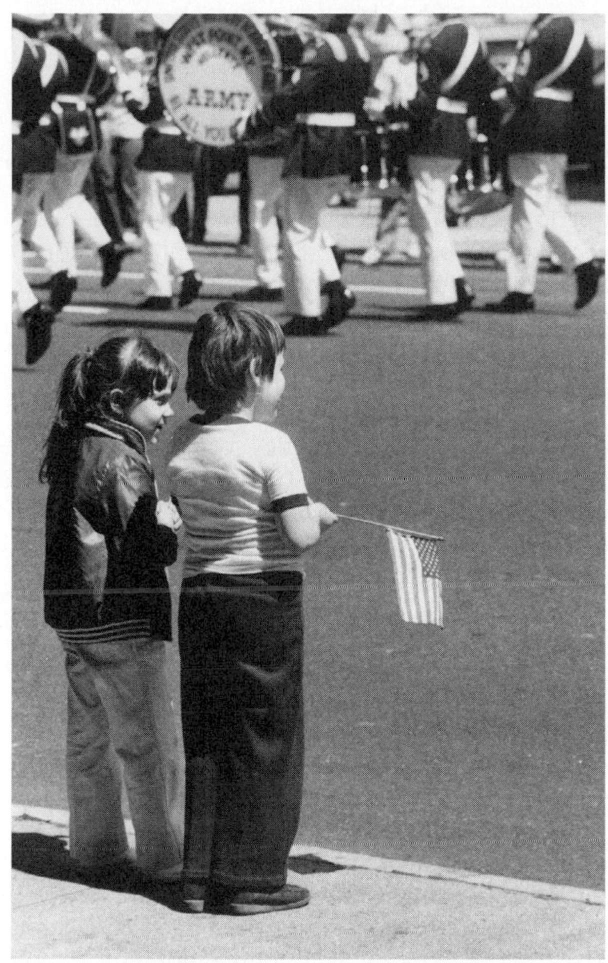

National pride soars as children take part in stirring national celebrations.

Day (February 14), April Fool's Day (April 1), and Halloween (October 31).

Critics of the proliferation of holidays complain that the sheer number of holidays often brings needless and potentially overpowering stimulation to the classroom. The result is a flood of holiday busywork frequently resulting in such trivial pattern projects as turkeys in November, green and red paper chains in December, snowmen in January, hearts in February, and shamrocks in March. Very little significant information is connected to these holiday projects; month after month, the children cut, glue, draw, and paint long-established holiday prototypes. The emptiness of such an approach is epitomized in Victor's (a first-grader) response when asked why he was gluing feathers on a vegetable can to make a tin can turkey: " 'Cause my teacher said I had to."

Learning about holidays must shift the center of attention from the "20 matching turkeys on the window" type of arts and crafts projects to learning about how and when holidays are celebrated, their origins, and their meanings. However, in some cases, this is a highly sensitive topic loaded with a great deal of uncertainty. Because the United States is such a highly diverse society, its public schools are caught up in a necessary effort to figure out how to deal fairly and sensitively with the growing diversity of its population. Take, for example, the legal issues related to the observance of our nation's only religious federal holiday—Christmas. How do public schools deal with related religious themes or religious beliefs? To begin, it is important to understand that any instructional decisions must be based on a commitment to the constitutional guarantee of freedom of religion. That is, public school teachers must steadfastly support the idea that the function of public education is to neither promote nor thwart any particular religious belief. Does this mean that learning about religious holidays such as Christmas or Hanukkah should not be carried out in our public schools?

To answer that question, we must first consider the influence of religion throughout history and its role in cultures. If we want to examine the significance of holidays while learning about cultural heritage, the instruction is considered appropriate. However, teachers must stay away from promoting any religion, religious celebration, or worship. Instruction must focus on the cultural aspect of the holiday, with an instructional focus on religious traditions only. With that perspective, it would seem wise to devise an instructional program that serves the needs and backgrounds of all students. Teachers should remember that December is not only the month for the Christian holidays of Christmas, the Jewish holiday of Hanukkah, and the African American holiday of Kwanzaa (nonreligious), but it is also when the Mahayana Buddhists celebrate the Enlightenment of Buddha, Eastern Europeans celebrate Saint Nicholas Day, Mexicans celebrate the Fiesta of Our Lady of Guadalupe, Swedes celebrate Saint Lucia Day, people in several countries celebrate Boxing Day on December 26 (an old holiday based on the tradition of giving gifts to the less fortunate members of society), and Japanese celebrate Omisoka (New Year's Eve), a very important day in Japan. In our multicultural society, public schools must regard all of these as possibilities for instruction (depending on the nature and needs of the school community), or none; the role of our schools is to neither promote nor malign any religion or culture. Art, drama, literature, and music with religious themes are all permissible, so long as they have a sound educational goal and are not used to encourage or discourage any particular religious beliefs.

Up to recent times, children from other cultures were to some extent disregarded with the traditional celebration of Christmas in the classroom. As multicultural awareness and sensitivity had grown and questions regarding religious holidays and public schools were raised, many schools reacted by excluding all Christmas activities to avoid offending people from other cultures. Recently, schools have drawn back from that extreme reaction to the point where current approaches to the situation appear to be recognizing holidays, including Christmas, not to inject religious beliefs, but as opportunities for teaching about cultural heritage.

Recognizing religious holidays is one area of controversy, but even traditional, nonreligious holidays have had their contemporary critics. Take Thanksgiving, for example. Most of us think of this national holiday as a commemoration of the feast held in the autumn of 1621 by the Pilgrims and the Wampanoag to celebrate the colony's first successful harvest. Critics ask the question, "What did the Europeans give in return?" and tell us that a mere 20 years later, European disease and treachery had decimated the Wampanoag. And, most of us think of Columbus Day as a holiday to celebrate Columbus's unsuccessful effort to find an all-water route to India, but stumbling, instead, on an entire continent that was mostly unknown to Europe. Critics of the holiday protest that Columbus and many of the Europeans who followed treated the Native American Indians cruelly, and they ultimately caused the deaths of countless people caused by diseases that until that time were unheard of in the Americas.

In a multicultural society such as ours, public schools try hard to be politically correct and make every effort to deal sensitively with these issues. However, issues like these will continue to be passionately debated, for that is the nature of our free democratic society. Citizens have historically championed the worth and dignity of all individuals since our nation began: "We hold certain Truths to be self-evident, that all men are created equal, that they are endowed by their Creator with certain unalienable Rights, that among these are Life, Liberty and the Pursuit of Happiness." The words of our founding fathers still ring loud and true in our schools today.

Sensitive school policies, then, note and celebrate key holidays that are significant to our many cultures, communities, and nation. Commemorating holidays not only provides children with a chance to reflect on and better understand our rich and cherished heritage, but also to learn from the mistakes we have made. Teaching our children about our country's holidays is important because everyone needs to know and appreciate that our heritage is a bequest from past generations; it took immense courage, loss of life, pain, sacrifice, and a great deal of hard work to arrive at where we are today. Our children will soon be entrusted as the caretakers of this cherished land and must be ready to assume that duty willingly and capably. Cultivating love of one's country by commemorating important public holidays is one way teachers help students bond to the land and people, its customs and traditions, its history, and its commitment to the welfare of all citizens.

We all agree that patriotic national holidays help build a feeling of national pride and loyalty. The same can be said for classroom spirit; special classroom "holidays" help add a deeper appreciation for group cohesiveness. It is fun and instructive to immerse the class totally into the day it is celebrating by gearing your curriculum to the theme, reading appropriate books, displaying suitable pictures, and playing fitting music: Book Readers Day, Diversity Day, Animal Respect Day, or Native American Day (a day set aside to help children acquire a deeper appreciation for Native people and their contributions to our country) are but a few creative classroom holidays that students have planned and observed in some elementary schools.

Elections and Voting

One of the best ways to educate young people about what it means to be a citizen in a democratic society is to get them involved in voting and other responsibilities of citizenship. Voting offers an excellent opportunity to learn civic responsibility and shared decision making in a meaningful and motivating context. By participating in the entire voting process (determining voting issues, suggesting possible choices, casting and tallying votes, and confirming the outcome of the vote), children directly experience how a democracy works.

First voting experiences should involve issues of interest for the entire class. It is no secret that unless people are interested in a voting issue, they will not be motivated to participate in the voting process and will likely come away from the experience with a feeling that voting is not important to them. Therefore, first votes should be taken on issues such as favorite storybook character, a class mascot, foods to serve at a classroom party, which animal makes the best pet, or who will win the Super Bowl.

Children should be encouraged to consider the issue carefully before they take a vote, making arguments in support of the position they are willing to defend and trying to persuade their classmates to vote in their favor. It should be emphasized that opposing points of view should be presented with self-control and easiness. The children must realize that it is normal for people to hold different opinions about things and that these differences should not break down friendly relationships.

The vote itself should be carried out deliberately. Try to remember that young children do not understand the voting process as adults do, so some of the measures we are comfortable with may be confusing to them. Take, for example, the common classroom practice of having the children vote by raising their hands. Oftentimes young children will let them fly as soon as a teacher says, "Raise your hands if . . ." whether they want to vote that way or not. Others will lower their hands before their votes are counted, and some may raise their hands more than once (even though they're directed not to). Instead of raising hands, it might be best to:

- *Poll children.* You can list the children's names on a chart and ask each child how he or she votes. The children can then cast votes by placing a tally mark next to their names. The class can then count the votes for each option.
- *Construct name graphs.* Have the children print their names on 3 × 5 inch index cards. Ask each child how he or she votes and then place the index cards in a line or a stack corresponding to the option. Again, the entire class will be involved in counting the votes.
- *Use secret ballots.* If children exert excessive pressure on others to vote their way, it might be best to give each child one piece of paper, ask her or him to secretely make a choice, and drop it into a box. Again, the entire class should count the votes.

Voting should be a part of the older child's classroom, too, for it exemplifies one of the duties and responsibilities of citizenship in a democratic society and demonstrates why voting matters. In the upper grades, however, it is common to extend the students' understandings of the voting process as it applies to the election of officials at the local, state, and national levels.

Gordon Palmer, for example, focused on the question, "So how does one get to be president of the United States?"

"We back Rex!" "A. Pat Osaurus in 2008!" Do these sound like strange election slogans to you? Not if you were visiting Gordon Palmer's fifth-grade classroom!

Mr. Palmer kicked off the election activities for the 2008 presidential election by having his fifth-graders search through an easy-to-read version of the United States Constitution for the three requirements a candidate for the presidency must meet: (1) at least 35 years old, (2) a natural-born citizen of the United States, and (3) a resident of the United States for a minimum of

14 years. "But how does one actually get to be president of the United States?" challenged Mr. Palmer. Finding that his children were fairly uninformed about the process, Mr. Palmer put to advantage his students' interest in dinosaurs to help them learn the election process.

To begin, Mr. Palmer reviewed with the children that dinosaurs can be classified in many ways, but the two most popular categories seem to be meat eaters (carnivores) and plant eaters (herbivores). By randomly picking slips of paper from a box, students were then assigned to the carnivore or herbivore "party." Each party met and selected a party name: the herbivores decided to call their party the Herbocrats while the carnivores favored the Carnublicans. Mr. Palmer explained that each party would meet to select a candidate for "dinosaur president." However, in order to vote, each student was required to register.

NCSS STANDARDS

VI. *Power, Authority, and Governance*

X. *Civic Ideals and Practice*

Mr. Palmer distributed 5 × 8 inch index cards to the students and asked them to print their names and addresses on the cards. The students then signed their cards. The Herbocrats and Carnublicans designed symbols for their parties and drew them on their registration cards. To be properly registered, the students went to a prearranged area in the classroom where an instructional aide checked their signatures on the class list, stamped their cards, and crossed their names off the list. They were told to put the cards in a safe place, as they would need to be presented as verification of registration when it came time to vote.

Each party was allowed to select three prospective candidates for dinosaur president. This process was compared to the primaries held during the actual presidential election process. During the primaries, party members vote for the candidate that will represent their party in the upcoming general election. Therefore, the Herbocrats selected Stegosaurus, Triceratops, and Apatosaurus. The Carnublicans went with Tyrannosaurus Rex, Deinonychus, and Raptor. The party members were divided on the issue of which dinosaur would represent them best, so each party mounted a primary campaign, including buttons, stickers, and hats to wear at a rally. Of course, countless speeches, posters, and mock TV commercials extolled the virtues of each potential dinosaur candidate.

While the primary campaign was running its course, Mr. Palmer and his students made a voting booth from a large packing crate the custodians had rescued from the trash pile. They placed an appropriate "United States Polling Place" at the top and decorated it with various patterns of red, white, and blue. It was important that the students had a place to vote in privacy. At last, it was time to complete the first step of the election process, with each party selecting its candidate!

Each party held its election, with officials making sure to check the registration cards and that each registered voter picked up only one ballot. After the election committee tabulated the results, Tyrannosaurus Rex emerged victorious from the Carnublican Party while the Herbocrats selected Apatosaurus. It was then time to focus on the national convention, step two in the election process. During the national convention, the party finalizes its selection for one presidential nominee and each presidential candidate chooses a dinosaur running mate.

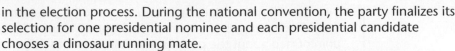

After each dinosaur party selected one presidential candidate, step three—the general election process—began. Candidates campaigned in an attempt to win the support of voters in the other fifth-grade classrooms. In November, the voters were to go to the polls to cast their ballots. Each party published an election newsletter containing background information about the candidates. They made campaign buttons, bumper stickers, and posters. As in the primaries, they wrote campaign songs and slogans. Most importantly, each party was directed to write a platform that presented its candidate's view on all issues of importance. The highlight of the whole experience was a spirited "dinosaur debate" with all the protocol observed during regular presidential television debates.

On voting day, students in Mr. Palmer's class lined up at their packing box voting booth to elect the first dinosaur president. The other classrooms followed. They all clutched their registration cards and voted for their choice, again by secret ballot. The votes were counted and the winner was announced later that afternoon. Tyrannosaurus Rex won in a landslide—the students felt that since this was the fiercest meat-eating land animal that ever lived, it would be most suitable to rule the land of the reptiles. Of course, a huge victory celebration took place that afternoon (arranged and hosted by aides and parents). Everyone had a great time. In addition, the voting booth stayed in the classroom and was used for all other important classroom votes that school year.

Mr. Palmer certainly understood that when a person casts a vote in the general election, he or she is not voting directly for a candidate. Instead, that person is actually casting a vote for a group of people known as *electors*. The electors are part of the Electoral College and are supposed to vote for their state's popularly elected candidate. However, the Electoral College system can confuse even many adult voters, so Mr. Palmer chose not to include it in his election simulation. Should you try the simulation in your classroom, it would be interesting to find a way to make the Electoral College a part of the process.

Children should learn that one of the most important ways they can participate in their government is to exercise their right to vote. By voting, people have a voice in their government.

The Actions and Attitudes of Civic Responsibility

Today's civics education takes on a much different character than it did in the past. The ultimate goal of civics education has shifted from the primary instructional goal of passing on knowledge to producing citizens who are not only knowledgeable but also committed to the principle of *civic responsibility*. Civic responsibility can be defined as accepting the "duties of a citizen"—becoming an active contributor to public life in a committed and productive manner. Civic responsibility can be displayed in many ways: being active in the school litter and recycling program; organizing a clothing or toy drive in school; writing letters to public officials to get a traffic signal placed at a busy intersection; visiting the elderly in assisted living facilities; volunteering in animal shelters, churches, or food banks; planting shrubs, flowers, and trees in the community; and so on. The character essential for becoming involved in situations like these sprouts at an early age and blossoms into adulthood as children learn that they can make a difference in their community and that their contributions are truly helpful and appreciated. Alleman and Brophy (2002) advise, "After students begin to understand and appreciate the importance of government and how its work is reflected in our lives, [they should be helped to understand] that governments cannot do everything . . . and appreciate the value of [civic action]. . . . Even children can do things . . . to make their community a better place" (p. 10).

The concern for encouraging public service and involvement is mushrooming today and, with growing community support, many schools have been quick to adopt community service programs. In a sense, they concur with the sentiments of one astute 11-year-old who observed, "We have freedom in this country but it stinks. Drugs . . . alcohol . . . crime . . . war. There's no good news anymore. We need someone to come in and clean out America!"

Education for civic responsibility means we must practice what we preach in our social studies classrooms. Informing students about the significance of civic participation is one thing; involving them in community service is better. When students roll up their sleeves and get involved, they understand what we really mean by citizenship responsibilities. A major goal of community service programs is to promote among elementary school children an understanding of how their interest and efforts can influence local public policy issues. Most classroom programs designed to promote civic awareness and public action operate in accord with this general instructional pattern: *selecting a local issue to investigate, examining the issue, considering the alternatives, agreeing on a course of action,* and *becoming active participants.* The process starts as children confront an issue that genuinely affects them—litter, homelessness, global warming, land-use issues, childhood obesity, immigration, or bicycle safety. The issue then serves as a springboard for careful study and direct action. The students consider strategies to tackle the issue, similar to the way Helena Rubin's students did at the beginning of this chapter.

Mirka Warczka's sixth-graders exhibited comparable effort and determination as they grew to be particularly troubled about a newspaper story about the accidental discovery of a mass grave as a construction crew was excavating a site for a new office complex. After a great deal of careful research, a university professor found that the remains were all that was left of 57 Irish immigrants who died of Black Diphtheria while working as

railroad laborers in the late summer of 1853. Their job was to use their picks and shovels to clear and straighten out a portion of hilly land through which a set of new train tracks were to run. It was grueling, dangerous work and these men labored from dawn to dusk during their 6-day work week. If a worker became sick or was injured on the job, he was fired immediately. Firings happened quite frequently, for safety measures and standards for cleanliness and sanitation at that time were dreadful. Unfortunately, a combination of these unhealthy conditions and terrible accidents helped contribute to a familiar expression of that time: "An Irishman buried under every tie."

NCSS STANDARDS

- **II.** *Time, Continuity, and Change*
- **III.** *People, Places, and Environments*
- **X.** *Civic Ideals and Practice*

The 57 Irish immigrants had been working here only six weeks before they got sick and died. They had developed Black Diphtheria, a bacterium that infects the nose and throat, causing a black, tough covering that eventually blocks the airways. "Their throats would swell up and kill them," it was reported. The 57 men were callously dumped in a mass grave between two of the hills they worked to clear. This location was now at the center of a busy crossroad where the office complex was going to rise.

"I cannot believe it," blurted Charles. "Those poor men didn't mean anything to the company that hired them."

"Yeah," agreed Katrice. "They were wiped off the face of the Earth and nobody even cared."

"It's like they were treated worse than animals. They were willing to work hard and look how bad they were treated!" protested Tyreke.

"I wish there was something we could do to give them the respect they deserve," offered Diane.

"Maybe there is," suggested Mr. Warczka. "Let's think about it."

The students researched the situation a bit further and found that a group of interested people had planned to gather at a dedication ceremony in about a month to honor the workers. The group's goal was to locate as many of the workers' remains as possible and provide the men with a proper burial near the construction site. Today, there is a small plot of land near the office site where the 57 Irish workers are buried; the stones surrounding the tiny burial ground are the exact blocks the workers put down as the base for the tracks.

The students wanted to attend the dedication ceremony and received permission to do so. Mr. Warczka suggested the students contact the local historical association and ask if there was any way they might add to the ceremony other than simply attend. They were given permission to plant an oak sapling at the site to commemorate the occasion. It now grows proudly next to a dignified historical marker that honors the workers.

"I cannot believe this happened to the workers the way it did," whispered Katrice at the dedication ceremony.

"Yeah," agreed Wesley. "It makes you sad to think how many other immigrant workers were treated like this."

"To know and to not do is to not know" is a very old Chinese proverb that sums up the situation that attracted the attention of these children. What the old saying means is that if these children were aware of this tragic civic injustice and failed to respond to it, then they may as well have not known about it at all. Children must be helped to become knowledgeable of public and political issues, pay attention to them, and embark on a path of participation that leads to positive change through civic action: "I would not have known how much a kid like me could help if we didn't have a chance to read about the Irish railroad workers," reflected Freddy.

Learning about the Civic Responsibility of Model Citizens

It is not easy to prepare young children for their roles as active citizens in a participatory democracy. Libresco (2002) stresses that many different learning experiences and sound educational resources must engage children in fundamental activities that teach not just information such as "How a bill becomes a law" but also "How can I participate effectively in the public life of my community?" Libresco goes on to explain: "Accordingly, I believe that students must study historical (and current) events in which small groups of citizens joined forces to make change; for example, to gain civil rights or to stop a war, or (at the neighborhood level) to curb driving drunk or to have a crosswalk installed. *The so-called experts rarely solve such problems; rather, the collective effort of citizens who realized they are not powerless is more likely to realize real change. . . . We are all public officials*" (italics mine) (p. 12).

Stephanie Koszalka, a fifth-grade teacher, was tremendously influenced by these kinds of well-reasoned commentaries. She immediately searched for enjoyable and productive strategies that might personally involve her children in the lives of people who have demonstrated exemplary civic dispositions. Ms. Koszalka was already aware that the power of superbly written biographies and their enduring themes of sacrifice and responsibility, power and oppression, failure and achievement. And she knew that these stories vicariously engage students in the lives of others, help them see the world through others' eyes, and make them aware of human potential. But, her major stumbling block was finding a theme that would grab the children's imagination and draw them into the stories of people who made a difference.

Ms. Koszalka's quandary was resolved as she watched the opening of the 2002 Winter Olympics on television. She looked on in admiration and respect as New York City police officer Daniel Rodriguez sang *God Bless America* with determined patriotism. The thought raced through her mind that if the shocking events of September 11, 2001, had not transpired, she would probably be listening to a popular recording artist instead of Officer Rodriguez. However, September 11 refocused our nation's collective image on civic heroes and their importance in our lives. Heroes help us aspire to civic action—their character traits and important contributions serve as distinctive models of good citizenship.

"That's it—heroes. That's exactly the theme I was looking for!" thought Ms. Koszalka. She then pulled together a series of dynamic learning experiences, including a text set of five different titles on the theme of "Heroes" and carried out an exemplary course of action.

Ms. Koszalka kicked off "Hero Week" in her classroom by inviting real-life local heroes to visit—a retired teacher who was also a Holocaust survivor, a former pilot who flew bombing raids over Germany during World War II, an ex-Negro League baseball player, and a former member of a nonviolent civil rights group who once was jailed for 21 days for her activities.

Then, convinced of the power of good books to exemplify wisdom, courage, and inner character, Ms. Koszalka gathered five copies each of five different books about people who made a difference—male and female, various cultures, the famous and not-so-famous, adults and children. Ms. Koszalka introduced these books to her young citizens during a short minilesson that began with Ms. Koszalka's oral reading of Barbara Cooney's picture book, *Eleanor* (Puffin). The book tells of how Eleanor Roosevelt overcame difficult childhood experiences to develop into the great person she turned out to be. When she finished reading, the children talked in great length about how different experiences during Eleanor's childhood helped her grow into a brave and loyal adult.

After the discussion, it was time for the students to go to work and select their own hero books from the text set Ms. Koszalka had pulled together:

- *Through My Eyes* by Ruby Bridges (Scholastic)
- *Clemente: The Passion and Grace of Baseball's Last Hero* by David Maraniss (Simon & Schuster)
- *Susan B. Anthony: Champion of Women's Rights* by Helen Albee Monsell (Aladdin)
- *Gandhi: Great Soul* by John B. Severance (Clarion)
- *General James Longstreet: The Confederacy's Most Controversial Soldier* by Jeffry D. Wert (Simon & Schuster)

NCSS STANDARDS

II. *Time, Continuity, and Change*
V. *Individuals, Groups, and Institutions*
X. *Civic Ideals and Practice*

Ms. Koszalka offered a brief description of each book and then turned the students loose. Her simple directions were that they were to look at the different books, but not select the first one they came to. They were to sample the different offerings to see which ones they might eventually like to read (she called this a "gallery tour"). As the students examined the books, Ms. Koszalka circulated throughout the area, informally talking with them and making a few timely suggestions to students who needed extra guidance.

After they completed their "gallery tour," Ms. Koszalka passed out slips of paper and asked the students to write their names at the top. They were then instructed to list their first through third book choices. Then, after school that day, Ms. Koszalka spread out all the slips and began assigning books according to choice. Because Ms. Koszalka had so many books to select from, most children would get their first choice. However, there were some adjustments that needed to be made, as a few children were assigned their second or third choices.

The next day, the children got their books, sat together in groups having the same book title, and began reading about their civic heroes. When they were finished, Ms. Koszalka devised a plan that would encourage the students to talk thoughtfully and intelligently about their books.

To bring together the entire literature-based experience, Ms. Koszalka organized the construction of a paper bag timeline. She modeled the process by showing the students a completed bag she had constructed for Eleanor Roosevelt. Each text set group was then given a strong paper bag and asked to print the name of its hero in bold letters at the top. The groups were to use this bag to show what they learned about their heroes through writing, drawing, and collage. The students were first given an outline of a coat-of-arms with four blank segments. They were directed to draw an appropriate picture or symbol (or print a word) in the segments that best answered the following questions:

1. What is your greatest personal accomplishment?
2. If you could compare yourself to an animal, what would it be?
3. What is one lesson others can learn from you?
4. What is one word you would most like people to use to describe you?

These coats-of-arms were taped to the front of the bags. The students labeled the bags with dates underneath the hero's name to show when their hero lived and printed two questions at the bottom of the bag. The students were to use questions that could be answered by looking at the coats-of-arms on the front of their bags.

One group completed Figure 6.5 for Ruby Bridges, who, in 1960 at age 6, was the first African American student to enter William Frantz Elementary School in New Orleans. The students explained that they drew a school in the first section because it showed that Ruby helped integrate the elementary school by passing through a mob of racist protestors shouting insults and threats. They selected a sheep as an animal to represent Ruby in section two because they felt Ruby had a wonderful smile and remained calm and peaceful throughout this unusual challenge. In the third section, the students explained that they depicted an African American child holding hands with a white child because Ruby Bridges would want to teach others that white people and black people should respect and love each other. Finally, the students wrote the word *courage* in the last section because they felt Ruby bravely faced a very difficult situation with very strong character. The story of Ruby Bridges showed that even small children can be heroes for each other.

When all the bags were finished on the outside, the students were asked to consider three important events from their heroes' lives and explain their significance; they were to find an artifact, make a model, or draw an

FIGURE 6.5 Coat of Arms for Ruby Bridges

illustration as a representation of each event. The items were then packed into the paper bags. One item placed in the Ruby Bridges bag was a small student-drawn sign reading "Whites Only" that signified the signs the angry white people carried in protest as they gathered outside the Frantz Elementary School. A baseball, toy airplane, and can of food helped another group represent a part of baseball star Roberto Clemente's life when he died in an airplane crash trying to bring people medical supplies and food to people in Nicaragua when their city was destroyed by a terrible earthquake in 1972.

After each group decided on its three artifacts and placed them into the bags, they sequenced the bags in chronological order. Next, each group prepared a short story that told about the events represented by their artifacts and presented the stories to their classmates. Afterwards, everyone had a chance to explore the fun questions, coats-of-arms, and artifacts.

To consider the contributions of each civic hero a bit more deeply, Ms. Koszalka introduced a list of five traits, called the "five themes of citizenship," that seemed to capture the major attributes of the heroic people the students had read about: *honesty, responsibility, compassion, respect*, and *courage*. She offered examples and discussed these traits with the class, making sure they understood each. Ms. Koszalka then challenged the students to think carefully about which of the five attributes best described their heroes. She then taped signs labeled with the five themes to the classroom walls at even intervals around the room. The students were asked to go with their books to the area designated by the theme they thought best defined their heroes. It was interesting to see that students reading the same biography tended to split away from their partners to position themselves at different signs. For example, one member of the Ruby Bridges group went to *responsibility* while three others went to *courage*. Knowing that open discussions often disintegrate into idle chatter, Ms. Koszalka directed their conversations with a printed conversation guide: (1) briefly summarize the actions or values that made your person a civic hero; (2) explain why you selected this trait to associate with your civic hero, reading a short selection from the book to support your point; and (3) make a connection between what you had read and your own lives. Of course, Ms. Koszalka modeled these responsibilities by first offering an example of what she would say based on the book she had read aloud to the class, *Eleanor*.

Ms. Koszalka brought her biographical study of heroes to a close by asking the students to consider three questions: "If you could bring any real-life hero from the past to the present, which would you choose?" "What five questions would you ask the person?" "What kind of hero will our country need in the year 2050?"

Good citizenship requires a clear understanding of core citizenship dispositions and virtues and a willingness to partake in responsible action directed toward the welfare of one's community. To portray the fundamental nature of heroes through their voluntary civic actions invites students to emulate their strengths and spirit in their own lives.

Civic Dispositions and Virtues

Up to this point, we have restricted our discussion of civics education to experiencing citizenship processes as members of a democratic classroom community, helping students construct subject matter concepts, and facilitating connections between what students learn in school and their civic responsibility. But the vision of contemporary civics education transcends even these three noble goals; an essential part of civics education deals with making a commitment to civic dispositions and virtues—the core values necessary to nurture and strengthen the ideals of American democracy. In its Curriculum Standards for Social Studies, the NCSS (1994) described this realm of instruction as going beyond the content of civics to the formation of dispositions required of effective citizenship. Standard X (Civic Ideals & Practices) states: "Social studies programs should include experiences that provide for the study of the ideals, principles, and practices of citizenship in a democratic republic" (p. 30).

In the elementary grades, students are introduced to civic dispositions and virtues throughout the day as they experience life in democratic classrooms. The dispositions and values of our nation are exemplified by the sense of community created in a democratic classroom—students functioning as young citizens making helpful decisions for the good of the group. In addition to those informal experiences, the Center for Civic Education (1994) established this standard: "Students should be able to explain the importance of the fundamental values and principles of American democracy" (p. 22). To achieve this standard, the center advised that students should be able to explain the importance for themselves, their school, their community, and their nation each of the following fundamental values of American democracy:

- Individual rights to life, liberty, property, and the pursuit of happiness
- The public or common good
- Justice
- Equality of opportunity
- Diversity
- Truth
- Patriotism (p. 22)

There has been a resurgence of concern during the past decade that patriotic values like these have fallen out of favor. However, Ryan (1993) comments that this realm of civics education has reemerged as a popular trend "because people are banging on the schoolhouse door. The invitation is coming from the outside. Parents and policymakers are disturbed by a total inability of our culture to pass on its values" (p. 1). Society is now turning back to the schools and demanding that certain widely held core values or virtues underlying American democratic society should be at the heart of the school curriculum, the purpose of which is to systematically develop the character of our students.

Critical Thinking

Early in our nation's history, reading aloud passages from the Bible helped carry out what we now call citizenship education. Even into the 1800s, instructional materials reflected a strong religious character, as we see in this selection from *The Boston Primer* (Hersh, 1980):

> Let children who would fear the LORD,
> Hear what their Teachers say,
> With rev'rence meet their Parents' word,
> And with Delight obey. (p. 16)

Children were required to read passages like this over and over again until they committed them to memory. Educators of the time thought that civic values were best instilled in this manner because young children were considered incapable of making their own decisions; they were simply unable to think rationally. Therefore, their thinking had to be done for them.

Certainly, distinguishing good from evil remains an important goal of citizenship education, but there is current agreement that simply committing virtuous anecdotes to memory could be described more as brainwashing than as learning. To replace the time-worn memorization strategy, today's teachers are advised to involve students in higher-order thinking exercises—asking questions, solving problems, judging, making personal decisions. In short, civic values should be taught in a classroom setting that supports the development of critical thinkers.

What is critical thinking? That is a tough question to answer, for critical thinking is such a complex process that psychologists have not yet been able to see eye to eye on a definition. Although there are many competing views, this definition is particularly appropriate for dynamic social studies instruction: the higher-order thought processes used to conceptualize and assess information for the purpose of deciding what to believe or what to do. Critical thinking involves the process of examining words and illustrations for the purpose of detecting accuracy, bias, fairness, or favoritism. In effect, the critical thinker asks, "What do I already know about this issue or person that helps me decide whether the statements I am taking in are legitimate or fair?" So, instead of simply taking in someone's words and accepting them as perfect, students learn to study the issues carefully, gather information, consider alternative points of view, uncover any biases, and suspend judgments, actions, or decisions until they view the issues from all sides.

More important than a definition of critical thinking by itself, however, is the idea that there is a better instructional road to take in social studies education than rote memorization. The NCSS Curriculum Standards for Social Studies (NCSS, 1994) supports this ambition by addressing citizenship in the context of civic action: "Social studies educators have an obligation to help students explore a variety of positions in a thorough, fair-minded manner. As each position is studied and discussed to determine the strongest points in favor of it, the strongest points in opposition to it, and the consequences that would follow from selecting it, students become better able to improve the ways in which they deal with persistent issues and dilemmas and participate with others in making decisions about them" (p. 10). The NCSS Task Force on Early Childhood/Elementary Social Studies (1989) takes a similarly strong position on the role of critical thinking and civic action in social studies: "For children to develop citizenship skills appropriate to a democracy, they must be capable of thinking critically about complex societal problems and global problems. . . . Children need to be equipped with the skills to cope with change" (p. 16).

How do elementary school teachers help build critical thinking skills in dynamic social studies programs? Perhaps because there is so much disagreement about what critical thinking is, and because it encompasses such a variety of sophisticated thinking skills, suggestions for classroom use are sketchy at best. However, if we want our students to be critical thinkers, then the answer lies in thinking about content in ways that evoke strong feelings. Children must know the topic in depth, question and challenge the ideas that confuse or disturb them, and, with thinking at its peak, establish personal decisions and judgments. Critical thinking, as you can see, cannot happen in a vacuum; you first teach for understanding. If students do not understand, they have no framework on which to reason and reflect.

Reflecting on Meaningful Content

Critical thinking is most commonly associated with the act of reading—taking in ideas in print and ultimately forming opinions and judgments. Young children get most of their social studies content from a variety of sources, but words-in-print seem to predominate. Written resources often contain the problems, issues, or ideas that become the lifeblood of meaningful classroom discussions. Short stories rather than "meaty" contemporary issues or controversial historical events supply the early grade children with content for critical thinking. Story books are better matched to their interests and abilities than newspaper clippings or magazine articles. Consider this example from Imelda Zavala's first-grade classroom. It draws content from a popular childhood story, but asks children to think beyond the actual story events by distinguishing between good acts and bad acts, or good thoughts and bad thoughts.

Today, Ms. Zavala read *The Little Red Hen Big Book* by Paul Galdone (Clarion) to her eager group of first-grade classroom youngsters. She knew that the book was useful for many instructional purposes, not the least of which was to offer an opportunity for critical thinking. After she finished reading the book, Ms. Zavala wanted to make sure that the children understood the story, so she helped the children complete a graphic organizer to activate and organize their thinking. The organizer ended with the hen's decision to not share her bread with the animals that refused to help her. To go beyond the content and encourage the children to form judgments, Ms. Zavala asked a key question: "Did the Little Red Hen do the right thing?" Ms. Zavala encouraged the class to think about why the animals refused to help the hen and whether they might have had good reasons. The children discussed what they thought about the hen's decision not to share her bread and considered other choices she could have made.

NCSS STANDARDS

IV. *Individual Development and Identity*

X. *Civic Ideals and Practice*

Finally, Ms. Zavala displayed a chart divided into three columns: (1) the child's name, (2) a "yes" column, and (3) a "no" column. Ms. Zavala explained the chart to the children and asked them to predict whether there would be more yes or no votes in response to the question, "Did the Little Red Hen do the right thing?" The children were invited to write their names and mark their votes answering the question (see Figure 6.6). Afterward, the class discussed the results, for the value of discussion and sharing is perhaps more important than the graphic organizer or chart itself.

As children experience opportunities for higher-order thinking throughout the primary grades, they will learn to consider issues more directly related to social studies content. Much of the subject matter contains issues and events that offer students an opportunity to weigh evidence and arrive at good/bad or pro/con judgments. Should the colonies have revolted against Great Britain? What are the so-

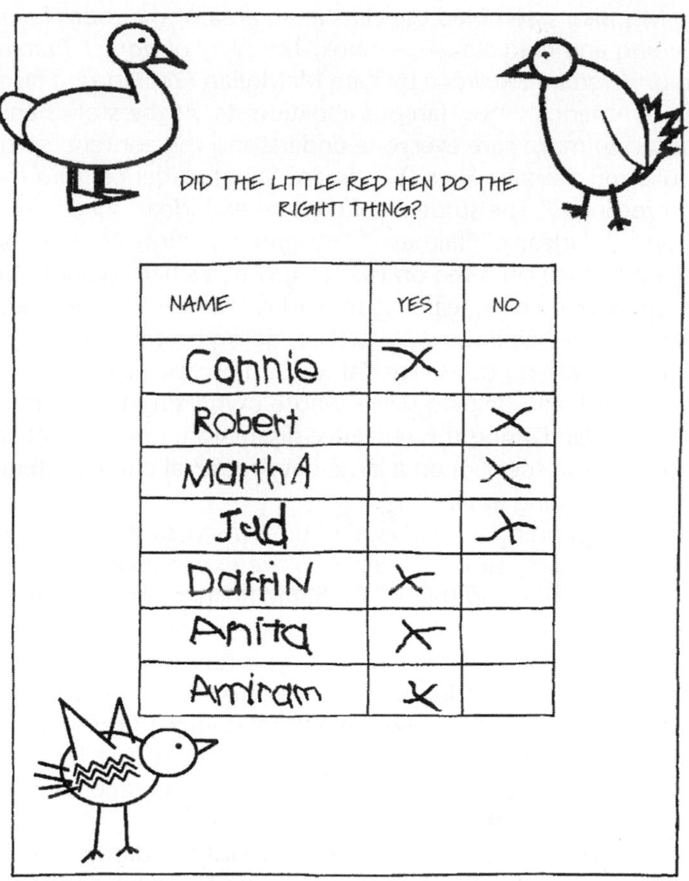

DID THE LITTLE RED HEN DO THE RIGHT THING?

NAME	YES	NO
Connie	X	
Robert		X
MarthA		X
Jad		X
DarriN	X	
Anita	X	
Amiram	X	

FIGURE 6.6 *Little Red Hen* Graph

lutions to illegal immigration in America? Should felons be allowed to vote? Of all former presidents, who was the best?

An upper-grade scenario begins as Maura Biko's fifth-graders return to their classroom after recess. The soft, plaintive strains of "Negro spirituals" fill the room. Ms. Biko will help her students understand that slaves created these songs not only to express their deep longing for freedom but also as coded messages that passed on secret information for escape, such as where to find escape routes and hideaways: *Steal Away to Jesus, Go Down, Moses, The Drinking Gourd*, and *Swing Low, Sweet Chariot.* The meaning of these spirituals was quite often hidden. For example, *Swing Low, Sweet Chariot* referred directly to the Underground Railroad, a secret organization that helped many slaves flee their masters.

Ms. Biko assembled the class at an area of the room favorable for good listening and read aloud the book, *The Story of Harriet Tubman: Conductor of the Underground Railroad* by Kate McMullan (Yearling), a fascinating story of one of America's most famous abolitionists. At the story's end, Ms. Biko wanted to make sure everyone understood the content, so she asked, "How would you describe Harriet Tubman? What evidence from the story supports your feelings?" The students offered several ideas, most of which revolved around the ideas of "fairness," "toughness," "intelligence," and "courage." Their evidence centered on Harriet Tubman's hard work in the fields, being whipped by owners, learning to read without her owner's knowledge, being injured while helping a slave escape, going on many Underground Railroad journeys, learning to use special ways to escape (such as navigating by the North Star), and helping slaves whose owners refused to release them after the Civil War. During this reflective discussion, one student served as a scribe, recording the specifics on a large data-retrieval chart strategically placed near the story reading area.

NCSS STANDARDS

- **I.** *Culture*
- **II.** *Time, Continuity, and Change*
- **X.** *Civic Ideals and Practice*

After spending a good deal of time discussing the story in this manner, Ms. Biko added a new dimension to the experience. "So far," she said, "we have been discussing the many characteristics and accomplishments that made Harriet Tubman stand out as a special person. Now I would like you to do some deeper thinking. Certainly, you have identified several of Harriet Tubman's major contributions to humankind, but now I want you to decide which you regard as her *most important* contribution of all." After much serious debate, small groups of students agreed that Tubman's most important contribution was her attempts to hide and transport slaves to freedom through the Underground Railroad.

Ms. Biko then shared a few ideas about the dangers of running away from slavery and aiding fugitives. She explained how the spirituals the children had listened to as they entered the room helped the slaves find their way to the North. She then read this dilemma faced by Sie, a slave from Maryland in 1825, when his extremely troubled master came to his cabin with an unusual request:

> One night in the month of January . . . he came into my cabin and waked me up. . . . For awhile he said nothing and sat . . . warming himself at the fire. "Sick, massa?" said I. "Can't I help you in any way, massa?" I spoke tenderly for my heart was full of compassion at his wretched appearance. At last . . . he cried, "Oh, Sie! I'm ruined, ruined, ruined. . . . They've got a judgment against me, and in less than two weeks every [slave] I've got will be . . . sold." I sat silent. . . . "And now, Sie," he continued, "there's only one way I can save anything. You can do it; won't you, won't you?" In his distress he rose and actually threw his arms around me . . . "I want you to run away, Sie, to . . . Kentucky,

and take all the servants along with you." . . . My master proposed to follow me in a few months and establish himself in Kentucky. (Henson, 1935, pp. 162–167)

After discussing the situation to make sure the students understood what it was all about, Ms. Biko said, "Isn't it interesting that after being Sie's master for over 30 years, the plantation owner became so dependent on him? Should Sie help out the owner?"

Ms. Biko divided the children into discussion groups and asked them to decide what Sie should do. She provided a graphic organizer for them to organize their divergent viewpoints (see Figure 6.7). Each group was to consider the owner's request and discuss whether to help him. Every time they listed a reason to help, they had to follow it with a reason not to help; the students must always have an equal number of items in both columns. When the groups finished their lists, they told whether they would help and supported their decision with reasons why.

PROS AND CONS

SOMETIMES AN ISSUE IS SO COMPLICATED IT'S HARD TO TAKE SIDES. HERE'S A WAY TO HELP YOU MAKE A DECISION.

SIE SHOULD HELP OUT THE OWNER.

AGREE	DISAGREE

FIGURE 6.7 Pro and Con Visual Organizer

Throughout this lesson, Ms. Biko employed refined instructional strategies designed to move her students beyond the realm of content itself and into higher-order thinking processes using rich, thought-provoking content. Thought-provoking content sets in motion adventures in critical thinking, for it provides the essential substance of productive discussions dealing with feelings and civic ideals.

Graphic Organizers

As the case with Maura Biko, teachers often use graphic organizers, visual representations of knowledge or ideas, to help their students manage their higher-order thinking. Graphic organizers assist students in arranging content or ideas in an orderly fashion, becoming aware of how ideas are connected, and participating in active, meaningful learning. For example, let us suppose that you are going to be teaching the idea that a stable food supply was one of the prerequisites of early settled civilizations. The specific content you must first help the children understand centers on the idea that as early gatherer-hunters learned to domesticate wild animals and to sow seeds, they gradually settled down and became farmers and herders. Then, as farming methods improved, people often found themselves with food surpluses. This unexpected bounty led to trade. A village with an overabundance of grain, for example, exchanged it for tools, pottery, cloth, or other goods from nearby villages. An overabundance of anything is called a *surplus*, and early civilizations had to learn how to face important decisions regarding surpluses—it wasn't always the best move to trade them for other goods.

By helping develop these understandings, your next step is to use it to encourage higher-order thinking. How can you do that? Omar Nemchick believes it can be effectively accomplished by using graphic organizers to help students arrive at a judgment. Here is the way he did it.

Mr. Nemchick had his students assume the role of citizens of an ancient village living on the land between the Tigris and Euphrates Rivers. Their village is fortunate; unlike others whose farmland has been scorched by the sun, theirs has an irrigation system that helped produce an abundance of grain. While other villages faced a devastating famine, theirs is thriving. Mr. Nemchick held a discussion focused on the following questions: "How do you feel about having surplus food while your neighbors are starving? Is it fair that one village should have so much while the others face famine? Do wealthy civilizations have a responsibility to help those that have less?"

To delve more deeply into these issues, Mr. Nemchick started a cooperative learning activity in which students considered the problem of what a village should do with its surplus grain. He divided the class into base groups of three, and assigned the students a number from one to three. Mr. Nemchick directed all the ones, twos, and threes to move from their base groups into expert groups, with each expert group assigned to examine the positive and negative consequences of one of these alternatives: All the ones

NCSS STANDARDS

II. *Time, Continuity, and Change*
III. *People, Places, and Environments*
X. *Civic Ideals and Practice*

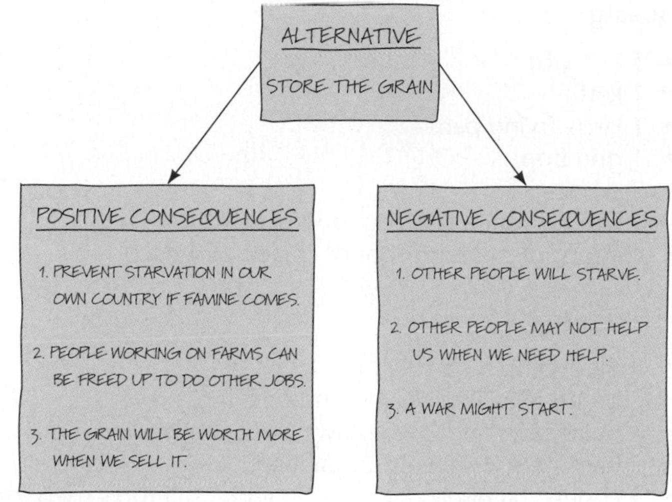

FIGURE 6.8 Decision-Making Graphic Organizer

will study the "store the grain" alternative, twos will study the "sell the grain" alternative, and the threes will study the "give it away" alternative. Completing a graphic organizer helped each group consider the positive and negative consequences of their alternatives. The "Store the Grain" group's completed organizer is shown in Figure 6.8.

After completing their graphic organizers, each member of the expert groups returned to his or her base group to share the conclusions. Each base group, after listening to the positive and negative consequences of each alternative, was directed to arrive at a decision.

There are many suitable graphics that can be used to help students organize items in this fashion. Alfonso Garces, for example, selected a 12-inch ruler graphic he called the "measuring stick" to involve his fifth-graders in making important decisions during a simulated seventeenth-century voyage from England to Massachusetts Colony.

To start, Mr. Garces asked his students to imagine themselves in the year 1625 as members of a Pilgrim family setting sail from England to Massachusetts Colony. He divided the class randomly into seven families, or groups. Their ship was large, so each family was given the luxury of packing whatever they wanted. The children were directed to search the Mayflower History website (www.mayflowerhistory.com/History/voyage6.php) and found everything that the Pilgrims would like to have taken:

NCSS STANDARDS

II. *Time, Continuity, and Change*
III. *People, Places, and Environments*
X. *Civic Ideals and Practice*

Cooking

- 1 iron pot
- 1 kettle
- 1 large frying pan
- 1 grid iron
- 2 skillets
- 1 spit (to rotate cooking food over a fire)
- Platters, dishes, and spoons (made of wood)

Work Tools

- 5 broad and 5 narrow hoes
- 2 broad axes, 2 pickaxes, and 5 felling axes
- 4 hand saws and 2 whipsaws (with sharpening file)
- 2 hammers, 3 shovels, 2 spades
- 2 augers, 6 chisels, 1 percer, 1 gimlet (all tools used for boring/drilling/chiseling wood)
- 2 hatchets
- 1 frow (a sharp tool used to split wood for fence posts)
- 1 grindstone
- Nails "of all sorts"

Weapons and Hunting

- Complete (but light) body armor
- Long-barreled musket (Captain Smith recommends 5 feet 6 inches long)
- 1 sword and belt
- 1 bandolier (a leather belt that was worn from the right shoulder across the breast and under the left arm, to support the musket)
- 20 pounds of gunpowder
- 60 pounds of shot

Food (for one person, intended to last one year)

- Beer (the primary drink for everyone, water was often considered unsafe)
- About 2 barrels of wheat (a barrel held 36 gallons)
- About ½ barrel of peas, and ½ barrel of oats
- 2 gallons of vinegar
- 1 gallon aqua-vitae (a strong liquor made from distilling beer or wine)
- 1 gallon salad oil
- Bacon
- Cheese
- Sugar, spice, and fruit

Bedding and Furniture

- 1 pair of canvas sheets
- About 26 feet of canvas to make a bed and bolster for two
- About 18 feet of canvas to make a bed for the sea voyage
- 1 rug
- 12 sewing needles
- Wooden chest
- Cradle
- Books

Animals

- Chickens
- Pigs
- Goats
- Oxen
- Horses
- Cattle
- Dogs

As the day of departure grew near, the ship's captain met with the voyagers and passed on some very distressing news—the original ship had been severely damaged in a storm at sea and could not be repaired in time for its scheduled launch. Instead, the Pilgrims would be required to sail on a ship half as big and incapable of holding large stores of cargo. Unfortunately, the Pilgrims would be forced to do away with most of their intended cargo. Each family was directed to meet together in order to prioritize the items from each category, placing the least important item at the bottom and the most important at the top of a "measuring stick." Mr. Garces developed the graphic organizer to help the students whenever they were challenged to sequence items using *most important* to *least important* criteria (see figure 6.9). Each family group was informed that it would will be able to take along only the top three items in each group (cooking, work tools, and so on), so family members were required to defend their choices with high quality reasons.

In this context, the families understood that they would find no shopping centers, malls, department stores, or supermarkets in Massachusetts, so they were forced to make hard choices about what to take with them. Through this exercise, the students not only learned the intended content (what the Pilgrims took on their voyage to America) but did so in an active, decision-making manner; almost as if they were living the experience themselves.

Tools	Food	Animals
4 Hand saws	Beer	Cattle
5 Broad hoes	Wheat	Horses
2 Hammers	Peas	Oxen
Nails	Oats	Goats
3 Shovels	Bacon	Chickens
2 Pick axes	Cheese	Pigs
1 Grind stone	Sugar	Dogs
1 Frow	Fruit	
2 Whipsaws	Vinegar	
2 Hatchets	Salad oil	
5 Felling axes	Spices	
2 Augers		

FIGURE 6.9 Graphic Organizer

The possibilities for using graphic organizers and cooperative learning strategies are endless. One of my favorite graphic organizers is the *Decision Tree*. Richard Remy and his associates (no date) at the Mershon Center of the Ohio State University developed this interesting graphic organizer. To begin climbing the Decision Tree, ask how many students notice that they make decisions every day, such as when they actually climb a tree or when they decide what to wear to school that day. Explain that decisions are not always as easy as those; in fact, many decisions require meaningful thought and careful planning. All decisions require choosing carefully from among competing alternatives. Select a decision such as deciding what to wear to school that day. "What alternatives (options) did you have?" In addition to identifying alternatives, decisions also involve studying the consequences (possible results) of each alternative. "What are the possible advantages and disadvantages of choosing either alternative?"

Next, inform the students that they are going to use their ability to use alternatives and consequences in an imaginative situation by helping Sir Lottalance decide what to do about Dingbat the Dimwitted, a fierce dragon causing the villagers severe problems. Tell the students to put themselves in the place of the knight, Sir Lottalance, as they listen to the following story:

> One day very long ago, the country's bravest knight, Sir Lottalance, was riding along on his horse, minding his own business, when he came across some very sad townspeople. They were upset because the nasty dragon, Dingbat the Dimwitted, had lumbered out of his dark cave and carried off the beautiful princess from the king's castle. The brokenhearted king had offered a huge reward for anyone who could destroy the dragon and save his daughter's life. But the first knight to try was barbecued by Dingbat's blazing breath. The second knight to try ran away in panic at the sight of the hulking creature, tripped over his own sword, and became the

dragon's shish kabob. Sir Lottalance could hear the princess beating her fists angrily against the dragon and calling him the nastiest names you ever heard. He could hear Dingbat's empty tummy rumbling as the dragon waited for another tasty meal of fried knight. Sir Lottalance was the fastest, strongest, and bravest knight in the kingdom. What could he do?

Now point to a bulletin board display showing Dingbat, Lottalance, and a large construction-paper decision tree bedecked with the sign "Occasion for Decision" (as in Figure 6.10). The "Alternative" and "Consequences" areas on the tree are initially blank. For the children to climb the tree, they will have to think of Sir Lottalance's alternatives. Ask them for alternatives. When they have described

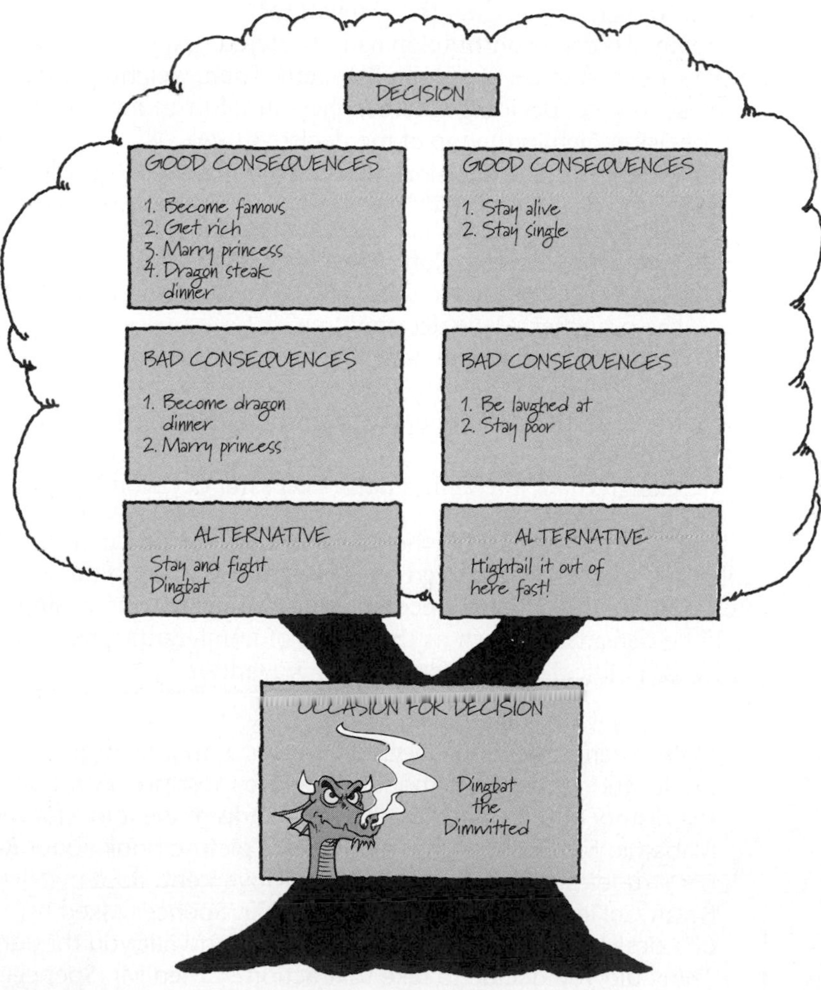

FIGURE 6.10 The Decision Tree

fighting or fleeing, write the responses on the alternative branches of the tree and congratulate the children for starting their climb up the decision tree.

Help the students climb higher into the branches of the tree by looking at the consequences of Sir Lottalance's decision. Ask, "What would be a good (or positive) consequence of getting out of there fast? What would be a bad (or negative) consequence of getting out of there fast?"

When the students have suggested ideas corresponding to "stay alive," "enjoy dragon burgers for life," or "be called Lottalance the Sissy," add them to the blank areas above the "getting out of here fast" alternative. Again, reinforce your students for doing a good job of climbing and remind them they still have an alternative branch to explore. Ask, "What would be some bad (or negative) consequences of fighting Dingbat the Dimwitted? What would be some good (or positive) consequences of fighting Dingbat the Dimwitted?"

Again, list each contribution as it is offered. Examine the whole tree and look for the students' sense of accomplishment. Then, weighing the consequences, ask the class to vote, deciding whether they should run away or fight. Finally, place their decision high in the top of the decision tree.

To summarize, the decision-tree strategy involves the following steps:

1. Decide what question to examine and label it at the base of the tree.
2. Abbreviate the decision in the "Occasion for Decision" sign.
3. Encourage children to think up alternatives and write them in the boxes on the branches of the decision tree.
4. Discuss positive and negative consequences of each alternative, one at a time.
5. Write in the consequences, ask the children to weigh each, and write in their goal.
6. Congratulate the children as successful decision makers.

Initial experiences with the decision tree should center on relatively simple problems, such as where to go on a field trip or what to do with friends on a free afternoon. As the children become more competent, increasingly complex issues could be considered, such as the status of immigrants, great historical decisions, voting for political candidates, or drug prevention.

Myles Spencer used the Decision Tree as a graphic organizer as his fifth-grade students learned about one of the most significant decisions made in the history of the United States. Rosa Parks made it in Montgomery, Alabama. Mr. Spencer read a children's picture book about Rosa Parks and her struggles during the Civil Rights Movement: *Rosa* by Nikki Giovanni and Bryan Collier (Square Fish). To begin, Mr. Spencer asked his students, "Think of a time you took a big risk to stand up for what you thought was right." "Why did you decide to take that action?" Then Mr. Spencer read Giovanni's account of Rosa Parks's famous act of disobedience on a bus in Montgomery,

Alabama, stopping the story at the point that she was confronted by the bus driver and directed to give up her seat.

The first question Mr. Spencer asked at that point focused on Rosa's decision: "Should Rosa Parks decide to protest an unfair rule by remaining seated on the bus?" Next, Mr. Spencer split the children into groups and asked them to think about what that decision meant. They were to list her alternatives and the consequences of each alternative on the Decision Tree. As they deliberated, Mr. Spencer moved from group to group and offered prompts to guide the children's thinking: "Why do you think some cities had rules establishing separate facilities for blacks and whites? Did Rosa Parks have a right to break those rules? Were the rules fair? What could happen if she did not give up her seat to the white person?" When they finished deliberating, each group shared its Decision Tree with the class.

The children were naturally curious about the real outcome of this event, and their questions flowed spontaneously: "What did Rosa Parks really do? What happened to her?" Mr. Spencer read the rest of the story to explain what happened. And, the questions made a perfect starting point for investigations into other struggles of the African American community against Jim Crow laws.

NCSS STANDARDS

II. *Time, Continuity, and Change*
IV. *Individual Development and Identity*
X. *Civic Ideals and Practice*

Separating Fact from Opinion

Learning to differentiate between *fact*, statements that can be proven true, and *opinion*, statements that convey personal beliefs, makes it possible for youngsters to critically evaluate what they read and listen to. Facts are defined as statements that are generally accepted as true and can be substantiated by firm evidence, such as, "George Washington was the first President of the United States." Opinions tell us what people personally feel or believe about something; opinions cannot be substantiated. For example, the statement, "George Washington was the greatest of all United States presidents," is, as stated, an opinion. It is true that George Washington is considered by many to be an exemplary figure among United States presidents, but the idea that he was "the *greatest* president of all" is an opinion. It cannot be proven; it simply tells how some people feel about Washington's importance. Opinions represent an individual's feelings, people's opinions may differ even when they are presented the same set of facts. Very few examples can make this point clearer than the well-known Dred Scott Decision of 1858. In 1846, Dred Scott's strong opinions about slavery caused him to sue his owner, Irene Emerson, for his freedom. His argument was based on the fact that although he and his wife Harriet were slaves, they had lived in states and territories where slavery was illegal. Therefore, their opinion was that they should be emancipated. Eleven years later, the Supreme Court issued its own opinion—Dred Scott must remain a slave because, in the words of Justice Roger Taney, blacks were beings "of an inferior order" and "had no rights which white men were bound to respect." Anti-slavery northerners were incensed. Frederick Douglass called the decision "a most scandalous and devilish perversion of the Constitution." Abraham Lincoln reacted with disgust to the ruling and was spurred to publicly speaking out against it. Their opinions brought greater attention to the issue and helped widen the political and social gap between the North and the South. The heated controversy moved the nation closer to the brink of Civil War and, by 1861, differences of opinion had grown to a boiling point. Seven southern states seceded from the Union; the Civil War had begun. It is important for the students to see that two people or two groups of people, faced with the same set of facts, often form incredibly different opinions. In this case, the strong contrasting opinions of northerners and southerners helped to ignite the Civil War.

Children must be helped to sort out factual from judgmental statements. Start out by explaining that a statement is considered a fact if you can answer yes to this question: "Can it be proven?" Write factual statements such as these on the chalkboard:

- The national capital of the United States is Washington, DC.
- The national motto of the United States is "In God We Trust."
- The national bird of the United States is the American bald eagle.
- The national flower of the United States is the rose.
- The national anthem of the United States is *The Star-Spangled Banner.*

Ask students if these statements are true. How do they know? What are some reliable sources of information they might use to check if these statements are factual? Ask the children to list additional statements of fact. Then explain that opinions are not factual; they are personal beliefs or judgments that cannot be verified by checking dependable sources of information; although they are often thought out very carefully, opinions are always open to disagreement.

Help the children spot opinions by encouraging them to look for words that a sentence is likely to express an opinion:

- *I think* the national capital of the United States should be moved close to the nation's geographic center, perhaps near Lebanon, KS (the center point of the 48 contiguous states).
- *I do not think* most children are aware of our national motto.
- *I feel,* just as Benjamin Franklin did, that the turkey is a more appropriate national bird than the bald eagle.
- *In my opinion,* the rose is the most fitting choice as national flower.
- If you ask me, *God Bless America* would make a better choice as our national anthem.

Have the students help you brainstorm other signal words that indicate that a judgment is about to be made—*I believe, I suggest, my point of view, if you ask me, perhaps, usually, bad, good, best, worst, most*. Children must be helped to realize that facts and opinions are all around them—in the books they read, on television, in advertisements, on the Internet, and in everyday conversations. Teachers in many classrooms use newspaper stories for teaching citizenship and critical thinking, especially the editorials and political cartoons. The power of their imagery and the force of their messages make them valuable classroom resources.

Political Cartoons and Editorials

Political cartoons and editorials use words and illustrations to influence one's opinion about a particular issue. Children should know that this is okay; it is certainly appropriate to voice an opinion, even if it differs from the opinions of others. Have the students search for political cartoons and editorials in the newspaper and compare these to the front page. Compare the difference between fact and opinion by examining how the cartoons and editorials are different from the front-page stories.

Sometimes the message of a political cartoon is just plain fun—an illustrated joke. Other times, however, political cartoons carry serious messages intended to influence a reader's opinion about an important issue, even though they use humor or sarcasm to make their point. Cartoonists use few words to express ideas because the illustrations themselves are intended to communicate the message. The cartoon characters tell the story. Cartoonists will exaggerate certain physical characteristics of people not only for comic effect but also to communicate an idea. George Washington's hair or Abe Lincoln's lanky, tall frame, beard, and stovepipe hat are examples of the kind of distinguishing traits cartoonists select to highlight the central cartoon figure. Cartoonists also use standard, quickly recognized symbols (e.g., Uncle Sam, dollar signs, the Republican elephant and the Democratic donkey, and the hawk and the dove) to quickly communicate an idea or feeling. To understand this aspect of cartooning, show the students a photograph of a

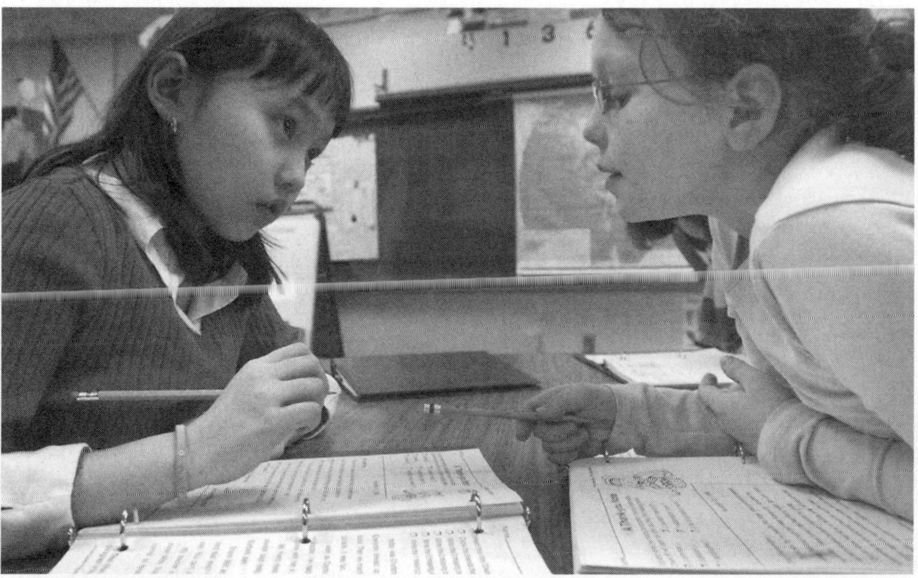

There are so many valuable thoughts that freely flow from our children's minds when they are asked to go beyond the content of social studies.

well-known news figure. Then display a caricature of the same person and have the students compare both images. What has the cartoonist done to exaggerate the features of the person? Does it portray the person in a favorable or unfavorable way? How does the cartoonist bring wit and humor to the caricature?

Next, show the children some political cartoons, making sure to choose those that get across the simplest ideas in the most uncomplicated style possible. Help the children identify the standard symbols and central characters, recognize the activity in which the characters are engaged, analyze the cartoonist's point of view, determine the cartoonist's purpose, and decide whether they agree or disagree with the cartoonist.

You could lead a discussion about the political cartoon shown in Figure 6.11 with the following prompts:

- What do you see here? Are these real people? Can you recognize any of the people in the cartoon?
- What is happening? Describe the action that is taking place.
- What issue do you think the cartoonist is trying to highlight? What point is he making about the issue? Whose viewpoint does it represent?
- Have you ever had anything like this happen to you?
- How would you react to this situation if you were a tourist? How would you feel if you were someone in the Amish family?
- Who is the intended audience? What is the purpose of the cartoon? What is its message? Is it effective?
- What techniques or devices does the artist use? Caricature? Symbolism?
- Do you agree or disagree with the cartoon's message? Why?

FIGURE 6.11 Political Cartoon

There are bound to be diverse opinions expressed during such discussions. Children should understand that everyone's ideas must be respected and nothing should be done to hurt someone else or create hostile feelings. Boehm, Ziven, and Schoenfeldt (2000), after using political cartoons in their classroom, reported that, "reading, interpreting, and drawing cartoons is a refreshing alternative to worksheets, workbooks, and textbooks for teachers and students alike. . . . [S]tudents enjoyed learning in a different, more active way. . . . We had challenged them to think critically" (p. 16).

Newspaper editorials serve the same purpose as political cartoons, but editorials use words rather than illustrations to convey a particular opinion. An editorial is not about news; it is about expressing an opinion. Like political cartoons, editorials should be discussed carefully. Help the students interpret the main issue, and then they can separate fact from opinion by highlighting the facts in one color marker and the opinions in another. They should see that editorials contain a combination of both. You might want to have the children re-examine the facts and write an editorial countering the opinions expressed by the original writer.

As students begin to understand the nature of editorials and cartoons as persuasive media, they develop strong interests in creating their own. John Kerrigan, for example, became deeply concerned about his principal's decision to remove the hallway door to the boy's restroom as a move to curb vandalism. To express his feelings about the principal's maneuver, John wrote a stinging editorial. After he read it aloud to the class, his friend Chris drew an accompanying political cartoon. Figure 6.12 displays their joint effort.

Critical thinking could and should be an important part of the elementary school social studies classroom. Children should be helped not only to comprehend social studies content but also to make judgments about people, events, and issues. Critical thinking is a crucial attribute that citizens need to participate competently in our contemporary democratic society.

A Final Thought

The primary reason for educating our youth has been, and continues to be, developing proud citizens who make up a rich nation—a unique combination of cultures we call American. Americans have come from everywhere and for every reason—some were brought against their will in chains as slaves; others came willingly to search for gold, to find land, to flee famine, or to escape religious or political discrimination. Even today, America continues to be a sanctuary for the oppressed as well as a haven for the ambitious. Forefathers of consummate wisdom created a new kind of government for America—of the people, by the people, and for the people. To maintain this prized inheritance, all elementary school teachers must stand up and accept their responsibility to protect, nurture, and renew our healthy democratic society. They can do this by supporting and enacting the influential declaration of the NCSS (1993): "The primary purpose of social studies is to help young people develop the ability to make informed and reasoned decisions for the public good as citizens of a culturally diverse, democratic society in an interdependent world" (p. 3).

Classrooms for young citizens should have a distinctly democratic flavor. Children should know what our country is now, and envision the best our country can be. As a teacher of young children, you will be an important nurturer of maximum civic growth. You will help make society. You must have a vision of good citizenship—much the same kind of vision as Michelangelo had when he peered intently

"Are bathrooms private anymore

Mr. Towson has a great scence of hummer, his last joke was the funnyest of of all. You better sit down for this Ready? Okay- He took... you sure your ready for this... Well, he took the bathroom door off See! I tould you should sit down. Now you propalley think all the resonibillaty has gone to his head. Well for once I think he's absolutely almost right. Heres his side. Someone took three rolls of tolite paper in the toilet and flush it. It flooded the bathroom and the boys locker room. But taking the bathroom door off is to much. I mean you ever try and go in the bathroom with about 50 girls standing in front. But, there is a good part, the vandalism has gone down.
Now Mr. Towson has something to worry about that is weather the school board impeaches him and if the health board calls the school a health hazard.

Har! A littel town with a littel school has there own Watergate. I can see the head of linds now "First Princepal to be Impeached." I thought Mr. Towson is a nice guy (sometimes). But the health hazard is yet a nother thing. But don't worry Mr. Towson will figure out some and we hop bathrooms are still private

Chris

got any toilet paper?

OH The Bathroom, first open Door on the right

FIGURE 6.12 Children's Version of an Editorial and Political Cartoon at a monumental slab of Carrara marble and saw within it the *Pieta*, waiting to be liberated. Will you work with the fervor of Michelangelo to release responsible democratic citizens? Should society expect anything less?

REFERENCES

Alleman, J., & Brophy, J. (2002). How to make government a class favorite. *Social Studies and the Young Learner, 15,* 6–10.

Boehm, L. M., Ziven, J. R., & Schoenfeldt, M. (2000). Cartoons during class? *Social Studies and the Young Learner, 13,* 16.

The Boston Primer. (1808). In R. H. Hersh (Ed.), *Models of moral education* (1980). New York: Longman.

Center for Civic Education. (1994). *National standards for civics and government.* Calabasas, CA: Author.

Darigan, D. L., Tunnell, M. O., & Jacobs, J. S. (2002). *Children's literature: Engaging teachers and children in good books.* Upper Saddle River, NJ: Merrill/Prentice-Hall.

Ennis, R. H. (1985). Goals for a critical thinking curriculum. In A. Costa (Ed.), *Developing minds: A resource book for teaching thinking.* Alexandria, VA: Association for Supervision and Curriculum Development.

Henson, J. (1935). A slave's dilemma. In B. Brawley (Ed.), *Early negro American writers* (pp. 162–167). Chapel Hill, NC: University of North Carolina Press.

Johnson, D. W., & Johnson, R. T. (1999). *Learning together and alone.* Boston: Allyn & Bacon.

Kahne, J., & Middaugh, E. (2008). High quality civic education: What is it and who gets it? *Social Education, 72,* 34–39.

Lesser, E. J. (2006). Constitution Day: Start the school year with civics. *Social Education, 70,* 294–300.

Libresco, A. S. (2002). Nurturing an informed citizenry: Three lessons for second graders. *Social Studies and the Young Learner, 15,* 11–16.

Lindquist, T. (1995). *Seeing the whole through social studies.* Portsmouth, NH: Heinemann.

McClurg, L. G. (1998). Building an ethical community in the classrooms: Community meeting. *Young Children, 53,* 30–35.

National Council for the Social Studies. (1993, January/February). *The social studies professional.* Washington, DC: Author.

National Council for the Social Studies. (1994). *Curriculum standards for social studies: Expectations of excellence.* Bulletin 89. Washington, DC: National Council for the Social Studies.

National Council for the Social Studies. (2001). Creating effective citizens: A position statement of National Council for the Social Studies. *Social Education, 65,* 319.

National Council for the Social Studies Task Force on Early Childhood/Elementary Social Studies. (1989). Social studies for early childhood and elementary school children preparing for the 21st century. *Social Education, 53,* 16.

Parker, W. C. (1989). Participatory citizenship: Civics in the strong sense. *Social Education, 53,* 353.

Parker, W. C. (2006). Talk isn't cheap: Practicing deliberation in school. *Social Studies and the Young Learner, 19,* 12–15.

Remy, R. C. (no date). *Skills in making political decisions.* Columbus, OH: Mershon Center, The Ohio State University.

Ryan, K. (1993). In M. Massey, Interest in character education seen growing. *Update, 35,* 1.

Social Education Staff. (2005). The civic mission of schools. *Social Education, 69,* 414.

Sterling, D. (1968). *Tear down the walls!* New York: Doubleday.

PART III Constructivist Approaches to Classroom Instruction

CHAPTER 7

The Learning Cycle
Teacher Scaffolded Social Constructivism

What Does Social Constructivism Look Like?

On a clear, crisp day just before Halloween, students from Mary Jo Mahoney's sixth-grade class learned there's more to cemeteries than cold gravestones and chilling ghost stories. The scene is Oaklands Cemetery, a venerable setting where young imaginations take wing at this time of year. Ms. Mahoney has been taking her students on field trips to Oaklands Cemetery for the past three autumns, always around Halloween; her students' motivation to explore the graveyard, for some mysterious reason, seems to peak during this spooky season.

To prepare her students for what they would experience on the trip, Ms. Mahoney showed them what she begins most social studies lessons with—objects she calls "interest-grabbers." In this instance, Ms. Mahoney's "interest-grabber" was a bronze metal star with an American flag attached, the kind used to decorate the graves of soldiers who had died in battle. The star had the letters GAR (Grand Army of the Republic) on it. Along with the star and flag, Ms. Mahoney showed the students a crayon rubbing of a grave marker she had made from a local cemetery. The worn, very simple stone had only the name of the deceased: J. R. McTavish, Co. B. 9th Pa. Inf. Nothing else was written. The students were encouraged to examine the flag and marker and to make comments or ask questions to see what they might know about them or what questions they might have. Initially, they didn't know that these items were from the Civil War era, but Richard finally spoke up: "Grand Army of the Republic! That was what they called the Union Army during the Civil War. I bet this is a soldier who died in the Civil War."

"Yeah!" added Molly. "Look at the grave rubbing. It says the soldier was from the 9th Pa. Inf. He must have been a Union soldier from Pennsylvania."

II. *Time, Continuity, and Change*
IV. *Individual Development and Identity*
X. *Civic Ideals and Practice*

Persistent observations eventually led them to the conclusion that the items on display had something to do with the Civil War. Ms. Mahoney operates with a conviction that connecting pre-trip, personalized experiences like these to the cemetery visit helps students more effectively attain valuable understandings and sensitivities.

When the class arrived at the cemetery, they were greeted by Fred Hubbert, a caretaker who led them on a walking tour past obelisks, shrines, sarcophagi, and ornate gravestones. "Look at the names; they're sure different from our names today!" commented Herschel. Mr. Hubbert picked up on Herschel's comment and explained how several of these people had helped shape their community's history. "That big old shrine over there belongs to Cyrus Hadfield. When he returned from fighting in the Civil War, he opened a carriage factory on Front Street. It became one of the country's largest carriage manufacturers. Hadfield Street is named in honor of Cyrus Hadfield." As they walked, Mr. Hubbert pointed out more of the cemetery's interesting features. At one rather plain gravestone, Mr. Hubbert explained, "Jonathan Taylor was the village physician in the mid-1800s. He stopped riding his bicycle after he turned 90. He said the streets were getting too busy."

How Global is the Curriculum *Go to MyEducationLab, click on Resources, then Web Destinations, and then select "The Association for Gravestone Studies."*

"Some of the earliest monuments date back to before the Civil War," Mr. Hubbert explained. A bronze statue of a Union soldier sitting on his horse guarded the cemetery's fenced-in Civil War section. The students counted 24 soldiers buried there. "Here's a Union soldier who was only 14 years old when he was shot," commented Kendra sadly. "That's not much older than we are."

"We used to plant tulips at the base of the statue guarding this section of the cemetery, but the deer and squirrels ate them all," explained Mr. Hubbert. "We're looking into something safer that could be planted."

After this interesting introduction by Mr. Hubbert, each young historian was assigned a partner, and the dyads were sent off to different sections of the cemetery to carry out their study. The students carefully filled out their observation sheets with responses to the tasks they talked about in the classroom, and made dozens of gravestone rubbings by placing large sheets of newsprint against the gravestones and carefully rubbing crayons over the paper. Everything on the gravestone (names, dates, epitaphs) transferred to the paper and provided excellent research material that could be taken back to the classroom. For example, one pair found a marker that read: "Sibyl—A little refugee from N.C. who died in 1865."

"What's a refugee?" they asked Mr. Hubbert. After he explained that a refugee is someone who seeks protection from something harmful, the young historians inquired further: "What kind of refugee would come to Pennsylvania from North Carolina in 1865? What kind of harm would this person face in North Carolina?" Mr. Hubbert explained that Sibyl was a slave who was brought to southeastern Pennsylvania and given her freedom by the Hastings family, members of the Society of Friends (a religious group strongly opposed to slavery).

Returning to the classroom, Ms. Mahoney's young historians analyzed their data and shared their findings. Perhaps the most inspiring upshot of the entire experience took place when several of the students expressed concern about the tulip bulbs in the Civil War section that were eaten by the wildlife. "I wish there was something we could do," lamented Bryce.

"Maybe there is," suggested Ms. Mahoney. "Let's check with a local nursery to see if they can suggest something to grow that the animals won't bother."

The class phoned a local nursery the next day and was informed that deer, squirrels, and other wildlife love tulip bulbs, but that they have an aversion to daffodil bulbs. The students mounted a fund-raising drive, earning enough money to buy 150 daffodil bulbs and a small plaque that was placed at the entrance to memorialize their efforts. Each member of the class planted 8 bulbs that autumn; now, each spring, the base of the Civil War monument is awash in a glorious blanket of brilliant yellow flowers.

Ms. Mahoney doesn't bother to quiz her children on these cemetery adventures. "That's one story I'm sure they'll remember," she proudly declares.

In this classroom example, Mary Jo Mahoney used a variety of strategies associated with *constructivism*, an instructional approach frequently linked with the works of two leading authorities—Jean Piaget and Lev Vygotsky. Ms. Mahoney feels strongly about basing her classroom practices on such time-honored authoritative support because she is convinced that social studies teachers cannot be effective unless their classroom practices rest on a firm foundation of established pedagogical principles. This point of view has been supported by Piaget (1948/1973) himself, who wrote that a teacher "should know not only his own science, but also be well versed in the details of the development of the child's . . . mind" (pp. 16–17).

Constructivist teachers such as Ms. Mahoney reject the "toss-and-catch" approach to education where a teacher tosses out the knowledge and waits for the students to grab hold of it and cram it into their memory cache. They also reject the argument that young children are basically "ignorant adults" and that the major purpose of education is to fill their empty or semi-empty minds with a glut of information. Instead, they embrace the principle that children's minds are different

from adults' minds. Children's minds develop through a series of stages that become gradually more complex as they move from infancy into adulthood. Intelligence develops in different ways throughout these stages, each stage having a particular set of characteristics that make only certain types of thinking possible. Throughout each stage, children develop intelligence not by being told about things, but by building (constructing) their own understandings. Brooks and Brooks (1993) elaborate: "Constructivism stands in contrast to the more deeply rooted ways of teaching that have long typified American classrooms. Traditionally, learning has been thought to be a 'mimetic' activity, a process that involves students repeating, or miming, newly presented information. . . . Constructivist teaching practices, on the other hand, help learners to internalize and reshape, or transform, new information" (p. 15).

What Is Constructivism?

When we address the topic of constructivism, we refer not to "what" the children know, but to "how" they acquire and organize information in their minds, the process by which they think and reason. We have discovered a great deal about how this happens from the work of Jean Piaget (1952), whose major contributions to our understanding of children's thinking now spans 60 years. During those years, he and his followers observed numbers of children and systematically detailed the manner by which they progressed through periods of intellectual growth from birth to adolescence. During distinct developmental periods, Piaget explained, children build specialized mental structures we often refer to as *concepts*, but which he called *schemata* (the singular is *schema*). Schemata help us organize and make sense of our world and serve as frameworks for constructing new understandings. Think of a single schema much as a file folder into which information can be sorted out and categorized. The schema represents some aspect of the world and can be as relatively uncomplicated as "bicycle" or as complex as "justice." Regardless of the level of their complexity, new life experiences help us construct new schemata and continually expand those that already exist.

How Global is the Curriculum *Go to MyEducationLab, select the topic Teaching Strategies, view the artifact entitled "Hand Stand," complete the questions that accompany it.*

As children grow and develop, schemata gradually become more complex and more differentiated in order to manage the information amassed from multifaceted life experiences. This is accomplished through a process Piaget calls *adaptation*. To understand the process of adaptation as it relates to mental functioning in social studies classrooms, we need to examine three essential components: assimilation, accommodation, and equilibrium. *Assimilation* is the mental process that takes place when individuals attempt to "file" new life experiences into an existing schema; in other words, learners try to connect new information to something they already know. If a meaningful connection is made to their existing view of the world, children are said to rest in a state of cognitive comfort, or *equilibrium*. In other words, they have successfully "assimilated" the new information into their existing view of the world—it makes sense. However, when children encounter a life experience that cannot be connected to an existing schema, their "disequilibrium" can cause three things to happen: (1) they attempt to construct a new schema into which the new information can be filed, (2) they are driven to alter an existing schema in such a way that the new information can be connected to it, or (3) they simply ignore or reject the new information inherent in the new life experience.

Whenever a new schema is constructed, or an existing schema altered, we say *accommodation* has taken place. Therefore, when learners encounter life experiences incompatible with what they already know, their cognitive comfort is disturbed and they try hard to bring it back in balance; that is, they will attempt to alter, or *accommodate*, existing schemata to fit in the new information.

Piaget explains motivation for learning, then, not as any external force such as receiving praise or a star from the teacher for a doing good job, but as a deep inner-drive to either *assimilate* into or *accommodate* schemata in response to new experiences in their environment. This process happens during each of Piaget's developmental stages: Children react to new experiences in their environment using whatever schemata they have constructed. If the experience is a familiar one, it fits easily—or is effortlessly assimilated—into the children's schemata so that they maintain mental equilibrium. If the new experience is dissimilar or novel, children seek equilibrium, and alter their cognitive structure to accommodate the new circumstances. This way, individuals construct progressively more complex schemata throughout their lifetimes. Constructivists would say that cognitive growth continues this way throughout one's lifetime.

The following paragraph, describing one day in 1620 when a Native American Indian encountered a group of pilgrims, may help illustrate this process:

> [Of] course the Pilgrims couldn't understand the Indian's language.
>
> But this Indian spoke English! Before the Pilgrims could shoot, he said in a loud voice, "Hello, Englishmen!" The Englishmen were astonished.
>
> His name was Samoset. He acted like a friend. But was he one?
>
> The Pilgrims gave Samoset some food to eat. They gave him a place to sleep. They watched him carefully.
>
> The next day he returned to the forest. But soon he came again, and this time he brought with him another Indian named Squanto. He [too] could speak English well. (Penner, 1991, pp. 26–27)

To attach meaning to this paragraph, students must have previously started building a "mental file" into which they have sorted information about the Pilgrims as they came to America: The Pilgrims wanted to pray in their own way; the Pilgrims decided to leave England and find a new home; the Pilgrims decided to sail across the Atlantic Ocean to America; the Pilgrims were afraid of what they would find in America; on September 6, 1620, the *Mayflower* raised anchor and the Pilgrims sailed for 66 days across the Atlantic; America was a wild place—wolves howled fiercely during the dark nights; the Pilgrims encountered an out-of-the-

ordinary, new civilization; the Pilgrims were afraid of an attack; the Native Americans approached the Pilgrims in a friendly manner.

However, if the students had no previous schema into which the new information about the Pilgrims' voyage to America could be incorporated, the paragraph would be beyond their understanding; they will probably either lose interest in the topic or reject it completely. Let us say, though, that the information contained in the paragraph was easily assimilated into an existing schema and incorporated into their current understanding of the world. In that case, the students would comfortably move on through the rest of the reading selection. However, if the paragraph contained information that conflicted with the students' understanding of the world, they would become energized to change (accommodate) their schemata so the new knowledge might fit somewhere. When the challenge of the unknown lies close enough to what students already know, they become motivated to construct new meaning from the life experience. What about you? As you read the paragraph, which of the descriptions best fit your reaction to the material: Were you comfortable with all the information or did the paragraph contain something that conflicted with what you already knew about the arrival of the Pilgrims? Is there anything in the paragraph that does not fit your existing schemata? Do you sense an urge to change existing schemata so that new information can fit in?

When I gave this selection to a group of fourth-graders, they asked this question at once: "How did the Indians learn to speak English before the Pilgrims came to Plymouth?" Mental conflict was created and the students were genuinely eager to reshuffle their schemata of the Pilgrims and Indians at Plymouth. Were *you* aware that Samoset and Squanto spoke English? How did they learn to do that if this was their first contact with outsiders? Are you in the least bit interested in finding out how they did it? If so, you are experiencing a constructivist moment—truly determined to uncover real meaning about your world rather than simply receiving or storing knowledge. (FYI: Squanto had actually been to England twice prior to 1620. Earlier English explorers had brought him back to England and he learned to speak English well.)

Constructivists seem to agree that learning takes place in this general way, but disagree on whether the process occurs within the individual learner *(cognitive constructivism)* or whether it takes place as a result of people working together *(social constructivism)*. The cognitive constructivists, supported by Piaget, believe that students learn best through instructional practices such as "discovery learning," "problem solving," or "inquiry;" learning is primarily an individualistic enterprise. Most social constructivists, supported by Vygotsky, agree that learning happens as Piaget described (so there is an important overlap between the two constructivist viewpoints), but stress that children create meaning through their interactions with teachers and with their peers; it is primarily a social enterprise. Because both viewpoints have important implications for social studies instruction, Chapters 7 and 8 will detail the social constructivist view and Chapter 9 will clarify the cognitive constructivist view.

What Is Social Constructivism?

A major element of both social and cognitive constructivism is stimulating children's reasoning through active methods of instruction. Although some constructivist devotees suggest that children learn best on their own, social constructivists advise that children thrive in situations where they are assisted by their teachers or peers; learning is an interactive, cooperative, and collaborative process. Some social constructivist strategies, such as cooperative learning, stress the value of interactions among the students, whereas others, such as classroom conversations, emphasize the importance of teacher and student interactions. Therefore, social constructivist teachers are concerned not only with selecting the materials best suited for promoting exploration and thinking, but also with cementing positive adult–student and student–student relationships, especially with regard to a specific focus on efforts that lead to initiative, experimentation, and collaboration.

Throughout the example at the beginning of this chapter, for example, Mary Jo Mahoney offered a type of assistance that bolstered children's learning by organizing challenging projects; making available uninterrupted time to work; offering ample opportunities for cooperative and collaborative learning; arranging for an on-site experience where meaningful research could be carried out; and using a variety of questions, probes, prompts, reminders, and encouragement until students gained the confidence to do more and more on their own. In the most general sense, Ms. Mahoney based her social studies program on the belief that anything that is learned must be actively taught and that students learn most effectively through social contact.

Educators like Ms. Mahoney have made use of Lev Vygotsky's ideas to furnish theoretical support for their social constructivist classroom practices. Basic to Vygotsky's thinking is the idea that humans are fundamentally different from animals because they make and use tools. Tools make work less difficult and help people solve problems. Tools can be classified as *physical tools* (implements such as hammers, spears, or wheels that were invented to help master the environment) or *mental tools* (complex cognitive processes used to solve all kinds of problems). Because physical tools and mental tools are both critical for human survival, cultures have insisted that they be passed on from generation to generation—that is, skills, understandings, and beliefs critical to the survival of the culture must be taught to others by those who are more knowledgeable or skilled. Passing on valued skills and knowledge is where language enters Vygotsky's thinking. According to Vygotsky, learning about one's culture is most appreciably influenced by children's verbal interactions with more capable or experienced adults or peers. Whether they are learning that a red light signals one to stop at an intersection or that certain freedoms are protected by the Constitution of the United States, language is the primary tool that makes it possible for individuals to grow as informed citizens. So, for Vygotsky, language and learning are indisputably entwined. Concepts and skills grow as children interact with more capable members of the culture—family, friends, teachers, classmates, casual acquaintances, and all human beings.

Zones of Development

Since the essence of social constructivism involves regular classroom interactions between teacher and students or among the students themselves, we must examine the issue of what kinds of interactions are considered most productive. According to Vygotsky, children at any age have a specific range, or zone, within which they can learn. One zone consists of the learning tasks that students can complete successfully with no help. Vygotsky calls this the *Zone of Actual Development (ZAD)*. When the teacher assigns a task and the children can accomplish it independently, the task is said to lie within their ZAD—they have already learned the information or mastered the skills associated with the task at hand. For example, if a teacher asks her students to identify the coordinates for five major cities on the globe and they all are able to carry out the task, we say the activity was within their ZAD.

At the other extreme are the learning tasks that students cannot complete successfully even if there was someone to give them help. No amount of outside assistance, for example, will foster much learning from a group of low-achieving first-graders faced with the challenge of considering the consequences of global warming on the economic, social, and cultural structure of the United States. Such unreasonable expectancies are sure to generate feelings of hopelessness and disappointment for the students as well as the teacher.

Somewhere in between these two extremes lies the most productive zone for learning—a cognitive region that enables students to come very close to completing learning tasks successfully, but they are unable to do so without the help of a teacher or more advanced peer. This cognitive region is known as the *Zone of Proximal Development (ZPD)*. The ZPD can be thought of as a "construction zone" where just the right amount of assisted support helps the student master a targeted skill and/or comprehend the planned content.

Scaffolding

How Global is the Curriculum *Go to MyEducationLab, select the topic Teaching Strategies, watch the video entitled "Peer Scaffolding," and complete the questions that accompany it.*

In order to implement assisted learning within the ZPD, teachers must learn how to offer just the right amount of help as students try to bridge the gap between what they already know (or can do) and the intended learning outcome. This kind of adult assistance is called *scaffolding*, a type of assistance adults or more competent/knowledgeable peers might provide that enables students to execute tasks within their ZPD. A flotation device for a child who cannot swim is a simple example of scaffolding. It is facilitative, supportive, but transitory, providing the novice with the support he or she needs only during the early stages of learning how to swim. Without an aid of this sort, the complex task of coordinating all the elements necessary to stay afloat would be practically impossible for many youngsters. The scaffold (flotation device) offers just the right amount of support until the "little guppies" are able to toss away their water wings and swim away on their own.

Although teachers take on several roles in a social constructivist classroom, their major responsibility is to stimulate and guide.

An educational scaffold, much like a flotation device, provides temporary support as students work to bridge the gap between what they already know or can do and the intended instructional outcome. Wood, Bruner, and Ross (1976), who were the first to use the term *scaffolding* in an educational context, defined it as "a process that enables a child or novice to solve a problem, carry out a task, or achieve a goal which would be beyond his unassisted efforts" (p. 90). As children demonstrate increasing awareness of a problem situation, the adult gradually relinquishes the supportive role and eventually turns over full responsibility of the learning experience to the child. Scaffolding allows teachers to provide the cueing, questioning, coaching, and support needed to allow students to complete a task before they are able to complete it independently. It is based on a problem-solving approach to learning consistent with the Curriculum Standards for Social Studies (NCSS, 1994): "Knowledge is constructed by learners as they attempt to fit new information, experiences, feelings, and relationships into their existing or emerging intellectual . . . constructs. . . . If we want our students to be better thinkers and better decision-makers, they must have contact with those accustomed to thinking with precision . . . and clarity" (p. 7).

The Learning Cycle: What Is the Teacher's Role in a Social Constructivist Classroom?

A frequently recommended strategy designed to facilitate learning through a teacher's supportive assistance is called the *Learning Cycle*. The Learning Cycle is a student-centered, problem-solving–based teaching approach intended to help children learn through peer or teacher support. It recognizes the students' current understanding of the world and helps them use what they know to construct new knowledge. In general, the Learning Cycle pattern selected for this text consists of three major elements, or phases, each requiring distinctive student and teacher actions and interactions: exploration, concept/skill development, and concept/skill application. See Figure 7.1.

A Learning Cycle begins with the exploration phase during which the teacher creates interest in the topic and generates curiosity; this is the time for disequilibrium. Next, during the concept/skill development phase, the children work individually or in small groups while the teacher facilitates such processes as observation, research, and experimentation. Finally, during the concept/skill application phase, the children use what they have learned to design meaningful models of the ideas they explored.

The Exploration Phase

A Learning Cycle begins with an *exploration phase* that connects with the students' previous experiences and provides a common background activity that helps students relate to the new experience. This initial phase has two vital purposes: (1) activating the students' prior knowledge while drawing the students into the lesson, and (2) focusing the students' attention on the instructional task by establishing a clear purpose for learning. In planning this phase of the Learning Cycle, the teacher must address questions such as: What prior knowledge do my students have of the

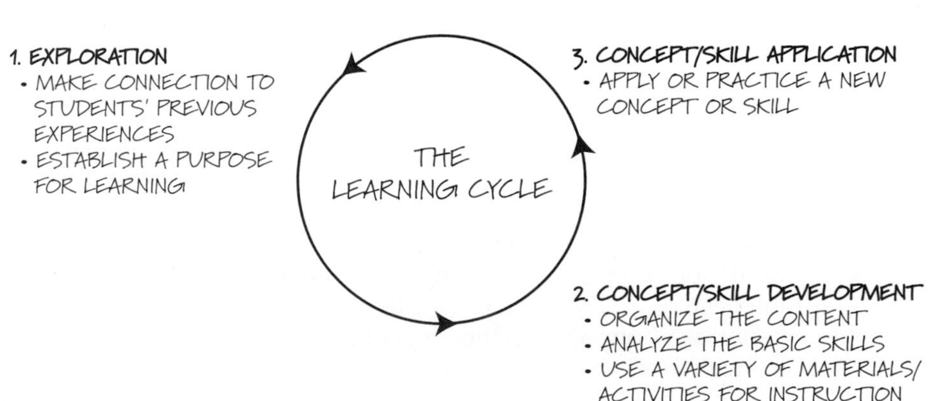

FIGURE 7.1 The Learning Cycle

concept targeted for instruction? Is the material too difficult or too easy? What activities can I use to encourage them to connect to their previously established understandings? How might I motivate the students and focus their attention on the material? How can I relate the learning material to the students' lives?

Activating Prior Knowledge

A good Learning Cycle is launched when students are helped to establish a connection between what they already know or can do to the new information or skill to be learned. David Ausubel (1961) offers historically respected support of the importance of this viewpoint, stating, "If I had to reduce educational psychology to just one principle, I would say this: The most important single factor influencing learning is what the learner already knows" (p. 16). Ausubel used the term *advance organizer* to refer to the prompts employed by teachers as they assist students to retrieve past knowledge in order to connect it to the new material. In addition to Ausubel's advance organizer, there are other terms commonly used to describe this process. You may have heard of Madeline Hunter's time-honored expression *anticipatory set,* or Lev Vygotsky's term *external mediator*. (Since our social constructivist strategy is primarily grounded in the works of Vygotsky, we will use the term *external mediator* in this text.) Consider the external mediator to be an initial prompt, task, or activity that provides a general overview of the new material and connects the new content to the students' prior experiences (or to what they have already learned).

Teachers use a variety of external mediators when they introduce Learning Cycles, but the most conventional are (1) class discussions that include thought-provoking questions, (2) stimulating objects or events, and (3) graphic organizers.

Class Discussions. Certainly the most common advance organizer is the use of introductory statements about the content to be learned, or asking a key question, followed by a general conversation that helps connect the students' existing knowledge to the new material. This discussion-type external mediator is not intended to become an extensive conversation, but only a quick connection to what the children already know. It should not develop into something so comprehensive that it ends up being a separate lesson in itself. The following strategy, an adaptation of Judith Langer's (1981) widely recognized PReP, is appropriate for helping children connect their background knowledge to any kind of learning activity involving social studies subject matter, whether it is a folktale, textbook selection, Internet site, guest speaker, or field trip:

1. *Identify the targeted concept or skill.* This will help you keep the ensuing conversation focused on the appropriate topic.
2. *Encourage free association and divergent thinking.* Ask the students to brainstorm anything that comes to their mind related to the central concept of the learning experience with a prompt like this: "Tell me anything that comes to your mind when you (see this picture, read this title, observe this object, hear this word, etc.)." Here are five useful types of prompts you

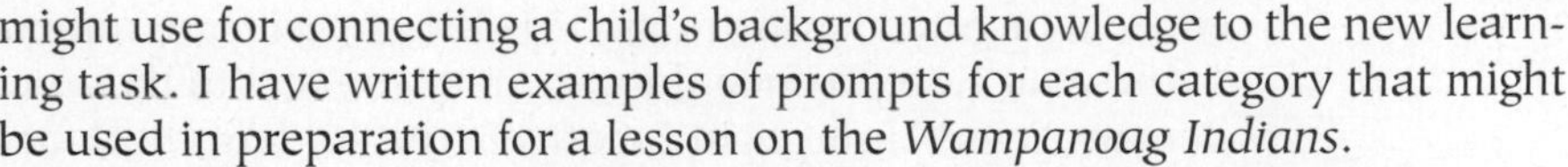

might use for connecting a child's background knowledge to the new learning task. I have written examples of prompts for each category that might be used in preparation for a lesson on the *Wampanoag Indians*.

- *Existing knowledge.* "Tell me what you now know about the Wampanoag Indians."
- *Thought association.* "When you hear the term *Wampanoag,* what do you think of?"
- *Rapid recognition.* Display key terms and ask the students to tell what they already know about them—*wigwams, longhouses, deer stew, breeches, loincloths,* and *petticoats.*
- *Quick lesson review.* Ask questions that help connect the new learning experience to information that was learned in previous lessons: "Yesterday, we learned about a native people called the Wampanoags. Who were the Wampanoags? Describe daily life in a Wampanoag village."
- *Open discussion.* Sometimes an open-ended question will offer the best connection to past experiences—"We are going to read about the Wampanoag Indians. What do you know about the Wampanoags?"

  The children's responses should be listed on the chalkboard or a chart as they are offered. This initial brainstorming activity can be carried out in small groups or with the entire class. If carried out in small groups, the ideas should be listed by a scribe from each group and then shared with the entire class.

3. *Have the students reflect on their initial associations.* Give the children an opportunity to explain their ideas as well as listen to the explanations of their classmates. At this point, the students interact and accept, reject, or revise their original associations. Ask the following question: "What made you think of . . . ?"
4. *Encourage children to adapt their schemata.* Give the children an opportunity to reflect on the shared explanations. They should be encouraged to revise what they already know or integrate new information into their current mental structures. Ask: "Based on our discussion, do you have any new ideas about (the picture, word, etc.)?" or "Can you tell me more about . . . ?" This gives the students an opportunity to elaborate on the degree to which any of their original associations were changed as a result of the explanation phase.
5. *With the list of brainstormed associations in full view, have the children participate in the learning activity.* Afterwards, they should return to the list of associated terms and evaluate how well their prior knowledge related to the new information contained in the learning experience.

The best way to understand how this is carried out is to visit a social studies classroom where a teacher is introducing a lesson on different types of pumps that are used in the oil industry.

Luke Bednarz's sixth-graders had been involved in the study of the oil industry and are about to learn about the different ways oil is pumped from the ground. Mr. Bednarz begins today's lesson by making a short introductory statement connecting what has gone on before to the new material to be covered: "Yesterday, we discovered where some of Earth's major oil fields are located. Today we will find out how the oil is drawn out from under the ground in those fields." Instead of giving a definition of the kind of oil pump they were going to be reading about, Mr. Bednarz asked the students to think about anything they might associate with grasshoppers. Immediately, students began to talk about the familiar insect they all knew as denizens of the lush fields in and about their rural community. Some talked about its thin, powerful back legs and how far grasshoppers are able to leap; others mentioned the antennae, the oddly shaped head, the long, thin body, and the wings. Most children volunteered something, whether they merely watched the grasshoppers jump and fly around in the barren fields or used them for something rather practical—fishing bait! Mr. Bednarz displayed a large illustration of the insect and asked if the students would agree that this was the bug they were all speaking of. The students agreed that it was and went on to talk more about its unique characteristics. Next, Mr. Bednarz asked a question that raised a few eyebrows: "Here's a question I want you to think deeply about: How do you suppose grasshoppers might be used in the oil industry?" The students glanced silently at one another and in due course giggled in disbelief. "Are you serious, Mr. Bednarz?" they asked suspiciously. "Of course, I'm serious," countered Mr. Bednarz, "I know it's hard to believe, but grasshoppers actually are used in the oil industry. Turn to a partner and talk about how you think that could be."

NCSS STANDARDS

III. *People, Places, and Environments*
VII. *Production, Consumption, and Distribution*
VIII. *Science, Technology, and Society*

After a few minutes, Mr. Bednarz invited the students to list their predictions on the chalkboard: "The oil workers put them in small cages and walk around a field that might have oil in it. The grasshoppers have a special sense that causes them to jump around real fast if oil is underground."

"The brown 'tobacco' that they spit on your hand when you hold them can be collected and used to lubricate the machinery until the well begins to produce oil."

"You'll find that more grasshoppers live in fields where there is oil underground."

After writing each prediction on the chalkboard, Mr. Bednarz made a direct connection to the forthcoming learning experience: "Your ideas are very interesting. Please search through the resources in the classroom research center to determine which, if any, of your thoughts explain how grasshoppers are actually used in the oil industry." The children quickly gathered at the center, using various books as well as the classroom computers to search for data to test their claims. Shortly, they returned to the discussion area and bellowed incredulously: "You tricked us, Mr. Bednarz! The oil industry doesn't use the grasshopper insects, they use grasshopper pumps!"

The students discovered that oil industry "grasshoppers" were large low-pressure pumps shaped somewhat like the actual insect. Mr. Bednarz displayed a large illustration of a grasshopper pump, as well as a model pump, next to the insect illustration and invited the students to discuss the similarities and differences. Although the oil "grasshoppers" weren't of the insect variety, signs of learning were obvious as the students continued to talk about the oil industry grasshoppers during a lively and informative discussion.

Luke Bednarz pursued this line of instruction because he knew it was important for students to connect their prior knowledge of "grasshoppers" to this new topic before they were asked to learn more about them, and to create the type of mental "conflict" that energizes students to want to learn. Compare Mr. Bednarz's approach with another teacher who began his class discussion with the statement, "Yesterday, we read about where the major oil fields are located throughout the world. Today we're going to keep on learning about the oil industry." Then, "How many of you have ever seen a grasshopper? Today we're going to learn about how oil is pumped from the ground with a special pump called a grasshopper. Read pages 78 to 81 to find out how this special pump works."

Notice that the second teacher's background development was somewhat related to the main concept of the book, but the mystery and intrigue associated with Mr. Bednarz's problem-based approach was missing. His strategy ended up to be much more productive because it created a puzzle in the children's minds and challenged them to think. Disequilibrium brought the students' existing knowledge to the forefront, offered the teacher some insight into the students' current level of cognitive functioning, and furnished a base from which to construct new concepts.

Stimulating Objects or Events. Ideally, whatever children do in our social studies classrooms would grow from an inner drive to do it—to meet all coursework with complete interest, focus, and concentration. Although this is a best possible scenario, it is seldom realized. A child, like all of us, often needs to be drawn into experiences, and social studies is no exception. Teachers must provide motivational activities to arouse enthusiasm, a desire to discover what the social studies activity has to offer. These motivational activities should involve many kinds of hands-on experiences. Mr. Bednarz, for example, used a brainteaser to motivate his students to read about the grasshoppers. But, if he did that every time he offered an external organizer, the students would quickly tire of the routine. Therefore, for another lesson, he might select a hands-on experience to pique his students' interests: Knowing they would be much more interested in viewing a video about coal mining in Appalachia if a few lumps of coal, a bandanna, and a miner's helmet were placed in a prop box, he would encourage his students to examine the items and tell what they brought to mind. Likewise, children would be spellbound as they handled a real Akua-ba doll from Ghana while you tell the story of how it is tucked into a skirt at the waist and carried by girls who hope to have children in the future. And what child wouldn't enjoy twirling a cowboy lariat prior to studying America's Old West? Real items inspire fascination for any social studies topic.

This is not meant to imply that teachers should never talk, but only to stress that they enhance learning by presenting students an opportunity to interact with something real. Think about all the possibilities for bringing in realia (real things) to introduce new ideas during any unit of study:

- Clothing (Indian sari, Japanese happi coat, fringed deerskin shirt of the Iroquois).
- Money (ruble, yen, mark, peso)
- Documents (wills, letters, newspapers, court records)
- Household items (colonial butter churn, Asian wok, African calabash)
- Musical instruments (Mexican guiro, Japanese den den, Zulu marimba)
- Tools (stethoscope, mortar and pestle, fishing net)
- Food (Pueblo Feast Day cookies, Mexican wedding cakes, Nigerian peanut soup)
- Toys (Chinese kites, Colonial "buzz saw," Jewish dreidel)

Oftentimes, teachers make collections of objects related to a theme and store them in boxes so they are kept well organized from year to year. These "prop boxes" can represent countries, cultures, community helpers, or most any other social studies topic. In selecting items for cultural boxes, be sure that you incorporate "present-day" samples whenever you include traditional items such as kimonos, kilts, or sombreros. If you want to put together a box containing only serapes, sombreros, and other traditional Mexican attire, for example, you will give an unfair picture of what people dress like in Mexico today unless you also include examples or photos of contemporary clothing.

NCSS STANDARDS
I. *Culture*
III. *People, Places, and Environments*
IX. *Global Connections*

To make a prop box, get a large, sturdy container that can be easily decorated (preferably by your students). Place real objects inside; some can be bought, others might be donated by businesses, and parents are always willing to contribute items (if they're returned in the condition you received them).

Orpha Diller, a student in one of my social studies methods classes, was assigned by her field experience teacher to plan and teach a one-week mini-unit of her choice. After considering several topics, Orpha eventually chose "Cultures and Traditions of Kenya" as the topic for her unit. Being convinced that the best way to learn about a culture is to examine ordinary objects used in daily life, Orpha obtained from fellow students, parents, relatives, friends, and local ethnic stores objects that would help her students learn more about Kenya and its people.

On the opening day of the unit, Orpha hauled in an antique-like trunk that she called "Grandma's Trunk." She told the students that she comes from a very close family and everyone felt duty-bound to help her get this important unit ready for her first significant teaching project. She went on to

explain that the trunk was a gift from her grandmother who was so very proud that Orpha was about to become a teacher. It was a special trunk, her grandmother explained, because whenever Orpha needed something special to use in her classroom, all she had to do was wish real hard, say the magic word (the children decided it should be "Shazam!"), open up the trunk, and look inside.

In anticipation, the students and Orpha chanted the magic word together, Orpha slowly opened up grandma's trunk, and, feigning great surprise at finding each, Orpha removed the following objects one by one: shanga (beaded jewelry), batik fabric, a skafu (head scarf), a mkeka (straw mat), a kikapu (straw basket), pesa (Kenya shilling—money), stempu (stamps), and kinu na mchi (mortar and pestle). Orpha introduced the objects singly, inviting the students to examine each as she talked about them and fielded comments and questions from her students. Orpha arranged the objects on a table display and added large-size index cards labeling the objects. The items served as models as the students made their own masks, baskets, and beaded jewelry throughout the unit.

Real experiences can serve as valuable external mediators as they raise questions in the students' minds and help draw them into the learning task. When we make early learning experiences positive and pleasurable, we stand a good chance of producing students who will be enthusiastic about, and willing to become actively involved in, learning throughout their lives.

Graphic Organizers. In addition to arousing attachment to the new content through carefully planned discussion strategies and thought-provoking materials, teachers often find it helpful to use graphic organizers such as diagrams, charts, drawings, and other visual displays. Graphic displays of information help students consciously connect their past experiences to the targeted skills or concepts under study.

Perhaps the most widely used graphic organizer is the *K–W–L chart*. Each letter represents a different activity that guides learners not only prior to but also during and after the learning experience. K represents what the students already know about the topic. Before the learning experience actually takes place, students discuss and brainstorm all the ideas they can associate with the topic and record their ideas on a chart, as shown in Figure 7.2. During a geography unit on oceans, a teacher might elicit suggestions with a question such as, "Before we read this material on oceans, let's take a few moments to jot down some of the things we already know about today's topic, 'beach sand.' " You may need to model one or two suggestions so that students begin to see what you mean. W represents what the students want to know. As the students reflect on what they already know about the topic, they form questions related to gaps in their understanding. Again, the teacher might need to model a personal question and write it down on the chart to give the children an idea of what they are expected to do. L represents

K = What We Know	W = What We Want to Find Out	L = What We Learned
waves wash sand onto beach made from tiny chips of rock some made from ground-down shells or coral sand is tiny, like salt you can make castles when it's wet	Where does sand come from? Why do some beaches have rocks instead of sand? What animals live in the sand? How can sand be different colors? How did sand get in deserts?	

FIGURE 7.2 K-W-L Chart

How Global is the Curriculum
Go to MyEducationLab, select the topic Teaching Strategies, watch the video entitled "Building Background Knowledge," and complete the questions that accompany it.

what students learned about the topic. After participating in the learning experience, students record what they discovered. They check their questions to see if each has been answered; if not, you may want to suggest other sources of information.

To illustrate, the following sequence of activities was used by Beatice Anderson to help her students understand how beach sand is created.

1. Begin by calling the children's attention to a study print of a typical seaside landscape. Discuss what the children see and invite them to talk about the times they have visited the beach. Encourage them to consider the vastness of the beach. Ask, "Who would care to guess how many grains of sand are on the beach?"
2. Hold up a large plastic jar filled with sand. Ask, "How many grains of sand are in this jar?" Add, "We may never know the answers to these questions, but we do know one thing—how sand is made."
3. Help students generate a list of all they know about how beach sand is made on a K-W-L chart. Write everything they know (or think they know) in the K column.
4. Have the students list what they want to know about the topic under the W column.
5. Read the book *Sand and Soil* by Beth Gurney (Crabtree). Invite the students to add questions to the W column if they wish.
6. Direct the students to record in the L column all they learned about how sand is made. In addition, any erroneous information listed in the first column should be corrected.
7. To bring closure, ask students to make an entry in their social studies journals summarizing what they have learned about beach sand.

The K–W–L strategy is a superior social studies activity because it helps students actively associate their previous knowledge and experiences while establishing personalized purposes for becoming involved in a new learning experience.

Establishing a Clear Purpose

"Why does my teacher want me to do this?" "What am I supposed to get out of it?" Students have asked questions like these in classrooms all around the country when given unclear reasons for becoming involved in a learning experience: "Read pages 43 to 45 in your textbook. Be prepared to answer my questions when you're done." Students who are on the receiving end of such insipid instructions often ask themselves: "Why?" "What's in it for me?" They do not sense a clear need for the assignment and often consider it impractical, unnecessary, or completely frustrating; they are confused by a lack of direction, so they do not push themselves into the learning experience with any degree of interest or importance. However, students who are informed about the reasons why they are to take on a learning experience are more likely to leap into the learning material actively, knowing what is expected at the end.

Keep in mind that this purpose-setting phase of the Learning Cycle must be linked to all that has gone on previously and, since it is the last part of the introductory phase of the lesson, purpose setting serves as the launching pad that propels the students into the main learning experience. Therefore, after showing her children a ship's bell, having them to handle it and ring it, and drawing out predictions about what it might be used for on a ship, a group of primary-grade children are directed to watch a video "to find out why bells ring every half-hour on a ship." After showing a large illustration of a mushroom cloud and holding an intense discussion of the horror of the atomic bomb, upper-grade students are directed to read the picture storybook *Hiroshima No Pika* (Translation: *The Flash of Hiroshima*) by Toshi Maruki. (This book vividly portrays in words and pictures the horror of an atomic attack with hopes that it will never happen again.) "Read the book to learn about the pain and suffering one family experiences when the flash interrupts their breakfast of sweet potatoes on August 6, 1945, at exactly 8:15 a.m." These purpose statements focus students' attention on what to look for as they proceed through the learning activity, directing them to a particular aspect or several aspects of importance. Sometimes these will simply be oral statements; at other times, they could be written on a chalkboard, chart, or handout so students can periodically refer to them.

With just the right amount of scaffolding, students will eventually learn to set their own purposes for learning. For example, they examine the photos in their textbook and wonder, "Why do banana farmers cut the stalks while the fruit is still green?" They then read to find out. Students also set their own purpose when they scan the headline in a newspaper, "The Outrage over Fake Indian Crafts," and turn it into a question, "Are cheap imitations being passed off as handmade American Indian crafts?"

The teacher appears pleased as this middle school student contributes to a K-W-L chart about Abraham Lincoln.

The Concept/Skill Development Phase

The *development phase* builds on the exploration phase by putting forward the main learning experience that will help develop the targeted concept or skill. During this second phase of the Learning Cycle, the teacher's role switches from that of "setting the table" to that of "sharing in the feast"—doing whatever it's going to take to assist the students in their quest to learn. During the second, or concept/skill development phase of a Learning Cycle, the teacher uses a variety of learning activities to make the topic or skill meaningful to students.

It is important that teachers address a number of key questions in order to carry out this second part of the Learning Cycle: What basic outcomes are targeted for instruction? What learning materials or activities hold the greatest potential for accomplishing the targeted outcomes? What strategies can best help students achieve the targeted outcomes? How can I help facilitate the construction of key learning outcomes? These questions are quite complicated and coming up with comprehensive responses for each can be a book in itself! This shows that teaching is hard work and that good teachers spend massive amounts of time preparing lessons that help students take in, process, and organize information.

Basic Content

In order to use the Learning Cycle well, teachers must be tuned in to subject matter. They must have a deep background of information, for each concept targeted for instruction has its own body of subordinate facts; each has a precise set of data. Teachers must be in command of this knowledge and use it to help students process and organize the information. After all, if teachers don't know the content, how can they hope to assist students in their efforts to construct new, accurate understandings of the world? To appreciate how important it is for a teacher to fully understand the content, let us imagine that you are teaching about the native people of the past who lived in Far North and were commonly referred to as *Eskimos*. Furthermore, let us assume that you have already helped the students learn about the food of the Eskimos from the past: the cold waters of the Arctic provided Eskimos with seals, salmon, whales, and other sea life. On land, there were caribou and geese in the summer and during the winter the Eskimos hunted bears, fox, and hares. Their favorite foods were seal and caribou meat, walrus liver, and the skin of whales.

The purpose of today's lesson is to help students understand the kind of homes the Eskimos lived in long ago. Focus for a minute on the first image of an Eskimo home that comes to your mind: If you are like most people, you have most likely shaped a mental picture of an *igloo*, a dome-shaped snow house sitting on a frigid, treeless, barren blanket of snow and ice. And, a more detailed picture might include spear-wielding whale hunters nearby, dressed in heavy fur clothing and standing near a sled ready to be pulled by a team of huskies. If you are like most, this conventional image would most likely guide your instruction, perhaps to the point of concluding the study of Eskimo igloos with the construction of tabletop models from sugar cubes or marshmallows. With such keen, clear-cut insight into Eskimos and their igloos, there wouldn't be any need to dig up much additional information, would there? You bet there would! If you had been meticulous enough to do an information search, you would have found that the people from the Far North who we've been calling Eskimos do not use the word *Eskimo* when speaking of themselves. They are offended by that expression, primarily because it was an unpleasant word anthropologists borrowed from American Indians meaning "eaters of raw meat." Instead, the people of the Far North prefer to use a name that simply means "the people." In Canada, that name is *Inuit*. In Alaska, it could be either *Inupiat* or *Yupik*. The name *Yuit* is used in Mongolia.

Furthermore, focusing solely on the dome-shaped snow houses many people picture as the primary shelter of the people of the Far North would have been both illogical and culturally insensitive. In the past, the people of the Far North lived in various types of shelters. Tents made of skin (seal or caribou) and whale bones provided shelter during the summer months, whereas in winter, most built semi-subterranean sod houses. And some permanent shelters were built from logs. Yes, a dome-shaped snow house consisting of blocks cut from snow and built upward in a spiral shape was built by some groups, especially by people of Canada's Central Arctic area, but most served mostly as temporary shelter while traveling or hunting. Many people mistakenly think exclusively of these dome-shaped snow structures as the Eskimos' primary igloos; actually, the people of the Far North call any place for living by that name, including the dormitory room, house, or apartment you are sitting in right now. In point of fact, *iglu* is the Inuit word for "house," and Inuit now live in modern houses, or split-level, colonial, condo, or apartment iglus, just like the ones you and I live in. And, like you and me, they live in towns and villages, work at contemporary jobs, wear modern clothing, eat food purchased in stores, and instead of kayaks and dogsleds, they use motorboats and snowmobiles.

What would children have learned about the Inuit if they were offered what we *thought* we knew about this fascinating culture? In this case, the result certainly would be unjust, stereotypical, and incorrect, abusing all the major responsibilities of a contemporary multicultural society. In any lesson, we must uncover and verify considerable information so that students acquire a genuine concept of the culture, period of time, or phenomenon being studied. Consider how one experienced teacher highlights the need for a spirit of continuous learning:

> The biggest surprise of teaching, for me, was that I didn't know my subject matter. That was the one thing I had been most confident about. I had almost an "A" average in my major and felt really on top of my field. When I began teaching and had to explain concepts, I found that I had only a very superficial understanding of them. I knew stuff in kind of a rote way and when I had to explain it to someone else I kind of just fell on my face. I learned more about my subject in my first four months of teaching than I did in my four years of college. (Ryan, Burkholder, & Phillips, 1983, p. 177)

As a teacher in a social constructivist classroom, this means that you must not only have much information at your fingertips but you should also have access to resources that supplement your knowledge. The computer and a wide variety of print sources are the places to start. Check with your school or public librarian for references on a concept you wish to pursue. Constantly search for information to bolster what you already know; you should find yourself saying, "I'll look it up," many times a day. Books and the computer will provide most of the needed information, but you will also want additional resources. Consult specialists both in person and by telephone, visit museums and other sites, view films or filmstrips, listen to audiotapes, and seek other opportunities to broaden your background. You will need to spend a great deal of time uncovering and organizing information, and love doing it.

Concept Analysis. In addition to knowing the content, teachers in social constructivist classrooms must also be able to organize it so that the content has most meaning. The most common way to organize the content is to classify it into *concept categories (schemata).* Because concept development takes place over a lifetime, we say that it is a dynamic process; that is, our understanding of the world keeps growing and changing as we file away new information throughout our

lifetimes. For example, as a youngster my "mental file folder" labeled *mound* contained very few items. One of the first bits of knowledge I filed away in my "mound" concept folder was the "mound of dirt" I used to play in at the far reaches of our back yard. Next, as a Little League pitcher, I learned that the slightly elevated pitcher's area in the center of a baseball diamond that I stood on was called a mound. So, my mental "concept folder" grew a bit as I added a new understanding of my world. When I got older, I learned that any raised mass, such as a pile of hay could be referred to as a mound and even that a large artificial pile of earth or stones marking a burial site can be called a mound. I'm sure most of you have similar data in your *mound* "concept folders," and will use that "folder" throughout your lifetime to sort out any new information you feel will be important enough to store there.

Think about the following information as a possible addition: In AD 1200, the Mississippians (an American Indian culture living along the banks of the river that now bears their name) built the town of Cahokia around a huge, steep platform called a *mound*. Because it was so huge (1,000 feet long by 700 feet wide), historians estimate that the mound would have taken the Mississippians more than 200 years to complete. The mound was so colossal, in fact, that it would dwarf even the Great Pyramids of Egypt. What do you think? Will you expand your mound "mental folder" with that information? What factors do you feel would cause some to say, "Yes, I will!" or "Sorry, try again!?"

Concepts are designated by a label, a word that helps us catalog incoming information conveniently. In the Learning Cycle model, learning depends a great deal on the teacher's ability to identify the defining features of the concept being taught. Many concepts, such as *mound, coin, flag, iceberg, fjord, merchant,* and *shelter,* have well-defined characteristics and are relatively easy to analyze and teach. They are called *concrete concepts* because they are easily recognized by their physical appearance. Others, such as *democracy, peace, freedom, justice, equal opportunity, liberty,* and *war,* have characteristics that are much less concrete and, therefore, are much more difficult to analyze and teach. These terms, called *abstract concepts*, are much more difficult to conceptualize because we cannot visibly observe their physical characteristics. That is why you will find concepts like *family* or *home* or *firefighter* taught at the first-grade level, yet *democracy* and *freedom* rarely find their way into the instructional program in a formal sense before the upper-elementary school grades or even middle school.

Concept analysis is the process of breaking down a concept by identifying its defining features. To better understand how this relates directly to social studies instruction, take a minute and think about a concept many fifth-graders learn about in their social studies classes—*Buddhism*. Our first responsibility is to come up with a brief definition for it—for example, "*Buddhism*: the teaching ascribed to Siddhartha Gautama holding that one can enter into nirvana by mental and moral self-purification." You need not come up with an original definition for each concept you will teach; they are easily found in dictionaries, encyclopedias, textbooks, and other reference materials. The concept label and definition are important, but the process of concept analysis is not complete until we break down its defining characteristics, or subordinate details, that help us distinguish Buddhism from Christianity, Hinduism, Judaism, Confucianism, Islam, or any other religion. Think about Buddhism for a moment; what particulars come to your mind? Are you picturing a sculpture of the Buddha? Maybe you see a mental image of a Buddhist monk. Perhaps words such as *Siddhartha Gautama, the Buddha, India, religion, Four Noble Truths*, and *dharma* pop into your head. We store information in our minds in a number of different ways; images and words are two of the most common. The images and symbols you associated with Buddhism are a result of your past experiences with Buddhism. The forms they took were determined by the way you sorted out, ordered, connected, and made sense of the details of those past experiences.

Factstorming

The first step in expanding the concept, then, is a process of finding the relevant details associated with a concept—a process commonly called *factstorming*. Virtually any concept can be factstormed; all that is required is to create a graphic representation of what you already know about the concept. First, label your selected concept at the top of a large sheet of paper and draw a circle around it. Then, by asking probing questions (for example, "What are the teachings of Buddhism?"), list all the relevant details you can think of. Write them on the paper, too, draw a circle around each, and draw lines to connect them to the central concept. Repeat the process with each relevant detail. The chart is only the beginning. As we learned with the Eskimo illustration, we do not know enough at this initial stage of the planning process to identify all the necessary content, but are only brainstorming "starters," or ideas to launch the planning process. You will need to exhaustively add to and refine the starter information, for the defining features of a concept must be complete and accurate if instruction is to succeed. An analysis of the defining characteristics of the concept of Buddhism as it was researched and organized by one teacher to serve as the content source for a mixed group of fifth- and sixth-graders is depicted in Figure 7.3.

Notice how the most general category (Buddhism) is at the top of the teacher's paper. It is the concept label under which the teacher diagrammed relevant details. Taken together, these comprise the defining features that will be used to teach about Buddhism. If the teacher were to offer a narrative explanation of the hierarchy, it would include statements such as those that follow:

- Buddhism is one of the world's great religions.
- Buddhism was started in India somewhere between 563 and 483 BC.
- Siddhartha Gautama established Buddhism.
- Siddhartha was called "the Buddha," or the "enlightened one."
- Buddhist laws and teachings are called the dharma.
- The Four Noble Truths explain the Buddha's beliefs about suffering.
- The Buddha preached "The Middle Way"—moderation.

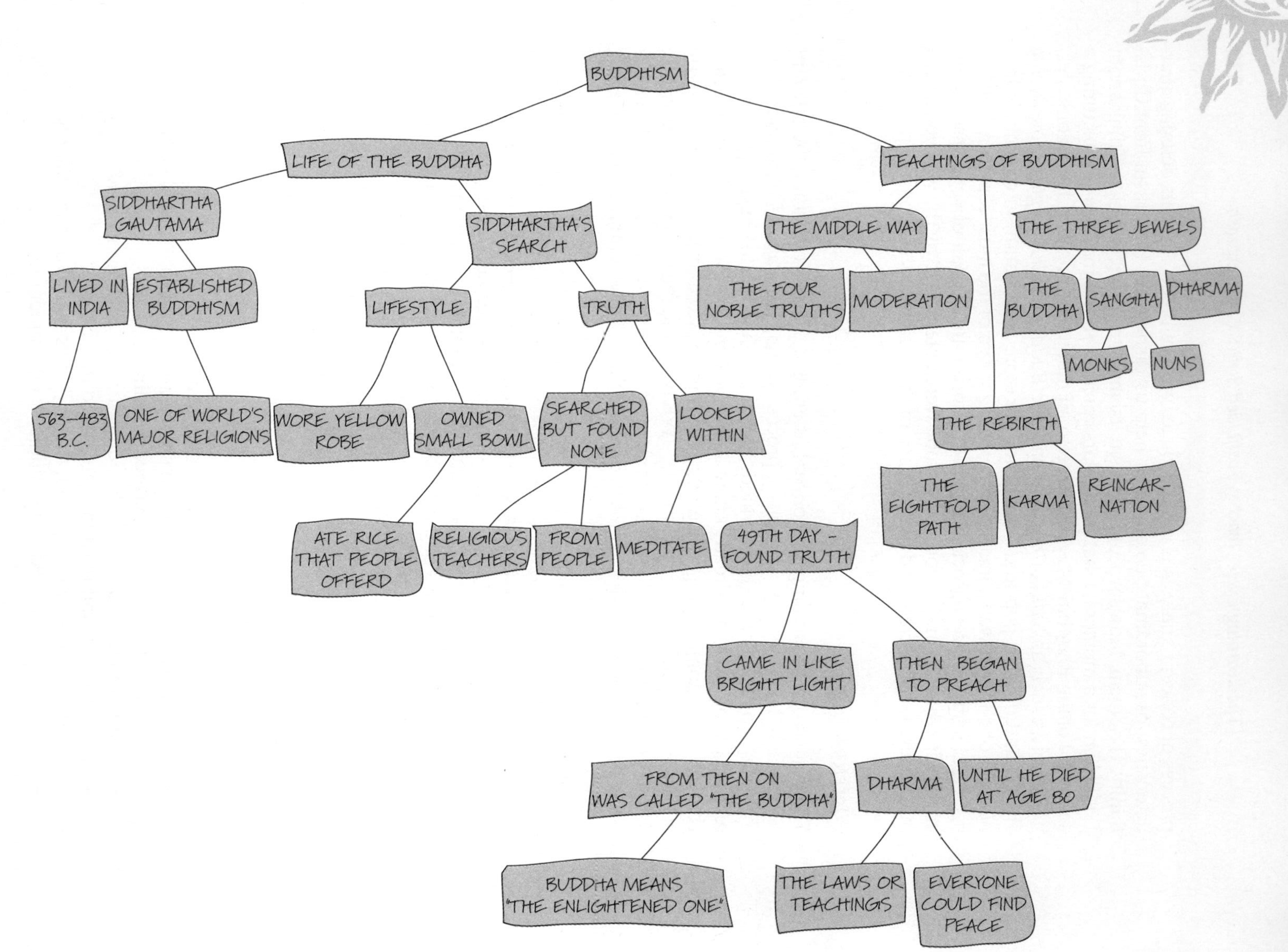

FIGURE 7.3 Concept Map for Buddhism

- Buddhists believe that the Eightfold Path leads to enlightenment. The deeds a person performs during his or her lifetime are called karma.
- Buddhists believe in a process called reincarnation.
- The good or bad karma travels with a person to the next life.
- The Buddhist tradition is made up of three parts called the Three Jewels: (1) the Buddha, (2) the dharma, and (3) the sangha (religious community, including nuns and monks).

Although they have been abused by overly excessive rote, drill, or practice exercises, facts are highly necessary ingredients of concept development. They help learners distinguish continents from countries, glaciers from icebergs, and Buddhism from Hinduism. Concepts grow from facts; facts are what give concepts their defining features. Facts serve as building blocks, furnishing the details necessary to develop concepts. Concepts do not materialize magically out of thin air; students gradually construct them as knowledge accumulates through varied life experiences. Without a system of organizing the wealth of information about our world, though, each fact becomes isolated and students have very few options other than to memorize it—and to complain that "social studies is boring!"

A word of caution about the defining characteristics of concepts must be given here, however: Although facts provide the defining features that make a concept what it is, they must be selected carefully. For example, details of George Washington's $60 dentures (made from ivory, wild animal teeth, or lead covered with gold), as interesting as they may be, would not contribute much to enriching the concept of the nation's presidency. However, they could provide interesting content to help construct an understanding of health care during colonial times. Concepts are superb organizational devices, but they can be formed accurately only when learners gather meaningful information through sound, developmentally appropriate activities. Concept learning is a process of learning what key features (defining characteristics) are essential components of a concept and what other features (irrelevant characteristics) are nonessential. Learning to differentiate defining features from irrelevant features takes time and experience; this process only takes longer and becomes more difficult to master when teachers present students with unclear examples.

Basic Skills (Task Analysis)

In addition to building concepts, another major goal of social studies instruction is helping children acquire specific skills such as constructing and interpreting charts and graphs, using the computer, composing a meaningful written report, making a timeline, reading a map, creating a model, outlining information from reference books, planning an interview, making a mural, learning the steps of an ethnic dance, comprehending textbook material, collecting data, or testing hypotheses. *Skills* are mental or physical operations having a specific set of actions that are developed through practice. Those who support the social constructivist

philosophy claim that students cannot learn skills without a teacher's help; these necessary skills are best taught and reinforced as separate lessons with clear assistance from the teacher followed by numerous opportunities for practice. This process begins by carefully breaking down the skill into a number of separate components, each of which provides the foundation for the next. The process through which the component parts of the skill are identified and sequenced is referred to as *task analysis*. In learning to read maps, for example, understanding what a map is would certainly come before a lesson requiring students to locate their state capital. In other words, instruction is sequenced so that more complex processes grow from less complex ones.

Many social constructivist teachers believe that social studies skills can be best acquired through the process of *modeling*—that is, observing someone more highly skilled and attempting to copy her or his behaviors. These teachers emphasize, for example, that it is no coincidence that better readers come from homes where parents read frequently—if children see their parents reading the morning newspaper or a book, they will be inspired to follow their lead.

Nadya Luca felt it was important to model certain reading skills from the social studies text so that her students could best develop subject area literacy. The question, "What must my students be able to do in order to learn effectively from their social studies text?" served as the basis for analyzing the specific skills that would be necessary for developing subject area literacy. Look carefully at the following list that Ms. Luca assembled. It served as the basis for subsequent instruction in her classroom.

Students must be able to:

1. Identify what they already know about the topic.
2. Raise questions about what they do not know.
3. Predict what the text will be about.
4. Predict what information will be found in the passage.
5. Relate new information to previous knowledge.
6. Focus their attention on the reading task.

First, Ms. Luca wanted her fourth-graders to relate their personal experiences to the textbook topic, so she began the social studies lesson by displaying a photograph of a small rural community and the rich, lush farmland that surrounded it. She used the photograph as a springboard for discussion of the ways people interact with and adapt to their environment, focusing especially on the need to protect natural resources: "How do people and animals rely on the fertile topsoil? How do they rely on trees? Water?" Ms. Luca and the class discussed wasteful practices such as overwatering lawns and using paper unwisely. She then asked the class how they might protect Earth's topsoil, trees, and water supply.

NCSS STANDARDS

III. *People, Places, and Environments*
X. *Civic Ideals and Practice*

Following this short discussion, Ms. Luca directed her students to turn to a specific page in their social studies text. She pointed to and read aloud the chapter title, "Saving Our Land." Ms. Luca explained that when she sees a new chapter title, she always thinks for a moment about what it might mean. "It seems to me that the chapter could be about ways of protecting our natural resources such as water and topsoil and trees," she suggested. "What do you suppose gave me that idea?" After they discussed Ms. Luca's idea for a short while, she asked the class to talk with a partner and produce an original idea about the chapter title. Then, as the pairs shared their original ideas, Ms. Luca wrote their suggestions on the chalkboard. Next, Ms. Luca asked the students to look at the text photos and the first major heading, "The Need to Protect Our Land." She said to the class, "I find that examining the illustrations and headings before I read raises questions in my mind about what might be ahead. For example, one question I had about the photo at the top of the page is, 'Why is conserving topsoil so important?' What are some other questions I might have asked myself about the heading and the photos?" Ms. Luca went through the next section, "Conservation Efforts," the same way and continued with the succeeding sections, writing each set of comments and questions on the chalkboard.

Although modeling is recognized as a highly effective and efficient method of helping students learn a specific skill or behavior, it must be emphasized that not just any model will do. Students have a greater tendency to accept their teachers as high-quality models if they perceive them as competent and capable professionals. I'm sure, for example, that you would have much more faith in a golf pro teaching you the nuances of the game than in a friend whose experiences consisted of watching the PGA Championship on television. Likewise, children learning how to use the Internet as a research tool are more likely to place their faith in a teacher who exhibits technological savvy rather than one who calls in sick with a computer virus!

In addition to a quality model, students are more likely to become engaged in certain tasks when they are convinced that they can be successful—that is, when they have a high degree of *self-efficacy*. For example, you may have a high degree of self-efficacy for teaching social studies to elementary school children. That is, you are quite capable of taking the information from this course and using it to carry out effective classroom practices. On the other hand, your self-efficacy for filling the cracks on Mount Rushmore might be slightly less sophisticated. Likewise, not all of your students will experience an equal degree of self-efficacy for everything you want them to learn. Some will have high efficacy for performing the Blackfoot Buffalo Dance, while others will prefer composing a poem. Students tend to bring greater effort to tasks that they think they will do well with and avoid those that they think they might have difficulty with. So, it is important to provide just the right amount of assistance to students. More assistance than the student actually needs sends the implied message that "I don't really think you can ever do this on your own." Not enough assistance has a high probability of resulting in failure and weakened self-confidence. And, verbal encouragement with little or no further assistance such as, "If at first you don't succeed, try and try again!" or, "I know you can do it. Don't give up" is questionable in providing a boost in self-efficacy. The key is to find the point at which your students can succeed at a task with your assistance (ZPD). At this point, they will have greater confidence in their ability to succeed and apply greater effort and determination to the task.

Materials for Instruction

Selecting learning materials and activities must be consistent with the ways children learn. For example, Jerome Bruner and colleagues (1966) identified three levels of learning that children move through as they encounter new information—enactive, iconic, and symbolic (see Figure 7.4). The *enactive level* includes objects, people, places, trips, visitors, and real-life classroom experiences. Within this level, children represent and understand the world through direct experience and actions on objects. For example, suppose your goal for today is to help students learn about the emergence of cotton as an important cash crop in the Southeast during the late 1700s. Your enactive level possibilities include bringing in cotton bolls for the children to handle as they examine the soft fibers, observe the tiny seeds, and touch the prickly shell. By handling the real item, the students can appreciate the agony slaves experienced as they were forced to spend immeasurable hours picking out the little seeds from within the boll in order to free the attached fibers.

The *iconic level* is a representation of real objects. For example, there is no way to have your students directly observe the slaves picking cotton in the hot fields all day and emptying their sacks until they built up a huge heap of cotton.

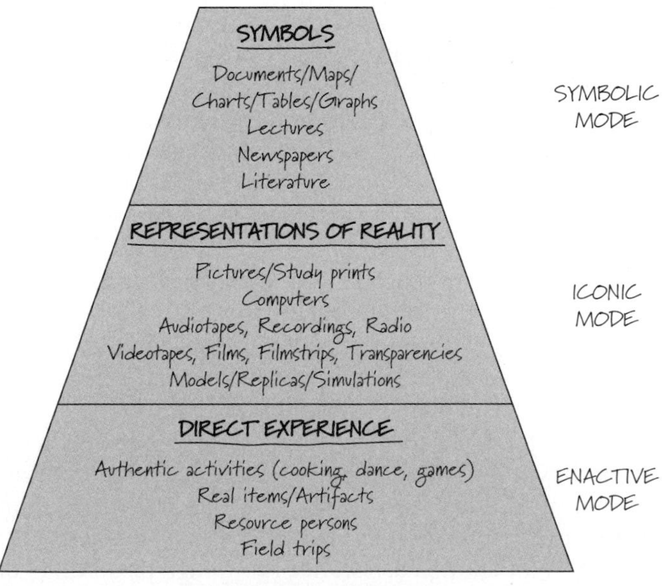

FIGURE 7.4 Bruner's Three Modes of Knowing

And, you cannot have them observe the next 8 to 10 hours when the slaves would clean the fiber out of the cotton bolls. Moment-in-time limitations make this impossible. A well-produced video documentary or possibly a set of study prints with clear explanations would then be a useful substitute for the real experience. Representations of reality help children construct new understandings when real things are not available. Although pictures and models are not always as motivating as something real, these learning resources are much more effective than trying to connect new learning to words alone. Good pictures, especially large poster-size photographs and prints, will deepen children's concepts of people and places. Dynamic social studies teachers build substantial picture files by searching hard for just the right pictures to furnish experiences that students can connect to new ideas. Models, too, bring valuable stimulation to the classroom. A good social studies classroom contains models that mirror displays found in our best museums—not a hands-off place where students simply stand and gawk, but one that invites handling and touching.

The *symbolic level* involves using abstract ideas, symbols, language, and logic to represent the world. For example, good information books and other sources of children's literature can enliven and deepen the children's knowledge of how cotton is grown and processed and how the Southeast became an important cotton-growing region.

Understanding Bruner's three levels of learning is important for planning and organizing the development phase of the Learning Cycle. They help you recognize the need for balance among the activities you choose, so that there is not too much symbolism (workbooks, practice sheets, talking, reading) nor too little realia—or vice versa—in your program. As a rule of thumb, you should remember that all students thrive on a balance of solid learning experiences, but that younger students need direct contact and real experiences (a visit to an orchard) and visual representations (a videotape of apple-growing procedures). Older students still require concrete experiences but are increasingly able to gain knowledge from abstract sources (listening to a well-planned lecture).

Assisting Students as They Construct Key Concepts

According to social constructivists, the act of learning about one's world cannot take place simply by handing children some learning materials and asking them to draw out the important understandings all by themselves. Piaget (1964) writes, "Experience is . . . necessary for intellectual development . . . but I fear that we may fall into the illusion that being submitted to an experience . . . is sufficient. . . . But more than this is required . . ." (p. 4). Piaget stressed the something "more" is the crucial role of the teacher; teachers must not only be effective organizers who select rich materials and intriguing situations that arouse interest in learning but they must also be thought-provoking guides who encourage students to use language to organize their thinking. Under their leadership, social constructivist classrooms become communities of learners working together to organize

knowledge and construct learning, and this goal cannot be accomplished unless there is talk.

If teachers expect the *concept development phase* of the Learning Cycle to play a major role in knowledge construction, they must encourage students to use language—to think and talk about what they have been trying to accomplish. These language-based strategies not only help students organize and explain what they have been learning but they also give teachers an idea of where students need supportive assistance or additional experience. Three familiar language-based strategies that help teachers build scaffolds for the construction of new knowledge include *general instructional conversations, small-group instructional conversations,* and *graphic organizers*. Using either or all of these three language-based strategies completes the crucial *development phase* of the Learning Cycle.

General Instructional Conversations. Scaffolding as a process of assisting students to construct knowledge occurs most effectively in classrooms where students come together to talk, listen, and learn from one another. Conversation is the system by which they share knowledge with one another and the primary method for developing higher-order thinking. One particular form of classroom conversation, called *instructional conversations,* has received a great deal of attention for its potential value in social constructivist classrooms (Gallimore & Tharp, 1990). Through instructional conversations, a teacher builds on the learning experiences the students have had and guides them toward the construction of new knowledge and understandings. Instructional conversations are *instructional* because they help assist learning; they are *conversations* because the interaction pattern is more varied than in typical classroom discussions. The course of dialogue flows from teacher to students, from students to teacher, and among students—the way a true conversation develops. When instructional conversations are used in social studies classrooms, the outcome is noticeably less teacher talk and more student talk.

Instructional conversations take place in a classroom environment where students can talk freely, presenting their ideas and opinions in whole-class or small-group situations. Teachers set off instructional conversations with well-planned questions and prompts that provoke students to think and reason about the content. Then, as the students respond, teachers listen and react to their ideas in a supportive, considerate manner.

If instructional conversations are to be productive, we must force from our minds any thoughts of traditional classroom dialogue where teachers use questions as tools of "interrogation" rather than as prompts to help students search for meaning. *Interrogations* can best be described as peppering students with closed-ended questions that require them simply to retrieve from memory any piece of specific information that was a part of the learning experience. For example, a question such as "In what year did a German submarine sink the *Lusitania?*" is considered to be closed-ended because there is only one possible answer. And, once a student responds, all further dialogue stops—discussion is closed. Monotonously, closed-ended questions after closed-ended questions flow in a steady stream until all the facts are recited. Through this type of fruitless exchange, students learn very early in their schooling that their role in classroom discussions is to send back what the teacher wants to hear rather than talk about what is truly important to them. One study reported on the wasteful nature of restrictive, traditional classroom interrogations: "When students . . . respond, typically they provide only simple information recall statements. This pattern of teacher–student interaction not only limits a student's opportunity to create and manipulate language, but it also limits the student's ability to engage in more complex learning" (Ramirez, Yuen, & Ramey, 1991, p. 8).

Instructional conversations are an alternative to restrictive, traditional teacher-centered classroom interrogations. The teacher is viewed more as a facilitator than an interrogator, using effective questions and prompts to help students think deeply about a learning experience. Although teachers may use closed-ended questions during instructional conversations, the purpose for these questions is to ensure that students have adequate prior knowledge about a topic to discuss it wisely. Conversely, open-ended questions such as "What culture other than your own do you admire most and why?" lead to more complex thinking. They challenge students to go beyond the content by engaging higher-order thought processes such as critical and analytical thinking. Students are usually more involved in class discussions when open-ended questions are asked because those kinds of questions are much more thought provoking. Check your ability to distinguish open-ended from closed-ended questions by categorizing each of the following examples as one or the other:

1. What was the name of the ship that brought the Pilgrims to Plymouth Colony in 1621?
2. The Pilgrims at Plymouth Colony had very strong religious beliefs. How do you think these beliefs affected their ability to survive the hardships of the first winter?
3. When spring came, many Indians visited the Pilgrims. What questions do you suppose the Indians wanted to ask the Pilgrims? What questions do you suppose the Pilgrims wanted to ask the Indians?
4. What was the name of the Indian tribe that visited the Pilgrims at Plymouth Colony that first spring?
5. Squanto showed the Pilgrims how to plant corn. What did he teach them to use as fertilizer?

I trust you selected questions 2 and 3 as open-ended or divergent questions. Those two questions are considered to be open-ended because they are thought-provoking and intended to pull out more than a single factual response. Discussion usually is extended because students will enjoy the challenge of using the

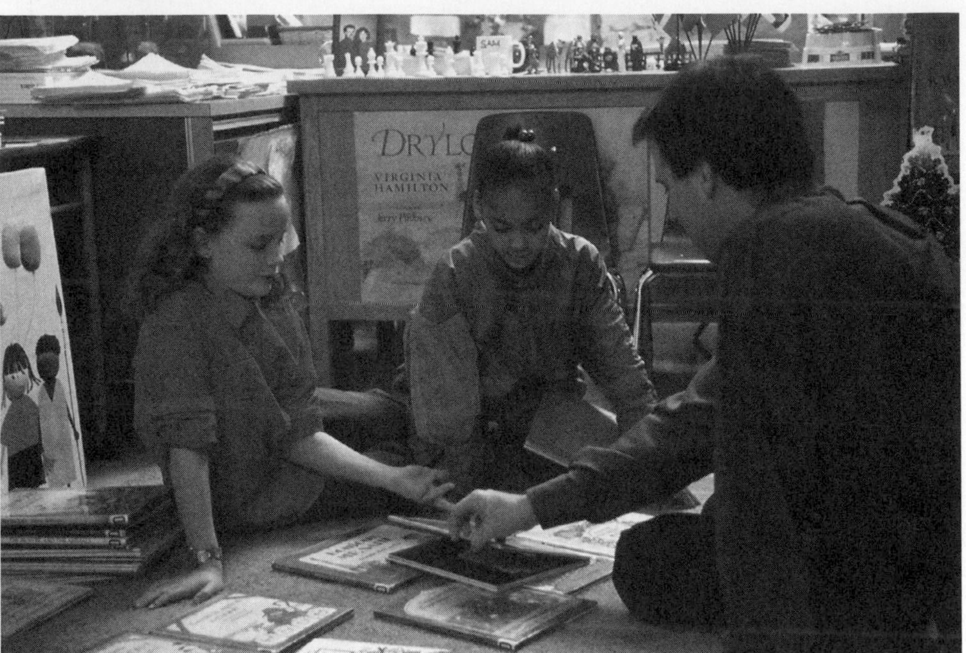

Effective instructional conversations establish a community spirit in which students are encouraged to share their ideas.

content to support their own beliefs and to question the beliefs of their classmates. Questions 1, 4, and 5 are closed-ended questions because they converge on a single, correct response. Unfortunately, when one student gives the correct response, discussion swiftly comes to a halt because there is nothing more one can think or talk about.

Asking good questions, as important as the process is, represents only one critical concern in leading instructional conversations. Teachers must also be skilled at sequencing or *patterning* the questions so that students can be systematically guided toward intended learning outcomes. Questions should never be randomly selected; it is important that they have a focus because discussions happen for different reasons. Perhaps you want your students to organize and elaborate on what they've learned. Maybe you would like them to critique a controversial issue. Whatever the reason for designing a questioning plan, the purpose must be kept foremost in mind so that you are able to maintain focus throughout the instructional conversation. So, as you begin to think about the kinds of questions to ask during this phase of the Learning Cycle, ask yourself these questions: "What do I want my students to gain from this discussion?" "How will the questions contribute to the overall purpose of the lesson?" Your replies will assist you to design worthwhile questions and help guide your students to deeper understanding of the targeted concept or skill.

To illustrate, let us examine the questioning patterns of two teachers, both of whom shared the same instructional purpose: *to help the students understand how the migration of white settlers changed the lives of the Plains Indians.*

Paul Resuta decided to launch his instructional conversation by asking an open-ended question intended to draw out personal feelings: "The Plains Indians had deep respect for nature and the land. Do you think the settlers shared this point of view?" The students eagerly offered several different viewpoints, and Mr. Resuta challenged them to support each of their beliefs with appropriate information: "What evidence do you have to support your position?" So, even though Mr. Resuta began the instructional conversation with an open-ended question, students were required to use relevant information to back up their arguments.

Grace Chacho, by contrast, preferred to set her instructional conversation in motion with a question that called for her students to summarize the content: "In what ways did the settlers upset the Plains Indians' way of life?" As the students volunteered a number of responses, Ms. Chacho transcribed each fact on an information summary chart. At the point when her students were unable to add further information, Ms. Chacho suggested, "Let's examine what you've come up with. What does this information tell you about how the Plains Indians and the settlers felt about the land? Do you think Americans of today have attitudes similar to the settlers at that time?"

Mr. Resuta asked an open-ended question to start the instructional conversation and then challenged the students to support their views with relevant details. Ms. Chacho did just the opposite; she started by asking the students to recall details with closed-ended questions and then encouraged them to draw their own conclusions from the data. Which approach is best for elementary school social studies instruction? Both are acceptable; each sequence was driven by a logical purpose, was patterned to address that purpose, and helped students cite evidence to support critical thinking. Rather than worrying about whether your sequence begins with an open- or closed-ended question, it is more important to become skilled at applying John Dewey's (1933) helpful "art of questioning," as proposed over 75 years ago:

- Questions should not elicit fact upon fact, but should be asked in such a way as to delve deeply into the subject; that is, to develop an overall concept of the selection.
- Questions should emphasize personal interpretations rather than literal and direct responses.
- Questions should not be asked randomly so that each is an end in itself, but should be planned so that one leads into the next throughout a continuous discussion.
- Teachers should periodically review important points so that old, previously discussed material can be placed into perspective with that which is presently being studied.

- The end of the question-asking sequence should leave the children with a sense of accomplishment and build a desire for that which is yet to come.

Interrogations, employed simply to quiz the students about facts associated with a learning experience, gives the illusion of teaching to the uninitiated. First-rate teachers, however, know that questions must be planned so that one leads to the other throughout a logical sequence, deliberately provoking deeper thought or creating new understandings. If teachers are able to effectively guide instructional conversations, students will discover that questions can serve as a useful tool of the mind that help organize their thinking now and throughout their lifetimes.

In addition to patterning questions, it is equally important to know how to *frame* questions; that is, to provide students enough time to think of a response and to transform their thoughts into a comment that they could share with their classmates. The fundamental system for framing questions is: (1) ask the question, (2) pause for 3 to 5 seconds (wait time I), (3) call on a student to respond, and (4) pause again for 3 to 5 seconds to give the student some time to think about and share a response (wait time II). There are a number of benefits associated with giving students ample time to think. First, a larger number of students will respond. Second, their responses tend to be longer, more complex, and more precise. Third, a pause provides the teacher with time to study the students' body language. With experience, you will be able to pick up their satisfaction, delight, concern, or boredom. Fourth, teachers who pause after asking questions become more patient while waiting for answers and the students become more comfortable while sharing their thoughts.

In addition to Learning Cycle applications, verbal interactions (scaffolds) with a teacher can be quite beneficial when it becomes necessary to help students clarify ideas or complete a task. For example, during a unit in "Famous Inventors," groups of students were challenged to do some of their own inventing. Their teacher showed them a pencil full of teeth marks, broken lead, chipped paint, and a ragged eraser: "We have a problem here . . . look at this mess! What's wrong with this pencil? How can we improve it? What could we add or change to make a pencil more appealing and useful?" Several groups launched themselves directly into the activity, bringing to life such ideas as a pencil that could also be used to write on the chalkboard, a pencil that could be safely eaten, a pencil with a transparent covering so you could see inside, a pencil that glows in the dark, and one that changes color as it wears down. One group, however, seemed to be stumped. The teacher approached and engaged its members in the following dialogue:

Teacher: How is the pencil project going, Travis?

Travis: We can't seem to come up with a good idea. I just don't know why we're stuck.

Teacher: Did you think about the things that might be wrong with the pencil that I showed to the class?

Travis: Yes. Here's our list. We thought of things like the lead breaks too easily, it's ugly, it's easy to lose, the eraser wears down too fast, it's boring, and you can only write on paper with it.

Teacher: That's an impressive list. Now, it would help if you examine the list and talk together about this question: "What bugs us most about the pencil?"

Natalie: I think the pencil's boring!

Geraldo: Me, too. Let's think of something really wild to make the pencil more fun.

Matt: How about making music as it moves across a page? That way we could write and have fun at the same time!

Geraldo: There, we did it! We finally got some good ideas going.

In the Vygotskian scheme, an educational dialogue is similar to a Socratic dialogue where there is give and take among all participants. As the teacher gradually relinquishes control of the learning situation (begins to "remove the scaffolding"), her questions should become internalized by the students and they should in due course achieve self-regulation, or personal control over the instructional dialogue. Notice, however, that throughout the entire progression of the sample experience, the teacher did not furnish the students with any answers, but supported them in solving the problem themselves. Experiencing success under such positive teacher guidance leads to strong feelings of competence and confidence rather than weakness or inferiority.

Although it is a valued strategy, assisted learning in the social studies classroom should not be limited to teacher–student interactions. Equally as important are the exchanges that go on among peers; although casual talking can help some children, learning can often be haphazard and the children can be misled by another child's misunderstandings. Teachers must understand that assisted learning involves many complex interactions, so to be a worthwhile experience, the situation must be deliberately structured and the types of interactions must be carefully spelled out. This means that during the early stages of a learning episode, when a concept is yet undeveloped, a teacher may find it more highly productive to lead the verbal interactions. As the children learn a skill or deepen concepts, peer interaction in small-group instructional situations can become more conducive to intellectual growth.

Small-Group Instructional Conversations. One of the best ways to incorporate language-based instruction into the Learning Cycle is to offer opportunities for cooperative and collaborative learning through *small-group instructional conversations*. Such conversations have become increasingly popular in social studies classrooms because, of all school subjects, social studies seems to be most fitting for group discussions. Students meet to talk about a field trip they had just taken, to respond to a biography their teacher just read to them, to plan a mural

project, to compare the actions of two historical figures, to explore the ramifications of harvesting the world's rainforests, or to summarize information presented in a video.

Typically, small-group instructional conversations are sparked by a meaningful question or problem offered by the teacher or another student. The subsequent talk allows for the exchange of observations, explanations, clarifying comments, and differing points of view. Although students do most of the talking in small-group instructional conversations, teachers nonetheless have vital responsibilities. To begin, they must make sure students have a sound background of information necessary to discuss the topic intelligently. They must model good dialogic behaviors and work to create a climate of mutual respect in the classroom. Social studies teachers must communicate expectancies like these to guide small-group instructional conversations:

- Everyone should take part in the conversation.
- Think before you speak.
- Speak honestly and openly about your thoughts and feelings.
- Listen carefully and politely to what others are saying, even if you disagree.
- Feel free to extend and expand another student's ideas.
- Ask clarifying questions if you do not understand something.
- Criticize ideas, not other students.

After the ground rules are well established and understood by all, teachers find it useful to use strategies like these to initiate good small-group instructional conversations:

- Select a topic with multiple perspectives.

  Example: "Who should take care of the elderly when they are no longer able to care for themselves?"

- Clarify the time frame.

  Example: "We'll meet in small groups for 15 minutes and then come back together as a whole class."

- Explain the procedures in manageable steps.

  Example: "Each group will be made up of four students. Each group of four will subdivide into two pairs. Each pair of students will discuss the issue and present its position to the other two students. The group of four will hold an open discussion on the issue, making sure each student has an opportunity to voice her or his viewpoint. The group of four will then attempt to reach consensus on the issue in a way that incorporates everyone's reasoning and explanations."

- After the small groups have talked about the topic for the specified time, or if they have thoroughly explored the topic before the time expires, the class can be brought back together and each group can share its results. The teacher should write key points on the board, and the final conclusion can then be examined by the entire class for common themes.

Example: "What did you learn from the conversation?" "What did you find you had in common with other members of the group?" "Are there any ways in which the conversation could be improved?"

Small-group instructional conversations seem to be more effective when they are structured in ways similar to those illustrated in the strategy outlined above. Additional examples of useful small-group conversation arrangements can be found in Chapter 8, *Cooperative and Collaborative Learning*.

To summarize, it is possible to provide language-based instructional scaffolding by involving students in general instructional conversations based on Dewey's "art of questioning" or by engaging them in small-group instructional conversations. These opportunities for constructive classroom talk provide the scaffolding needed to move a student from a dependent to an independent learner. Another widespread language-based scaffolding technique involves the use of *graphic organizers*. Graphic organizers provide students a framework for processing information, whether recognizing relationships, outlining processes, or identifying needed information.

How Global is the Curriculum *Go to MyEducationLab, select the topic Teaching Strategies, watch the video entitled "Mapping," and complete the questions that accompany it.*

Graphic Organizers. Most of us learned to outline information when we were in school, so when we hear or read the term *graphic organizer*, the idea of an outline or summary paragraph often pops into our heads. If you find this happening, clear your mind and think instead of replacing outlines or summary paragraphs with visual representations called *graphic organizers*. Graphic organizers are sketches or illustrations that help students represent key ideas and organize information. Often, graphic organizers are called *concept maps* because they help teachers and students "map out" their ideas pictorially. Graphic organizers help students detect helpful patterns and relationships within the content. They are able to see how ideas are connected and how information can be stored in an orderly fashion.

Graphic organizers, like instructional conversations, are considered to be language-based scaffolding experiences because students need not only draw and write in order to complete an organizer but they must also talk, listen, and think. Let's consider some of the most well-known varieties of graphic organizers. Four basic patterns, with endless variations, appear to have the greatest utility in social studies classrooms: conceptual, sequential, cyclical, and hierarchical.

Conceptual graphic organizers (also known as *concept maps*) are simple diagrams that spotlight a central topic or concept and show the relationship between the supporting details and the spotlighted topic or concept. A favorite concept map of social studies teachers is the *semantic web*. Semantic webs are graphic organizers that look much like a spider's web when complete—hence their name. Semantic webs are comprised of three basic elements: core concept, web strands, and strand supports.

The *core concept*, or concept of central importance to the learning experience, serves as the focus of the web. An example of a core concept associated with the study of the New England Colonies might be "Daily Life." Place the core concept in the center of a growing matrix (see Figure 7.5) and initiate an instructional conversation with a prompt like this: "As you think about the video, try to recall the different kinds of activities that made up daily life of the New England colonists."

The students then brainstorm details about the daily activities of early New England colonists. Their ideas are listed randomly on the chalkboard or a chart; the teacher probes and extends the students' suggestions as she or he finds it reasonable to do so. When the students have no more information to offer, the teacher asks them to organize the details into meaningful categories such as jobs, school, food, furniture, entertainment, religion, games, or any other label they suggest. The students' suggestions are placed at various points around the core to represent different categories of information. These points are referred to as *web strands*.

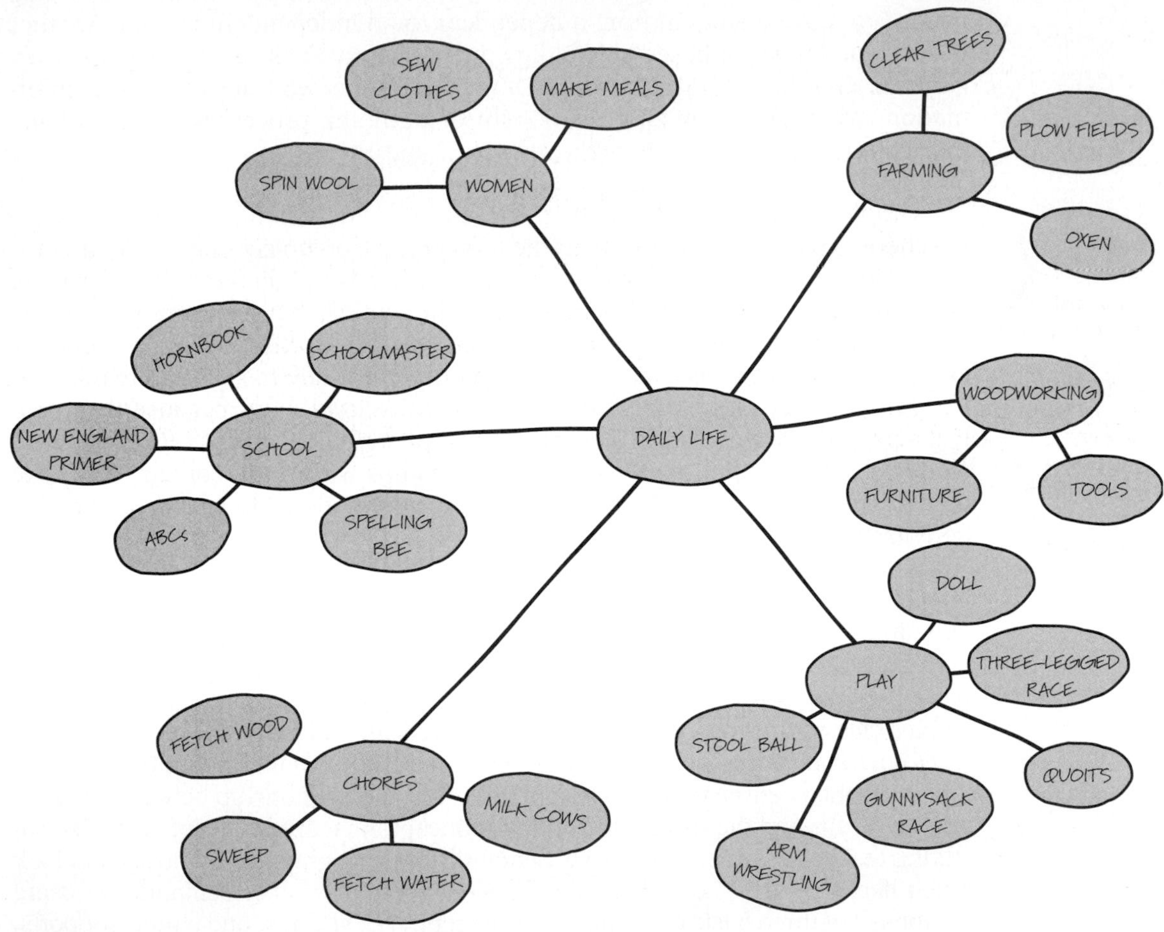

FIGURE 7.5 Web: Daily Life in Colonial America

The details used by the students to support each web strand are called *strand supports*. The strand supports surround each web strand, organizing the important information. The students continue to classify and categorize ideas until a graphic representation similar to Figure 7.5 emerges. The map construction phase involves active scaffolding encounters as students must talk together in order to create and interpret the classification and categorization systems.

Sequential graphic organizers arrange processes or events in steps or chronological order. They are usually formed as a straight line; timelines, as discussed in Chapter 3, are good examples.

Cyclical graphic organizers help students visualize a series of connected events that occur in sequence but produce a repeated result. See Figure 7.6 for an example. The months and seasons of a year, for example, demonstrate a cyclical process, as do the water cycle and the metamorphosis of a caterpillar. One cyclical process taught in most dynamic social studies classrooms is the practice of

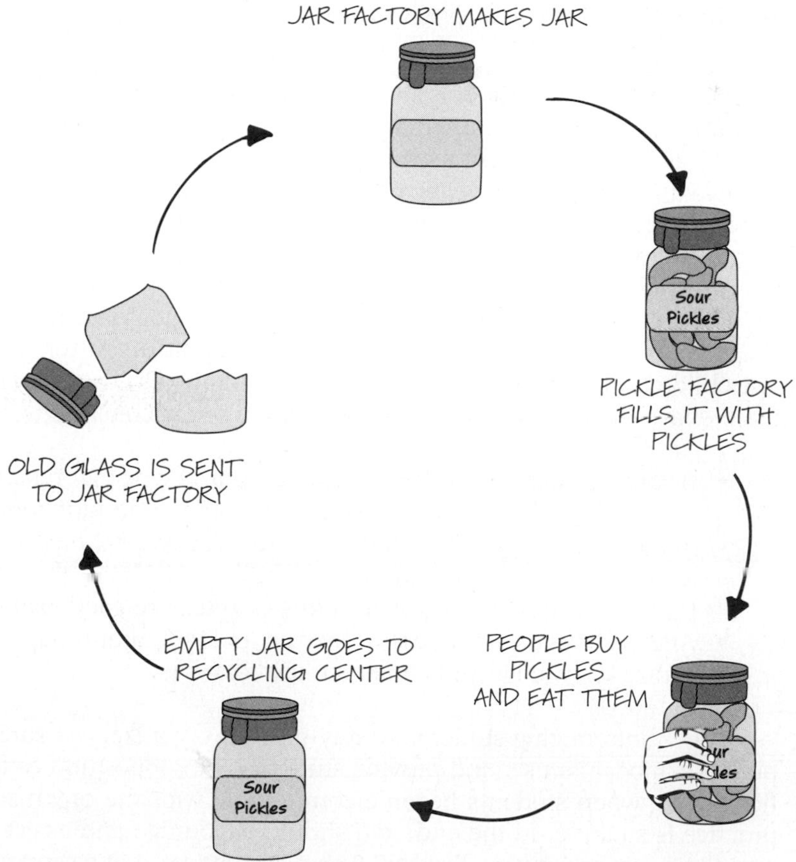

FIGURE 7.6 Cycle Graphic Organizer

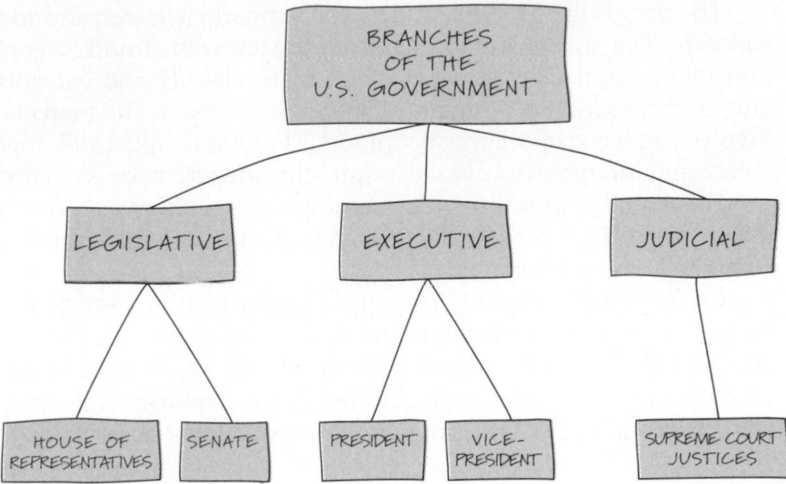

FIGURE 7.7 Hierarchical Graphic Organizer

recycling. Help your students understand this process by first writing the word *recycling* on the chalkboard. Then have the students complete a cyclic graphic organizer as they learn about recycling.

Hierarchical graphic organizers center on a main concept or process and the subcategories under it. For example, students in one fifth-grade classroom were learning about the three branches of the U.S. government—the legislative, executive, and judicial. Their hierarchical diagram of the branches is shown in Figure 7.7.

Graphic organizers are elemental to knowledge construction. Clearly, you should offer opportunities to develop and use graphic organizers whenever you assist children in developing relationships among ideas. In general, there are two major ways teachers use graphic organizers in social constructivist classrooms:

- *Before instruction:* When introducing a new topic, teachers may use a graphic organizer to make visually clear the important concepts and ideas that will be covered. Teachers can also use a graphic organizer to get a good idea of the background knowledge the students have about the topic. K-W-L charts, as described earlier in this chapter, are good examples.
- *After instruction:* Students construct individual or group organizers to organize knowledge and construct key concepts.

When introducing students to any graphic organizer, be sure to describe its purpose, model its use, and provide students with opportunities for guided practice. Then, when students become comfortable with the organizer, independent practice is suitable. In the end, you should encourage and assist students to design their own organizers. Figure 7.8 shows a variation of a sequential graphic organizer Jean Linton came up with when she and her fourth-grade classmates were given the assignment to write about a special talent or skill that makes them an "ex-

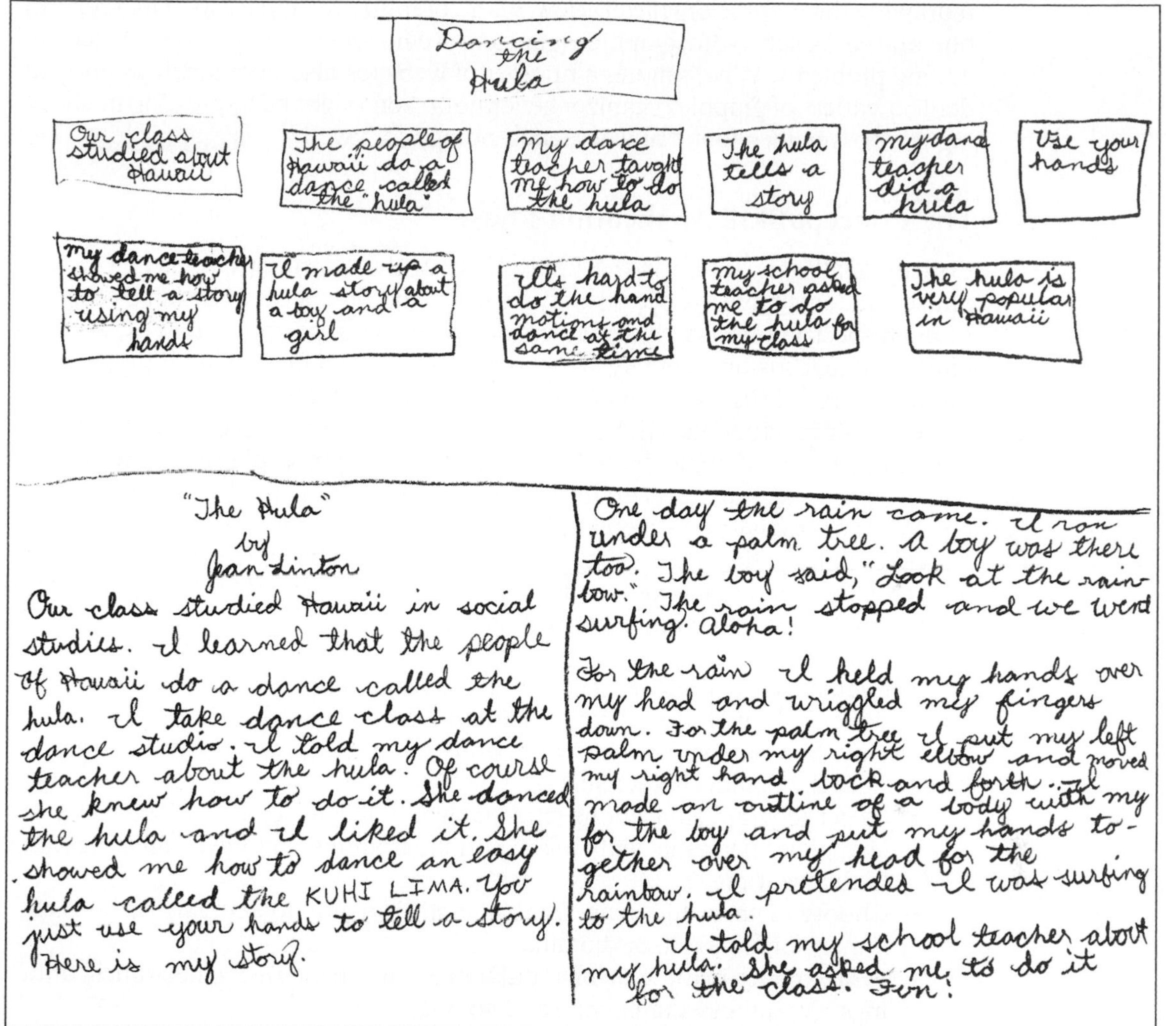

FIGURE 7.8 Using Cards to Organize a Sequential Graphic Organizer

pert." Instead of using a single sheet of paper to build her sequential graphic organizer, Jean recalled a hula she had created, jotted the major elements of the process on a number of index cards, and arranged the index cards in order. Using the cards as "organizational handles," Jean then expanded on each and wrote her story. Figure 7.8 illustrates the steps of Jean's writing project. You can easily see how the graphic organizer helped Jean write a clear, descriptive account of the steps involved in creating her new hula.

Traditionally, graphic organizers like the ones described in this section have been drawn as large wall charts or illustrated in a student's notebook. Revisions are often difficult; changes can be made only by crossing out, erasing, or even redrawing the graphic organizer. Now, with computer resources such as Kidspiration and Microsoft Word, graphic organizers are no longer hampered by space and editing problems. What's more, a number of websites also offer teachers and students a variety of graphic organizer generators. You might be interesting in checking the possibilities found at www.teach-nology.com/web_tools/graphic_org/.

The Concept/Skill Application Phase

Concept/skill application is the final phase of the Learning Cycle. During this phase, students have the opportunity to apply and practice a new skill or concept through special projects or independent activities. Because application experiences often tend to focus on creativity and choice, they may include such things as group murals, story writing, construction projects, drama, puppetry, and music. In all of these activities, students will be asked to use what they have learned while constructing deeper meaning. The key to success in this phase of the Learning Cycle is the same as was appropriate for success in all of social studies teaching—variety. Vary your activities to keep interest and motivation high. Because social studies topics differ in their complexity, some strategies will be more useful than others for enriching, reinforcing, or extending the targeted concepts or skills. Some examples of concept/skills application strategies follow.

- Dramatize the firing of the "shot heard around the world."
- Bake and eat Harry S Truman's favorite food, brownies.
- Give first-person accounts of famous historical events as if the students were the actual characters.
- Select geographic locations students would like to "cheer" about. Then design paper pennants with colors and illustrations that have some meaning to the location.
- Choose a favorite scene from a historical era to recreate in a three-dimensional model, or diorama.
- Write articles in the style of popular news magazines using headlines, drawings, eyewitness statements, and so on.
- Construct puppets and present a show depicting something interesting that was learned.

To illustrate, Bonnie Sullivan asked her students to design postage stamps to honor the various presidents they had been studying. One student submitted the design shown in Figure 7.9 to honor the president she had been researching, Abraham Lincoln. Another time, Ms. Sullivan and her students organized an "Inventor's Hall of Fame" to culminate their study of inventors and inventions. Figure 7.10 shows one of the plaques that was on display at the Hall of Fame.

By reading professional magazines and organizing an idea file, you will begin to accumulate ideas for functional application experiences. Remember, though, that these experiences must be an integral part of the total direct instruction lesson, not "extra busy work" or a cutesy "icing on the cake" activity tacked on at the

FIGURE 7.9 Postage Stamp Design as a Culminating Activity

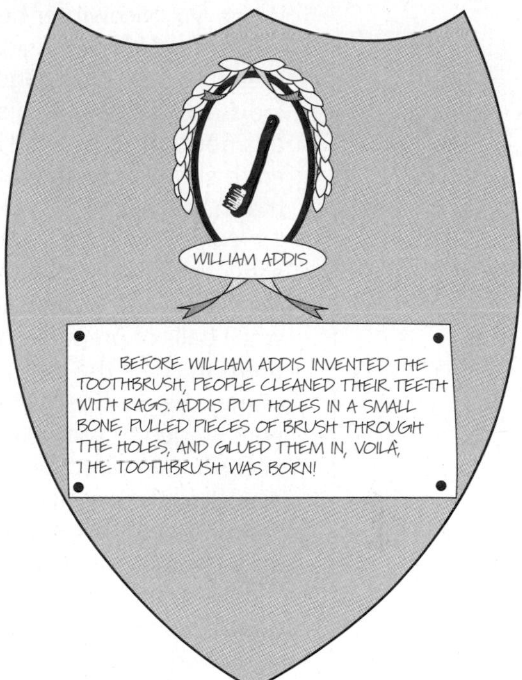

FIGURE 7.10 "Hall of Fame" Plaque as a Culminating Activity

end. This final activity uses the concepts constructed by the students to discover potential relevance or usefulness.

Written reports have wide acceptance as a culminating activity at all grade levels in social studies programs around the country. However, you cannot expect students to compose good written reports simply by announcing, "Write a report on Sitting Bull for next Tuesday," or handing out a list of topics related to the Civil War and assigning students to pick one and write a report about it. Assigning these kinds of tasks only frustrates many students and encourages them to copy every bit of information from a written resource or Internet site. Report writing itself isn't the problem, however. The real problem with social studies reports lies in our methods of assigning them. We need to show students how to investigate questions and communicate their findings, how to go beyond plagiarism to genuine communication. That's where scaffolding comes in. Good teachers know that all writing must be supported by models to imitate, so they offer their students quality children's literature as they develop into more mature writers. No matter what point they want to demonstrate about writing, there are good books to help make it clear. Good models produce good results.

Gary Nicewinter understood this point, so he included a good book as he organized a learning sequence that culminated in a report writing experience.

When Mr. Nicewinter began his unit on "bread," he showed his children an assortment of real bread, as well as pictures of bread and plastic models of bread: bagels, pita, baguette, paska, challah, tortillas, rye bread, cornbread, croissants, fry bread, injera, and chapatti, to name a few. Mr. Nicewinter did this not only to provide his students with a direct experience but also to generate enthusiasm and interest, to prime the pump for the flurry of activity that naturally follows.

NCSS STANDARDS

I. *Culture*
IX. *Global Connections*

Mr. Nicewinter invited the children to taste the real breads and, as a class activity, had the children mark the country of origin of each on a large map. Mr. Nicewinter added another hands-on experience by giving the children small balls of prepared bread dough (available in supermarkets) and asked them to place the dough balls on sheets of aluminum foil labeled with their names. Before they put their dough into the oven, the children were encouraged to shape the balls any way they wished. The bread was baked according to directions, and the children discussed their sensory experiences as well as the physical changes they observed from start to finish. Everyone responded to this activity with enthusiasm and interest; a wealth of questions and comments followed the activity.

To begin the actual writing phase, Mr. Nicewinter formed committees around common topics of interest which, after much discussion, were narrowed down to four: bread bakers and bakeries, bread from around the world, what bread is eaten with (condiments), and homemade bread. The children wrote on a piece of paper the two topics they would most like to pursue. Mr. Nicewinter then formed interest committees that would meet the next day.

The next day, Mr. Nicewinter assigned to each committee the task of writing its own information booklet on its chosen topic. He specified the form the writing would take, but the children would eventually determine the content. To familiarize the children with the form that their booklets were to take, Mr. Nicewinter brought to class a very simple model of informational writing: *Bread, Bread, Bread* by Ann Morris (HarperTrophy). The book contains impressive photographs and short descriptions of various breads being made around the world. As the class and Mr. Nicewinter surveyed the book together, they paid particular attention to the way the photographs and text were presented on each page. Mr. Nicewinter and the students agreed that their information pages would include a drawing and a sentence with some information about the drawing—just like the literature model.

The children worked on their bread books for about three days during social studies period. Most of the committees decided that their books should be about five pages long (one page for each child), but a few committees wrote more. To help the committees find information about bread, Mr. Nicewinter located suitable trade books and inserted bookmarks at the proper places. He could find no useful Internet sites for his young researchers. At the end of the first day, Mr. Nicewinter and the children sat in a circle with their papers and the books they had used to uncover information. They shared what they had done and how things had gone for them. Most had gotten as far as locating something they wanted to write about and starting their illustration. The second day was spent completing the illustrations and the associated text.

On the third day, Mr. Nicewinter talked to the children about book titles and discussed how the covers of several of the books the children had been reading contained illustrations that represented the main idea of the text. The children illustrated the covers of their own books, added titles, listed their names as authors, put the pages in order, and stapled them together. The committees shared their books with one another, and the final copies were ceremoniously added to the classroom library.

The "Bread From Around the World" committee compiled this book, along with appropriate illustrations, which they proudly titled *The Bread Book:*

Page 1:	Navajos eat fry bread almost every day. It is fried in shortening, not baked.
Page 2:	People from France eat baguettes. They are long loaves of bread with a thin golden crust.
Page 3:	Paska is a traditional round Easter bread decorated with fancy dough. It is very special bread from Ukraine.
Page 4:	Mexican people like to eat a flat bread called tortillas. Tortillas can be made from flour or corn. Some tortillas are spiced and flavored.
Page 5:	Chapatti is bread from India. It is flat and round like a pancake. It is made without yeast.

What follows are several key points to keep in mind while planning to stimulate children's cognitive development through the Learning Cycle:

- *Begin by attaching the children's background to the targeted concept.* Suppose *plantation* was selected as the central concept for today's lesson. You will want to help the students attach their previous knowledge of the topic to the content of this lesson: Southern *Plantation* Society. Specifically, plantations in the early 1800s consisted of three interdependent elements: the plantation owners, the slaves, and cotton (the crop that made the plantation possible).
- *Present numerous and varied examples of the concept.* Students must experience many examples that clearly illustrate the defining features of the concept through a variety of learning materials. In teaching about Southern Plantation Society, the children would use books, pictures, videos, Internet websites, and a variety of other resources to learn such defining features as *cotton, cotton gin, cotton fields, big house, gardens, more than 100 acres, slave quarters, slaves, slave labor, abolitionists,* and *plantation owners*.

- *Present nonexamples to demonstrate what the concept is not.* Students construct stronger concepts when they are able to contrast negative instances of the concept with positive examples. Nonexamples help students delineate a concept's limits by knowing what fits and doesn't fit into its boundaries. For example, southern farmers who did not own slaves primarily made a living growing corn and other vegetables because their land was not fertile enough to grow cotton. So, nonexamples of Southern Plantation Society would include small crop farmers whose defining features would include *corn, vegetables, log cabins, poverty,* and *less than 100 acres of land.*
- *Facilitate learning through the use of instructional conversations and graphic organizers.* Instructional conversations involve the practice of asking questions or offering information, clues, reminders, demonstrations, and encouragement at just the right time and in the proper amount. Graphic organizers serve as handy instructional tools that help students organize and illustrate the attributes of a process or concept.
- *Complete a task or project that helps students apply or extend the skills or concepts.* This must help achieve a logical purpose as a continuation of the learning experience, not as a frivolous add-on that was selected because it looked "cute" or "fun."

A Final Thought

Children learn through a combination of physical and mental activity; they "mess about" and naturally want to get into or try out everything. They may come to elementary school knowing a little bit about a lot of things, but one quality they all share is a thirst for experiences that will help them find out more. When these enthusiastic, energetic youngsters come to school, they expect to learn about all that interests them in much the same way, through activity and involvement. They are not much interested in memorizing information or in sedentary activities such as completing ditto sheets or workbook pages. They want to try things out.

Helping elementary school students construct meaningful concepts is one of the foremost challenges to social studies teachers. A major part of this challenge is to help learners attach their backgrounds to the learning experience and to organize new information into appropriate schemata. As Piaget and Vygotsky emphasize, meaningful learning takes place only when learners are able to bridge the gap between the unknown and the known. To that end, this chapter has described the Learning Cycle as a system of instruction through which the teachers are able to effectively direct their students through the process of concept construction.

Developing a Learning Cycle plan is a complex professional responsibility involving a great deal of knowledge, hard work, and skill. As a new teacher, you might question whether the results are worth the effort. In effect, you might wonder, "Why bother? After all, the textbook and teacher's manual were written by experts in the field who really know the social studies." To an extent, you are correct.

Manuals can be very helpful, especially for student or beginning teachers. As guides, though, they must be viewed as suggestions, not as prescriptions. You will probably want to start your career by using the teacher's guide closely, but as you gain experience, you will adapt it to the changing needs of the different groups of children you will teach each year. The constructivist approach described in this chapter allows you the flexibility to constantly change your teaching approach within a framework of sound planning.

REFERENCES

Ausubel, D. P. (1961). In defense of verbal learning. *Educational Theory, 2,* 16.

Bodrova, E., & Leong, D. J. (1996). *Tools of the mind: A Vygotskian approach to early childhood education.* Upper Saddle River, NJ: Merrill/Prentice-Hall.

Boyer, E. L. (1982). Seeing the connectedness of things. *Educational Leadership, 39,* 384.

Brooks, J. G., & Brooks, M. G. (1993). *In search of understanding: The case for constructivist classrooms.* Alexandria, VA: Association for Supervision and Curriculum Development.

Bruner, J. S., Olver, R. R., & Greenfield, P. M. (1966). *Studies in cognitive growth.* New York: John Wiley.

Dewey, J. (1933). *How we think.* Boston: D. C. Heath.

Gallimore, R. & Tharp, R. (1990). Teaching mind in society: Teaching, schooling, and literate discourse. In L.C. Moll (Ed.), *Vygotsky and education,* Cambridge: Cambridge University Press.

Hunter, M. (1982). *Mastery teaching.* El Segundo, CA: TIP Publications.

Langer, J. (1981). From theory to practice: A prereading plan. *Journal of Reading, 25,* 152–156.

National Council for the Social Studies. (1994). *Curriculum standards for social studies: Expectations of excellence.* Washington, DC: National Council for the Social Studies.

Ormrod, J. E. (2000). *Educational psychology: Developing learners.* Upper Saddle River, NJ: Merrill.

Penner, L. R. (1991). *Eating the plates.* New York: Macmillan.

Piaget, J. (1948/1973). *To understand is to invent.* New York: Grossman.

Piaget, J. (1952). *The origins of intelligence in children.* New York: International Universities Press.

Piaget, J. (1964). Three lectures. In R. E. Ripple & U. N. Rockcastle (Eds.), *Piaget rediscovered.* Ithaca, NY: Cornell University Press.

Piaget, J. (1971). *Understanding causality.* New York: Norton.

Ramirez, J., Yuen, S., & Ramey, D. (1991). *Executive summary: Longitudinal study of structured English immersion strategy, early-exit, late-exit transitional bilingual education programs for language minority children.* San Mateo, CA: Aguirre International.

Remy, R. C. (1990). The need for science/technology/society in the social studies. *Social Education, 54,* 204.

Ryan, K., Burkholder, S., & Phillips, D. H. (1983). *The workbook.* Upper Saddle River, NJ: Merrill/Prentice-Hall.

Wood, D., Bruner, J. S., & Ross, G. (1976). The role of tutoring in problem solving. *Journal of Child Psychology and Psychiatry, 17,* 89–100.

CHAPTER 8

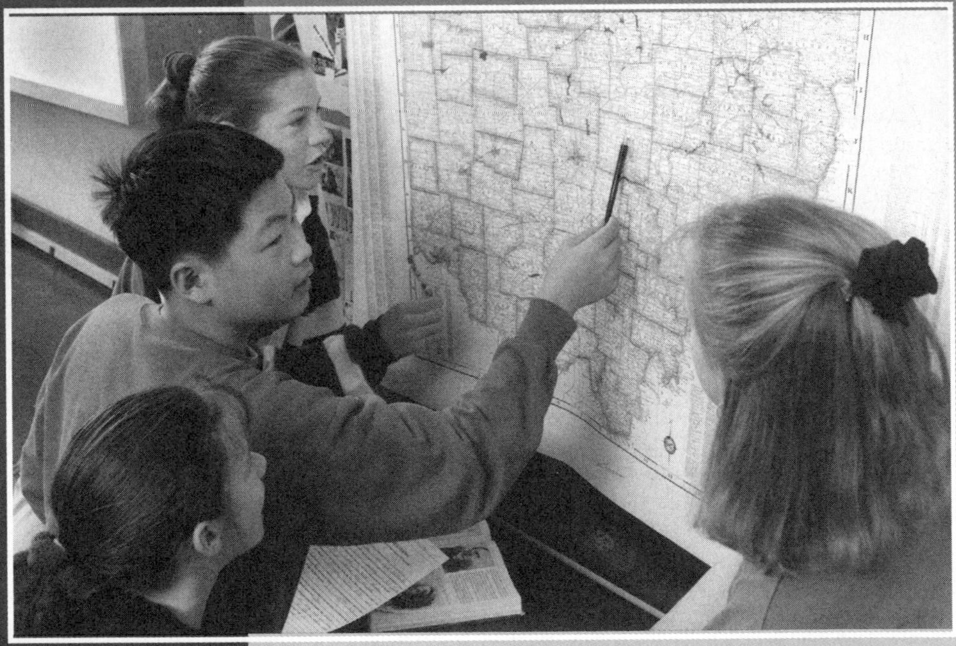

Collaborative and Cooperative Learning:
Student-Assisted Social Constructivism

What Does Collaborative/Cooperative Learning Look Like?

One day Jennifer Puksta's fourth-grade students returned from lunch upset about watching their peers unload huge amounts of food from their trays into the trash containers. The subsequent discussion inspired a searching "why" from the students. Antonio thought that the explanation was simple—most children just didn't like meat loaf, the meal served that day. His classmates offered other explanations; most students agreed, however, that the overall quality and nutritional value of the food needed to be improved. Ms. Puksta sensed that student interest in this situation was deep and that their concerns centered about two fundamental questions: "What is the least favorite food served for lunch?" and "What is the favorite food served for lunch?" Ms. Puksta's fourth-grade students offered guesses such as, "Spaghetti is the favorite of most kids. They hardly throw any away," "Tacos are number one! Everybody likes tacos." "No one likes meatloaf. It ends up in the trash every time," and "Chicken fingers are yucky. The stuff inside doesn't even look like chicken!"

Ms. Puksta now had two choices: She could extend the impassioned class discussion a few more minutes and then move on to spelling class, or she could seize the opportunity and use her students' deep interest in the situation as a springboard for applying their emerging problem-solving talents. Rather than limit the experience to a short, heated exchange about why so many lunches ended up in the trash, Ms. Puksta decided to help her students substantiate their claims about what the children "really liked" by turning their problem into a group-oriented project.

NCSS STANDARDS

IV. *Individual Development and Identity*
VII. *Production, Distribution, and Consumption*
VIII. *Science, Technology, and Society*

The students decided to find out exactly what their peers preferred for lunch, so they chose to conduct a quick survey. To begin, they considered several questions that might focus their data-finding efforts before settling on the two that they felt would yield the needed data: "Of the following, what is your favorite lunch served in the lunchroom?" and "Of the following, what is your least favorite lunch served in the lunchroom?" On the other hand, they decided that a question such as "What do you think of the food served at school?" was too general and could not yield the data they wanted.

Once the clear-cut polling questions were chosen, an authentic survey instrument needed to be constructed. Should the students poll their peers orally and keep a running record of the results, or should they distribute written questionnaires? Could voting be arranged on classroom computers? The students settled on a written questionnaire. Next, the students needed to select a sample population for their investigation. Should they question every child who eats lunch in the cafeteria? Should only a small portion of the student body be surveyed? They determined that it would not be necessary to obtain data from every child eating lunch in the cafeteria, so they considered a sampling strategy. Should they interview every third child in the lunch line? Someone suggested that they may want an equal boy/girl distribution; if so, should they poll every third boy, every third girl, and so on. Perhaps they should randomly select 50 fourth-graders by drawing names out of a hat? The students concluded that, whatever their choice, they must do all they could to ensure that their survey data is gathered from a representative sample of the larger population.

Once small groups of students gathered the data, Ms. Puksta helped them pull it together and interpret it. This was a major task, but Ms. Puksta helped the class construct tables, charts, graphs, and other visual displays of their data.

After they had recorded the information, the children examined and analyzed it. Naturally, they didn't need to use a complex chi-square analysis, but they did need to look at the numbers simply and accurately. Ms. Puksta's students examined the figures and concluded that most of the children preferred tacos; chicken fingers were almost as popular as tacos; and meatloaf and hot dogs were tied as least favorite.

"Look," exclaimed Alex, "we were right about the meatloaf. Nobody likes it!"

"Yeah," added Laura, "and most of the kids liked tacos—just like we thought!"

"You guys are right," interrupted Caesar, "but before you get too carried away, take a look at the chicken fingers. We said they were awful, but a lot of kids like them." Group discussion of the data was a valuable experience for Ms. Puksta's students; they were encouraged to examine and argue the results at length.

While considering how to share the results of their lunchroom survey with others, it was first necessary for Ms. Puksta's students to determine who would benefit most from seeing their results. Should they compose an oral response and deliver it to the cafeteria manager? Should they write an article for the school newspaper so that everyone in the school could see the results? Perhaps a letter to the school principal would be most appropriate? Ms. Puksta's students deliberated these possibilities and finally decided to break up into groups and complete each one.

A valuable and direct outgrowth of the group work was the development of a deep concern for a point brought up by Beatrice: "We've been talking about what food is our favorite, but shouldn't we think about how good the food is for us, too?" This was all that was needed to propel the students into an analysis of the nutritional value of foods served in the lunchroom: "How does eating the food usually served in the lunchroom affect our health and growth?"

Because the federal government was in the process of raising standards for food served in schools, the school principal and cafeteria manager were especially interested in the students' awareness of the issue as well as in the results of their collaborative research efforts. Working together with Ms. Puksta's class (who broke up into groups to sample various selections), they mulled over options that might become new lunchroom menu items. After considering Yadier's claim that his classmates were "programmed to like fried stuff," the school made a change to baked chicken bits with whole grain breading that the groups agreed "tasted real good and looked like real chicken." The groups also approved whole wheat crust pizza, but rejected breaded baked fish. They ditched hotdogs as being too unhealthy and replaced them with healthier tuna and turkey wraps. Little did the students foresee that their group-oriented investigation into lunchtime favorites would lead to a major overhaul of the lunchroom menu. So, in addition to facilitating children's collaboration and use of an assortment of research and communication skills, educational benefits of this classroom venture included empowering youngsters to change their behaviors in matters that affected their lives.

In Chapter 7, we examined the components of the Learning Cycle, a teaching strategy that clarifies the teacher's role while scaffolding, or facilitating, children's efforts during instructional tasks. In this chapter, we will look at the many ways peers can support each other's learning. In the preceding example, Ms. Puksta used collaborative learning as her primary instructional strategy becauses she believes that many important concepts can emerge from joint peer interaction. Ms. Puksta believes that her students learn more and learn better when they support each other's attempts to solve problems or construct new knowledge.

Although Ms. Puksta is convinced that group experiences support social studies learning, she also knows that casual peer interactions can often be so unfocused and haphazard that important attributes of selected concepts may not grow as planned or shared misconceptions may mislead the students. However, Ms. Puksta is aware that by structuring group experiences, peer interactions have greater potential for success. Therefore, peer interactions in Ms. Puksta's social studies classroom are clearly defined so that essential and meaningful understandings can best be accomplished. The strategies and tactics she employs require specific types of small groups of students joining together to explore a significant concept or question or to create a meaningful project. This chapter will describe how teachers can successfully facilitate peer interaction in social studies classrooms by planning, controlling, and monitoring productive collaborative and cooperative learning groups.

What Are Collaborative and Cooperative Groups?

How Global is the Curriculum *Go to MyEducationLab, select the topic Teaching Strategies, watch the video entitled "Cooperative Learning and Teaching," and complete the questions that accompany it.*

The overall purpose of group work in social studies is to support interactions with more knowledgeable peers. Working in groups gives students an opportunity to learn from and teach each other. Various names have been given to this type of teaching and learning; the two most currently in fashion are *cooperative learning* and *collaborative learning*. Although many people have trouble differentiating between the two, you should think of collaborative learning as a somewhat informal method of teaching and learning where students join together to further certain learning goals or create a major project. The process of collaborative learning is based on the idea that learning is a natural social act in which the participants talk, share, plan together, and work together. A team of students constructing a topographic map of their state, sets of students from schools in different parts of the country communicating over the Internet to compare prices of gasoline, or even two students helping each other with homework are each an example of collaborative learning. Collaborative learning takes place any time students work productively together, whether they are practicing a basic skill or solving a complex problem. Gallavan and Juliano (2007) point out that collaborative learning allows freedom and creativity; groups function in various ways and produce assorted outcomes.

Cooperative learning, on the other hand, is a type of collaborative learning where students work together in small teams in a more highly prescribed manner. Gallavan and Juliano (2007) explain that, although both collaboration and cooperation feature groups working together, "learners organized into cooperative learning groups tend to be more closely directed and managed by the teacher. . . . The teacher establishes specific guidelines and detailed operating procedures based on one set of expectations. . . . In general, all cooperative learning groups function the same way and generate similar outcomes or separate pieces of an overall cohesive product" (p. 13).

How Does Group Learning Work?

How Global is the Curriculum *Go to MyEducationLab, select the topic Teaching Strategies, watch the video entitled "Group Work: Elementary," and complete the questions that accompany it.*

Few of us feel comfortable at work or play without some kind of contact with other people. Surely, we need our moments of privacy but, as social creatures, we seek companionship. Group learning is a great way to satisfy this need for social engagement; it is not only a natural and enjoyable experience but it also provides a powerful context for learning. To use group work effectively, however, you need to teach your students what it takes to work as members of a group.

Getting Started

Working in groups is often a real challenge for students and teachers alike, especially if all they have experienced is traditional whole-class instruction. Because these students will often be unskilled at working with others in a small-group setting, it is essential to begin the process with activities designed to boost interpersonal skills and team awareness. The skills required for group work are quite different from those required to meet the demands of most whole-class seatwork assignments. Sometimes the transition process goes smoothly, but it can easily turn out to be chaotic. Students must learn how to get their ideas across to others, ask questions, listen to the ideas of others, encourage everyone to participate, monitor and manage group efforts, and communicate effectively. The key to increasing the productive times is to understand the major factors that contribute to successful group performance:

- Following directions
- Keeping focused on the task
- Completing responsibilities on time
- Asking for help when you need it
- Listening attentively to others
- Contributing ideas when you have them
- Considering the ideas and feelings of others
- Offering encouragement to others
- Making sure everyone has a chance to participate

Selma Wasserman (1989) recalls her frustrations as she attempted to transition sixth-grade children into responsible cooperative groups before many had the opportunity to acquire related skills: "The first weeks of so-called 'cooperative' group work was anything but. All manner of uncooperative behavior emerged. . . . They couldn't focus on the tasks; they didn't care about each other; they didn't understand 'what they were supposed to do.' In the absence of clear and specific teacher direction (i.e., 'Do this now and do it THIS way!'), they fell apart" (p. 204).

Wasserman described her biggest disappointment in watching her students become unruly: "My biggest disappointment was not that the children were unable to function in . . . sophisticated, mature and self-disciplined ways. . . . The killing blow was that the children wanted, asked, begged for a return to 'the way we did it in Grade 5' " (p. 203).

It was at that point that Wasserman realized that she needed to help the children learn the skills required to function as thoughtful, responsible, supportive learners. She needed to *teach* those skills. This was not an easy task either, for as she admits, "It may be a lot easier to teach children to read and spell than it is to teach them to behave cooperatively . . . with each other" (p. 204).

If your goal is to engage students in group work, then you must help them gain an understanding of themselves as group members and of what it takes to function effectively as group members. This is good news—group work skills can be taught and learned just like any other skill. In addition, like any other skill, you will need to be patient while offering meaningful opportunities to help children learn. It may be October or November before you are able to recognize any major shift in the way your students approach group work, but you must follow the children's lead, never moving so fast that students are overwhelmed by your efforts.

It may be most productive to begin with game-oriented tasks when you target a special group skill to work on. A game I have found to be particularly useful is "Puzzle Squares," which is described here. Fortunately, many books and professional magazines contain suggestions for similar cooperative games.

Puzzle Squares

Goal

Each child in a group must use the puzzle pieces to complete a 5-inch square consisting of only three pieces.

Materials

1. Cut out five heavy tagboard squares, each about 5 inches square.
2. Cut each square into three segments using the following patterns (see Figure 8.1).
3. Scramble the 15 pieces and put them into a large manila envelope.
4. Repeat the procedure for each set of five children in your classroom.

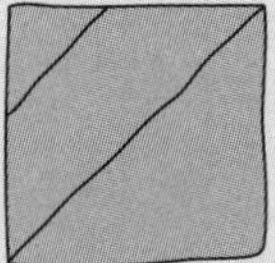
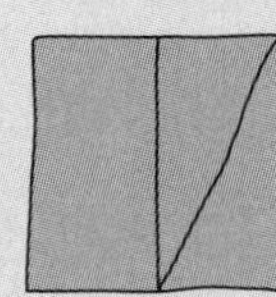
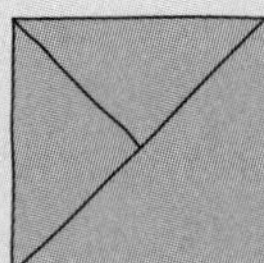
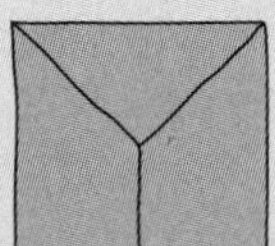
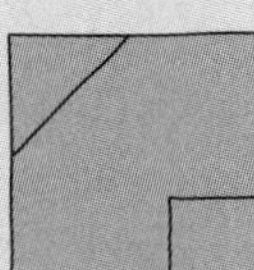

FIGURE 8.1 Puzzle Squares

Procedure

1. Place children into groups of five and have them select a group leader.
2. Give each group leader one of the envelopes containing 15 puzzle pieces.
3. On signal, the group leader opens the envelope and randomly passes three puzzle pieces to each group member.
4. Direct the students to examine their puzzle pieces and try to make a square from them. Signal the students to begin. Most groups will complete this task within 20 minutes; therefore, allow the proper amount of working time. If the students discover their segments will not form a perfect square, they may exchange pieces with other members of their group, but only with these rules:
   (a) No talking. The game must be played in complete silence.
   (b) No eye signals, hand signals, or gestures. Communication of any kind is discouraged.
   (c) No taking another puzzle piece from another player, unless he or she first offers it to you.

When the time is up and several puzzles have been completed, discuss questions such as, "How did you feel when you first started working with the group? Did you find it difficult to work together with others? What were some of the problems that your group experienced? How could they be resolved? What feelings did you have toward the other members of your group? What made you feel that way?"

As you provide additional activities to help students acquire important group work insights, you will need to keep a number of important suggestions in mind:

1. *Define the skill clearly and specifically.* Be sure the students understand their responsibilities. For example, "When I say, 'Talk in quiet voices,' I mean that you will need to use your foot voices.'" You can then show your students a 12-inch ruler to demonstrate how far a "foot voice" should carry.
2. *Ask students to characterize the skill.* A version of the "T-chart" can effectively demonstrate what is meant by skill characterization (see Figure 8.2). To construct a T-chart, draw a horizontal bar and write the skill above it in question form. Draw a vertical line down from the middle of the bar. On one side, list student responses to the question, "What would this skill look like?" On the other side, list their responses to the question, "What would this skill sound like?" You then model the skill until all students have a clear idea of what its correct performance looks and sounds like.

Looks Like	Sounds Like
• wait for a signal to go • gather all materials • stand up and push chair in smoothly • walk slowly and softly to your group area • wait for all members to arrive before you start your work	• silence • quiet • peacefulness • stillness • noiseless movements • hushed voices

FIGURE 8.2 T-Chart

3. *Practice and reinforce the skill.* You cannot teach students to work cooperatively after only a single lesson or experience. Growth occurs over time with meaningful practice and effective reinforcement.

One teacher's effort to help her students acquire the skill of "encouraging others to contribute" is exemplified by Barbara Wertz, who formed eight three-member groups, each of which was given this problem to address: "What makes a person great?" Ms. Wertz handed out five plastic counters to each student. The students were directed to place a counter in a container at the center of their table each time they spoke. When a student had "spent" all her or his counters, she or he could speak no longer.

After everyone's counters were "spent," each group member received another set of five and started again. A few students became quite flustered when their five counters were spent and they had something important to say! But, they playfully placed their hands over their mouths and followed the rules of the activity until they received a new set.

This type of game usually works very well with elementary school students and needs to be used only once or twice to get the message across (although first-graders can become strongly attached to counters and are sometimes reluctant to give them up). Can you imagine this method being used for a student or faculty meeting on your campus? Five counters are handed to each student or professor when they come in. When they speak . . . .

If we are to prepare students for group work in social studies classrooms, we must first help them acquire the skills and strategies required to function effectively as group members. Rather than lecturing students about those behaviors, we must offer opportunities to practice the skills that will encourage children to understand their various roles. Group work, then, can truly become a prime vehicle of social constructivism. By *social,* I mean that participants engage in peer interactions and coordinated efforts to accomplish a goal. By *constructivist,* I mean that the peer interactions and coordinated efforts help children build carefully detailed understandings and skills.

Collaborative and Cooperative Learning Groups

Teachers frequently organize small groups, or teams, of children with similar needs or interests in their social studies so they can support one another socially and academically. This form of instruction has been referred to by assorted, often confusing, labels: *cooperative learning, collaborative learning, team-based learning, learning communities, peer tutoring, peer learning, literature circles, study groups,* and *work groups*. But, for our purposes, let's examine the two major types of group work in social studies classrooms—informal groups and formal groups. First, collaborative learning will be considered the informal approach to using groups in social studies classrooms. Next, since student roles and responsibilities are much more highly prescribed and controlled in cooperative groups, they will be regarded as the formal system of grouping.

Collaborative Learning

Collaborative learning can be carried out within a wide-ranging assortment of alternative structures; some are short in duration, and others can last for weeks. Three of the most widely used and simplest to manage short-term groups are buzz groups, brainstorming groups, and peer tutoring groups. The most widely used long-term group arrangement seems to be the project-oriented investigative group.

Buzz Groups

Buzz groups consist of two or three students who meet for just a few minutes to quickly pool their knowledge or ideas related to a topic or problem under study. To start, a teacher gives specific directions such as, "Turn to a person sitting next to you and take two minutes to talk about this question: 'Is it ever okay to break the law?'" The teacher makes sure everyone understands the question or challenge, and then signals the groups to start "buzzing." It is helpful to write the question on the chalkboard or chart paper, for groups will frequently refer to it to stay on track. One child should serve as a recorder who is responsible for keeping accurate notes of the key items discussed as well as recording the final proposal of the group. Because the recorders are most closely linked with the written record, they should stand up one by one and report the group's information to the whole class.

Brainstorming Groups

Brainstorming is a highly useful collaborative group strategy designed to generate large numbers of ideas as potential solutions to a problem. The process is particularly helpful when teachers want to draw out original and novel ideas. Brainstorming works best when groups are small and manageable (4 to 6 students are suggested) and when ample time is allocated (10 to 15 minutes is recommended).

Brainstorming challenges must be easily understood by the children or they will quickly lose interest in dealing with them. The challenges should be worded clearly and concisely: "In what ways might our modern society become 'more civilized?"' The students should take a few moments to think silently about the challenge and, once the brainstorming starts, propose their ideas freely and openly while a recorder writes them down on the chalkboard or chart. Teachers should keep the session focused on the problem; however, the purpose is not to come up with an immediate solution but to generate a lot of promising ideas. Teachers must provide an adequate orientation of the brainstorming process to ensure that the students will work productively toward generating a helpful plan of action:

1. *Produce a large number of ideas.* The goal of brainstorming is to generate quantity, for a large number of ideas seem more likely to produce a first-class idea. One teacher referred to this idea generation phase of brainstorming as "Popcorn Thinking" and encouraged her students to "just keep the ideas popping." Don't worry about quality yet; that will be considered at a later time.
2. *Discourage criticism.* Accept every idea that is offered, no matter how outlandish or impractical it may appear to be at first. To create an atmosphere essential for original thinking, everyone must be assured that their ideas are valued and respected. So, regardless of how unworkable or impractical a suggestion might originally appear, it should be recorded. Children often find that seemingly "silly" ideas they were originally tempted to reject turn into the most fascinating, imaginative solutions. All types of verbal and nonverbal criticism (eye rolling, face making, groaning, and cynical smiles) are disallowed.
3. *Encourage "hitchhiking."* The children should feel comfortable latching onto and improving other students' ideas, or to use other ideas as a base from which to dream up their own. Combining an idea with someone else's often produces possibilities that are more interesting and useful than either by itself.
4. *Challenge students to stretch themselves.* Many students will exert only nominal effort before announcing, "I just can't think of anything else." However, children should display the courage to stay in the battle beyond this point of "idea exhaustion." Sometimes the most original ideas pop out after students think they don't have anything left, so I like to challenge them to add five new ideas after they come up with their final list.

In addition to buzz groups and brainstorming groups, there are many other variations of relatively short-lived grouping patterns that use student interaction as the major strategy for stimulating thinking about important social studies topics. The number and variety of options are too numerous to include in this text, but by searching through instructional resources you will easily find many different possibilities that match the targeted goals and objectives of your lesson as well as the unique characteristics of your children.

NCSS STANDARDS

II. *Time, Continuity, and Change*
VIII. *Science, Technology, and Society*

Peer Tutoring

When a competent peer, with help and guidance from a teacher, helps a novice acquire a skill or build a concept, we are drawing on a special collaborative process referred to as *peer tutoring*. In peer tutoring, the students work together as a team as the "expert" gives just the right amount of assistance to master the information or skill without doing the work for the novice. Because both students are at the same grade level, advice is often more openly accepted from the novice through a type of peer rapport that the teacher finds difficult to establish.

Althea Gridley's class has been studying about transcontinental rail travel during the 1800s for the past week. The students were organized into study groups to explore areas of interest such as the risks of rail travel or how luxurious the rail travel experience could be. The children enjoyed searching for solutions to questions or problems and arrived at a deep understanding of the content. Each study group considered different plans to demonstrate knowledge of their selected topic. Some eventually decided to write and illustrate a storybook, others wrote and performed a short skit, and still others made a timeline of the milestones in transcontinental rail travel.

One student, Doreen, decided to use PowerPoint, Microsoft's popular presentation software, to organize her group's presentation on the influence of railroads on early American Indian culture. She planned to design an interactive story using the hyperlink features of PowerPoint. First, Doreen planned her story on paper, creating a storyboard depicting words and scenes from her story, and then she selected a design template and typed the story's text on each slide, leaving room for the action buttons. Ms. Gridley noticed that Doreen was having trouble adding the hyperlinks, so she asked Shirley, the "Class Computer Expert," to help. Shirley's job was not to carry out the task for Doreen, but rather to explain the process and offer encouragement until Doreen was able to do it herself.

"Here is what I do," explained Shirley. "First, I bring up the slide that I want to add the buttons to. Then I select Action Buttons from the Slide Show menu. Now, see the blue bar above the action buttons? You do the next job. . . . Ready? Now, click the blue bar and drag the box. . . ." Shirley guided Doreen through the next few steps of the process and then stood by for support as Doreen confidently went through the process by herself and added hyperlinks to the next two slides. Through her tutoring help and individualized support, Shirley helped Doreen acquire a skill through carefully designed instruction called peer tutoring, or peer scaffolding. In other words, Shirley provided the necessary support for Doreen until she was able to master the task by herself.

The peer tutoring process must be carefully planned to make the process work in elementary school social studies classrooms. The teacher must carefully instruct

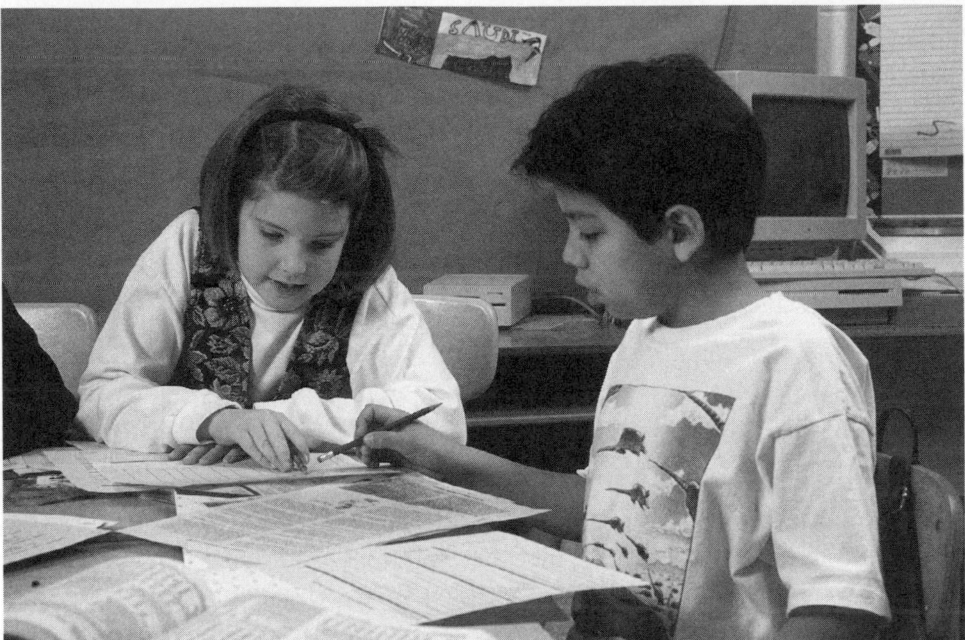

Many benefits for both partners result from peer tutoring programs; oftentimes, the tutor receives the most gains!

tutors in the proper techniques to assist learning. If this isn't done, you will often find the tutor giving an answer or performing the skill rather than modeling helpful strategies. Explain and demonstrate what to do if the novice makes mistakes, and how to encourage the novice to practice and learn. Show the tutors how to be encouraging as their partners make progress toward achieving their goal. And make sure every child has an opportunity to be a peer tutor. In that regard, teachers should think of themselves as talent scouts, searching for the special abilities hidden within each child. Speaking? Planning? Writing? Singing? Human relations? Dancing? Reading? Organizing? Constructing? Discover the many gifts concealed within the children in your classroom and give each a chance to shine!

How Global is the Curriculum *Go to MyEducationLab, select the topic Teaching Strategies, and read the lesson plans entitled "Model Lesson: Using Cooperative Learning Groups in Bill Graham's Class" and "A Cooperative Learning Lesson."*

Project-Oriented Investigative Groups

The life of buzz groups, brainstorming groups, and peer tutoring pairings is relatively short and their work is usually appended to a teacher's whole-class lesson. Long-term groups differ because the group works together for a longer period of time and addresses its goals through sustained, supportive investigations. The teacher's role shifts from that of delivering whole-class lessons to that of facilitator—intervening only to make certain that student efforts stay focused and that the students maintain a shared responsibility in carrying out their tasks.

Project-oriented investigative groups begin their work after they confront a challenging question or problem. For example, while initiating a study of the different types of shelters representative of cultures around the world, George White first read an interesting picture book to his class—Ann Grifalconi's *The Village of Round and Square Houses* (Little, Brown).

Grifalconi's book tells the fascinating tale of Tos, an actual village built on the side of an inactive volcano in Central Africa. Mr. White selected this book for its power to stimulate the children's interest in dwellings representative of cultures around the world. The legend explains why the women of Tos in reality dwell in round thatch-roofed huts while the men live separately in square ones. After a short discussion of the story, Mr. White informed his students that they were about to break from the normal classroom routine and try something different: "We're going to try something different in social studies class today—working together as investigative teams to uncover more interesting information about dwellings around the world. I know we'll learn a great deal about the topic as we work with each other." He directed the students' attention to pictures of homes pinned to the bulletin board: Mongolian yurts, Inuit igloos, water villages of Malaysia, Navajo hogans, and others. They spent several minutes inspecting the pictures and reading the short description beneath each.

NCSS STANDARDS

I. *Culture*
III. *People, Places, and Environments*
IX. *Global Connections*

"Write your name on a piece of paper," Mr. White directed, "then list three types of homes you're most interested in learning about. I'll check the requests and let you know tomorrow what dwelling you'll be working on." As he studied the requests, Mr. White was mindful of the possible problems that might crop up if he brought together incompatible students. Therefore, his decision was guided not only by the number of students assigned to each group, but the group's composition as well. Because these investigative groups will probably write reports and construct models to exhibit what they have uncovered, Mr. White made certain each had a good investigator as well as a well-organized student to help with the writing and a skilled builder to help with model construction. The goal of any group investigation provides Mr. White with the criteria for selecting team members.

The groups were formed the next day and the team members gathered together for the first time. Mr. White asked the team members to interview each other: "Find out why your teammates are interested in the home they chose and what they already know about those homes." As soon as the interviewing buzz subsided, Mr. White announced, "Our next job is to think about the kinds of questions you should ask about your dwellings and where you might be able to find the information you'll need." Mr. White helped the students locate reference books, storybooks, videos, Internet sites, and other useful information sources to help with their research. For the next four days, the students worked together to establish a plan of action and carry out their investigative tasks so that everyone had a fair chance to contribute. They weren't too far into their research before the first true test of collaboration surfaced.

While considering a way to build their Navajo village, the "hogan" group members disagreed about what shape their model Navajo hogans should take. Addie was convinced that the hogan she had started with her partner was the best, but Nate felt that something was just not right. Addie's hogan was a replica of a crude mud structure that the Navajo built up around three main wooden poles. A little piece of cloth covered the opening in the model, much as a woolen blanket covered the entry of the traditional Navajo structure. "Wait a minute," groused Nate. "I read that a hogan was built a lot like a log house, but the shape was different. You don't have any logs on your hogan. The Navajo stacked logs on top of one another to make a building with eight sides. It actually looks like a big round log house. How can your hogan be so different?" Addie tried to support her position by showing Nate a picture she was using as a guide; Nate, a different book in hand, stood by, eager and ready to prove his point.

After comparing their sources, Addie and Nate were shocked to discover some similarities between the Navajo hogans and the round and square houses from Tos. They learned that Addie's model was actually a replica of the earliest Navajo hogans—the "male" pole and mud structures. Nate's eight-sided log hogan is known as the "female" hogan, modern versions of which are seen today on Navajo reservations.

"Even though they lived on two different continents, the Navajo had male and female houses just like the villagers of Tos!" Addie and Nate agreed. After a quick but noteworthy meeting, Addie and Nate decided that their model village should have both types of dwellings, one set of hogans designated "male" and the other "female."

Like Nate and Addie, children should be helped to deal with their own disagreements while working together in groups, for cognitive discord often leads to intellectual growth. However, you should always be near just in case appropriate guidance becomes necessary.

After the groups complete their projects, they should present them to an authentic audience; they can display the models and written reports for their classmates and other classrooms to inspect, or make the displays available for their parents on Parent Night at school. Whatever the choice, the important outcome is that students share a physical product with someone by pulling together an informative and interesting presentation.

You will need to keep the following principles in mind as you plan and implement project-oriented investigative groups.

- *Groups must be carefully established and managed.* The largest collaborative groups should be four members. Children should not choose their own teams, since friendship groups often result in factions that can exclude some individuals. Otherwise, groups should be selected using three criteria: *a student's interest* in the topic, *the goal of the activity*—so that special student strengths and talents can be distributed among groups, and *diversity*—groups should be balanced in terms of race, ethnicity, and gender. Most of the problems that crop up in collaborative learning groups can be directly linked to poorly designed group makeup.

- *Assign nonoverlapping roles.* The teacher motivates students' curiosity and interest with a stimulating question or a problem. The children then begin their group task by clarifying its goal, agreeing on the resources they will need, and settling on a plan of action. Once they make these decisions, the students will need to identify their roles and responsibilities. Who will be responsible for drawing together the background information? Who will write the report? Who will check the writer's work? Who will make the model? Who will present the final product? Who will be responsible for monitoring the group's behavior?
- *Complete the task.* When the students are sure of their roles and have established a plan of attack, they are free to embark on the longest phase of the shared group activity—carrying out its responsibilities through constructive social interactions.
- *Share the results.* Groups or individuals take the information gathered and organize it into some type of presentation. PowerPoint presentations, written reports, and poster displays are but three examples of presentations that could be considered. The groups should present information in clear and interesting ways to an authentic audience and allow time for any questions that may arise.

A large number of different grouping configurations are associated with *collaborative learning*, for the term generally covers an assortment of strategies that call for shared efforts among students to achieve a common goal. The grouping examples shared so far are among the most popular of all techniques in elementary school social studies classrooms. But, like Bill Pancoast, you might also someday create a collaborative learning technique you can call all your own. Mr. Pancoast's unique collaborative strategy designed to stimulate writing in social studies is outlined for you.

1. Bring in a number of objects related to a topic or theme of instruction. For example, after reading about the traditions of Hanukkah during a thematic unit on Winter Holidays, Mr. Pancoast brought in six objects: a menorah, a dreidel, latkes, an oil lamp, a replica Torah scroll, and a picture of a Jewish temple. One item was displayed at each of six tables spread around the room. Taped to the wall near each table were two large sheets of chart paper.
2. Divide the class into groups of four students each. Mr. Pancoast explained that the items were to be used for an activity that would take place in

stages, each lasting for about five minutes. One group would start out at each of the tables, brainstorming words associated with the object on the table and writing them down on one of the sheets of chart paper.

3. Rotate each group to the next table. Each group will now have an object different than the one it had brainstormed. The menorah group, for example, moves to the oil lamp table, the oil lamp table moves to the Torah table, and so on. The groups must now write a short story about their object on the second sheet of chart paper, using the brainstormed words of the previous group.
4. Rotate again to the next table. This time, each group revises the story written by the previous group—adding to, deleting, or revising ideas.
5. Rotate once again. Now each group edits the work of the previous groups, checking for such mechanics as spelling, punctuation, and grammar.
6. On this fourth rotation, students examine the edited piece and compose a final copy on a clean sheet of chart paper (leaving room for an illustration).
7. Rotate still one more time, assigning each group the responsibility to create an illustration for the final written piece.
8. On the last rotation, each group should be back at its original table, examining the story written for its object and sharing their reactions. The separate pages are then read aloud to the whole class, and then bound together as a chapter in a class-generated big book about winter holidays.

A field especially open and ready to experience innovative group collaboration strategies involves utilizing the new technologies. Sending and receiving e-mail messages can connect children to classrooms all over the world. Students can collaborate to publish a classroom website that presents student projects or outcomes of their social studies investigations. The ability for students to leave comments in an interactive format is an important part of many blogs. Commercial software makes it possible for classrooms around the country to collaborate on group projects. This exciting new field is open for innovation. In what ways do you see technology being used with collaborative learning?

How Global is the Curriculum
Go to MyEducationLab, select the topic Teaching Strategies, watch the video entitled "Cooperative Learning," and complete the questions that accompany it.

Cooperative Learning

Cooperative learning is the instructional use of small teams, consisting of students of various ability levels, working together to accomplish an instructional goal. Each coworker is responsible not only for her or his own learning but also for helping teammates. The cooperative learning concept is rather straightforward. Class members are organized heterogeneously into small teams whose members work together until all group members successfully understand a concept, solve a problem, or complete a task. It is only under certain conditions, however, that a group is considered a cooperative group. According to Johnson, Johnson, and Holubec (1993), those conditions are:

1. Positive interdependence
2. Face-to-face interaction
3. Individual and group accountability
4. Interpersonal and small-group skills
5. Group processing

Positive Interdependence

The first requirement for a cooperative group is that students believe they are connected with teammates in such a way that the group cannot succeed unless everybody succeeds—they "sink or swim together." Cooperative learning specialists refer to this kind of teamwork as *positive interdependence*. Think of positive interdependence as the type of teamwork we see on a basketball court when one player passes the ball to a teammate who, in turn, slams it through the basket with a crashing dunk. The actions of both players were independent of each other (they both did completely different things) but the points could not have been scored without the essential contributions of both. Without positive interdependence, there would have been no basket; likewise, without positive inderdependence, there is no cooperative learning. Teachers structure positive interdependence by establishing *mutual goals* (learn and make sure all other group members learn), *joint rewards* (if all group members achieve above the criteria, each will receive bonus points), *shared resources* (one paper for each group or each member receives part of the required information), and *assigned roles* (summarizer, encourager of participation, elaborator).

Face-to-Face Interaction

Positive interdependence is heightened through face-to-face communication where group members support and assist each other's efforts while striving to achieve the group's goals. Face-to-face interactions are all those interpersonal classroom exchanges that provide help and encouragement; the idea here is that teams perform best when motivation and teamwork are high. So, the general feeling of team spirit is encouraged—help each other out, encourage each other's efforts, and applaud the successes of everyone in the group. *Teams, teamwork,* and *team spirit* are not meaningless terms; they represent something very noteworthy in the cooperative learning process. Teachers configure cooperative groups so that students sit knee-to-knee and talk face-to-face through each aspect of the group's assignment.

Individual and Group Accountability

Two levels of accountability, or responsibility, must be accepted by all members of a cooperative group. First, since everyone contributes to the group's success, each member must contribute her or his fair share of work. So, all team members are held accountable for their effort, and their effectiveness is monitored throughout the cooperative learning process. Second, the group is accountable for achieving its goals. The main reason that teachers use cooperative learning is so students will achieve greater success than they experienced while working on their own. Consequently, each student and each team is accountable through such formal and informal assessment strategies as testing, calling on one student randomly to present the group's work to the teacher, observing each group and recording each member's contributions, assigning one student in each group the role of checker who asks other group members to explain the reasoning and rationale underlying group answers or solutions, and having students teach what they learned to someone else.

How Global is the Curriculum *Go to MyEducationLab, select the topic Teaching Strategies, and read the Case Study entitled "Coping With Problems Effectively—Elementary School," and complete the question that accompanies it.*

Interpersonal and Small-Group Skills

The fourth essential element of cooperative groups has to do with the interpersonal and small-group social skills that help the teams function effectively. Those skills include (1) getting to know each other and building trust, (2) communicating accurately and clearly, (3) accepting and supporting each other, and (4) resolving conflict constructively. Simply organizing students into groups and telling them to cooperate with each other would be ideal if that's all it took, but elementary school children must be taught the interpersonal and small-group skills for cooperative groups to be productive. Several cooperative group games and other activities were shared with you earlier in this chapter, and numerous professional resources contain strategies and materials for teaching these social skills. Be sure to base your cooperative learning program on a foundation of interpersonal and social skills, for these are the fundamental keys to group efficiency and effectiveness.

Group Processing

The final essential element of cooperative learning is group processing, a course of action through which groups reflect on how well they are working toward achieving their goals and consider whether they are maintaining effective working relationships. Group processing involves describing the actions considered helpful and unhelpful and deciding what behaviors to continue or change. The purpose of group processing is to clarify and improve the effectiveness of each member's efforts in helping to achieve the group's goals.

Although most pre- and in-service teachers are aware that cooperative learning is quite different from collaborative learning, the procedures required to implement the model are much less known. For that reason, even expert teachers often cringe at the suggestion of managing cooperative group efforts. However, all this uneasiness is unfounded. Successful cooperative groups flourish when teachers address the major decisions that account for a successful implementation: *determining group membership, selecting a cooperative learning approach,* and *deciding on a reward system.*

Determining Group Membership

As with moving toward any form of group work, it is often best to wait until at least October or November before plunging students into cooperative groups, especially if they have never before experienced group work. This extra time gives teachers an opportunity to know their students and to help forge a community classroom spirit. After about 6 to 8 weeks of whole-group social studies lessons interspersed with activities specifically designed to introduce group responsibilities, students will then readily entertain the idea of cooperative group work. To be successful, the method of assigning team members must be deliberately planned. There is no magic recipe to help all teachers arrive at the ideal number of students for a cooperative learning group; experts differ on the ideal makeup of cooperative groups, so you will need to experiment to see what works best for you. Often, the larger the group, the more skilled the members of the group must be to function well. Initial cooperative learning groups for primary-grade children or older children with little prior group-work experience should consist of pairs, or *dyads*, because young children find it difficult to involve more than one other person while making a decision. By grade 3 or 4, as the children become more skilled at working together, you can think about assigning them heterogeneously to three-member teams. Students through middle school can function as quartets, but they need much success working in dyads and trios before they can work in groups of four. Freiberg and Driscoll (1992) have examined the common group sizes found in elementary school social studies classrooms and detail some of the benefits of each:

> *Two-Person Group.* This size promotes a relationship and generally ensures participation. This is a good way to begin with inexperienced "groupies" (students who have not been grouped before). In a pair, students gain experience and skill before working in a complex group arrangement.
>
> *Three-Person Group.* This arrangement allows for a changing two-person majority. Participation is very likely because no one wants to be the odd person out. Roles in this size group can be those of speaker, listener, and observer, and learners can experience all three roles in a brief period of time. This size group is appropriate for creating descriptions, organizing data, drawing conclusions, and summarizing ideas.
>
> *Four-Person Group.* In a four-person group, there will likely be different perspectives. This size is small enough that each member will have a chance to express himself and can be comfortable doing so. Often this size group emerges as two pairs when opinions are expressed. A group of four people requires basic communication and cooperation skills, but offers ideal practice for learning group process. (p. 277)

In addition to group size, the actual "coming together" of cooperative learning groups begins when students are carefully assigned to teams. For most tasks, you should use heterogeneous grouping, placing "high," "middle," and "low" achievers

Sometimes cooperative groups can be as small as two members; oftentimes dyads are the most effective beginning cooperative groups.

in the same learning group. This can be done easily by assigning numbers to your students corresponding to the number who will be assigned to each group. Figure 8.3 illustrates one teacher's heterogeneous breakdown of students into four-member teams. Darcee is the top-ranked student in this classroom, and Donald is the lowest, so they are both members of Team 1. Warren and Robin are next at both extremes, so they are together in Team 2. In like manner, the rest of the class is divided into heterogeneous teams based on achievement.

Notice that even though the teacher carefully divided the teams on the basis of academic ability, minor adjustments needed to be made as each group's composition was examined more closely: "Are all the talkative (or quiet) children in one group? Have I put together children who act up? Did I balance gender, race, or ethnic factors? In order to complete the group's goal, must I add someone with a special skill (e.g., to draw an illustration)?"

To assure success, then, teachers must select the two-, three-, and four-member groups so that students are mixed heterogeneously, with consideration for academic ability and for balance of ethnic backgrounds, race, and gender. And, in all cases, teachers should never create groups based on friendship or cliques. In heterogeneous groups, students are more prone to work together to achieve success, more tolerant of diverse points of view, and more genuinely considerate of the thoughts and feelings of others.

STUDENT	GROUP	STUDENT	GROUP
1. DARCEE	1	11. JEFFWAN	1
2. WARREN	2	12. INEZ	2
3. HOLLY	3	13. PATTY	3
4. AHMAD	4	14. GINA	4
5. JOHNNY	5	15. LINDA	5
6. PENNY	5	16. MACK	5
7. MIKE	4	17. BOBBY	4
8. LUIS	3	18. LAURA	3
9. NATE	2	19. ROBIN	2
10. CARLA	1	20. DONALD	1

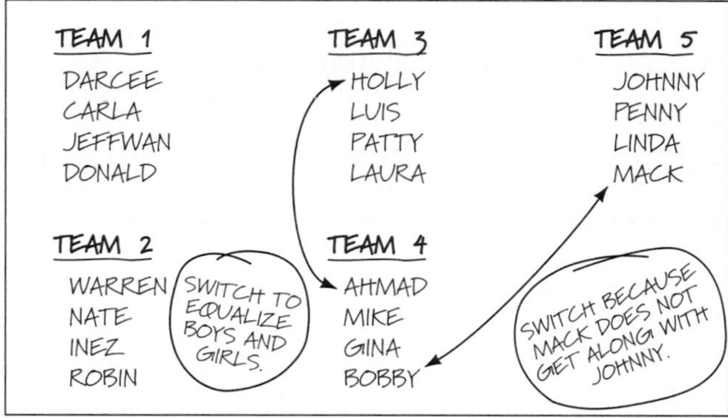

FIGURE 8.3 Establishing Heterogeneous Groups

When first groups are established, it is a good idea to assign individual responsibilities. As children gain experience, they will be able to select their own roles. Different tasks call for different roles; you will need to shift team roles as the demands of unique group tasks change from assignment to assignment. Here are some examples of roles team members can play:

Group Captain: Reads the task aloud to the group. Checks to make sure everyone is listening. Makes the task as clear as possible. Coordinates the group's efforts; provides leadership.

Materials Manager: Gathers, distributes, and collects all research books and other supplies.

Recorder: Fills out forms and writes down and edits the group's report. Shares the group's result with the class.

Illustrator: Draws any pictures, graphs, charts, or figures that help communicate the group's findings.

Monitor: Keeps the group focused on the task. Makes sure each member of the group can explain the answer or information and tell why it was selected.

Coach: Sees that everyone has an equal chance to participate; offers praise and encouragement to members as they work.

Cooperative learning groups vary in duration, depending on the task to be accomplished. Some groups remain together for only a short time—until they complete a special project, study new material, or solve a problem. Others change frequently throughout the day (dyads, for example), especially those formed quickly when teachers ask questions that have numerous possible answers. And others, called *base groups*, stay together for an entire year or semester, therefore providing a means by which students can offer stability and support.

Selecting a Cooperative Learning Approach

Teachers interested in using cooperative learning in their classrooms are free to select from among a wide variety of strategies. The following are but a few of the more successful alternatives. They are examples of specific, tried-and-true strategies that you might find useful.

Think-Pair-Share. This is one of the simplest cooperative learning techniques. The teacher stops at natural "break" points during a lesson and poses a question. The students are given a short time to *think* about the question silently. The teacher then tells the students to *pair* up: "Turn to your partner and . . ." (think about what makes the San Joaquin Valley a good place for farming; predict where the Mississippi River begins; tell why the Cheyenne held Medicine Dances). The teacher gives the students a minute or two to talk together and discuss their ideas. The teacher then asks a few groups to *share* their ideas with the whole class or another group, but all groups are not required to share each time.

Think-Pair-Square. Like Think-Pair-Share, the teacher poses a problem and then the students *think* about it and *share* their thoughts with a partner. Instead of then sharing with the entire class, however, two dyads join together and *share* together as a foursome—a *square*.

Numbered Heads Together. Numbered Heads Together entails a simple four-step course of action:

1. The teacher divides the class into groups of four and assigns a number to each student: 1, 2, 3, or 4.
2. The teacher asks a question related to a topic under study. For example, while studying Medieval England, one teacher asked, "What were some of the responsibilities of the women inside a castle?"
3. The teacher tells the students to "put their heads together" and work until she gives them a signal to stop.

4. The teacher calls a number (1, 2, 3, or 4). The students with that number raise their hands, become the groups' representatives, and can be called on by the teacher to respond.

Kagan (1989) reports that positive interaction and individual accountability are both included in this Numbered Heads Together technique. The high achievers share answers because they know their number might be called, and they want their team to do well. The lower achievers also listen carefully because they know their number might be called. Therefore, students work together and help one another find answers, and all students learn what is being studied.

Jigsaw. Jigsaw is a cooperative learning technique developed by Elliot Aronson and his colleagues (1978). The process starts when the teacher assigns students heterogeneously to groups of four, called their *home group*. Each home group works on content material that the teacher has broken down into sections. Each home group member is responsible for one of the sections.

Members of the different home groups who are responsible for the same sections leave their home groups and meet in *expert groups* to study and discuss their specialized sections. These students then return to their original home groups and take turns sharing with their teammates about their respective sections.

To better understand the Jigsaw technique, it is best to describe it being used in Jack Cosgrove's social studies classroom. Mr. Cosgrove and his fifth-graders use Jigsaw frequently in social studies. To introduce the activity, Mr. Cosgrove divided his students into home groups of four members each. The home groups followed this procedure for a lesson on Helen Keller:

1. The class started out with five home groups, each consisting of four team members.
2. Mr. Cosgrove gave each member of a home group a sheet of writing paper with a different-colored adhesive dot (red, yellow, blue, green) at the top. The dots signified membership in different expert groups.
3. Students left their home groups and went to a section of the room designated by sheets of colored construction paper that matched their dots, and joined the other members of their expert groups. Mr. Cosgrove had four expert groups, each focused on a different aspect of the life of Helen Keller: Helen's childhood, Helen's early accomplishments, Helen's adult life, and Helen's influence on history.
4. While in their expert groups, the students studied the contents of several resources and selected important information, becoming "experts" on that part of Helen Keller's life. Finally, they summarized the information on their writing paper so it could be used to teach the members of their home groups about what they learned. The experts then returned to their home groups, and there was an expert on every section in each home group.

5. Every expert shared information on his or her part of Helen Keller's life with other members of the home group. Because students were able to learn about other parts of Helen Keller's life only by listening carefully to their teammates, they were motivated to attend to one another's work.
6. Each home group planned a special presentation to share its collective learning about Helen Keller.

Pick Your Spot. Pick Your Spot is a useful cooperative learning technique that helps students to think about and share their preferences or choices on a variety of issues or topics in social studies. Developed by Ellis and Whalen (1990), the strategy is comprised of the following four steps:

1. Ask the students a question from which they are to select an answer from among alternatives—for example, "Which former president would be most able to lead our country from its troubles today: George Washington, Abraham Lincoln, Franklin D. Roosevelt, or John F. Kennedy?"
2. Identify "spots" in the room that offer alternatives. Word or picture cards identifying each president could be attached to the wall. Ask students to quickly pick a spot and quietly congregate there.
3. Tell students at each spot to give the reasons for taking their position. Have a large sheet of chart paper available so the students can record their responses.
4. After allowing sufficient time to build a strong case, call on one student from each group to share the group's results with the rest of the class. After each group has reported, ask if any students would like to switch and pick a new spot. If they do, ask which argument persuaded them. Inviting questions or challenges from each group can expand and enrich this step.

Choosing a Reward System

When cooperative learning works as intended, students acquire a strong team attachment with each other and take tremendous pride in celebrating their victories with meaningful recognition and rewards. Cooperative teamwork results in greater success when it incorporates *reward interdependence*—group members receive a reward only if the whole group accomplishes its objective. For example, one group may be assessed on the total or average of individual test scores and another on the average rubric evaluation of products such as a report, mural, or dramatic skit. Teachers may choose to recognize a group's accomplishments with praise, extra recess time, free homework passes, or bonus points tacked onto children's grades. Or they may award prizes such as stickers, erasers, inexpensive toys, pencils, or snacks, or give public recognition as a team picture on the classroom "Wall of Fame" or article in the class newspaper. You must remember, though, that all group members must be given a reward for the accomplishment; everyone is rewarded or no one is rewarded. For example, every group member gets 10 minutes extra re-

Teachers in cooperative classrooms spend a great deal of time observing learning groups to assess the students' academic progress as well as their use of interpersonal and group work skills.

cess time when group members correctly match all United States capital cities with their states. The rewards should be both enticing and inexpensive.

The Benefits of Cooperative Learning

Is cooperative learning worth the time and effort in your social studies classroom? Or is cooperative learning a fad that will come and go like so many others in recent years? After more than 30 years of research involving over 80 research studies and a series of extensive reviews of research on cooperation and learning (more than 800 dating back to the late nineteenth century), Roger and David Johnson (2002) have no doubts: Cooperative learning works to the benefit of students, teachers, schools, and communities. Roger Johnson asserts, "Human beings learn more, flourish, and connect more when they're cooperating and less when they're competing or working in an isolated fashion" (p. 1). In short, research seems to indicate that the benefits of cooperative learning activities, done well, help students improve their learning and experience joy and satisfaction in helping one another. Watching students take to cooperative learning is something like watching survivors on a lifeboat. They quickly realize that they'll either sink or swim together.

They learn to be patient, less critical, and more compassionate. If they see a teammate in need, they go to her or his aid. Cooperative learning seems to be here to stay because evidence indicates it does what people say it will do. Teachers can use it with confidence in a variety of ways because the benefits of the approach are considerable.

There are no shortcuts to learning how to use cooperative learning in your social studies classroom; gaining expertise requires years of effort and long-term commitment to self-improvement. Seek help from colleagues, attend professional workshops, exchange ideas, and read widely.

A Final Thought

Group learning may be broadly defined as any classroom learning situation in which students work together toward a joint or common goal. Of all the student-centered instructional options available for social constructivist classrooms, teachers seem to prefer this form of teaching to any other. Collaborative and cooperative learning form an ideal partnership with social constructivism primarily because those strategies require students to work together to achieve goals in ways they could not attain individually. Instead of working in competition with other students in the classroom, children are assigned the task of building a learning community where everyone contributes in important and meaningful ways.

Collaborative and cooperative classrooms do not emerge spontaneously; they are the product of teacher-led transitions from whole-class instruction to the establishment of joint learning teams. Once students learn to assume active roles in group efforts and begin to take responsibility for their own learning, they are likely to achieve higher levels of academic success. But group work goes beyond academic success; it helps form the foundation on which strong democratic communities can be built and maintained—it enhances self-esteem and builds the kinds of lifelong interpersonal and communication skills considered necessary to function as productive members of society.

Managing a cooperative learning classroom changes the social constructivist teacher's role from that of directing whole-class learning through the Learning Cycle to that of managing small learning teams. Gone for the most part is the planning and presentation of three-part lessons; in its place teachers become primarily concerned with helping students grow into a community of learners.

REFERENCES

Aronson, E., Blaney, N. T., Stephan, C., Sikes, J., & Snapp, M. (1978). *The jigsaw classroom.* Beverly Hills, CA: Sage.

Bodrova, E., & Leong, D. (1996). *Tools of the mind.* Columbus, OH: Merrill.

Ellis, S. S., & Whalen, S. F. (1990). *Cooperative learning: Getting started.* New York: Scholastic.

Freiberg, H. J., & Driscoll, A. (1992). *Universal teaching strategies.* Boston: Allyn & Bacon.

Gallavan, N. P., & Juliano, C. M. (2007). Collaborating to create future societies with young learners. *Social Studies and the Young Learner, 19,* 13–16.

Johnson, D. W., & Johnson, R. T. (2002). *Research WORKs: Cooperative learning.* University of Minnesota: College of Education and Human Development. [Online]. http://cehd.umn.edu/Pubs/ResearchWorks/coop-learning.html.

Johnson, D. W., Johnson, R. T., & Holubec, E. J. (1993). *Cooperation in the classroom.* Edina, MN: Interaction Book Company.

Kagan, S. (1989). The structural approach to cooperative learning. *Educational Leadership, 47,* 12–15.

Slavin, R. E. (1984). Students motivating students to excel: Incentives, cooperative tasks and student achievement. *The Elementary School Journal, 85,* 53–62.

Slavin, R. E. (1995). *Cooperative learning* (2nd ed.). Boston: Allyn & Bacon.

Wasserman, S. (1989). Children working in groups? It doesn't work! *Childhood Education, 5,* 204.

CHAPTER 9

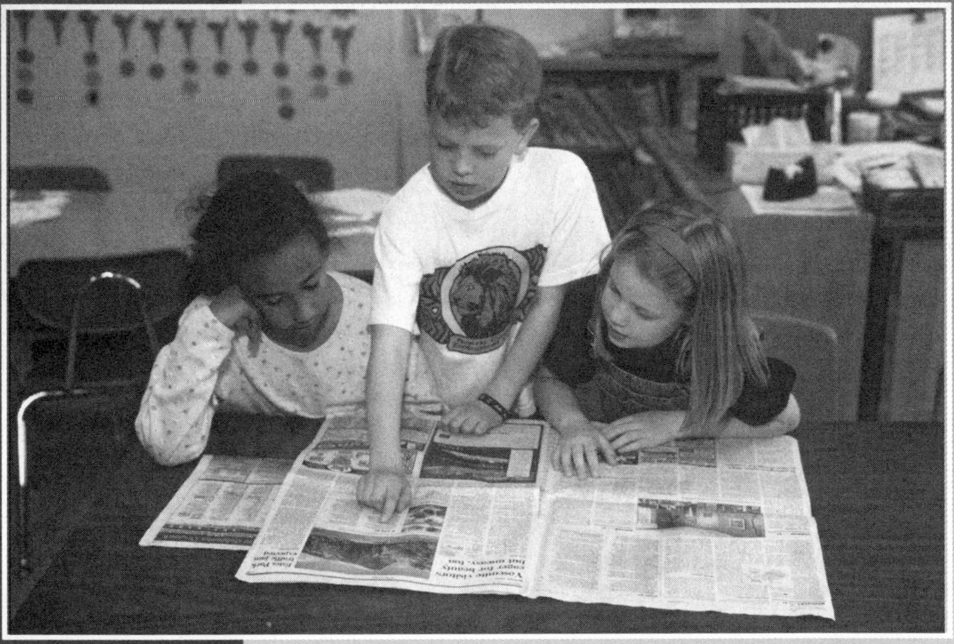

Inquiry and Problem Solving
Cognitive Constructivism in Action

What Does Cognitive Constructivism Look Like?

Students in Sheila Kirtland's fifth-grade social studies class have been investigating various customs of people around the world. One day, as they were watching a video on diverse cultural traditions, the students became particularly interested in the historically popular Muslim greeting of keeping the palm of one's hand open and touching the breast, forehead, and lips, signifying endearment in heart, thoughts, and words. Traditional greetings of various cultures around the world became the rage in Ms. Kirtland's class as the students engaged in a spontaneous and productive discussion of the many interesting ways people greet one another: "The people of Japan bow politely when greeting someone." "The French and other continentals 'kiss' one another on both cheeks." "Boy Scouts in America shake left-handed—the hand nearest the heart—with the three middle fingers extended to the other person's wrist." The highest degree of curiosity in the topic surfaced, however, after some students demonstrated the handshaking styles of present-day athletes. The main question was, "Who started all of this?"

Ms. Kirtland encouraged her students to pursue their interest by helping them locate and explore various resources that might assist them with an answer. Some searched the Web, using *Yahooligans* (www.yahooligans.com/) as a starting point. Others looked through books and magazines. A few students thought they might uncover information by interviewing parents, teachers, and other adults. Their research produced some fascinating information, such as discovering that the practice of grasping and shaking hands goes back to earliest civilizations when the right hand normally held a weapon. If empty, however, the extended right hand became a gesture of welcome and peace. They also learned that although the handshake has been by far the most popular greeting throughout the United States, it is viewed as senseless and inconvenient in other parts of the world. Many countries believe it is the most potent means of spreading disease and, for sanitary reasons, prefer the bow as practiced by the people of Asia. The students discovered that, in terms of handshaking, as far back as the sixteenth century the Ashanti of Africa had a handshake and an expression of greeting: "Five must lie within five." The Dutch of old ended business negotiations with a ritualistic hand slapping, high and low, which served as a basis for the expression "striking a bargain."

NCSS STANDARDS

I. *Culture*
V. *Individuals, Groups, and Institutions*

As far as identifying the source of the modern "shaking" variations practiced by present-day athletes, Ms. Kirtland's students discovered that, although they are rooted in African American culture, the evidence was inconclusive as to who actually started the practices. Basketball player Magic Johnson claimed to have originated the "high five" at Michigan State in 1980, but long jumper Ralph Boston argued that the "slap five" began among African American track athletes on the international track circuit prior to 1968. Some insist that revolutionary handshakes started as far back as the 1940s when African American musicians greeted each other with a special shake accompanied by the jive phrase, "Gimme a little skin, man." Regardless of their origin, Ms. Kirtland's students became convinced that the new handshakes were not just a a passing trend.

"They're not just a fad," argues Kareem. "I've high-fived a million times! No contest."

"People will keep inventing handshakes until the end of time," added Lillian in support. "The possibilities are endless."

"I agree," volunteered Nicole, "but by the time you learn all the handshakes, the season is over!"

Ms. Kirtland supported her students throughout this thought-provoking investigation because she is convinced that the most worthwhile learning in social studies occurs when children work at what *they* want to know. Her viewpoint is based on a belief that elementary school students are naturally inclined to dive headlong into whatever excites their interests and that social studies teachers should be a little more flexible, a little more spontaneous, and a little more willing to help them explore their interesting world. In this classroom episode, for example, Ms. Kirtland recognized that her students' interest in the handshaking matter was quite powerful so it was important to risk a temporary departure from the regular curriculum so they could resolve their absorbing problem. Such a strong inner drive to unlock for themselves the mysteries of their world is clearly exemplified by the comments

I once overheard a second-grader make after his teacher asked the class, "What would it be like to know *everything*?"

"Awful!" the little boy blurted out right away.

"Awful?" inquired the teacher in disbelief. "Why do you think knowing everything would be awful?"

"'Cause then there'd be nothin' left to wonder 'bout!" answered the youngster.

In the vein of this astute second-grader, teachers in dynamic social studies classrooms inspire their students to look at their social world with a sense of wonder. "If teachers are reluctant to take risks, how will they ever inspire risk-taking in their students?" Ms. Kirtland asks. "It is the job of social studies teachers to arouse, not suppress, the natural curiosity their students carry to school. The students are often their own best teachers." In that single persuasive statement, Ms. Kirtland summed up the beliefs of those who contend that social studies education should be "student run." These educators draw a majority of their support from cognitive constructivists who propose that knowledge is best constructed through self-initiated inquiry and individual problem-centered investigations.

Cognitive constructivists and social constructivists have much in common, but they differ noticeably in one key area—the extent and type of involvement of both students and teachers. Although each model requires effort and responsibility on the part of both, *social constructivists* stress the organization of "communities of learners" in which "more expert" adults or peers provide assistance to the less skilled learners. *Cognitive constructivists*, on the other hand, propose a learner-centered environment where the construction of knowledge is carried out by individual students in a fashion that supports their interests and needs. For cognitive constructivists, learning is primarily an individual venture.

What Is Cognitive Constructivism?

You have read in Chapter 7 that constructivists fundamentally agree that learning can be most reasonably explained as an active process that Piaget referred to as *equilibration*—a path of action by which students try to make sense of the world either by fitting new experiences into an existing schema (*assimilation*) or by revising an existing schema as a result of a new experience (*accommodation*). In this perspective, learning is always driven by the learner as she or he moves to assimilate or accommodate new experiences into existing schemata. So, students learn by fitting, or attempting to fit, new information into what they already know. Although they agree on those principles, constructivists are split into two camps on their views of how constructive activity should take place. You will recall that the social constructivist camp (Vygotsky) claims that learning is embedded in *social situations*. The cognitive constructivists, on the other hand, explain learning from the perspective of the *individual*. A social constructivist would describe a sociable mind that prefers to pull out beyond the limits of one's body into her or his social environs; a cognitive constructivist would depict the mind as being more solitary,

confining its sphere of learning to an individual's head. Internal development is the focus of teaching, and the social context is to some extent played down.

Instruction seeks to capitalize on the wondering and exploring nature of children through such methods as inquiry and problem-centered instruction. The cognitive constructivist teacher functions as a "facilitator" who provides something meaty for the children to sink their teeth into and then sits back to wait for their results. These teachers do not check the teacher's manual to see what to do next; they go to where the action is. Only one thing matters: a teacher who is tuned into and encourages the exploration of the interests and curiosities of the students. Students are recognized as "young social scientists"— learning about their world by using strategies employed by real social scientists—addressing questions or problems, gathering data, and searching for answers.

Cognitive constructivism centers on *problem-centered learning*, a term that has been used by various writers to cover a number of things we do in social studies, from putting puzzles together to coming up with solutions to everything from war to global warming. However, no description of problem-centered instruction has had more impact on elementary school social studies instruction than the one expressed by John Dewey (1916) during the early part of the twentieth century. At that time, Dewey proposed that *problems can be thought of as anything that creates doubt and uncertainty in learners*. Because Dewey's description has maintained acceptance over the years, it will serve to guide our discussion of problem-centered instruction.

How Do Teachers Facilitate Inquiry and Problem Solving?

Problem-centered learning is a term that encompasses two teaching approaches generally considered appropriate for cognitive constructivist classrooms—*inquiry* and *creative problem solving*. Although each is characterized by its own set of distinctive processes, they share one very important similarity—helping students solve problems. As you read on about what distinguishes these two approaches, you will address these important questions: What are the characteristics of inquiry and creative problem solving? How are these two strategies similar? How are they different? How does each alternative contribute to contructivist learning? What roles do teachers and students carry out in each?

The Inquiry Process

The term *inquiry* has received widespread recognition as an important instructional strategy through the years. For example, the influential publication, *Curriculum Standards for Social Studies* (NCSS, 1994) recommends that "teachers model seriousness of purpose and a thoughtful approach to inquiry and use instructional strategies designed to elicit and support similar qualities from students. . . . Teachers gradually move from providing considerable guidance . . . to a less directive role that encourages students to become independent and self-

How Global is the Curriculum *Go to MyEducationLab, select the topic Teaching Strategies, watch the video entitled "The Inquiry Method," and complete the questions that accompany it.*

regulated learners" (p. 12). Some people consider inquiry to be an instructional approach that is undeniably new. Others consider it to be at least as old as ancient Greece and that it has previously traveled under such names as the *Socratic method, problem solving, critical thinking, scholarly investigation,* and *scientific thinking*. Despite this ambiguity, the characteristic that sets inquiry apart from other teaching strategies is that it is the only approach designed to teach students how to carry out independent investigations through a systematic process of gathering and analyzing data. The most common pattern of inquiry seems to be the time-honored process recommended by John Dewey (1916):

1. The students identify a problem or question that can be investigated.
2. The students generate hypotheses, or tentative answers that can be verified.
3. The students collect data.
4. The students analyze the data and form generalizations that can be applied to this problem and to similar ones encountered in their lives.
5. The students share their results with an audience.

Do you remember learning about the method of scientific inquiry in elementary school or high school? People who do often tell me that it left them with the impression that social scientists never deal with a problem until they put on their horn-rimmed glasses, sharpen their pencils, pull out a paper pad listing the steps of the inquiry process, and carefully check off each step as they complete it. In the real world, however, this version is erroneous. Sometimes social scientists follow the scientific method to the letter, but more often they work in a slightly more unmethodical way, grubbing around and hunting for answers through trial and error. Doesn't this informal approach remind you of the way children tackle problems, too? Children, by their very nature, are curious about their world and love to explore and investigate until they arrive at answers to their questions—sometimes unsystematically and sometimes in a more organized manner, just like certified social scientists.

The Essence of Inquiry-Based Learning

Social studies instruction capitalizes on the natural curiosity of children—wondering, asking questions, probing possible answers, and constructing their own awareness of the world. One of the primary goals of social studies teachers is to understand how to channel the children's spontaneous investigations and help them acquire the confidence and skill to carry out the processes of constructivist inquiry in the classroom. Although children are effectual natural inquirers, they often lack the expertise required to carry out a wide variety of content area investigations. Children's first experiences with constructivist inquiry are intended to serve as a bridge between their free, natural childhood explorations and the acquisition of an interconnected set of organized processes and skills that children will need to employ as they raise questions about their social world.

As with collaborative and cooperative learning, there must be a transition period during which students change over from traditional teacher direction to more independence and inquiry-centered learning. It may take several weeks or months to reach the point where you and your students are able to work together while investigating problems productively. I have heard teachers give up after only one unsuccessful try, saying, "I knew it! These kids just can't think for themselves!" and go through the rest of the year doing the children's thinking for them. But would these teachers ever say, "These children cannot add and subtract by themselves," and thereafter remove any further opportunity for them to learn those important skills the rest of the school year? Before you make the same mistake and end up crying, "Bring back the textbook! Give me back my worksheets! This business of inquiry-centered learning just doesn't work!" you must know that children change direction slowly; the processes of inquiry will not magically emerge after a single exposure to the process. Introducing new expectancies all at once is distracting and produces a situation in which the children's cognitive systems collapse under an overload of input. Time, patience, and your belief in the importance of student-directed learning are the key ingredients of a successful transition.

Teachers help students on the road to self-directed learning by offering early, hands-on, problem-based experiences that incorporate the following elements: (1) designing captivating classroom displays (mini-museums), (2) discussing the displays, and (3) encouraging children's questions.

Informal Classroom Displays (Mini-Museums)

Classroom displays, or what I like to call "mini-museums" when they are arranged for social studies purposes (also referred to as *interest areas, curiosity centers*, and *theme tables*), are essentially exhibit areas designed to encourage children to explore, question, think, and talk. Today's exhibit might be origami, a Chilean rain stick, foreign coins, a butter churn, a powder horn, shark's teeth, campaign buttons, a tape recording of city sounds, or a sombrero. Whatever you select for the mini-museum should be treated like exhibits in the best public children's museums—with a policy that invites touching, exploration, and investigation.

To begin, take your students to a local museum where a museum educator can lead a gallery tour and explain how objects are displayed in the exhibits. Observing exhibit designers laying out an exhibit area can be especially helpful if you plan to involve the students in designing and putting together the classroom exhibit area. Back in the classroom, review what a museum is—a place where interesting objects of historic or cultural significance are displayed. Lead a class conversation by offering prompts such as: "What exhibit do you remember best?" "Why do you think that particular exhibit stands out in your mind?" "How might objects be exhibited in a classroom museum?" and "What would you call the classroom museum?" It is important to remember that these collections should be neither haphazardly displayed nor should they be looked at briefly and then put on a shelf and forgotten.

Explain that research is an important part of setting up a museum exhibition area. Curators must study the objects in their care so they can provide visitors with accurate information—where, when, and by whom it was used as well where it was found and who made it.

One teacher modeled the curator's research responsibilities by placing a seemingly odd object on a table—a stiff brush used by dog groomers. On the wall above the table was a sign that read "Classroom Museum." Almost instantly the children began looking at the brush, touching it, and talking about what it might be. The teacher watched and listened, occasionally asking open-ended questions and making comments to stimulate the children to think more about the object. One child tried to use the brush on her own hair. She was surprised to see just how stiff the bristles were. Naturally, the other children had to try, too.

Rosa eventually identified the object. Her mother was a veterinarian and Rosa often helped around the office. She was obviously thrilled to share her knowledge with her classmates; their interest became much deeper as they listened to the knowledgeable description by their friend. To capitalize on this growing fascination with the brush and what veterinarians do, the teacher invited Rosa's mother to visit the class to talk about her profession.

You can see from this example that it is a good idea to plan what you display at the mini-museum rather than select items in a hit-or-miss fashion. You want something to happen at the center—interests to grow and concepts to deepen as the activity extends in the direction of the children's interests.

Planned Observational Experiences

Rather than making the mini-museum an informal observation/conversation place as Rosa's teacher did, some teachers prefer to introduce the mini-museum during planned meeting times. The following dialogue illustrates one such meeting. That teacher, Thomas Fant, opens the meeting by calling the students' attention to a large picture of an archaeologist studying some interesting artifacts.

Mr. Fant: Today we're going to discover some fascinating things at our social studies mini-museum. First, look carefully at this photo. The person you see is called an archaeologist. Have you ever heard that word? (Mr. Fant holds up a word card for archaeologist.) What is it that archaeologists do?

Adam: She seems to be looking at something.

Mr. Fant: Yes, she's looking at, or examining, something. What kinds of things do you suppose archaeologists examine?

Denise: Fossils?

Tamara: Yeah. To see what Earth was like a long time ago.

Mr. Fant: Yes, they examine old objects and use that information to describe what people were like very long ago. That's a good start. Does anyone else have an idea?

Patrick: They dig for old tools and things—even bones.

NCSS STANDARDS

I. *Culture*
II. *Time, Continuity, and Change*
III. *People, Places, and Environments*

Mr. Fant: Yes, they might study fossils, bones, tools, paintings, clothes, furniture, and other objects. These objects are called *artifacts*. Studying artifacts can help us understand the lives of people. Have you ever seen an archaeologist examine artifacts?

Nelson: I saw a picture of an archaeologist in a museum. It was in an exhibit about China.

Lucinda: On a TV show once, I saw some archaeologists looking in old pyramids for mummies.

Mr. Fant: Yes, archaeologists study many things to learn about the lives of people. Artifacts can tell about the games they play, the tools they use, and even the way they eat their meals. Many of the artifacts archaeologists uncover find their way to museums where curators and conservators study the objects and arrange them in galleries. From now on, this table will be called the mini-museum. It is a gallery where you can come to discover things about the lives of people by doing some of the important jobs museum curators do—examining them and keeping a "museum fact sheet" that provides information about the artifact. (Mr. Fant brings out a cornhusk doll.) I've brought an artifact for you to examine today. Look at it carefully and see what kinds of discoveries you might make. Amour, what are some things you notice?

Amour: It looks like a toy—a doll, maybe?

Mr. Fant: What makes you think it's a doll, Amour?

Amour: It looks like it has arms and legs. The top is like a head.

Mr. Fant: It is shaped like a doll. What do you notice, Raphael?

Raphael: I think it might be made out of corn. It feels and looks like the dried corn plants we put out at Halloween.

Mr. Fant: That part of a corn plant is called a husk. Here, look at this. It is a cornhusk before it was made into a doll. (Shows cornhusk.)

Moira: How do people ever make dolls out of cornhusks?

Mr. Fant: Here, I'll show you. It's quite simple. (Takes a few minutes and demonstrates how to construct a cornhusk doll as the children follow his lead to make their own. He explains that the husks he is using were soaked in warm water for about an hour until they become soft. Mr. Fant takes them out of the water and dries them with paper towels. Then he puts about five cornhusks together and ties a string around the middle for a waist. As Mr. Fant continues the process, he demonstrates that people can be a very important source of information. He emphasizes the importance of checking other sources, too, calling the children's attention to a set of five books, each of which contains information about cornhusk dolls.) What does the doll tell you about the people who used it? (The craft activity continues for several more minutes.) You've been examining our artifact very carefully today. You made some interesting discoveries. Archaeologists don't stop with discoveries, though. They must keep careful records of everything they do so their findings can be shared with other people. We will use a special way of recording our discoveries—"museum fact sheets." (Mr. Fant passes out the fact sheets.) There's a place for your name and the date, and then the paper says, "What I Know About" followed by a long blank. What words should I put in the blank?

Martha: Cornhusk dolls!

Mr. Fant: That's right, Martha. There is also a big box on the paper for you to draw an illustration of what you studied. Please make a careful drawing there. Finally, at the bottom you will find some space to write. What are some things curators might write about this cornhusk doll?

Denise: The doll is made from dried cornhusks.

Amanda It was made in a place where people grew lots of corn.

Martin: It could have been a gift for a boy or a girl.

Louise: There weren't many stores around selling toys then. People had to make their toys from things around them. (The suggestions keep coming for several minutes. The children then complete their observation sheets. Figure 9.1 shows a completed museum fact sheet.)

As important as they are, observational experiences by themselves do not guarantee the acquisition of constructivist inquiry skills. Mr. Fant also used

These children are thoroughly engaged in a well-planned investigative activity—exploring dried corn husks.

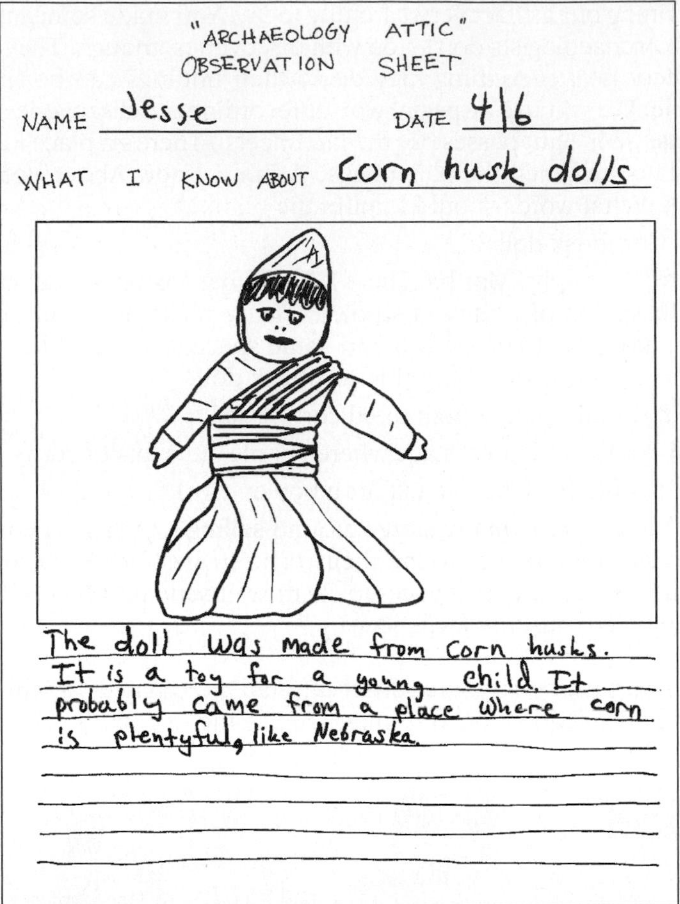

"ARCHAEOLOGY ATTIC"
OBSERVATION SHEET
NAME Jesse
DATE 4/6
WHAT I KNOW ABOUT corn husk dolls
The doll was made from corn husks. It is a toy for a young child. It probably came from a place where corn is plentyful, like Nebraska.

FIGURE 9.1 Completed Student Observation Sheet

carefully worded questions or comments to help the children unlock meaning from the mysteries that confronted them:

- "What do you see here?"
- "How do you suppose it is used?"
- "I wonder what would happen if . . . ?"
- "If we try it again, do you think the same thing will happen?"
- "Is this like anything you've ever (used, seen, tried out) before?"
- "How can we find out more about . . . ?"
- "Can we find out if we watch it carefully?"
- "What makes you think so?"
- "Who do you think might use this?"

- "Where do they live? What makes you think so?"
- "What can you tell about the people who use this?"
- "What do you think of the people who use this?"

Some of these questions and comments help children look for specific things; others are more open and encourage higher thought processes such as predicting and discovering relationships. Through such thought-provoking observational experiences, children develop the basic observation skills required for sophisticated scientific investigations.

Encouraging Children's Questions

How Global is the Curriculum *Go to MyEducationLab, select the topic Teaching Strategies, watch the video entitled "The Indirect Instruction Model," and complete the questions that accompany it.*

Making careful observations in informal classroom exhibit areas and taking part in planned observational experiences are two important components of early inquiry-centered learning and make an excellent transition from more teacher-directed instructional approaches. A third important component of this process is encouraging children to ask their own questions about their experiences. Children often have a lot of questions of their own to ask. For example, Thomas Edison's last day in school came when he asked, "How can water run uphill?" after he noticed that a river in Ohio did just that. Young Tom was then expelled for expressing himself in ways that were unacceptable at the time. Children come to us with a strong need to ask questions and often come up with incredible examples. Respect their questions and support your students in using this childhood gift. Here are a few questions and comments I remember while working with children:

- "Do caterpillars *know* they're going to turn into butterflies?"
- "Are babies born with brains?"
- "Look! That man has a hole in his hair (he was balding)."
- "Why are museums called museums?"
- "What do they call earthquakes on Mars?"

Wouldn't it be interesting to know what the children had in mind when they asked their questions? When such splendid expressions explode from inquiring minds, ask yourself, "Am I listening as carefully and sensitively as I can?" When you do listen, you communicate to the child that she or he is a worthwhile individual whose extra-special thoughts are valued. This is something the children need to know, for question asking is an indispensable part of the problem-solving process. Don't be afraid to admit you don't know the answer when children ask questions like these: "I don't know the answer, but that's a very good question." Then, go forward and encourage the children to seek out an answer: "Let's look that up on the Internet." "Let's look that up in the library." "Do we know anyone who might have the answer to that?"

The goal of these preliminary experiences is to help children acquire the skills needed for self-directed learning. Self-directed learning emerges when students are aware that a problem or question exists and attack it in a systematic, thorough manner—understanding what they need to know and devising strategies to find out what they don't. Self-directed learners have the ability to find out something by themselves by using these three questions whenever they encounter a perplexing problem or situation: (1) What do I already know about this? (2) What else do I need to find out? and (3) Where can I find this information?

Focused Personal Investigations

Second-grade teacher Robert Kurzinsky introduces his children to the important concepts and skills of the constructivist inquiry process by taking advantage of happenings in the world around them. "Children have an instinctive curiosity that compels them to probe their world," he says. "The very nature of childhood drives youngsters to explore, and this need must be taken advantage of through focused investigations in social studies classrooms."

"Teachers play an important role in facilitating the construction of early inquiry skills and concepts," advises Mr. Kurzinsky, "that's why I use various instructional strategies that begin with where the children are right now. What's interesting is that they don't even know they're in social studies class. They think they're just having fun!"

Mr. Kurzinsky bases this developmental emphasis on the works of Alfie Kohn (1999), who recommends that teachers should value children for who they are right now rather than seeing them as adults-in-the-making. Therefore, what we ask children to do in school should have what Kohn refers to as *horizontal relevance;* instruction ought to be meaningful to them at the time, such as something that could happen at home or in school. This is in contrast to *vertical relevance*, Kohn explains, which justifies learning something simply because the children will need to know it later—for example, "You'll need to know how to use inquiry because your third-grade teacher will expect it."

When Mr. Kurzinsky's second-graders came back to school in the fall, they were excited to share all the interesting things that happened to them during summer vacation. Hands flew into the air during sharing time in eager anticipation of who would be the first to talk. Teri's words exploded as she told about helping her parents take care of their vegetable garden. Agostino's eyes sparkled with pride as he described the new furniture that arrived at his house in the middle of summer ("A beautiful yellow sofa, just beautiful!"). Wendy sadly recounted her family's heavy-hearted task of saying good-bye to their 10-year-old beagle who was struck down by a speeding car. Kun Hwan happily described his seventh birthday party, and Frey told of his family's trip to the state aquarium.

After they shared their experiences, Mr. Kurzinsky passed out drawing paper and asked each child to draw a picture of his or her special event. After the children finished their drawings, Mr. Kurzinsky directed them to print

NCSS STANDARDS

IV. *Individual Development and Identity*
V. *Individuals, Groups, and Institutions*

their stories in the space above or below each drawing. Figure 9.2 is Frey's story about his family's trip to the state aquarium. Frey was particularly interested in the dolphins; when asked about his written piece, he explained that the dolphin was saying, "Ouch!" Then he read what he had written above the drawing: "Animals should definitely not wear clothing because a dolphin might have trouble with its fin." One of Frey's favorite books was *Animals Should Never Wear Clothing* by Judi Barrett and Ron Barrett (Aladdin), a humorous picture book that explains why an animal's clothing is perfect just as it is and the problems they would likely encounter if they tried wearing human clothing (a snake, for example, might lose its clothing, or a billy goat might eat its clothes for lunch). Frey modeled his writing and illustrating approach after the style found in the book. Mr. Kurzinsky explains the importance of these early drawing/writing experiences: "As the blank pages come alive with drawings and words telling of their experiences, I could see these children were showing me what they knew as well as what they needed to know."

The children enjoyed sharing the pictures and stories of their summer, but Wendy's tragic beagle mishap seemed to regain the most interest. Her classmates felt sorry for Wendy and were very supportive, and everyone seemed quite relieved as Wendy described the new floppy-eared, sad-eyed basset hound puppy her family adopted from a local rescue organization. Soon, they began talking about their own pets at home. Their interest seemed to reach its peak when Moira speculated aloud, "I wonder what kind of pet most of us have."

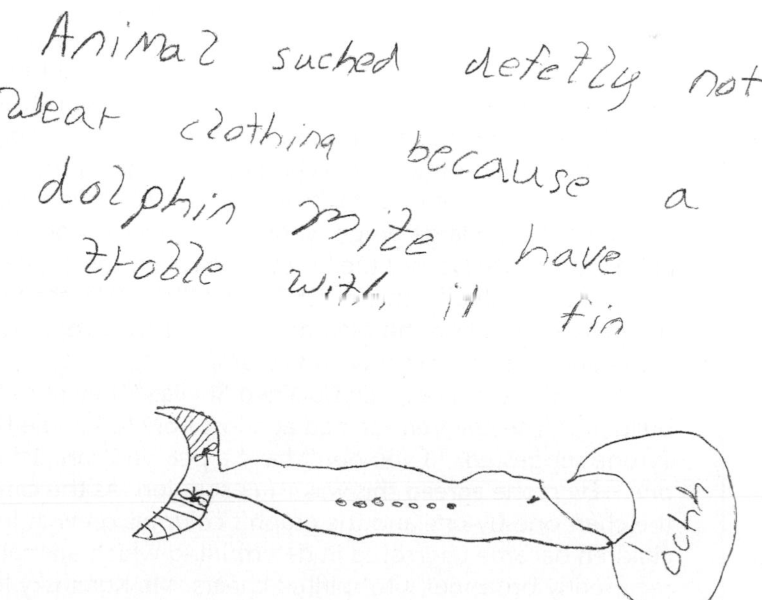

FIGURE 9.2 The Drawing/Writing Connection

"Yeah," the children all seemed to agree.

Knowing that the spark for inquiry is often set off during such gripping discussions, Mr. Kurzinsky decided that the time was ripe for an introduction to the processes involved in carrying out constructivist inquiry: "That's a good question, Moira. Let's try to find an answer for it."

Mr. Kurzinsky could have simply asked for a show of hands to indicate the most common pets but he decided that a survey would probably be the best investigative tool to acquire the data. Also, a graph would be a good tool to help them see relationships among the data because they had been learning about graphs in math class. Mr. Kurzinsky knew that initial attempts at conducting surveys should reflect student interests in things closest to their lives, so their spontaneous question was a wonderful invitation to start. The first step of the constructivist inquiry process, then, evolved naturally; the students settled on an interesting question to explore.

When a clear-cut question is raised, children are invited to offer hypotheses, or reasoned guesses, about a likely end result: "I think fish are most popular. One of my friends has an aquarium in her house and there are lotsa fishes in there!" "I think cats are most popular because me and my friend have cats." "More will pick dogs 'cause everybody likes dogs."

Once the hypotheses are offered and reasons for them have been shared, help the children decide on the most helpful data to seek as they worked to solve a problem or answer a question. Because Mr. Kurzinsky decided that conducting a survey would be the method of data collection the class will use for this question, his challenge to the students was: "Let's settle on the five animals we think most of our classmates might have at home." The students decided that their comparisons should include cat, dog, bird, fish, and other animals (turtles, snakes, rabbits, gerbils).

Mr. Kurzinsky next presented the actual survey instrument the class would use to test the hypotheses. He reproduced a set of cards for each child with separate illustrations depicting each animal in the survey. On a large sheet of chart paper with the heading "Our Most Popular Pets," Mr. Kurzinsky drew a large graph whose boxes were large enough to enclose the animal cards. He labeled the bottom boxes on the chart "Cat," "Dog," "Bird," "Fish," and "Other Animals." Mr. Kurzinsky then had each child tell the class about her or his pet and then glue the proper illustrated card onto the chart in the correct row and column.

"I don't have a pet," complained Sheila. "They're not allowed in our building." The children seemed at a loss how to handle the situation until Tyrone suggested, "If you don't have a pet, you can just pretend you have one." Everyone agreed this was a fair solution. As the cards were pasted to the chart one-by-one and the graph's columns grew at irregular intervals, the children became engrossed in determining which animal was "winning" and recurrently broke out into spirited cheers. Mr. Kurzinsky led a running discussion of the data, regularly asking the children how many more cards there were in one column than another, how many cards were shown altogether, whether the data were or were not supporting their hypotheses, and how many cards still needed to be placed. Eventually, to the relief of at least half the children, the cat column surged ahead and convincingly overtook the others.

After a short informal class conversation, Mr. Kurzinsky helped the children examine and analyze the data:

- Which column has the most?
- Which column has the least?
- Are there more fish or more dogs?
- How many _____ are there?
- How many more _____ are there than _____?
- How many fewer _____ are there than _____?
- Are any columns the same?
- What does the graph tell us?
- What do we know about our favorite pets?

To make the introductory inquiry activity more authentic, it is advantageous to share the results publicly in some manner. In this case, the students' findings were published in the school newspaper under the heading, "What We Discovered about Our Pets."

This was a valuable hands-on, minds-on way to learn how to carry out the steps of constructivist inquiry. First, the children had a meaningful question to investigate. All inquiry starts with a question. Second, they made reasoned guesses, or predictions, about what they thought would happen. Reasoned guesses are called *hypotheses*. Third, they designed a survey-based experiment with their teacher to test the hypotheses. They decided to poll each child in the class, even those without pets. Fourth, they conducted the experiment and collected data in the form of a graph. Fifth, they carefully examined and analyzed the data. Sixth, they explained what happened to an interested audience. They learned all these processes by being immersed in the method; the children "owned" the problem, truly cared about it, and had a deep desire to resolve it.

After experiencing the success of this introductory inquiry episode, Mr. Kurzinsky offered many other opportunities for scientific investigation. The children wanted to collect pet data from other classes to see if it agreed with theirs. But this venture raised some important issues: "Must we poll every child in school?" Mr. Kurzinsky's young social scientists thought it would be wise to use some type of sampling strategy instead. Perhaps they might interview every third child who moved through the lunch line at noon? If so, they decided it would be best to have an equal boy/girl distribution and decided to alternate every third boy, every third girl, and so on. As that suggestion became too complicated, Artis suggested they might want to randomly select 50 pet owners from the general grade-level population by drawing names out of a hat (not quite in those exact words, however).

Inquiry capitalizes on young social scientists' needs and desires to figure something out by themselves.

The students continued to debate this point quite exhaustively, for they were very determined to make certain that their survey data were gathered from a fair, representative sample of the larger population.

The children went on to carry out constructive inquiries on a variety of other "favorites"—fruit, shoe, crayon color, birthday present, Halloween costume, book, and even presidential candidate. Thus, Mr. Kurzinsky reinforced the idea that the most valuable investigations are those that develop spontaneously; teachers must learn to recognize these natural opportunities and value their impact on children's learning.

Content-Focused Constructivist Inquiry

There are many ways to introduce students to inquiry in social studies; no single approach can or should be considered universally appropriate. It does seem apparent, however, that there is some type of developmental continuum through which teachers can move students until they reach the point where they are able to search out and discover content-focused knowledge for themselves. That continuum begins with interesting classroom mini-museums, moves on to focused personal investigations, and ultimately includes opportunities for students to take part in active investigations through which they construct and represent subject matter concepts.

Both process skills and content knowledge become critical as teachers move children toward instructional episodes, for both are hallmarks of capable social scientists. The processes the children will use to accomplish this goal are quite similar to those an actual social scientist uses while studying important questions, issues, or problems. Children will learn to identify and refine questions about key issues, collect and analyze information from various resources, and discover new information or construct new concepts. And, as a social scientist might write and publish a paper on her or his findings, children will make their results known to others in a fitting manner.

How Global is the Curriculum
Go to MyEducationLab, select the topic Teaching Strategies, watch the video entitled "Field Trip," and complete the questions that accompany it.

Most inquiry episodes are carried out in accord with the broad-based suggestions that follow. Of course, teachers will need to modify any procedure as the age, skills, and interests of their children dictate. However, the acquisition of content-focused inquiry skills will assist students not only in dealing with everyday life problems but also in refining the problem-solving, decision-making, and research skills that are essential for discharging the duties of the office of citizen in our contributory democracy.

Formulating Key Problems, Issues, or Questions

To begin, students must meet an attention-grabbing problem in order for content-focused inquiry to work. The problem should hold a high degree of mystery and intrigue, for children find it difficult to attach themselves to anything they do not care about. One youngster's reaction to a teacher who passed out a list of 12 topics related to the Civil War and directed the students to select one to work on for a written research report was uninspired, to say the least: "Social studies can be so boring when the teacher makes you do research on stuff you don't even care about!"

What *are* good social studies problems? Obviously, the best are those that arouse interest. Herein lies the real crux of inquiry: "How can I find out just what it is that my students are interested in?" First and foremost, students will become interested if they are able to connect themselves to the problem; they must be certain that the problems they come across are worth thinking about. The problems must be clear, understandable, and meaningful, and involve a high degree of mystery. Additionally, the problem must lie within the students' range of ability, offering just the proper amount of intrigue to challenge previously established ideas, but not so much that it is either too easy or too difficult to understand. If the problem is too difficult, students will be intimidated by it; they have too little or no background knowledge to help make sense of it. By contrast, if the problem can be easily unraveled with information the students already have, it is obviously not a challenge and the students will quickly discard it.

Teachers have a crucial role in creating the spirit to solve a problem. One of their most important functions is to perform as models, thinking aloud about

fascinating things and exhibiting the behaviors they would like to see used by their students. They ask questions: "What's going on here? What do we need to know more about?" They prompt students to ask similar questions. Teachers must show they are open to new experiences. Students welcome teachers who reach out for the different and unusual—teachers who look at life with passion. Teachers stop, look, and listen; they feel, taste, and smell. They ask, "What is it? Where does it come from? What is it for?" They perform their own absorbing classroom investigations and, through their passion for new discoveries, offer the greatest form of encouragement to their students. We must do our best in dynamic social studies programs to nurture curiosity for life; one of the best ways to do this is to be a teacher who responds to the world with a probing, wondering mind and regularly proposes, "What do you think? Let's find out!" The discovery of solutions to problems is usually accompanied by a strong feeling of delight. This is what drives people to explore and investigate: It feels good!

The problem, often stated as a question, is the initial spark for further investigation. This first step of the inquiry process is very important, because only when the students experience a felt need to confront the problem, will they be stimulated to move on and search for a solution. In general, there are two fundamental sources of problems to set off inquiry episodes in dynamic social studies classrooms: (1) problems sparked by a teacher and (2) problems proposed by the students. It is hard to tell when either source is most powerful, but an interesting consideration can be associated with the professional responsibilities of actual social scientists during the early part of their careers. Many report that during their first research assignments the majority of the research questions were created by supervisors or more advanced coworkers. Their job was to assemble and assess information in a competent way until they were ultimately entrusted to design their own questions. Could teacher-sparked questions, then, be a useful way to set off content-focused inquiry in social studies classrooms?

During the earliest stages of content-focused inquiry, a personal need to know will often be effectively created by a teacher's attention-grabbing question or problem. Steve Nafe, for example, initiated an inquiry into tropical rain forests by first having his fifth-graders read Tim Knight's fascinating book about what to wear and what to expect when traveling to the world's rain forests—*Journey into the Rainforest* (Oxford University Press). After assisting them to process key information from the book, Mr. Nafe showed the class an official-looking letter from the director of a zoo. It seems the zoo was planning to redesign its rain forest exhibit and was looking for input about how the lives of the plants and animals of the rain forest are entwined. Could the class please consider developing a guide book that would be used by visitors to the zoo describing this aspect of the rain forest? This was all it took to launch Mr. Nafe's students into something they really wanted to learn about.

As students participate in similar teacher-initiated inquiry experiences, their own curiosities will begin to inspire forthcoming investigations. Maybelle Page, for example, had just finished reading Lynne Cherry's heartrending picture book *The Great Kapok Tree* (Harcourt Brace). In this story, a number of Amazon rain forest animals plead with a woodcutter not to destroy their home. Each appeal presents a scientifically accurate and convincing case for preserving our natural environment. The message of this preservationist book was clear: "Save the rain forest!" The open discussion that followed the book-reading experience focused squarely on that message; students talked about plight of the animals in the book as well as a wide variety of other animals in danger of disappearing forever—the giant panda, the green sea turtle, and the African elephant, for example. Their main concern had to do with the human actions that have endangered the earth's wildlife, largely by destroying natural habitats. The children's interest in the topic was well indicated by the number of spontaneous questions they raised: "When are certain animals considered endangered?" "What animals are regarded as endangered today?" "What caused the extinction of animals in the past?" "How are humans a threat to animals?" "Are there any laws to protect endangered animals?" "What are some ways we can help protect endangered animals?"

"Those are quite interesting questions," observed Ms. Page as she hastily recorded each on a large sheet of chart paper. "Now, wouldn't it be great to know the answers?" For the next week or two, students looked up information in the classroom, the library, and on the Internet, and even took it upon themselves to search for all they could on their own at home in the evening. Having generated their own questions for inquiry, the students couldn't stop looking for answers until they were satisfied they had done all they could. So, Ms. Page capitalized on a deep personal concern and used the students' questions as a base for initiating an inquiry into the ways human beings have affected the planet's fragile ecosystem. Using this most basic self-initiated course of action, Ms. Page's students personified what it means to operate as natural social scientists.

Teachers must support their students as autonomous investigators whether the question is student initiated or teacher initiated. Regardless of the source, there are several factors that help determine the quality of the questions designed to initiate student inquiry:

- *Most importantly, the question should be something the children are sincerely interested in.* Addressing good questions about things of interest is the heart of effective lifelong thinking.
- *The answer is open to investigation.* It cannot result in obtaining a simple fact such as, "Who designed the first American flag?" The question must engage students in finding answers or solutions by conducting meaningful research: "Did Betsy Ross really make the first U.S. flag?"
- *The question should have a clear focus.* The question should be unambiguous so that the students will have a clear direction of where to proceed with their research. For example, the question "What is government?" is much too broad. Where would a student start? The question could be refined by breaking it up into several smaller questions such as, "What do we consider to be the five most important government documents in the history of the United States?"

Generating Hypotheses

Once the problem is understood by the students and accepted as interesting and worthwhile, they are ready for action; it is now time to work toward a solution. I hesitate to use the word *hypothesis* to explain what is done during this component of the inquiry process because many future teachers feel intimidated by such jargon, thinking that such a big word most certainly entails some sort of complicated activity. But, for elementary school students, the hypothesis is simply an "educated guess" or a "feeling," "prediction," "hunch," or "suspicion" based on partial evidence. You can help your students come up with a hypothesis by asking questions such as these: "What do you already know about this situation? What have you already learned that we might be able to use now? How could this information help us come up with an answer to our problem? What ideas can you suggest as a solution based on what we've just discussed?" The purpose of these questions is to help students attach information they already know to the problem.

Formulating hypotheses involves a certain amount of risk for students, so you must be especially careful to attach importance to each individual's input. It is easy for teachers to acknowledge hypotheses they might agree with or those that they think might be "sensible." However, responding to incomplete or unusual suggestions is not quite as easy. Remember that the students' ideas are nothing more than presumptions, so you don't want students to drop out of the rest of the process because they feel rejected. Honor all responses by offering comments and/or questions such as these:

- "I heard you say . . ."
- "What I believe you are telling me is . . ."
- "That is a very interesting idea. I never thought of it that way."
- "You have an intriguing idea, but I'm a bit confused. Could you enlarge on it a bit?"
- What if I told you (add some information)? How would that change your hypothesis?

Definitive solutions and opportunities to accept or reject hypotheses will come as students go on to gather and analyze data. The main purpose of making hypotheses is to steer the students as they enter into the next phase of the inquiry process: *data gathering*.

Gathering the Data

During the data-gathering phase, students initiate an active search for information that helps find an answer for, solution to, or explanation about that which they are curious. What resources are available? Where can they be found? As students answer these questions, they embark on the process of gathering and assessing the information they will require to answer the question or resolve the problem. In most elementary school classrooms, research is conducted in either of three major ways: library research, descriptive research, and historical research.

Library Research. *Library research*, perhaps the most common source of information for inquiry-based questions and problems, includes materials such as encyclopedias, informational books, computers, magazines, newspapers, pamphlets, almanacs, catalogs, dictionaries, travel brochures, atlases, guides and timetables, posters, films, videos, photographs, and even the phone book. Library research also embraces Internet research, especially the World Wide Web. The Internet provides practically instant information on almost every topic the children will be studying. Surfing through the wealth of educational sites on the Web is fun and can be instructive as students follow links from page to page hoping to uncover useful information. But surfing can also be overwhelming when young children seek out focused information. Therefore, it would be wise to encourage appropriate use of "child-specific" search engines such as Ask Jeeves for Kids (http://ajkids.com), which allows students to search for information by asking broad questions. Or you might furnish reference links on the Internet start page to get the young researchers moving in the right direction. Other child-friendly search engines include:

42eXplore by Topic
ALA | Great Web Sites for Kids
AOL@SCHOOL
Awesome Library—K–12 Education Directory

School librarians know the Web well, so you will find excellent results when you check with your library personnel. It must also be emphasized that inquiry-oriented instruction does not necessarily preclude the use of textbooks as important information sources, too, for even textbooks can do much to enliven the spirit of inquiry.

How Global is the Curriculum *Go to MyEducationLab, select the topic Teaching Strategies, watch the video entitled "Experiential Learning," and complete the questions that accompany it.*

The students must carefully examine each resource to determine its helpfulness in addressing the research question and then remove any unnecessary or redundant information. What is left should be organized into a rough draft or information summary chart that will serve as an outline for the final product: "How does this information help answer my research question?" "How does it relate to what I already know?" Does it support my hypotheses?" "What new questions does it raise?"

Descriptive Research. *Descriptive research* helps students uncover important information about the question under study by seeking answers to the questions *who, what, when, where,* and *how*. There are several different types of descriptive research but the three most useful in elementary school classrooms are observational research, surveys, and interviews.

Observational research can include all the experiences through which students observe, handle, participate in, or try out genuine objects or events. For example, while investigating significant Native American Indian cultural traditions, one class visited a display of authentic Native American Indian arrowheads, beaded items, pottery, stone artifacts, and other items from the past. An outing to the commuter train station to observe the "crunch" of rush hour is also considered observational research, as is a field trip to the water-powered grist mill where grain was ground to the customer's order, and a classroom visit by a Civil War reenactor.

Survey research, discussed earlier in this chapter, consists of a series of questions designed to ascertain the feelings or beliefs people hold about a question or problem. The first responsibility in conducting a survey is to design clear, understandable survey questions. Next, the students must decide if they want to ask the questions orally and record responses on a notepad or whether they want to construct a paper questionnaire and hand it out to be completed privately. Then, the students must agree if they should ask the questions to their classmates, all the classes at the same grade level, randomly selected students from the entire school, students in the school band, support staff at school, adults in their neighborhood, or teachers at the school. After collecting the data, the students must then organize and analyze it. The most common way elementary school children organize and display survey information is by making large, chart-size bar graphs or picture graphs. But, many tech-savvy teachers like to select from among the free graph-making tools available online. The students culminate the survey process by presenting the results of their research to an authentic audience.

Interviews can be a productive way of acquiring useful information about almost any question or problem. Interviewees bring both a depth of information and the power of personal experience to a story that makes it attention-grabbing and realistic. Just about every child has seen an interview carried out on television, and they will clearly welcome the opportunity to try to do what a reporter does. It would be wise to have your children review their knowledge of interviews and together discuss the processes involved in conducting an actual interview. The steps are presented here.

1. *Preparing for the Interview.* Be sure to research the topic to be discussed. Then make a list of questions to get more in-depth information about the topic under study. Questions should focus on *who, what, when, why,* and *how,* but those requiring simple "yes" or "no" answers should be avoided. The questions should be reexamined; redundant or ineffective questions should be discarded and those remaining should be logically ordered. Be sure to set up a mutually convenient time for the interview and inform the interviewee how the information will be used.
2. *Conducting the Interview.* Greet the interviewee warmly and make sure she or he is comfortable. (Sometimes, however, it is necessary or more convenient to conduct the interview over the telephone or in an alternative electronic format.) If conducting the interview in person, it is helpful to tape record or video record the session. Be sure to get the interviewee's permission to tape it, however. Ask the questions in a conversational style

instead of mechanically reading them word for word. The interviewee's interesting ideas and insights may lead to extra questions, or follow-up questions might be needed to explain points that are not clear. Be sure to treat the interviewee with respect; always pay attention to what is being said, do not interrupt, and be careful not to push the interviewee into answering a question if she or he appears uncomfortable. Finally, be sure to thank the person for participating in the interview.

3. *Sharing the Results of the Interview.* Students often think their work is over once they complete the interview, but they are only part way finished. Now is the time to check all the information and pull it all together in a meaningful way. Will they now write a story? Compose a newspaper article? Make an oral presentation to another class or even a community group? Regardless of choice, a copy should be shared with the interviewee not only to make sure everything is accurate but also because the interviewee will be pleased to see the finished product.

Historical Research. When children delve into conditions of "long ago," they must gather and evaluate relevant traces of the past. *Historical research* is the process of searching for answers to questions about the past by examining and interpreting such evidence as artifacts, diaries, newspapers, pictures, letters, music, oral history, advertisements, or speeches. The student's job is to find evidence, analyze it, and use it to create an explanation of past events. Sadly, however, their explanations often end up as a pointless outline of dates, names, and events. Social studies teachers expect more than this; they want their students to carry out research in such a way that historical facts come to life and gain personal meaning through the construction of new ideas. Ideas to accomplish this goal were detailed in Chapter 4; please refer to that portion of the book if you need to refresh relevant understandings. For now, however, students should think about using historical research when they have these kinds of questions for inquiry:

- What happened?
- When did it happen?
- Why did it happen?
- To whom did it happen?
- What did it mean to the people at that time?
- What does it mean to people today?
- What do historians have to say about what happened?

Organizing and Analyzing the Data

At this point in the inquiry process, students are faced with the challenge of organizing the information and deriving some meaning from it. In essence, they ask themselves, "What do all of these data mean to me?" They have located information related to the question, and now must examine and group the information

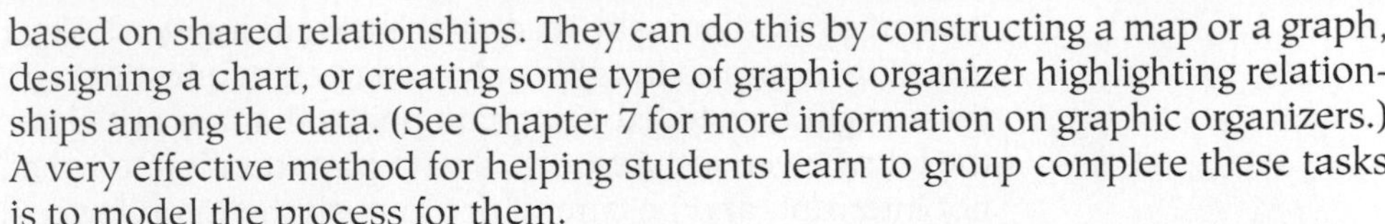

based on shared relationships. They can do this by constructing a map or a graph, designing a chart, or creating some type of graphic organizer highlighting relationships among the data. (See Chapter 7 for more information on graphic organizers.) A very effective method for helping students learn to group complete these tasks is to model the process for them.

This next-to-final stage of the inquiry process is a time for reflection—looking back at the problem or question, revisiting the hypotheses, studying the data gathering effort, and making observations: "Has a solution or an answer been found?" Do new questions come to light?" This is a major task of the inquiry process and teachers must be prepared to help the students through it.

Sharing Results

How Global is the Curriculum
Go to MyEducationLab, select the topic Teaching Strategies, watch the video entitled "Inquiry Learning," and complete the questions that accompany it.

The final step of an inquiry episode is sharing the results with an authentic audience by using appropriate vehicles of communication. In the adult world, much of the satisfaction gained from research comes from having an impact on desired audiences; professors of education experience great pleasure after receiving approval from their peers while delivering a speech about their research into a revolutionary new instructional approach, and medical researchers are thankful for the recognition they receive from other health care professionals after publishing a paper describing a new treatment for some difficult-to-control disease. Each of these individuals appreciates the resulting respect for their research labors and experiences an immeasurable amount of inner satisfaction for their accomplishments. Likewise, young learners take pleasure and pride in the recognition they receive after sharing the results of their research with an authentic audience.

Keep in mind that sharing authentic research goes beyond the traditional formal written report by engaging children in varieties of communication possibilities—oral presentations, graphic representations, photographs, audio- or videotapes, debates, dramatic skits, bulletin board displays, and a variety of other forms. A special area of interest that has contributed greatly to social studies programs today has been the use of *hypermedia*, a communications tool that combines video, graphics, animation, and text. Known also as *presentation software*, hypermedia authoring programs enable students to organize and communicate information in innovative and thought-provoking ways, accessing and integrating information from such diverse sources as the Internet, sounds or clip art pulled from public domain software, photographs from a digital camera or scanner, and clips from a video camera or a CD-ROM. Three widely used presentation software programs are Microsoft's *PowerPoint*, Google's *Google Presentations* (docs.google.com), HyperStudio, ClarisWorks, and, especially for the younger set, the SlideShow portion of KidPix. These are not the only hypermedia tools available to teachers and students, but they are excellent possibilities.

Lifelong learners get their start in elementary school social studies classrooms as teachers arouse curiosity for stimulating problems and propel their students into research to obtain answers. The resulting outcomes lead to the intellectual independence we so often find in lifelong learners.

These students are looking at a display of written and drawn stories that a group investigating the lives of the Lakota Sioux had composed as a way to share what they had learned.

Two classroom examples of inquiry-based learning will now be presented. Examine each carefully, for they represent the diverse ways that inquiry is commonly practiced by different teachers. The first example is launched from a problem initiated by the students. The second emerges from a situation contrived by the teacher. Notice that the first vignette illustrates a spontaneous, less formal approach to inquiry, whereas the second follows the steps of the inquiry process much more deliberately. These examples show that sometimes a question will arise from the class and the teacher must be alert and sensitive to seize such opportunities when they occur. Other opportunities for carefully planned, full-scale inquiry lessons can be planned by teachers to get the inquiry process rolling. Both approaches are important components of quality social studies programs. Besides their ability to provoke curiosity and wonder, they each do much to help students understand how knowledge is produced.

"Spontaneous" Inquiry Example

At present, the Clarksville Senior Center has a serene new flower garden—thanks to Debra Wood's fifth graders. While visiting the center in early autumn to bring gifts of potted chrysanthemums they had started from seeds as a science project a few weeks earlier, the students noticed that an area between the main building and a shed looked desolate and depressing.

Subsequent to returning to the classroom, the students asked Ms. Wood if they could do something to improve the area. After much discussion, the class eventually decided on a flower garden. "A garden is so restful and peaceful," explained Jana. "Yeah," added Vance, "a garden could even bring back memories of World War II victory gardens."

Ms. Wood is an avid gardener and the president of the largest local garden club. She invited several members of the club to visit the class to recommend plants that would need a minimum amount of upkeep in their hot and dry climate. The garden club donated the flowers for the children's project and offered advice to the children as they cleaned up the area and planted the flowers. A parent who owned a landscaping company wanted to help, too, so the students dressed the flower area with his donated mulch. The class then solicited other local businesses for help; several chipped in to help as the garden expanded beyond their wildest dreams. A retired carpenter volunteered his time and expertise to make benches. A local lumberyard supplied the gravel and decorative block for a patio where the beautiful wooden benches now rest. An individual donor contributed a birdbath and feeder. In addition, the students took up a collection for a butterfly bush that added to the overall ambiance of the garden.

NCSS STANDARDS

III. *People, Places, and Environments*
V. *Individuals, Groups, and Institutions*
X. *Civic Ideals and Practice*

The garden is wheelchair accessible, a definite plus for seniors with restricted mobility. The senior adults are now responsible for the general upkeep of the garden and have passionately accepted that responsibility. "It gives them something to take pride in," explains Ms. Wood. "Some senior adults like the tranquility of the garden and will sit on the benches and reminisce. Others find the garden a great place to socialize. I'm so glad the students thought of this wonderful idea."

One child's response to the project is shown in Figure 9.3.

"Planned" Inquiry Example

Heidi Vonder's sixth-grade class had been working at the sand table (borrowed from the kindergarten classroom) digging up and brushing off replicas of artifacts their teacher had hidden beneath the soil she had substituted for the kindergartners' sand. Acting as "apprentice archaeologists," the students divided the surface of the site into squares with grids made from yarn. Then they carefully removed the soil from their own section, layer by layer, to dig up the remains from an unknown past civilization. As they dug, students deliberately recorded the exact location of everything they found. Jenny uncovered what looked like an old coin. She examined it closely and searched for any information that might tell her where the coin might have been from. She observed what she thought was a likeness of a Roman emperor wearing a laurel crown. The word *AUGUSTUS* was printed above the likeness. "Hmmm," reflected Jenny, "Where could this coin be from?"

NCSS STANDARDS

I. *Culture*
II. *Time, Continuity, and Change*

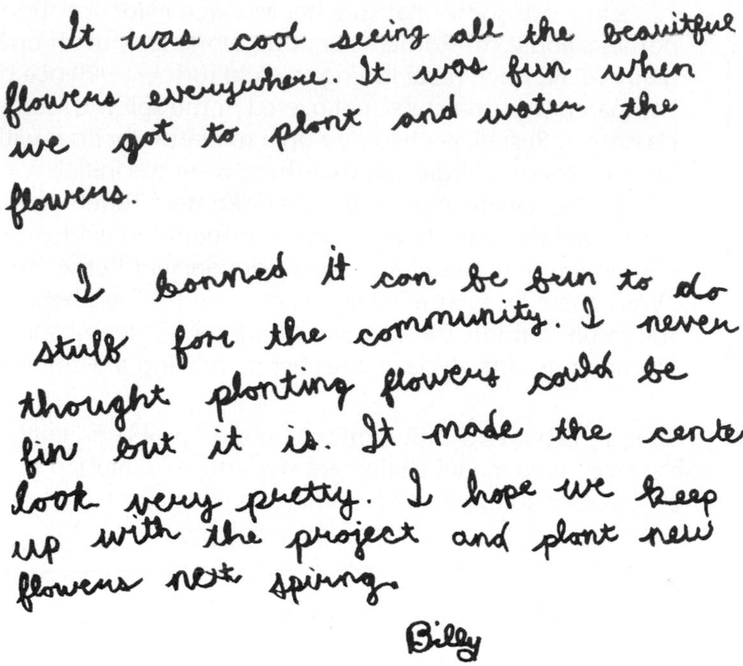

It was cool seeing all the beauitfue flowers everywhere. It was fun when we got to plont and water the flowers.

I lonned it con be fun to do stuff fore the community. I never thought plonting flowers could be fun but it is. It made the center look very pretty. I hope we keep up with the project and plant new flowers next spiring.

Billy

FIGURE 9.3 Student's Reaction Letter

"That's it! I'll prove to Ms. Vonder that this mystery coin is from ancient Rome!" The excitement in Jenny's voice was as clear as the pleasure reflected in her face. She saw what she believed to be a Roman emperor wearing a head decoration that looked like leaves. Based on this observation, Jenny guessed that the coin could have come from ancient Rome. So, Jenny deftly formulated a reasonable hypothesis while observing the coin and deliberately searching for any clues that she might associate with previous experiences.

Jenny next used an indirect observation strategy to gather data for the purpose of testing her hypothesis. She searched through a series of reference books arranged beforehand by her teacher and learned about the history of Roman coins. She also consulted an electronic encyclopedia available on the classroom computer. She found that Roman coins were decorated with the likeness of the emperor in power at the time. She also discovered that laurel crowns were used to adorn emperors and also that the title *AUGUSTUS* was given to the popular Roman leader Octavian when he succeeded Julius Caesar following his death at the hands of Brutus. There was no date on the coin, but Jenny compared her information about Roman coins and emperors with what was on the coin she uncovered and made an educated guess that this coin was made in Rome between 31 BC and AD 14.

Jenny was somewhat sure her research evidence supported her initial hypothesis about the Roman coin, but, working with an open mind, she stood ready to alter her initial feelings should further evidence demand it. She compared the artifact she uncovered in the soil with something found by a classmate, Russell. He had dug up a miniature banner with the letters *SPQR*. Russell's research indicated that these were the initials for Latin words translated, "The senate and the people of Rome." Together, Jenny and Russell concluded that they had enough corroborating evidence to substantiate a contention that these items were from ancient Rome. The question was, "Were these artifacts from Rome, or were they left behind in foreign lands as the result of trade, travel, war, or migration?" Jenny and Russell would await the findings of their classmates before making a definitive conclusion.

Inquiry is but one important variation of problem-centered learning. Another problem-centered model challenges students to explore problems and to generate novel, creative solutions, rather than conclusions based on hard data. We will refer to this model as creative problem solving.

Creative Problem Solving (CPS)

We once saw a tyrannosaurus.
And we feared he'd end our lives faurus.
But, "Look!" said my friend,
"He's rubber, can bend!"
Then we realized we were in Toysaurus.

My son Jeff wrote this limerick in elementary school as part of an integrated thematic unit on dinosaurs. His teacher sent the poem home along with a note telling us that she felt the limerick was remarkably creative. Of course, Jeff's "impartial" parents thought likewise and displayed it proudly in the middle of the refrigerator door. What do you think of Jeff's limerick? Would you say it is creative? If so, what makes it creative? If not, you've just failed this course (only kidding)!

Creative Thinking

What do we mean by *creativity*? Like other inner-directed, deeply personal phenomena such as love, patriotism, or intelligence, the term *creativity* means different things to different people and is virtually impossible to define precisely. However, most definitions of creativity include two major components:

- *Novel or Original Behavior.* Behavior that has not been learned from anyone else; it is fresh, new, and unique.
- *An Appropriate and Productive Result.* Coming up with a suitable or worthwhile product or an effective solution to a problem.

How does Jeff's poem reflect these two components? Is it fresh and original or did he get the idea from somewhere else? Is it an appropriate response to the teacher's assignment to write a limerick about the dinosaurs they had been studying?

What prompts some children to create in such engaging ways, while others struggle to move beyond the ordinary? Although a certain degree of intelligence is helpful, something more is required. In Jeff's case, that "something more" was the ability to "play" with ideas—to see things in a new way. Identifying what that something more might be has been debated over the years, but consensus seems to exist that an individual's creativity is influenced by the intermingling of four cognitive traits: fluency, flexibility, originality, and elaboration:

- *Fluency* is the ability to produce a large number of ideas. The child who responds to "What things are crops?" with "Wheat, corn, beans, peas, and tomatoes" is more fluent than the child who responds "Wheat and corn."
- *Flexibility* is the ability to produce a number of different categories of responses. The child who responds to "What things are crops?" with "Wheat, tomatoes, apples, peanuts, and tobacco" is a more flexible thinker than the child who responds "Wheat, rye, oats, and barley (all grains)."
- *Originality* is the ability to produce unusual or clever responses. The child who responds to "What can you do with an empty cereal box?" with "Make a snowshoe out of it" is more original than the child who says "Store things in it." Originality is usually determined statistically; the response is considered original if it is offered by less than 10 percent of those responding.
- *Elaboration* is the ability to expand on a simple idea to make it richer. The child who responds to a teacher's request to draw a picture of the geographical area where the Sioux lived with a simple landscape drawing shows less elaboration than the child who includes buffalo, tipis, and Sioux farmers working in the fields.

If we hope to help students enhance their creativity in dynamic social studies classrooms, we need to examine the kinds of classroom activities and practices that are supportive of creativity. Certainly, a major responsibility of social studies instruction is teaching the content, and, up to now in this text, we have examined various ways to challenge students to explore and discover new information. However, creativity takes knowledge a step further; it "puts knowledge to work." Creativity allows students to express and use what they know in unique ways. The remainder of this chapter examines how the content of social studies relates to creativity and the processes of thinking creatively.

Creative Problem Solving in Dynamic Social Studies Classrooms

Perhaps the oldest and most widely used strategy to support creative thinking in social studies classrooms is the *creative problem solving (CPS)* model developed by Alex Osborn (1963) and Sidney J. Parnes (1981) during the 1960s and 1970s. To

understand CPS, it would be instructive to contrast it with what we now know about inquiry. Remember that the goal of inquiry is to systematically search for facts and information to answer questions or solve problems. Some students do this well; they sort out the clues, pull them together, look for patterns, and deliberately arrive at valid conclusions. Others, however, attack problems in quite different ways. This variation of a well-known story helps illustrate the difference between the two:

> An engineering major and an elementary education major were hiking in the woods when they came across a grizzly bear. Both were terrified and quickly began to search for an escape route, each in her/his own way.
>
> The engineering major took out his pocket calculator and quickly computed the mathematical differential between his speed and the bear's. His face turned ashen as he stared at the results.
>
> The elementary education major simply took off her hiking boots, opened her backpack, slipped on a pair of jogging shoes, and took off.
>
> "Boy, you are WRONG," the engineering major yelled to the elementary education major as she sprinted down the trail. "My calculations show you can't outrun a grizzly bear!"
>
> "I don't have to," the elementary education major shouted back. "I only have to outrun YOU!"

This story demonstrates how two people can respond very differently to the same problem. The two response categories in this example are generally referred to as *systematic* (the engineering major who relied on facts and logical thought) and *intuitive* (the elementary education major who relied on gut feelings and intuition). Original, creative solutions to problems come from an ability to shift directions in thought—to move beyond the obvious to the subtle. Some would say that the elementary education major's solution was more creative than the engineering major's. Do you agree? What made it so? Regardless of whether you are trying to figure out how to study for an exam when your friends want you to go to a movie or where to get money for next year's tuition hike, you are likely to rely on one of those cognitive styles.

Traditionally, most schoolwork has called for systematic rather than intuitive thinking, so we find that schools tend to overemphasize logic-related skills at the expense of intuitive-related skills, giving our children an apparently "lopsided" education. Teaching for creativity does not minimize the importance of a solid background of information; creativity in social studies is more likely to occur when students have mastered the content. Neither interesting problems nor their solutions often pop up without having substantial background knowledge. Teresa M. Amabile (1989) emphasizes this partnership in her acclaimed model of creativity. Her model has three components; in order for creativity to occur, all three must be in place:

1. *Domain Knowledge and Skills.* This component includes the technical skills and content needed to solve a given problem. A student who is to design a creative problem or make a creative contribution in geography, for example, will need to know something about geography. Creative ideas do not spring forth from a vacuum.
2. *Creative Thinking and Working Skills.* Knowledge is but one component of creative thinking, but is not sufficient by itself. Creative thinking and working skills add that "something extra" that forms the creative personality. The four cognitive traits of creativity described earlier explain the kinds of thinking abilities that help students take new perspectives on problems and come up with unusual ideas. These are required for creative ideas.
3. *Intrinsic Motivation.* Intrinsic motivation comes from within the person, not from an outside source. Intrinsically motivated students enjoy the pleasure and satisfaction of the work itself, not the external recognition or reward.

The Creative Problem-Solving Model

The original CPS model is comprised of six steps, each driving the creative process. That model works well with high school students and adults, but I prefer a simplified three-step method for elementary school students. A unique feature is that each of these steps, in turn, involves both a *divergent phase* during which students generate lots of ideas and a *convergent phase* during which they select only the most promising idea(s) for further exploration.

The divergent phase of each CPS step makes use of brainstorming strategies. Brainstorming is an appropriate strategy when you want to generate a large number of ideas, particularly new and original ones. In traditional brainstorming, students work in groups of three to five members with a recorder to keep track of ideas and an encourager to monitor the rules. The basic ground rules that help students brainstorm were discussed in Chapter 7. You (and your students) should become familiar with them because they are an integral component of the CPS approach.

The three steps of CPS are outlined here; an example of how they might be implemented in a dynamic social studies classroom will follow.

The Mess. This step involves saying all that can be said about a problem situation—factual statements as well as feelings. For example, Lalitha Amani created a pretend community environmental tragedy as shown in Figure 9.4. She divided her class into five-member groups and asked each group to stand in line in front of charts that were taped at even intervals around the room. The first student in line was to write a word, short phrase, or statement about the "mess" in which the community found itself. These can be factual statements or feelings

FIGURE 9.4 Environmental Pollution Problem

Timberland is a small village in rural Forest County with a population of just over 5,000. It is a friendly place to live with characteristics common to most villages—homes, stores, places to worship, restaurants, a movie theater, service stations, schools, government, and a few miscellaneous businesses. People are genuinely happy with their lives in Timberland, but a problem of great concern has surfaced recently and has grown in scope during the past year.

The problem is how to capture what the village residents describe as a "new breed of vermin"—illegal garbage dumpers. Village officials have identified 17 illegal dumpsites in the 85,000-acre forest that surrounds Timberland. They have noticed rubbish and junk accumulating along the roadsides, stream banks, and hollows.

The problem has grown in part because communities surrounding Timberland have grown in size the past few years and there is more and more rubbish to dispose of. The Departments of Sanitation of these communities have been overworked and the local landfill is nearly filled to capacity, so each household is limited to the removal of two trash containers per week.

Hoping to help solve the problem, the local Unspoiled Forest Club organized a campaign that prompted the village government to post signs threatening fines or possible arrests for those caught dumping junk illegally. The junk piles kept spreading, however, and the forest faces the danger of becoming an unhealthy eyesore.

The condition of the forest is a topic of daily conversation among the residents of Timberland. Some have suggested that more drastic actions be taken toward the solution of their problem.

about the issue. Basically, the students were advised not to hold back, for everything about the problem should be said whether they think it fits or not. In turn, the rest of the students rotated to the chart, writing as quickly as they could the things they knew, felt, or thought about the "mess." Some groups wrote in excess of 20 entries in the 5 minutes allotted for this task. This was the divergent phase.

Examining each list, Ms. Imani directed the students to talk together and converge on one item that "bugs" them most or seems to capture the situation best. Each group then rewrote the selection as a problem statement. The Osborn/Parnes model suggests that the problem statement begin with an "IWWMW. . . . ?" phrase, or "<u>I</u>n <u>w</u>hat <u>w</u>ays <u>m</u>ight <u>w</u>e . . . ?" For example, if a concern about the unspoiled magnificence of the forestland was the most troublesome aspect for one group, its problem statement might read, "In what ways might we control the junk that is being dumped in the forest?" If health concerns were the most worrisome facet for another group, it might write, "In what ways might we avoid infestation by dangerous vermin and avoid contagious diseases?"

Idea Finding. This step involves brainstorming dozens of possible remedies for the problem. What are all the possible ways to address the problem statement? Using a clean sheet of chart paper and employing the same "relay" strategy as they used in the previous section, Ms. Imani encouraged the students to write whatever came to mind, even if it seemed to have nothing to do with a solution at this time. No idea would be critiqued until after all ideas had been written down. The students then looked over their lists and determined which one or two ideas might best be made into an interesting solution. The students considered all possible ways that the tentative solution might be elaborated on or improved. The convergent phase of this step required the groups to restate the problem and narrow down the lists of suggestions by addressing such concerns as Will this idea actually solve the problem? Will it create new problems? What are the chances it will work? Is it practical? Will we be able to use it in the near future? What are the strengths and weaknesses? Can any of the ideas be combined into one useful solution? After narrowing their lists, each group works toward an agreed-on decision. The ultimate choice might contain one idea or a combination of ideas.

Ms. Imani prodded the students' thinking with thought-provoking questions such as these:

- *New Ideas*
  Can it be used in new ways as it is?
  Can it be put to other uses if it is changed in some way?
- *Adaptation*
  What else is like this?
  What other idea does this make us think of?
  What new twist could we add to the idea?
  Could we change the color, shape, sound, or odor?
- *Enlargement*
  What can we add?
  Should we make it longer, wider, heavier, faster, more numerous, or thicker?
- *Condensation*
  What can we take away?
  Should we make it smaller, shorter, narrower, lighter, slower, or thinner?
- *Substitution*
  What else can we use to do the same thing?
  What other materials or ingredients might we use?

One group suggested making big signs such as "*Spruce* Up Around Here!" (*Spruce* was their play on words!) Another thought it would be constructive to establish a community "clean-up" festival. Still a third announced that it would in-

stall surveillance video cameras in secret locations throughout the affected areas with the goal of identifying and prosecuting violators, and forcing them to pay fines or spend time in jail.

Action Planning. This step involves expanding the interesting idea or combining interesting ideas into a statement that outlines an action plan that details the steps necessary to implement the solution: What course of action will we take? Does this plan depend on someone else's approval or support? What steps are needed? Who will do what? When must the steps be completed? The video camera group, for example, suggested that its program would need to be approved by the village council and could be paid for with a grant from the state Department of Environmental Protection.

Three major benefits result when students are involved in CPS in dynamic social studies classrooms: (1) higher feelings of self-confidence, self-esteem, and compassion result; (2) wider exploration of traditional content subjects and skills are undertaken; and (3) higher levels of creative invention in content and skills are used by the students. Therefore, our classrooms must encourage not only the systematic problem-centered efforts associated with inquiry but also the inventive, intuitive thinking associated with creative problem solving.

Creative problems differ from inquiry problems in that they call for divergent thinking as opposed to convergent thinking as students search for solutions to problems. Both types of problems, however, are crucial to today's dynamic social studies classrooms in that they encourage children to dig into things, turn over ideas in their minds, try out alternative solutions, search for new relationships, and struggle for new knowledge.

A Final Thought

It often happens that when the word *research* is mentioned to college students, groans and steely glares accompany the predictable questions: "How long does the paper have to be? How many references do we need? What's the topic?" Exposing students exclusively to this type of forced research often builds negative attitudes toward the processes of problem solving and inquiry. Written reports on teacher-determined topics using secondary sources not only produce downbeat attitudes in students but also present an unrealistic view of research in the real world. Although this kind of research has a place, to present it as the only form of research does students a disservice. We cannot limit elementary school research to such practices either; remember that most elementary school youngsters are natural problem finders. They take pleasure in investigating the mysteries of their world. On their own, they deftly uncover problems of interest—the important first step of research: "Why do farmers cut off the corn and leave the lower part of the plants behind?" "How many ears grow on each corn plant?" What students need at school is to learn the methods through which these questions can be explored. All the particular problems children bring to school may not be particularly significant, but the processes they go through and the feelings they gain about themselves as capable researchers are. Therefore, authentic research associated with creative problem-solving and inquiry processes teaches students that they have the skill and ability to pursue knowledge in a meaningful way and that their efforts have real value now and in the future.

REFERENCES

Amabile, T. M. (1989). *Growing up creative*. New York: Crown.

Dewey, J. (1916). *Democracy and education*. New York: Free Press.

Kohn, A. (1999). *The schools our children deserve*. New York: Houghton Mifflin.

National Council for the Social Studies. (1994). *Curriculum standards for social studies: Expectations for excellence* (Bulletin 89). Washington, DC: Author.

Osborn, A. F. (1963). *Applied imagination: Principles and procedures of creative problem-solving*. New York: Charles Scribner's Sons.

Parnes, S. J. (1981). *The magic of your mind*. Buffalo, NY: Creative Education Foundation and Bearly Limited

PART IV Key Organizational Decisions

CHAPTER 10

Managing Instruction
Planning Lessons and Units

Marge Feeney, a student teacher eager to spread her teaching wings, had spent her first two weeks in Mr. Willmore's third-grade classroom impatiently observing the daily routine, correcting papers, taking lunch count, assisting individuals in need of special help, and getting to know the children. At last, the day she had been longing for had arrived. Marge's cooperating teacher assigned her to teach her first lesson—a social studies lesson! The class had been involved in an interdisciplinary unit on Russia, and the students were having a wonderful time discovering some of the unique aspects of Russian culture. To enrich their understandings, Marge's job was to prepare a lesson about Russian currency. In a twinkling of an eye, her eager anticipation turned to sudden alarm. "Russian currency?" Marge's mind shrieked silently. "Why, I don't know anything about Russian currency! How does Mr. Willmore expect me to teach something I don't have a clue about? Even worse, what kind of activity can I possibly use to teach something I don't know anything about?" Trying to maintain a coolness that wouldn't betray her inner panic, Marge swallowed hard and choked out the words, "I'd love to teach tomorrow's lesson about Russian currency!"

Marge was jolted into a sudden realization that dynamic social studies teachers need a lot of information—much more than they can store in their minds. She learned that to be effective, she must be ready to say many times a day, "I don't know. I'll look it up." So Marge went back to her college library, sat down at a computer, and found a useful website with the information she needed for her lesson.

When she felt comfortable with the content for her lesson, Marge took on the next challenge—finding a developmentally suitable instructional strategy. Because she had only 40 minutes for the entire lesson, Marge was forced to utilize a time-efficient model. Since she was unable to obtain actual Russian currency to show the children, she decided it was best to have the children find related information on an appropriate website and follow it with a game to reinforce the information (www.math.mit.edu/∼igorvp/Russia/Other/Currency/currency.html).

NCSS STANDARDS

I. *Culture*
VII. *Production, Distribution, and Consumption*
IX. *Global Connections*

Mr. Willmore required his student teachers to write very detailed daily plans. "With a plan in place," he advised, "you'll feel better prepared to face the students." Therefore, Marge set to work writing a rough draft detailing the content as well as the step-by-step procedures she intended to carry out during the lesson. After an hour of jotting down and organizing ideas, a lesson finally took shape (see Figure 10.1).

Theme: Russia

Grade: 4

Teacher: Marge Feeney

Long-Term Goal

1. The children will understand the Russian monetary system.

Short-Term Goal

1. The student will identify Russian coins and state their value.
2. The student will solve problems that require the regrouping of kopeks into rubles.

Performance Standards

1. The students will differentiate among various forms of exchange and money.

Materials

1. Duplicate for each of five groups: 1 game card; ten 1-kopek coins, ten 10-kopek coins, and one ruble.
2. One die for each group.
3. A set of four small toys such as a plastic car, box of crayons, ball, and spinning top.

Procedure

1. Divide the class into five groups of four students each.
2. Give each group an envelope containing Russian coin cards and ask them to empty the contents on their table.
3. Ask: "Does anyone know the country these coins are from?" "What are they called?" Have them examine the coin cards, calling special attention to the Cyrillic letters.
4. After the students have made their predictions, direct them to examine the information on the preaccessed website.
5. Explain that the coins depicted on the cards are from Russia and that a ruble is much like the dollar in the United States, a 10-kopek coin is like a dime, and a 1-kopek coin is like a penny. (There are also 2-, 3-, 5-, 15-, 20-, and 50-kopek coins and 3-, 5-, 10-, 25-, and 100-ruble bills.)

6. Invite the students to examine the money for a short period of time. Then introduce them to the Kopek/Ruble Game. In each group:
   a. Players take turns rolling the dice.
   b. Count the sum of the dice and ask for the amount in kopeks.
   c. Take the designated amount of kopeks and place them on the kopek section of the game board.
   d. When a group has 10 kopeks in the first column, it must exchange them for a 10-kopek coin and place it in the second column. When a group has ten 10-kopek coins, it exchanges them for a ruble.
   e. See which team can be first to trade ten 10-kopek coins for a ruble.
7. To bring closure, tell the students that you will show them a small toy and the price of the toy in Russian money. Each child in the group numbers off from one to four. Assign each child a toy and ask him or her to select the duplicated coins necessary to buy the assigned toy. Ask, "What are the important Russian coins and bills?"

Assessment

1. Observe the students during the game to see if they are selecting the appropriate coins and whether the coins have been correctly regrouped.
2. Check to see if each student has selected the correct Russian coins to pay for his or her toy.
3. Students write in their journals about Russian money.

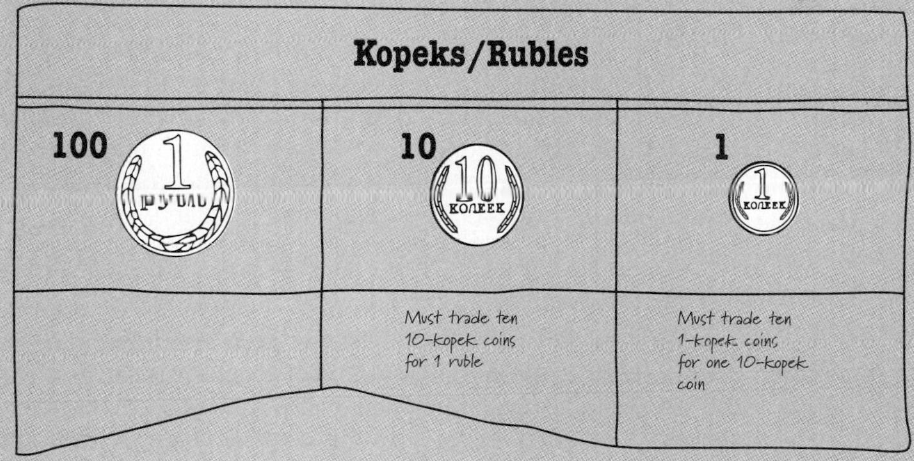

FIGURE 10.1 Continued

Although she had already worked for over an hour on her planning, Marge wasn't close to being finished. "All I have left is to make and collect the game materials and bring together all the other necessary supplies! Who said teaching was easy?" joked Marge.

One could easily see that the growth in confidence Marge experienced from carrying out such a demanding professional challenge far outweighed the hard work she found herself caught up in. "I can do it," acknowledged Marge, "It's not easy, but like 'The Little Engine That Could,' I think I can . . . I think I can do it."

"It worked!" Marge bellowed to no one in particular as she returned from school the next day. "The lesson actually went well. It wasn't perfect, but it went well. I lost my train of thought once or twice, but the lesson plan kept me on track. I had the children explore Russian currency on the website and they learned all about kopeks and rubles. We played the "Kopek/Ruble Game" and they loved it. When they got excited and I told them to calm down, they actually did. I feel like a real teacher, like I'm ready to step in and take over my own classroom. After all the course work, and all the worries, and all the dreaming, I think I'm ready to take the next step."

Why Is Planning Important?

How Global is the Curriculum *Go to MyEducationLab, select the topic Planning Lessons and Units, watch the video entitled "The Importance of Planning," and complete the questions that accompany it.*

Can you imagine a lawyer going to court without a legal summary (brief) of the case? How about a football coach going into the Super Bowl without a game plan? Would you allow a builder to assemble your house without a set of blueprints? And, what could you expect from a financial advisor who fails to set up a well-defined investment plan? I think you would agree that the results in each case would be catastrophic. Yet, whenever the topic of planning for instruction comes up in my methods course, students are likely to whine, complain, gripe, and mutter their most melancholic objection: "Do we *have* to write lesson plans?"

I have found that one of the reasons why so many pre-service teachers underestimate the value of careful planning is that a great portion of their lives has been spent as students in classrooms. From this student-oriented perspective, teaching can look so smooth and effortless that the hours of background preparation and planning are undetectable. However, effective teaching is not a hit-or-miss process; teachers do plan ahead—formally or informally—to create an environment that sets learning in motion. Careful planning brings about such a command of content and mastery of teaching strategies that a well-prepared teacher's actions appear instinctive. This message comes across loud and clear to skeptics who stand in front of the classroom for the first time. They are often shocked to realize that when the spotlight is on them, the classroom (which they saw previously as an orderly domain) suddenly starts spinning with confusion and chaos lurking at every turn.

Luckily, Marge Feeney learned that the framework on which successful social studies teaching rests is deliberate planning. After she experienced just how much the planning process contributed to the success of her Russian currency lesson, active planning became a high priority in Marge's professional life. "Plans help keep me on course—just like a roadmap for a trip, plotting out a sound route to a destination," explains Marge. "A friend of mine went into a lesson stone cold and the whole thing ended up a joke. The kids were bored and confused, and he kept wandering off track. I know my friend learned his lesson. I'm not so naïve to think that a plan in itself guarantees success, but it does give you a good guide for instruction and serves as a record of what should be kept for the future and what should be improved on next time."

To be fair, planning can be a tiring and time-consuming process; however, all good social studies teachers plan their daily lessons. Although experienced teachers will not spend the time and energy writing out the step-by-step, formal plans that you will at this early stage of your career, they nevertheless understand the importance of planning. They think deeply about what needs to be done, even though their efforts may seem unsystematic (for example, jotting down their ideas on a note pad or in the small squares of large weekly planning books). They can record their lesson plans like this because their experience has helped them sense what methods and materials work best in certain situations. You do not yet have these experiences; therefore, you must be much more deliberate in outlining step-by-step plans.

Effective social studies teachers do not teach day to day, but their planning starts at the beginning of the school year when they examine what is expected to be taught during the entire year. They open up the textbook and examine the important topics to be covered. They look at the district curriculum guide for an idea of the concepts and skills that must be mastered. They become familiar with professional, state, and local standards that specify what students should know, understand, and be able to do. These sources are like a steering wheel on a car; they maneuver teachers in the right direction and guide the planning process. The planning process itself is carried out on two different levels. On one level, we have long-range plans called *unit plans* that usually last for about two to three weeks. *Lesson plans* spell out how daily instruction will be carried out. Unit plans describe long-term plans; lesson plans outline short-term or daily plans.

How Are Unit Plans Constructed?

Unit plans contain an orderly sequence of lessons that provide a sense of cohesiveness, or unity, to long-term social studies instruction. The actual design of a unit plan varies from school to school; some are merely a chapter from the textbook supplemented with a few additional activities jotted down in the margins of the instructor's manual, but others are finely detailed outlines for instruction incorporating content and processes from across subject area lines (math, science, literature, creative writing, music, art, and others).

How Global is the Curriculum *Go to MyEducationLab, select the topic Planning Lessons and Units, watch the video entitled "Planning for and Managing Learning Centers," and complete the questions that accompany it.*

Understanding by Design, a book by Grant Wiggins and Jay McTighe (2005), offers a helpful process for planning units called the *backward design*. Their design is considered backward because it reverses the direction teachers normally move in as they plan units. The authors claim that teachers often start the planning process by selecting the materials and activities; then they end with some type of assessment plan. Wiggins and McTighe (2005) explain that such units may be organized around a theme and provide interdisciplinary connections, but questions about the value of the work remain: "To what end is the teaching directed?" "What are the big ideas and important skills to be developed during the unit?" Although the students are participating in loads of activity, there seems to be no clear-cut intellectual goals: What is important here? What is the point?

At the outset of the backward design planning process, by contrast, teachers first identify the big ideas that will engage the students in the unit, as well as the strategies to assess performance. Only after these critical decisions have been made are teachers advised to begin selecting the instructional materials and activities. Wiggins and McTighe (2005) assert that it is inappropriate to think about *how* you're going to teach until you know exactly *what* you want your students to learn. Backward design shifts teacher perspectives by focusing on goal setting and assessment first and instructional materials and activities last. Wiggins and McTighe (2005) explain: "One starts with the end—the desired results (goals or standards)—and then derives the [unit] from the evidence of learning (performances) called for by the standard and the teaching needed to equip students to perform" (p. 8). The authors are careful to point out that the backward design approach is not a prescriptive, step-by-step program, but a general way to design any unit to make student understanding more likely. Therefore, although the suggestions that follow are closely aligned with the backward design model, I have deleted or minimized some sections that were beyond the scope of this book.

The backward design planning framework is comprised of three stages, each guided by central questions:

- *Stage 1: Identify Desired Results.* What should students know, understand, or be able to do? What content is worthy of understanding?
- *Stage 2: Determine Acceptable Evidence.* How will you know if students have achieved the targeted results?
- *Stage 3: Plan Learning Experiences and Instruction.* What activities and materials will help the students construct the targeted understandings and skills?

We will follow the progress of fifth-grade teacher Nina Zook as she moves through these three stages while implementing the backward design model into her social studies planning.

Stage 1: Identify Desired Results

A teacher's initial responsibility in designing a unit of instruction is deciding on the learning outcomes: "What content is worthy of understanding?" "What should students know, understand, or be able to do?" You must target what the students are expected to take away from the unit by addressing four important considerations : (1) curriculum expectations, (2) instructional goals, (3) established performance standards (national professional organizations, state, school district), and (4) content expectations.

Curriculum Expectations

Although it may appear deceptively simple on the surface, selecting a theme or topic for a unit is one of the most understated of all responsibilities associated with unit planning. The amount of freedom teachers have to select topics for study varies from district to district, so it is possible to encounter any number of freedoms and constraints. Consider the following curriculum expectations:

- *School district A* has developed a districtwide, textbook-based social studies curriculum in its effort to meet state standards. It expects every teacher to follow the curriculum so closely that all teachers must be on the same page of the book at the same date; at times a subject area supervisor may check plan books to see that this is being done. There is very little room for individual planning; the district feels that the textbook alone most effectively ensures achievement of state standards.
- *School district B* supplies a comprehensive curriculum guide and a set of textbooks for each teacher. Teachers are permitted to extend and enrich the specific topics so long as the basic subject matter and sequence of topics do not change. Conformity to specific content among all teachers is considered the most effective way to achieve state standards.
- *School district C* furnishes a curriculum guide and textbook program, but considers these more as suggestions for attaining standards than as "the final word." Standards guide the curriculum, but the formality associated with a text-based program is missing. Topics and instructional strategies are modified as growing interests and needs dictate. This is a middle-of-the-road approach, moving away from textbook-dominated instruction, although not yet completely.
- *School district D* has developed a philosophy that the social studies curriculum should be planned by the teacher in response to state standards, but content is guided by student interests and backgrounds. Based on the standards, teachers formulate their own goals and objectives, learning activities, and assessment strategies. However, a great deal of emphasis is placed on integrating the curriculum and on the use of a variety of instructional resources, including individualized instruction, learning centers, self-paced materials, learning packets, and specialized research projects.

Regardless of the pattern you find yourself in, however, you will reach a point in your professional development where you will be motivated to try new things and to make your classroom a special place for yourself and your students. How can you accomplish these goals in such a way that learning cuts across subject matter lines and reflects the real world in which we live? As you begin planning your first social studies unit, select a topic that has a high interest factor. What trips have you taken? What are you passionate about? What do you enjoy reading about or watching on television? Do you have a rich knowledge of a particular culture? Likewise, what are your students excited about? What are some of their favorite stories, movies, television shows, and things to talk about? What questions do they ask? What are their ethnic/cultural backgrounds? In addition to interest, make sure that the topic is rich in literature, both fiction and nonfiction, and that it has natural links to other areas of the curriculum.

A lot of a teacher's time and energy go into selecting a topic. Nonetheless, the value of a personalized social studies program is obvious: It is chosen with your children in mind. And who knows your children better—you or the developers of a textbook series?

Nina Zook developed a fifth-grade thematic unit, "Great Inventors and Their Inventions," for five good reasons: (1) "Inventors" was a required topic of study in her school district's fifth-grade curriculum. (2) The textbook treatment of "Inventors" by itself was unsatisfactory and needed to be enhanced. (3) She visited Washington, DC, last summer and was fascinated by the presentations and exhibits at the Lemelson Center for the Study of Invention and Innovation at the Smithsonian Institution's National Museum of American History. She was impressed with the center's mission to document, interpret, and disseminate information about invention and innovation; to encourage inventive creativity in young people; and to foster an appreciation for the central role invention and innovation play in the history of the United States. (4) She had collected assorted souvenirs, photos, videos, and print materials during her visit to the Smithsonian. (5) Her students were enthusiastic learners and had a keen interest in inventions and enjoyed expressing their inventive creativity.

A short summary paragraph usually follows the unit title, like the one that will be used in Ms. Zook's sample unit, "Great Inventors and Their Inventions:"

Summary of the Unit

This is a thematic unit based on knowledge of inventors and their inventions. The lessons will introduce students to famous inventors, their inventions, and the process of formulating an invention. It is a learner-centered experience designed to motivate students to build on their knowledge of inventors, their inventions, and the invention process to create their own inventions. Emphasis will be placed on the problem solving and analytical skills involved in inventing. The culminating event will be an Invention Convention, where students will display their inventions for other students and their parents.

Instructional Goals

What do you hope to personally accomplish this semester? Make the dean's list? Find your soulmate? Stick to a budget? Get organized? Lose/gain weight and get into better physical shape? Enrich your life by volunteering and helping others? Whether your plans include personal enrichment, academic success, or significant life changes, goal setting is a handy process that helps you decide where you want to go in life and what the best path might be to get you there.

Rather than describing personal targets, instructional goals are general statements describing the desired knowledge, skills, and attitude outcomes of an instructional unit. Instructional goals tell us what students should know and be able to do as a result of the unit of instruction; they guide the selection of assessment methods and help determine the most appropriate instructional activities, materials, and strategies. Goals are usually stated in such broad terms that most cannot be brought about during the unit or even during a school year. Rather, students often work toward achieving some goals throughout all 12 years of schooling, and maybe throughout their entire lives.

A suitable goal statement would be written like this: "The students shall acquire understandings about the human experience from the past." An improper goal statement would look like this: "The students shall be able to select and defend the ten greatest inventions of all time." Can you see how the second statement defines specific understandings that are essentially limited to a single unit while the first is broader and more sweeping, appropriate for a lifetime? Because goals are so wide-ranging, expecting to address more than three or four in any unit can become an exercise in futility.

When applied to the principles of backward design, teachers are required to first center their attention on the learning goals. For sake of illustration, let us look at the goals Nina Zook wrote for the sample social studies unit, "Great Inventors and Inventions":

1. The students will understand that every change, every invention, begins with the recognition of a problem or opportunity that somebody finds meaningful.
2. The students will understand that everyone has problems and challenges that need to be addressed, and that most of them can be overcome using a simple, focused program of invention.
3. The students will think logically, analytically, and creatively while forming reasoned judgments and solving real-world problems.

Short-Term Goals The *long-term goals* you have just examined furnish a "big picture" of what we want to do with the unit, but their attainment is so far off in the future that we often have trouble understanding their focus. To clarify the direction of our unit, then, we must break down these long-term goals into the smaller targets so that we can identify precisely what we want to achieve in the near future—in a day, a week, or by the end of the unit. This is why it is important now to set up *short-term* or *enabling goals*, written to help us clarify a long-term goal and measure our progress toward reaching them.

Short-term goals are statements that target the specific outcomes students will accomplish as a result of experiencing the unit of instruction. There are many recommended formats for writing short-term goals, but Norman Gronlund (1991) developed a style that seems particularly useful for our purposes and is perhaps the most popular among curriculum writers and teachers today. Gronlund's approach starts with writing a long-term goal and then clearly breaking that goal down into smaller targets. To illustrate, one of the long-term goals for Nina Zook's unit, "Great Inventors and Their Inventions," is delineated below:

Long-Term Goal

The students will understand that everyone has problems and challenges that need to be addressed and that most of them can be overcome using a simple, focused program of invention.

Short-Term Goals

1. The students shall explain that an inventor is someone who works hard to solve problems.
2. The students shall explain that some inventions are inspired by the desire to help people; others to make money.
3. The students shall discover many of the world's great inventors and their amazing inventions.
4. The students shall think like an inventor and create their own inventions.
5. The students shall describe and apply advertising techniques to market their inventions.

It is beyond the scope of this book to break down the remaining long-term goals in Ms. Zook's unit plan, but she would employ the same clarifying process for each. Although this is very time consuming, it is important to begin your unit plan with carefully selected and clearly articulated instructional goals. These statements pinpoint what students should be able to know or do as a result of taking part in the unit. They also serve as handy guides for teachers as they begin to organize the content, make plans to assess student understanding and proficiency, and select instructional activities and materials.

Established Performance Standards

Since nearly every teacher works in a standards-based classroom, she or he will be required to use professional organization, state, and/or school district standards as a basis for unit planning. The standards define the outcomes of instruction—not only the big ideas that the students are expected to develop by the end of the unit but also the discrete knowledge (facts and concepts) that should be acquired. The following example is taken from the social studies standards of the Rhode Island Department of Elementary and Secondary Education (1997). It is appropriate for inclusion in Nina Zook's evolving unit plan on inventors and inventions. Although the standard may initially appear to be too large-scale, performance indicators (designated by bullets) spell out more precisely what the students should know or be able to do.

> **STANDARD 1—Problem Solving**
>
> The student applies problem solving strategies in purposeful ways, both in situations where the problem and the desirable solutions are clearly evident and in situations requiring a creative approach to achieve outcome.
>
> - DESIGNING—The student designs and creates a product, service or system to meet an identified need.
> - IMPROVING SYSTEM—The student troubleshoots problems in the operation of a system in need of repair or devises and tests ways of improving the effectiveness of a system in operation.
> - PLANNING AND ORGANIZING—The student plans and organizes an event or activity. (p. 58)

Ms. Zook will continue the process of examining and including endorsed standards until she clearly defines what her students will be expected to learn after being engaged in the unit. The standards will serve not only to define the outcomes of instruction but will also help Ms. Zook focus on the discrete content of the unit and ultimately provide the basis for unit assessment and ensuing instructional decisions. If we do not take time to find a focus for the unit, we can run the risk of flitting about from one activity to another without getting much out of any, or of spending so much time on one or two things that we run out of interest, time, and energy. Learning goals and standards pinpoint what you want to accomplish from the unit, and helps prevent the instructional sequence from wandering aimlessly or from becoming stalled in one place too long.

Content Expectations

Wiggins and McTighe (2005) suggest that the content should be organized around "big ideas" or *umbrella concepts*, terms that can be compared to the discussion of concepts and schemata in Chapter 7. Some teachers think of concepts as being a lot like "conceptual Velcro" in that they help children know where to attach related facts and make them more understandable. "Big ideas" can be found in the goals and standards listed for the unit. Take, for example, the short-term goal we examined earlier:

> The students shall describe and apply **advertising techniques** to **market** their **inventions**.

The "big ideas" are highlighted in the statement. They will not only furnish the students with a conceptual tool to help connect discrepant facts but they will also provide teachers with a framework for selecting the unit content.

How do teachers stay focused on the big ideas throughout the planning process? How can they help students bring meaning to the mass of related subject matter content? Wiggins and McTighe (2005) suggest that unit developers frame the desired outcomes in terms of Essential Questions. These are broad questions that are not answerable with a brief statement, but their aim is to stimulate thought, to provoke inquiry, and to spark more questions. These are the Essential Questions Ms. Zook listed as she worked toward constructing a meaningful framework for the learning experiences that will follow:

- What is an invention?
- What are the 25 most significant inventions in history?
- What conditions/problems motivated these inventions?
- What were the positive and negative consequences of the inventions?
- Why do people invent?
- Do all inventions help people?
- How do inventors get their ideas?
- How do inventors bring their ideas to reality?
- Can I be an inventor?

After stating the goals and standards for instruction, then, the process of building a unit of instruction continues with a thorough search of the big ideas and content required to help achieve the targeted goals and standards. Each unit has so much potential content that beginning teachers often become frustrated as they try to decide what information should be included and what should be left for another time. The goals, standards, and big ideas prevent teachers from trying to include too much by giving them a clear idea of where to focus the content search.

A helpful way to begin selecting and organizing virtually any unit topic content is by *factstorming*. Just think about what you already know and ask questions about the topic or big ideas (for example, "How does someone dream up an invention?"). Repeat the process with each potential subtopic ("What are the steps to inventing?"). Most teachers do not know enough about the topic at this time to plan a good unit. But that's not the overall purpose of this activity; it is designed simply to help you realize what more needs to be done.

Once you exhaust the information you already have on a big idea, you will need to know more in order to enlarge it. Toward that goal, you must have access to a variety of resources (surfing the Web and scanning a wide variety of print sources are good places to start). Check with your school or public librarian for references on a topic you wish to pursue. You should find yourself saying, "I'll look it up," many times a day.

The background material you unearth should be extensive. You will not use all of it, but when you teach elementary school children, it's best to learn all you can find out about a subject. As they progress through the unit, children will ask many questions. It certainly is okay to reply, "I don't know. Let's find out together," to some of the children's questions, but teachers who can answer a great many questions are the ones who gain their students' confidence and respect.

Immediately following the summary paragraph, goal statements, and targeted standards, Ms. Zook organized an outline of the content. For the content outline, it helps to record the big ideas and then list the key content below each. You can guide the selection by asking a series of key questions: "What are the 'big ideas' in this goal or standards statement?" "What knowledge must a student have to understand this concept?" Again, it is beyond the scope of this book to outline all the content appropriate for this unit, but the following example illustrates how the content outline for one "big idea" (*marketing*) central to Ms. Zook's unit, "Great Inventors and Their Inventions," could be outlined:

Content Outline

Big Idea:

Marketing an Invention (Advertising techniques commonly used to persuade a buyer to purchase a product)

To attract the attention of consumers, advertisers usually select one or more of the following basic marketing techniques:

- *Bandwagon:* An appeal to follow the crowd
- *Buzz Words:* Words that have suddenly become popular with consumers (like "low-carb" or "natural")
- *Testimonial:* Someone you admire or respect endorses the product (like Tiger Woods endorsing a certain brand of clothing)
- *Snob Appeal:* An attempt to convince buyers that owning a certain product is a status symbol
- *Facts and Figures:* Trying to convince a buyer that "nine out of ten families" prefer a certain product (without telling you who those families are)
- *Plain Folks:* A suggestion that the product is a good value for ordinary people (such as an automobile manufacturer showing an ordinary family piling into a minivan)

- *Wit and Humor:* Giving customers a reason to laugh or to be entertained by clever use of visuals or language
- *Patriotism:* The suggestion that purchasing this product shows your love of your country (a company brags about its product being made in the United States by American workers)
- *Demonstration:* Simply showing the product in action
- *Problems:* The product can help the buyer solve a problem (like cleaning out the rain gutters)

Ms. Zook will continue to examine the major concepts (big ideas) and prioritize the content considered essential for student understanding. Clarity and comprehensiveness during this element of unit planning helps assure Ms. Zook not only that she will effectively plug in appropriate knowledge and skills, but also minimize the amount of useful content that might fall between the cracks.

Stage 2: Determine Acceptable Evidence

In the second phase of backward design, teachers consider what they will use as evidence of successful learning. The core of the "backward design" process is pinpointing assessment strategies *before* selecting the learning experiences, and identifying what is essential for the students to know *before* determining how they will

It is helpful when teachers work together while developing instructional plans designed to meet the needs of all their students.

demonstrate their understanding. It is not until these critical decisions have been made that the learning experiences should be considered. Wiggins and McTighe (2005) suggest three important questions to guide planning at this stage:

- What evidence can be used to indicate whether or not students have achieved the desired results as outlined in Stage 1?
- What assessment tasks will anchor our curricular unit and thus guide our instruction?
- What should we look for to determine the extent of student understanding? (p. 146)

Teachers must constantly assess their children's work in order to determine to what degree they are achieving the intended instructional outcomes. *Assessment* is the process by which teachers collect clear, timely, and focused data on how well their students are meeting intended instructional outcomes in light of stated goals and standards. The purpose of assessment is to supply teachers and students with information and insights essential for improving learning quality and teaching effectiveness. Wiggins and McTighe (2005) elaborate: "Given the likelihood that learners will misunderstand key ideas and make performance errors (not necessarily signs of poor teaching or learning), the design must make sure that teachers as well as learners get the feedback they need to rethink, revise, and refine. As on the field, the stage, or in the studio, building in feedback and the opportunity to use it is a vital aspect of a good learning plan" (p. 192).

Knowing what and how well students learn has been and continues to be an important part of educational practice in social studies and a catalyst for strengthening and improving instruction. Standardized tests have been the customary measuring tool for gauging student growth and are considered to be among the most reliable and objective ways to measure academic performance. If used properly, standardized tests provide teachers with solid evidence of academic growth. They can be used to compare the achievement of students in a school district, reveal how students in one school district compare to students across the state or nation, indicate the degree to which a school is meeting standards of instruction, provide support for grouping and placement decisions, help identify students in need of special services, and aid teachers in making curricular decisions.

How Global is the Curriculum
Go to MyEducationLab, select the topic Assessment, watch the video entitled "Standardized Tests," and complete the questions that accompany it.

Standardized Tests

One of the most hotly debated assessment strategies is called the *standardized test*. Standardized tests are commercially prepared, machine-scored, "norm-referenced" instruments. *Norm referencing* means that the test is administered to a sampling of students selected according to such factors as age, gender, race, grade, or socioeconomic status. Their average scores then serve as "norm scores" and become the basis for comparing the performance of all the students who will subsequently take the test.

How do we use the results of standardized achievement tests in social studies? What do they offer that we can't get without them? Comparability in the context of the "big picture" is the major thing. It isn't very useful, for example, for one teacher to compare her or his students' results with those of a classroom next door and then to make decisions about instruction based on that comparison. To many, it is more important to get a broader, more comprehensive picture: "In general, are my fourth-graders learning basic social studies content as well as other fourth-graders in our school district?" "Compared to fifth-graders throughout the United States, how well are those in our school district doing in map skills?" "How does our district's social studies curriculum compare with others in the state?" Despite the fact that standardized tests can determine only a small fraction of any student's total achievement in social studies, the public assigns standardized test scores great weight: "Are our students making 'normal' progress?" "Is their overall achievement above or below average?"

When test scores have serious consequences—and they often do—teachers will teach to the test. This devalues good classroom instruction and undercuts the authenticity of scores as measures of what children really know. "Test-generated" instruction often leads to repeated drill and practice on skills and content because teachers are pressured to prove that what they are doing produces good test scores. Challenging activities such as problem solving and creative thinking are deemphasized; learning centers, literature, art, and music are pushed aside to make more time for daily drill and practice. One first-year teacher described the stress produced by such pressure: "I was petrified that my class would do so poorly that I wouldn't be back next year. So I taught what the other teachers recommended to get them ready for the test. After the test I started teaching, good teaching. The class enjoyed it, and I think they learned more the last three weeks of school than they did the first six months, because I was more relaxed, the students were more relaxed, and I was able to hone in on those areas where they needed help" (Livingston, Castle, & Nations, 1989, p. 24).

Such reactions only help to support the contention that "what gets tested gets taught"—that is, the system of assessment dictates the system of instruction.

Classroom Quizzes and Tests

Many social studies units use quizzes and short tests as part of their overall assessment strategy. If used for the proper reasons, quizzes and tests can provide important evidence for students to use as they identify their strengths as well as areas of misunderstanding, and they can furnish teachers with timely feedback on student learning. The form of classroom quizzes and tests varies from unit to unit. Some units focus on the creation of tangible products, so they tend to utilize a wide range of performance tasks, demonstrations, and portfolios. Content-oriented units, on the other hand, will rely on several quizzes or tests as the primary means of assessment, and these tests will often be focused on the recall of essential information. Without debate, students must acquire a rich content background in social studies, but tests must move beyond simple recall and include the use of higher-order thinking skills such as making predictions or defending a personal point of view.

The National Council for the Social Studies affirms that some instructional goals and standards may be most fittingly assessed with standardized tests as well as classroom quizzes and tests. Knowledge is a necessary and valued outcome of social studies instruction, for it serves as the foundation for critical thinking and civic decision making.

Performance Assessment

Other outcomes, however, lend themselves to multiple assessments that require higher-order thinking, writing, and connecting social studies knowledge to applications in the world outside of school. For those results, NCSS recommends *performance assessments* that are intended to reflect real-life situations, including open-ended test questions, portfolios, essays, presentations, exhibitions, and large projects carried out over a period of time. Performance assessment in social studies is designed to further the goal of preparing students to become active citizens who make informed and reasoned decisions as citizens in a democratic society. In the global world of the twenty-first century, students need not only know the basics but they also must think creatively, critically, inferentially, and analytically. Educators and parents alike have recognized that the basics are no longer good enough and are calling for a closer match between what students learn in school and what they will need know or be able to do as adults in a democratic community. As a result, performance assessment is evolving into a process that goes beyond the results of formal tests to an examination of skills and understandings applicable in real-life, or *authentic situations*.

How Global is the Curriculum *Go to MyEducationLab, select the topic Assessment, watch the video entitled "Performance Assessment," and complete the questions that accompany it.*

Authentic assessment, another term for *performance assessment,* is a form of assessment where students are asked to complete tasks that demonstrate meaningful application of targeted knowledge and skills. The tasks involve students in challenging situations where they must use social studies knowledge and/or skills to produce effective and creative exhibits or presentations. If, for example, your university's football coach had just opened a preseason try-out camp to assess athletes for a possible spot on the team, he would be interested in finding out whether they have a good understanding of the game as well as the skills necessary to perform at a high level on the playing field. Would it be wiser for the coach to assess the athletes' knowledge and abilities by administering a multiple-choice test or by observing them perform on the gridiron? Although a coach's decision is obvious when it comes to judging athletic talent, teachers find that they, too, are better able to assess some goals and standards if they ask their students to perform authentic tasks.

To begin the assessment process, you must first pinpoint the desired learning outcomes: "What should my students know or be able to do after they have completed this unit?" You have clearly identified those outcomes in the goals and standards for the unit, and should use them as a measuring stick to select assessment options. High-quality authentic assessment usually begins with a set of standards in mind. Standards are important because they set reasonable expectations for what teachers need to teach and students need to learn. They also inform parents and teachers what is expected of their students and offer a guide for measuring each student's performance and achievement.

Connecticut has become a leader in the use of diversified assessments to assess social studies instruction. Its assessment plan is driven by a carefully articulated vision of learning, *Connecticut's Common Core of Learning (CCL)*, a standards document that sets forth what students should know and be able to do as they prepare for productive adult life and responsible citizenship (www.state.ct.us/sde/dtl/curriculum/currkey2.htm). Based on the standards contained in its Common Core of Learning, the Connecticut State Department of Education has initiated a multifaceted assessment program designed to measure outcomes delineated in the Core—a new model that includes, in addition to formal tests, authentic measures such as exhibitions, hands-on performance experiences, student portfolios, and other tasks that require students to demonstrate knowledge-in-use.

It is important for teachers to base their assessment practices on the learning targets as specified by the goals and standards. For example, if a content standard specifies an outcome such as "Students will demonstrate an understanding of how the federal government works," then a written test question could yield useful feedback. On the other hand, a standard such as "Students will locate the homes of classmates on a map" requires students to demonstrate their knowledge and skills in more multifaceted ways. A 25-item multiple-choice test will not work. Clearly stated outcomes help teachers match assessment methods to the targets of instruction.

The way to find out if Lamont can meet a targeted objective of reciting the Pledge of Allegiance is to have him recite it. And, if a lesson objective is to teach children how to fill out a patent application, then filling one out would be considered an appropriate assessment strategy. If you want to find out whether Belinda can sketch a blueprint of an invention idea, it would be appropriate to observe her at work to see if she can complete the process. By gathering information from situations and contexts like those in which students normally learn, the results may be more meaningful to you, to them, and to their families.

Two of the most common performance-based assessment tasks are those that result in some type of student-made product:

- *Group or individual projects* where a number of students plan and work together on a problem that requires planning, research, collaboration, creating a product, and group presentation.
- *Writing tasks* reflecting students' understanding of social studies content through description, analysis, or summary.

Group Projects. As assessment tools, group projects allow for both the examination of content outcomes and for the evaluation of students' ability to function as a group member. Social studies projects that involve making a product and/or delivering an oral report provide especially worthwhile contexts for authentic assessment. A teacher and peers can evaluate the performance and contribution of each group member during project work. Groups may be organized informally—random pairs of students helping one another learn—or formed to carry out a well-defined task. Before groups begin their work, however, you must make sure that students are not only skilled at working collaboratively but that they also have clear guidelines for their projects and presentations. You must inform them of the purpose of the group activity as well as the criteria that will be used for assessment. Students can then use the assessment criteria to help them develop the product or presentation.

Projects can take many forms, from designing posters and pamphlets to building models and displays. Projects and presentations function as important assessment tools, as well as invite students to connect with important knowledge and processes as they construct new ideas.

Writing Tasks. Writing tasks have long been used to assess a student's understanding of social studies through a written description, analysis, explanation, or summary. Writing tasks can readily demonstrate how well a student uses facts in context, expresses her or his ideas in creative ways, or structures a clear argument or discussion. Most writing tasks are expository in nature and can be easily assessed with observational checklists and rubrics that describe levels of content focus and writing mechanics. However, many opportunities for expressive (creative) writing are also found in social studies.

Because a student's performance in either of these situations is judged against a set of criteria, we refer to the assessment tasks as *criterion-referenced measures.* Teachers usually select from among several different types of criterion-referenced scales that contain the essential criteria for the task and appropriate levels of performance for each criterion. Two of the most common are observation checklists and rubrics.

Observation Checklists

Observation checklists offer social studies teachers one of the most versatile and time-efficient tools in their assessment repertoire. A carefully constructed checklist or rating scale should be used during observations of students as they are involved in performance tasks. Checklists are particularly helpful when you want to determine the degree to which students have demonstrated specific skills, behaviors, or competencies. To construct a checklist, first list the specific outcomes to be assessed and then record the occurrences of each. A sample checklist for behaviors considered important for cooperative learning is shown in Figure 10.2.

	Sometimes Present	Mastered
Assists co-workers when needed		
Follows group-established rules		
Does fair share of group work		
Respects group decisions		
Shares materials willingly		

Directions:

(✓) Place a check in the "Sometimes Present" column if the characteristic is occasionally observed.

(+) Place a plus in the "Mastered" column if the characteristic occurs habitually.

( ) Make no mark if the characteristic is observed seldom or not at all.

FIGURE 10.2 Observation Checklist for Cooperative Learning Skills

Rubrics

Teachers often use rubrics to identify important strengths and weaknesses in student learning. *Rubrics* consist of two primary components: *performance criteria* and *level of performance*. They are constructed by listing the behaviors associated with an assessment task and describing various qualities of those behaviors. The criteria, or characteristics of performance, are usually listed in the left-hand column of a rubric. A number or other indicator of the quality of work is often placed at the top of the rubric. To design a rubric, a teacher would include at least two criteria and at least two levels of performance.

The rubric shown in Figure 10.3 may give you a sense of one way rubrics are used to assess written reports. It was created online at RubiStar, a free Internet site supported by a grant from the U.S. Department of Education (www.rubistar.4teachers.org).

Portfolios

Portfolios have come to the forefront as a valued technique of collecting assessment evidence. *Portfolios* are collections of student work that document their efforts, progress, and achievements over a period of time. There is no single list of items recommended for portfolios; they may include items such as student writings, art products, photographs, independent research reports, projects, favorite books, and work samples.

Nina Zook liked the idea of using portfolios to assess her students' progress in the unit, "Great Inventors and Their Inventions," but felt that her students required a model before they were able to put together their own. so she used a special introductory plan.

FIGURE 10.3 Rubric for Written Research Report

Category	4	3	2	1
Organization	Information is very organized with well-constructed paragraphs and subheadings.	Information is organized with well-constructed paragraphs.	Information is organized, but paragraphs are not well constructed.	The information appears to be disorganized.
Quality of Information	Information clearly relates to the main topic. It includes several supporting details and/or examples.	Information clearly relates to the main topic. It provides 1–2 supporting details and/or examples.	Information clearly relates to the main topic. No details and/or examples are given.	Information has little or nothing to do with the main topic.
Sources	All sources (information and graphics) are accurately documented in the desired format.	All sources (information and graphics) are accurately documented, but a few are not in the desired format.	All sources (information and graphics) are accurately documented, but many are not in the desired format.	Some sources are not accurately documented.
Internet Use	Successfully uses suggested Internet links to find information and navigates within these sites easily without assistance.	Usually able to use suggested Internet links to find information and navigates within these sites easily without assistance.	Occasionally able to use suggested Internet links to find information and navigates within these sites easily without assistance.	Needs assistance or supervision to use suggested Internet links and/or to navigate within these sites.
Paragraph Construction	All paragraphs include introductory sentence, explanations or details, and concluding sentence.	Most paragraphs include introductory sentence, explanations or details, and concluding sentence.	Paragraphs included related information but were typically not constructed well.	Paragraphing structure was not clear and sentences were not typically related within the paragraphs.
Mechanics	No grammatical, spelling, or punctuation errors.	Almost no grammatical, spelling, or punctuation errors.	A few grammatical, spelling, or punctuation errors.	Many grammatical, spelling, or punctuation errors.
Diagrams & Illustrations	Diagrams and illustrations are neat, accurate and add to the reader's understanding of the topic.	Diagrams and illustrations are accurate and add to the reader's understanding of the topic.	Diagrams and illustrations are neat and accurate and sometimes add to the reader's understanding of the topic.	Diagrams and illustrations are not accurate OR do not add to the reader's understanding of the topic.

Ms. Zook wrote the word *portfolio* on the chalkboard. She asked if anyone had an idea of what a portfolio might be. Anticipating that not many would have a clue, Ms. Zook brought out a box containing items that, in effect, created her biographical sketch. She informed her students that portfolios tell a story and that she chose objects that helped tell a story about herself as a person.

The first item in Ms. Zook's portfolio was a photograph of her family. "I love my family," she announced proudly and showed that her husband and young children were in the picture (along with Barkley and Betty Basset Hound, the family pets). Next came a not-so-new golf ball: "I got my first hole-in-one the summer after I graduated from college," she said proudly. Several ribbons followed—they were awarded to her as a youngster for winning a local geography bee. Ms. Zook then held up a favorite book and explained, "In my spare time, I enjoy reading." The most fascinating items came next—a photo of Ms. Zook taken when she was a fifth-grader and her report card from the same grade. "I wanted to show you the best report card I ever received," she explained. "I had a fabulous fifth-grade teacher." The last article she removed from the box was a children's book, *The Little Engine That Could*. "This is one of my favorite books. From the first time my parents read it to me as a child, I loved it. It taught me that a person could accomplish almost anything if he or she tried hard enough."

Comparing her collection of personal memorabilia to a social studies portfolio, Ms. Zook asked the class what might be included in their portfolios for the unit. She received several suggestions: daily assignments, drawings, illustrated plans, their writings and reports, group projects, individual projects, journal entries, oral reports, and so on. The class then discussed the format of a good portfolio. They decided it should be housed in a suitable container—boxes, file folders, or binders. File folder "Inventor's Portfolios," all agreed, made excellent containers. The class also decided the portfolio should be neat and include a table of contents. Furthermore, each item should have with it a short personal statement about why it was important to the learner. Following this discussion, Ms. Zook gave her students two days to select the works to be placed in the portfolios.

There are countless ways to put together portfolios; the important consideration is that the students take an active role in selecting material for and organizing them. Of course, the portfolios must address instructional standards and goals. When students create their portfolios, their exhibits become a means through which you may provide evaluative feedback and monitor progress. You should hold individual conferences with the students during which you guide portfolio review with such questions as the following:

- "How has your work in social studies changed since last year (or last month)?"
- "What do you now know about ________ that you didn't know before?"

- "What are the special items in your portfolio?"
- "What would you most like me to understand about your portfolio?"
- "How did you decide to organize the items?"
- "What are the strengths as displayed in the portfolio? What needs improvement?"

The conference should focus not just on subject-matter accomplishments but also on planning strategies, personal reflections, and evidence of progress. Assuming active roles in the learning process goes beyond simply recognizing that the students have made mistakes to receiving feedback from others and finding practical ways to do something about it. Portfolios provide evidence of performance that goes far beyond command of factual knowledge by offering a clear and understandable picture of how a student's works evolved. Although this is all important, the greatest benefit of portfolios may be in self-evaluation. Portfolio assessment offers students the opportunity to set individual goals, select the items for evaluation, and reflect on their work. In this way it encourages pride in learning and helps students develop the motivation to improve.

An important point to remember about assessment is that no single instrument or technique can adequately measure the range of performances and behaviors contained in social studies units. For this reason, educators today strongly recommend obtaining a variety of assessment data and making assessment an integral part of the learning process rather than something that happens at the end.

Ms. Zook proposes to use the following assessments for understanding and performance throughout her unit:

- Daily teacher observations to monitor the children's progress
- Oral responses to literature discussions
- Rubrics to judge core performance tasks, such as a Rube Goldberg machine, a group inventor report, and an individual invention design
- Portfolios containing evidence of performance tasks

Stage 3: Plan for Learning

At long last, you have pinpointed the outcomes of the unit and determined how you will know the degree to which your students are moving toward the desired results. Now you have the green light to embark on the task teachers seem to get most pleasure from—the learning activities! As you approach this task, however, Wiggins and McTighe (2005) suggest that your efforts be guided with this question: "Given the goals, standards, and targeted performances, what kind of instructional approaches, resources, and experiences will be most productive?"

Learning experiences are the instructional activities we employ to achieve the content goals and standards, the actual experiences that involve children in puzzling, wondering, exploring, experimenting, finding out, and thinking. Not all learning experiences need to be new or unique; highest priority should be placed on

Much as physicians translate physiological knowledge into medical practice, goals and objectives help teachers translate into educational practice.

balance and variety. Do not choose activities because they are "cute" or "entertaining"; select them because they stand the best chance of accomplishing your targeted outcomes.

Although this is always the most highly anticipated section of unit plans, it is often the most puzzling section for first-year teachers. Some instructional models advise teachers to involve the entire class in the same experiences at the same time. Other models invite students to actively pursue individual interests. Some models place the teacher in the spotlight; others are student centered. Project based? Problem based? Textbook based? Literature based? Cooperative learning? Collaborative learning? Social models? Radical models? All these choices can set even the calmest mind spinning. Which model works best? That is a question that has baffled educators since the onset of formal education, and one that has not yet been persuasively answered. It is important to consider that teaching is such a multifaceted responsibility that it is impossible to identify any distinctly best way to teach in all situations and for all purposes. Good teachers do not single-mindedly draw on but one model of instruction; rather, they make choices from among the rich repertoire of choices after analyzing educational goals and standards and the linked assessment strategies.

The nature of backward design calls for flexible, adaptable teachers. You may be surprised to know that not all contemporary teaching methods are original; most are adaptations or reworked versions of older, more traditional methods. The crux of successful teaching lies not in whether a method is new or old, but in flexibility; the younger the children, the greater the variety should be. Sometimes you will:

- Lecture to your children, but this should occur rarely. The younger the child, the less you should talk.
- Use good questioning and discussion techniques to hold discussion sessions with the entire class.
- Lead whole-group learning experiences from the textbook or another common source of information; such experiences offer balance and proportion to the program.
- Bring to class objects such as jewelry, clothing, dolls, toys, books, catalogs, containers, tools, and other realia. These items help to form classroom connections to other people, times, and places.
- Choose books, computer applications, videos, slides, tapes, filmstrips, records, pictures, bulletin boards, and other learning aids to provide a variety of essential learning materials.
- Encourage children to solve problems and search for answers to their own questions; an independent quest for information is a lifelong asset.
- Encourage children to work together collaboratively and cooperatively; children learn a great deal from one another. However, sometimes children will work alone; meeting personal interests and needs must assume high priority in all classrooms.

Wiggins and McTighe (2005) explain that in order for a unit plan to be a good unit plan, it must be engaging and effective: "By *engaging*, we mean a design that the (diverse) learners find truly thought provoking, fascinating, energizing. It pulls them all deeper into the subject and they *have* to engage by the nature of the demands, mystery, or challenge into which they are thrown. . . . By *effective*, we mean that the learning design helps learners become more competent and productive at worthy work" (p. 195).

There are many ways to organize the learning experiences for a unit; the outline that follows is only a suggested guide. It should be adapted or restyled to suit your personal preferences and the needs of your students.

Phase One: Introductory Activities

Establishing classroom conditions that motivate children to learn is a major mission during this initial portion of the unit. What kind of "bait" can you cast out to "hook" students on the topic so they will participate as eager and involved learners? Usually encompassing the first day or two of instruction, the "hook" for a social studies unit can be cast out in a number of ways. Wiggins and McTighe (2005) suggest that the "implications of the 'hook' are clear enough: It is in *our* interest to hook students early and often through *their* interests and by what is inherently

Instructional activities must be aligned with goals, standards, and assessment if they are to achieve targeted outcomes.

intellectually provocative. Thus, the better [sequences of learning experiences] immerse learners early on in intriguing issues, problems, situations, or other experiences" (p. 220).

There are many good introductory experiences (field trips, community visitors, videos, realia, and the like); however, in my opinion, one of the most important ingredients is a good book or a well-told story. I call stories, either read or told, that are used during the introductory phases of social studies units *literacy launchers*. Their purpose is to sweep up the students and carry them off into our captivating, enchanting world. As powerful as they are for this purpose, however, good stories should not be limited only as the introductory experiences. They are powerful instructional tools when used at strategic points throughout the unit, too. A good unit is rich in literature, both fiction and nonfiction.

Phase Two: Developmental Experiences

Following the introductory activities, you enter into what is often described as the "brass tacks" of the unit. Activities may be done independently, in small groups, or by the whole class, but what really matters is that you stay within the periphery of the children's interests. You must choose worthwhile experiences that are neither mere entertainment nor busywork, but are gripping and rich and powerful in potential learning. As you set this phase in motion, the students go to work; you may retreat a bit, since your initial teaching responsibilities as a stimulator and arranger are now over. You will have more teaching to do, but in other ways; you must now analyze the unit objectives and ask, "What learning experiences will most effectively help me achieve the unit's objectives?"

The developmental experiences, then, offer students opportunities to wrestle with real problems. The whole point is to help them comprehend the interrelationships among phenomena that can make this nation and the world better places to live. We do this not only from the social studies alone, but by utilizing experiences that cut across all subject lines.

Phase Three: Culminating Activity

While the preceding phases of the unit were content or process specific, the culminating activity allows students to review, summarize, or bring closure to the topic. This concluding portion of the unit usually takes the form of a whole-class project that gives students an opportunity to apply or extend what they have learned. The culmination might be a time during which group projects are shared; a festival where dance performances, creative skits, and cultural meals are enjoyed; a "readers forum" where written reports are read; or a construction project, such as a model community, where children represent the major concepts learned.

Sometimes the unit that will follow is such a natural transition that neither a culminating activity for the first unit nor an introductory experience for the second is necessary. If one unit deals with "The First Americans" (Native Americans), for example, and is followed by "Settling the Land" (early settlers), continuity from one unit to the next need not be broken.

You must carefully orchestrate the three major phases of activities, because each activity flows from preceding experiences and furnishes the foundation for those that follow. Think of the entire collection of activities as being much like a beautiful symphony that is made up of separate movements which, when woven together, shape a grand masterpiece.

Teachers usually describe the specific learning activities they have selected for the unit using either (or a combination) of two formats: unit blueprints and daily lesson plans. A *unit blueprint* gives a brief description, in paragraph form, of all the daily activities a teacher intends to provide throughout the unit. *Daily lesson plans,* by contrast, are detailed; they expand on the blueprint's brief description by clearly and comprehensively explaining how things will be done. The following material shows Ms. Zook's blueprint. Any of the parts of her blueprint can be easily expanded into a lesson plan, or detailed description of intended daily instruction. Although each course instructor has her or his preferred design for writing a lesson plans, most contain some or all of the elements shown in Figure 10.4.

Phase One: Introductory Experiences

1. Prepare an "Invention Box" with several unusual items that reflect both traditional and contemporary life, such as a "buttoneer" (a gadget that replaces buttons in seconds) or a fake soda pop can that has secret storage for valuables.

FIGURE 10.4 "Rube Goldberg Inventions" Lesson Plan

Topic: Rube Goldberg Invention

Grade: 5

Teacher: Nina Zook

Long-Term Goal

1. The students will understand that every change, every invention, is the result of someone's imagination and creativity.

Short-Term Goal

1. The students shall use their ingenuity and creativity to build their own Rube Goldberg machine.
2. The students shall understand the basic steps involved in the invention process.

Performance Standards

1. Students will identify and describe examples of how inventions have changed the lives of people.

Materials

1. Gather items from the junk drawer, garage, schoolroom, or home: cardboard tubes, string, old play figurines, jar lids, paper cups, rubber bands, thread spools, wire, small wheels, any junk.

Procedure

1. Review the information about Rube Goldberg, especially examples of his "real" Rube Goldberg machines depicted in his wacky cartoons.
2. Divide the class into groups of three and give each group a "junk" box (referred to as "Inventor's Kit").
3. Tell the students that they will use the materials in their Inventor's Kits to create a distinctive Rube Goldberg machine that will burst a balloon (the last step of the machine). Their inventions should consist of six actions in a chain of events; the last event is the burst balloon.

   The Rube Goldberg project rules are:
   - There must be six events.
   - The events must be clearly visible.
   - The goal is to burst a balloon.
   - Safety is important. Fire is prohibited. Any pointed objects such as a dart, nail, or pin cannot travel a distance of more than a foot.
4. Encourage the students to play with the things in their boxes. Can a toy car bump into something and knock it down? Can a string pull something up or knock it down? Can a ball roll down a ramp to set something else in motion? Use your creativity!
5. The students should sketch their ideas on a piece of drawing paper. Draw simple pictures of things that seem to work well so they won't be forgotten. Is there a theme that might be used (perhaps some toy military figures can be central to a battlefield scene or a toy trac-

FIGURE 10.4 Continued

tor and toy cow can be part of a farm theme?) Start building the machine. Don't overlook a major element of Rube Goldberg's inventions—wackiness!

6. The students should remember what they have been learning in science class—levers, inclined planes, and other simple machines. They should also be reminded that many ideas they come up with might not be used and that they will change their minds quite a bit in the beginning.
7. Creativity cannot be forced out in a short time. The students may need two or three class periods to complete this project.
8. After the inventions are completed, have the students gather for an informal get-together where they will exhibit their inventions and demonstrate how they work. The Rube Goldberg inventions will remain on display on a table in the classroom throughout the entire unit.

Assessment

1. Observe students during the invention activity to determine the degree to which they are achieving the lesson objectives.
2. Use a rubric to assess the effectiveness of the invention: Is it unique? Does it have the right number of events? Does it work consistently? Have all the conditions been met?

Obtain inexpensive items from friends, parents, restaurants, gift shops, or specialty stores. Wrap the box in plain brown wrapping paper and address it to the class. Next, ask a colleague or staff member to deliver the box to your classroom at a designated time. Looking surprised, bring the students to your group conversation area and say, "What do you suppose is in this special delivery package? Where did it come from?" Examine the box together for clues. Open the box and use these questions as you share each item: "What is it? How do you think it is used?"

Establish the point that an invention doesn't have to be something radically new or historically important—even the simplest or more unusual items have an impact on our lives. Divide the class into groups of four. Ask the groups to think of all the appliances, medicines, and conveniences that have made a difference in their lives, and compose a class list for discussion.

2. Share Maynard Frank Wolfe's book, *Rube Goldberg: Inventions* (Simon & Schuster), which includes the famous author's inventions and ingenious editorial cartoons with captions. These drawings show the most complicated ways that you can think of to complete the most ordinary tasks such as "Golf Inventions," "Simple Orange-Squeezing Machine," and "Idea for Dodging Bill Collector." Wheels, gears, handles, balls, and paddles are set in motion by canaries, boots, brooms, and shears to perform simple tasks like closing a window in case it starts to rain before you get home. Anyone who has played the game "Mousetrap" has witnessed a "Goldberg" invention. The inventions were a tongue-in-cheek commentary on the Machine Age in which Goldberg lived as well as on the strong interest Americans displayed toward inventions and inventors of the time. A sample is shown in Figure 10.5. If the book is unavailable, you can sample some of Goldberg's clever inventions online at www.rube-goldberg.com.

3. Before doing this activity with your class, gather containers full of various recycled objects such as dominoes, magnets, balls, cardboard tubes, funnels, yarn, thread, popsicle sticks, balloons, tape, cupcake paper tins—basically anything that could be found laying around the house or garage or in a junk box! Then show the class a Rube Goldberg invention that you invented the night before from items that were lying around the house. Give a bag of "stuff" to each group. Invite them to use the materials to create their own Rube Goldberg invention that might turn the page of a book, drop a coin in a bank, pop a balloon, or perform some other common task in a complicated way.

After the inventions have been made, have the students gather for an informal get-together where they will exhibit their inventions and demonstrate how they work. The Rube Goldberg inventions will remain on display in the classroom throughout the entire unit.

Phase Two: Developmental Experiences

1. Read to your students from the book, *Mistakes That Worked* by Charlotte Foltz Jones (Doubleday). There are 40 stories in this book about inventions that were made by mistake. For example, Ruth Wakefield invented the "Toll House" (chocolate chip) cookie while running the Toll House Inn in New Bedford, Massachusetts. Having an imaginative touch, Mrs. Wakefield thought it would be interesting to make a special kind of cookie for her customers. She broke apart a chocolate candy bar and dropped the pieces into regular cookie batter. As the cookies were baking, Mrs. Wakefield thought the pieces would melt and marble into the cookie. However, when she bit into a finished cookie, Mrs. Wakefield was amazed—the chocolate chips were still intact, just a little softened. By accident, a delicious new cookie had been invented and quickly became a "Toll House" favorite.

After discussing the story of the Toll House cookie, divide your class into small groups. Challenge them to invent their own special cookies. The students must agree on what special new ingredient (à la the chocolate chips) will be in their cookie, the shape their cookie will take after it is baked, and its name. They should draw an illustration of their new invention. Finally, the groups should share their cookie inventions with each other. Display the illustrations in the room throughout the invention unit.

2. Now that the students have had a "fun" introduction to the inventing process, they will be motivated to spend time learning about various inventors. It is now time for the students to research the lives of inventors and prepare presentations for each. Organize a text set of four books for five or six different great inventors. These were used by Ms. Zook:

- Russell Freedman's biography of Orville and Wilbur Wright, *The Wright Brothers: How They Invented the Airplane* (Holiday House). This biography tells the story of the lives of the Wright brothers, from the time they were little boys tinkering with toys, to when they finally sold their marvelous invention to the United States government. This book shows how the airplane started out as a glider and developed into a plane that eventually stayed in the air for an hour and 13 minutes. The book is illustrated with a large number of photographs, many taken by the Wright Brothers themselves.

- Laurie Carlson's *Boss of the Plains: The Hat That Won the West* (DK Publishing), is a story of how John Batterson Stetson invented the "ten-gallon hat." As a boy, John Stetson dreamed of going west. When at last he went, he found that everyone wore whatever hats they'd worn back home: knit caps, wool derbies, straw sombreros. Stetson found that the sun blistered his face because his derby did not provide enough protection so the young hat maker invented the wide-brimmed "Boss of the Plains." Others struck gold or blazed trails through unknown territory, but John Stetson made his mark with a hat.
- Catherine Thimmesh's *Girls Think of Everything: Stories of Ingenious Inventions by Women* (Houghton Mifflin) is a compilation of inspiring stories of successful women and girl inventors. Students will learn about what inspired these women and girls and how they turned their ideas into reality.
- Eva Moore's *The Story of George Washington Carver* (Scholastic) is a biography of one of the most distinguished individuals of our time. Born into slavery, he grew up to become a world-famous scientist and inventor. Carver is best known for his invention of hundreds of ways to use peanuts and sweet potatoes.
- Keith Elliot's *Steven Jobs & Stephen Wozniak: Creating the Apple Computer* (Blackbirch Marketing Partners Series) highlights the importance of cooperation and teamwork in the invention process. The book tells the story of two contemporary inventors who were daring leaders in the personal computer revolution.
- Bruce Koscielniak's *Johann Gutenberg and the Amazing Printing Press* (Houghton Mifflin) is a fact-filled book that starts out by explaining how books were handmade and individually penned to order in fifteenth-century Europe. After this overview, Gutenberg's revolutionary idea for a printing press is introduced and the story of this famous printer's successes and difficulties is told.

Assign small groups of students to each text set. As they read, the students should uncover the following information:

- When the inventor lived
- The inventor's most famous invention
- Why she or he invented it
- The details of the invention
- Other interesting inventions by the inventor (if there were any)
- An explanation of the significance of the invention

Make a large chart with the headings related to the categories of information researched above. Have each group fill in a summary of the data it had uncovered. Discuss the results.

The students in each group should work together to design a costume that one member might wear to share information with the rest of the class. Did he have a moustache? Then the speaker should have one, too. Did she wear a hat? So should the speaker. In addition to looking and acting like the inventor, the students should try to use some type of aid in describing the invention. Would a large illustration work? What about a model or the actual invention?

3. Involve the students in the actual steps of inventing something. First, lead a brainstorming session during which small groups identify as many problems as they can about their home, school, neighborhood, or any other location. Next, they should examine only three problems and focus on one that bugs them the most. Centering on that problem, students should brainstorm ideas for an invention that could solve it. For example, one group may decide that they become quite uncomfortable playing outdoors on cold winter days. After running around for awhile, their noses inevitably begin to run. It is not easy for them to sort through layers of coats and sweaters to find a tissue or handkerchief. So, after considering several alternatives, including a handkerchief that could be attached temporarily to a coat sleeve and used to swipe away the drops (and removed to wash), it suggested an invention called the "Stop Dripping Mitten." The mitten carried a supply of tissues inside a dispenser built into its palm.

4. Next, the students must plan and design their inventions. Distribute large sheets of drawing paper that could be used to sketch their designs. The drawings should show every feature of the inventions. It would be instructive to show students examples of actual sketches of inventions made by their inventors. If your students can do it, they might be interested in using the guidelines for making patent sketches. There are regulations for the size of the paper and the format, the color of the drawings, their proportion, how they are numbered and referred to, and how they are included in the patent application. You can find the specific guidelines on the official website of the United States Patent and Trademark Office (www.uspto.gov/web/offices/pac/design/index.html#drawings). Sample illustrations drawn by actual inventors can be found on various other sites, too. They serve as effective models for the students.

5. After the groups have planned and designed their inventions, they have the chance to give them names. Students should not underestimate the importance of coming up with a good name, for the name has a very important purpose—it helps sell the product. A good product name will help get attention, especially if it is catchy, easy to remember, or clever. When students have created a name, they should make sure it will do all it can to bring attention to the product:

- Does the name adequately describe the product?
- Will the name project the idea you want people to get?
- Is the name easy to remember?

The next step in the invention process entails applying for a patent. A patent is an agreement between the U.S. government and an inventor that protects anyone from stealing the inventor's idea. For the purposes of this unit, however, group members will file a joint "application" for their inventions—a simplified version that asks them to name their inventions, describe them, explain the things they feel are unique and useful, attach the sketches, and verify that the works are theirs by placing their signatures in the spaces provided: "We, the undersigned, affirm that we are the original and first inventors of the ______________________." Of course, like the real patent application, the inventors must obtain signatures from two witnesses who can substantiate their claims.

When the applications are complete, they are sent to the Commissioner of Patents and Trademarks at the U.S. Patent Office (the teacher) who will check them to see if everything is complete and done according to the rules. The teacher will sign the applications, issue the inventions official patent serial numbers, and stamp them with the official acceptance date.

6. No one is going to come knocking at the door of our new patent holders to buy their new inventions unless they promote them. One way to find potential buyers is to advertise the product, and one of the best ways to advertise it is to examine newspaper or magazine ads to find items that are similar to theirs. Then, using the advertising techniques described earlier in this chapter, the students should find examples of the persuasive techniques. Discuss the ads with these prompts:

- Does the ad attract attention?
- Does it show the benefits of buying the produce?
- Does it create a desire to buy the product?

To make students aware of the power advertising has in the success of a new product, have each group select one technique that they think will help make their product successful. Then have them design and display their own advertisements.

Phase Three: Culminating Activity

Make known to others the products of the students' ingenuity by holding an "Invention Convention"—a display of student-generated inventions. Both the Rube Goldberg-style and patent-awarded inventions, along with related activities, will be organized on tables in different areas of the classroom. Send home an invitation so parents can enjoy seeing what can happen when their children's creative juices really get flowing. At the end of the event, award an Invention Convention certificate of achievement to each young inventor. The students will enjoy the pats on the back and encouragement that will pour their way on this big day!

How Global is the Curriculum *Go to MyEducationLab, select the topic Teaching Strategies, watch the video entitled "Culminating Event as an Evaluative Tool," and complete the questions that accompany it.*

The learning activities section brings to an end our discussion of unit and lesson planning. Planning at both levels is a crucial element of dynamic social studies instruction. Planning, either formally or informally, is a continuous process for everyone, for there is a constant need to keep materials, activities, and techniques up to date. As a new teacher, you will work hard to accumulate a rich teaching repertoire; ideas can be found in magazines and journals, and ready-made file cabinets (virtual file cabinets) are out there on the Internet, free for the taking. So, dive into the planning process, examine the many planning sources that are popping up

regularly, and experience the joy and satisfaction of creating a plan for a topic that has held your fascination. Perhaps you will make an important professional contribution that will become a rich source for future generations of teachers and students in your school district to enjoy.

A Final Thought

Creative teachers clearly demonstrate a key ingredient of first-rate instruction—a characteristic I call "stick-with-it-ness." This is a persistent, intense commitment to what they are doing. Teachers with stick-with-it-ness are thrilled with their professional responsibilities. Teaching is not only their job—it is their passion. It leaves them virtually starry-eyed and eager to devise experiences that activate children for learning. All children must believe that their teachers are captivated by what they are doing in the classroom. In social studies, this means that teachers view their world with fascination and inspire their children to accept theirs as a never-ending mystery. To do this, teachers must plan significant learning situations in which there is a little mystery, a bit of magic, and a dash of magnificence to confront the children. Elementary school children respond to these things; that is what makes their classrooms different from those for any other age.

Teachers achieve magic in the elementary school social studies program when they help each child become challenged by the activities and emotionally involved in the subject matter. They deliver the best for each youngster and make the most of their time every day. Teachers adapt instruction to meet the special needs and interests of all their students; they fully understand and are willing to work toward fulfilling the principles and assumptions that underlie learning carried out by small groups or individuals. Teachers use a large variety of learning tasks to meet their students' needs. Although thematic planning has become extremely popular in recent years, many elementary school social studies teachers continue to use a number of techniques that have been a part of the educational scene for years.

REFERENCES

Gronlund, N. (1991). *How to write and use instructional objectives.* New York: Macmillan.

Livingston, C., Castle, S., & Nations, J. (1989). Testing and curriculum reform: One school's experience. *Educational Leadership, 46,* 24.

National Council for the Social Studies. (1994). *Curriculum standards for social studies: Expectations of excellence* (Bulletin 89). Washington, DC: Author.

National Education Goals Report. (1995). Washington, DC: U.S. Government Printing Office.

Orlich, D. C., Harder, R. J., Callahan, R. C., Kauchak, D. P., Pendergrass, R. A., Keogh, A. J., & Gibson, H. (1990). *Teaching strategies: A guide to better instruction.* Lexington, MA: D. C. Heath.

Paulson, F. L., Paulson, P. R., & Meyer, C. A. (1991). What makes a portfolio a portfolio? *Educational Leadership, 48,* 60.

Rhode Island Department of Elementary and Secondary Education. (1997). *A standards-based guide for social studies programs in Rhode Island schools.* Providence, RI: Author.

Wiggins, G., & McTighe, J. (2005). *Understanding by design.* Upper Saddle River, NJ: Pearson Education by arrangement with the Association for Supervision and Curriculum Development.

APPENDIX A

Cited Children's Literature

Angeletti, Roberta. *The Cave Painter of Lascaux* (Crystal Productions).

Barrett, Marvin & Fogarty, Pat. *Meet Thomas Jefferson* (Random House).

Beatty, Patricia. *Charley Skedaddle* (Troll Communications).

Brett, Jan. *The Mitten: A Ukrainian Folktale* (Putnam).

Bridges, Ruby. *Through My Eyes* (Scholastic).

Brown, Jeff. *Flat Stanley* (HarperCollins).

Brown, Marc. *Arthur's Eyes* (Little, Brown).

Brown, Margaret Wise. *The Important Book* (HarperTrophy).

Bunting, Eve. *Moonstick: The Seasons of the Sioux* (HarperTrophy).

Burnham, Brad. *Cave of Lascaux: The Cave of Prehistoric Wall Paintings* (Powerkids Press).

Burton, Virginia Lee. *Katie and the Big Snow* (Houghton Mifflin).

Cherry, Lynne. *The Armadillo from Amarillo* (Voyager Books).

Cherry, Lynne. *The Great Kapok Tree: A Tale of the Amazon Rain Forest* (Gulliver Green).

Clifton, Lucille. *My Friend Jacob* (Dutton Juvenile).

Climo, Shirley. *The Egyptian Cinderella* (HarperTrophy).

Collier, Bryan. *Uptown* (Henry Holt).

Collier, James Lincoln and Collier, Christopher Collier. *Jump Ship to Freedom* (Dell Yearling).

Cooney, Barbara. *Eleanor* (Puffin).

de Paola, Tomie. *Now One Foot, Now the Other* (Puffin).

de Paola, Tomie. *The Popcorn Book* (Holiday).

Douglas, Lloyd G. *The American Flag* (Children's Press).

Forbes, Esther. *Johnny Tremain* (Houghton Mifflin).

Frank, Anne, Falstein, Mark, and Moore, Steve. *Anne Frank: The Diary of a Young Girl* (Tandem Library).

Fritz, Jean. *Shh! We're Writing the Constitution* (Putnam).

Fritz, Jean. *Stonewall* (Putnam).

Galdone, Paul. *The Little Red Hen Big Book* (Clarion).

Garcia, Guy. *Spirit of the Maya: A Boy Explores His People's Mysterious Past* (Walker).

Giovanni, Nikki and Collier, Bryan. *Rosa* (Square Fish).

Gregory, Kristina. *Across the Wide and Lonesome Prairie: The Oregon Trail Diary of Hattie Campbell, 1847* (Scholastic).

Grifalconi, Ann. *The Village of Round and Square Houses* (Little, Brown).

Hall, Donald. *Ox-Cart Man* (Viking).

Hill, Eric. *Spot's First Walk* (Puffin).

Hinshaw, Dorothy. *Mystery of the Lascaux Cave* (Benchmark).

Hirst, Robin, Hirst, Sally, and Harvey, Roland. *My Place in Space* (Orchard Books).

Hoobler, Dorothy and Hoobler, Thomas. *We Are Americans: Voices of the Immigrant People* (Scholastic).

Hoyt-Goldsmith, Diane. *Hoang-Anh: A Vietnamese-American Boy* (Holiday House).

Hutchins, Pat. *Rosie's Walk* (Puffin).

Isadora, Rachel. *Isadora Dances* (Puffin).

Johnson, Dolores. *Now Let Me Fly* (Aladdin).

Johnson, Phyllis Hacken. *Heather Hits Her First Home Run* (Lollipop Power Books).

Jones, Charlotte Foltz. *Mistakes That Worked* (Doubleday).
Keller, Helen. *The Story of My Life* (Doubleday).
Kian, Fereydoun. *Humpty Dumpty Sat on the Globe: Geotales from Around the World* (Wonderglades Kids).
Knight, Tim. *Journey into the Rainforest* (Oxford University Press).
Knowlton, Jack. *Maps and Globes* (HarperTrophy).
Kraft, Betsy Harvey. *Theodore Roosevelt: Champion of the American Spirit* (Clarion).
Lee, Carol Ann. *Anne Frank's Story: Her Life Retold for Children* (Troll).
Les Tina, Dorothy. *Flag Day* (Crowell).
Levy, Janice. *Celebrate! It's Cinco De Mayo* (Albert Whitman).
Litchfield, Ada Bassett. *A Button in Her Ear* (Albert Whitman).
Louie, Ai-Ling. *Yeh-Shen* (Putnam).
Maraniss, David. *Clemente: The Passion and Grace of Baseball's Last Hero* (Simon & Schuster).
McMullen, Kate. *The Story of Harriet Tubman: Conductor of the Underground Railroad* (Yearling).
Monsell, Helen Albee. *Susan B. Anthony: Champion of Women's Rights* (Aladdin).
Morris, Ann. *Bread, Bread, Bread* (HarperTrophy).
O'Dell, Scott. *Carlota* (Laurel Leaf).
Onyefulu, Ifeoma. *My Grandfather Is a Magician: Work and Wisdom in an African Village* (Frances Lincoln Children's Books).
Perrault, Charles. *Cinderella* (North-South Books).
Perrine, Mary. *Nannabah's Friend* (Houghton Mifflin).
Peterson, Katherine. *The Tongue-Cut Sparrow* (Dutton Juvenile).
Platt, Richard. *Castle Diary: The Journal of Tobias Burgess* (Candlewick).
Pryor, Bonnie. *The House on Maple Street* (HarperTrophy).
Quackenbush, Robert. *Stop the Presses, Nellie's Got a Scoop!* (Simon and Schuster).
Rabe, Tish. *There's a Map on My Lap!* (Dragonfly).
Robinet, Harriette Gillem. *Children of the Fire* (Aladdin Paperbacks).
Robinson, Jackie with Duckett, Alfred. *I Never Had It Made: An Autobiography of Jackie Robinson* (Harper Perennial).
Rosenberg, Maxine B. *My Friend Leslie* (Lothrop).
Rylant, Cynthia. *Appalachia: The Voices of Sleeping Birds* (First Voyager).
Saint James, Synthia. *The Gifts of Kwanzaa* (Albert Whitman).
San Souci, Robert D. *Cendrillon: A Caribbean Cinderella (Aladdin).*
Say, Allen. *Tree of Cranes* (Houghton Mifflin).
Severance, John B. *Gandhi: Great Soul* (Clarion).
Sobel, Sy. *The U.S. Constitution and You* (Barron's Educational Series).
Speare, Elizabeth George. *The Sign of the Beaver* (Yearling).
Steptoe, John. *Mufaro's Beautiful Daughters* (HarperTrophy).
Stier, Catherine. *If I Were President* (Albert Whitman).
Sweeney, Joan. *Me on the Map* (Dragonfly).
Taylor, Mildred D. *Mississippi Bridge* (Penguin).
Tompert, Ann. *Grandfather Tang's Story* (Dragonfly).
Turner, Ann. *Katie's Trunk* (Aladdin).
Venezia, Mike. *George W. Bush* (Children's Press).
Venezia, Mike. *George Washington: First President 1789–1797* (Children's Press).
Wallace, Ian. *Chin Chiang and the Dragon's Dance* (Groundwood).
Wert, Jeffry D. *General James Longstreet: The Confederacy's Most Controversial Soldier* (Simon & Schuster).
White, Ellen Emerson. *Voyage on the Great Titanic: The Diary of Margaret Ann Brady* (Scholastic).
Wilder, Laura Ingalls. *Little House on the Prairie* (HarperTrophy).
Winn, Marie. *Shiver, Gobble, and Snore* (Simon & Schuster).
Wolfe, Maynard Frank. *Rube Goldberg: Inventions* (Simon & Schuster).
Zion, Gene. *Harry the Dirty Dog* (HarperTrophy).
Zolotow, Charlotte. *William's Doll* (HarperTrophy).

Author Index

Subject Index